ESSAYS ON THE CIVIL WAR AND RECONSTRUCTION

HRW Essays in American History Series
  Paul Goodman, Editor

ESSAYS ON THE CIVIL WAR AND RECONSTRUCTION

EDITED BY

IRWIN UNGER

New York University

HOLT, RINEHART AND WINSTON, INC.

New York · Chicago · San Francisco · Atlanta
Dallas · Montreal · Toronto

Cover: Alfred R. Waud, "Brig. Gen. Francis
Barlow's Charge at Cold Harbor, June 3,
1864." Courtesy of the Library of Congress.

Copyright © 1970 by Holt, Rinehart and Winston, Inc.
All rights reserved
Library of Congress Catalog Card Number: 75–105542
SBN: 03–079640–7
Printed in the United States of America
1 2 3 4 5 6 7 8 9

*To Brooke David, Miles Jeremy, and Paul Joshua,
with love*

Preface

Americans never seem to lose interest in the Civil War. Although a century has passed, the war still exerts—and always will exert—its fascination for us. The reasons for this perennial attraction are fairly clear. The events of 1861 to 1865 are romantic. Cavalry charges and crinoline, plantation houses and bearded soldiers, Lincoln at the Gettysburg battlefield and the burning of Atlanta are brilliant images evoking days that were exciting and heroic and yet simpler and less ambiguous than our own. They are also sentimental. Side by side with the heroic tableaux we can place the sleeping sentry-boy pardoned by the harassed, careworn President; the fraternizing infantrymen of blue and gray warning each other of an impending artillery barrage; Grant's gracious gesture at Appomattox allowing the vanquished Confederates to take their horses for spring plowing. It is from such human material, romantic and sentimental, that Civil War myth and folklore are compounded.

But the war's hold over our imagination has deeper roots than these. The "War Between the States" was the most profound crisis in our national history. Any political jolt, if severe enough, may crack the hard surface that normally covers deep-running social and cultural currents and show us the inner workings of a society. In this role the Civil War was not unique in our past. The events following 1763, the crisis of the 1890's, the Great Depression of a generation ago, all served to provide uncommon views of our national workings. But none of these reveals more than the Great Crisis of the Union. The origins, the course, and the results of the Civil War tell us more about mid-nineteenth century American society than perhaps any other event of our past. The great crisis of 1861 to 1865 also tells us much about our own times, for the issues of the war, in spite of the North's victory on the battlefield, have still not been fully resolved. The conflict was closely intertwined with chattel slavery; the issue of race is still a painful problem in our lives. It involved states' rights, and federal power versus local autonomy is still a matter for argument. It was, of course, a confrontation between North and South, and sectional antagonism still exists in the United States. To some degree it pitted rural-agrarian values against urban-industrial ones; in the altered form of suburb versus central city that battle is still with us.

Filled with such modern resonance, it is not surprising that the war has provoked fierce contention among historians. The professional students have disagreed over almost every major characteristic of the conflict. Its causation—and historical causation is both endlessly fascinating and endlessly controversial—has probably been the most hotly contested issue. Ever since the actual outbreak of hostilities, men have argued over the fundamental reason for the tragic breakdown of peaceful means for adjusting sectional differences. As Thomas Pressly has noted, many of the explanations for the war that are popular today actually date from the war years themselves or the period immediately following.[1] During the conflict, particularly in the North, men asserted versions of the "slave conspiracy" argument, or the "two civilizations" argument, or the "irrepressible conflict" argument, or even the "conflict of economic interests" argument to explain the tragic events of the day. Equally controversial has been the nature of the Reconstruction period after 1865, and again almost every one of the currently popular hypotheses was foreshadowed by discerning contemporaries.

But there is more to the historiography of the Civil War than a series of arguments. Much of the best work of the last generation has been a process of discovering new dimensions to this immensely complicated human event. With the changing years and with altering perspectives, new concerns inevitably appear in a society as dynamic as ours. These concerns arise out of the shifts of social and intellectual outlook that emerge from our recent experiences. Crucial here, of course, is the civil rights movement and black militancy and the way in which these phenomena have directed our attention to racism in early America and to the role of black people in the nation's past. They also derive from new techniques or procedures made possible either by new technology or, often, by new concepts in the social sciences that are useful to historians. These new techniques and approaches are reflected in the awakened, or re-awakened, interest in the economic effects of slavery on the South and in recent attempts to test major historical conclusions by rigorous statistical analysis.

At first glance it might appear that historians who are influenced by the new approaches are merely following the intellectual fashions. It is equally disconcerting to discover that the experts seem to rewrite the past every 20 years and that at any one given time, reputable scholars disagree. To the uninitiated there appears, perhaps, to be no solid substratum of reality in history; history is merely the current tricks that we play on the dead. But such cynicism is unwarranted. Although young scholars, particularly, often think that their new insights have completely superseded and invalidated the older interpretations, the newer views generally merely modify or supplement what is already known. In this way through reexamination and reinterpretation, historical knowledge is advanced. History, as the actual events of the past, is so enormous, varied, and complex that differing interpretations, when stripped of their exaggerated claims to exclusiveness, often turn out to be mutually compatible and equally valid. It is possible, for example, that the Civil War was both a battle over slavery and at the same time a struggle between two societies. It is not inconceivable that Andrew Johnson was both a sincere and generous sympathizer with the defeated South and a bigot, easily flattered and manipulated by ex-Confederates.

In the following pages are some of the best interpretive articles written on the Civil War era. I have conceived the period rather broadly and have reprinted essays on the origins and background of the war, on the growing disparities between North and South in the years preceding the war, on the war itself, and on the Reconstruction period. Despite this breadth, I have not sought to assemble a connected history of the period between 1840 and 1880. While I have tried to cover the major components of the great sectional struggle, my chief criterion for selecting an article has been

[1] See Thomas J. Pressly, *Americans Interpret Their Civil War* (New York: Collier Books, 1962), p. 146.

quality, even if this entailed an over emphasis on certain themes and a relative neglect of others. I do not agree with every author included, but I have selected articles that I hope are provocative, interesting, significant, and well-argued, and that provide a convenient introduction to the literature of the Civil War period.

The collection is divided into six sections representing the major themes of the volume. An introduction precedes each selection in order to place it in its historical context, to contrast it with other views of the same subject, and, hopefully, to illuminate its contents. I have also affixed to each selection a brief bibliography of works on the same or closely related topics.

New York   Irwin Unger
February 1970

Contents

ESSAYS ON THE CIVIL WAR AND RECONSTRUCTION

Part I

FUNDAMENTAL CAUSES OF THE CIVIL WAR

1 / The American Civil War as a Constitutional Crisis

Arthur Bestor

Immediately following 1865, it was popular to treat the Civil War as a clash between two incompatible views of the relative power of the state and federal governments. Southerners, especially, found the constitutional analysis congenial. Southern apologists, even before the war ended, charged that the North had subverted the proper constitutional relations between state and national governments by expanding federal functions thereby driving the South to secession. When, after 1865, former Confederate officials such as President Jefferson Davis and Vice-President Alexander Stephens wrote their elaborate apologies for the South's course, they confined themselves almost entirely to a legalistic defense of the Southern interpretation of the Constitution as guaranteeing states' rights and permitting secession. Even Southerners who had seriously doubted the constitutional right of secession in 1860, came to defend the legality of that act in the postwar years and to believe that the North's disregard of the clear intent of the founding fathers had justified Southern withdrawal.

As time passed, the constitutional explanation came to seem peculiarly abstract and irrelevant. As the participants in the war, with their need for self-justification passed from the scene, and as social scientists probed beneath the skin of society to identify "forces" governing human affairs, the constitutional battles that preceded the outbreak of the war appeared increasingly to be merely rationalizations of positions ultimately determined not by some deep commitment to a particular interpretation of the federal Constitution but by "interest." Not the sacred principles of states' rights or federal

The American Historical Review, LXIX, No. 2 (January 1964). Reprinted by permission.

Mr. Bestor, professor of history at the University of Washington, presented a version of this paper, May 3, 1963, to a joint session of the Mississippi Valley Historical Association and the American Studies Association in Omaha. He has also incorporated a few passages from a paper read, August 28, 1963, to the Pacific Coast Branch of the American Historical Association in San Francisco. Mr. Bestor has examined certain points in the present discussion more fully in a previous article: "State Sovereignty and Slavery: A Reinterpretation of Proslavery Constitutional Doctrine, 1846–1860" (*Journal of the Illinois State Historical Society,* LIV [Summer 1961]).

supremacy, but the distribution of national power and wealth came to seem the heart of the matter, with states' rights doctrines serving to defend the weaker party and national supremacy to justify the stronger.

Yet in recent years the constitutional interpretation has regained some of its former standing. The events of our own day have helped this revival. The central role that the Supreme Court has played in revising our political and racial practices has turned the attention of serious men and scholars to constitutional matters. An interest in constitutional history, a field once seemingly moribund, has also been revived.

However, the new constitutional history is more subtle and sophisticated than the old. Its practitioners no longer purvey arid, abstract explanations for events. They are not logicians lost in a neat and orderly syllogistic world. The new breed of constitutional historians recognize the complex interactions of law, institutions, and interests, but insist that the legal and constitutional framework within which basic disputes over power and wealth occur are important elements in shaping their course.

If any major event in our history lends itself to a constitutional interpretation, it is surely the Civil War. That conflict most immediately grew out of the division of the federal domain into slave and free territories. Whether a given portion of the newly settled West would enter the Union as slave or free no doubt depended on such factors as climate, soil, and proximity to free or slave states. But since the process of creating new legal communities was a constitutional one, it inevitably also depended on the specific constitutional rules that were applied. Behind the constitutional issues were obviously such matters as slavery, cultural divergences, and differing economic interests, among others, but as Arthur Bestor argues in the selection that follows, without the special configuration of the federal Constitution, none of these tensions need have erupted into a civil war.

For further reading: Arthur Bestor, "State Sovereignty and Slavery: A Reinterpretation of Proslavery Constitutional Doctrine, 1846–1860," *Journal of the Illinois State Historical Society,* LIV (Summer 1961); Alexander H. Stephens, *A Constitutional View of the Late War Between the States* (Philadelphia: The National Publishing Company, 1868–1870); Charles G. Haines and Foster H. Sherwood, *The Role of the Supreme Court in American Government and Politics,* II (Berkeley, Calif.: University of California Press, 1957).

Within the span of a single generation—during the thirty-odd years that began with the annexation of Texas in 1845 and ended with the withdrawal of the last Union troops from the South in 1877—the United States underwent a succession of constitutional crises more severe and menacing than any before or since. From 1845 on, for some fifteen years, a constitutional dispute over the expansion of slavery into the western territories grew increasingly tense until a paralysis of normal constitutional functioning set in. Abruptly, in 1860–1861, this particular constitutional crisis was transformed into another: namely, that of secession. Though the new crisis was intimately linked with the old, its constitutional character was fundamentally different. The question of how the Constitution ought to operate as a piece of working machinery was superseded by the question of whether it might and should be dismantled. A showdown had come, and the four-year convulsion of Civil War ensued. Then, when hostilities ended in 1865, there came not the hoped for dawn of peace, but instead a third great constitutional struggle over Reconstruction, which lasted a dozen years and proved as harsh and divisive as any cold war in history. When the nation finally emerged from three decades of corrosive strife, no observer could miss the profound alterations that its institutions had undergone. Into the prodigious vortex of crisis and war every current of American life had ultimately been drawn.

So all-devouring was the conflict and so momentous its effects, that to characterize it (as I have done) as a series of constitutional crises will seem to many readers an almost irresponsible use of language, a grotesque belittling of the issues. Powerful economic forces, it will be pointed out, were pitted against one another in the struggle. Profound moral perplexities were generated by the existence of slavery, and the attacks upon it had social and psychological repercussions of incredible complexity. The various questions at issue penetrated into the arena of politics, shattering established parties and making or breaking the public careers of national and local leaders. Ought so massive a conflict to be discussed in terms of so rarefied an abstraction as constitutional theory?

To ask such a question, however, is to mistake the character of constitutional crises in general. When or why or how should they arise if not in a context of social, economic, and ideological upheaval? A constitution, after all, is nothing other than the aggregate of laws, traditions, and understandings—in other words, the complex of institutions and procedures—by which a nation brings to political and legal decision the substantive conflicts engendered by changes in all the varied aspects of its societal life. In normal times, to be sure, routine and recurrent questions of public policy are not thought of as constitutional questions. Alternative policies are discussed in terms of their wisdom or desirability. Conflicts are resolved by the ordinary operation of familiar constitutional machinery. A decision is reached that is essentially a political decision, measuring, in some rough way, the political strength of the forces that are backing or opposing some particular program of action, a program that both sides concede to be constitutionally possible, though not necessarily prudent or desirable.

When controversies begin to cut deep, however, the constitutional legitimacy of a given course of action is likely to be challenged. Questions of policy give place to questions of power; questions of wisdom to questions of legality. Attention shifts to the Constitution itself, for the fate of each particular policy has come to hinge upon the interpretation given to the fundamental law. In debating these constitutional questions, men are not evading the substantive issues. They are facing them in precisely the manner that the situation now requires. A constitutional dispute has been superadded to the controversies already present.

Should the conflict become so intense as to test the adequacy of exisiting mechanisms to handle it at all, then it mounts to the level of a constitutional crisis. Indeed the capability of producing a constitutional crisis is an ultimate measure of the intensity of the substantive conflicts themselves. If, in the end, the situation explodes into violence, then the catastrophe is necessarily a constitutional one, for its very essence is the failure and the threatened destruction of the constitutional framework itself.

The secession crisis of 1860–1861 was obviously an event of this kind. It was a constitutional catastrophe in the most direct sense, for it resulted in a civil war that destroyed, albeit temporarily, the fabric of the Union.

There is, however, another sense—subtler, but perhaps more significant—in which the American Civil War may be characterized as a constitutional crisis. To put the matter succinctly, the very form that the conflict finally took was determined by the pre-existing form of the constitutional system. The way the opposing forces were arrayed against each other in war was a consequence of the way the Constitution had operated to array them in peace. Because the Union could be, and frequently had been, viewed as no more than a compact among sovereign states, the dissolution of the compact was a conceivable thing. It was constitutional theorizing, carried on from the very birth of the Republic, which made secession the ultimate recourse of any group that considered its vital interests threatened.

Since the American system was a federal one, secession, when it finally occurred, put the secessionists into immediate possession of fully organized governments, capable of acting as no *ad hoc* insurrectionary regime could possibly have acted. Though sometimes described as a "Rebellion" and sometimes as a "Civil War," the American conflict was, in a strict sense, neither. It was a war between pre-existing political entities. But it was not (to use a third description) a "War between the States," for in war the states did not act severally. Instead, the war was waged between two federations of these states: one the historic Union, the other a Confederacy that, though newly created, was shaped by the same constitutional tradition as its opponent. In short, only the pre-existing structure of the American Constitution can explain the actual configuration even of the war itself.

The *configurative* role that constitutional issues played is the point of crucial importance. When discussed in their own terms and for their own sakes, constitutional questions are admittedly theoretical questions. One may indeed say (borrowing a phrase that even academicians perfidiously employ) that they are academic questions. Only by becoming involved with other (and in a sense more "substantive") issues, do they become highly charged. But when they do become so involved, constitutional questions turn out to be momentous ones, for every theoretical premise draws after it a train of practical consequences. Abstract though constitutional issues may be, they exert a powerful shaping effect upon the course that events will in actuality take. They give a particular direction to forces already at work. They impose upon the conflict as a whole a unique, and an otherwise inexplicable, pattern or configuration.

To speak of a configuration of forces in history is to rule out, as essentially meaningless, many kinds of questions that are popularly supposed to be both answerable and important. In particular, it rules out as futile any effort to decide which one of the various forces at work in a given historical situation was "*the most important cause*" of the events that followed, or "*the* decisive factor" in bringing them about, or "*the* crucial issue" involved. The reason is simple. The steady operation of a single force, unopposed and uninterrupted, would result in a development so continuous as to be, in the most literal sense, eventless. To produce an event, one force must impinge upon at least one other. The event is the consequence of their interaction. Historical explanation is, of necessity, an explanation of such interactions.

If interaction is the crucial matter, then it is absurd to think of assigning to any factor in history an intrinsic or absolute weight, independent of its context. In the study of history, the context is all-important. Each individual factor derives its significance from the position it occupies in a complex structure of interrelationships. The fundamental historical problem, in short, is not to measure the relative weight of various causal elements, but instead to discover the pattern of their interaction with one another.[1]

A cogent illustration of this particular point is afforded by the controversy over slavery, which played so significant a role in the crisis with which this paper deals. Powerful emotions, pro and con, were aroused by the very existence of slavery. Powerful economic interests were involved with the fate of the institution. Nevertheless, differences of opinion, violent though they were, cannot, by themselves, account for the peculiar configuration of events that historically occurred. The forces unleashed by the slavery controversy were essentially indeterminate; that is to say, they could lead to any number of different outcomes, ranging from simple legislative emancipation to bloody servile insurrection. In the British West Indies the former occurred; in Haiti, the latter. In the United States, by contrast with both, events took an exceedingly complicated course. The crisis can be said to have commenced with a fifteen-year dispute not over slavery itself, but over its expansion into the territories. It eventuated in a four-year war that was avowedly fought not over the issue of slavery, but over the question of the legal perpetuity of the Union. The slavery controversy, isolated from all other issues, cannot begin to explain why events followed so complex and devious a course. On the other hand, though other factors must be taken into account in explaining the configuration of events, these other factors, isolated from those connected with slavery, cannot explain why tensions mounted so high as to reach the breaking point of war.

No single factor, whatever its nature, can account for the distinctive form that the mid-nineteenth-century American crisis assumed. Several forces converged, producing a unique configuration. Men were debating a variety of issues simultaneously, and their various arguments intertwined. Each conflict tended to intensify the others, and not only to intensify them but also to alter and deflect them in complicated ways. The crisis was born of interaction.

The nature of these various converging conflicts is abundantly clear. They are

---

[1] A contrary view is advanced by Sidney Hook: "The validity of the historian's findings will . . . depend upon his ability to discover a method of roughly measuring the relative strength of the various factors present." (Social Science Research Council, Bulletin 54, *Theory and Practice in Historical Study: A Report of the Committee on Historiography* [New York, 1946], 113.) Hook, writing as a philosopher, insists that his criterion is part of the "pattern of inquiry which makes a historical account scientific." (*Ibid.*, 112.) But, as another philosopher, Ernest Nagel, points out, "the natural sciences do not appear to require the imputation of relative importance to the causal variables that occur in their explanations." On the contrary, "if a phenomenon occurs only when certain conditions are realized, all these conditions are equally essential, and no one of them can intelligibly be regarded as more basic than the others." (Ernest Nagel, "Some Issues in the Logic of Historical Analysis," *Scientific Monthly*, LXXIV [Mar. 1952], 162–69, esp. 167.)

spread at length upon the historical record. Documents, to be sure, are not always to be taken at face value; there are occasions when it is legitimate to read between the lines. Nevertheless, the documentary record is the foundation upon which historical knowledge rests. It can be explained, but it cannot be explained away, as many writers on the causes of the Civil War attempt to do. Most current myths, indeed, depend on such wholesale dismissals of evidence. Southern apologetics took form as early as 1868 when Alexander H. Stephens unblinkingly asserted that "this whole subject of Slavery, so-called, . . . was, to the Seceding States, but a drop in the ocean compared with . . . other considerations,"[2] by which he meant considerations of constitutional principle. The dogma of economic determinism can be sustained only by dismissing, as did Charles and Mary Beard in 1927, not merely that part of the record which Stephens rejected but also the part he accepted. Having decided, like Stephens, that "the institution of slavery was not the fundamental issue," the Beards went on to assert that constitutional issues likewise "were minor factors in the grand dispute."[3]

When the historical record is as vast as the one produced by the mid-nineteenth-century American crisis—when arguments were so wearisomely repeated by such multitudes of men—it is sheer fantasy to assume that the issues discussed were not the real issues. The arguments of the period were public ones, addressed to contemporaries and designed to influence their actions. If these had not touched upon genuine issues, they would hardly have been so often reiterated. Had other lines of argument possessed a more compelling force, they would certainly have been employed.

The only tenable assumption, one that would require an overwhelming mass of contrary evidence to rebut, is that men and women knew perfectly well what they were quarreling about. And what do we find? They argued about economic measures—the tariff, the banking system, and the Homestead Act—for the obvious reason that economic interests of their own were at stake. They argued about slavery because they considered the issues it raised to be vital ones—vital to those who adhered to the ideal of a free society and vital to those who feared to disturb the *status quo*. They argued about the territories because they felt a deep concern for the kind of social order that would grow up there. They argued about the Constitution because they accepted its obligations (whatever they considered them to be) as binding.

These are the data with which the historian must reckon. Four issues were mentioned in the preceding paragraph: the issue of economic policy, the issue of slavery, the issue of the territories, and the issue of constitutional interpretation. At the very least, the historian must take all these into account. Other factors there indubitably were. To trace the interaction of these four, however, will perhaps suffice to reveal the underlying pattern of the crisis and to make clear how one of these factors, the constitutional issue, exerted a configurative effect that cannot possibly be ignored.

Conflicts over economic policy are endemic in modern societies. They formed a recurrent element in nineteenth-century American political conflict. To disregard

[2] Alexander H. Stephens, *A Constitutional View of the Late War between the States* (2 vols., Philadelphia, 1868–70), I, 542.

[3] Charles A. and Mary R. Beard, *The Rise of American Civilization* (2 vols., New York, 1927), II, 40, 42.

them would be an even greater folly than to assume that they determined, by themselves, the entire course of events. Between a plantation economy dependent upon the sale of staples to a world market and an economy in which commerce, finance, and manufacturing were rapidly advancing, the points of conflict were numerous, real, and important. At issue were such matters as banks and corporations, tariffs, internal improvements, land grants to railroads, and free homesteads to settlers. In a general way, the line of division on matters of economic policy tended, at mid-century, to coincide with the line of division on the question of slavery. To the extent that it did so (and it did so far less clearly than many economic determinists assume), the economic conflict added its weight to the divisive forces at work in 1860–1861.

More significant, perhaps, was another and different sort of relationship between the persistent economic conflict and the rapidly mounting crisis before the Civil War. To put the matter briefly, the constitutional theories that came to be applied with such disruptive effects to the slavery dispute had been developed, in the first instance, largely in connection with strictly economic issues. Thus the doctrine of strict construction was pitted against the doctrine of loose construction as early as 1791, when Alexander Hamilton originated the proposal for a central bank. And the doctrine of nullification was worked out with ingenious thoroughness in 1832 as a weapon against the protective tariff. Whatever crises these doctrines precipitated proved to be relatively minor ones so long as the doctrines were applied to purely economic issues. Within this realm, compromise always turned out to be possible. The explosive force of irreconcilable constitutional theories became apparent only when the latter were brought to bear upon the dispute over slavery.

Inherent in the slavery controversy itself (the second factor with which we must reckon) were certain elements that made compromise and accommodation vastly more difficult than in the realm of economic policy. To be sure, slavery itself had its economic aspect. It was, among other things, a labor system. The economic life of many regions rested upon it. The economic interests that would be affected by any tampering with the institution were powerful interests, and they made their influence felt.

Nevertheless, it was the noneconomic aspect of slavery that made the issues it engendered so inflammatory. As Ulrich B. Phillips puts it, "Slavery was instituted not merely to provide control of labor but also as a system of racial adjustment and social order." The word "adjustment" is an obvious euphemism; elsewhere Phillips speaks frankly of "race control." The effort to maintain that control, he maintains, has been "the central theme of Southern history." The factor that has made the South "a land with a unity despite its diversity," Phillips concludes, is "a common resolve indomitably maintained—that it shall be and remain a white man's country."[4]

It was this indomitable resolve—say rather, this imperious demand—that lay at the heart of the slavery controversy, as it lies at the heart of the struggle over civil rights today. To put the matter bluntly, the demand was that of a master race for a completely free hand to deal as it might choose with its own subject population. The word "sovereignty" was constantly on the lips of southern politicians. The concept they were invoking was one that Blackstone had defined as "supreme, irresistible,

---

[4] Ulrich B. Phillips, *The Course of the South to Secession*, ed. E. Merton Coulter (New York, 1939), 152.

absolute, uncontrolled authority."[5] This was the kind of authority that slaveholders exercised over their chattels. What they were insisting on, in the political realm, was that the same species of power should be recognized as belonging to the slaveholding states when dealing with their racial minorities. "State Sovereignty" was, in essence, the slaveowner's authority writ large.

If slavery had been a static system, confined geographically to the areas where the institution was an inheritance from earlier days, then the demand of the slaveholding states for unrestricted, "sovereign" power to deal with it was a demand to which the majority of Americans would probably have reconciled themselves for a long time. In 1861, at any rate, even Lincoln and the Republicans were prepared to support an ironclad guarantee that the Constitution would never be amended in such a way as to interfere with the institution within the slaveholding states. An irrepealable amendment to that effect passed both houses of Congress by the necessary two-thirds vote during the week before Lincoln's inauguration.[6] The incoming President announced that he had "no objection" to the pending amendment,[7] and three states (two of them free) actually gave their ratifications in 1861 and 1862.[8] If the problems created by slavery had actually been, as slaveowners so vehemently maintained, of a sort that the slaveholding states were perfectly capable of handling by themselves, then the security offered by this measure might well have been deemed absolute.

As the historical record shows, however, the proposed amendment never came close to meeting the demands of the proslavery forces. These demands, and the crisis they produced, stemmed directly from the fact that slavery was *not* a static and local institution; it was a prodigiously expanding one. By 1860 the census revealed that more than half the slaves in the nation were held in bondage *outside* the boundaries of the thirteen states that had composed the original Union.[9] The expansion of slavery meant that hundreds of thousands of slaves were being carried beyond the territorial jurisdictions of the states under whose laws they had originally been held in servitude. Even to reach another slaveholding state, they presumably entered that stream of "Commerce . . . among the several States," which the Constitution gave Congress a power "to regulate."[10] If they were carried to United States territories that had not

[5] William Blackstone, *Commentaries on the Laws of England* (4 vols., Oxford, Eng., 1765–69), I, 49.

[6] Joint Resolution to Amend the Constitution, Mar. 2, 1861, 12 US Statutes at Large 251. It passed the House by a vote of 133 to 65 on February 28, 1861, and the Senate by a vote of 24 to 12 on the night of March 3–4, 1861. Technically, the sitting of March 2, 1861, was still in progress in the Senate, hence the date attached to the joint resolution as officially published. (*Congressional Globe*, 36 Cong., 2 sess., 1285, 1403 [Feb. 28, Mar. 2, 1861].)

[7] First inaugural address, Mar. 4, 1861, *The Collected Works of Abraham Lincoln*, ed. Roy P. Basler *et al.* (9 vols., New Brunswick, N. J., 1953–55), IV, 270.

[8] Ohio on May 13, 1861, Maryland on Jan. 10, 1862, Illinois on Feb. 14, 1862. (Herman V. Ames, *The Proposed Amendments to the Constitution of the United States during the First Century of Its History, Annual Report, American Historical Association, 1896* [2 vols., Washington, D. C., 1897], II, 363.)

[9] Of the 3,953,760 slaves in the United States in 1860, 2,174,996 were held in the 9 states of Kentucky, Tennessee, Florida, Alabama, Mississippi, Missouri, Arkansas, Louisiana, and Texas. (US, Ninth Census [1870], Vol. I, *The Statistics of the Population* [Washington, D. C., 1872], 3–8 [a corrected recompilation of previous census figures].)

[10] US Constitution, Art. I, Sec. 8 [clause 3].

yet been made states, their presence there raised questions about the source and validity of the law that kept them in bondage.

Territorial expansion, the third factor in our catalogue, was thus a crucial element in the pattern of interaction that produced the crisis. The timing of the latter, indeed, indicates clearly the role that expansion played. Slavery had existed in English-speaking America for two centuries without producing any paralyzing convulsion. The institution had been brought to an end in the original states of the East and North by unspectacular exercises of legislative or judicial authority. Federal ordinances barring slavery from the Old Northwest had operated effectually yet inconspicuously since 1787. At many other points federal authority had dealt with slavery, outlawing the foreign slave trade on the one hand and providing for the return of fugitive slaves on the other. Prior to the 1840's constitutional challenges to its authority in these matters had been few and unimportant. Indeed, the one true crisis of the period, that of 1819–1821 over Missouri, was rooted in expansionism, precisely as the later one was to be. The nation was awaking to the fact that slavery had pushed its way northward and westward into the virgin lands of the Louisiana Purchase. Only when limits were drawn for it across the whole national domain did the crisis subside.

Suddenly, in the election of 1844, the question of territorial expansion came to the fore again. Events moved rapidly. Within the space of precisely a decade, between the beginning of 1845 and the end of 1854, four successive annexations added a million and a quarter square miles to the area under undisputed American sovereignty.[11] Expansion itself was explosive; its interaction with the smoldering controversy over slavery made the latter issue explosive also.

The annexation of Texas in 1845, the war with Mexico that followed, and the conquests in the Southwest which that war brought about gave to the campaign against slavery a new and unprecedented urgency. Within living memory the plains along the Gulf of Mexico had been inundated by the westward-moving tide of slavery. Alabama and Mississippi, to say nothing of Arkansas and Missouri, furnished startling proof of how quickly and ineradicably the institution could establish itself throughout great new regions. Particularly telling was the example of Texas. There slavery had been carried by American settlers to nominally free soil beyond the boundaries of the United States; yet in the end the area itself was being incorporated in the Union. To guard against any possible repetition of these developments, antislavery forces reacted to the outbreak of the Mexican War by introducing and supporting the Wilmot Proviso. Originally designed to apply simply to territory that might be acquired from Mexico, it was quickly changed into an all-encompassing prohibition: "That there shall be neither slavery nor involuntary servitude in any territory on the

[11] The area of so-called "continental" United States (exclusive of Alaska as well as of Hawaii) is officially put at 3,022,387 square miles. It attained this size in 1854. More than two-fifths of this area, that is, 1,234,381 square miles, is conventionally regarded as having been acquired through the annexation of Texas by joint resolution in 1845, the partition of the Oregon country by agreement with Great Britain in 1846, the cessions from Mexico by the treaty ending the Mexican War in 1848, and the additional territory acquired from the latter country by the Gadsden Purchase of 1853–1854. The conventional reckoning (which disregards all the complex questions created by prior American claims) is given in US Bureau of the Census, *Historical Statistics of the United States, Colonial Times to 1957: A Statistical Abstract Supplement* (Washington, D. C., 1960), 236.

continent of America which shall hereafter be acquired by or annexed to the United States . . . in any . . . manner whatever." [12] The steadfast refusal of the Senate to accept the proviso did not kill it, for the prospect of continuing expansion kept the doctrine alive and made it the rallying point of antislavery sentiment until the Civil War.

This prospect of continuing expansion is sometimes forgotten by historians who regard the issue of slavery in the territories as somehow bafflingly unreal. Since 1854, it is true, no contiguous territory has actually been added to the "continental" United States. No one in the later 1850's, however, could know that this was to be the historic fact. There were ample reasons to expect otherwise. A strong faction had worked for the annexation of the whole of Mexico in 1848. Filibustering expeditions in the Caribbean and Central America were sporadic from 1849 to 1860. As if to spell out the implications of these moves, the notorious Ostend Manifesto of 1854 had announced (over the signatures of three American envoys, including a future President) that the United States could not "permit Cuba to be Africanized" (in plainer language, could not allow the slaves in Cuba to become free of white domination and control), and had defiantly proclaimed that if Spain should refuse to sell the island, "then, by every law, human and divine, we shall be justified in wresting it from Spain if we possess the power." [13] This was "higher law" doctrine with a vengeance.

Behind the intransigent refusal of the Republicans in 1860–1861 to accept any sort of compromise on the territorial question lay these all too recent developments. Lincoln's letters during the interval between his election and his inauguration contained pointed allusions to filibustering and to Cuba.[14] And his most explicit instructions on policy, written on February 1, 1861, to William H. Seward, soon to take office as his Secretary of State, were adamant against any further extension of slavery in any manner:

> I say now, . . . as I have all the while said, that on the territorial question— that is, the question of extending slavery under the national auspices,—I am inflexible. I am for no compromise which *assists* or *permits* the extension of the institution on soil owned by the nation. And any trick by which the nation is to acquire territory, and then allow some local authority to spread slavery over it, is as obnoxious as any other.

[12] This was the form in which the proviso was adopted by the House on February 15, 1847. (*Congressional Globe*, 29 Cong., 2 sess., 424–25 [Feb. 15, 1847].) In its original form, as moved by David Wilmot of Pennsylvania on August 8, 1846, and adopted by the House the same day, it spoke only of "the acquisition of any territory from the Republic of Mexico." (*Ibid.*, 29 Cong., 1 sess., 1217 [Aug. 8, 1846].)

[13] Ostend Manifesto (actually dated at Aix-la-Chapelle), Oct. 18, 1854, *The Ostend Conference, &c.* (*House Executive Documents*, 33 Cong., 2 sess., X, No. 93), 131. Though the Secretary of State, William L. Marcy, was forced by public opinion to repudiate the manifesto, James Buchanan was helped to the presidency in 1857 by the fact that his signature was on it.

[14] *Collected Works of Lincoln*, ed. Basler *et al.*, IV, 154, 155, 172. It should be noted that Stephen A. Douglas, in his third debate with Lincoln, at Jonesboro, Illinois, on September 15, 1858, declared in forthright language that the doctrine of popular sovereignty ought to apply "When we get Cuba" and "when it becomes necessary to acquire any portion of Mexico or Canada, or of this continent or the adjoining islands." (*Ibid.*, III, 115.) The word was "when," not "if."

The obnoxious "trick" that Lincoln feared was, of course, the acceptance of Stephen A. Douglas' doctrine of popular sovereignty. The supreme importance that Lincoln attached to the territorial issue was underlined by the final paragraph of his letter, wherein he discussed four other issues on which antislavery feeling ran high: the Fugitive Slave Act, the existence of slavery in the national capital, the domestic slave trade, and the slave code that the territorial legislature of New Mexico had enacted in 1859. Concerning these matters, Lincoln wrote Seward:

> As to fugitive slaves, District of Columbia, slave trade among the slave states, and whatever springs of necessity from the fact that the institution is amongst us, I care but little, so that what is done be comely, and not altogether outrageous. Nor do I care much about New-Mexico, if further extension were hedged against.[15]

The issues raised by territorial expansion were, however, not merely prospective ones. Expansion was a present fact, and from 1845 onward its problems were immediate ones. Population was moving so rapidly into various parts of the newly acquired West, most spectacularly into California, that the establishment of civil governments within the region could hardly be postponed. Accordingly, within the single decade already delimited (that is, from the beginning of 1845 until the end of 1854), state or territorial forms of government were actually provided for every remaining part of the national domain, except the relatively small enclave known as the Indian Territory (now Oklahoma). The result was an actual doubling of the area of the United States within which organized civil governments existed.[16] This process of political creation occurred not only in the new acquisitions, but it also covered vast areas, previously acquired, that had been left unorganized, notably the northern part of the old Louisiana Purchase. There, in 1854, the new territories of Kansas and Nebraska suddenly appeared on the map. With equal suddenness these new names appeared in the newspapers, connected with ominous events.

The process of territorial organization brought into the very center of the crisis a fourth factor, the last in our original catalogue, namely, the constitutional one. The organization of new territories and the admission of new states were, after all, elements in a constitution-making process. Territorial expansion drastically changed the character of the dispute over slavery by entangling it with the constitutional problem of devising forms of government for the rapidly settling West. Slavery at last became, in the most direct and immediate sense, a constitutional question, and thus a question capable of disrupting the Union. It did so by assuming the form of a question about the power of Congress to legislate for the territories.

[15] Lincoln to Seward, Feb. 1, 1861, *ibid.,* IV, 183.

[16] At the beginning of 1845 the United States comprised approximately 1,788,000 square miles (exclusive of its claims in the Oregon country). Of this total, 945,000 square miles were within the boundaries of the 26 full-fledged states of the Union; another 329,000 square miles belonged to organized territories; and the remaining 514,000 square miles were without organized civil governments. At the end of 1854 the total area had increased to approximately 3,022,000 square miles, of which 1,542,000 lay within the 31 states that were now members of the Union (Florida, Texas, Iowa, Wisconsin, and California having been admitted during the decade); another 1,410,000 square miles belonged to organized territories; and only 70,000 square miles remained in the unorganized Indian Territory. Boundaries are shown in Charles O. Paullin and John K. Wright, *Atlas of the Historical Geography of the United States* (Washington, D. C., 1932), plates 63A and 63B (for the situation in 1845), plates 63B, 64A, and 64C (for 1854).

This brings us face to face with the central paradox in the pre-Civil War crisis. Slavery was being attacked in places where it did not, in present actuality, exist. The slaves, close to four million of them, were in the states, yet responsible leaders of the antislavery party pledged themselves not to interfere with them there.[17] In the territories, where the prohibition of slavery was being so intransigently demanded and so belligerently resisted, there had never been more than a handful of slaves during the long period of crisis. Consider the bare statistics. The census of 1860, taken just before the final descent into Civil War, showed far fewer than a hundred slaves in all the territories,[18] despite the abrogation of restrictions by the Kansas-Nebraska Act and the Dred Scott decision. Especially revealing was the situation in Kansas. Though blood had been spilled over the introduction of slavery into that territory, there were actually only 627 colored persons, slave or free, within its boundaries on the eve of its admission to statehood (January 29, 1861). The same situation obtained throughout the West. In 1846, at the time the Wilmot Proviso was introduced, the Union had comprised twenty-eight states. By the outbreak of the Civil War, more than two and a third million persons were to be found in the western areas beyond the boundaries of these older twenty-eight states, yet among them were only 7,687 Negroes, free or slave.[19] There was much truth in the wry observation of a contemporary: "The whole controversy over the Territories . . . related to an imaginary negro in an impossible place." [20]

The paradox was undeniable, and many historians treat it as evidence of a growing retreat from reality. Thus James G. Randall writes that the "larger phases of

---

[17] In his first inaugural, Lincoln reiterated a statement he had made earlier in his debates with Douglas: "I have no purpose, directly or indirectly, to interfere with the institution of slavery in the States where it exists. I believe I have no lawful right to do so, and I have no inclination to do so." (Collected Works of Lincoln, ed. Basler et al., IV, 263.) The statement was originally made in the debate at Ottawa, Illinois, August 21, 1858. (Ibid., III, 16; see also the discussion of the proposed constitutional amendment of Mar. 2, 1861, above, notes 6–8.)

[18] US, Eighth Census (1860), Preliminary Report on the Eighth Census, 1860 (Washington, D. C., 1862), 131; confirmed in the final report, Population of the United States in 1860 (Washington, D. C., 1864), 598–99. Slaves were recorded in only three territories: fifteen in Nebraska, twenty-nine in Utah, and two in Kansas; a total of forty-six. Certain unofficial preliminary reports gave slightly higher figures: ten slaves in Nebraska, twenty-nine in Utah, twenty-four in New Mexico, and none in Kansas; a total of sixty-three. (American Annual Cyclopaedia, 1861 [New York, 1862], 696.) It should be noted that the census figures for 1860 were tabulated in terms of civil divisions as they existed early in 1861. Thus Kansas was listed as a state, though it was not admitted until January 29, 1861, and statistics were presented for the territories of Colorado, Dakota, and Nevada, though these were organized only in February and March 1861.

[19] Census figures for the six states admitted from 1846 to 1861, inclusive (Iowa, Wisconsin, California, Minnesota, Oregon, and Kansas), and for the seven organized territories enumerated in the census of 1860 (Colorado, Dakota, Nebraska, Nevada, New Mexico, Utah, and Washington) showed an aggregate of 2,305,096 white persons, 7,641 free persons of color, and 46 slaves; making a total (including also "civilized Indians" and "Asiatics") of 2,382,677 persons. (Eighth Census [1860], Population, 598–99.) Ironically enough, the aborigines in the Indian Territory held in slavery almost as many Negroes as were to be found, slave or free, in the entire area just specified. (Eighth Census [1860], Preliminary Report, 136.) This special tabulation for the Indian Territory (not incorporated in the regular census tables) showed 65,680 Indians, 1,988 white persons, 404 free colored persons, and 7,369 slaves.

[20] James G. Blaine, Twenty Years of Congress (2 vols., Norwich, Conn., 1884), I, 272, quoting an unnamed "representative from the South."

the slavery question . . . seemed to recede as the controversies of the fifties developed." In other words, "while the struggle sharpened it also narrowed." The attention of the country was "diverted from the fundamentals of slavery in its moral, economic, and social aspects," and instead "became concentrated upon the collateral problem as to what Congress should do with respect to slavery in the territories." Hence "it was this narrow phase of the slavery question which became, or seemed, central in the succession of political events which actually produced the Civil War." As Randall sees it, the struggle "centered upon a political issue which lent itself to slogan making rather than to political analysis." [21]

Slogan making, to be sure, is an important adjunct of political propaganda, and slogans can easily blind men to the relatively minor character of the tangible interests actually at stake. Nevertheless, a much more profound force was at work, shaping the crisis in this peculiar way. This configurative force was the constitutional system itself. The indirectness of the attack upon slavery, that is to say, the attack upon it in the territories, where it was merely a future possibility, instead of in the states, where the institution existed in force, was the unmistakable consequence of certain structural features of the American Constitution itself.

A centralized national state could have employed a number of different methods of dealing with the question of slavery. Against most of these, the American Constitution interposed a barrier that was both insuperable and respected.[22] By blocking every form of frontal attack, it compelled the adoption of a strategy so indirect as to appear on the surface almost timid and equivocal.[23] In effect, the strategy adopted was a strategy of "containment." Lincoln traced it to the founding fathers themselves. They had, he asserted, put into effect a twofold policy with respect to slavery: "restricting it from the new Territories where it had not gone, and legislating to cut off its source by the abrogation of the slave trade." Taken together, these amounted to "putting the seal of legislation against its spread." The second part of their policy was still in effect, but the first, said Lincoln, had been irresponsibly set aside. To restore it was his avowed object:

> I believe if we could arrest the spread [of slavery] and place it where Washington, and Jefferson, and Madison placed it, it would be in the course of ultimate ex-

[21] James G. Randall, *The Civil War and Reconstruction* (Boston, 1937), 114–15. In a later work, Randall described the issue of slavery in the territories, when debated by Lincoln and Douglas in 1858, as "a talking point rather than a matter for governmental action, a campaign appeal rather than a guide for legislation." (*Lincoln the President* [4 vols., New York, 1945–55], I, 125.)

[22] As I have written elsewhere: "The fact that the controversy of 1846–1860 turned on the extension of slavery to the territories (and, to a lesser extent, on the fugitive-slave law) showed that antislavery leaders, far from flouting the Constitution, were showing it a punctilious respect. Had they been disposed, as their opponents alleged, to ride roughshod over constitutional limitations, they would hardly have bothered with the question of the territories or the question of fugitive slaves." (Arthur Bestor, "State Sovereignty and Slavery," *Journal of the Illinois State Historical Society,* LIV [Summer 1961], 127.)

[23] The failure of the Republicans to mount a frontal attack upon slavery in the slaveholding states seemed to the Beards sufficient reason for treating the attack upon slavery as hardly more than a sham battle. Secession, they argued, was the southern planters' "response to the victory of a tariff and homestead party that proposed nothing more dangerous to slavery itself than the mere exclusion of the institution from the territories." (Beard, *Rise of American Civilization,* II, 37, see also 39–40.)

tinction, and the public mind would, as for eighty years past, believe that it was in the course of ultimate extinction. The crisis would be past.[24]

Whether or not slavery could have been brought to an end in this manner is a totally unanswerable question, but it requires no answer. The historical fact is that the defenders of slavery regarded the policy of containment as so dangerous to their interests that they interpreted it as signifying "that a war must be waged against slavery until it shall cease throughout the United States."[25] On the other hand, the opponents of slavery took an uncompromising stand in favor of this particular policy because it was the only one that the Constitution appeared to leave open. To retreat from it would be to accept as inevitable what Lincoln called "the perpetuity and nationalization of slavery."[26]

To understand the shaping effect of the Constitution upon the crisis, one must take seriously not only the ambiguities that contemporaries discovered in it, but also the features that all alike considered settled. The latter point is often neglected. Where constitutional understandings were clear and unambiguous, responsible leaders on both sides accepted without serious question the limitations imposed by the federal system. The most striking illustration has already been given. Antislavery leaders were willing to have written into the Constitution an absolute and perpetual ban upon congressional interference with slavery inside the slaveholding states. They were willing to do so because, as Lincoln said, they considered "such a provision to now be implied constitutional law," which might without objection be "made express, and irrevocable."[27]

Equally firm was the constitutional understanding that Congress had full power to suppress the foreign slave trade. On the eve of secession, to be sure, a few fire-eaters proposed a resumption of the importation of slaves. The true index of southern opinion, however, is the fact the Constitution of the Confederate States outlawed the foreign trade in terms far more explicit than any found in the Constitution of the United States.[28]

Far more surprising, to a modern student, is a third constitutional understanding that somehow held firm throughout the crisis. The Constitution grants Congress an unquestioned power "To regulate Commerce with foreign Nations, and among the several States, and with the Indian Tribes."[29] Employing this power, Congress had outlawed the foreign slave trade in 1808, with the general acquiescence that we have just noted. To anyone familiar with twentieth-century American constitutional

[24] First debate with Douglas, Ottawa, Ill., Aug. 21, 1858, *Collected Works of Lincoln,* ed. Basler *et al.,* III, 18 (italics of the original not reproduced here).

[25] "Declaration of the Immediate Causes which Induce and Justify the Secession of South Carolina from the Federal Union," Dec. 24, 1860, *Journal of the Convention of the People of South Carolina, Held in 1860, 1861 and 1862* (Columbia, S. C., 1862), 465.

[26] *Collected Works of Lincoln,* ed. Basler *et al.,* III, 18.

[27] First inaugural, Mar. 4, 1861, *ibid.,* IV, 270; see also above, notes 6–8.

[28] In the US Constitution the only reference to the slave trade is in a provision suspending until 1808 the power of Congress to prohibit "the Migration or Importation" of slaves. (Art. I, Sec. 9 [clause 1].) The power itself derives from the commerce clause (Art. I, Sec. 8 [clause 3]), and Congress is not required to use it. By contrast, the Confederate Constitution not only announced that the foreign slave trade "is hereby forbidden," but also went on to *require* its Congress to pass the necessary enforcement laws. (Constitution of the Confederate States, Art. I, Sec. 9 [clause 1]; text in Jefferson Davis, *The Rise and Fall of the Confederate Government* [2 vols., New York, 1881], I, 657.)

[29] US Constitution, Art. I, Sec. 8 [clause 3].

law, the commerce clause would seem to furnish an obvious weapon for use against the domestic slave trade as well. Since the 1890's the power of Congress to regulate interstate commerce has been directed successively against lotteries, prostitution, child labor, and innumerable other social evils that are observed to propagate themselves through the channels of interstate commerce.

The suppression of the domestic slave trade, moreover, would have struck a far more telling blow at slavery than any that could possibly have been delivered in the territories. Only the unhampered transportation and sale of slaves from the older seaboard regions can account for the creation of the black belt that stretched westward through the new Gulf States. By 1840 there were already as many slaves in Alabama and Mississippi together, as in Virginia. During the twenty years that followed, the number of slaves in the two Gulf States almost doubled, while the number of slaves in Virginia remained almost stationary.[30]

The migration of slaveholding families with the slaves they already possessed can account for only part of this change. The domestic slave trader was a key figure in the process. His operations, moreover, had the indirect effect of pouring money back into older slaveholding states like Virginia, where slavery as an economic system had seemed, in the days of the Revolution, on the verge of bankruptcy. Furthermore, a direct attack upon the domestic slave trade might well have aroused less emotional resentment than the attack actually made upon the migration of slaveholders to the territories, for the slave trader was a universally reprobated figure, the object not only of antislavery invective but even of southern distrust and aversion.

No serious and sustained effort, however, was ever made to employ against the domestic slave trade the power of Congress to regulate interstate commerce. The idea was suggested, to be sure, but it never received significant support from responsible political leaders or from public opinion. No party platform of the entire period, not even the comprehensive, detailed, and defiant one offered by the Liberty party of 1844, contained a clear-cut proposal for using the commerce power to suppress the interstate traffic in slaves. Public opinion seems to have accepted as virtually axiomatic the constitutional principle that Henry Clay (who was, after all, no strict constructionist) phrased as follows in the set of resolutions from which the Compromise of 1850 ultimately grew:

> Resolved, That Congress has no power to prohibit or obstruct the trade in slaves between the slaveholding States; but that the admission or exclusion of slaves brought from one into another of them, depends exclusively upon their own particular laws.[31]

Careful students of constitutional history have long been at pains to point out that the broad interpretation that John Marshall gave to the commerce clause in 1824 in

---

[30] In 1840 there were 448,743 slaves in Alabama and Mississippi, as against 448,987 in Virginia. In 1860 there were 871,711 slaves in the two Gulf States, as against only 490,865 in Virginia. During the same twenty years there was a net increase of 365,911 in the white population of the two Gulf States, and a net increase of 306,331 in the white population of Virginia. (US, Ninth Census [1870], I, Population, 3–8.)

[31] Last of the eight resolutions introduced in the Senate by Henry Clay, Congressional Globe, 31 Cong., 1 sess., 246 (Jan. 29, 1850). According to Clay himself, the resolution proposed no new legislation, but merely asserted "a truth, established by the highest authority of law in this country." He expected, he said, "one universal acquiescence." (Ibid.)

the notable case of *Gibbons* v. *Ogden*[32] represented a strengthening of federal power in only one of its two possible dimensions. The decision upheld the power of Congress to sweep aside every obstruction to the free flow of interstate commerce. Not until the end of the nineteenth century, however, did the commerce power begin to be used extensively for the purpose of regulation in the modern sense, that is to say, restrictive regulation. The concept of a "federal police power," derived from the commerce clause, received its first clear-cut endorsement from the Supreme Court in the Lottery Case,[33] decided in 1903. These facts are well known. Few scholars, however, have called attention to the dramatic illustration of the difference between nineteenth- and twentieth-century views of the Constitution that is afforded by the fact that the commerce clause was never seriously invoked in connection with the slavery dispute. This same fact illustrates another point as well: how averse to innovation in constitutional matters the antislavery forces actually were, despite allegations to the contrary by their opponents.

Various other constitutional understandings weathered the crisis without particular difficulty, but to catalogue them is needless. The essential point has been made. The clearly stated provisions of the Constitution were accepted as binding. So also were at least two constitutional principles that rested upon no specific written text, but were firmly ingrained in public opinion: the plenary authority of the slaveholding states over the institution within their boundaries and the immunity of the domestic slave trade to federal interference.

In the Constitution as it stood, however, there were certain ambiguities and certain gaps. These pricked out, as on a geological map, the fault line along which earthquakes were likely to occur, should internal stresses build up to the danger point.

Several such points clustered about the fugitive slave clause of the Constitution.[34] Clear enough was the principle that slaves might not secure their freedom by absconding into the free states. Three vital questions, however, were left without a clear answer. In the first place, did responsibility for returning the slaves to their masters rest with the states or the federal government? As early as 1842, the Supreme Court, in a divided opinion, placed responsibility upon the latter.[35] This decision brought to the fore a second question. How far might the free states go in refusing cooperation and even impeding the process of rendition? The so-called "personal liberty laws" of various northern states probed this particular constitutional question. Even South Carolina, originator of the doctrine of nullification, saw no inconsistency in its wrathful denunciation of these enactments, "which either nullify the Acts of Congress or render useless any attempt to execute them."[36] A third question arose in connection with the measures adopted by Congress to carry out the constitutional provision, notably the revised Fugitive Slave Act of 1850. Were the methods of enforcement prescribed by federal statute consistent with the procedural guarantees and underlying spirit of the Bill of Rights? From the twentieth-century viewpoint, this was perhaps the most profound of all the constitutional issues raised by the slavery dispute. It amounted to a direct confrontation between the philosophy of freedom and the incompatible philosophy of slavery. Important and disturbing though the

[32] 9 Wheaton 1 (1824).

[33] *Champion v. Ames*, 188 US Reports 321 (1903).

[34] US Constitution, Art. IV, Sec. 2 [clause 3].

[35] *Prigg v. Pennsylvania*, 16 Peters 539 (1842).

[36] South Carolina, "Declaration," Dec. 24, 1860, *Journal of the Convention*, 464.

issues were, the mandate of the fugitive slave clause was sufficiently clear and direct to restrain all but the most extreme leaders from outright repudiation of it.[37]

Of all the ambiguities in the written Constitution, therefore, the most portentous proved in fact to be the ones that lurked in the clause dealing with territory: "The Congress shall have Power to dispose of and make all needful Rules and Regulations respecting the Territory or other Property belonging to the United States."[38] At first glance the provision seems clear enough, but questions were possible about its meaning. Eventually they were raised, and when raised they turned out to have so direct a bearing upon the problem of slavery that they would not down. What did the Constitution mean by mingling both "Territory" and "other Property," and speaking first of the power "to dispose of" such property? Was Congress in reality given a power to govern, or merely a proprietor's right to make regulations for the orderly management of the real estate he expected eventually to sell? If it were a power to govern, did it extend to all the subjects on which a full-fledged state was authorized to legislate? Did it therefore endow Congress with powers that were not federal powers at all but municipal ones, normally reserved to the states? In particular, did it bestow upon Congress, where the territories were concerned, a police power competent to deal with domestic relations and institutions like slavery?

This chain of seemingly trivial questions, it will be observed, led inexorably to the gravest question of the day: the future of slavery in an impetuously expanding nation. On many matters the decisions made by territorial governments might be regarded as unimportant, for the territorial stage was temporary and transitional. With respect to slavery, however, the initial decision was obviously a crucial one. A single article of the Ordinance of 1787 had eventuated in the admission of one free state after another in the Old Northwest. The omission of a comparable article from other territorial enactments had cleared the way for the growth of a black belt of slavery from Alabama through Arkansas. An identical conclusion was drawn by both sides. The power to decide the question of slavery for the territories was the power to determine the future of slavery itself.

In whose hands, then, had the Constitution placed the power of decision with respect to slavery in the territories? This was, in the last analysis, the constitutional question that split the Union. To it, three mutually irreconcilable answers were offered.

The first answer was certainly the most straightforward. The territories were part of the "Property belonging to the United States." The Constitution gave Congress power to "make all needful Rules and Regulations" respecting them. Only a definite provision of the Constitution, either limiting this power or specifying exceptions to

---

[37] In 1844, to be sure, the Liberty party solemnly repudiated this specific obligation: "We hereby give it to be distinctly understood, by this nation and the world, that, as abolitionists, . . . we owe it to the Sovereign Ruler of the Universe, as a proof of our allegiance to Him, in all our civil relations and offices, whether as private citizens, or as public functionaries sworn to support the Constitution of the United States, to regard and to treat the [fugitive slave clause] of that instrument . . . as utterly null and void, and consequently as forming no part of the Constitution of the United States, whenever we are called upon, or sworn, to support it." (*National Party Platforms, 1840–1956,* ed. Kirk H. Porter and Donald B. Johnson [Urbana, Ill., 1956], 8.) Lincoln, on the other hand, solemnly reminded the nation in his first inaugural that public officials "swear their support to the whole Constitution—to this provision as much as to any other." (*Collected Works of Lincoln,* ed. Basler *et al.,* IV, 263.)

[38] US Constitution, Art. IV, Sec. 3 [clause 2].

it, could destroy the comprehensiveness of the grant. No such limitations or exceptions were stated. Therefore, Congress was fully authorized by the Constitution to prohibit slavery in any or all of the territories, or to permit its spread thereto, as that body, in exercise of normal legislative discretion, might decide.

This was the straightforward answer; it was also the traditional answer. The Continental Congress had given that answer in the Ordinance of 1787, and the first Congress under the Constitution had ratified it. For half a century thereafter the precedents accumulated, including the precedent of the Missouri Compromise of 1820. Only in the 1840's were these precedents challenged.

Because this was the traditional answer, it was (by definition, if you like) the conservative answer. When the breaking point was finally reached in 1860–1861 and four identifiable conflicting groups offered four constitutional doctrines, two of them accepted this general answer, but each gave it a peculiar twist.

Among the four political factions of 1860, the least well-organized was the group that can properly be described as the genuine conservatives. Their vehicle in the election of 1860 was the Constitutional Union party, and a rattletrap vehicle it certainly was. In a very real sense, however, they were the heirs of the old Whig party and particularly of the ideas of Henry Clay. Deeply ingrained was the instinct for compromise. They accepted the view just stated, that the power of decision with respect to slavery in a particular territory belonged to Congress. But they insisted that one additional understanding, hallowed by tradition, should likewise be considered constitutionally binding. In actually organizing the earlier territories, Congress had customarily balanced the prohibition of slavery in one area by the erection elsewhere of a territory wherein slaveholding would be permitted. To conservatives, this was more than a precedent; it was a constitutional principle. When, on December 18, 1860, the venerable John J. Crittenden offered to the Senate the resolutions summing up the conservative answer to the crisis, he was not in reality offering a new plan of compromise. He was, in effect, proposing to write into the Constitution itself the understandings that had governed politics in earlier, less crisis-ridden times. The heart of his plan was the re-establishment of the old Missouri Compromise line, dividing free territories from slave.[39] An irrepealable amendment was to change this from a principle of policy into a mandate of constitutional law.

That Congress was empowered to decide the question of slavery for the territories was the view not only of the conservatives, but also of the Republicans. The arguments of the two parties were identical, up to a point; indeed, up to the point just discussed. Though territories in the past had been apportioned between freedom and slavery, the Republicans refused to consider this policy as anything more than a policy, capable of being altered at any time. The Wilmot Proviso of 1846 announced, in effect, that the time had come to abandon the policy. Radical though the proviso may have been in a political sense, it was hardly so in a constitutional sense. The existence of a congressional power is the basic constitutional question. In arguing for the existence of such a power over slavery in the territories, the Republicans took the same ground as the conservatives. In refusing to permit mere precedent to hamper the discretion of Congress in the use of that power, they broke with the conservatives. But the distinction they made between power and discretion, that is, between constitutional law and political policy, was neither radical nor unsound.

One innovation did find a place in antislavery, and hence in Republican, con-

[39] *Congressional Globe,* 36 Cong., 2 sess., 114 (Dec. 18, 1860).

stitutional doctrine. Though precedent alone ought not to hamper the discretion of Congress, specific provisions of the Constitution could, and in Republican eyes did, limit and control that discretion. With respect to congressional action on slavery in the territories, so the antislavery forces maintained, the due process clause of the Fifth Amendment constituted such an express limitation. "Our Republican fathers," said the first national platform of the new party in 1856, "ordained that no person shall be deprived of life, liberty, or property, without due process of law." To establish slavery in the territories "by positive legislation" would violate this guarantee. Accordingly the Constitution itself operated to "deny the authority of Congress, of a Territorial Legislation [sic], of any individual, or association of individuals, to give legal existence to Slavery in any Territory of the United States." [40] The Free Soil platform of 1848 had summed the argument up in an aphorism: "Congress has no more power to make a SLAVE than to make a KING; no more power to institute or establish SLAVERY, than to institute or establish a MONARCHY." [41] As a doctrine of constitutional law, the result was this: the federal government had full authority over the territories, but so far as slavery was concerned, Congress might exercise this authority in only one way, by prohibiting the institution there.

The conservatives and the Republicans took the constitutional system as it stood, a combination of written text and historical precedent, and evolved their variant doctrines therefrom. By contrast, the two other factions of 1860—the northern Democrats under Stephen A. Douglas, and the southern Democrats whose senatorial leader was Jefferson Davis and whose presidential candidate was John C. Breckinridge—appealed primarily to constitutional theories above and beyond the written document and the precedents. If slogans are meaningfully applied, these two factions (each in its own way) were the ones who, in 1860, appealed to a "higher law."

For Douglas, this higher law was the indefeasible right of every community to decide for itself the social institutions it would accept and establish. "Territorial Sovereignty" (a more precise label than "popular sovereignty") meant that this right of decision on slavery belonged to the settlers in a new territory fully as much as to the people of a full-fledged state. At bottom the argument was one from analogy. The Constitution assigned responsibility for national affairs and interstate relations to the federal government; authority over matters of purely local and domestic concern were reserved to the states. So far as this division of power was concerned, Douglas argued, a territory stood on the same footing as a state. It might not yet have sufficient population to entitle it to a vote in Congress, but its people were entitled to self-government from the moment they were "organized into political communities." Douglas took his stand on what he regarded as a fundamental principle of American political philosophy: "that the people of every separate political community (dependent colonies, Provinces, and Territories as well as sovereign States) have an inalienable right to govern themselves in respect to their internal polity." [42]

Having thus virtually erased the constitutional distinction between a territory and a state—a distinction that was vital (as we shall see) to the state sovereignty inter-

[40] *National Party Platforms*, eds. Porter and Johnson, 27. This argument from the due process clause went back at least as far as the Liberty party platform of 1844. (*Ibid.*, 5.) It was reiterated in every national platform of an antislavery party thereafter: in 1848 by the Free Soil party, in 1852 by the Free Democrats, and in 1856 and 1860 by the Republicans. (*Ibid.*, 13, 18, 27, 32.)

[41] *Ibid.*, 13. Repeated in the Free Democratic platform of 1852. (*Ibid.*, 18.)

[42] Stephen A. Douglas, "The Dividing Line between Federal and Local Authority: Popular Sovereignty in the Territories," *Harper's Magazine*, XIX (Sept. 1859), 519–37, esp. 526.

pretation—Douglas proceeded to deal with the argument that since a territorial government was a creation of Congress, the powers it exercised were delegated ones, which Congress itself was free to limit, to overrule, or even to exercise through direct legislation of its own. He met the argument with an ingenious distinction. "Congress," he wrote, "may institute governments for the Territories," and, having done so, may "invest them with powers which Congress does not possess and can not exercise under the Constitution." He continued: "The powers which Congress may thus *confer* but can not *exercise,* are such as relate to the domestic affairs and internal polity of the Territory." [43] Their source is not to be sought in any provision of the written Constitution, certainly not in the so-called territorial clause,[44] but in the underlying principle of self-government.

Though Douglas insisted that the doctrine of popular sovereignty embodied "the ideas and principles of the fathers of the Revolution," his appeal to history was vitiated by special pleading. In his most elaborate review of the precedents (the article in *Harper's Magazine* from which quotations have already been taken), he passed over in silence the Northwest Ordinance of 1787, with its clear-cut congressional ban on slavery.[45] Douglas chose instead to dwell at length upon the "Jeffersonian Plan of government for the Territories," embodied in the Ordinance of 1784.[46] This plan, it is true, treated the territories as virtually equal with the member states of the Union, and thus supported (as against subsequent enactments) Douglas' plea for the largest measure of local self-government. When, however, Douglas went on to imply that the "Jeffersonian Plan" precluded, in principle, any congressional interference with slavery in the territories, he was guilty of outright misrepresentation. Jefferson's original draft (still extant in his own hand) included a forthright prohibition of slavery in all the territories.[47] The Continental Congress, it is true, refused at the time to adopt this particular provision, a fact that Douglas mentioned,[48] but there is no evidence whatever to show that they believed they lacked the power to do so. Three years later, the same body exercised this very power by unanimous vote of the eight states present.[49]

Disingenuousness reached its peak in Douglas' assertion that the Ordinance of

[43] *Ibid.,* 520–21.

[44] Douglas insisted that this clause referred "exclusively to property in contradistinction to persons and communities." (*Ibid.,* 528.)

[45] He likewise ignored all subsequent enactments of the same sort, save to register agreement with the dictum of the Supreme Court, announced in the Dred Scott opinion, that the Missouri Compromise had always been unconstitutional. (*Ibid.,* 530.)

[46] *Ibid.,* 525–26.

[47] Report to Congress, Mar. 1, 1784, and revised report, Mar. 22, 1784, *The Papers of Thomas Jefferson,* ed. Julian P. Boyd *et al.* (16 vols., Princeton, N. J., 1950–   ), VI, 604, 608.

[48] Douglas, "Federal and Local Authority," 526. The antislavery provision came to a vote in the Continental Congress on April 19, 1784, under a rule requiring the favorable vote of the majority of the states for adoption. Six states voted in favor of the provision, only three against it. One state was divided. Another state could not be counted, because a quorum of the delegation was not present, but the single delegate on the floor voted "aye." (*Journals of the Continental Congress,* ed. Worthington C. Ford *et al.* [34 vols., Washington, D. C., 1904–37], XXVI, 247.)

[49] *Ibid.,* XXXII, 343. This was the vote on July 13, 1787, adopting the Ordinance of 1787 with its antislavery article; only one member voted against the ordinance. There is no evidence of opposition to the antislavery article itself, which was added as an amendment in the course of the preceding debate.

1784 "stood on the statute book unrepealed and irrepealable . . . when, on the 14th day of May, 1787, the Federal Convention assembled at Philadelphia and proceeded to form the Constitution under which we now live."[50] Unrepealed the ordinance still was, and likewise unimplemented, but irrepealable it was not. Sixty days later, on July 13, 1787, Congress repealed it outright and substituted in its place the Northwest Ordinance,[51] which Douglas chose not to discuss.

Despite these lapses, Douglas was, in truth, basing his doctrine upon one undeniably important element in the historic tradition of American political philosophy. In 1860 he was the only thoroughgoing advocate of local self-determination and local autonomy. He could justly maintain that he was upholding this particular aspect of the constitutional tradition not only against the conservatives and the Republicans, but also (and most emphatically) against the southern wing of his own party, which bitterly repudiated the whole notion of local self-government, when it meant that the people of a territory might exclude slavery from their midst.

This brings us to the fourth of the parties that contested the election of 1860, and to the third and the last of the answers that were given to the question of where the Constitution placed the power to deal with slavery in the territories.

At first glance there would appear to be only two possible answers. Either the power of decision lay with the federal government, to which the territories had been ceded or by which they had been acquired; or else the decision rested with the people of the territories, by virtue of some inherent right of self-government. Neither answer, however, was acceptable to the proslavery forces. By the later 1850's they were committed to a third doctrine, state sovereignty.

The theory of state sovereignty takes on a deceptive appearance of simplicity in most historical accounts. This is because it is usually examined only in the context of the secession crisis. In that situation the corollaries drawn from the theory of state sovereignty were, in fact, exceedingly simple. If the Union was simply a compact among states that retained their ultimate sovereignty, then one or more of them could legally and peacefully withdraw from it, for reasons which they, as sovereigns, might judge sufficient. Often overlooked is the fact that secession itself was responsible for reducing the argument over state sovereignty to such simple terms. The right to secede was only one among many corollaries of the complex and intricate doctrine of the sovereignty of the states. In the winter and spring of 1860–1861, this particular corollary, naked and alone, became the issue on which events turned. Earlier applications of the doctrine became irrelevant. As they dropped from view, they were more or less forgotten. The theory of state sovereignty came to be regarded simply as a theory that had to do with the perpetuity of the Union.

The simplicity of the theory is, however, an illusion. The illusion is a consequence of reading history backward. The proslavery constitutional argument with respect to slavery in the territories cannot possibly be understood if the fifteen years of debate prior to 1860 are regarded simply as a dress rehearsal for secession. When applied to the question of slavery, state sovereignty was a positive doctrine, a doctrine of power, specifically, a doctrine designed to place in the hands of the slaveholding

---

[50] Douglas, "Federal and Local Authority," 526.

[51] *Journals of the Continental Congress,* ed. Ford *et al.,* XXXII, 343. As if anticipating Douglas' contention that the earlier ordinance was "irrepealable," the Congress that had adopted it not only repealed it, but declared it "null and void."

states a power sufficient to uphold slavery and promote its expansion *within* the Union. Secession might be an ultimate recourse, but secession offered no answer whatever to the problems of power that were of vital concern to the slaveholding states so long as they remained in the Union and used the Constitution as a piece of working machinery.

As a theory of how the Constitution should operate, as distinguished from a theory of how it might be dismantled, state sovereignty gave its own distinctive answer to the question of where the authority lay to deal with matters involving slavery in the territories. All such authority, the theory insisted, resided in the sovereign states. But how, one may well ask, was such authority to be exercised? The answer was ingenious. The laws that maintained slavery—which were, of course, the laws of the slaveholding states—must be given extraterritorial or extrajurisdictional effect.[52] In other words, the laws that established a property in slaves were to be respected, and if necessary enforced, by the federal government, acting as agent for its principals, the sovereign states of the Union.

At the very beginning of the controversy, on January 15, 1847, five months after the introduction of the Wilmot Proviso, Robert Barnwell Rhett of South Carolina showed how that measure could be countered, and proslavery demands supported, by an appeal to the *mystique* of the sovereignty of the several states:

> Their sovereignty, unalienated and unimpaired . . . , exists in all its plenitude over our territories; as much so, as within the limits of the States themselves. . . . The only effect, and probably the only object of their reserved sovereignty, is, that it secures to each State the right to enter the territories with her citizens, and settle and occupy them with their property—with whatever is recognised as property by each State. The ingress of the citizen, is the ingress of his sovereign, who is bound to protect him in his settlement.[53]

Nine years later the doctrine had become the dominant one in proslavery thinking, and on January 24, 1856, Robert Toombs of Georgia summed it up succinctly: "Congress has no power to limit, restrain, or in any manner to impair slavery: but, on the contrary, it is bound to protect and maintain it in the States where it exists, and wherever its flag floats, and its jurisdiction is paramount."[54] In effect, the laws of slavery were to become an integral part of the laws of the Union, so far as the territories were concerned.

Four irreconcilable constitutional doctrines were presented to the American people in 1860. There was no consensus, and the stage was set for civil war. The issues in which the long controversy culminated were abstruse. They concerned a seemingly minor detail of the constitutional system. The arguments that supported the various positions were intricate and theoretical. But the abstractness of constitutional issues has nothing to do, one way or the other, with the role they may happen to play at a moment of crisis. The sole question is the load that events have laid upon them. Thanks to the structure of the American constitutional system itself, the abstruse issue of slavery in the territories was required to carry the burden of well-nigh all the emotional drives, well-nigh all the political and economic tensions, and well-

---

[52] These terms were suggested, and their propriety defended, in my article, "State Sovereignty and Slavery," 128–31, 147.

[53] *Congressional Globe*, 29 Cong., 2 sess., Appendix, 246 (Jan. 15, 1847).

[54] Speech in Boston, reprinted in an appendix to Stephens, *Constitutional View*, I, 625–47, esp. 625.

nigh all the moral perplexities that resulted from the existence in the United States of an archaic system of labor and an intolerable policy of racial subjection. To change the metaphor, the constitutional question of legislative authority over the territories became, so to speak, the narrow channel through which surged the torrent of ideas and interests and anxieties that flooded down from every drenched hillside upon which the storm cloud of slavery discharged its poisoned rain.

2 / The Causes of the Civil War

Arthur Schlesinger, Jr.

Slavery is at least as venerable an explanation for the Civil War as are conflicting constitutional principles. If the constitutional structure of the United States molded the form of the sectional struggle, much of the actual content of the dispute consisted of passionate disagreement over black servitude.

Slavery had been introduced into British North America in the early seventeenth century and had spread throughout the English mainland colonies. By the eve of the Revolution it legally existed from Maine to Georgia and would soon cross the mountains into the Mississippi Valley with the first massive thrust of Americans westward.

Had the institution remained continental in scope, it obviously could not have become a bone of contention between the sections. But slavery had always been weaker in the North than in the South and was further weakened in both sections by the liberating ideology of the Revolution. By the opening of the nineteenth century, it had been partially extinguished everywhere north of the Ohio River and the Mason-Dixon line. By 1818, when Illinois, the last Northern state, officially outlawed it, slavery had become the "peculiar institution" of the American South, and the ground cleared for a bitter sectional battle.

For more than a century, historians have argued over the connection between slavery and the bloody events of 1861 to 1865. Once the war began, few Northerners doubted that it had been the cause of the conflict, although even at that time its exact link with the tumultuous event was controversial. Some men saw secession as the conspiracy of a militant "slavocracy" intent on destroying the Union to further a drive for power. Others emphasized the divergent economic interests of slave and free society. Still others claimed that intemperate agitators on both sides of the slavery question had driven the sections apart.

These, and still other versions of the slavery argument, were widely held at least until the early twentieth century. Then, in an era of growing nativism, sectional reconciliation, and increasing cynicism, historians found them less credible. As Arthur Schlesinger, Jr., notes, they were largely displaced by explanations that emphasized the failure of statesmanship or mass

Partisan Review, XVI, No. 10 (October 1949), 969–981. Reprinted by permission.

irrationality or the clash of economic interests. Slavery was not entirely ignored by these analyses. No one denied the underlying importance of the division of the nation into slave and free. What distinguished the newer schools from the old was their disregard of the moral dimension of the slavery struggle. Most nineteenth-century proponents of the view that slavery caused the war considered the peculiar institution evil, its destruction warranted, and the war itself a necessary and successful crusade for social justice. But as the new arguments of the "revisionists" were elaborated in the earlier years of this century, the moral component in the war virtually disappeared. Whether in sectional interpretations such as Frederick Jackson Turner's, or economic interpretations such as Charles Beard's, or largely political and psychological ones such as James G. Randall's and Avery Craven's, the war seemed a tragic mistake, or at best a brutal if inevitable act of aggression. Rather than a successful struggle to extirpate a retrograde, exploitive institution, it was either an avoidable catastrophe caused by agitators and incompetents or the triumph of naked power. The revisionists were not indifferent to injustice, but they were skeptical of moral professions and cynical about men's motives.

With onset of the 1940's, World War II, and the Civil Rights struggle, the current once more reversed. A new generation of historians, hostile to segregation and ashamed of the wrongs committed for generations against black Americans, were keenly alive to the antislavery origins of the Civil War. Holding racism immoral in their own day, they felt an intense horror toward slavery and saw in the sectional battle of 1861 to 1865 a great struggle for human freedom. Men such as Arthur Schlesinger, Jr., whose essay follows, insisted that we view the moral as well as other aspects of the war. Whatever the motives of the agitators and the politicians, the war achieved the immense and indispensable result of destroying slavery.

As if in response to Schlesinger's manifesto, more recently Staughton Lynd has sought to place slavery and the race issue at the very center of the nation's history from at least the beginnings of the federal government under the Constitution. According to Lynd, Northern capitalists and Southern planters "joined hands" in 1776 to win independence and again in 1787 to create the Constitution. They "then drifted, almost immediately into [a] sectional cold war" that culminated in the firing on Fort Sumter. This interpretation is clearly within the Beard-Turner mode; however, at the same time, as a young historian deeply committed to a radical reorientation of American society, Lynd has been strongly influenced by the fight for racial justice of the last decade. Clearly, the issues of the Civil War continue to be relevant to contemporary Americans.

For further reading: Staughton Lynd, "On Turner, Beard and Slavery," *Journal of Negro History*, XLVIII (October 1963); *Thomas Pressly, *Americans Interpret Their Civil War* (Princeton, N. J.: Princeton University Press, 1954); James G. Randall, "The Blundering Generation," *Mississippi Valley Historical Review*, XXVII (June 1940); Avery Craven, *The Repressible Conflict, 1830–1861* (Baton Rouge, La.: Louisiana State University Press, 1939) and "Slavery and the Civil War," *The Southern Review*, IV

(Autumn 1938); David Donald, "American Historians and the Causes of the Civil War," *South Atlantic Quarterly*, LIX (Summer 1960).

The Civil War was our great national trauma. A savage fraternal conflict, it released deep sentiments of guilt and remorse—sentiments which have reverberated through our history and our literature ever since. Literature in the end came to terms with these sentiments by yielding to the South in fantasy the victory it had been denied in fact; this tendency culminated on the popular level in *Gone with the Wind* and on the highbrow level in the Nashville cult of agrarianism. But history, a less malleable medium, was constricted by the intractable fact that the war had taken place, and by the related assumption that it was, in William H. Seward's phrase, an "irrepressible conflict," and hence a justified one.

As short a time ago as 1937, for example, even Professor James G. Randall could describe himself as "unprepared to go to the point of denying that the great American tragedy could have been avoided." Yet in a few years the writing of history would succumb to the psychological imperatives which had produced *I'll Take my Stand* and *Gone with the Wind*; and Professor Randall would emerge as the leader of a triumphant new school of self-styled "revisionists." The publication of two vigorous books by Professor Avery Craven—*The Repressible Conflict* (1939) and *The Coming of the Civil War* (1942)—and the appearance of Professor Randall's own notable volumes on Lincoln—*Lincoln the President: Springfield to Gettysburg* (1945), *Lincoln and the South* (1946), and *Lincoln the Liberal Statesman* (1947)—brought about a profound reversal of the professional historian's attitude toward the Civil War. Scholars now denied the traditional assumption of the inevitability of the war and boldly advanced the thesis that a "blundering generation" had transformed a "repressible conflict" into a "needless war."

The swift triumph of revisionism came about with very little resistance or even expressed reservations on the part of the profession. Indeed, the only adequate evaluation of the revisionist thesis that I know was made, not by an academic historian at all, but by that illustrious semi-pro, Mr. Bernard De Voto; and Mr. De Voto's two brilliant articles in *Harper's* in 1945 unfortunately had little influence within the guild. By 1947 Professor Allan Nevins, summing up the most recent scholarship in *Ordeal of the Union,* his able general history of the 1850's, could define the basic problem of the period in terms which indicated a measured but entire acceptance of revisionism. "The primary task of statesmanship in this era," Nevins wrote, "was to furnish a workable adjustment between the two sections, while offering strong inducements to the southern people to regard their labor system not as static but evolutionary, and equal persuasions to the northern people to assume a helpful rather than scolding attitude."

This new interpretation surely deserves at least as meticulous an examination as Professor Randall is prepared to give, for example, to such a question as whether or not Lincoln was playing fives when he received the news of his nomination in 1860. The following notes are presented in the interests of stimulating such an examination.

The revisionist case, as expounded by Professors Randall and Craven, has three main premises. First:

(1) that the Civil War was caused by the irresponsible emotionalization of poli-

tics far out of proportion to the real problems involved. The war, as Randall put it, was certainly not caused by cultural variations nor by economic rivalries nor by sectional differences; these all existed, but it was "stupid," as he declared, to think that they required war as a solution. "One of the most colossal of misconceptions" was the "theory" that "fundamental motives produce war. The glaring and obvious fact is the artificiality of war-making agitation." After all, Randall pointed out, agrarian and industrial interests had been in conflict under Coolidge and Hoover; yet no war resulted. "In Illinois," he added, "major controversies (not mere transient differences) between downstate and metropolis have stopped short of war."

Nor was slavery the cause. The issues arising over slavery were in Randall's judgment "highly artificial, almost fabricated. . . . They produced quarrels out of things that would have settled themselves were it not for political agitation." Slavery, Craven observed, was in any case a much overrated problem. It is "perfectly clear," he wrote, "that slavery played a rather minor part in the life of the South and of the Negro."

What then was the cause of war? "If one word or phrase were selected to account for the war," wrote Randall, ". . . it would have to be such a word as fanaticism (on both sides), misunderstanding, misrepresentation, or perhaps politics." Phrases like "whipped-up crisis" and "psychopathic case" adorned Randall's explanation. Craven similarly described the growing sense of sectional differences as "an artificial creation of inflamed minds." The "molders of public opinion steadily created the fiction of two distinct peoples." As a result, "distortion led a people into bloody war."

If uncontrolled emotionalism and fanaticism caused the war, how did they get out of hand? Who whipped up the "whipped-up crisis"? Thus the second revisionist thesis:

(2) that sectional friction was permitted to develop into needless war by the inexcusable failure of political leadership in the fifties. "It is difficult to achieve a full realization of how Lincoln's generation stumbled into a ghastly war," wrote Randall. ". . . If one questions the term 'blundering generation,' let him inquire how many measures of the time he would wish copied or repeated if the period were to be approached with a clean slate and to be lived again."

It was the politicians, charged Craven, who systematically sacrificed peace to their pursuit of power. Calhoun and Adams, "seeking political advantage," mixed up slavery and expansion; Wilmot introduced his "trouble-making Proviso as part of the political game"; the repeal clause in the Kansas-Nebraska Act was "the afterthought of a mere handful of politicians"; Chase's Appeal to the Independent Democrats was "false in its assertions and unfair in its purposes, but it was politically effective"; the "damaging" section in the Dred Scott decision was forced "by the political ambitions of dissenting judges." "These uncalled-for moves and this irresponsible leadership," concluded Craven, blew up a "crack-pot" crusade into a national conflict.

It is hard to tell which was under attack here—the performance of a particular generation or democratic politics in general. But, if the indictment "blundering generation" meant no more than a general complaint that democratic politics placed a premium on emotionalism, then the Civil War would have been no more nor less "needless" than any event in our blundering history. The phrase "blundering generation" must consequently imply that the generation in power in the fifties was *below* the human or historical or democratic average in its blundering. Hence the third revisionist thesis:

(3) that the slavery problem could have been solved without war. For, even if slavery were as unimportant as the revisionists have insisted, they would presumably admit that it constituted the real sticking point in the relations between the sections. They must show therefore that there were policies with which a non-blundering generation could have resolved the slavery crisis and averted war; and that these policies were so obvious that the failure to adopt them indicated blundering and stupidity of a peculiarly irresponsible nature. If no such policies could be produced even by hindsight, then it would seem excessive to condemn the politicians of the fifties for failing to discover them at the time.

The revisionists have shown only a most vague and sporadic awareness of this problem. "Any kind of sane policy in Washington in 1860 might have saved the day for nationalism," remarked Craven; but he did not vouchsafe the details of these sane policies; we would be satisfied to know about one.[1] Similarly Randall declared that there were few policies of the fifties he would wish repeated if the period were to be lived over again; but he was not communicative about the policies he would wish pursued. Nevins likewise blamed the war on the "collapse of American statesmanship," but restrained himself from suggesting how a non-collapsible statesmanship would have solved the hard problems of the fifties.

In view of this reticence on a point so crucial to the revisionist argument, it is necessary to reconstruct the possibilities that might lie in the back of revisionism. Clearly there could be only two "solutions" to the slavery problem: the preservation of slavery, or its abolition.

Presumably the revisionists would not regard the preservation of slavery as a possible solution. Craven, it is true, has argued that "most of the incentives to honest and sustained effort, to a contented, well-rounded life, might be found under slavery. . . . What owning and being owned added to the normal relationship of employer and employee is very hard to say." In describing incidents in which slaves beat up masters, he has even noted that "happenings and reactions like these were the rule [sic], not the exception." But Craven would doubtless admit that, however jolly this system might have been, its perpetuation would have been, to say the least, impracticable.

If, then, revisionism has rested on the assumption that the nonviolent abolition of slavery was possible, such abolition could conceivably have come about through internal reform in the South; through economic exhaustion of the slavery system in the South; or through some government project for gradual and compensated emancipation. Let us examine these possibilities.

(1) *The internal reform argument.* The South, the revisionists have suggested, might have ended the slavery system if left to its own devices; only the abolitionists spoiled everything by letting loose a hysteria which caused the southern ranks to close in self-defense.

This revisionist argument would have been more convincing if the decades of alleged antislavery feeling in the South had produced any concrete results. As one judicious southern historian, Professor Charles S. Sydnor, recently put it, "Although the abolition movement was followed by a decline of antislavery sentiment in the

---

[1] It is fair to say that Professor Craven seems in recent years to have modified his earlier extreme position; see his article "The Civil War and the Democratic Process," *Abraham Lincoln Quarterly,* June, 1947.

South, it must be remembered that in all the long years before that movement began no part of the South had made substantial progress toward ending slavery. . . . Southern liberalism had not ended slavery in any state."

In any case, it is difficult for historians seriously to suppose that northerners could have denied themselves feelings of disapproval over slavery. To say that there "should" have been no abolitionists in America before the Civil War is about as sensible as to say that there "should" have been no anti-Nazis in the 1930s or that there "should" be no anti-Communists today. People who indulge in criticism of remote evils may not be so pure of heart as they imagine; but that fact does not affect their inevitability as part of the historic situation.

Any theory, in short, which expects people to repress such spontaneous aversions is profoundly unhistorical. If revisionism has based itself on the conviction that things would have been different if only there had been no abolitionists, it has forgotten that abolitionism was as definite and irrevocable a factor in the historic situation as was slavery itself. And, just as abolitionism was inevitable, so too was the southern reaction against it—a reaction which, as Professor Clement Eaton has ably shown, steadily drove the free discussion of slavery out of the South. The extinction of free discussion meant, of course, the absolute extinction of any hope of abolition through internal reform.

(2) *The economic exhaustion argument.* Slavery, it has been pointed out, was on the skids economically. It was overcapitalized and inefficient; it immobilized both capital and labor; its one-crop system was draining the soil of fertility; it stood in the way of industrialization. As the South came to realize these facts, a revisionist might argue, it would have moved to abolish slavery for its own economic good. As Craven put it, slavery "may have been almost ready to break down of its own weight."

This argument assumed, of course, that southerners would have recognized the causes of their economic predicament and taken the appropriate measures. Yet such an assumption would be plainly contrary to history and to experience. From the beginning the South has always blamed its economic shortcomings, not on its own economic ruling class and its own inefficient use of resources, but on northern exploitation. Hard times in the 1850s produced in the South, not a reconsideration of the slavery system, but blasts against the North for the high prices of manufactured goods. The overcapitalization of slavery led, not to criticisms of the system, but to increasingly insistent demands for the reopening of the slave trade. Advanced southern writers like George Fitzhugh and James D. B. DeBow were even arguing that slavery was adapted to industrialism. When Hinton R. Helper did advance before the Civil War an early version of Craven's argument, asserting that emancipation was necessary to save the southern economy, the South burned his book. Nothing in the historical record suggests that the southern ruling class was preparing to deviate from its traditional pattern of self-exculpation long enough to take such a drastic step as the abolition of slavery.

(3) *Compensated emancipation.* Abraham Lincoln made repeated proposals of compensated emancipation. In his annual message to Congress of December 1, 1862, he set forth a detailed plan by which states, on an agreement to abolish slavery by 1900, would receive government bonds in proportion to the number of slaves emancipated. Yet, even though Lincoln's proposals represented a solution of the problem conceivably gratifying to the slaveholder's purse as well as to his pride, they got

nowhere. Two-thirds of the border representatives rejected the scheme, even when personally presented to them by Lincoln himself. And, of course, only the pressure of war brought compensated emancipation its limited hearing of 1862.

Still, granted these difficulties, does it not remain true that other countries abolished slavery without internal convulsion? If emotionalism had not aggravated the situation beyond hope, Craven has written, then slavery "might have been faced as a national question and dealt with as successfully as the South American countries dealt with the same problem." If Brazil could free its slaves and Russia its serfs in the middle of the nineteenth century without civil war, why could not the United States have done as well?

The analogies are appealing but not, I think, really persuasive. There are essential differences between the slavery question in the United States and the problems in Brazil or in Russia. In the first place, Brazil and Russia were able to face servitude "as a national question" because it was, in fact, a national question. Neither country had the American problem of the identification of compact sectional interests with the survival of the slavery system. In the second place, there was no race problem at all in Russia; and, though there was a race problem in Brazil, the more civilized folkways of that country relieved racial differences of the extreme tension which they bred in the South of the United States. In the third place, neither in Russia nor in Brazil did the abolition of servitude involve constitutional issues; and the existence of these issues played a great part in determining the form of the American struggle.

It is hard to draw much comfort, therefore, from the fact that other nations abolished servitude peaceably. The problem in America was peculiarly recalcitrant. The schemes for gradual emancipation got nowhere. Neither internal reform nor economic exhaustion contained much promise for a peaceful solution. The hard fact, indeed, is that the revisionists have not tried seriously to describe the policies by which the slavery problem could have been peacefully resolved. They have resorted instead to broad affirmations of faith: if only the conflict could have been staved off long enough, then somehow, somewhere, we could have worked something out. It is legitimate, I think, to ask how? where? what?—at least, if these affirmations of faith are to be used as the premise for castigating the unhappy men who had the practical responsibility for finding solutions and failed.

Where have the revisionists gone astray? In part, the popularity of revisionism obviously parallels that of *Gone with the Wind*— the victors paying for victory by pretending literary defeat. But the essential problem is why history should be so vulnerable to this literary fashion; and this problem, I believe, raises basic questions about the whole modern view of history. It is perhaps stating the issue in too portentous terms. Yet I cannot escape the feeling that the vogue of revisionism is connected with the modern tendency to seek in optimistic sentimentalism an escape from the severe demands of moral decision; that it is the offspring of our modern sentimentality which at once evades the essential moral problems in the name of a superficial objectivity and asserts their unimportance in the name of an invincible progress.

The revisionists first glided over the implications of the fact that the slavery system was producing a closed society in the South. Yet that society increasingly had justified itself by a political and philosophical repudiation of free society; southern thinkers swiftly developed the anti-libertarian potentialities in a social system whose cornerstone, in Alexander H. Stephens's proud phrase, was human bondage. In theory and in practice, the South organized itself with mounting rigor against ideas of human dignity and freedom, because such ideas inevitably threatened the basis of their own system. Professor Frank L. Owsley, the southern agrarian, has described inadvertently but accurately the direction in which the slave South was moving. "The abolitionists and their political allies were threatening the existence of the South as seriously as the Nazis threaten the existence of England," wrote Owsley in 1940; ". . . Under such circumstances the surprising thing is that so little was done by the South to defend its existence."

There can be no question that many southerners in the fifties had similar sentiments; that they regarded their system of control as ridiculously inadequate; and that, with the book burning, the censorship of the mails, the gradual illegalization of dissent, the South was in process of creating a real machinery of repression in order more effectively "to defend its existence." No society, I suppose, encourages criticism of its basic institutions. Yet, when a democratic society acts in self-defense, it does so at least in the name of human dignity and freedom. When a society based on bond slavery acts to eliminate criticism of its peculiar institution, it outlaws what a believer in democracy can only regard as the abiding values of man. When the basic institutions are evil, in other words, the effect of attempts to defend their existence can only be the moral and intellectual stultification of the society.

A society closed in the defense of evil institutions thus creates moral differences far too profound to be solved by compromise. Such a society forces upon every one, both those living at the time and those writing about it later, the necessity for a moral judgment; and the moral judgment in such cases becomes an indispensable factor in the historical understanding.

The revisionists were commendably anxious to avoid the vulgar errors of the post-Civil War historians who pronounced smug individual judgments on the persons involuntarily involved in the tragedy of the slave system. Consequently they tried hard to pronounce no moral judgments at all on slavery. Slavery became important, in Craven's phrase, "only as a very ancient labor system, probably at this time rather near the end of its existence"; the attempt to charge this labor system with moral meanings was "a creation of inflamed imaginations." Randall, talking of the Kansas-Nebraska Act, could describe it as "a law intended to subordinate the slavery question and hold it in *proper* proportion" (my italics). I have quoted Randall's even more astonishing argument that, because major controversies between downstate and metropolis in Illinois stopped short of war, there was reason to believe that the Civil War could have been avoided. Are we to take it that the revisionists seriously believe that the downstate-metropolis fight in Illinois—or the agrarian-industrial fight in the Coolidge and Hoover administrations—were in any useful sense comparable to the difference between the North and South in 1861?

Because the revisionists felt no moral urgency themselves, they deplored as fanatics those who did feel it, or brushed aside their feelings as the artificial product of emotion and propaganda. The revisionist hero was Stephen A. Douglas, who always thought that the great moral problems could be solved by sleight of hand. The phrase "northern man of southern sentiments," Randall remarked, was "said opprobriously . . . as if it were a base thing for a northern man to work with his southern fellows."

By denying themselves insight into the moral dimension of the slavery crisis, in other words, the revisionists denied themselves a historical understanding of the intensities that caused the crisis. It was the moral issue of slavery, for example, that gave the struggles over slavery in the territories or over the enforcement of the fugitive slave laws their significance. These issues, as the revisionists have shown with cogency, were not in themselves basic. But they were the available issues; they were almost the only points within the existing constitutional framework where the moral conflict could be faced; as a consequence, they became charged with the moral and political dynamism of the central issue. To say that the Civil War was fought over the "unreal" issue of slavery in the territories is like saying that World War II was fought over the "unreal" issue of the invasion of Poland. The democracies could not challenge fascism inside Germany any more than opponents of slavery could challenge slavery inside the south; but the extension of slavery, like the extension of fascism, was an act of aggression which made a moral choice inescapable.

Let us be clear what the relationship of moral judgment to history is. Every historian, as we all know in an argument that surely does not have to be repeated in 1949, imports his own set of moral judgments into the writing of history by the very process of interpretation; and the phrase "every historian" includes the category "revisionist." Mr. De Voto in his paraphrases of the revisionist position has put admirably the contradictions on this point: as for "moral questions, God forbid. History will not put itself in the position of saying that any thesis may have been wrong, any cause evil. . . . History will not deal with moral values, though of course the Republican radicals were, well, culpable." The whole revisionist attitude toward abolitionists and radicals, repeatedly characterized by Randall as "unctuous" and "intolerant," overflows with the moral feeling which is so virtuously excluded from discussions of slavery.

An acceptance of the fact of moral responsibility does not license the historian to roam through the past ladling out individual praise and blame: such an attitude would ignore the fact that all individuals, including historians, are trapped in a web of circumstance which curtails their moral possibilities. But it does mean that there are certain essential issues on which it is necessary for the historian to have a position if he is to understand the great conflicts of history. These great conflicts are relatively few because there are few enough historical phenomena which we can confidently identify as evil. The essential issues appear, moreover, not in pure and absolute form, but incomplete and imperfect, compromised by the deep complexity of history. Their proponents may often be neurotics and fanatics, like the abolitionists. They may attain a social importance only when a configuration of nonmoral factors—economic, political, social, military—permit them to do so.

Yet neither the nature of the context nor the pretensions of the proponents alter the character of the issue. And human slavery is certainly one of the few issues of whose evil we can be sure. It is not just "a very ancient labor system"; it is also a betrayal of the basic values of our Christian and democratic tradition. No historian can understand the circumstances which led to its abolition until he writes about it in its fundamental moral context. "History is supposed to understand the difference between a decaying economy and an expanding one," as Mr. De Voto well said, "between solvency and bankruptcy, between a dying social idea and one coming to world acceptance. . . . It is even supposed to understand implications of the difference between a man who is legally a slave and one who is legally free."

"Revisionism in general has no position," De Voto continues, "but only a vague

sentiment." Professor Randall well suggested the uncritical optimism of that sentiment when he remarked, "To suppose that the Union could not have been continued
or slavery outmoded without the war and without the corrupt concomitants of war
is hardly an enlightened assumption." We have here a touching afterglow of the
admirable nineteenth-century faith in the full rationality and perfectibility of man;
the faith that the errors of the world would all in time be "outmoded" (Professor
Randall's use of this word is suggestive) by progress. Yet the experience of the
twentieth century has made it clear that we gravely overrated man's capacity to solve
the problems of existence within the terms of history.

This conclusion about man may disturb our complacencies about human nature.
Yet it is certainly more in accord with history than Professor Randall's "enlightened"
assumption that man can solve peaceably all the problems which overwhelm him.
The unhappy fact is that man occasionally works himself into a logjam; and that the
logjam must be burst by violence. We know that well enough from the experience
of the last decade. Are we to suppose that some future historian will echo Professor
Nevins' version of the "failure" of the 1850s and write: "The primary task of statesmanship in the 1930s was to furnish a workable adjustment between the United
States and Germany, while offering strong inducements to the German people to
abandon the police state and equal persuasions to the Americans to help the Nazis
rather than scold them"? Will some future historian adapt Professor Randall's
formula and write that the word "appeaser" was used "opprobriously" as if it were a
"base" thing for an American to work with his Nazi fellow? Obviously this revisionism of the future (already foreshadowed in the work of Charles A. Beard) would
represent, as we now see it, a fantastic evasion of the hard and unpleasant problems
of the thirties. I doubt whether our present revisionism would make much more sense
to the men of the 1850s.

The problem of the inevitability of the Civil War, of course, is in its essence a problem devoid of meaning. The revisionist attempt to argue that the war could have been
avoided by "any kind of sane policy" is of interest less in its own right than as an expression of a characteristically sentimental conception of man and of history. And the
great vogue of revisionism in the historical profession suggests, in my judgment, ominous weaknesses in the contemporary attitude toward history.

We delude ourselves when we think that history teaches us that evil will be "outmoded" by progress and that politics consequently does not impose on us the necessity
for decision and for struggle. If historians are to understand the fullness of the social
dilemma they seek to reconstruct, they must understand that sometimes there is no escape from the implacabilities of moral decision. When social conflicts embody great
moral issues, these conflicts cannot be assigned for solution to the invincible march
of progress; nor can they be bypassed with "objective" neutrality. Not many problems
perhaps force this decision upon the historian. But, if any problem does in our history, it is the Civil War.

To reject the moral actuality of the Civil War is to foreclose the possibility of an
adequate account of its causes. More than that, it is to misconceive and grotesquely
to sentimentalize the nature of history. For history is not a redeemer, promising to
solve all human problems in time; nor is man capable of transcending the limitations
of his being. Man generally is entangled in insoluble problems; history is consequently a tragedy in which we are all involved, whose keynote is anxiety and frustration, not progress and fulfillment. Nothing exists in history to assure us that the

great moral dilemmas can be resolved without pain; we cannot therefore be relieved from the duty of moral judgment on issues so appalling and inescapable as those involved in human slavery; nor can we be consoled by sentimental theories about the needlessness of the Civil War into regarding our own struggles against evil as equally needless.

One must emphasize, however, that this duty of judgment applies to issues. Because we are all implicated in the same tragedy, we must judge the men of the past with the same forbearance and charity which we hope the future will apply toward us.

3 / The American Civil War: The Last Capitalist Revolution

Barrington Moore, Jr.

Primitive versions of an economic interpretation date from the Civil War itself. A few journalists and politicians in the early 1860's discussed the economic origins of sectional conflict. Karl Marx and Friedrich Engels proposed a class conflict analysis during the war that forms the basis for much subsequent Marxist interpretation. In a series of newspaper articles and letters, the founders of modern Socialism pictured the crisis of the Union as a confrontation of a bourgeois-capitalist North and a semifeudal, agrarian South. Owing to the peculiar development of the United States, the struggle between the progressive Northern capitalists and reactionary Southern planters had become sectionalized and converted into a war of two geographically compact entities. But the American experience was not a struggle for Southern national independence; it was really a fundamental class conflict comparable to the English Puritan Revolution and the European upheavals after 1789.

By the early years of the twentieth century, Charles A. Beard had begun his lifelong work of interpreting the American past in terms of conflicting economic interests. Beard's clearest statement on the Civil War appears in his sweeping and dramatic text, the *Rise of American Civilization* (1927). Beard was an American Progressive who argued that the Civil War was a "Second American Revolution" by which the industrial Northeast defeated the agrarian South and imposed on it and the unsuspecting West a settlement that assured the triumph of industrial capitalist values and interests. Unlike the Marxists who regarded the victory of the business classes as a progressive stage of the development toward Socialism, Beard's sympathies were with the agrarian interests, because he believed they represented "the people." Their defeat in 1865 represented a defeat for democracy.

Beard's views had their greatest vogue during the Great Depression when business leadership was discredited and class conflict was considered a serious threat. World War II restored class harmony and postwar affluence, and the Cold War with the Soviet Union placed a premium on consensus

From *Social Origins of Dictatorship and Democracy: Lord and Peasant in the Making of the Modern World* (Boston: The Beacon Press, 1966), Chap. III. Reprinted by permission of the Beacon Press. Copyright © 1966 by Barrington Moore, Jr.

in American values. Inevitably these events colored the way historians viewed the American past, and class struggle and economic explanations of historical events fell into disfavor. Then, with the advent of the "New Left" at the end of the 1960's, came a resurgence of Marxist interpretations. One of the most notable of these interpretations is Eugene Genovese's *The Political Economy of Slavery*, an interesting neo-Marxist analysis of the Old South. Although he is primarily intent on dissecting slavery and the slave economy, Genovese underscores the economic contradictions within the slave society and holds these contradictions and dilemmas responsible for the South's secession. A more precisely focused Marxist treatment of the origins of the Civil War is the following chapter from Barrington Moore, Jr.'s, book, *Social Origins of Dictatorship and Democracy*, a work that attempts to explain why some nations have achieved modernization via the democratic route while others have relied on totalitarian methods.

For further reading: Charles and Mary Beard, *The Rise of American Civilization* (New York: The Macmillan Company, 1927), II, Chaps. XVII, XVIII, XX; Algie M. Simons, *Class Struggles in America* (Chicago: C. H. Kerr and Company, 1903); Richard Enmale (ed.), *The Civil War in the United States* by Karl Marx and Frederick Engels (New York: International Publishers, 1937); * Eugene Genovese, *The Political Economy of Slavery* (New York: Pantheon Books, Inc., 1965); George O. Virtue, "Marxian Interpretation of the Civil War," *Nebraska History*, XXX (March 1949); * Louis Hacker, *The Triumph of American Capitalism* (New York: Columbia University Press, 1947).

PLANTATION AND FACTORY: AN INEVITABLE CONFLICT?

The main differences between the American route to modern capitalist democracy and those followed by England and France stem from America's later start. The United States did not face the problem of dismounting a complex and well-established agrarian society of either the feudal or the bureaucratic forms. From the very beginning commercial agriculture was important, as in the Virginian tobacco plantations, and rapidly became dominant as the country was settled. The political struggles between a precommercial landed aristocracy and a monarch were not part of American history. Nor has American society ever had a massive class of peasants comparable to those in Europe and Asia.[1] For these reasons one may argue that American history contains no revolution comparable to the Puritan and French Revolutions

---

[1] Like many such terms it is impossible to define the word peasantry with absolute precision because distinctions are blurred at the edges in social reality itself. A previous history of subordination to a landed upper class recognized and enforced in the laws, which, however, need not always prohibit movement out of this class, sharp cultural distinctions, and a considerable degree of *de facto* possession of the land, constitute the main distinguishing features of a peasantry. Hence Negro sharecroppers in the present-day South could be legitimately regarded as a class of peasants in American society.

nor, of course, the Russian and Chinese twentieth-century revolutions. Still there have been two great armed upheavals in our history, the American Revolution and the Civil War, the latter one of the bloodiest conflicts in modern history up to that time. Quite obviously, both have been significant elements in the way the United States became the world's leading industrial capitalist democracy by the middle of the twentieth century. The Civil War is commonly taken to mark a violent dividing point between the agrarian and industrial epochs in American history. Hence in this chapter I shall discuss its causes and consequences from the standpoint of whether or not it was a violent breakthrough against an older social structure, leading to the establishment of political democracy, and on this score comparable to the Puritan and French Revolutions. More generally I hope to show where it belongs in the genetic sequence of major historical upheavals that we can begin arbitrarily with the sixteenth-century peasant wars in Germany, that continues through the Puritan, French, and Russian Revolutions, to culminate in the Chinese Revolution and the struggles of our own time.

The conclusion, reached after much uncertainty, amounts to the statement that the American Civil War was the last revolutionary offensive on the part of what one may legitimately call urban or bourgeois capitalist democracy. Plantation slavery in the South, it is well to add right away, was not an economic fetter upon industrial capitalism. If anything, the reverse may have been true; it helped to promote American industrial growth in the early stages. But slavery was an obstacle to a political and social democracy. There are ambiguities in this interpretation. Those that stem from the character of the evidence are best discussed as the analysis proceeds. Others lie deeper and, as I shall try to show at the end of the chapter, would not disappear no matter what evidence came to light.

Aside from questions of space and time at the reader's disposal as well as the author's, there are objective reasons for passing over the American Revolution with but a few brief comments. Since it did not result in any fundamental changes in the structure of society, there are grounds for asking whether it deserves to be called a revolution at all. At bottom it was a fight between commercial interests in England and America, though certainly more elevated issues played a part as well. The claim that America has had an anticolonial revolution may be good propaganda, but it is bad history and bad sociology. The distinguishing characteristic of twentieth-century anticolonial revolutions is the effort to establish a new form of society with sub-stantial socialist elements. Throwing off the foreign yoke is a means to achieve this end. What radical currents there were in the American Revolution were for the most part unable to break through to the surface. Its main effect was to promote unification of the colonies into a single political unit and the separation of this unit from England.

The American Revolution can be trotted out from time to time as a good example of the American (or sometimes Anglo-Saxon) genius for compromise and concilia-tion. For this, the Civil War will not do; it cuts a bloody gash across the whole record. Why did it happen? Why did our vaunted capacity for settling our differ-ences fail us at this point? Like the problem of human evil and the fall of Rome for Saint Augustine, the question has long possessed a deep fascination for Ameri-can historians. An anxious if understandable concern seems to underlie much of the discussion. For some time, it often took the form of whether or not the war was avoidable. The present generation of historians has begun to show impatience with this way of putting the problem. To many the question seems merely a semantic one, since if either side had been willing to submit without fighting there would have been no war.[2] To call it a semantic problem dodges the real issue: why was there an unwillingness to submit on either side or both?

It may be helpful to put the question in less psychological terms. Was there in some objective sense a mortal conflict between the societies of the North and the South? The full meaning of this question will emerge more clearly from trying to answer it on the basis of specific facts than through theoretical discussion at this point. Essentially we are asking whether the institutional requirements for operating a plantation economy based on slavery clashed seriously at any point with the corresponding requirements for operating a capitalist industrial system. I assume that, in principle at any rate, it is possible to discover what these requirements really were in the same objective sense that a biologist can discover for any living organism the conditions necessary for reproduction and survival, such as specific kinds of nourishment, amounts of moisture, and the like. It should also be clear that the requirements or structural imperatives for plantation slavery and early industrial capitalism extend far beyond economic arrangements as such and certainly into the area of political institutions. Slave societies do not have the same political forms as those based on free labor. But, to return to our central question, is that any reason why they have to fight?

One might start with a general notion to the effect that there is an inherent conflict between slavery and the capitalist system of formally free wage labor. Though this turns out to be a crucial part of the story, it will not do as a general proposition from which the Civil War can be derived as an instance. As will appear shortly, cotton produced by slave labor played a decisive role in the growth not only of American capitalism but of English capitalism too. Capitalists had no objection to obtaining goods produced by slavery as long as a profit could be made by working them up and reselling them. From a strictly economic standpoint, wage labor and plantation slavery contain as much of a potential for trading and complementary political relationships as for conflict. We can answer our question with a provisional negative: there is no abstract general reason why the North and South had to fight. Special historical circumstances, in other words, had to be present in order to prevent agreement between an agrarian society based on unfree labor and a rising industrial capitalism.

For clues as to what these circumstances might have been, it is helpful to glance at a case where there was an agreement between these two types of subsocieties within a larger political unit. If we know what makes an agreement possible, we also know something about circumstances that might make it impossible. Once again the German record is helpful and suggestive. Nineteenth-century German history demonstrates quite clearly that advanced industry can get along very well with a form of agriculture that has a highly repressive system of labor. To be sure, the German Junker was not quite a slave owner. And Germany was not the United States. But

[2] Donald in the preface to Randall and Donald, *Civil War,* vi. Fully documented and with an excellent bibliography, this general survey provides a most helpful guide to the present state of historical opinion. An enlightening general survey of past discussions may be found in Beale, "Causes of the Civil War" (1946). Stampp, *Causes of the Civil War* (1959), provides an illuminating collection of contemporary and modern historical writings about the reasons for the war. In his editorial preface (p. vi) Stampp repeats Beale's observation, made more than a dozen years before, that the debate remains inconclusive while modern historians often merely repeat partisan themes set out at the time.

where precisely did the decisive differences lie? The Junkers managed to draw the independent peasants under their wing and to form an alliance with sections of big industry that were happy to receive their assistance in order to keep the industrial workers in their place with a combination of repression and paternalism. The consequence in the long run was fatal to democracy in Germany.

German experience suggests that, if the conflict between North and South had been compromised, the compromise would have been at the expense of subsequent democratic development in the United States, a possibility that, so far as I am aware, no revisionist historian has explored. It also tells us where we might look with profit. Why did Northern capitalists have no need of Southern "Junkers" in order to establish and strengthen industrial capitalism in the United States? Were political and economic links missing in the United States that existed in Germany? Were there other and different groups in American society, such as independent farmers, in the place of peasants? Where and how were the main groups aligned in the American situation? It is time now to examine the American scene more closely.

THREE FORMS OF AMERICAN CAPITALIST GROWTH

By 1860 the United States had developed three quite different forms of society in different parts of the country: the cotton-growing South; the West, a land of free farmers; and the rapidly industrializing Northeast.

The lines of cleavage and cooperation had by no means always run in these directions. To be sure, from the days of Hamilton and Jefferson there had been a tug-of-war between agrarians and urban commercial and financial interests. The expansion of the country westward made it seem for a moment, under President Jackson in the 1830s, that the principles of agrarian democracy, in practice an absolute minimum of central authority and a tendency to favor debtors over creditors, had won a permanent victory over those of Alexander Hamilton. Even in Jackson's own time, however, agrarian democracy had severe difficulties. Two closely related developments were to destroy it: the further growth of industrial capitalism in the Northeast and the establishment of an export market for Southern cotton.

Though the importance of cotton for the South is familiar, its significance for capitalist development as a whole is less well known. Between 1815 and 1860 the cotton trade exercised a decisive influence upon the rate of growth in the American economy. Up until about 1830 it was the most important cause of the growth of manufacturing in this country.[3] While the domestic aspect remained significant, cotton exports became an outstanding feature at about this time.[4] By 1849, sixty-four percent of the cotton crop went abroad, mainly to England.[5] From 1840 to the time of the Civil War, Great Britain drew from the Southern states four-fifths of all her cotton imports.[6] Hence it is clear that the plantation operated by slavery was no anachronistic excrescence on industrial capitalism. It was an integral part of this system and one of its prime motors in the world at large.

[3] North, *Economic Growth*, 67, 167, 189.
[4] North, *Economic Growth*, 194.
[5] Gates, *Farmer's Age*, 152.
[6] Randall and Donald, *Civil War*, 36.

In Southern society, the plantation and slave owners were a very small minority. By 1850 there may have been less than 350,000 slave owners in a total white population of about six million in the slaveholding areas.[7] With their families, the slaveholders numbered perhaps a quarter of the white population at the most. Even within this group, only a small minority owned most of the slaves: a computation for 1860 asserts that only seven percent of the whites owned nearly three-quarters of the black slaves.[8] The best land tended to gravitate into their hands as well as the substance of political control.[9]

This plantation-owning élite shaded off gradually into farmers who worked the land with a few slaves, through large numbers of small property owners without slaves, on down to the poor whites of the back country, whose agriculture was confined to a little lackadaisical digging in forlorn cornpatches. The poor whites were outside of the market economy; many of the smaller farmers were no more than on its periphery.[10] The more well-to-do farmers aspired to owning a few more Negroes and becoming plantation owners on a larger scale. The influence of this middling group may have declined after the Jacksonian era, though there is a whole school of Southern historians that tries to romanticize the yeomen and "plain folk" of the old South as the basis of a democratic social order.[11] That, I believe to be utter rubbish. In all ages and countries, reactionaries, liberals, and radicals have painted their own portraits of small rural folk to suit their own theories. The element of important truth behind this particular notion is that the smaller farmers in the South by and large accepted the political leadership of the big planters. Writers tinged with Marxism claim that this unity within the white caste ran counter to the real economic interests of the smaller farmers and came about only because fear of the Negro solidified the whites. This is possible but dubious. Small property owners in many situations follow the lead of big ones when there is no obvious alternative and when there is some chance of becoming a big property holder.

Since plantation slavery was the dominant fact of Southern life, it becomes necessary to examine the workings of the system to discover if it generated serious frictions with the North. One consideration we can dispose of rapidly. Slavery was almost certainly not on the point of dying out for internal reasons. The thesis is scarcely tenable that the war was "unnecessary" in the sense that its results would have come about sooner or later anyway by peaceful means and that therefore there was no real conflict. If slavery were to disappear from American society, armed force would be necessary to make it disappear.

On this question the best evidence actually comes from the North, where peaceful emancipation during the Civil War faced nearly insuperable difficulties. Union states that had slavery dragged their feet and expressed all sorts of apprehension when Lincoln tried to introduce a moderate scheme of emancipation with compensation for the former owners. Lincoln had to drop the plan.[12] The Emancipation Proclamation (January 1, 1863), as is well known, excluded slave states in the Union and those

[7] Randall and Donald, Civil War, 67.

[8] Cited by Hacker, Triumph of American Capitalism, 288. Randall and Donald's figures are close to these.

[9] Gates, Farmer's Age, 151, 152.

[10] North, Economic Growth, 130.

[11] Owsley, Plain Folk, 138–142. This study impresses me as folklorish sociology that misses nearly all the relevant political and economic issues.

[12] Randall and Donald, Civil War, 374, 375.

areas of the South within Union lines; that is, it emancipated slaves, in the words of a contemporary English observer (Earl Russell, ancestor of Bertrand Russell) only "where the United States authorities cannot exercise any jurisdiction."[13] If peaceful emancipation faced these difficulties in the North, those in the South scarcely require comment.

These considerations point strongly toward the conclusion that slavery was economically profitable. The author of a recent monograph argues cogently that slavery persisted in the South primarily because it was economically profitable. Southern claims that they were losing money on the operation he dismisses as part of the rationalizations through which Southern spokesmen tried to find a higher moral ground for slavery, an early version of the white man's civilizing burden. Ashamed to justify slavery on crude economic grounds, which would have made them resemble money-grubbing Yankees, Southerners preferred to claim that slavery was the natural form of human society, beneficial both to the slave and the master.[14] More recently still, two economists dissatisfied with the evidence upon which previous studies rested, mainly fragmentary and incomplete accounting records from early plantation activities, have tried to find the answer by examining more general statistical information. In order to find out whether slavery was more or less profitable than other enterprises, they have collected statistics about average slave prices, interest rates on prime commercial paper, costs of maintaining slaves, yields per prime field hand, cotton marketing costs, cotton prices, and other relevant facts. Though I am moderately skeptical about the reliability and representative value of the original statistics, their conclusions are in line with other considerations and about as close to reality as we are likely to get in this fashion. They, too, conclude that plantation slavery paid, moreover that it was an efficient system which developed in those regions best suited to the production of cotton and other specialized staples. Meanwhile, less productive areas in the South continued to produce slaves and export the increase to the main regions producing staple crops.[15]

To know that plantation slavery as a whole was a money-making proposition is important but insufficient. There were differences of time and place among the plantation owners that had significant political consequences. By the time the war broke out, plantation slavery had become a feature of the lower South. It had disappeared from the tobacco plantation before 1850 mainly because there were no great advantages to large-scale operations. In Maryland, Kentucky, and Missouri even the term "plantation" had become almost obsolete before the Civil War.[16] Around 1850 really fat pickings were to be had, chiefly in virgin areas; at first such places as Alabama and Mississippi provided such opportunities; after 1840, Texas. Even in virgin lands, the best way to make money was to sell out and move on before the soil gave out.[17]

To the extent that plantation slavery migrated from the South toward the West, it did create a serious political problem. Large parts of the West were still unsettled or sparsely settled. Though cotton growing had obvious limitations of climate

---

[13] Randall and Donald, *Civil War,* 380–381.

[14] Stampp, *Peculiar Institution,* esp chap IX.

[15] Conrad and Meyer, "Economics of Slavery," 95–130; see esp 97 for the general thesis.

[16] Nevins, *Ordeal,* I, 423.

[17] Gates, *Farmer's Age,* 143; Gray, *Agriculture in Southern United States,* II, chaps XXXVII, XXXVIII for more detail.

and soil, no one could be certain just what the limitations were. If slavery spread, the balance between slave and free states might be upset—something that mattered of course only if the difference between a society with slavery and one without mattered. By 1820 the problem was already acute, though a settlement was reached in the Missouri Compromise, balancing the entry of Missouri as a slave state by that of Maine as a free state. From then on the problem erupted intermittently. Solemn and statesmanlike political bargains hopefully settled the question for good, only to become unstuck after a short while. The issue of slavery in the territories, as partly settled areas that had not yet become states were called, played a major part in bringing on the war. The inherent uncertainty of the situation very likely magnified economic conflicts out of all proportion.

The migratory tendency of the plantation economy was important in other ways as well. As cotton planting declined in the old South, there was some inclination to adapt to the situation by breeding slaves. The extent to which this took place is difficult to determine. But there are at least moderately clear indications that it was not enough to meet the demand. The costs of slaves rose rather steadily from the early 1840s until the outbreak of the war. The price of cotton also tended to rise, but with much more marked fluctuations. After the financial panic of 1857, the price of cotton fell off, while the price of slaves continued to climb steeply.[18] Slaves could not be legally imported, and the blockade seems to have been moderately effective. Together with Southern talk about reopening the slave trade, talk that became fairly vigorous just before the final outbreak of hostilities, such evidence points in the direction of a serious labor shortage facing the plantation system. How serious? That is much harder to tell. Since capitalists are nearly always concerned about the prospect that labor may be short, it will be wise to treat Southern laments on this count with a touch of skepticism. It is very doubtful that the plantation system was about to expire from Northern economic strangulation.

So far the argument that the requirements of the plantation economy were a source of economic conflict with the industrial North does not turn out to be very persuasive. After all, was not the plantation owner just another capitalist? Nevins observes correctly: "A great plantation was as difficult to operate as a complicated modern factory, which in important respects it resembled. Hit-or-miss methods could not be tolerated; endless planning and anxious care were demanded."[19] Might it not therefore have been perfectly possible for the plantation owner to get along with his equally calculating capitalist brethren in the North? In my estimation it would have been quite possible had strictly rational economic calculations been the only issue. But, *pace* Max Weber, the rational and calculating outlook, the viewing of the world in terms of accounts and balances, can exist in a wide variety of societies, some of which may fight one another over other issues.[20] As we have already noticed in examining the French nobility, this type of outlook is not by itself enough to generate

[18] See table in Phillips, *Life and Labor,* 177, and the discussion of alleged overcapitalization of the labor force in Conrad and Meyer, "Economics of Slavery," 115–118. Even if the plantation owner was not caught in a net of his own making—Phillips's thesis that Conrad and Meyer combat—it seems clear enough, and not denied by these two authors, that many planters did face increasing labor costs. See further, Nevins, *Ordeal,* I, 480, for some contemporary views.

[19] *Ordeal,* I, 438.

[20] Nevins' description of the plantation is strikingly similar to the rational methods of calculation that prevailed, even without the use of writing, on the medieval English manor. See the vivid description in Bennett, *Life on the English Manor,* 186–192, esp 191.

an industrial revolution. Certainly it did not in the South, where urban growth, outside of a few major entrepôts such as New Orleans and Charleston, remained far behind that in the rest of the country. The South had a capitalist civilization, then, but hardly a bourgeois one. Certainly it was not based on town life. And, instead of challenging the notion of status based on birth, as did the European bourgeoisie when they challenged the right of aristocracies to rule, Southern planters took over the defense of hereditary privilege. Here was a real difference and a real issue.

The notion that all men were created equal contradicted the facts of daily experience for most Southerners, facts that they had themselves created for good and sufficient reasons. Under the pressure of Northern criticism and in the face of worldwide trends away from slavery, Southerners generated a whole series of doctrinal defenses for the system. Bourgeois conceptions of freedom, those of the American and the French Revolutions, became dangerously subversive doctrines to the South, because they struck at the key nerve of the Southern system, property in slaves. To grasp how a Southern planter must have felt, a twentieth-century Northerner has to make an effort. He would do well to ask how a solid American businessman of the 1960s might feel if the Soviet Union existed where Canada does on the map and were obviously growing stronger day by day. Let him further imagine that the communist giant spouted self-righteousness at the seams (while the government denied that these statements reflected true policy) and continually sent insults and agents across the border. Southern bitterness and anxiety were not just the expressions of a fire-eating minority. In his appeal for compromise among the sections Henry Clay, the most famous of Southern moderates, made this revealing and much quoted statement: "You Northerners are looking on in safety and security while the conflagration I have described is raging in the slave States. . . . In the one scale, then, we behold sentiment, sentiment, sentiment alone; in the other, property, the social fabric, life, and all that makes life desirable and happy." [21]

As industrial capitalism took more and more hold in the North, articulate Southerners looked about themselves to discover and emphasize whatever aristocratic and preindustrial traits they could find in their own society: courtesy, grace, cultivation, the broad outlook versus the alleged money-grubbing outlook of the North. Shortly before the Civil War, the notion took hold that the South produced in cotton the main source of American wealth upon which the North levied tribute. As Nevins points out, these ideas parallel physiocratic doctrines to the effect that the profits of manufacture and trade come out of the land.[22] Such notions crop up everywhere as industrialization takes hold, even to some extent without industrialization. The spread of commercial agriculture in a precommercial society generates various forms of romantic nostalgia, such as Athenian admiration of Sparta or that of late Republican Rome for the supposed virtues of early days.

Southern rationalizations contained a substantial portion of truth. Otherwise they would have been too hard to believe. There were differences between Northern and Southern civilizations of the type suggested. And Northerners did make profits, big ones too, in marketing cotton. There was no doubt a much larger proportion of sheer fake in the Southern rationalizations. The supposed aristocratic and precommercial or anticommercial virtues of the plantation aristocracy rested on the strictly commercial profits of slavery. To try to draw the line between what was true and

[21] Quoted after the version in Nevins, *Ordeal,* I, 267.
[22] Nevins, *Emergence of Lincoln,* I, 218.

what was fake is extremely difficult, probably impossible. For our purposes it is not necessary. Indeed to do so may darken counsel by obliterating important relationships. It is impossible to speak of purely economic factors as the main causes behind the war, just as it is impossible to speak of the war as mainly a consequence of moral differences over slavery. The moral issues arose from economic differences. Slavery was the moral issue that aroused much of the passion on both sides. Without the direct conflict of ideals over slavery, the events leading up to the war and the war itself are totally incomprehensible. At the same time, it is as plain as the light of the sun that economic factors created a slave economy in the South just as economic factors created different social structures with contrasting ideals in other parts of the country.

To argue thus is not to hold that the mere fact of difference somehow inevitably caused the war. A great many people in the South and the North either did not care about slavery or acted as if they did not care. Nevins goes so far as to assert that the election of 1859 showed that at least three-quarters of the nation still opposed radical proslavery and antislavery ideas at what was almost the last moment.[23] Even if his estimate exaggerates the strength of neutral sentiment, one of the most sobering and thought-provoking aspects of the Civil War is the failure of this mass of indifferent opinion to prevent it. It is also this substantial body of opinion that has led intelligent historians such as Beard to doubt the importance of slavery as an issue. That I hold to be an error, and a very serious one. Nevertheless the failure and collapse of moderation constitute a key part of the story, one on which those with Southern sympathies have shed valuable light. For a situation to arise in which war was likely to occur, changes had to take place in other parts of the country besides the South.

The main impetus behind the growth of Northern capitalism itself through the 1830s came, as we have seen, from cotton. During the next decade the pace of industrial growth accelerated to the point where the Northeast became a manufacturing region. This expansion ended the dependence of the American economy on a single agricultural staple. The Northeast and the West, which had in the past supplied the South with much of its food and continued to do so, became less dependent on the South and more on each other. Cotton remained important to the Northern economy, but ceased to dominate it.[24] Measured by the value of its product, cotton still ranked second among Northern manufactures in 1860. On the other hand, the North by this time produced a wide variety of manufactured goods, generally, to be sure, in small factories. A high proportion of the output was to meet the needs of an agricultural community: flour milling, lumber, boots and shoes, men's clothing, iron, leather, woolen goods, liquor, and machinery.[25] As we shall see in a moment, Northern manufacturing output came to be exchanged very heavily with the rapidly growing Western areas of the country.

Though the diminution of Northern dependence on Southern cotton and the development of some economic antagonisms were the dominant trends, there are others that deserve our attention. It will not do to overemphasize the divisive tendencies. In its relation to the plantation economy, the Northeast provided the services

---

[23] *Emergence of Lincoln*, II, 68.
[24] North, *Economic Growth*, 204–206.
[25] North, *Economic Growth*, 159–160.

of financing, transportation, insurance, and marketing.[26] The bulk of the cotton exported left from Northern ports, of which New York was the most important. Thus—and this was a source of friction—Southern incomes were spent very largely in the North to purchase services for the marketing of cotton, to buy what was needed on the plantation that could not be produced on the spot, and, no small item, for holidays from the heat by rich planters. Furthermore both the North and the West still sold manufactured goods and food to the South. The 1850s were the heyday of the Mississippi steamboat trade.[27] Most important of all, the relative efficiency of New England cotton textile mills in relation to foreign competition improved between 1820 and the outbreak of the war. From 1830 onward, they enabled the United States to enter the export market.[28] Had this push been stronger, Northern and Southern interests might have come closer, and conceivably the war might not have taken place. In any event Northern business interests were very far from bellicose advocates of a war of liberation or even war for the sake of the Union. An adequate study of the political attitudes and activities of Northern industrialists remains to be written.[29] It seems wide of the mark, however, to entertain any notion to the effect that Northern industrialists were itching to work the levers of the federal government on behalf of their purely economic interests.

What Northern capitalism needed from any government was the protection and legitimation of private property. It took some very special circumstances, however, to make the owners of Southern plantations and slaves appear as a threat to this institution. What Northern capitalists also wanted was a moderate amount of government assistance in the process of accumulating capital and operating a market economy: more specifically, some tariff protection, aid in setting up a transportation network (not all of which need be strictly ethical—though many of the big railway scandals came later), sound money, and a central banking system. Above all, the ablest Northern leaders wanted to be able to do business without bothering about state and regional frontiers. They were proud of being citizens of a large country, as of course others were too, and in the final crisis of secession reacted against the prospect of a balkanized America.[30]

The economic issue that aroused the most excitement was the tariff. Since American industry made remarkable progress under relatively low tariffs after 1846, the Northern demand for a higher tariff and Southern opposition to it look at first like a false issue, one that people quarrel about when they are really mad about something else. If Northern industry was booming, what earthly need did it have for political protection? The whole thesis that the South was trying to exercise some sort of veto on Northern

[26] North, *Economic Growth*, 68.

[27] North, *Economic Growth*, 103.

[28] North, *Economic Growth*, 161.

[29] As in the case of the French bourgeoisie prior to the bourgeois revolution, I have not found a good monograph that deals with the decisive political and economic questions. Foner, *Business and Slavery,* is very helpful as far as it goes but cannot be depended on for a general analysis because it concentrates on New York business interests closely connected with the South. The author is a well-known Marxist but in this study seems quite undogmatic. Industrial interests in Pennsylvania and Massachusetts need to be considered, but no adequate studies exist here either.

[30] On sentiment about the Union see Nevins, *Ordeal,* II, 242, and on contemporary editorial opinion Stampp, *Causes of Civil War,* 49–54. The selection from the Buffalo *Courier,* April 27, 1861 (pp. 52–53), is interesting for its protofascist language.

industrial progress begins to look very dubious as soon as one asks this question. A closer look at the time sequence dispels much of the mystery, though it will be necessary to discuss the point again after other relevant facts have appeared. There was a very rapid industrial growth after 1850. But trouble became acute in certain areas, iron and textiles, during the middle of the last decade before the war. By the end of 1854 stocks of iron were accumulating in every market of the world, and the majority of American mills had shut down. In textiles Lancashire had learned to produce low-priced goods more cheaply than New England mills; between 1846 and 1856 imports of printed dyed cotton leaped from 13 million yards to 114 million, those of plain calico from 10 million to 90 million. In 1857 came a serious financial crash. A tariff passed in that year, reflecting Southern pressures, gave no relief and actually reduced duties in these two areas.[31] Partly *because* they followed a period of prosperity and rapid growth, it seems, these events aroused sullen indignation in Northern industrial circles.

Northern capitalists also needed a reasonably abundant force of laborers, to work at wages they could afford to pay. Here was a serious sticking point. Free land to the west tended to draw off laborers, or at least many people thought so. And a major thrust behind the Jacksonian system had been a working coalition of planters, "mechanics" or workers, and free farmers on the one hand against finance and industry in the Northeast. Where then was the labor to come from? And how was Northern capital to break out of its economic and political encirclement? Northern political and economic leaders found a solution that enabled them to detach the Western farmers from the South and attach them to their own cause. Significant alterations in the economy and social structure of the West made these changes possible. It will be necessary to examine them more closely in a moment. But we may perceive their significance at once: by making use of these trends, the Northern capitalists freed themselves from any need to rely on Southern "Junkers" in order to keep labor in its place. Perhaps more than any other factor, these trends set the stage for armed conflict and aligned the combatants in such a way as to make possible a partial victory for human freedom.

Between the end of the Napoleonic Wars and the outbreak of the Civil War what is now known as the Midwest, but was then simply the West, grew from the land of pioneers to that of commercial farming. Indeed many of those who lived through the rugged age of the pioneer seem to have left it rapidly behind for others to praise. Marketable surpluses of food with which to buy a few necessities and still fewer amenities appeared quite early. Up until the 1830s the bulk of this surplus made its way South to feed the more specialized economy of that area, a trend that was to continue but lose its significance when the Eastern market became more important.[32] Thrown heavily still on their own resources, the small independent farmers in the first third of the nineteenth century were keen to wrest control over the public lands from politicians in Washington who either speculated in land on a large scale or were otherwise indifferent to the claims and needs of the West. They sought local autonomy sometimes at the expense of slim ties that connected them to the Union.[33]

---

[31] Nevins, *Emergence of Lincoln*, I, 225–226. In his final assessment of the causes of the war, Nevins deprecates the role of the tariff and economic factors generally. See *Emergence of Lincoln*, II, 465–466. More on this later, but at least on the tariff his argument seems to me contradictory.

[32] North, *Economic Growth*, 143, 67–68, 102.

[33] Beard and Beard, *American Civilization*, I, 535–536.

They were sympathetic to Andrew Jackson's attacks on the Eastern citadels of wealth and formed one wing of the superficially plebeian coalition that then ruled the country.

The growth of manufacturing in the East and the consequent rise in an effective demand for Western grain and meat changed this situation. Waves of expansion into the West in 1816–1818, 1832–1836, 1846–1847, and 1850–1856 reflect the increasing profitability of wheat, corn, and their derivatives.[34] From the 1830s onward, there was a gradual redirection of Western produce toward the Eastern seaboard. The "transportation revolution," the rise of canals and railroads, solved the problem of cross-mountain haulage, making possible a new outlet for Western farm products. The West's trade with the South did not decline absolutely, but actually increased. It was the proportions that shifted and helped to draw the West closer to the North.[35]

The demand for farm products gradually transformed the social structure and psychological attitudes of the West in such a way as to make a new alignment possible. The outlook of the early individualist and small-scale capitalist, characteristic of the Northeast, spread to the dominant upper stratum of the Western farmers. Under the technological conditions of the day, the family farm was an efficient social mechanism for the production of wheat, corn, hogs, and other marketable products.[36] "As quick transportation carried farm produce to eastern markets and brought ready cash in return," says Beard in one of the many passages that capture the essence of a basic social change in a few rolling sentences, "as railways, increasing population, and good roads lifted land values, brick and frame houses began to supplant log cabins; with deep political significance did prosperity tend to stifle the passion for 'easy money' and allay the ancient hatred for banks. At last beyond the mountains the chants of successful farmers were heard above the laments of poor whites. . . ."[37] A further consequence was the spread and deepening of antislavery sentiment, probably traceable to the rooting of the family farm as a successful commercial venture in Western soil.[38] There are puzzles here, since the family farm run without slaves was very common in the South as well, though it seems to have been less of a commercial affair and more of a subsistence undertaking. In any case it is clear that growing up outside the shadow of the plantation, and depending mainly on family members for labor, the Western system of farming generated considerable fear of competition from slavery.[39]

Before the middle of the nineteenth century, Southern planters who had once welcomed Western farmers as allies against the plutocracy of the North came to see the spread of independent farming as a threat to slavery and their own system. Earlier proposals to divide up Western lands on easy terms for the small farmer had antagonized Eastern seaboard areas that feared emigration and loss of labor, including even some in the South, such as North Carolina. Initiatives in support of free land

[34] North, Economic Growth, 136, and chart on 137.

[35] North, Economic Growth, 103, 140–141.

[36] North, Economic Growth, 154.

[37] Beard and Beard, American Civilization, I, 638. Nevins, Ordeal, II, chaps V, VI, tells essentially the same story.

[38] A map of the distribution of Abolition Societies in 1847 (Nevins, Ordeal, I, 141) shows them to be nearly as thick in Ohio, Indiana, Illinois as in Massachusetts.

[39] See Nevins, Ordeal, II, 123. As support for Seward was strong in rural New York (Nevins, Ordeal, I, 347), there is reason to suspect that the same sentiment was strong among Eastern farmers.

had come from the Southwest. With the establishment of commercial farming in Western areas, these alignments altered. Many Southerners dug in their heels against "radical" notions of giving land away to farmers that would "abolitionize" the area.[40] Plantation interests in the Senate killed the Homestead Bill of 1852. Eight years later President Buchanan vetoed a similar measure, to the delight of nearly all Southern congressmen who had been unable to prevent its passage.[41]

The response in the North to the changes in Western agrarian society was more complex. Northern mill owners were not automatically ready to give away land to anyone who asked for it, since doing so might merely diminish the number of willing hands likely to appear at the factory gates. Southern hostility to the West gave the North an opportunity for alliance with the farmer but one that Northerners were slow to grasp. The coalition did not become a political force until very late in the day, in the Republican platform of 1860 that helped to carry Lincoln to the White House, even though a majority of the country's voters opposed him. The rapprochement appears to have been the work of politicians and journalists rather than businessmen. The proposal to open up Western lands for the smaller settlers provided a way that a party attached to the interests of those with property and education could use to attract a mass following, especially among urban workers.[42]

The essence of the bargain was simple and direct: business was to support the farmers' demand for land, popular also in industrial working-class circles, in return for support for a higher tariff. "Vote yourself a farm—vote yourself a tariff" became Republican rallying cries in 1860.[43] In this fashion there came to be constituted a "marriage of iron and rye"—to glance once more at the German combination of industry and Junkers—but with Western family farmers, not landed aristocrats, and hence with diametrically opposite political consequences. On into the Civil War itself, there were objections to the wedding and calls for a divorce. In 1861 C. J. Vallandigham, an advocate of the small farmers, could still argue that "the planting South was the natural ally of the Democracy of the North and especially of the West," because the people of the South were an agricultural people.[44]

But these were voices from the past. What made the realignment possible, in addition to the changes in the character of Western rural society, were the specific circumstances of industrial growth in the Northeast. The existence of free land gave a unique twist to the relations between capitalists and workmen in the beginning stages of American capitalism, stages which in Europe were marked by the growth of violent radical movements. Here energies that in Europe would have gone into building trade unions and framing revolutionary programs went into schemes providing a free farm for every workman whether he wanted it or not. Such proposals sounded subversive to some contemporaries.[45] The actual effect of the Westward trek, nevertheless, was to strengthen the forces of early competitive and individualist capitalism by spreading the interest in property. Beard is too colorful when he speaks of the

[40] Zahler, *Eastern Workingmen*, 178–179, 188, esp note 1, p. 179.

[41] Beard and Beard, *American Civilization*, I, 691–692; more details on the attitudes in Congress in Zahler, *Eastern Workingmen*, chap IX.

[42] Zahler, *Eastern Workingmen*, 178.

[43] Beard and Beard, *American Civilization*, I, 692. For further information on the background of this rapprochement, which represented a significant reversal of earlier notions prevalent in the East, see Zahler, *Eastern Workingmen*, 185; Nevins, *Emergence of Lincoln*, I, 445.

[44] Beard and Beard, *American Civilization*, I, 677.

[45] Beard and Beard, *American Civilization*, I, 648–649.

Republicans' flinging the national domain to the hungry proletariat "as a free gift more significant than bread and circuses," after which the socialist movement sank into the background.[46] There was hardly time for all that to happen. The Civil War itself, as he remarks a few sentences later, cut short the drift to radicalism. And just how much help Western land may have been to the Eastern workingman before the Civil War remains a very open question. Already speculators were getting their hands on big chunks of it. Nor is it likely that the really poor in Eastern cities could leave the mine shaft and the factory bench to buy a small farm, equip it even with simple tools, and run it profitably, even if they benefited from the prospect that others might be able to do so.

Despite all these qualifications, there is a vital remnant of truth in the famous Turner thesis about the importance of the frontier for American democracy. It lies in the realignment of social classes and geographical sections that the open West produced at least temporarily. The link between Northern industry and the free farmers ruled out for the time being the classic reactionary solution to the problems of growing industrialism. Such an alignment would have been one of Northern industrialists and Southern planters against slaves, smaller farmers, and industrial workers. This is no abstract phantasy. Quite a few forces pushed in this direction before the Civil War, and it has been a prominent feature in the American political landscape ever since the end of Reconstruction. In the circumstance of midnineteenth-century American society, any peaceful solution, any victory of moderation, good sense, and democratic process, would have to be a reactionary solution.[47] It would have had to be at the expense of the Negro, as it was to be eventually anyway, unless one is ready to take seriously the notion that more than a hundred years ago both Northerners and Southerners were ready to abandon slavery and incorporate the Negro into American society. The link between Northern industry and Western farmers, long in preparation if sudden in its arrival, for the time being did much to eliminate the prospect of a straightforward reactionary solution of the country's economic and political problems on behalf of the dominant economic strata. For the very same reason, it brought the country to the edge of Civil War.

TOWARD AN EXPLANATION
OF THE CAUSES OF THE WAR

The alignment of the main social groupings in American society in 1860 goes a long way toward explaining the character of the war, or the issues that could and could not come to the surface—more bluntly what the war could be about. It tells us what was likely *if* there was to be a fight; by itself the alignment does not account very well for *why* there actually was a fight. Now that some of the relevant facts are before us it is possible to discuss with greater profit the question of whether or not there was an inherent mortal conflict between North and South.

Let us take up the economic requirements of the two systems one by one in order

---

[46] Beard and Beard, *American Civilization*, I, 751.

[47] Drawing on Latin-American experience, Elkins, *Slavery*, 194–197, presents a "catalogue of preliminaries" that might have helped to eliminate slavery without bloodshed: to bring the slaves under Christianity, safeguard the sanctity of the slave family, allow the slave use of free time to accumulate his purchase price. These measures still seem to me highly reactionary, a form of tokenism within the framework of slavery.

of 1) capital requirements, 2) requirements for labor, and 3) those connected with marketing the final product.

Though the point is open to some dispute, it is possible to detect definite expansionist pressures in the plantation economy. Fresh virgin lands were necessary for the best profits. Thus there was some pressure on the side of capital requirements. There are corresponding indications that the labor supply was tight. More slaves would have been very helpful. Finally, to make the whole system work, cotton, and to a lesser extent other staples, had to fetch a good price in the international market.

Northern industry required a certain amount of assistance from the government in what might be called overhead costs of capital construction and the creation of a favorable institutional environment: a transportation system, a tariff, and a sufficiently tight currency so that debtors and small men generally did not have undue advantages. (Some inflation, on the other hand, that would keep prices moving up would probably be rather welcome, then as now.) On the side of labor, industry needed formally free wage laborers though it is not easy to prove that free labor is necessarily superior to slavery in a factory system, except for the fact that someone has to have money in order to buy what industry produces. But perhaps that is a sufficient consideration. Finally, of course, growing industry did need an expanding market, provided still in those days quite largely by the agricultural sector. The West furnished much of this market and may be regarded as part of the North for the sake of this crude model.

It is difficult to perceive any really serious structural or "mortal" conflict in this analysis of the basic economic requirements, even though I have deliberately tried to bias the model in that direction. Here it is indispensable to remember, as revisionist historians of the Civil War correctly point out, that any large state is full of conflicts of interest. Tugging and hauling and quarreling and grabbing, along with much injustice and repression, have been the ordinary lot of human societies throughout recorded history. To put a searchlight on these facts just before a violent upheaval like the Civil War and call them the decisive causes of the war is patently misleading. To repeat, it would be necessary to show that compromise was impossible in the nature of the situation. From the analysis so far this does not seem to be the case. The most one can say along this line is that an increase in the area of slavery would have hurt the free farmers of the West badly. Although the areas where each kind of farming would pay were determined by climate and geography, no one could be sure where they were without trying. Still this factor alone does not seem sufficient to account for the war. Northern industry would have been as happy with a plantation market in the West as with any other, if such considerations were all that mattered, and the conflict could very likely have been ironed out. The other points of potential and actual conflict seem less serious. Northern requirements in the area of capital construction, the demand for internal improvements, a tariff, etc., cannot be regarded as threatening a crushing burden for the Southern economy. To be sure quite a number of marginal planters would have suffered, a factor of some importance. But if Southern society was run by the more successful planters, or if this influence was no more than very important, the smaller fry could have been sacrificed for the sake of a deal. In the question of slave labor versus free there was no real economic conflict because the areas were geographically distinct. Every account that I have come upon indicates that Northern labor was either lukewarm or hostile to the antislavery issue.

In addition to the conflict between free farmers in the West and the plantation system, about the strongest case one can make in strictly economic terms is that for the South secession was not an altogether unreasonable proposal mainly because the South did not need much that the North really had to offer. In the short run the North could not buy much more cotton than it did already. The most that the North could have offered would have been to reopen the slave trade. There was talk about taking over Cuba for slavery, and even some desultory action. As quite recent events have shown, under other circumstances such a move might be an extremely popular one in all parts of the country. At that time it seems to have been both impractical and impolitic.

To sum up, the strictly economic issues were very probably negotiable. Why, then, did the war happen? What was it about? The apparent inadequacy of a strictly economic explanation—I shall argue in a moment that the fundamental causes were still economic ones—has led historians to search for others. Three main answers are distinguishable in the literature. One is that the Civil War was fundamentally a moral conflict over slavery. Since large and influential sections of the public in both the North and the South refused to take a radical position either for or against slavery, this explanation runs into difficulties, in effect the ones that Beard and others tried to circumvent in their search for economic causes. The second answer tries to get around both sets of difficulties by the proposition that *all* the issues were really negotiable and that the blunderings of politicians brought on a war that the mass of the population in the North and in the South did not want. The third answer amounts to an attempt to push this line of thought somewhat further by analyzing how the political machinery for achieving consensus in American society broke down and allowed the war to erupt. In this effort, however, historians tend to be driven back toward an explanation in terms of moral causes.[48]

Each of the explanations, including that stressing economic factors, can marshal a substantial body of facts in its support. Each has hit at a portion of the truth. To stop at this observation is to be satisfied with intellectual chaos. The task is to relate these portions of the truth to each other, to perceive the whole in order to understand the relationship and significance of partial truths. That such a search is endless, that the discovered relations are themselves only partial truths, does not mean that the search ought to be abandoned.

To return to the economic factors, it is misleading, if at times necessary, to take them separately from others with the traditional labels political, moral, social, etc. Similarly, it is a necessity for the sake of comprehensible exposition to break the issues down one by one in some other series—such as slavery as such, slavery in the territories, tariff, currency, railroads and other internal improvements, the alleged Southern tribute to the North. At the same time, the breakdown into separate categories partially falsifies what it describes because individual people were living

---

[48] Nevins stresses moral causes at the same time that he reports most people were unconcerned about them, a paradox that, as far as I can see, he does not directly confront. See *Emergence of Lincoln*, II, 462–471, for his general explanation; on the widespread desire for peace, ibid., 63, 68. But Nevins does give much factual material helpful in trying to resolve the paradox. For a succinct statement of the thesis that the politicians were responsible, see the extract from Randall's *Lincoln the Liberal Statesman*, reprinted in Stampp, *Causes of the Civil War*, 83–87. Nichols, *Disruption of American Democracy*, and Craven, *Growth of Southern Nationalism*, present versions of the third thesis. No one author, it should be noted, presents a pure version or a lawyer's brief for a specific explanation. It is a matter of emphasis, but very strong emphasis.

through all these things at once, and persons who were apathetic about one issue could become excited about another. As the connection among issues became apparent, the concern spread among articulate people. Even if each individual issue had been negotiable, a debatable point, collectively and as a unit they were almost impossible to negotiate. And they were a unit, and so perceived by more than a few contemporaries, because they were manifestations of whole societies.

Let us begin the analysis afresh with this viewpoint in mind. Primarily for economic and geographical reasons, American social structure developed in different directions during the nineteenth century. An agrarian society based on plantation slavery grew up in the South. Industrial capitalism established itself in the Northeast and formed links with a society based on farming with family labor in the West. With the West, the North created a society and culture whose values increasingly conflicted with those of the South. The focal point of the difference was slavery. Thus we may agree with Nevins that moral issues were decisive. But these issues are incomprehensible without the economic structures that created and supported them. Only if abolitionist sentiment had flourished in the South, would there be grounds for regarding moral sentiments as an independent factor in their own right.

The fundamental issue became more and more whether the machinery of the federal government should be used to support one society or the other. That was the meaning behind such apparently unexciting matters as the tariff and what put passion behind the Southern claim that it was paying tribute to the North. The question of power at the center was also what made the issue of slavery in the territories a crucial one. Political leaders knew that the admission of a slave state or a free one would tip the balance one way or another. The fact that uncertainty was an inherent part of the situation due to unsettled and partly settled lands to the West greatly magnified the difficulties of reaching a compromise. It was more and more necessary for political leaders on both sides to be alert to any move or measure that might increase the advantages of the other. In this larger context, the thesis of an attempted Southern veto on Northern progress makes good sense as an important cause of the war.

This perspective also does justice, I hope, to the revisionist thesis that it was primarily a politician's war, perhaps even an agitator's war, if the terms are not taken to be merely abusive epithets. In a complex society with an advanced division of labor, and especially in a parliamentary democracy, it is the special and necessary task of politicians, journalists, and only to a somewhat lesser extent clergymen to be alive and sensitive to events that influence the distribution of power in society. They are also the ones who provide the arguments, good and bad alike, both for changing the structure of society and for maintaining things as they are. Since it is their job to be alert to potential changes, while others keep on with the all-absorbing task of making a living, it is characteristic of a democratic system that politicians should often be clamorous and intensify division. The modern democratic politician's role is an especially paradoxical one, at least superficially. He does what he does so that most people do not have to worry about politics. For that same reason he often feels it necessary to arouse public opinion to dangers real and unreal.

From this standpoint too, the failure of modern opinion to halt the drift to war becomes comprehensible. Men of substance in both North and South furnished the core of moderate opinion. They were the ones who in ordinary times are leaders in their own community—"opinion makers," a modern student of public opinion would be likely to call them. As beneficiaries of the prevailing order, and mainly interested in making money, they wanted to suppress the issue of slavery rather than seek structural reforms, a very difficult task in any case. The Clay-Webster Compromise of 1850 was a victory for this group. It provided for stricter laws in the North about the return of fugitive slaves and for the admission of several new states to the union: California as a free state, New Mexico and Utah at some future date with or without slavery as their constitutions might provide at the time of admission.[49] Any attempt to drag the slavery issue out into the open and seek a new solution made large numbers of these groups cease being moderates. That is what happened when Senator Stephen A. Douglas put an end to the Compromise of 1850 only four years later by reopening the question of slavery in the territories. Through proposing in the Kansas-Nebraska Act that the settlers decide the issue for themselves one way or the other, he converted, at least for the time being, wide sections of Northern opinion from moderation to views close to abolitionism. In the South, his support was not much more than lukewarm.[50]

By and large the moderates had the usual virtues that many people hold are necessary to make democracy work: willingness to compromise and see the opponent's viewpoint, a pragmatic outlook. They were the opposite of doctrinaires. What all this really amounted to was a refusal to look facts in the face. Trying mainly to push the slavery issue aside, the moderates were unable to influence or control the series of events generated by the underlying situation.[51] Crises such as the struggles

[49] On social groupings that supported the Compromise in the South, see Nevins, *Ordeal,* I, 315, 357, 366, 375. On 357 he remarks, "the . . . largest element was a body of moderates . . . who believed both in Southern Rights and the Union, but hoped they could be reconciled." In other words, they wanted to have their cake and eat it too. On general reactions and those in the North, see Nevins, *Ordeal,* I, 346, 293–294, 348; more detail on selected Northern business reaction in Foner, *Business and Slavery,* chaps 2–4. Excitement about fugitive slaves in both the North and the South seems to have been greatest in states where the problem was least likely to occur. But it was Clay and Webster who provided the evidence for this thesis. See Nevins, *Ordeal,* I, 384.

[50] On reactions to Douglas's proposal in the North and the South see Nevins, *Ordeal,* II, 121, 126–127, 133–135, 152–154, 156–157. A sympathetic treatment of Douglas may be found in Craven, *Coming of the Civil War,* esp 325–331, 392–393. On the Kansas-Nebraska affair Craven makes a plausible case for the thesis that dishonest Northern politicians stirred up slavery as a false issue. On the Lincoln-Douglas debates he argues that Lincoln's own high-sounding moral ambiguities had the effect of making Douglas appear thoroughly indifferent to moral issues. This treatment is diametrically opposite to that in Nevins. Commenting on Douglas's action in reopening the issue of slavery by the Kansas-Nebraska bill, Nevins remarks (*Ordeal,* II, 108), "When indignation welled up like the ocean lashed by a hurricane, he [Douglas] was amazed. The fact that the irresistible tidal forces in history are moral forces always escapes a man of dim moral perceptions." This is commencement oratory, not history. Successful political leaders have to be morally ambiguous in their efforts to cope with conflicting moral forces. Subsequent historians make the politicians that win into moral heroes. Generally Nevins does not succumb to such nonsense.

[51] During the winter of 1858–1859 plans were afoot in the South to create a new party, characterized by Nevins, *Emergence of Lincoln,* II, 59, as "a conservative, national, Union-exalting party which should thrust aside the slavery issue, denounce all secessionists, push a broad program of internal improvements, and on constructive grounds overthrow the Democrats." It drew on men of substance, political leaders, journalists, tried to appeal to small farmers versus big slaveholders, but made hardly any dent. During the last phase, when secessionists were in charge of events, the main opposition seems to have come from those who had direct trade connections

over "bleeding Kansas," the financial panic of 1857, John Brown's melodramatic attempt to put himself at the head of a slave insurrection, and many others eroded the moderate position, leaving its members increasingly disorganized and confused. The practicality that tries to solve issues by patiently ignoring them, an attitude often complacently regarded as the core of Anglo-Saxon moderation, revealed itself as totally inadequate. An attitude, a frame of mind, without a realistic analysis and program is not enough to make democracy work even if a majority share this outlook. Consensus by itself means little; it depends what the consensus is about.

Finally, as one tries to perceive American society as a whole in order to grasp the causes and meaning of the war, it is useful to recall that searching for the sources of dissension necessarily obscures a major part of the problem. In any political unity that exists for a long time, there must be causes to produce the unity. There have to be reasons why men seek accommodation for their inevitable differences. It is difficult to find a case in history where two different regions have developed economic systems based on diametrically opposite principles and yet remained under a central government that retained real authority in both areas. I cannot think of any.[52] In such a situation there would have to be very strong cohesive forces to counteract the divisive tendencies. Cohesive forces appear to have been weak in the midnineteenth century in the United States, though there is always the risk of exaggerating their weakness because the Civil War did happen.

Trade is an obvious factor that can generate links among various sections of a country. The fact that Southern cotton went mainly to England is almost certainly a very important one. It meant that the link with the North was so much the weaker. English partiality to the Southern cause during the war itself is well known. But it will not do to put too much weight on the direction of trade as an aspect of disunity. As pointed out earlier, Northern mills were beginning to use more cotton. When the Western market fell off sharply after the crash of 1857, New York merchants relied for a time more heavily on their Southern connections.[53] In a word, the situation in trade was changing; had the war been averted, historians who look first for economic causes would have had no difficulty in finding an explanation.

Though the fact that cotton still linked the South with England more than with the North was significant, two other aspects of the situation may have been more important. One has already been mentioned: the absence of any strong radical working-

---

with the North, i.e., merchants and professional men in some Southern ports, and the smaller farmers. See Nevins, *Emergence of Lincoln*, II, 322, 323, 324, 326. New York business circles blew hot and cold. After being vigorous defenders of the Compromise of 1850, they turned nearly abolitionist over Douglas's Kansas-Nebraska action, reversing themselves again shortly afterward. As Foner remarks (*Business and Slavery*, 138), "Ever since 1850, the great majority of New York merchants had operated under the illusion that the sectional struggle would right itself in time if 'politicians and fanatics' would only leave the controversial incidents alone." This desire to dodge the issues seems to be the one constant theme in their outlook. Excitement was bad for business. On October 10, 1857, the *Herald* predicted (Foner, *Business and Slavery*, 140–141): "The nigger question must give way to the superior issues of a safe currency, sound credits, and solid and permanent basis of security upon which all the varied commercial and business interests of the country may repose." On this platform, at least, moderates North and South could agree. In time it became the one upon which the Civil War and its aftermath were liquidated.

[52] The British Commonwealth may be the most obvious candidate. Its breakup into independent units in the last fifty years supports the above generalization.

[53] Foner, *Business and Slavery*, 143.

class threat to industrial capitalist property in the North. Secondly, the United States had no powerful foreign enemies. In this respect, the situation was entirely different from that facing Germany and Japan, who both experienced their own versions of political modernization crises somewhat later, 1871 in Germany, 1868 in Japan. For this combination of reasons, there was not much force behind the characteristic conservative compromise of agrarian and industrial élites. There was little to make the owners of Northern mills and Southern slaves rally under the banner of the sacredness of property.

To sum up with desperate brevity, the ultimate causes of the war are to be found in the growth of different economic systems leading to different (but still capitalist) civilizations with incompatible stands on slavery. The connection between Northern capitalism and Western farming helped to make unnecessary for a time the characteristic reactionary coalition between urban and landed élites and hence the one compromise that could have avoided the war. (It was also the compromise that eventually liquidated the war.) Two further factors made compromise extremely difficult. The future of the West appeared uncertain in such a way as to make the distribution of power at the center uncertain, thus intensifying and magnifying all causes of distrust and contention. Secondly, as just noted, the main forces of cohesion in American society, though growing stronger, were still very weak.

THE REVOLUTIONARY IMPULSE AND ITS FAILURE

About the Civil War itself, it is unnecessary to say more than a few words, especially since the most important political event, the Emancipation Proclamation, has already been mentioned. The war reflected the fact that the dominant classes in American society had split cleanly in two, much more cleanly than did the ruling strata in England at the time of the Puritan Revolution or those in France at the time of the French Revolution. In those two great convulsions, divisions within the dominant classes enabled radical tendencies to boil up from the lower strata, much more so in the case of the French Revolution than in England. In the American Civil War there was no really comparable radical upsurge.

At least in major outline the reasons are easy to see: American cities were not teeming with depressed artisans and potential *sans-culottes*. Even if only indirectly, the existence of Western lands reduced the explosive potential. In the second place, the materials for a peasant conflagration were lacking. Instead of peasants at the bottom of the heap, the South had mainly black slaves. Either they could not or they would not revolt. For our purpose it does not matter which. Though there were sporadic slave outbreaks, they had no political consequences. No revolutionary impulse came from that quarter.[54]

What there was in the way of a revolutionary impulse, that is, an attempt to alter by force the established order of society, came out of Northern capitalism. In the group known as the Radical Republicans, abolitionist ideals fused with manufacturing interests to ignite a brief revolutionary flash that sputtered and went out in a mire

[54] The well-known Marxist scholar Aptheker collects these instances in his *American Negro Slave Revolts,* chap XV.

of corruption. Though the Radicals were a thorn in Lincoln's side during the war, he was able to fight the war to a successful military conclusion mainly on the basis of preserving the Union, that is, without any serious offensive against Southern property rights. For a brief time, about three years after the end of the fighting, 1865–1868, the Radical Republicans held power in the victorious North and mounted an offensive against the plantation system and the remnants of slavery.

Leading members of this group perceived the war as a revolutionary struggle between a progressive capitalism and a reactionary agrarian society based on slavery. To the extent that the conflict between the North and the South really had such a character, a conflict some of whose most important struggles came after the actual fighting stopped, this was due to the Radical Republicans. From the perspective of a hundred years later, they appear as the last revolutionary flicker that is strictly bourgeois and strictly capitalist, the last successors to medieval townsmen beginning the revolt against their feudal overlords. Revolutionary movements since the Civil War have been either anticapitalist, or fascist and counterrevolutionary if in support of capitalism.

From abolitionist ideologues and Free Soil radicals, a small band of Republican politicians took over the conception of slavery as an anachronistic "remnant of a dying world of 'baron and serf—noble and slave.' " The Civil War itself they perceived as an opportunity to root out and destroy this oppressive anachronism in order to rebuild the South in the image of the democratic and progressive North, based on "free speech, free toil, schoolhouses, and ballot boxes." Though his public statements were somewhat milder, the leader of the Radical Republicans in the House of Representatives, Thaddeus Stevens, wrote privately to his law partner during the year that what the country needed was someone in power (i.e., *not* Lincoln) "with sufficient grasp of mind, and sufficient moral courage, to treat this as a radical revolution, and remodel our institutions. . . . It would involve the desolation of the South as well as emancipation, and a repeopling of half the Continent. . . ." What put steam behind this movement and lifted it out of the realm of noisy talk was the fact that it coincided with the interests of crucial segments of Northern society.[55] One was the infant iron and steel industry of Pennsylvania. Another was a set of railroad interests. Stevens acted as a Congressional go-between for both of these interests, from each of whom he received cash favors in accord with prevailing political morals.[56] The Radical Republicans also received substantial support from Northern labor. Even though Northern workers were very cool to abolitionist propaganda, fearing Negro competition and regarding New England abolitionists as hypocritical representatives of the mill owners, they were enthusiastic about Radical conceptions of tariff protection and going slow on the contraction of inflated Northern currency.[57] Financial and commercial interests, on the other hand, were unenthusiastic about the Radicals. After the war, principled Radicals turned against the "plutocracy of the North."[58]

Thus the Radical offensive did not represent a united capitalist offensive on the plantation system. It was a combination of workers, industrialists, and some railroad

---

[55] See the excellent study by Shortreed, "The Antislavery Radicals," 65–87, esp 68–69, 77, from which the remarks in quotations are taken.
[56] Current, *Old Thad Stevens*, 226–227, 312, 315–316.
[57] See Rayback, "American Workingman and Antislavery Crusade," 152–163.
[58] Sharkey, *Money, Class and Party*, 281–282, 287–289.

interests at the time of its greatest power. Still it would not be amiss to label it entrepreneurial and even progressive capitalism; it attracted the main creative (and philistine) forces that Veblen later liked in American society and repelled those that he disliked: snobbish financiers who made their money by selling instead of doing. In Thaddeus Stevens and his associates, this combination had skilled political leadership and sufficient minor intellectual talent to provide a general strategy. Radicals had an explanation of where society was heading and how they could take advantage of this fact. For them the Civil War was at least potentially a revolution. Military victory and Lincoln's assassination, which they welcomed with scarcely disguised joy, gave them a brief opportunity to try to make it a real one.

Thaddeus Stevens again provided the analysis as well as the day-to-day political leadership. Essentially his strategy amounted to capturing the machinery of the federal government for the benefit of the groups for which he was spokesman. To do so it was necessary to change Southern society lest the old type of plantation leadership return to Congress and frustrate the move. Out of this necessity came what little revolutionary impulse there was to the whole struggle. Stevens had enough sociological insight to see what the problem was and to cast about for a possible remedy, as well as enough nerve to make a try.

In his speeches of 1865 Stevens presented to the general public and to Congress a surprisingly coherent analysis and program of action. The South had to be treated as a conquered people, not as a series of states that had somehow left the Union and were now to be welcomed back. "The foundation of their institutions both political, municipal, and social *must* be broken up and *relaid,* or all our blood and treasure have been spent in vain. This can only be done by treating and holding them as a conquered people." [59] They should not be allowed to return, he asserted, "until the Constitution shall have been so amended as to make it what its framers intended; and so as to secure perpetual ascendency to the party of the Union," that is, the Republicans. [60]

If the Southern states were not "reconstructed"—the revealing euphemism for revolution from above has passed from contemporary usage into all subsequent histories—they might easily overwhelm the North, Stevens calculated carefully and openly, and thus enable the South to win the peace after losing the war. [61]

Out of these considerations came the program to rebuild Southern society from top to bottom. Stevens wanted to break the power of the plantation owners by confiscating estates over two hundred acres, "even though it drive (the Southern) nobility into exile." In this way, he argued, citing statistics, the federal government would obtain enough land to give each Negro household some forty acres. [62] "Forty acres and a mule" became in time the catchword slogan to discredit the supposedly utopian hopes of the newly freed Negroes. But the Radical Republicans were no utopians, not even Stevens. The demand for sweeping land reform reflected realistic awareness that nothing else would break the power of the planters. These had already set about to recover the substance of their old power by other means, something they were able to do because the Negroes were economically helpless. All this, at least a few Radicals

---

[59] Speech of September 6, 1865, in Lancaster, Pennsylvania, as given in Current, *Old Thad Stevens,* 215.

[60] *Reconstruction, Speech, December 18, 1865,* p. 5.

[61] *Reconstruction, Speech, December 18, 1865,* p. 5.

[62] Speech of September 6, 1865, in Current, *Old Thad Stevens,* 215.

saw quite clearly. And there are indications that dividing up the old plantations to give the Negroes small farms was feasible. In 1864 and 1865, Northern military authorities made two experiments along these lines in order to take care of the troublesome problem of thousands of destitute Negroes. They turned over confiscated and abandoned lands to more than 40,000 Negroes who are said to have been successful in working the land as small farmers until President Johnson returned the estates to their former white owners.[63] Still the experience of slavery was scarcely one to prepare Negroes to manage their own affairs as small rural capitalists. Stevens was aware of this and felt that the Negroes would need supervision by his friends in Congress for a long time to come. At the same time he saw that, without minimal economic security and minimal political rights, including the right to vote, they could do little for themselves or for Northern interests.[64]

In a nutshell, the Radical version of reconstruction came down to using the North's military power to destroy the plantation aristocracy and create a facsimile of capitalist democracy by ensuring property and voting rights for the Negroes. In the light of Southern conditions at the time, it was indeed revolutionary. A century later, the movement for civil rights for the Negroes seeks no more than this, indeed not quite all that, since the economic emphasis remains muted. If being ahead of the times is revolutionary, Stevens was that. Even sympathetic Northerners professed shock. Horace Greeley, editor of the *New York Tribune,* long sympathetic to the abolitionist cause, wrote in response to Stevens's speech of September 6, 1865, ". . . we protest against any warfare on Southern property . . . because the wealthier class of Southerners, being more enlightened and humane than the ignorant and vulgar, are less inimicable to the blacks." [65] Greeley's misgivings give a hint of what was to come when men of substance North and South were to bury their differences and, by another famous compromise, leave the Negroes to make what they could of their freedom.

It is not surprising therefore that defeat came soon to the Radicals, or more precisely to what was radical in their program, as soon as it encountered Northern property interests. The Radicals were unable to force confiscation into the reconstruction acts of 1867 against the wishes of more moderate Republicans. In the House, Stevens's "40 acres" measure received only 37 votes.[66] Influential Northern sentiment was in no mood to tolerate an outright attack on property, not even Rebel property and not even in the name of capitalist democracy. The *Nation* warned that "A division of rich men's lands amongst the landless . . . would give a shock to our whole social and political system from which it would hardly recover without the loss of liberty." The failure of land reform was a decisive defeat and removed the heart of the Radical program. Without land reform the rest of the program could be no more

[63] Stampp, *Reconstruction,* 123, 125–126.

[64] "Without the right of suffrage in the late slave States (I do not speak of the free States,) I believe the slaves had far better been left in bondage."—*Reconstruction, Speech, December 8, 1865,* pp. 6, 8.

[65] Quoted from the issue of September 12, 1865, by Current, *Old Thad Stevens,* 216–217. Greeley also criticized Stevens for failing to include a suffrage plank in this speech, which he did in the later one, mainly it seems in response to pressure from Senator Charles Sumner of Massachusetts. I have not tried to present differences of opinion within Radical ranks, but have concentrated on Stevens as its most revolutionary figure, as well as its most influential day-to-day strategist when the movement was at its height.

[66] Current, *Old Thad Stevens,* 233.

than palliatives or irritants, depending on one's viewpoint. To say that this failure cleared the way for the eventual supremacy of Southern white landholders and other propertied interests may nevertheless be an exaggeration.[67] The Radicals had never even really managed to bar the way. Their failure at this moment revealed the limits American society imposed upon the revolutionary impulse.

In the absence of confiscation and redistribution of land, the plantation system recovered by means of a new system of labor. At first there were attempts with wage labor. These failed, at least partly because Negroes were inclined to draw their wages in slack months and abscond when the cotton had to be picked. Hence there was a widespread turn toward sharecropping which gave the planters superior control of their labor force. The change was significant. As we shall see in due course, share-cropping in many parts of Asia has constituted one way of extracting a surplus from the peasant through economic rather than political methods, though the latter are often necessary to buttress the former. Hence it is instructive to see fundamentally similar forms appear in America without the prior existence of a peasantry.

The country merchant gave a local twist to the American situation, though similar devices occurred also in China and elsewhere. The country merchant was often the large planter. By making advances of groceries to tenant and sharecropper, charging much higher rates for them than ordinary retail prices, he kept control of the work force. Tenants and sharecroppers could trade at no other store, since they had credit at no other and were usually short of cash.[68] In this fashion economic bonds replaced those of slavery for many Negroes. How much real improvement, if any, the change meant is very difficult to say. But it would be a mistake to hold that plantation owners prospered greatly under the new system. The main effect appears to have been to make the South even more of a one-crop economy than before, as banker pressed planter, and planter pressed cropper to grow crops that could be quickly turned to cash.[69]

Political recovery proceeded along with economic recovery, reenforcing each other rather than in any simple relationship of cause and effect. There is no need to re-count here the political twistings and turnings of the successors to the antebellum ruling groups in the South as they sought for political leverage, though it is worth noticing that "scalawags"—white collaborationists they might be called today—included numerous planters, merchants, and even industrial leaders.[70] A good deal of violence, perhaps deprecated by the better elements, though skepticism is in order here, helped to put the Negroes "in their place" and reestablish overall white supremacy.[71] Meanwhile industrialists and railroad men were becoming increasingly influential in Southern affairs.[72] In a word, moderate men of substance were return-ing to power, authority, and influence in the South, as they were in the North as well. The stage was being set for an alliance of these across the former battle lines. It was consummated formally in 1876 when the disputed Hayes-Tilden election was settled by allowing the Republican Hayes to take office in return for removing the

[67] See the excellent account in Stampp, *Reconstruction*, 128–130; the quotation from the *Nation* occurs on 130.

[68] See Shannon, *American Farmers' Movements*, 53 for a succinct description.

[69] Randall and Donald, *Civil War*, 549–551.

[70] Randall and Donald, *Civil War*, 627–629, sketches these maneuvers.

[71] Randall and Donald, *Civil War*, 680–685.

[72] Woodward, *Reunion and Reaction*, 42–43. Chapter II provides a first-rate analysis of the whole process of moderate recovery.

remnants of the Northern occupational regime. Under attack from radical agrarians in the West and radical labor in the East, the party of wealth, property, and privilege in the North was ready to abandon the last pretense of upholding the rights of the propertyless and oppressed Negro laboring class.[73] When Southern "Junkers" were no longer slaveholders and had acquired a larger tincture of urban business and when Northern capitalists faced radical rumblings, the classic conservative coalition was possible. So came Thermidor to liquidate the "Second American Revolution."

THE MEANING OF THE WAR

Was it a revolution? Certainly not in the sense of a popular uprising against oppressors. To assess the meaning of the Civil War, to place it in a history that is still being made, is just as difficult as to account for its cause and course. One sense of revolution is a violent destruction of political institutions that permits a society to take a new course. After the Civil War, industrial capitalism advanced by leaps and bounds. Clearly that was what Charles Beard had in mind when he coined the famous phrase, "the Second American Revolution." But was the burst of industrial capitalist growth a consequence of the Civil War? And how about the contribution to human freedom that all but the most conservative associate with the word revolution? The history of the Fourteenth Amendment, prohibiting the states from depriving any person of life, liberty, or property, epitomizes the ambiguity on this score. As every educated person knows, the Fourteenth Amendment has done precious little to protect Negroes and a tremendous amount to protect corporations. Beard's thesis that such was the original intent of those who drafted the amendment has been rejected by some.[74] That in itself is trivial. About the consequence, there is no doubt. Ultimately the way one assesses the Civil War depends on the assessment of freedom in modern American society and the connection between the institutions of advanced industrial capitalism and the Civil War. Another whole book would scarcely serve to argue these issues. I shall do no more than try to sketch a few of the more important considerations.

Certain very important political changes did accompany and follow the Northern victory. They may be summed up in the remark that the federal government became a series of ramparts around property, mainly big property, and an agency to execute the biblical pronouncement, "To him that hath shall be given." First among the ramparts was the preservation of the Union itself, which meant, as the West filled up after the war, one of the largest domestic markets of the world. It was also a market protected by the highest tariff to date in the nation's history.[75] Property received protection from state governments with unsound inclinations through the Fourteenth Amendment. Likewise the currency was put on a sound footing through the national banking system and the resumption of specie payments. Whether such

---

[73] Woodward, *Reunion and Reaction*, 36–37.

[74] Randall and Donald, *Civil War*, 583; see also 783–784 for a review of the literature.

[75] The Morrill Tariff of 1861 was the beginning of a sharp upward climb in tariffs. It raised average tariff rates from 20 percent of value to 47 percent, more than double the rates prevailing in 1860. Designed at first to raise revenues for the wartime Union treasury, it established protectionism deeply in American economic policies. The acts of 1883, 1890, 1894, and 1897 granted even more protection. See Davis and others, *American Economic History*, 322–323.

measures hurt the Western farmers as much as was once supposed is dubious; there are indications that they were doing quite well during the war and for some time afterward.[76] At any rate they received some compensation through the opening of the public domain in the West (Homestead Act of 1862), though it is on this score that the federal government became an agency of the biblical statement just quoted. Railroads received huge grants, and disposal of public domains also formed the basis of great fortunes in timber and mining. Finally, as a compensation to industry that might lose laborers in this fashion the federal government continued to hold open the doors to immigration (Immigration Acts of 1864). As Beard puts it, "All that two generations of Federalists and Whigs had tried to get was won within four short years, and more besides." [77] "Four short years" is a rhetorical exaggeration; some of these measures were also part of Reconstruction (1865–1876), and the resumption of specie payment did not take place until 1879. But that is a small matter, since Reconstruction was definitely a part of the whole struggle. If one looks back and compares what happened with the planter program of 1860: federal enforcement of slavery, no high protective tariffs, no subsidies nor expensive tax-creating internal improvements, no national banking and currency system,[78] the case for a victory of industrial capitalism over the fetters of the plantation economy, a victory that required blood and iron to occur at all, becomes very persuasive indeed.

Reflection may make much of this conviction evaporate. It is worth noticing that Beard's own position is quite ambiguous. After recounting the victories of Northern capitalism just summarized above he remarks, "The main economic results of the Second American Revolution thus far noted would have been attained had there been no armed conflict. . . ." [79] But Beard's views are not in question except insofar as the provocative writings of a first-rate historian shed light on the issues. Three related arguments may be brought to bear against the thesis that the Civil War was a revolutionary victory for industrial capitalist democracy and necessary to this victory. First, one might hold that there is no real connection between the Civil War and the subsequent victory of industrial capitalism; to argue in favor of this connection is to fall victim to the fallacy of *post hoc, ergo propter hoc*. Second, one might hold that these changes were coming about of their own accord through the ordinary processes of economic growth and needed no Civil War to bring them about.[80] Finally, one could argue on the basis of evidence discussed at some length earlier in this chapter that the economies of North and South were not really in serious competition with one another: at best they were complementary; at worst, they failed to link up with each other due to fortuitous circumstances, such as the fact that the South sold much of its cotton to England.

All such arguments would receive an effective answer only if it were possible to

[76] Sharkey, *Money, Class, and Party,* 284–285, 303.

[77] Beard and Beard, *American Civilization,* II, 105; see pages 105–115 for a survey of the measures summarized here; also Hacker, *Triumph of American Capitalism,* 385–397, for a similar and in some ways more concise analysis.

[78] Beard and Beard, *American Civilization,* II, 29.

[79] Beard and Beard, *American Civilization,* II, 115.

[80] Cochran, "Did the Civil War Retard Industrialization?" 148–160 seems to me a version of this and the preceding argument. I do not find it persuasive because it merely shows on the basis of statistics that the Civil War temporarily interrupted industrial growth. It touches only briefly and tangentially on the problem of institutional changes, which I hold to be the center of the question.

demonstrate that Southern society, dominated by the plantation, constituted a formidable obstacle to the establishment of industrial capitalist democracy. The evidence indicates very clearly that plantation slavery was an obstacle to democracy, at least any conception of democracy that includes the goals of human equality, even the limited form of equality of opportunity, and human freedom. It does not establish at all clearly that plantation slavery was an obstacle to industrial capitalism as such. And comparative perspective shows clearly that industrial capitalism can establish itself in societies that do not profess these democratic goals or, to be a little more cautious, where these goals are no more than a secondary current. Germany and Japan prior to 1945 are the main illustrations for this thesis.

Once again the inquiry leads back toward political questions and incompatibilities between two different kinds of civilizations: in the South and in the North and West. Labor-repressive agricultural systems, and plantation slavery in particular, are political obstacles to a *particular kind* of capitalism, at a specific historical stage: competitive democratic capitalism we must call it for lack of a more precise term. Slavery was a threat and an obstacle to a society that was indeed the heir of the Puritan, American, and French Revolutions. Southern society was based firmly on hereditary status as the basis of human worth. With the West, the North, though in the process of change, was still committed to notions of equal opportunity. In both, the ideals were reflections of economic arrangements that gave them much of their appeal and force. Within the same political unit it was, I think, inherently impossible to establish political and social institutions that would satisfy both. If the geographical separation had been much greater, if the South had been a colony for example, the problem would in all probability have been relatively simple to solve at that time—at the expense of the Negro.

That the Northern victory, even with all its ambiguous consequences, was a political victory for freedom compared with what a Southern victory would have been seems obvious enough to require no extended discussion. One need only consider what would have happened had the Southern plantation system been able to establish itself in the West by the middle of the nineteenth century and surrounded the Northeast. Then the United States would have been in the position of some modernizing countries today, with a latifundia economy, a dominant antidemocratic aristocracy, and a weak and dependent commercial and industrial class, unable and unwilling to push forward toward political democracy. In rough outline, such was the Russian situation, though with less of a commercial emphasis in its agriculture in the second half of the nineteenth century. A radical explosion of some kind or a prolonged period of semireactionary dictatorship would have been far more probable than a firmly rooted political democracy with all its shortcomings and deficiencies.

Striking down slavery was a decisive step, an act at least as important as the striking down of absolute monarchy in the English Civil War and the French Revolution, an essential preliminary for further advances. Like these violent upheavals, the main achievements in our Civil War were political in the broad sense of the term. Later generations in America were to attempt to put economic content into the political framework, to raise the level of the people toward some conception of human dignity by putting in their hands the material means to determine their own fate. Subsequent revolutions in Russia and China have had the same purpose even if the means have in large measure so far swallowed up and distorted the ends. It is in this context, I believe, that the American Civil War has to be placed for its proper assessment.

That the federal government was out of the business of enforcing slavery was no small matter. It is easy to imagine the difficulties that organized labor would have faced, for example, in its effort to achieve legal and political acceptance in later years, had not this barrier been swept away. To the extent that subsequent movements toward extending the boundaries and meanings of freedom have faced obstacles since the end of the Civil War, they have done so in large measure because of the incomplete character of the victory won in 1865 and subsequent tendencies toward a conservative coalition between propertied interests in the North and the South. This incompleteness was built into the structure of industrial capitalism. Much of the old repression returned to the South in new and more purely economic guises, while new forms appeared there and in the rest of the United States as industrial capitalism grew and spread. If the federal government no longer concerned itself with enforcing the fugitive slave laws, it either acquiesced or served as an instrument for new forms of oppression.

As far as the Negro is concerned, only in quite recent times has the federal government begun to move in the opposite direction. As these lines are being written, the United States finds itself in the midst of a bitter struggle over the Negroes' civil rights, a struggle likely to ebb and flow for years to come. It involves a great deal more than the Negroes. Due to the peculiarities of American history, the central core of America's lowest class are people with dark skins. As the one major segment of American society with active discontents, the Negroes are at present almost the only potential recruiting ground for efforts to change the character of the world's most powerful capitalist democracy. Whether this potential will amount to anything, whether it will splinter and evaporate or coalesce with other discontents to achieve significant results, is quite another story.

At bottom, the struggle of the Negroes and their white allies concerns contemporary capitalist democracy's capacity to live up to its noble professions, something no society has ever done. Here we approach the ultimate ambiguity in the assessment and interpretation of the Civil War. It recurs throughout history. There is more than coincidence in the fact that two famous political leaders of free societies chose to express their ideals in speeches for their fallen dead given more than two thousand years apart. To the critical historian both Pericles and Lincoln become ambiguous figures as he sets what they did and what happened alongside what they said and in all likelihood hoped for. The fight for what they expressed is not over and may not end until mankind ceases to inhabit the earth. As one peers ever deeper to resolve the ambiguities of history, the seeker eventually finds them in himself and his fellow men as well as in the supposedly dead facts of history. We are inevitably in the midst of the ebb and flow of these events and play a part, no matter how small and insignificant as individuals, in what the past will come to mean for the future.

Part II

THE SLAVE SOUTH

4 / The Effects of Slavery upon the Southern Economy

Stanley L. Engerman

Whatever the role of slavery in lighting the fuse of civil war, it was clearly a fundamental element in defining the Old South. Men knew this before the great conflagration and have continued to recognize it ever since. The most emphatic statement of this viewpoint was U. B. Phillips' now classic article, "The Central Theme of Southern History," published in 1928. In this essay, Phillips, a distinguished historian of slavery and ante-bellum Southern society, denied that geography or economics or politics or even a common culture explained the distinctiveness of the South. Rather, he insisted, its bond of unity arose from "a common resolve indomitably maintained . . . that it [the South] shall be and remain a white man's country."

As a neutral statement of fact, few historians today would argue with this view. Both before and after the Civil War, the presence of large numbers of blacks, in many places outnumbering the whites, obviously had a profound effect on every aspect of Southern life. Unfortunately Phillips went on to defend the South's obsession with race and the conservative Southern view that Negroes should permanently remain an inferior caste. Although he was not a blatant bigot, Phillips nevertheless insisted on seeing slavery through the rose-colored glasses of the white Southern elite. In his version of the institution, drawn largely from surviving records of the planter class, relations between masters and slaves were generally benevolent. "Darkies" were generally happy, simple beings who seldom resented their bondage or experienced cruelty or harshness at the hands of their masters who were usually considerate men, more sinned against by their careless, irresponsible servants, than sinning. Slavery was generally an unprofitable enterprise both for the planters and the South. It persisted because the possession of slaves conferred prestige and because slavery protected the childlike Negro and at the same time preserved racial peace. Slavery survived, then, as a

Explorations in Entrepreneurial History, Second Series, IV, No. 2 (Winter 1967), 71–97. Reprinted by permission.

I am indebted to Robert Fogel, Robert Gallman, Sherman Rosen, and Edward Zabel for comments and suggestions. A modified and extended treatment of the issues raised in this paper will appear in Robert W. Fogel and Stanley L. Engerman, *The Economics of Slavery,* and an essay based on that monograph will appear in Fogel and Engerman (eds.), *The Reinterpretation of American Economic History.* [AU.]

system of social control, one marked by generosity and warm human relations, rather than as an exploitive labor system.

Phillips' views have come under heavy attack in the past 20 years from both historians and economists, who insist that slavery was profitable and consider Phillips an apologist for the slaveholding class. Reflecting modern concern with racial injustice, historian Kenneth Stampp of the University of California at Berkeley proclaims "that the slaves were merely ordinary human beings, that innately Negroes *are*, after all, only white men with black skins." Slavery, he argues, was neither a charitable enterprise nor a viable educational system, but a highly profitable labor system that made money for Southern white men and survived because of this fact.

Economists employing economic theory and statistical analysis have also demurred from Phillips' views. Alfred H. Conrad and John R. Meyer argue that, when one considers the price of slaves, their longevity, their natural increase, the price of cotton, and the returns on alternative investments, slavery was a profitable enterprise for the average slaveholder, and cotton culture with slaves was profitable for the entire South.

Although it was widely hailed when it first appeared, Conrad's and Meyer's essay has since been attacked as inadequate, particularly in regard to the impact of slavery on the Southern economy. Critics concede that the average planter may have made a profit, but they believe that slavery may well have held back Southern economic growth. Conrad and Meyer did not, they note, consider slavery's impact on social values and Southern attitudes toward work, and the poor morale, incentives, and education of the slave labor force. These vitally affected the growth possibilities of the South, and yet they are difficult if not impossible to quantify. In the review essay that follows, Stanley Engerman, who accepts the approach and the conclusions of the econometricians, reconsiders the impact of slavery on the ante-bellum Southern economy.

For further reading: Martin Fischbaum and Julius Rubin, "Slavery and the Economic Development of the American South," *Explorations in Entrepreneurial History*, Second Series, VI (Fall 1968); Alfred H. Conrad and John R. Meyer, *The Economics of Slavery and Other Studies in Econometric History* (Chicago, Ill.: Aldine Publishing Company, 1964); Alfred H. Conrad, Douglas Dowd, and others, "Slavery as an Obstacle to Economic Growth in the United States: A Panel Discussion," *The Journal of Economic History*, XXVII (December 1967); Harold D. Woodman, "The Profitability of Slavery: A Historical Perennial," *Journal of Southern History*, XXIX (August 1963); U. B. Phillips, "The Economic Cost of Slaveholding in the Cotton Belt," *Political Science Quarterly*, XX (June 1905).

The economic effects of slavery have long been a subject of great interest.[1] Hotly debated in the antebellum period, the question has been discussed extensively by

[1] For another critical review of the debate, from a different perspective, see Harold D. Woodman, "The Profitability of Slavery: A Historical Perennial," *Journal of Southern History*, 29:303–325 (August, 1963).

historians ever since. Over the years there emerged among historians a general consensus which held that slavery not only prevented the economic development of the South, but that by 1860 it had become unprofitable to the slaveholders. Consequently the slave system was economically decadent before the onset of the Civil War. The chief architects of this interpretation were Ulrich B. Phillips and Charles W. Ramsdell. Although challenged by several writers in the 1930's and 1940's, the Phillips-Ramsdell position continued to be dominant until the late 1950's. However, during the past decade a series of attacks on the views of Phillips, Ramsdell, and their main supporters has substantially modified the old consensus.

In this critical review of the long debate on the economics of slavery I shall discuss both the basic arguments of the Phillips-Ramsdell view and the recent attacks on it. It will be important to distinguish three related but different issues often confused in the debate. These are:

1. The profitability of slavery to the individual slave-owner.
2. The viability of slavery as an economic system.[2]
3. The effects of the slave system on the economic development of the South.

The answers to these questions do not necessarily fall into a simple pattern; a positive answer to any one does not imply the answer to the others. Much disagreement in the literature can be traced to the failure to recognize the differences among these questions.

THE PHILLIPS-RAMSDELL POSITION

Historical work on the slavery question has been dominated by the writings of Ulrich B. Phillips.[3] Phillips discussed almost all the economic aspects of slavery and much of the subsequent debate has been within the framework which he set forth. Phillips' study led him to conclude that slavery was economically unprofitable to the planter, was undoubtedly moribund on the eve of the Civil War, and that it was the crucial factor in the presumed retarded development of the southern economy. Phillips granted that his conclusions were not always true, since slavery had been established and initially expanded "because the white people were seeking their own welfare and comfort." However, he argued, "in the long run [private gain and public safety] were attained at the expense of private and public wealth and of progress."[4]

Central to this position was his view that the Negro slave was an innately ignorant savage and an inefficient worker who could handle only simple tasks and who re-

[2] Viability is defined as the ability of an industry to continue existing. In economic terms an industry would be considered viable if a market rate of return could be made on the replacement cost of capital used. In the case of slavery the test for viability is the equating of the present value of the future stream of income from slaves with the costs of rearing them. If the present value, computed on the basis of the market rate of interest, was less than the present value of rearing costs, slavery would have been economically unviable—there would have been no incentive for anyone to raise slaves.

[3] The most pertinent of these are: "The Economic Cost of Slave-holding in the Cotton Belt," *Political Science Quarterly*, 20:257–275 (June, 1905); and *American Negro Slavery* (New York, 1918).

[4] Phillips, "Economic Cost," p. 259.

quired constant control. To use such crude labor the plantation system, which provided the necessary supervision, was essential. Therefore, the slave system and the plantation system became identical in the South.

In an early article, Phillips presented his basic arguments for the conclusion that slavery had become unprofitable and moribund by the time of the Civil War.[5] His major piece of evidence was a comparison of the ratio between the price per pound of cotton and the price of male field hands. Observing a ten- to twelve-fold increase in the ratio of slave prices to cotton prices between 1800 and 1860, he stated (without supporting evidence) that such an increase was much too great to be explained by increased slave productivity. He went on to point out that the cost of using slave labor included: "expense of food, clothing and shelter"; interest on the capital invested in the slave; economic insurance against death, illness or escape; the "wear and tear" of years; and taxation on the capitalized value of the slave. While no conclusions were drawn concerning the sum of these costs, in context they seem clearly designed to buttress the argument of unprofitability. Phillips noted that account should have been taken of the market value of offspring, but he claimed this was offset by the cost of supporting the aged. The existence of high and rising slave prices he attributed to overspeculation—"an irresistible tendency to overvalue and overcapitalize slave labor."

Phillips stated that another important factor in bidding up the price of slaves was economies of scale in cotton production. This, he contended, would explain in part the high and rising slave prices since a price in excess of the value of each particular slave would be paid. It also explained why larger plantations expanded relative to smaller holdings, and how these larger plantations could have shown profits while losses were widespread. For this reason, according to Phillips, all funds that the planter could earn or borrow went to purchase slaves, "not into modern implements or land improvements."[6]

The existence of a demand for slaves for purposes of prestige and conspicuous consumption was also mentioned as a cause of high slave prices. Implicit is the statement that only part of the slave's price was based upon the value of production, the remainder representing a form of consumption expenditure by the owners of slaves.[7] If this were true, slavery could be viable even if it were an unprofitable investment as measured by the return from business operations alone. The large extent

[5] *Ibid., passim.*

[6] *Ibid.*, p. 272. The question of economies of scale in cotton production is one of the key questions concerning the plantation which remain to be answered. The primary evidence for increasing returns to scale is the increased plantation size and concentration of holdings in larger plantations before 1860. See Lewis Cecil Gray, *History of Agriculture in the Southern United States to 1860* (2 vols., Washington, 1933), 478–480, 530. William Parker apparently doubts the existence of economies in production attributable to the costs of management and equipment, or at least he doubts that they alone can explain the observed size distribution of plantations. William N. Parker, "The Slave Plantation in American Agriculture," First International Conference of Economic History, *Contributions and Communications* (Paris, 1960), 321–331.

[7] Rising slave prices in this period could be attributed to either increased consumption of prestige by slaveowners or to increased value of slave production in business operations (with the consumption expenditure remaining constant), or to some combination of the two. The observation that the price of slaves fluctuated with the price of cotton does not itself suggest that southerners were behaving to maximize profits from business operations alone. Such variations are consistent with the hypothesis that the expenditure for prestige remained constant.

of the prestige demand, however, was considered an important element in explaining the low rate of capital formation and economic growth in the southern economy.

Phillips argued that the slave system further retarded southern economic development because "the capitalization of labor and the export of earnings in exchange for more workmen, always of a low degree of efficiency," deprived the southern economy of capital which presumably could have been used for other (industrial) purposes, and made the South a chronic debtor to northern merchants and bankers.[8] Phillips' argument about labor capitalization and export of earnings is rather confusing. He realized that after the closing of the external slave trade in 1808 the export drain went to the Upper South rather than outside the southern states. However, he claimed, "there it did little but demoralize industry and postpone to a later generation the agricultural revival"—but the mechanism explaining this outcome was never clearly stated.[9] The capitalization of the labor force presumably reduced labor elasticity and versatility: "it tended to fix labor rigidly in one line of employment." [10] This was significant in the South's one-crop economy, particularly since the profitability of cotton production exhibited considerable cyclical variation. However, Phillips was not clearly on the side of those blaming the South's ills on agricultural specialization. At one point he argued that slavery "deprived the South of the natural advantage which the cotton monopoly should have given it." [11]

Given all the adverse effects, why maintain the system? Because it was essential to keep the "savage instincts from breaking forth"—in other words, for race control and protection.[12] Maintaining slavery and letting slaves produce agricultural commodities was, in Phillips' opinion, less expensive than sending slaves back to Africa or supporting the police and army which would have been required if the slaves were freed.

The Phillips position was modified and extended in an influential article by Charles W. Ramsdell, which claimed that while profitable before 1860, slavery had become unprofitable and moribund by that year.[13] Ramsdell held that economic factors would have made slavery unprofitable to the planting class and that slavery would have ended in the late nineteenth century without the Civil War. In his view, the decline of slavery was likely because the planters had reached the end of the land upon which cotton could be grown profitably. Ramsdell suggested that by 1860 the western limits of slavery had been reached in Texas, and no room existed for expansion northward. Geographic containment would have caused a rise in the labor/land ratio and, as a consequence, slave prices would have fallen until it became too expensive for the owners to maintain their slaves. The end result would have been manumission.

The Ramsdell position—frequently called the natural limits hypothesis—is theoretically plausible, but Ramsdell argued as if there were little room for downward

[8] Phillips, "Economic Cost," p. 275.

[9] *Ibid.*, p. 273.

[10] *Idem.* Phillips later argued that the slave system had the advantage of providing for mobility of the labor force (*Slavery*, p. 395). The distinction intended was apparently that between occupational mobility and geographic mobility.

[11] *Ibid.*, p. 275.

[12] *Ibid.*, p. 259.

[13] Chas. W. Ramsdell, "The Natural Limits of Slavery Expansion," *Mississippi Valley Historical Review*, 16:151–171 (September, 1929).

adjustment of slave prices before freedom of the slaves would become an attractive alternative to owners. He also exaggerated the potential pressure on slave prices by ruling out the possibilities that soil in the older areas might be refurbished or that slaves might be profitably employed in other agricultural or non-agricultural pursuits. Nevertheless the natural limits hypothesis has attracted a large number of adherents.

The Phillips position received new support during the 1930's when several southern historians turned to the records and diaries of individual plantations.[14] Focusing on the profitability of slavery to the planter, they uncovered evidence which appeared to indicate a low rate of return in most of the cases reviewed. Although the accounting techniques used were open to question, and it was never established whether those plantations whose records were used were representative, these studies were used to buttress the Phillips position.

The most recent support for the Phillips conclusion has come from writers who have revived antebellum arguments concerning the effects of slavery upon the course of southern economic development. While generally accepting the profitability of slavery to the planter, they argue that the socio-economic system associated with slavery nevertheless retarded the growth of the overall southern economy. Perhaps the most prominent exponent of this position is Eugene Genovese, who stressed the effects of the slave system upon the size of the internal market in the South.[15] Genovese posited that the skewed income distribution which slavery created made for low demand for domestically manufactured goods within the South; wealthy planters preferred to import goods, slaves had no purchasing power, and low income whites had little market impact. This situation contrasted with that of the North and Midwest where a large "middle-class" market was held to have led to the internal development of industry and a more diversified economy. Genovese argued that this restriction of the internal market deprived the South of economies of scale upon which to create an efficient industrial base. The result was a rural, agricultural southern economy dependent upon outsiders for modern industrial goods. An additional effect of the skewed income distribution was that it caused, or at least permitted, conspicuous consumption and lavish living on the part of the rich planters. Consequently savings and capital formation were reduced.

Douglass North has recently put forward the suggestion that the most important effect of slavery upon capital formation was to be found in the small amount of investment in human capital in the South.[16] Unlike Phillips, who had earlier made a similar point, North considered the South wasteful of the potential of both white and Negro workers. Phillips had argued that slavery prevented the development of a skilled labor force by discouraging the non-planter whites, but he dismissed the possibility of improving the skills or intelligence of the Negro.

[14] See, in particular: Ralph Betts Flanders, *Plantation Slavery in Georgia* (Chapel Hill, 1933); Charles Sacket Sydnor, *Slavery in Mississippi* (New York, 1933); and Charles S. Davis, *The Cotton Kingdom in Alabama* (Montgomery, 1939).

[15] Eugene D. Genovese, "The Significance of the Slave Plantation for Southern Economic Development," *Journal of Southern History*, 28:422–437 (November, 1962). Reprinted in his *The Political Economy of Slavery: Studies in the Economy and Society of the Slave South* (New York, 1965), 157–179.

[16] Douglass C. North, *The Economic Growth of the United States, 1790–1860* (Englewood Cliffs, 1961), 133–134. See also his *Growth and Welfare in the American Past: A New Economic History* (Englewood Cliffs, 1966), 90–97.

THE REVISIONS

The attack on the arguments of Phillips, Ramsdell, and their followers began in the thirties when Lewis Gray and Robert Russel presented strong arguments for the profitability and viability of slavery, although both did consider the South stagnant relative to the rest of the nation.[17] Gray's work was particularly important since it clearly set forth most of the general considerations to be found in the recent discussions of profitability and viability. However, Gray did conclude that slavery indeed retarded the growth of the southern economy. In the early forties Thomas P. Govan pointed to serious mistakes in several of the studies based on plantation records. He contended that correction of these mistakes led to the conclusion that slavery was profitable.[18] Kenneth Stampp, in his thorough study of slavery (published in 1956), reached the same conclusion as did Govan, and he went on to dismiss most of the arguments which had been used to connect slavery and the backwardness of the southern economy.[19] However, it apparently was not until after the appearance of the widely discussed essay on "The Economics of Slavery in the Antebellum South," by Alfred H. Conrad and John R. Meyer that the old interpretation lost its clearly dominant position.[20]

Profitability to the Planter

As noted above, Phillips' contention that slavery was unprofitable to the planters found support in several studies of plantation records. Recent attacks on these studies have come from two directions. First, the records were found to be incomplete and to contain a crucial conceptual error. Second, economists have applied the traditional tools of economic analysis to test for the profitability of slavery in a manner which removed the reliance upon the fortunes of those particular plantations whose complete records survived. The results of this analysis contradicted the Phillips hypothesis.

It was never clear how much reliance should be placed upon conclusions drawn from the analysis of those few plantations whose records survived. Not all plantations kept records and even fewer were preserved. Special factors could have affected each plantation, but no adjustment can be made without prior knowledge of the biases. It is therefore not certain that the existing sample of plantations is representative. There were long and short cycles in prices and output, regional variation was pronounced, and there were apparently differences based upon size of plantation. Conrad and Meyer did use these records, but they used only certain of the data they contained as sample observations in determining estimates of particular variables. They did not generalize from the profit position of a small number of plantations.

Moreover, the use of plantation records by Phillips and his followers contained several errors, the importance of which were first stressed by Govan, and later

[17] Robert R. Russel, "The General Effects of Slavery upon Southern Economic Progress," *Journal of Southern History*, 4:34–54 (February, 1938), and *Gray, op. cit.*, 462–480, 940–942.

[18] Thomas P. Govan, "Was Plantation Slavery Profitable?" *Journal of Southern History*, 8:513–535 (November, 1942).

[19] Kenneth M. Stampp, *The Peculiar Institution: Slavery in the Ante-Bellum South* (New York, 1956), 383–418.

[20] Alfred H. Conrad and John R. Meyer, "The Economics of Slavery in the Ante-Bellum South," *Journal of Political Economy*, 66:95–130 (April, 1958). Reprinted in their *The Economics of Slavery and Other Studies in Econometric History* (Chicago, 1964), 43–92.

reiterated by Stampp. A conceptual error in accounting technique led to an erroneous conclusion. Phillips included interest on the capital invested in slaves and land as costs in his discussion of the expenses of plantation owners. The later accounting studies similarly included the imputed interest on invested capital as a cost to be deducted from revenues in calculating net profits. This net profit figure was then divided by the capital value of the plantation to measure the average rate of return on capital. Since the rate of return computed in this manner was below the rate of return on alternative investments, slavery was considered unprofitable.

Govan and Stampp both pointed out that this was an illegitimate calculation, since it resulted in double-counting the cost of capital. Net profits are computed by deducting all expenses (including depreciation) from gross revenues. A positive residual includes the imputed return on the capital of the owner, as well as the wages of management and "pure profits." When imputations for capital cost and the wages of management are deducted any positive sum remaining would be "pure profits." The existence of such "pure profits" would indicate that the investment was profitable. There is no need to then compare this with the alternative rate of return, since deducting the imputed capital cost allows for this. The same test could be made by deducting from net profits the imputed wages of management, computing the rate of return upon this investment, and then comparing it with the rate of return upon alternative assets. If the rate of return on the investment exceeds that upon alternative assets, the investment is considered to be profitable. Both methods described provide the same answer; what is shown to be profitable by one computation is profitable under the other. (Accounting and economic approaches differ in the way costs are measured—the accounting calculations using historical costs and the economic current opportunity costs.)[21]

An important omission from plantation income was the capital gain derived from the reproduction of the slave labor force. As long as slave children could be sold or used on the plantation, this was an additional source of income. A capital gain was also to be derived from the increased value of existing slaves. The slaves held in the 1850's were usually purchased in earlier years at below their current market value. Other errors were the exclusion of slave household services and slave land clearing and maintenance services, and the treatment of the personal expenditures of planters as costs rather than as a use of profits. Govan and Stampp argued that correcting the omissions and errors of earlier historians showed that their samples clearly demonstrated high rates of return to slave ownership in the antebellum period.

The path-breaking essay by Conrad and Meyer was more general in scope, based on an economist's as opposed to an accountant's approach to the problem. Rather than confining their attention to measuring the rates of return of particular plantations, they asked whether, on the average, a planter who purchased slaves and land at an "average" price for the period (1830–1860) could have expected to make as high a rate of return as if he had invested in some alternative asset. While not arguing that every plantation made money, their important conclusion was that, on the average, profits were to be made from slave ownership.

In their analysis, Conrad and Meyer separated the slave economy into two sectors, and estimated the profitability of slave ownership in each. Male slaves were regarded

---

[21] For a criticism of the accounting calculations, based as they are upon historical cost, see Yasukichi Yasuba, "The Profitability and Viability of Plantation Slavery in the United States," *The Economic Studies Quarterly*, 12:60–67 (September, 1961).

as capital goods used in the production of marketable output of agricultural staples. Female slaves, however, not only were used to produce staples but also were the source of additional slaves. Thus the female slave could be considered a capital good who produced the capital goods used to produce final output.

By regarding both male and female slaves as capital goods, Conrad and Meyer were able to test for the profitability of slavery by computing the rate of return on the total investment in slaves, including the land and other assets which the slave used. The basic computation involved solving to find that rate of return which equated the cost of obtaining slaves with the net stream of earnings derived from using the slaves. Separate rates of return were computed for male and female slaves.

These calculations involved the estimation of four variables. First, the period over which the stream of earnings was obtained was estimated by using an average life expectancy drawn from mortality tables. Second, the total cost of the investment in the slave and the complementary assets was derived from information on slave prices collected by Phillips, with various sources providing the basic information for other assets. Third, the rates of return from bonds and commercial paper were used to compare with the rate of return on slaves. The fourth variable, the annual value of earnings from the slave's productive activities was computed differently for males and females. For the male, gross earnings were measured by multiplying the estimated quantity of cotton produced per slave by the farm price per pound of cotton. Net earnings were obtained by subtracting the costs of maintaining and supervising the slave from gross earnings. For the female, net earnings depended not only on the value of the cotton she produced but also on the market value of offspring. The computation involved estimates of the expected number of offspring, a deduction for nursery and other costs of raising the offspring to the age at which they were sold (assumed to be 18), and a deduction for maintenance and supervision costs. In effect, all the costs of raising slave children to productive age were charged against the female slaves, and all proceeds from sales were attributed to her.

Conrad and Meyer estimated the rate of return from slave ownership for different types of land using various selling prices of cotton. For the majority of plantations they estimated the return on male slaves to range between 4½ percent and 8 percent. On poor soils, such as upland pine or the worked-out lands of the east, the rate of return varied from 2.2 percent to 5.4 percent. On the best lands of the South the returns varied from 10 percent to 13 percent. These rates of return meant that males yielded a rate of return equal to or in excess of the return on alternative assets on all but the poorest lands.

For female slaves a rate of return was computed for land of average quality only. If the females had only five marketable offspring, the estimated lower limit, the rate of return was 7.1 percent. If there were ten offspring, the estimated upper limit, the rate of return was 8.1 percent. Conrad and Meyer then argued that slaveholders in the older regions of the South, where males were yielding a low rate in cotton production, were able to achieve a profitable rate of return by selling the offspring of their female slaves to the newer areas where profitable cotton production was possible. They demonstrated the existence of this type of slave reallocation by pointing out differences in the age structure of slaves in the newer and older states, as well as by citing testimony of contemporaries.[22]

[22] They also directly answered Phillips' charge that slaves were overpriced by pointing to a sharp rise in productivity in this period, justifying the rise in slave prices in terms of cotton

The computations of Conrad and Meyer have been attacked as showing too high a rate of return from investment in slaves. While their estimates of each of the four variables—slave life expectancy, capital costs, the rate of return on alternative assets, and the income obtained from slaves—have been criticized, the revision which most sharply challenges their conclusion is Edward Saraydar's downward adjustment of the productivity of prime male field hands in cotton production.[23]

Saraydar was interested in testing a more restricted hypothesis about slave profitability than were Conrad and Meyer. He was concerned only with the profitability of owning male prime field hands; thus ignoring the gains from slave offspring which Conrad and Meyer accounted for in computing the rate of return upon females. This means that Saraydar understated the profitability of slave ownership to the individual plantation owner (as well as to the southern economy) as long as female slaves were a profitable investment. The specific formulation of the test for the profitability of male slaves used by Saraydar was the same as that of Conrad and Meyer. He computed the rate of return from the use of males in cotton production using averages of the period 1830–1860. His one major change was to provide an alternative measure of physical productivity in cotton operations. Rather than an average of estimates presented in various "contemporary journals," Saraydar used a sample of counties taken from the 1849 census to estimate slave yields in various parts of the South. The particular year chosen, 1849, was justified as being one of average crop size for the 1830–1860 period. Saraydar selected counties in which little was produced besides cotton, and then adjusted the total slave population to obtain an estimate of the average number of field hands. Dividing total cotton output in these counties by the estimated number of field hands gave cotton productivity per field hand. This resulted in a lowering of the all-south average yield per field hand from Conrad and Meyer's 3.75 bales to 3.2, and the yield on alluvial soil from 7.0 bales to 3.6.[24] Using these lowered yields, Saraydar computed sharply lower rates of return on male slaves. On average land the computed rate of return was below that upon alternative assets, and only on the best alluvial land were field hands a profitable investment to the planter. Even there the rates of return were distinctly lower than the rates computed by Conrad and Meyer.

Both Saraydar's form of the test for the profitability of slavery and his specific productivity estimates were challenged in turn by Richard Sutch. Sutch incorporated into one production function the computations which Conrad and Meyer did

---

prices. (See *op. cit.*, pp. 116 and 117, particularly Table 17). However, the increase in productivity they show may be too large. First, their estimates ignore the secular and cyclical variations in the proportion of slave labor used in cotton production. Second, a published estimate of man-hours per bale of cotton shows a fall from 601 in 1800 to 439 in 1840 and 304 in 1880. Department of Agriculture, *Progress of Farm Mechanization* (Miscellaneous Publication No. 630, Washington, 1947), p. 3. This study, however, shows no change in yield per acre between 1800 and 1840, which is surprising given the move to presumably more fertile soils.

[23] Edward Saraydar, "A Note on the Profitability of Ante Bellum Slavery," *Southern Economic Journal*, 30:325–332 (April, 1964).

[24] Saraydar also claimed that Conrad and Mayer must have overstated alluvial yields since the average yield per acre for the nation didn't reach their implied level until after World War II. Richard Sutch pointed out that alluvial yields in 1879 exceeded those implied by Conrad and Meyer. Richard Sutch, "The Profitability of Ante Bellum Slavery—Revisited," *Southern Economic Journal*, 31:365–377 (April, 1965), with "Reply" by Saraydar, 377–383.

separately for males and females, thus providing for a single overall test of slave profitability. In effect, Sutch's formulation considered the plantation owner to purchase a slave whose price was determined by applying to Phillips' data the age-sex composition of the slave population and allowed the owner to benefit from the growth of the slave labor force. Unlike Conrad and Meyer, however, the benefits of the increased labor were not attributed to the female alone. This formulation meant that the purchase of a slave provided a permanent stream of income to the owners as long as average slave productivity exceeded average costs of rearing and maintenance. By applying this production function to Saraydar's figures, Sutch estimated rates of return on slave ownership roughly similar to those of Conrad and Meyer.

Sutch, however, also attacked Saraydar's estimates of income from slaves by preparing specific tests of profitability for the years 1849 and 1859. His main correction of Saraydar's 1849 figures was the use of the higher cotton price of that year, while for 1859 both the higher cotton price and increased physical productivity were used. However, these corrections provide too favorable an estimate of slave profitability for the thirty-year period studied. Although the 1849 crop was below that of the preceding two years, it was rather high for the decade of the 1840's, and Sutch's argument that the marked price rise that year is indicative of a small crop is weak. The 1849 price was unusually high—only one year of the seventeen from 1839 to 1855 had a higher cotton price. The 1859 crop, on the other hand, was abnormally large. It was almost half-again as large as that of the average of the 1850's, and was not exceeded until 1879. Thus, while they indicate that Saraydar's adjustments may not be relevant for those specific years, Sutch's corrections of price and yield seem excessive when applied to the years between 1830 and the outbreak of the Civil War.

There are several questions concerning the profitability of slaves in cotton production which require further analysis. First, the argument that profits should be measured using data from a large span of years to compute averages does create some problems and gives an element of arbitrariness to the calculations. Since prices and output of cotton varied considerably during the thirty years presumably averaged, and slave prices did move sharply, the measurement of profitability is sensitive to the particular numbers chosen. The use of averages also ignores the possibility of an upward trend in slave productivity above that attributable to the movement to newer soils. Computations for specific years may provide a better indication of profitability than does the thirty-year average, though sensitive to the particular years studied. Saraydar and Sutch, of course, may both be correct. Slavery may have been unprofitable in the earlier part of the interval studied, but profitable in the 1850's.

Second, the use of an average price of slaves for the entire South overlooks the fact that the market adjustment between the Upper South and the Lower South did not lead to price uniformity. Evans' data suggest an average price spread of about 25 percent in the years from 1830 to 1860, with no marked trend in the size of the differential over time.[25] The use of Lower South slave costs in all regions results in an understatement of the rate of return in the older regions, though the computations for the better soils are not affected.

[25] Robert Evans, Jr., "The Economics of American Negro Slavery," in National Bureau of Economic Research, *Aspects of Labor Economics* (Princeton, 1962), 185–243. The Phillips estimates do show an increased differential in favor of the Lower South after 1856.

Third, better estimates of slave productivity are necessary. To obtain these more detailed work on census manuscripts and plantation records is necessary. Questions as to the degree of self-sufficiency on plantations, the possible production of other marketed crops on what are primarily cotton producing plantations, the other functions of an income-yielding nature performed by slaves, and the quantity of cotton produced by whites both on and off plantations require further study, some of which is currently being undertaken.[26]

What Saraydar has done is to throw into some doubt the profitability of owning male slaves. This does not mean that slavery would be unprofitable to planters, as long as females were owned and produced marketable offspring. Saraydar's result, in fact, suggests that female slaves were underpriced, given the market value of slaves. If he were correct we would expect the price of male field hands to fall below that of females, since it is the offspring who are the source of profits. It is the maintenance of the higher price on male slaves which raises questions about the meaning of Saraydar's (and Conrad and Meyer's) separate production functions for male and female slaves, as well as the accuracy of Saraydar's yield estimates.

Moreover, a study by Robert Evans using a different set of data and testing the same hypothesis as did Saraydar, reached the same conclusion as Conrad and Meyer. Evans estimated the rate of return on male slaves only, excluding the value of offspring. He used data on the prices paid to hire slaves as estimates of the income to be derived from using slaves. If the slaves hired were equal in productivity to the slaves used elsewhere, the hiring rate should provide an estimate of the income produced per slave. Evans' treatment of the problem of slave mortality also differed from Conrad and Meyer's. Evans adjusted slave incomes for the proportion of deaths each year rather than using an average expected life span. Rates of return were computed for five-year periods between 1830 and 1860. They ranged from 9.5 percent to 14.3 percent in the Upper South, and between 10.3 percent and 18.5 percent in the Lower South. Evans further tested the sensitivity of his results to possible errors in the data, and concluded that it was improbable that his conclusion was in error. The maximum cumulation of probable errors would not be sufficient to reduce the rate of return from ownership of male slaves below the return from alternative assets.

We should be clear as to exactly what has been measured in these studies. If Conrad and Meyer and Evans are correct, a planter who purchased either a male or female slave at the market price could have made a rate of return equal to or better than that upon alternative investments. This would mean that prestige demand does not have to be used in explaining the price of slaves. It means further that regardless of how inefficient slave labor was relative to white labor, the planters who employed slaves were profiting from their use. The market price could be justified on the basis of the productivity of the male slave in market activities, and labor productivity plus the value of the slave offspring in the case of the female. By arguing that most planters made profits, these studies made a presumption of viability. The finding of profitability also means that any retardation the South experienced could not be attributed to sub-marginal investments made by slaveowners.

---

[26] Robert Gallman and William Parker have been studying the manuscript census for southern states in 1860. In a related study, James T. Foust and Dale Swan have been examining the effects upon measured productivity of owners of small plantations (six or fewer slaves) working in the field alongside their slaves.

Viability to the Economy

Yasuba, Evans, and Sutch have each pointed out that the conclusion that slavery was profitable to the planter did not prove the viability of the slave system. It is possible that a profitable rate of return be made on the market price of existing slaves although the system was moribund. If the value of slaves (as reflected in the market price) was below the rearing cost, there would be an adjustment over time, resulting in a decline in the number of slaves until the institution disappeared. If the demand for slaves fell, but the market price for a reduced number of slaves was equal to the rearing cost, the slave industry would decline without disappearing. However, not only was the market price of slaves in excess of rearing costs in the years before the Civil War, but as Yasuba has demonstrated, this surplus—or capitalized rent—was growing in the late 1840's and 1850's.[27]

Capitalized rent would exist in the price of slaves as long as the market price exceeded the cost of producing slaves—the cost of raising them to the age at which they became productive or were sold. This surplus was not eliminated because once the importation of slaves from Africa was forbidden, the increase in supply set by either biological or institutional constraints was not sufficient to reduce the market price of slaves to their rearing cost. The surplus of market price over cost of production is the measure of the potential fall in slave values which could have occurred without making slavery unprofitable to the southern economy.[28] A falling price of slaves due to a decline in demand would mean that it was possible for the same rates of return to be made on the market price of slaves before and after the decline in demand.[29] However, this price decline, resulting in a capital loss to those who owned the slaves, need not imply that slavery as an institution was not viable, as long as the lowered price still exceeded the costs of producing slaves.

Thus studies which indicate slave purchasers made a rate of return roughly equal to that upon alternative assets would not be surprising. Rather, since supply was inelastic at any moment of time, the price of slaves was set by the demand for them. It therefore would mean that the price of slaves was set at a figure which yielded the market rate of return to the purchaser.

The level of the price of slaves could be based upon elements of both prestige demand and demand for use in production. As long as the total price southerners were willing to pay for slaves exceeded rearing costs, the institution was viable. However, Conrad and Meyer and Evans argued that the market price could be justified on the basis of slave productivity alone. This means that slavery's viability was not attributable to an element (prestige demand) which caused apparent business losses and lowered southern capital formation. (If prestige demand were high it would not necessarily

[27] Yasuba's calculations are based on the estimates of Conrad and Meyer. Even if, as discussed above, the latter overstate cotton yields per slave the existence of rent and the trend remain.

[28] As Sutch pointed out, flexibility also existed in the price of land.

[29] This point is overlooked by Govan in his discussion of the Evans paper. He rejected as implausible Evans' finding that the profits of slave purchasers not only did not fall, but actually rose in the early 1840's. Thomas P. Govan, "Comments" in National Bureau of Economic Research, *Aspects of Labor Economics* (Princeton, 1962), 243–246. Yasuba found the capitalized rent in this period lower than in preceding and succeeding intervals, which meant that the market price of slaves fell more than their rearing costs. Thus it was possible for those who purchased slaves in this period to have made high rates of return, since they obtained slaves at a lower price. Apparently investors as a group were overly pessimistic.

mean that, properly defined, business losses occurred, or that capital formation was reduced. Rather, the profitability test should be based upon the business value of slaves—deducting the imputed consumption element—and the capital formation comparison would need to bring in the expenditures upon goods for conspicuous consumption in the North, which also reduced the investible surplus.)

Yasuba separately estimated the rent element in the price of male slaves and of female slaves. Since the form of the calculation attributes the value of the offspring to the female slave, the rent on the female is based not only upon her productivity in growing cotton, but also upon the future value of her marketable offspring. Thus, the demand for female slaves would be based upon expectations covering not only her life-span but also that of her offspring. If there was an anticipation of an early end to slavery, for economic or other reasons, the demand for female slaves would decline. That Yasuba finds the rent rising before 1860 implies that the southern planters did not expect slavery to decline, let alone be abolished, until at least several decades elapsed. Whatever merit there is in the natural limits hypothesis, its presumed effects were not anticipated in the South before the Civil War. Indeed the magnitude of the rent calculated by Yasuba makes it clear that a substantial decline in slave values would have had to occur for the institution to be threatened.[30]

Richard Sutch independently arrived at the same result concerning slavery's viability as did Yasuba, although he stated his argument differently. Sutch's analysis was based upon a comparison of the costs of using free labor with the costs of using slave labor to the economy (the annual "maintenance cost" plus the amortization of rearing costs). The value of the marginal productivity of the slave to the southern economy exceeded the costs of using the slave, thus creating an economic surplus. The free laborer was paid the value of the marginal product, so that no such surplus existed. If we assume that slave and free labor are equally productive, and that the cost of using slaves was at a subsistence level, then slavery would be viable as long as the free wage rate exceeded subsistence. (If the productivity of the two types of labor differed, the condition for viability is that the ratio of the cost of using slave labor to the wages paid free labor be less than the ratio of their marginal value products.) This would be equivalent to Yasuba's result if slavery were profitable to the planter, since the present value of the surpluses from the use of slave labor would then be equal to the capitalized rent in the price of the slave.[31]

The discussion of the viability of the slave economy points out that the rate of return to the southern economy from its investment in slave labor exceeded the rates of return earned by planters. This was because the latter studies measured the rate of return based upon the market price of the slave, while, as Yusuba notes, for the economy it would be based upon rearing costs. The difference between rearing costs and the market price resulted in capital gains for slaveholders—the question of who received the capital gains depending upon the foresight with which slave values were predicted once the importation of slaves was prohibited.

---

[30] John Moes has suggested another possible economic end to slavery. If the productivity of the freed Negro was sufficiently in excess of his productivity while enslaved he would have been able to compensate his owner for granting freedom. John E. Moes, "Comments," in National Bureau of Economic Research, *Aspects of Labor Economics* (Princeton, 1962), 247–256.

[31] If slavery were unprofitable this would mean that rent as measured by Yasuba, based upon the excess of market price at age 18 above rearing costs, would exceed that implied by Sutch, which is based upon the excess of productivity above rearing and maintenance costs.

A Stagnant Economy?

The strongest argument against slavery on economic grounds has been the image of a poor and stagnant southern economy in the antebellum period. Some historians have argued that slavery was both profitable and viable, but have introduced other factors to contend that the long-run effect of the slave system was to retard southern economic development. As described in Section I, major emphasis has been upon the presumed effects of the slave system upon income distribution (and thus the size of the internal market) and the rate of capital formation. Stagnation has also been attributed to southern specialization in the production of agricultural staples, particularly cotton, for export. A long debate has taken place as to whether slavery caused specialization, or whether specialization in cotton promoted slavery. In either case, analogy has been made with the supposed weak position of agricultural export producers in the world today. The argument is that a shift away from agricultural specialization would have led to a more rapid rate of economic growth in the South.

Many discussions of the antebellum southern economy start with the presumption of a low income, slow growing region. Thomas Govan had used the wealth estimates of the 1850 and 1860 censuses to question the concept of a stagnant southern economy, but it is only with the recent estimates of regional income by Richard Easterlin that this point can be examined in more detail. By applying Easterlin's estimates of the income shares by region to Robert Gallman's estimates of national income for 1840 and 1860 we can calculate the level of income by region for the two decades preceding the Civil War, and compute regional growth rates. The regional income estimates can be placed on a per capita basis by dividing by regional population.[32]

Easterlin's estimates of regional income include slaves as part of the population and their "incomes" (maintenance costs) in the income total for each region. On this basis the level of southern per capita income in 1860 was 80 percent of the national

[32] Richard A. Easterlin, "Regional Income Trends, 1840–1950," in Seymour Harris, ed., *American Economic History* (New York, 1961), 525–547; Robert E. Gallman, "Gross National Product in the United States, 1834–1909," in Conference on Research in Income and Wealth, Volume Thirty, *Output, Employment, and Productivity in the United States After 1800* (New York, 1966), 3–76; Department of Commerce, *Historical Statistics of the United States: Colonial Times to 1957* (Washington, 1961), Series A123-180, p. 13. There were a number of revisions applied to Easterlin's data in obtaining the estimates of Table 1. The major revision was the estimation of income for Texas in 1840, so that Texas could be brought into the southern region in both years. To downward bias the growth rate Texas per capita income in 1840 was assumed equal to the 1860 level. The 1840 population was interpolated between the 1836 and 1846 estimates presented in Lewis W. Newton and Herbert P. Gambrell, *A Social and Political History of Texas* (Dallas, 1932), p. 280. Thus the regional breakdown in Table 1 differs from Easterlin's in including Texas in the South, but accords with his placement of Delaware and Maryland in the Northeast. The Mountain and Pacific states were excluded from the national and regional totals in both years.

Easterlin's estimates are the most detailed available for this period, but, of course, may not be perfectly accurate for the conclusions made. Genovese, for example, has stressed the inferior quality of livestock in the South. (See "Livestock in the Slave Economy of the Old South— A Revised View," *Agricultural History*, 36:143–149 (July, 1962). Reprinted in his *The Political Economy of Slavery*, 106–123.) The importance of such biases awaits further study. However, two points should be made. First, it is improbable that such corrections could reverse the finding that growth did occur in the slave economy. Second, while it is possible that such corrections would reduce the level of southern income in 1860, it need not affect the relative growth rate if the same relative quality existed in 1840 and 1860.

average (Table I). While less than 60 percent of the per capita income in the Northeastern states, it was higher than the per capita income in the North Central states. Comparing rates of growth of per capita income between 1840 and 1860, the southern economy does not appear stagnant. The southern rate of growth, 1.6 percent, exceeded that of the rest of the nation, 1.3 percent.[33]

TABLE I

PER CAPITA INCOME BY REGION, 1840 AND 1860 (IN 1860 PRICES)

	Slaves as Consumers		Slaves as Intermediate Goods*	
	1840	1860	1840	1860
National Average	$ 96	$128	$109	$144
North:	109	141	110	142
Northeast	129	181	130	183
North Central	65	89	66	90
South:	74	103	105	150
South Atlantic	66	84	96	124
East South Central	69	89	92	124
West South Central	151	184	238	274

SOURCE: See text and footnotes 32 and 35.
* "Maintenance cost" equal to $20.

The pattern of income change within the southern economy is of interest. The per capita income within each component section grew at a rate below the national average. Nevertheless, it is clear that growth did occur within the period in each of the sections. The shift of southern population into the richer West South Central states, particularly Texas, explained the high southern growth rate. However, since it says nothing about the imminence of any possible decline in that area nor anything about declines in the older parts of the South, this population redistribution cannot be used to support the natural limits thesis. As Sutch has argued, the greater profitability of slavery in the New South immediately prior to the Civil War meant that land (and slave) prices had not reached equilibrium. The low level of land rent is indicative of a relative abundance of cheap lands.[34] Similarly the higher levels of land values in the Old South do not suggest that this area had lost economic potential.

The comparisons in the previous paragraphs included slaves in the population and their "incomes" in the income totals. For those imbued with twentieth-century mores this seems the obvious thing to do, but we should remember that to southern planters slaves were intermediate goods, used in the production process, not individuals for whom society was producing final output. From the viewpoint of these planters, the comparisons of per capita income should be based upon the income of the free

[33] As I have indicated elsewhere, southern backwardness appears to be mainly attributable to the effects of the Civil War and its aftermath. If per capita income in the South had grown as rapidly between 1860 and 1870 as it had between 1840 and 1860, the 1870 level would have been about twice the observed level. Stanley L. Engerman, "The Economic Impact of the Civil War," Explorations in Entrepreneurial History, Second Series, 3:176–199 (Spring, 1966).

[34] Sutch, op. cit., p. 377.

population only, deducting the "maintenance cost" as the expense of using slave labor.[35] This redefinition of "Southern society" raises both the level and rate of growth of southern per capita income relative to that of the rest of the nation. With the exclusion of slaves from "society" the level of southern per capita income in 1860 exceeds the national average. Southern per capita income was two-thirds again as large as the per capita income of the North Central states, and the gap between the South and the Northeast is reduced by over 50 percent. Treating slaves as intermediate goods also has an effect upon rates of growth. The southern growth rate becomes 1.8 percent, in contrast with the rest of the nation's 1.3 percent.

Given these findings, how do we account for the widespread impression of southern backwardness? Three factors seem most important. First, the fact that the South had only 33 percent of the nation's population in 1860 (24 percent of the free population) means that comparisons based upon total output (perhaps useful in discussing war potential) provide a less favorable comparison for the South than do the per capita measures.[36] Second, the commercial dependence upon the North for financial and transport services, as well as for manufactured goods, upset the southerners, who seemed unwilling to acknowledge fully their comparative advantage in the production of cotton and other staples. Third, if growth is equated with urbanization and industrialization, the South does compare unfavorably with the rest of the nation. Comparisons with the agricultural states of the North Central region, however, are less unfavorable to the South. The percentage of population in urban areas in 1860 was 36 percent in the Northeast, 14 percent in the North Central states, and 7 percent in the South. Of the total national employment in manufacturing in that year, 72 percent was in the Northeast, 14 percent in the North Central states, and 10 percent in the South. (The population shares were 36 percent, 29 percent, and 33 percent, respectively).[37]

The last two of the indicators have been widely used as proxy measures for southern economic development, in the absence of a more complete set of income estimates. Thus their usefulness as proxies has been superseded by Easterlin's measures, which directly give us the information we want. While it is true the South lacked industry and was not urbanized relative to the rest of the nation, this clearly did not mean that the South was a poor or a stagnant area.

[35] The "maintenance cost" per slave used in these calculations was $20 (see Gray, op. cit., p. 544). It should be noted that while a higher maintenance cost would reduce the relative per capita income of free southerners in 1860, it would raise the rate of growth of their income between 1840 and 1860. E.g., if a $30 figure were used the southern per capita income would have been $144, compared to the North's $142, but the growth rate would have risen to 1.9 percent, with that of the North remaining the same as in the previous calculation. For similar comparisons see Easterlin, op. cit., p. 527, and Robert William Fogel, "The Reunification of Economic History with Economic Theory," American Economic Review, 55:92–98 (May, 1965).

[36] Hinton Helper's classic attack was restricted to measures of total output, overlooking population differences. Hinton Rowan Helper, The Impending Crisis of the South: How to Meet It (New York, 1963). His comparison was based upon a more complicated model, since it is also intended to explain the net outflow of population from the South. Southern total income grew at 4.1 percent from 1840 to 1860 as contrasted with the rest of the nation's rate of 4.7 percent. The northeastern growth rate, however, was only 4.0 percent. (With slaves treated as intermediate goods, the southern growth rate becomes 4.2 percent, still below the rest of the nation's rate of 4.7 percent.)

[37] Bureau of the Census, Sixteenth, Population (Washington, 1942), Vol. I, p. 20. Census, Eighth, Manufactures of the United States in 1860 (Washington, 1865), p. 729.

Other of the arguments which have been used to suggest southern backwardness can also be misleading. The particular nature of cotton as a crop may explain the low level of farm mechanization in the South, since cotton was profitably farmed without mechanical equipment. It is of interest that no important cotton harvesting equipment was adopted until the middle of the twentieth century. Profitability of new lands can explain the frequent mention of presumably exhausted soil in the older areas of the South. Given a choice between investing in older soils (fertilizing) and in new soils (clearing), at the relative prices existing before the Civil War, movement to new soil was apparently economically rational. It is not clear, moreover, that this behavior would not have changed had the relative prices for these types of investment in land shifted.

Emphasis by Phillips on the effects of slavery upon capital formation has made this a standard argument for southern retardation. The slave system has been considered to be the cause of low southern investment in physical capital, since investment in slaves presumably absorbed capital which would have had other uses in the economy.[38] However, once the external slave trade was forbidden, there was no capital drainage out of the South—funds were merely being transferred from one region to another within the southern economy. Therefore, it is necessary to determine what the seller of the slave did with his funds.[39] It is, in fact, possible that slave ownership increased the ability of southerners to borrow from the North (as well as the planter's ability to borrow within the South) by providing a marketable asset which could be used for collateral on loans, and thus permitted increased capital formation.

Other explanations of low southern capital formation can also be questioned. That a skewed income distribution and the social climate attributable to slavery resulted in conspicuous consumption and waste of money on the part of the plantation owners has often been argued.[40] At present, however, no reliable income distribution statistics exist for the antebellum South which can be compared with other regions and years. For a rough indication of the inequality of the income of the free population in 1860, I have estimated the share of income going to the top approximately 1 percent of free southern families in 1860. The basic assumption is that all the top income earners were plantation owners. By using data on the size distribution of

[38] Moes has pointed out a theoretically plausible way in which such a decline in investment could have occurred. If in a non-slave society expenditures on rearing children are considered consumption to the parents while in a slave society such expenditures are considered part of capital formation, slave societies which have the same savings-income ratio as non-slave societies would devote less to non-human capital. However, if the ratio of savings to income was higher the more unequally income was distributed, the slave society might devote more to all types of capital formation than the non-slave. John E. Moes, "The Absorption of Capital in Slave Labor in the Ante Bellum South and Economic Growth," *American Journal of Economics and Sociology*, 20:535–541 (October, 1961).

[39] It is not clear in which direction within the South net capital flowed. If a slave was sold from an older region to a new region, there would be a net flow of funds to the older area in exchange for human capital. If the planter moved with his slaves there would be a net inflow of human and other capital into the new region, with no corresponding outflow. See William L. Miller, "A Note on the Importance of the Interstate Slave Trade of the Ante Bellum South," *Journal of Political Economy*, 73:181–187 (April, 1965).

[40] The distribution of income in the South is still debated. For an argument that inequality was not as great as often implied, see Frank Lawrence Owsley, *Plain Folk of the Old South* (Baton Rouge, 1949). For a rebuttal to this position see Fabian Linden, "Economic Democracy in the Slave South: An Appraisal of Some Recent Views," *Journal of Negro History*, 31:140–189 (April, 1946).

plantations by number of slaves owned, it was estimated that the share of free southern income going to the top 1 percent of the free population was about the same as the income share of the top 1 percent of the population in 1929.[41] While crude, it does suggest the need for more detailed examination of southern income distribution.

The essential point of the conspicuous consumption argument is not that planters purchased more land and slaves—this could represent a productive use of capital— but that they lived too lavishly. This is usually supported by fragmentary mentions of wasteful expenditures by planters. Unfortunately, we again lack sufficient data to determine if the spending propensities were higher in the South than in the North, as well as if the South had more and/or richer upper income families. We do know, however, that the large consumption expenditures do not imply low savings. In the somewhat atypical year of 1928, the per capita consumption of the top 1 percent of income earners in the United States population was about $5200, while that of the remaining 99 percent was under $600. Certainly this is a pronounced difference, and given normal human reactions this could (and did) lead to discussions of wasteful expenditures by the rich. Yet in this year the top 1 percent had a savings-income ratio of 43.3 percent, and accounted for over 100 percent of estimated personal savings.[42] This suggests the possibility that the effects of large consumption expenditures on southern capital formation may be overstated. That conspicuous consumption which did exist was probably carried on mainly by planters who were wealthy by the standards of the times. Their conspicuous consumption possibly absorbed only part of their incomes, and their saving rates could have exceeded the national average. Indeed, given what we now know about the relationship between income and savings, it is quite possible that savings in the South were higher than they would have been with a less skewed income distribution.

Another way in which slavery was presumed to have retarded southern capital formation was by necessitating debt payments to be made to the North. Payments on

[41] The key assumptions were that only plantation owners fell in the top 1 percent of income earners, and that dividing estimated plantation income by five (the average family size) does not change the rankings. Thus what is actually measured is the share of income going to families owning large plantations. The size distribution of plantations is in Census, Eighth, *Agriculture of the United States in 1860* (Washington, 1864), p. 247 and errata sheet. Each slave was considered to represent capital (including land, etc.) of $2500. Capital was then decapitalized at 6 percent, roughly the market rate of interest. If slavery were unprofitable, the capital estimate would be decapitalized at a lower rate, and the income amount and share would be correspondingly lower. Total free southern income was taken from the detail underlying Table I. The top 0.8 percent of free population, representing plantations with over 50 slaves, received 15 percent of income, while the top 1.2 percent (plantations with over 40 slaves) received 18.5 percent. In 1929 the top 1 percent of the population received 17.2 percent of income (economic variant). See Simon Kuznets, *Shares of Upper Income Groups in Income and Saving* (National Bureau of Economic Research Occasional Paper 35, New York, 1950), p. 67. For a study of the wealth distribution in 1860, based on census manuscripts, see Robert E. Gallman, "The Social Distribution of Wealth in the United States," unpublished paper presented to the International Economic History Conference, August, 1965.

[42] See Robert J. Lampman, *The Share of Top Wealth-Holders in National Wealth, 1922–56* (Princeton, 1962), p. 236. This is the boldest comparison, but more typical years of the 1920's can be used to demonstrate the same point. In 1925, e.g., the ratio of consumption per capita of the upper 1 percent to that of the rest of the population was 9:1; yet the upper income groups had a savings-income ratio of 42.9 percent, and accounted for 51 percent of personal savings.

loans led to a drain of funds from the South, as did southern purchases of services from the North. However, the existence of such flows are part of the costs to be paid for profitable borrowing and specialization. Certainly the existence of capital imports for the South need not result in any reduction in income or capital formation. If the capital imports permitted a higher level of investment in the South it could have raised, rather than lowered, the rate of growth of the economy.

It has been argued that the income estimates do not provide the relevant comparisons—that the South should have industrialized for long-term growth irrespective of its prewar condition. This implies that a deliberate effort should have been made to shift resources from agriculture to manufacturing. This policy has been advocated on two grounds. The first is that the southern entrepreneurs were backward, and therefore were unwilling or unable to take advantage of modern developments. It appears, however, that the South did not ignore all modern developments. The South had 31 percent of the nation's railroad mileage, with per capita mileage only slightly below the national average.[43] This network was financed predominantly by indigenous capital, a fact which is of interest for the capital formation hypothesis discussed above. While the track to area ratio was lower in the South than elsewhere, the southern economy was favored by a transportation network based upon navigable streams and rivers. Thus the absence of an entrepreneurial spirit within the confines of the slave system is not clearly established.

The second reason for advocating a shift to manufactures is the proposition that growth based upon an agricultural export commodity was doomed to ultimate failure. The more rapid the shift away from cotton, the better the longer-term prospects for the southern economy. Implicit in this is the statement that southern whites would not have responded to changing profit opportunities. This statement is usually justified by the argument that industrialization was prevented because it would have meant the end of slavery. While the hypothesis that with the existence of shifts in profitability the South would not have shifted into industry is widely debated, it should be repeated that cotton production was apparently profitable in most of the antebellum period, that geographic mobility in response to income differentials existed, and that, at least within agriculture, there were responses to changing profitability.

In concluding this section, we can raise further questions about two of the arguments previously given for slavery's deleterious effect upon southern economic development. The first, arguing for retarded development of the internal market, needs more justification. The question is not slave purchasing power but the amount of demand which existed for products the slaves consumed. Southern discussions of the clothing and shoes for slaves which were imported from the North suggest the existence of a substantial market for consumer goods on plantations. That the planters paid for these goods rather than the slaves does not diminish the effect on demand. It can be argued that the products ordered by planters were more standardized and amenable to mass production techniques than would have been the situation if the slaves were themselves the source of demand.

[43] See George Rogers Taylor, *The Transportation Revolution, 1815–1860* (New York, 1951), p. 79. Similarly, Allen Fenichel shows that in 1838 (the only ante bellum year for which data exist) the South had 38.2 per cent of the nation's total capacity of steam power in manufacturing. Allen H. Fenichel, "Growth and Diffusion of Power in Manufacturing, 1838–1919," in Conference on Research in Income and Wealth, Volume Thirty, *Output, Employment, and Productivity in the United States After 1800* (New York, 1966), 443–478.

Given the small optimal size of manufacturing plants in 1860, it seems probable that the southern market could have been large enough to support internal industry, if the South's comparative advantage had been manufacturing. Estimates presented by Genovese of cash expenditures per person in the South suggest that the region could have supported over 50 cotton textile plants and more than 200 boot and shoe establishments of Massachusetts size. While an admittedly crude calculation, it is more probable that the estimates are too low rather than too high.[44] For a more complete answer the important questions are those of plantation self-sufficiency and the nature of the products purchased by southerners. To settle this, detailed records of the magnitude and composition of southern purchases from other regions and from abroad are needed.[45]

The second argument, the relative deficiency of education in the South, is clearly supported by the relevant data. The education of slaves was forbidden by law, while that of the whites was certainly below that in the rest of the nation.[46] However, given the world demand for cotton and the rate of growth of income in the antebellum South, it may be that whatever costs it did impose were negligible relative to the effects in the late nineteenth and twentieth centuries. Here again, more research is needed in order to establish the size of the penalty paid by the South for its educational backwardness before the Civil War.

CONCLUSION

The recent works of historians and economists have resulted in revisions of the conclusions about the economics of slavery which derive from the pioneer works of U. B. Phillips. Indications are that on the eve of the Civil War slavery was profitable to the planters, viable, and consistent with a growing economy.

There are many aspects of the overall impact of slavery which have not been discussed. The effects on political decision-making, the psychology of the white population, and the propensity to innovate, for example, must be answered before a full determination of the social and economic effects of the slave system can be made.[47]

[44] Genovese estimates 1860 cash expenditure in Mississippi at about $25 per person (Genovese, *Political Economy*, p. 169). If we assume this amount to hold throughout the southern states, this amounts to about one-fourth of southern per capita income in that year. Making the extreme assumption that outside of the South all income went into cash expenditures, while the southern share was only one-fourth, and that expenditures on boots and shoes and cotton textiles were proportional to all cash expenditures, we can use the value of output of those sectors to estimate total southern cash expenditures on the specific goods. Total value of output and average output per Massachusetts plant are from Census, Eighth, *Manufactures*, pp. xxi and lxxiii. In 1860 there were 217 cotton textile plants and 1,354 boot and shoe establishments in Massachusetts.

[45] For an attempt to measure this trade see Albert Fishlow, *American Railroads and the Transformation of the Antebellum Economy* (Cambridge, 1965), 269–288, as well as the articles by Fishlow and Fogel in Ralph L. Andreano, ed., *New Views on American Economic Development* (Cambridge, 1965), 187–224.

[46] See Albert Fishlow, "The Common School Revival: Fact or Fancy?", in Henry Rosovsky, ed., *Industrialization in Two Systems: Essays in Honor of Alexander Gerschenkron* (New York, 1966), 40–67.

[47] For a study of some of these effects see Stanley M. Elkins, *Slavery: A Problem in American Institutional and Intellectual Life* (Chicago, 1959).

Perhaps the basic economic question would be the comparison of southern developments under free and slave labor. It is possible that growth might have been more rapid and the returns to investment higher had the slave system never been introduced. Yet we do know that up to the Civil War the South had a relatively high level of per capita income, that because of the surplus above subsistence costs the planters as a class made a return on their investments in slaves greater than that on alternative investments possible at that time, and that even if slave labor had been less efficient than free, its use probably did not cause losses to the owners. While the broader and more difficult questions are still unanswered, the recent revisions have improved the analytical and factual framework in which they can be pursued.

5 / Slavery and Personality: A Further Comment

Mary Agnes Lewis

In addition to challenging Phillips' views of plantation profits, historians have recently denied that slavery was benevolent or the slave contented. Here, too, Stampp has led the assault. In *The Peculiar Institution,* he views slavery not only as economically exploitive but also as cruel and harshly inhumane. Moreover, black men, he notes, bitterly resented it and struck back in every way possible for men living under a powerful, coercive system.

Taking a sharply different tack, Stanley Elkins of Smith College in his controversial work, *Slavery: A Problem in American Institutional and Intellectual Life,* accepts without question the fact that slavery was stern and repressive. He differs from Stampp, however, in doubting that the typical slave resisted the system at every turn. Stampp emphasized the overt anger and rage of the slave; Elkins stresses his essential dependence, passivity, and acquiescence. Unlike the black slave in Latin America who boldly resisted the system by participating in numerous revolts, the American slave became a "Sambo" who took refuge in a false, childlike, irresponsible, unthreatening personality. Unprotected by a powerful royal authority and an international church such as existed in Latin America, the slave in the United States was fully exposed to the naked force of capitalism. Like the Jews who passively went to their slaughter in the Nazi concentration camps during World War II, the black man in the Old South was reduced to a thing, his manhood systematically stripped away.

Elkins' analysis has caused considerable discomfort to some historians because it seems to paint an unflattering image of the Negro personality under slavery, and also seems to suggest that black men did little or nothing to achieve their own freedom. Inspired by such uneasiness, a number of scholars have been critical of Elkins, especially of his "Sambo" image. At least one historian has suggested that the meek, happy-go-lucky mien of the slave was merely a device to spare him punishment, and that beneath the surface and detectable in his humor and folklore, were deep angers and resentments. Mary Agnes Lewis in the following brief article takes a

American Quarterly, XIX, No. 1 (Spring 1967), 114–121. Copyright © 1967 by the Trustees of the University of Pennsylvania. Reprinted by permission.

somewhat different approach that draws on social psychology, much as Elkins did himself, but she reaches opposite conclusions.

For further reading: * Kenneth Stampp, *The Peculiar Institution: Slavery in the Ante-Bellum South* (New York: Alfred A. Knopf, Inc., 1956); * U. B. Phillips, *American Negro Slavery* (Gloucester, Mass.: Peter Smith, 1959); * Stanley Elkins, *Slavery: A Problem in American Institutional and Intellectual Life* (Chicago: University of Chicago Press, 1959); Kenneth W. Porter, "Negroes and the Seminole War, 1835–1842," *Journal of Southern History*, XXX (November 1964); * David B. Davis, *The Problem of Slavery in Western Culture* (Ithaca, N. Y.: Cornell University Press, 1966); Herbert S. Klein, *Slavery in the Americas: A Comparative Study of Cuba and Virginia* (Chicago, Ill.: University of Chicago Press, 1967); Eugene Genovese, "Rebelliousness and Docility in the Negro Slave: A Critique of the Elkins Thesis," *Civil War History*, XIII (December 1967).

This paper will explore Stanley Elkins' treatment of the American plantation system as a factor in the formation and perpetuation of distinct slave personality traits. In his book *Slavery*,[1] Elkins combines role psychology and the interpersonal approach to personality formation. The interpersonal theory asserts that in any group certain people are influential in the formation of the personalities of individual members of that group. Sullivan[2] has designated this influential or reference group *significant others*. The individual internalizes the reactions of others toward his performance of certain roles. Personality is acquired through social interaction as the individual continually adjusts his behavior to conform to the expectations and evaluations of significant others.

The role system, on the other hand, de-emphasizes the factor of individual choice since roles are defined and assigned by society and not by the individual. Role theory focuses on the ways in which a society determines how social intercourse is to be conducted.[3]

This paper was prepared as an independent study project in consultation with Dr. Robin Brooks, History Department, California State College at Hayward.

[1] Stanley M. Elkins, *Slavery: A Problem in American Institutional and Intellectual Life* (Chicago, 1959).

Elkins' much-debated thesis on individual and group adjustment has received considerable attention in recent years. The most important uses of the "Sambo" stereotype are to be found in the literature dealing with concepts of identity. The emergence of the slaveowner as the sole significant other within the American slave system is discussed in W. Haywood Burns, *The Voices of Negro Protest* (New York and London, 1963). The psychological consequences of the slave's and freedman's dependence on white authority-figures is summarized in Charles Silberman's *Crisis in Black and White* (New York, 1964) and Thomas F. Pettigrew's *A Profile of the Negro American* (Princeton, 1964). In *The New World of Negro Americans* (New York, 1963), Harold R. Isaacs finds the major element in Afro-American group identity to be "identification with the aggressor"—the desire to be white.

[2] Harry Stack Sullivan, *Conceptions of Modern Psychiatry* (Washington, D. C., 1947), pp. 95–96; see also Sullivan's *The Interpersonal Theory of Psychiatry* (New York, 1953).

[3] Theodore M. Newcomb, *Social Psychology* (New York, 1950), pp. 280–83.

Elkins writes, "In the slave system of the United States—so finely circumscribed and so cleanly self-contained—virtually all avenues of communication to the society at large, originated and ended with the master. The system was unique, *sui generis*."[4] The essence of this unique system was its "closedness," that is, the near-total domination of slaves by owners. The psychological consequence of this closed system was the creation and fostering of a distinct slave personality of which the principal element was the slave's "total" dependence on a single authority-figure, the owner.

Elkins characterizes this personality type: "Sambo, the typical plantation slave, was docile but irresponsible, loyal but lazy, humble but chronically given to lying and stealing; his behavior was full of infantile silliness and his talk inflated with childish exaggeration. His relationship with his master was one of utter dependence and childlike attachment: it was indeed this childlike quality that was the very key to his being."[5]

The assumption we are asked to accept is that a group of atomized, childlike individuals had no means by which to relate themselves and others save the integrative framework provided by the owner's authority. The Self (slave) they related to was a direct function of the Other (owner).

The owner, then, was the sole significant other in that he provided the ways in which the slave viewed himself and the rest of society. Moreover, the owner set the social goal to which the slave aspired—to become an obedient and "loved" servant. The slave manifested his gratitude for this love and approval by his loyalty and service to the owner.

For a paradigm of the effective "closed system" Elkins turns to the German concentration camps of the Second World War. Here, compliance and the appropriate patterns of behavior were exacted in a relatively short period of time. The effectiveness of the camp experience in structuring personality is measured by the lack of organized resistance among prisoners, the infrequency of suicides and the absence of hatred toward the guards.[6] Elkins acknowledges exceptions to submissive, childlike behavior among camp inmates. These were notably people who performed roles *other than* that of prisoner. They were orderlies, clerks and the like. Thus, even in such a "perverted patriarchy" many of the inmates escaped identification with the SS guards.[7]

Elkins also acknowledges that exceptions to "Sambo" obtained under plantation slavery. However, he insists that the most important factor in conditioning the personalities of the majority of slaves was identification with a benevolent patriarch. Elkins informs us that it was because the system was closed that "the individual, consequently, for his very psychic security, had to picture his master in some way as the 'good father,' even when, as in the concentration camp, it made no sense at all."[8]

As the plantation system became more elaborate, race relations came to be

[4] Elkins, p. 63.

[5] *Ibid.*, p. 82.

[6] *Ibid.*, pp. 114–15.

[7] *Ibid.*, pp. 134–35. Here Elkins writes that "to a prisoner so engaged, there were others who mattered, who gave real point to his existence—the SS was no longer the only one. Conversely, the role of the child was not the only role he played. He could take initiative; he could give as well as receive protection; he did things which had meaning in adult terms."

[8] *Ibid.*, pp. 128–29.

governed by patterns of behavior which differentiated black and white into distinct and irrevocable categories.[9] The crystallization of a truly "closed" structure was prevented by permitting two racially autonomous groups of people to exist. The link between the races was economic rather than one based on social reciprocity.[10]

Once the system sanctioned the existence of an independent slave community the possibility that the owner would remain the only significant other vanished. For, while the slave remained an object in his relations with whites, within his own community the slave performed roles other than those required by the "institution" of slavery. The structure and values of the slave community were sufficiently separate from those of whites. Kenneth Stampp has noted that "the resulting unique patterns of slave behavior amused, or dismayed, or appalled the whites and convinced most of them that Negroes were innately different."[11] It was possible for a woman to work all day in the fields and return to her cabin in the evening and poison her baby rather than have it live in bondage.[12] In the field she worked as did other slaves; in the cabin her considerations were those of a mother. Some of the roles validated only within the slave community were those of conjurer, teacher and parent.

Reports of ex-slaves indicate that considerations having no relation to the approval of a benevolent patriarch were instrumental in shaping the aspirations of slaves. Of these aspirations, the most notable was, of course, the desire for freedom. Any slave who conceived of freedom was, at that moment, outside the system.[13] James L. Smith reported that on his escape several friends accompanied the escape party part of the way—thus, vicariously participating in the escape each may have wished for himself.[14] There are also numerous reports of slaves rendering assistance to fugitives.[15] The danger of these ventures should indicate that participation on any

---

[9] These behaviors served to separate rather than to join people together. See E. Franklin Frazier, *The Negro in the United States* (New York, 1949), chap. iii, "The Plantation as a Social Institution"; and Bertram W. Doyle, *The Etiquette of Race Relations in the South* (Chicago, 1937), chaps. ii and iii.

[10] Slave and owner were bound together in an economic venture and its failure could have grave consequences for both parties. "The most grotesque aspect of plantation paternalism lay in the fact that if a planter took *too* complaisant an attitude toward the performance of field work, he courted financial failure, and with failure would come the sale of his slaves to pay his indebtedness." Willie Lee Rose, *Rehearsal for Reconstruction: The Port Royal Experiment* (Indianapolis, 1964), p. 127.

[11] Kenneth Stampp, *The Peculiar Institution* (New York, 1964), p. 334.

[12] Such an incident is recorded in *Lay My Burden Down: A Folk History of Slavery*, ed. B. A. Botkin (Chicago, 1945), p. 154.

[13] Compare with concentration camp inmates, who, according to Bruno Bettleheim, "frequently admitted that they could no longer visualize themselves living outside the camps, making free decisions, taking care of themselves and their families." "Individual and Mass Behavior in Extreme Situations," *Journal of Abnormal and Social Psychology*, XXXVIII (Oct. 1943), 439.

It appears that the major difference between camp inmates and slaves was a vitality that the former entirely lacked. Harvey Wish has noted that while "ex-slaves took issue with the impression of plantation visitors that the slaves must have been contented, . . . the constant outbreak of hearty Negro laughter, the improvised singing and the vigorous dancing. . . . All this did show an impressive zest for life and a level of existence undoubtedly higher than that of the inmates of a twentieth-century concentration camp." *Slavery in the South: First-Hand Accounts of the Ante-Bellum American Southland*, ed. Harvey Wish (New York, 1964), p. xix.

[14] James L. Smith, *Autobiography* (Norwich, 1881), p. 41.

[15] For activities of the underground railroad see Austin Bearse, *Remembrances of Fugitive Slave*

level was more meaningful to the slave than the presumed "total" identification with the values of the owner and his household.

Frederick Douglass, like many slaves, had a variety of black significant others. These ranged from "Doctor" Isaac Cooper, the slave who taught him "religion," to the artisans on the plantation.[16] Along this continuum were also to be found those who persisted in defying the authority of the owner and his underlings.[17]

Nichols has rightly observed that "the Negro lived in two worlds in both of which he strove to gain status. Among other Negroes he was often expected to act against his owner's interest or to show a manliness which the master would not permit. To his owner the slave was forced to act with the deference expected of the subordinate caste."[18] The conflict emerging between self and role assignment intensified as the slave community defined "freedom" in terms that opposed the interests of the owner. Suicide, escape and rebellion were some of the consequences of this conflict.

There were those who, after escaping, regrouped in stable communities in the United States and Canada. Any slave having knowledge of successful escapes, uprisings, and especially communities in which black men lived together in freedom had ties beyond slavery. He had significant others who had not only outwitted the owner but with whom he could intimately identify.

Elkins refuses to accept compliance (accommodation) as a valid defensive function of slave personality.[19] To view compliance as a convenient mechanism employed by several generations would necessarily destroy his assumption of the slave's internalization of the "Sambo" role. Consequently, the possibility that conformity and compliance might be extorted without significant personality distortion is not considered. If the "Sambo" role were internalized then the use of force would not have been as prevalent as the literature reveals. The use and significance of force is well documented in both judicial records and the reports of ex-slaves.[20] Many fugitives commented on the seemingly paradoxical phenomenon that those individuals who most humbly submitted to punishment and the wrath of the owner or overseer were thereafter most frequently and harshly punished:

> They prefer to whip those who are most easily whipped. The doctrine that submission to violence is the best cure for violence did not hold good as between slaves and overseers. He was whipped oftener who was whipped easiest. That slave who had the courage to stand up for himself against the overseer, although he might have many hard stripes at first, became virtually a freeman. "You can

---

Days (Boston, 1880); William Wells Brown, Narrative (London, 1849); and William Still, The Underground Railroad (Philadephia, 1872).

[16] Frederick Douglass, Life and Times of Frederick Douglass (New York, 1962), p. 62.

[17] Successful or not, these rebels became the slave's heroes: "When Nat Turner's insurrection broke out, the colored people were forbidden to hold meetings among themselves. Nat Turner was one of the slaves who had a quite large army; he was the captain to free his race." Smith, p. 30.

[18] Charles H. Nichols, Many Thousand Gone (Leiden, 1963), p. 74.

[19] Elkins, pp. 132–33, n. 106.

[20] See James Roberts, Narrative (Chicago, 1858), pp. 11–12; Austin Stewart, Twenty-Two Years a Slave and Forty Years a Freeman (New York, 1867), pp. 17–18; Judicial Cases Concerning American Slavery and the Negro, ed. Helen T. Catterall (5 vols.; Washington, D. C., 1926–37), I, 216–21, 247.

shoot me," said a slave to Rigby Hopkins, "but you can't whip me," and the result was he was neither whipped nor shot.[21]

Evidently the slave with whom the owner and overseer could most readily relate was one who performed the role of submissive slave. Confrontations with recalcitrant slaves were avoided; they could be ignored, hired out, sold or killed, but not confronted.[22]

A concept dealing with the reinforcement of stereotypes is the "self-fulfilling prophecy." [23] This concept treats social perception as an integral part of transactions people define as being real. By predicting the outcome of any situation the perceiver is aware of and responds to only those things relevant to his initial judgment. He is never conscious of the contribution of his behavior and attitudes to the final outcome. He has, in effect, psychological investments in the maintenance of the initial perception. In this and similar ways slaveholders could remain *selectively inattentive* to anything that might lead to their interacting with slaves in terms other than those provided by the stereotype.

An interesting example of selective inattention is provided in the following letter to an escaped slave from his former owner:

> I write you these lines to let you know the situation we are in,—partly in consequence of your running away and stealing Old Rock, our fine mare. Though we got the mare back, she never was worth much after you took her,—and, as I now stand in need of some funds, I have determined to sell you, and I have had an offer for you, but did not see fit to take it. If you will send me one thousand dollars, and pay for the old mare, I will give up all claim I have to you. . . . If you do not comply with my request, I will sell you to some one else, and you may rest assured that the time is not far distant when things will be changed with you. . . . You know that we reared you as we reared our own children; . . . that shortly before you ran away, when your master asked you if you would like to be sold, you said you would not leave him to go with any body.
>
> Sarah Logue[24]

The man to whom this letter was addressed was certainly no "Sambo"! He replied:

> you never could have insulted a brother by telling him you sold his only remaining brother and sister, because he put himself beyond your power to convert him into money. . . . Now you have the unutterable meanness to ask me to return and be your miserable chattel, or, in lieu thereof, send you $1000 to enable you to redeem the *land*, but not to redeem my poor brother and sister! . . . you say, 'You know we raised you as we did our own children.' Woman, did you raise your *own children* for the market? . . . Did you raise them to be driven off, bound to a coffle in chains? Where are my poor bleeding brothers and sisters? Can you tell? Who was it that sent them off into sugar and cotton fields, to be kicked and cuffed, and whipped, and to groan and die; and where no kin can hear their groans, or attend and sympathize at their dying bed, or follow in their funeral? . . . But, by the way, where is your husband? You don't speak of him.

---

[21] Douglass, p. 52.

[22] The concentration camp system did not tolerate these alternative methods of dealing with difficult prisoners. Bettleheim, *Jour. of Abnormal & Soc. Psychology*, XXXVIII, 436.

[23] Robert K. Merton, "The Self-Fulfilling Prophecy," *Antioch Review*, VIII (Summer 1948), 193–210.

[24] *The Mind of the Negro as Reflected in Letters Written During the Crisis, 1800–1860*, ed. B. A. Botkin (Chicago, 1945), p. 154.

I infer, therefore, that he is dead; that he has gone to his great account, with all his sins against my poor family upon his head. . . . If you or any other speculator on my body and rights, wish to know how I regard my rights, they need but come here, and lay their hands on me to enslave me. . . .

Yours, etc.,

J. W. Loguen[25]

Another example of the pervasiveness of selective inattention within the plantation system is given by James "Lindsey" Smith who reported:

My master came as far as Philadelphia to look for me; and my brother says, when he came back without me, he became a very demon on the plantation, cutting and slashing, cursing and swearing at the slaves till there was no living with him. He seemed to be out of his head; and for hours would set looking straight into the fire; when spoken to, he would say: "I can't understand what made Lindsey leave me." [26]

This last example is perhaps the best instance of the self-fulfilling prophecy of the benevolent patriarch. Smith was not a favorite slave. He was lame, had a record of shunning work, feigning illness and all the other mechanisms employed to "trick" the owner. Why the owner would have gone to so much bother to retrieve Lindsey becomes clear when one considers the psychological investment in the performance of the role of patriarch. For his owner, "Lindsey" remained the dependent ward whose behavior in running away was unintelligible. In interaction with the slave-holder only that part of Lindsey associated with "Sambo" was recognized. The slave's true self could be affirmed only by his fellows.

Finally, Elkins' analysis, far from offering new insights into the American slave system, falls comfortably within traditional approaches to the subject. We have been asked to accept the same syndrome of cultural assumptions and have been guided to the same conclusion: though slavery, per se, was "wrong" it did provide the deculturalized African and his progeny with those valuable cues which enabled them to make appropriate adjustments to their situation.[27] Elkins asks that we accept, on the basis of the evidence, the validity of the "Sambo" stereotype so that the debate can finally be closed.[28]

However, the closed construct employed by Elkins is inapplicable to slavery as it existed in the United States. So long as there was the possibility of the emergence of alternative significant others the owner's control over the psychological security of slaves was not absolute, or even near-absolute. A viable, self-perpetuating slave culture did emerge to compete with the slaveowner's authority and significance. It was from this society that the slave sought approval and affirmation of himself as a man.

In applying his theory of a closed society to slavery, Elkins is forced to treat escapees, rebels and the like as deviants. From his established framework, he could not recognize that those he would call deviants fulfilled the ideals and aspirations of many slaves, that day to day resistance could be manifested in any number of

[25] *Ibid.*, pp. 218–19.

[26] Smith, p. 23.

[27] Elkins, pp. 88–89.

[28] Rose, pp. 129–30: "although 'Sambo' finds many illustrations . . . he remains a statistical concept, and the record contains as many stories of protest, disloyalty to the late masters, and manly independence as of servile acquiescence. . . ."

ways. "Occasional sabotage, self-maiming, and inadequate workmanship were common enough to bring complaints from owners and employers. More frequent still was the slow-down. Masters could never be certain how much of this was a vote against the system itself and how much simply reflected the low incentives that characterized slavery."[29] The "Sambo" stereotype does not provide any cues to the readiness of slaves to leave the plantation during and after the Civil War. Nor does it explain the behavior of those who remained but who were engaged in subversive activities.

Elkins assumed that the condition of slavery was similarly experienced and responded to by most American slaves. However, the evidence suggests that there were numerous ways in which black people reacted to slavery and exclusion from the larger society. It also suggests that the concept of the self-fulfilling prophecy offers a preferable explanation of the creation and pervasiveness of the "Sambo" stereotype by revealing the psychological investment of slaveowners (and, indeed, most whites) in its perpetuation.[30]

[29] Richard C. Wade, *Slavery in the Cities: The South 1820–1860* (New York, 1964), pp. 225–26.

[30] "There was the hope on the part of most of the non-slaveholders that they would some day become owners of slaves. Consequently, they took on the habits and patterns of thought of the slaveholders before they actually joined that class." John Hope Franklin, *From Slavery to Freedom* (2nd ed.; New York, 1956), p. 185.

6 / Southern Society: A Reinterpretation

Frank L. Owsley

If historians have argued over the nature of slavery, they have also disagreed about its impact on Southern society. Hinton R. Helper's antebellum work, *The Impending Crisis of the South,* pilloried slavery for degrading the nonslaveholding whites and for hindering Southern economic progress. Modern versions of Helper's critique focus largely on the "poor whites." This argument states that since Southern society degraded work and enabled the planter class to engross the best land, most Southern whites were reduced to a brutalized subsistence existence at the margins of society. Few men of middle rank survived in this system, and the Old South consisted of a planter elite, slaves, and "poor white trash."

In the following selection, Frank Owsley seeks to refute this view. Owsley, who taught for many years at Vanderbilt University in Nashville, Tennessee, has a perspective similar to that of the Nashville "agrarians," a group that flourished in the 1920's and 1930's and was largely composed of literary men antagonistic to the predominant materialism of their day. Disgusted by the crude, exploitive commercialism of modern America, they depicted the Old South as a just society where black men and white men accepted their established roles and treated one another with respect and dignity. Owsley also seeks to rehabilitate the Old South, but he does so by arguing that it was essentially democratic in its social structure, with a large group of yeomen who possessed all of the sturdy, democratic virtues that we associate with nineteenth-century America.

Owsley and his students at Vanderbilt undertook immensely detailed analyses of the manuscript census returns to prove their point. They claimed that this data showed clearly that a large yeoman element existed in the Old South and that landless, poor whites were relatively uncommon. Going beyond the census material, they also sought to demonstrate that far from being a shiftless, immoral fellow, as he is so often depicted, the Southern small farmer was a respectable and intelligent husbandman whose life revolved about his family, his friends, and old-time evangelical religion.

In 1946, Fabien Linden arrived at quite different conclusions using similar source material. In his long and closely argued article, "Economic

Plain Folk of the Old South (Baton Rouge, La.: Louisiana State University Press, 1949), pp. 1–22. Reprinted by permission.

Democracy in the Slave South: An Appraisal of Some Recent Views,"
Linden conceded that the old "planter-poor white stereotype of southern
society" was invalid, but he insisted that the white middle class "shared . . .
a relatively small proportion of the south's property, while conversely an
almost negligible segment of the population owned a very significant portion of the productive lands and slave labor."

The truth of the matter probably lies between these two views.

For further reading: Fabien Linden, "Economic Democracy in the Slave
South: An Appraisal of Some Recent Views," *Journal of Negro History,*
XXXI (April 1946); Blanche H. Clark, *The Tennessee Yeoman, 1840–1860*
(Nashville, Tenn.: Vanderbilt University Press, 1942); Herbert Weaver,
Mississippi Farmers, 1850–1860 (Nashville, Tenn.: Vanderbilt University
Press, 1945); Paul H. Buck, "The Poor Whites of the Ante-Bellum South,"
American Historical Review, XXXI (October 1925); *Hinton R. Helper,
The Impending Crisis of the South: How to Meet It (New York: Burdick
Brothers, 1857).

Most travelers and critics who wrote about the South during the late antebellum
period were of the opinion that the white inhabitants of the South generally fell
into two categories, namely, the slaveholders and the "poor whites." Moreover,
whether or not they intended to do so, they created the impression in the popular
mind that the slaveholder was a great planter living in a white-columned mansion,
attended by a squad of Negro slaves who obsequiously attended his every want and
whim. According to the opinion of such writers, these "cavaliers" were the great
monopolists of their day; they crowded everyone not possessed of considerable wealth
off the good lands and even the lands from which modest profits might be realized;
they dominated politics, religion, and all phases of public life. The six or seven
million nonslaveholders who comprised the remainder of the white population and
were, with minor exceptions, considered "poor whites" or "poor white trash" were
visualized as a sorry lot indeed. They had been pushed off by the planters into the
pine barrens and sterile sand hills and mountains. Here as squatters upon abandoned
lands and government tracts they dwelt in squalid log huts and kept alive by hunting and fishing, and by growing patches of corn, sweet potatoes, collards, and
pumpkins in the small "deadenings" or clearings they had made in the all-engulfing
wilderness. They were illiterate, shiftless, irresponsible, frequently vicious, and nearly
always addicted to the use of "rot gut" whiskey and to dirt eating. Many, perhaps
nearly all, according to later writers, had malaria, hookworm, and pellagra. Between
the Great Unwashed and the slaveholders there was a chasm that could not be
bridged. The nonslaveholders were six or seven million supernumeraries in a slaveholding society.[1]

Frederick Law Olmsted, perhaps, contributed more than any other writer to the
version of Southern society sketched above; for he was possessed of unusual skill

[1] See A. J. N. Den Hollander, "The Tradition of the Poor White" in W. T. Couch (ed.),
Culture in the South (Chapel Hill, 1934), 403, 415, for a criticism of the traditional view of
society in the antebellum South.

in the art of reporting detail and of completely wiping out the validity of such detail by subjective comments and generalizations. For example, despite the fact that he saw little destitution and almost constant evidence of well-being among the poorer folk, he was still able to conclude "that the majority of the Negroes at the North live more comfortably than the majority of whites at the South"; that, indeed, the majority of the people of the South were poor whites. It was not, in his opinion, sterile soil and unhealthful climate that created the great mass of poor whites, but slavery. These people would not work because work was identified with slavery, "For manual agricultural labor . . . ," Olmsted wrote, "the free man looking on, has a contempt, and for its necessity in himself, if such necessity exists, a pity quite beyond that of the man under whose observations it has been free from such an association of ideas." Olmsted could make this generalization despite the fact that throughout his extensive travels in the South he had constantly observed Negro slaves and whites working in the fields together. Indeed, the degradation of free labor by slavery was Olmsted's major premise from which all conclusions flowed regardless of the factual observations that he conscientiously incorporated in his books.[2]

Other writers, who had little or no firsthand knowledge of the South, quite naturally relied on the writings of travelers, and particularly Olmsted, who was regarded as dispassionate and authoritative. Their tendency was to seize upon the generalizations rather than the detailed reporting of the travel literature, with the result that they further simplified the picture of Southern society. George M. Weston's *Poor Whites of the South* and his *Progress of Slavery in the United States* are excellent examples of this process of simplification. "The whites of the South not connected with the ownership or management of slaves," he wrote, "constituting not far from three fourths of the whole number of whites, confined at least to the low wages of agricultural labor, and partly cut off even from this by the degradation of a companionship with black slaves, retire to the outskirts of civilization, where they lead a semisavage life, sinking deeper and more hopelessly into barbarism with each succeeding generation. The slave owner takes at first all the best lands, and finally all the lands susceptible of regular cultivation; and the poor whites, thrown back upon the hills and upon the sterile soils—[are] mere squatters without energy enough to acquire the title even to the cheap lands they occupy, without roads, and at length, without even a desire for education. . . ."[3]

J. E. Cairnes, the British economist, presented the final stereotype of Southern society in his book *The Slave Power*. Cairnes appears to have rested his generalizations about the social structure of the South largely upon those of Olmsted, Weston, and Hinton Rowan Helper. It was a pyramid upon a pyramid. But it was a picture of Southern society that made a deep and lasting impression, for as late as 1947 Allan Nevins drew upon Cairnes's *Slave Power* in his *Ordeal of the Union*. "The constitution of a slave society . . . resolves itself into three classes," writes Cairnes, "broadly distinguished from each other and connected by no common interest—the slaves on whom devolves all the regular industry, the slaveholders who reap all its

---

[2] Frederick L. Olmsted, *A Journey in the Back Country* (New York, 1863), 237, 297, 298, 299, *passim*. See also *id., A Journey in the Seaboard Slave States, with Remarks on Their Economy* (New York, 1856), and *A Journey Through Texas* (New York, 1857), *passim*.

[3] George M. Weston, *The Poor Whites of the South* (Washington, 1856), 5. His *Progress of Slavery* was published in 1857.

fruits, and an idle and lawless rabble who live dispersed over vast plains in a condition little removed from absolute barbarism."[4] "These mean whites . . . are the natural growth of the slave system"; "regular industry is only known to them as the vocation of slaves, and it is the one fate which above all others they desire to avoid."[5] "In the Southern States no less than five million human beings [who have been expelled from the good lands by the slaveholders] are now said to exist . . . in a condition little removed from savage life, eking out a wretched subsistence by hunting, fishing, by hiring themselves out for occasional jobs, by plunder."[6]

The generalization that these writers made about the Old South—which may well be considered the first version of *Tobacco Road*—should be kept in mind, for they have been subjected to frequent examination in preparing this study and will be points of reference in it.

A few Southern historians have accepted in whole or in part the picture of the society of the Old South, as portrayed by such writers as those quoted previously; but most of them, without doubt, have regarded it as fantastic. Sometimes with an expression of indignation on their faces they will say "folks are just not like that in the South. Society is not and never has been divided into rich and poor." Those who were born before 1890 had a firsthand acquaintance with one and often two generations who had lived before 1860 and who were not—nor had they ever been —either poor whites or planters. For example, outstanding Southern historians such as J. G. de Roulhac Hamilton, Charles W. Ramsdell, George Petrie, and Walter Lynwood Fleming grew up in communities where heads of many families, including their own, had been reared before 1860. It will, perhaps, drive home the idea as to how well antebellum Southern society was known by those born prior to the close of the last century if it is remarked that Confederate soldiers in 1900 were about the average age of veterans of World War I in 1949.

Possessed of this firsthand acquaintance with numerous representatives of the Old South, Southern historians have, with few exceptions up until this time, strongly maintained that the white people of the antebellum rural South were not divided into the simple categories of rich planter and poor white. As time has passed, and with it the older generations, even stronger assertions are being made concerning the plain folk of the Old South and, indeed, concerning the whole society in that region. The tone of some of these claims, as I have suggested, is somewhat indignant just as the tone of anyone tends to grow indignant when he knows from his own observations and experiences whereof he speaks, but discovers that his star witnesses have disappeared from the court. The truth of the matter is that for good reasons, such as a lack of trained historians in the South until well after the opening of the present century, the testimony of these star witnesses, the survivors of the old regime, was not taken while they were numerous enough and young enough for their evidence to be both full and valid. It has been assumed, too, quite naturally, that since the farmers and small planters, unlike the large planters and businessmen, seldom preserved their private papers and business accounts, no record of their manner of life and their place in the Southern society remained after they passed on.

But these millions of people did leave records of their lives: the church records,

[4] J. E. Cairnes, *The Slave Power: Its Character, Career and Probable Designs* (New York, 1862), 60.
[5] *Ibid.*, 78, 79.
[6] *Ibid.*, 54.

wills, administration of estates, county-court minutes, marriage licenses, inventory of estates, trial records, mortgage books, deed books, county tax books, and the manuscript returns of the Federal censuses. Other important sources from which much can be learned not only about the plain folk, but about society as a whole in the South, are the older county and town histories, biographies, autobiographies, and recollections of men and women of only local importance—preachers, lawyers, doctors, county newspaper editors, and the like, who knew every family in the county and frequently in a much wider area. Last but not least must be mentioned the writings of those sojourners in the South, who remained in one place long enough to become acquainted with the country and the people. Out of such documents a picture of the whole people can be constructed, not just that of the great planter and merchant, but, in the words of an old jingle: "Rich man, poor man, beggar man, thief, doctor, lawyer, merchant, chief. . . ."

Of all these sources, the county records and the unpublished census reports, which are made by county for each individual, are the most valuable documents from which to study the life of the people as a whole. It is only by employing them in great volume, however, and receiving a cumulative effect that they can at all be usefully employed.

Upon reading page after page of tax lists and census returns, both of which give the landholdings and much of the personal property of all individuals, the picture of the economic structure of the Old South gradually takes form. These sources reveal the existence of a society of great complexity. Instead of the simple, two-fold division of the agricultural population into slaveholders and nonslaveholding poor whites, many economic groups appear. Among the slaveholders there were great planters possessed of thousands of acres of land and hundreds of slaves, planters owning a thousand or fewer acres and two score slaves, small planters with five hundred acres and ten or fifteen slaves, large farmers with three or four hundred acres and five to ten slaves, small farmers with two hundred or fewer acres and one or two slaves. Among the nonslaveholders were large farmers employing hired labor who owned from two hundred to a thousand acres; a middle group which owned from one hundred to two hundred acres; "one horse farmers" with less than one hundred acres; and landless renters, squatters, farm laborers, and a "leisure class" whose means of support does not appear on the record. But the core of the social structure was a massive body of plain folk who were neither rich nor very poor. These were employed in numerous occupations; but the great majority secured their food, clothing, and shelter from some rural pursuit, chiefly farming and livestock grazing. It is the plain country folk with whom I am most concerned here—that great mass of several millions who were not part of the plantation economy. The group included the small slaveholding farmers; the nonslaveholders who owned the land which they cultivated; the numerous herdsmen on the frontier, pine barrens, and mountains; and those tenant farmers whose agricultural production, as recorded in the census, indicated thrift, energy, and self-respect.

It is impossible to convey the picture thus formed by comprehensive examination of tax lists and census reports to those who have not scrutinized these documents to some extent; but, as is so often true under such circumstances, it becomes necessary to resort to abstractions. In this case that means, of course, a statistical analysis, which will be presented later. Only general conclusions and a few sample exhibits from the census reports will be presented here concerning the extent of slave ownings and the spread and sizes of the landholdings of both slaveholders and nonslaveholders.

The slaveholding families composed nearly one third of the white population of the South, and most of them were small slaveowners and small landowners. As estimated, 60 percent owned from one to five slaves, and another large group held from five to ten. Most slaveholders whose chief occupation was agriculture owned their farms, and the small slaveholders, as would be expected, were small landowners. At least 60 percent of the small slaveholders had farms ranging in size from fifty to three hundred acres. Over 60 percent of the nonslaveholders outside the upper seaboard states—who, it will be recalled, were classed as poor white trash—were also landowners. In the lower South and in portions of the upper south central states an estimated 70 percent owned farms. The sizes of their holdings differed very little from those of the small slaveholders. About 75 percent ranged from a few to two hundred acres, and the other 25 percent were above two hundred acres in size. The following table (I–V inclusive) from the agricultural census returns,

TABLE I

HEADS OF AGRICULTURAL FAMILIES,
ROBERTSON COUNTY, TENNESSEE, 1850

Name	Slaves	Acres Imp.	Acres Unimp.	Value of Farm
1. Marvel Lowe	8	200	415	$3,600
2. Caleb Keeler (millwright)	0	50	146	1,000
3. Alexander Lowe	8	150	400	4,000
4. W. E. Felts (blacksmith)	0	50	150	800
5. Whitwell Dowlin	1	50	46	400
6. Harris Dowlin	11	70	60	600
7. Joseph McCormick	0	50	50	300
8. Jno. B. Fiser	29	400	455	5,000
9. B. W. Bradley	5	250	635	3,500
10. Lucy Harris (tenant)	4	40	87	200
11. Jno. C. Balthrop	3	60	200	1,000
12. W. H. Farmer	0	60	187	650
13. James Head	0	40	58	650
14. Mathew Woodruff	1	75	125	325
15. Jas. Gower	0	20	30	150
16. Jacob Bell	6	100	800	2,000
17. Jas. O. Whited	0	60	80	420
18. Geo. Head	0	60	132	150
19. David Alley	0	40	222	200
20. Josiah Winters	0	75	107	675
21. W. H. Head	0	40	60	200
22. Jas. J. Wilson	12	100	163	1,000
23. Jas. Elliott	4	35	15	200
24. Thos. B. Williams	6	60	140	600
25. Geo. W. Farmer	0	30	79	500
26. M. W. Winters (tenant)	0	77	135	700

with data from the slave schedule added, are examples of the type of material used in making the statistical analyses of land and slave ownership. These tables consist of heads of families engaged in agriculture together with their slaves and landhold-

TABLE II

HEADS OF AGRICULTURAL FAMILIES,
WILSON COUNTY, TENNESSEE, 1860

Name	Slaves	Acres Imp.	Acres Unimp.	Value of Farm
1. Sumner Hamilton	4	75	9	$ 2,000
2. Allen Wilson	0	175	30	2,500
3. S. F. Anderson	7	125	150	2,800
4. Noel Keyton	0	100	10	2,000
5. Thomas Keyton	0	120	80	4,000
6. Josiah Davis	0	180	100	7,000
7. Chistifer Cobb	0	50	80	1,500
8. Sarah Hatley	0	20		400
9. Antony Owens	18	500	200	25,000
10. William E. Lacks	8	175	180	8,400
11. M. Lacks (renter)	0	15	5	300
12. W. Lacks (renter)	0	30	10	600
13. Chistifer Owens	2	100	50	3,000
14. Mary Owens	0	125	100	5,675
15. W. D. Jennings	3	120	82	6,000
16. James Bryant	0	150	175	7,000
17. Mary Bryant	0	40	20	1,200
18. John H. Byrn	5	200	200	8,000
19. John Owen	0	75	30	2,000
20. J. W. Williams	0	25	15	800
21. John Sneed	4	100	93	4,825
22. S. N. Thomas	1	100	137	5,925
23. L. V. Cannada	0	40	78	2,300
24. G. L. Smith	0	40	20	1,200
25. William Jewell	0	75	25	2,000
26. J. B. Thomas	0	300	233	10,660
27. Thomas Barkley	0	75	50	2,600
28. H. N. Thomas	0	60	70	4,500
29. Henry Darity	3	100	140	4,800
30. Hanthis Baxter	0	35	30	1,950
31. John G. Thomas	2	100	92	5,760
32. John C. Byrn	0	75	30	3,000
33. Sterling Sugs	0	50	50	1,500

ings. They were transcribed from Schedule IV (Productions of Agriculture) in the exact order as written in the manuscript census returns of 1850 and 1860. The slaves were added from Schedule II (Slave Inhabitants). The vast data on the census sheets, relating to the agricultural productions, the livestock, slaughtered animals, and home manufactures of each farm operator, had to be omitted because of the impracticability of devising a chart large enough for such data and not too large for use in this volume. Each table represents, in a general way, a rural community or settlement; for the census enumerator usually listed each farm and plantation as he came to it, riding horseback along a neighborhood road. These charts are not intended to be used for any mathematical analysis—that matter has been reserved for the final chapter in this volume—but they are placed at this point to convey a general picture of the social and economic structure of a rural community, and to serve as an introduction to the type of material on which all statistical matter relat-

TABLE III

HEADS OF AGRICULTURAL FAMILIES, LOWNDES COUNTY, MISSISSIPPI, 1860

Name	Slaves	Acres Imp.	Acres Unimp.	Value of Farm
1. James Wood	4	100	60	$1,600
2. John M. Basmore	1	60	140	1,000
3. James Wood	1	100	220	1,500
4. Joseph Morris	0	14	26	200
5. Robert Miller	0	12	78	400
6. W. F. Malloy	0	20	220	1,000
7. J. M. Dotson	0	60	100	800
8. R. Worthington	0	50	70	600
9. J. W. Gosa (guardian)	5	80	80	1,500
10. John Morris	10	100	100	2,000
11. Henry Wills	1	80	80	1,600
12. J. W. Lysles	0	60	200	2,000
13. Thomas Smith	9	100	500	4,000
14. Charles Revels	0	55	65	600
15. James Smith	0	40	270	1,200
16. Joseph Slown	0	40	80	500
17. Everard Downey	8	100	320	3,000
18. Jemison Loftis	1	80	120	600
19. William Hudson	0	30	90	600
20. J. C. Lawrence	2	40	50	300
21. W. L. Betts	1	22	51	1,000
22. C. H. Lance	0	50	30	400
23. W. E. Verner	16	200	280	2,000
24. J. W. Denton	0	40	40	800
25. John G. Gaston	0	50	150	1,000
26. F. A. McCown	0	30	90	1,000
27. E. M. Minter	0	60	140	1,000
28. Richard Wood	24	300	100	2,400
29. Ann Morris	0	36	50	800
30. Susan Minter	0	47	73	600
31. James C. Oden	3	20	60	400
32. John L. Kidd	0	45	75	1,000
33. James Eggar	0	65	95	8,000
34. Robert Stephenson	4	80	160	3,000
35. Ruffin Webb	0	50	230	3,000

ing to the ownership of land and slaves has been based. The sizes of farms and plantations and of slaveholdings can be seen at a glance to have been more modest in the rich land areas than tradition has it; and outside the delta the same hasty glance reveals the thorough intermingling of small and large slaveholders and of all slaveholders and nonslaveholders. These factors, in the very beginning, cast doubt upon the validity of the old stereotype of a white society made up of rich planters and poor whites, the former living in the fertile lands and the latter in the sand hills.

Wilson and Robertson counties in middle Tennessee and Lowndes County in eastern, north-central Mississippi are selected as representative of soil areas of intermediate fertility, being neither extremely fertile nor extremely poor, and well suited for general farming as well as the growing of money crops such as cotton

TABLE IV

HEADS OF AGRICULTURAL FAMILIES,
HINDS COUNTY, MISSISSIPPI, 1860

Name	Slaves	Acres Imp.	Acres Unimp.	Value of Farm
1. J. G. Lee	5	150	290	$ 3,520
2. A. Dulaney	4	95	65	1,600
3. J. J. Dees	6	35	85	1,200
4. W. Hand (renter)	11	220	100	4,800
5. R. Umderwood (renter)	3	75	121	2,352
6. A. C. Fletcher	10	100	132	2,480
7. R. McGowen	5	100	91	1,520
8. J. Ainsworth (renter)	23	250	150	6,000
9. J. Gallman	11	175	185	5,400
10. M. Holliday	14	200	59	2,815
11. M. Griffith	4	30	58	704
12. Z. Holliday	26	230	300	6,480
13. A. Gallman	11	160	160	3,440
14. L. Sinclair	6	150	160	3,840
15. C. B. Jones	37	250	135	7,700
16. J. T. Biggs	5	60	20	1,200
17. W. Wise	16	200	150	5,250
18. S. M. Miller	23	250	110	4,500
19. L. W. Carraway	25	500	360	11,335
20. T. G. Ford	15	265	494	11,385
21. J. W. Paterson	35	400	246	10,000
22. J. C. Sims	29	450	500	12,000
23. A. F. Granberry	35	500	660	10,000
24. J. A. Morgan	24	260	220	9,600
25. W. Biggs	18	300	200	6,000
26. W. S. Alsop	15	200	160	3,600
27. E. Coker	21	400	550	14,250
28. J. E. Moncure	66	1,200	1,000	18,900
29. C. E. Wolfe	27	220	100	3,200
30. F. A. Wolf	14	200	236	10,000
31. J. H. Miller	0	50	110	1,600
32. W. B. Smart	56	950	350	26,000
33. L. N. Wolfe	2	155	195	3,200

and tobacco. Plantations dveloped in each of these counties, especially in Lowndes; but the operating units were, as a rule, farmers rather than planters. In the Robertson County table of twenty-six farmers John B. Fiser, with four hundred acres under cultivation and twenty-nine slaves, is the only person who could be classed as even a small planter. Of the thirty-three persons listed in the Wilson County table, Antony Owens, with eighteen slaves and five hundred acres under cultivation, and J. B. Thomas, nonslaveholder, with three hundred acres under cultivation, are the only two who could be considered planters. Of the thirty-six persons in the Lowndes County census table, Richard Wood is the only one who can be ranked as a planter.

Hinds and Bolivar counties were selected as typical of the most fertile soils in the South. Hinds is in the loess-soil region and Bolivar is in the delta. The former, though skirted by the Big Black and Pearl rivers along which there was considerable swampy land, was, on the whole, high and dry and its soil easily brought under cul-

TABLE V

HEADS OF AGRICULTURAL FAMILIES,
BOLIVAR COUNTY, MISSISSIPPI, 1860

Name	Slaves	Acres Imp.	Acres Unimp.	Value of Farm
1. Geo. W. Walton	26	400	560	$ 36,000
2. Iverson Gayden	74	410	400	32,000
3. T. B. Lenore	46	240	880	44,000
4. Chas. Clark	149	1,200	1,760	100,000
5. Jno. B. Flowers	0		960	10,000
6. T. J. Childres	14		440	4,000
7. C. G. Coffee	44	500	1,500	84,000
8. Polk and Rawls	86	1,400	800	70,000
9. Ike S. Robinson	0		2,000	20,000
10. Fielding B. Lewis	29	150	490	20,000
11. S. D. Harris	13	300	820	26,000
12. C. C. S. Farrar	86	500	143	30,000
13. G. L. and R. M. Lewis	53	425	550	50,000
14. Orrin Kingsley	40	1,000	380	20,000
15. F. A. Montgomery	0	200	600	3,200
16. Joseph Sellers	36	230	410	3,200
17. Livingston & Leddell	29	100	700	30,000
18. Dickerson Bell	55	360	1,950	65,250
19. A. and J. A. Rawls	9		308	3,000
20. James M. Owen	0	80	220	6,000
21. A. D. Luck	0	200	230	30,000
22. Wm. E. Starke	35	300	820	32,000
23. E. J. Girault	0	450	590	45,000
24. Wm. Kirk	0	60	1,040	35,000

tivation. It is not surprising, therefore, to find numerous small slaveholders and an occasional nonslaveholding small farmer in this county. Indeed, if one goes back to the settlement of this county he will discover that many of the slaveholders and large planters were originally nonslaveholders, in poor or moderate circumstances in the beginning, and that their wealth was developed from the richness of the soil (at the present time much depleted by erosion). Of the thirty-three men listed in the table, one had no slaves, seven held from two to five, three from six to ten, eight from eleven to sixteen, eight from twenty-three to twenty-nine, three from thirty-five to thirty-seven, and two held fifty-six and sixty-six.

Bolivar County was low and swampy, and large outlays of capital were required to bring the soil under cultivation. Swamps had to be drained, levees built, and the ground cleared of gigantic hardwood forests and jungles of canebrakes. The result was that only those possessed of considerable wealth would undertake to open up a farm or plantation in this region. It will be observed, however, that of the twenty-four men listed, seven were nonslaveholders, three of whom may be classed as planters. Indeed, the nonslaveholder, E. J. Girault, had 450 acres under cultivation and grew 400 bales of cotton and 5,000 bushels of corn according to the census returns, while F. A. Montgomery, another nonslaveholder, with 200 acres under cultivation made 103 bales of cotton and 2,500 bushels of corn. Both grew numerous other crops and owned livestock valued at $5,000 and $3,000 respectively. These nonslaveholders, of course, probably found it less expensive—and certainly less hazardous in a malarial country—to hire slaves rather than own them. Compared to the size of plantations in the delta region today, these plantations were quite modest in acreage, and some would be classed as farms if the land under cultivation is used as an index.

From these tables it will be observed that there was very little tenancy. Most of the operators owned their land. Outside of the Carolinas and Virginia, which have not as yet been systematically examined, from 80 to 85 percent of the agricultural population owned their land.

If one considers the landed resources that were available to the Southern people between the Revolution and the Civil War, it will become apparent why the bulk of the Southern rural population, nonslaveholder and slaveholder alike, acquired the ownership of farmsteads and plantations, and how it was that the herdsmen had such ample pasturage for their livestock. A goodly portion of the Federal public domain, which totaled 1,309,591,680 acres,[7] and over 200,000,000 acres of state lands in Virginia, the Carolinas, Georgia, and Texas had been open to Southerners during this period.[8] The opportunity of acquiring land was greater in the South than in the North. For example, in 1848, before the creation of Oregon Territory the area of the states and organized territories of the South was more than twice as great as that of the North, whereas the population of the South was scarcely half that of the North.[9] At all times during the interval between the Revolution and the Civil War the combined Federal and state public domains in the South were greater than those open to settlement in the North, and the population was increasingly less. But the Southern farmers had another great advantage over the Northerners in that the grain, livestock, and tobacco farmers of the upper South and the Southern highlands could and did move into the lower parts of the Northwest, whereas the Northern farmers could not profitably move South.

The tax lists and census reports enable us to determine with reasonable accuracy the social structure of the rural South, and they are in some degree a measure of the economic struggle of the people. They give us, however, only an impersonal, external view; they furnish, let us say, a picture of the economic man, not the social, gregarious human. It is such documents as grand-jury reports, trial records, court minutes, and wills that furnish the vital spark and recreate the individual, the family, and the community. The wills especially, often so personal and intimate, go far toward supplying a substitute for the private letters and diaries which the common folk, unlike the planters, failed to preserve. The wills also reveal many family customs. A few excerpts should demonstrate the value of such documents in reconstructing the thoughts and attitudes and family relationships and customs of the Southern folk. The will of John Davidson of Dickinson County, Tennessee, nonslaveholder, substantial farmer, and owner of about three hundred acres of land, numerous horses and work stock, swine, and cattle, is given in part.

[7] Benjamin H. Hibbard, *A History of the Public Land Policies* (New York, 1924), 78; Thomas C. Donaldson, *The Public Domain; Its History, with Statistics* (Washington, 1884); table on page 13.

[8] Samuel G. McLendon, *History of the Public Domain of Georgia* (Atlanta, 1924), *passim*; Roy M. Robbins, *Our Landed Heritage; the Public Domain* (Princeton, 1942), 9; Reuben McKitrick, *The Public Land System of Texas, 1823–1910* (Madison, 1918); and Aldon S. Lang, *Financial History of the Public Lands in Texas* (Waco, 1932), *passim*.

[9] See Donaldson, *Public Domain*, 28–29, for areas of states and territories.

> In the name of God, Amen. I, John Davidson Sen'r being of sound mind but in a low state of health do make and publish this my last will and testament. First I desire that all my debts be paid as soon as possible out of the first money that comes into the hands of my beloved wife or my executor. Second, as to what property we have, we in the bonds of affection have labored for it lovingly. We have enjoyed it and now with a glad heart do I will and bequeath all that I die possessed of whether it be lands, crops of any kind, household and kitchen furniture or fowls of all kinds to my beloved wife during her natural life or widowhood for the support of herself and family.

Following this he makes the customary parting gifts to his adult children who seem already to have been given a portion of their inheritance. Then he selected two of his elder sons to manage the farm and care for their mother and the younger children, as was the custom. Thus, this plain man of the Old South in simple eloquence of Biblical flavor bade farewell to his beloved family and all his earthly possessions without a word of regret or complaint. Here was a nonslaveholder, obviously a very literate person, who, together with his family, did not regard labor in the fields as degrading.[10] Davidson's will also illustrates the custom of deeding the land to the widow during her lifetime or widowhood, and the designation of the older sons to manage the farm for her.

The will of James Davis of Harris County, Georgia, which I quote in part, illustrates the conditional granting of land in return for support. It is an example of the method used by the Southern folk to provide social security.

> Whereas my said daughter Sarah Jane and her husband James Lysle has agreed to live with and take care of me during my natural life and also during the lifetime or widowhood of my beloved wife Judith I therefore give and bequeath unto my daughter Sarah Jane Lysle. . . . .for her sole and separate use during her natural life free and exempt from the debts and liabilities of her present or any future husband the following property. . . . .containing one hundred and a fourth acres more or less, and on her decease to her children.

But the ownership of the property was not to pass to Sarah Jane, cautioned the father "unless her and her husband shall remain with us until the time above mentioned," that is, until their deaths. If "they do not remain till said time, the said land is to revert back to my estate." [11]

One finds in the wills many personal touches. Often the testator had the last word in an old quarrel with his children or his wife or sweetheart. Sometimes it would be in the form of an invocation of the blessings of the Almighty upon a den of iniquity; and sometimes it would be in plain, unadorned, illiterate English. Green Sorrell of Chambers County, Alabama, disinherited what he, at least, regarded as a quarrelsome and unregenerate brood of sons and daughters by leaving most of his property to his grandchildren, and ended his will on this pious note: "last and not least of all my requests—I earnestly request my family to live in peace with each other as far as possible for my sake and pray the blessings of God on them all." [12] William Burriss of Campbell County, Tennessee, had obviously been "feuding" with his wife— possibly a second or third wife, somewhat on the young and flirtatious side. After referring to her as "Elizabeth Burriss" rather than "my beloved wife" as was the

[10] Dickinson County (Tennessee) Will Book A, 140, W.P.A. Copy, 76.
[11] Harris County (Georgia) Wills, 1850–1875, February 5, 1849.
[12] Chambers County (Alabama) Wills, II, 1842–1855, June 27, 1842.

usual practice, he grimly stated that the property he left for her support should be hers only "as long as she lives single and behaves herself." [13] Christine Calhoun of Tallapoosa County, Alabama, never liked sons-in-law in general and her sons-in-law in particular. Two of them she held in contempt. If they were not aware of this fact while the old lady was alive they were informed of it after she was buried and they could not talk back to her. "It must be understood," she explains in her will,

> that the moneys [from the estate] will be paid each of the five [daughters] in their hands but not to any of the husbands. . . . But [above all] it is my wish and desire that no part of my estate shall go into the hands of David and William Paul as they have already proved so very sorry particularly David Paul.[14]

The will of Thomas Coy of Franklin County, Tennessee, bears the marks of tragedy. It was in the form of a personal letter to intimate friends who had stood by Coy in need. Coy was laboring under great mental stress brought on by an unjust accusation. He had been accused of unfaithfulness by his sweetheart, Martha, and had been discarded by her. His lack of literacy, made to seem even worse by the strain under which Coy labored, did not conceal an underlying eloquence and sensitiveness. Certainly Coy had the last word with his sweetheart:

> Friend Willick you and wife have bin friends to me through adversity as well as prosperity and will prove my thankfulness to you for it   it is no use to Raise my voice or to say a word in my defense   i am condemned by all for unfaithfulness of friendship   there was never any one more unjustly condemned to my best friends I leave my best respects   Except the Boon I offer you   there is about Fifteen hundred Dollars   Give Ben Spyker my gun and watch   the remainder keep your self   you will pay W Pryor for washing   let Dr Borrough have my tools   make it write with him   Dock does not owe me anything   perhaps I owe him something   Keep all the rest yourself   O pardon me for this vast act   I cannot Buffet the waves any longer   God knows there is nobody tries harder to do right than I do   tell Martha I still think of her till death Martha you judged me wrong   But I forgive   you only misunderstood me   fairwell to all for I am not mad at nobody   God knows it   Missis Spyker as a last token of my friendship for you except the small sum of five hundred Dollars from your unworthy friend Coy. I should have made you a much better present But I burnt it in a mistake a long with some letters and papers. Miss Spyker i am unjustly and ungreatfully [accused] i have not the strength of mind to [bear] it any longer. I am going to the mountains there to wander the balance of my Days. I give Ben my watch   Good Ben I bid you all goodby   I am mad at none of you   God knows it.

Poor Thomas Coy had only a short time to wander in the mountains; indeed, he probably leaped off one of the Cumberland mountain tops, for his will was soon probated as a sign of his death.[15]

Ofttimes some little item in the will revealed the loving care of the testator. James Whitehead of Harris County, Georgia, after providing for the comfortable support of his wife added this thoughtful sentence: "I give and bequeath to my wife Jane my horse and buggy in order that she may go to meeting and visit in the neighbor-

---

[13] Campbell County (Tennessee) Wills and Inventories, 1807–1841, 420–21, W.P.A. Copy, 70.

[14] Tallapoosa County (Alabama) Wills, I, 1838–1866, 21.

[15] Franklin County (Tennessee) Will Book I–II, 238, W.P.A. Copy, 274.

hood." John J. Claxton of the same county, without imposing any conditions, left his entire estate to his "dear wife" Nancy. "My motive for giving all this," explained Claxton, "is to prevent her from [the cares] of this world to enable her to visit her friends and connections." [16]

[16] Harris County (Georgia), Wills and Bonds A, 1833–1849, 18, 19.

7 / The Tragic Southerner

Charles G. Sellers, Jr.

In addition to analyzing the social structure of the Old South, historians have also closely examined its culture and values. Many have concluded that the existence of a retrograde institution such as slavery, condemned by the liberal sentiment of the entire Western world, stultified the South by forcing Southerners into sterile and repressive intellectual postures. During the Revolutionary generation, men such as George Washington and Thomas Jefferson opposed slavery and championed freedom of thought. Southern leaders and statesmen who subscribed to the noble principle that "all men are created equal," enunciated in the Declaration of Independence, accepted slavery only as a necessary evil because there seemed to be no practical way to get rid of it. For a while, abolition societies flourished in the South and Southern states legalized voluntary emancipation. But by the 1820's, the South was becoming a closed society. Slavery was proclaimed "a positive good," and Southerners who disagreed were muzzled or forced to flee.

As the following selection by Charles Sellers suggests, it was not easy for the South to surrender its democratic and egalitarian ideals. But surrender them it did; and this capitulation was costly to the South. It sapped the intellectual and literary creativity of the section, drove into exile some of its most talented and sensitive spirits, and encouraged a hysterical and strident attack on all free institutions. By the eve of the Civil War, it has been said, two distinct cultures had emerged in the United States, one committed to liberty and progress and the other to slavery and the past.

For further reading: *Clement Eaton, *Freedom of Thought in the Old South* (Durham, N. C.: Duke University Press, 1940); William S. Jenkins, *Pro-Slavery Thought in the Old South* (Chapel Hill, N. C.: University of North Carolina Press, 1935); John Hope Franklin, *The Militant South, 1800–1861* (Cambridge: Harvard University Press, 1956); Ralph E. Morrow, "The Proslavery Argument Revisited," *Mississippi Valley Historical Review,* XLVIII (June 1961); Kenneth M. Stampp, "The Fate of the Southern

"The Travail of Slavery," in Charles G. Sellers, Jr. (ed.), *The Southerner as American* (Chapel Hill, N.C.: The University of North Carolina Press, 1960), pp. 40–71. Reprinted by permission.

Antislavery Movement," *Journal of Negro History,* XXVIII (January 1943);
*William Freehling, *Prelude to Civil War: The Nullification Controversy in
South Carolina, 1816–1836* (New York: Harper and Row, Publishers,
1966).

The American experience knows no greater tragedy than the Old South's twistings
and turnings on the rack of slavery. Others suffered more from the "peculiar institution," but only the suffering of white Southerners fits the classic formula for
tragedy. Like no other Americans before or since, the white men of the antebellum
South drove toward catastrophe by doing conscious violence to their truest selves.
No picture of the Old South as a section confident and united in its dedication to
a neo-feudal social order, and no explanation of the Civil War as a conflict between
"two civilizations," can encompass the complexity and pathos of the antebellum
reality. No analysis that misses the inner turmoil of the antebellum Southerner
can do justice to the central tragedy of the southern experience.*

The key to the tragedy of southern history is the paradox of the slaveholding
South's devotion to "liberty." Whenever and wherever Southerners sought to invoke
their highest social values—in schoolboy declamations, histories, Fourth of July
orations, toasts, or newspaper editorials—"liberty" was the incantation that sprang
most frequently and most fervently from their lips and pens. "The love of liberty
had taken deep root in the minds of carolinians [sic] long before the revolution,"
explained South Carolina's historian David Ramsay in 1809. The "similarity of state
and condition" produced by the early settlers' struggle to subdue the wilderness had
"inculcated the equality of rights" and "taught them the rights of man." [1]

The Revolutionary struggle made this implicit colonial liberalism explicit and
tied it to patriotic pride in the new American Union. From this time on, for
Southerners as for other Americans, liberty was the end for which the Union existed,
while the Union was the instrument by which liberty was to be extended to all
mankind. Thus the Fourth of July, the birthday of both liberty and Union, became
the occasion for renewing the liberal idealism and the patriotic nationalism which
united Americans of all sections at the highest levels of political conviction. "The
Declaration of Independence, and the Constitution of the United States—Liberty
and Union, now and forever, one and inseparable," ran a Virginian's toast on July
4, 1850. The same sentiment and almost the same phrases might have been heard
in any part of the South in any year of the antebellum period.[2]

Now "liberty" can mean many things, but the Old South persistently used the
word in the universalist sense of the eighteenth-century Enlightenment. At Richmond
in 1826 John Tyler eulogized Jefferson as "the devoted friend of man," who "had
studied his rights in the great volume of nature, and saw with rapture the era near

* My interpretation of the Old South draws heavily on the brilliant insights of Wilbur J.
Cash in *The Mind of the South* (New York, 1941), and also on Clement Eaton's *Freedom of
Thought in the Old South* (Durham, 1940).

[1] David Ramsay, *The History of South-Carolina, from Its First Settlement in 1670, to the
Year 1808* (2 vols.; Charleston, 1809), II, 384.

[2] Fletcher M. Green, "Listen to the Eagle Scream: One Hundred Years of the Fourth of July
in North Carolina (1776–1876)," *North Carolina Historical Review,* XXXI (July, October,
1954), 36, 534.

at hand, when those rights should be proclaimed, and the world aroused from the slumber of centuries." Jefferson's fame would not be confined to Americans, said Tyler, for his Declaration of Independence would be known wherever "man, so long the victim of oppression, awakes from the sleep of ages and bursts his chains." The conservative, slave-holding Tyler would soon be indicted by northern writers as a leader of the "slave power conspiracy" against human freedom; yet in 1826 he welcomed the day "when the fires of liberty shall be kindled on every hill and shall blaze in every valley," to proclaim that "the mass of mankind have not been born with saddles on their backs, nor a favored few booted and spurred to ride them. . . ."[3]

Although a massive reaction against liberalism is supposed to have seized the southern mind in the following decades, the Nullifiers of the thirties and the radical southern sectionalists of the forties and fifties did not ignore or reject the Revolutionary tradition of liberty so much as they transformed it, substituting for the old emphasis on the natural rights of all men a new emphasis on the rights and autonomy of communities. It was ironic that these slaveholding defenders of liberty against the tyranny of northern domination had to place themselves in the tradition of '76 at all, and the irony was heightened by their failure to escape altogether its universalist implications. Even that fire-eater of fire-eaters, Robert Barnwell Rhett, declaimed on "liberty" so constantly and so indiscriminately that John Quincy Adams could call him "a compound of wild democracy and iron bound slavery."[4]

Indeed the older nationalist-universalist conception of liberty remained very much alive in the South, and Southerners frequently used it to rebuke the radical sectionalists. Denouncing nullification in 1834, a Savannah newspaper vehemently declared that Georgians would never join in this assault on America's Revolutionary heritage. "No!" said the editor, "the light of the 4th of July will stream across their path, to remind them that liberty was not won in a day. . . ." Even a Calhounite could proudly assure an Independence Day audience in Virginia a few years later that American principles were destined "to work an entire revolution in the face of human affairs" and "to elevate the great mass of mankind." In North Carolina in the forties, citizens continued to toast "The Principles of the American Revolution —Destined to revolutionize the civilized world"; and editors rejoiced that the Fourth sent rays of light "far, far into the dark spots of oppressed distant lands." In Charleston itself a leading newspaper proclaimed that Americans were "the peculiar people, chosen of the Lord, to keep the vestal flame of liberty, as a light unto the feet and a lamp unto the path of the benighted nations, who yet slumber or groan under the bondage of tyranny."[5]

Throughout the antebellum period the South's invocation of liberty was reinforced by its fervent devotion to the Union. "America shall reach a height beyond the ken of mortals," exclaimed a Charleston orator in the 1820s; and through the following decades Southerners continued to exult with other Americans over their

[3] *A Selection of Eulogies Pronounced in the Several States, in Honor of Those Illustrious Patriots and Statesmen, John Adams and Thomas Jefferson* (Hartford, 1826), 6–7. For an indication of the currency of similar sentiments, see Green, "Listen to the Eagle Scream," *North Carolina Historical Review*, XXXI, 303, 305, 548.

[4] Laura A. White, *Robert Barnwell Rhett, Father of Secession* (New York, 1931), 50–52; Merle Curti, *The Roots of American Loyalty* (New York, 1946), 137–38, 153–54.

[5] Curti, *American Loyalty*, 68, 154; R. M. T. Hunter, *An Address Delivered before the Society of Alumnia of the University of Virginia . . . on the 4th of July, 1839* (Charlottesville, 1839), 4.

country's unique advantages and brilliant destiny. The Old South's Americanism sometimes had a surprisingly modern ring, as when a conservative Georgia newspaper called on "True Patriots" to join the Whigs in defending the "American Way" against the "Red Republicanism" of the Democratic party. Even that bellwether of radical Southernism, *De Bow's Review*, printed article after article proclaiming the glorious destiny of the United States.[6]

To the very eve of the Civil War the Fourth of July remained a widely observed festival of liberty and union in the South. By 1854, a hard-pressed orator was complaining that there was nothing fresh left to say: "The Stars and Stripes have been so vehemently flourished above admiring crowds of patriotic citizens that there is hardly a rhetorical shred left of them. . . . The very Union would almost be dissolved by eulogizing it at such a melting temperature." The rising tide of sectional antagonism did somewhat dampen Independence Day enthusiasm in the late fifties, but even after the Civil War began, one southern editor saw "no reason why the birth of liberty should be permitted to pass unheeded wherever liberty has votaries. . . . The accursed Yankees are welcome to the exclusive use of their 'Doodle' but let the South hold on tenaciously to Washington's March and Washington's Principles and on every recurring anniversary of the promulgation of the Declaration, reassert the great principles of Liberty."[7]

What are we to make of these slaveholding champions of liberty? Was the antebellum Southerner history's most hypocritical casuist? Or were these passionate apostrophes to the liberty of distant peoples a disguised protest against, or perhaps an escape from, the South's daily betrayal of its liberal self? Southerners were at least subconsciously aware of the "detestable paradox" of "our every-day sentiments of liberty" while holding human beings in slavery, and many Southerners had made it painfully explicit in the early days of the republic.[8]

A Virginian was amazed that "a people who have declared 'That all men are by nature equally free and independent' and have made this declaration the first article in the foundation of their government, should in defiance of so sacred a truth, recognized by themselves in so solemn a manner, and on so important an occasion, tolerate a practice incompatible therewith." Similarly, in neighboring Maryland, a leading politician expressed his astonishment that the people of the Old Free State "do not blush at the very name of Freedom." Was not Maryland, asked William Pinkney, "at once the fair temple of freedom, and the abominable nursery of slaves; the school for patriots, and the foster-mother of petty despots; the asserter of human rights, and the patron of wanton oppression?" "It will not do," he insisted, "thus to talk like philosophers, and act like unrelenting tyrants; to be perpetually sermonizing it with liberty for our text, and actual oppression for our commentary."[9]

Still another leading Marylander pointed out that America's Revolutionary struggle

[6] Curti, *American Loyalty*, 41, 43, 61, 72, 102–3, 152; Horace Montgomery, *Cracker Parties* (Baton Rouge, 1950), 3.

[7] Green, "Listen to the Eagle Scream," *North Carolina Historical Review*, XXXI, 314, 319–20, 534–36.

[8] Daniel R. Goodloe, *The Southern Platform: or, Manual of Southern Sentiment on the Subject of Slavery* (Boston, 1858), 91.

[9] William S. Jenkins, *Pro-Slavery Thought in the Old South* (Chapel Hill, 1935), 37–38.

had been "grounded upon the *preservation of those rights* to which God and nature entitled *us,* not in *particular,* but in common with *all the rest of mankind.*" The retention of slavery, declared Luther Martin in 1788, was "a solemn mockery of, and insult to, that God whose protection we had then implored, and could not fail to hold us up to detestation, and render us contemptible to every true friend of liberty in the world." During the Revolution, said Martin, "when our liberties were at stake, we warmly felt for the common rights of men."[10]

Martin did not exaggerate the inclusiveness of the liberal idealism that had accompanied the Revolutionary War in the southern states. Many of the Revolutionary county committees had denounced slavery, and Virginia's Revolutionary convention of 1774 had declared its abolition to be "the greatest object of desire in those colonies where it was unhappily introduced in their infant state." The implications of universalist liberalism for slavery were recognized most clearly, perhaps, by the Georgia county committee which resolved early in 1775 "to show the world that we are not influenced by any contracted motives, but a general philanthropy for all mankind, of whatever climate, language, or complexion," by using its best endeavors to eliminate "the unnatural practice of slavery."[11]

It is well known that the South's great statesmen of the Revolutionary generation almost unanimously condemned slavery as incompatible with the nation's liberal principles. Though these elder statesmen proved incapable of solving the problem, Thomas Jefferson consoled himself with the thought that it could safely be left to the "young men, grown up, and growing up," who "have sucked in the principles of liberty, as it were, with their mother's milk."[12] Such young men did indeed grow up, and they kept most Southerners openly apologetic about slavery for 50 years following the Declaration of Independence.

When, in the mid-thirties, John C. Calhoun declared on the floor of the Senate that slavery was "a good—a great good," one of Jefferson's protégés and former law students was there to denounce "the obsolete and revolting theory of human rights and human society by which, of late, the institution of domestic slavery had been sustained and justified by some of its advocates in a portion of the South." Slavery was "a misfortune and an evil in all circumstances," said Virginia's Senator William C. Rives, and he would never "deny, as has been done by this new school, the natural freedom and equality of man; to contend that slavery is a positive good." He would never "attack the great principles which lie at the foundation of our political system," or "revert to the dogmas of Sir Robert Filmer, exploded a century and a half ago by the immortal works of Sidney and Locke."[13]

Though open antislavery utterances grew infrequent after the 1830s, the generation which was to dominate southern life in the forties and fifties had already come

[10] Goodloe, *Southern Platform,* 94.

[11] *Ibid.,* 3–5.

[12] Hinton Rowan Helper, *The Impending Crisis of the South: How to Meet It* (New York, 1860), 197.

[13] *Register of Debates,* 24th Cong., 2d Sess., 719–23. Almost as significant as Rives' own position is the fact that he touched Calhoun at a tender point when he associated him with the anti-libertarian Filmer. The South Carolinian "utterly denied that his doctrines had any thing to do with the tenets of Sir Robert Filmer, which he abhorred." "So far from holding with the dogmas of that writer, he had been the known and open advocate of freedom from the beginning," Calhoun was reported as saying. "Nor was there any thing in the doctrines he held in the slightest degree inconsistent with the highest and purest principles of freedom."

to maturity with values absorbed from the afterglow of Revolutionary liberalism. On the eve of the Civil War *De Bow's Review* was to complain that during these earlier years, "when probably a majority of even our own people regarded the existence of slavery among us as a blot on our fair name . . . our youth [were allowed] to peruse, even in their tender years, works in which slavery was denounced as an unmitigated evil." [14] Some of these youngsters had drawn some vigorous conclusions. "How contradictory" was slavery to every principle of "a republican Government where liberty is the boast and pride of its free citizens," exclaimed the son of a slave-holding family in South Carolina. Similarly a 15-year-old Tennessee boy called slavery "a foul, a deadly blot . . . in a nation boasting of the republicanism of her principles" and owing allegiance to "the sacred rights of man." [15]

A whole generation cannot transform its most fundamental values by a mere effort of will. Though Southerners tended during the latter part of the antebellum period to restrict their publicly voiced libertarian hopes to "oppressed distant lands," the old liberal misgivings about slavery did not die. Instead they burrowed beneath the surface of the southern mind, where they kept gnawing away the shaky foundations on which Southerners sought to rebuild their morale and self-confidence as a slave-holding people.

Occasionally the doubts were exposed, as in 1857, when Congressman L. D. Evans of Texas lashed out at the general repudiation of liberalism to which some defenders of slavery had been driven. The doctrine of human inequality and subordination might do for the dark ages of tyranny, he declared, "but emanating from the lips of a Virginia professor, or a statesman of Carolina, it startles the ear, and shocks the moral sense of a republican patriot." But Evans only illustrated the hopelessness of the southern dilemma by his tortured argument for transforming slavery into a kind of serfdom which would somehow preserve the slave's "natural equality," while gradually evolving into a state of "perfect equality." [16]

The same year a Charleston magazine admitted that "We are perpetually aiming to square the maxims of an impracticable philosophy with the practice which nature and circumstances force upon us." Yet on the very eve of war, few Southerners were ready to resolve the dilemma by agreeing with the writer that "the [liberal] philosophy of the North is a dead letter to us." [17]

If the Southerner had been embarrassed by his devotion to liberty and Union alone, he would have had less trouble easing his mind on the subject of slavery. But as a Virginia legislator exclaimed in 1832, "This, sir, is a Christian community." Southerners "read in their Bibles, 'Do unto all men as you would have them do unto you'; and this golden rule and slavery are hard to reconcile." [18] During those early decades of the nineteenth century, when the South was confessing the evils of slavery, it had been swept by a wave of evangelical orthodoxy. Though the wave

---

[14] Russel B. Nye, *Fettered Freedom: Civil Liberties and the Slavery Controversy, 1830–1860* (East Lansing, Mich., 1949), 72.

[15] Lillian A. Kibler, *Benjamin F. Perry, South Carolina Unionist* (Durham, 1946), 31; Pulaski *Tennessee Beacon and Farmers Advocate*, June 16, 1832.

[16] W. G. Bean, "Anti-Jeffersonianism in the Ante-Bellum South," *North Carolina Historical Review*, XII (April, 1935), 111.

[17] John Hope Franklin, *The Militant South, 1800–1861* (Cambridge, 1956), 222.

[18] Goodloe, *Southern Platform*, 49.

crested about the time some Southerners, including some clergymen, began speaking of slavery as a positive good, it does not follow that the evangelical reaction against the eighteenth century's religious ideas contributed significantly to the reaction against the eighteenth century's liberalism with regard to slavery.

On the contrary, the evangelical denominations had strong antislavery tendencies. Methodists, Quakers, and Baptists nurtured an extensive abolitionist movement in the upper South during the twenties, when the rest of the country was largely indifferent to the slavery question; and the Presbyterians were still denouncing slavery in Kentucky a decade later. It would be closer to the truth to suggest that as Southerners wrestled with their consciences over slavery, they may have gained a firsthand experience with the concepts of sin and evil that made them peculiarly susceptible to Christian orthodoxy. At any rate, as late as 1849, a proslavery professor at the University of Alabama complained to Calhoun that no one had yet published a satisfactory defense of slavery in the light of New Testament teachings. The "many religious people at the South who have strong misgivings on this head," he warned, constituted a greater threat to the peculiar institution than the northern abolitionists.[19]

Even the irreligious found it hard to resist the claims of simple humanity or to deny that slaves, as one Southerner put it, "have hearts and feelings like other men." And those who were proof against the appeals to Revolutionary liberalism, Christianity, and humanity, still faced the arguments of Southerners in each succeeding generation that slavery was disastrous to the whites. Jefferson's famous lament that the slaveholder's child, "nursed, educated, and daily exercised in tyranny . . . must be a prodigy who can retain his manners and morals undepraved," was frequently echoed. George Mason's lament that slavery discouraged manufactures, caused the poor to despise labor, and prevented economic development, found many seconders in Virginia's slavery debate of 1831–32 and received elaborate statistical support from Hinton Rowan Helper in the fifties. The seldom mentioned but apparently widespread practice of *miscegenation* was an especially heavy cross for the women of the South. "Under slavery we live surrounded by prostitutes," wrote one woman bitterly. ". . . Any lady is ready to tell you who is the father of all the mulatto children in everybody's household but her own. . . . My disgust sometimes is boiling over."[20]

It is essential to understand that the public declarations of Southerners never revealed the full impact of all these antislavery influences on the southern mind. Fear of provoking slave insurrections had restrained free discussion of slavery even in the Revolutionary South, and an uneasy society exerted steadily mounting pressure against antislavery utterances thereafter. Only when Nat Turner's bloody uprising of 1831 shocked Southerners into open debate over the peculiar institution did the curtain of restraint part sufficiently to reveal the intensity of their misgivings. Thomas Ritchie's influential Richmond *Enquirer* caught the mood of that historic moment when it quoted a South Carolinian as exclaiming, "We may shut our eyes and

[19] E. Mitchell to John C. Calhoun, February 5, 1849, John C. Calhoun Papers (Clemson College Library).

[20] Goodloe, *Southern Platform*, 49; Helper, *Impending Crisis*, 195, 208–9; John J. Flournoy, *An Essay on the Origin, Habits, &c. of the African Race . . .* (New York, 1835), 25; Kenneth M. Stampp, *The Peculiar Institution: Slavery in the Ante-Bellum South* (New York, 1956), 356.

avert our faces, if we please, but there it is, the dark and growing evil at our doors; and meet the question we must, at no distant day. . . . What is to be done? Oh! my God, I do not know, but something must be done." [21]

Many were ready to say what had to be done, especially a brilliant galaxy of the liberty-loving young Virginians on whom the dying Jefferson had pinned his hopes. "I will not rest until slavery is abolished in Virginia," vowed Governor John Floyd; and during the winter of 1831–32 a deeply earnest Virginia legislature was wrapped in the Old South's only free and full debate over slavery. Not a voice was raised to justify human servitude in the abstract, while a score of Virginians attacked the peculiar institution with arguments made deadly by the South's endemic liberalism and Christianity. Two years later a Tennessee constitutional convention showed a tender conscience on slavery by admitting that "to prove it to be an evil is an easy task." Yet in both states proposals for gradual emancipation were defeated.[22]

The outcome was no surprise to the editor of the Nashville *Republican*. Few would question the moral evil of slavery, he had written back in 1825, "but then the assent to a proposition is not always followed by acting in uniformity to its spirit." Too many Southerners believed, perhaps from "the exercise of an interested casuistry," that nature had ordained the Negro to slavery by giving him a peculiar capacity for labor under the southern sun. Furthermore southern white men would have to "be convinced that to labor personally is a more agreeable, and desirable occupation, than to command, & superintend the labor of others." Consequently, "as long as slavery is conceived to advance the pecuniary interests of individuals, they will be slow to relish, and reluctant to encourage, any plan for its abolition. They will quiet their consciences with the reflection that it was entailed upon us—that it has grown up with the institutions of the country—and that the establishment of a new order of things would be attended with great difficulty, and might be perilous." [23]

Thus when Nat Turner frightened Southerners into facing squarely the tragic ambiguity of their society, they found the price for resolving it too high. The individual planter's economic stake in slavery was a stubborn and perhaps insurmountable obstacle to change; and even Jefferson's nerve had failed at the task of reconstituting the South's social system to assimilate a host of Negro freedmen.

The whole South sensed that a fateful choice had been made. Slowly and reluctantly Southerners faced the fact that, if slavery were to be retained, things could not go on as before. The slaves were restive, a powerful antislavery sentiment was sweeping the western world, and southern minds were not yet nerved for a severe struggle in defense of the peculiar institution to which they were now committed. The South could no longer ease its conscience with hopes for the eventual disappearance of slavery, or tolerate such hopes in any of its people. "It is not enough for them to believe that slavery has been entailed upon us by our forefathers," proclaimed Calhoun's national newspaper organ. "We must satisfy the consciences, we must allay the fears of our own people. We must satisfy them that slavery is of itself right—that it is not a sin against God—that it is not an evil, moral or political. . . . In this way, and this way only, can we prepare our

[21] Joseph C. Robert, *The Road from Monticello: A Study of the Virginia Slavery Debate, 1832* (Durham, 1941), 17–18, and *passim*.

[22] Charles H. Ambler, *The Life and Diary of John Floyd* (Richmond, 1918), 172; Jenkins, *Pro-Slavery Thought*, 88n.

[23] Nashville *Republican*, October 22, 1825.

own people to defend their institutions."[24] So southern leaders of the Calhoun school began trying to convince themselves and others that slavery was a "positive good," while southern legislatures abridged freedom of speech and press, made manumission difficult or impossible, and imposed tighter restrictions on both slaves and free Negroes. The Great Reaction was under way.

Yet the Great Reaction, for all its formidable facade and terrible consequences, was a fraud. Slavery simply could not be blended with liberalism and Christianity, while liberalism and Christianity were too deeply rooted in the southern mind to be torn up overnight. Forced to smother and distort their most fundamental convictions by the decision to maintain slavery, and goaded by criticism based on these same convictions, Southerners of the generation before the Civil War suffered the most painful loss of social morale and identity that any large group of Americans has ever experienced.

The surface unanimity enforced on the South in the forties and fifties by the Great Reaction concealed a persistent hostility to slavery. It is true that large numbers of the most deeply committed antislavery men left the South. They were usually men of strong religious conviction, such as Levi Coffin, the North Carolina Quaker who moved to Indiana to become the chief traffic manager of the Underground Railroad, or Will Breckinridge, the Kentucky Presbyterian who declared, "I care little where I go—so that I may only get where every man I see is as free as myself." In fact the national banner of political antislavery was carried in the forties by a former Alabama slaveholder, James G. Birney, who had rejected slavery for the same reasons that bothered many other Southerners—because it was "inconsistent with the Great Truth that all men are created equal . . . as well as the great rule of benevolence delivered to us by the Savior Himself that in all things whatsoever ye would that men should do unto you do ye even so to them."[25]

Many zealous antislavery men remained in the South, however, to raise their voices wherever the Great Reaction relaxed its grip. If this almost never happened in the lower South, a dissenter in western Virginia could exult in 1848 that "antislavery papers and anti-slavery orators are scattering far and wide the seeds of freedom, and an immense number of persons are uttering vaticinations in contemplation of a day of emancipation"; while the reckless courage of Cassius Clay and his allies kept the antislavery cause alive in Kentucky. "The contention of planter politicians that the South had achieved social and political unity," concludes the ablest student of the peculiar institution, "appears, then, to have been the sheerest of wishful thinking."[26]

Far more significant than outright antislavery opinion was the persistent disquietude over slavery among the many white Southerners who found the new proslavery dogmas hard to swallow. The official southern view held that slaveholders "never inquire into the propriety of the matter . . . they see their neighbors buying slaves, and they buy them . . . leaving to others to discuss the right and justice

[24] Washington (D. C.) *United States Telegraph*, December 5, 1835.

[25] Walter B. Posey, "The Slavery Question in the Presbyterian Church in the Old Southwest," *Journal of Southern History*, XV (August, 1943), 319; Betty Fladeland, *James Gillespie Birney: Slaveholder to Abolitionist* (Ithaca, 1955), 83.

[26] Kenneth M. Stampp, "The Fate of the Southern Antislavery Movement," *Journal of Negro History*, XXVIII (January, 1943), 20, 22, and *passim*.

of the thing." In moments of unusual candor, however, the proslavery propagandists admitted the prevalence of misgivings. Calhoun's chief editorial spokesman thought the principal danger of northern abolitionism was its influence upon "the consciences and fears of the slave-holders themselves." Through "the insinuation of their dangerous heresies into our schools, our pulpits, and our domestic circles," Duff Green warned, the abolitionists might succeed in "alarming the consciences of the weak and feeble, and diffusing among our own people a morbid sensitivity on the question of slavery."[27]

Slavery's apologists were particularly irritated by the numerous instances "in which the superstitious weakness of dying men . . . induces them, in their last moments, to emancipate their slaves." Every manumission was an assault on the peculiar institution and a testimony to the tenacity with which older values resisted the proslavery dogmas. "Let our women and old men, and persons of weak and infirm minds, be disabused of the false . . . notion that slavery is sinful, and that they will peril their souls if they do not disinherit their offspring by emancipating their slaves!" complained a Charleston editor in the fifties. It was high time masters "put aside all care or thought what Northern people say about them."[28]

Yet the manumissions went on, despite mounting legal obstacles. The census reported more than 3,000 for 1860, or one manumission for every 1,309 slaves, which was double the number reported ten years before. If this figure seems small, it should be remembered that these manumissions were accomplished against "almost insuperable obstacles"—not only southern laws prohibiting manumission or making it extremely difficult, but also northern laws barring freed Negroes. The evidence indicates that there would have been many more manumissions if the laws had been more lenient, and if masters had not feared that the freed Negroes would be victimized.[29]

The explanations advanced by men freeing their slaves illustrate the disturbing influence of liberalism and Christianity in the minds of many slaveholders. A Virginia will affirmed the testator's belief "that slavery in all its forms . . . is inconsistent with republican principles, that it is a violation of our bill of rights, which declares, *that all men are by nature equally free;* and above all, that it is repugnant to the spirit of the gospel, which enjoins universal love and benevolence." A North Carolinian listed four reasons for freeing his slaves: (1) "Agreeably to the rights of man, every human being, be his colour what it may, is entitled to freedom"; (2) "My conscience, the great criterion, condemns me for keeping them in slavery"; (3) "The golden rule directs us to do unto every human creature, as we would wish to be done unto"; and (4) "I wish to die with a clear conscience, that I may not be ashamed to appear before my master in a future World." In Tennessee, one man freed his slave woman because he wanted her to "Enjoy Liberty the birthright of all Mankind." Another not only believed "it to be the duty of a Christian to deal with his fellow man in a state of bondage with humanity and kindness," but also feared that his own "happiness *hereafter*" depended on the disposition he made of his slaves. Still another, after ordering two slaves freed, hoped that "no one will offer to undo

---

[27] Stampp, *Peculiar Institution,* 422–23; Washington (D. C.) *United States Telegraph,* December 5, 1835.

[28] Stampp, *Peculiar Institution,* 234, 423.

[29] Clement Eaton, *Freedom of Thought in the Old South* (2d ed.; New York, 1951), xii–xiii; J. Merton England, "The Free Negro in Ante-Bellum Tennessee," *Journal of Southern History,* IX (February, 1943), 44–45. Cf. Stampp, *Peculiar Institution,* 234–35.

what my conscience tole me was my duty," and that "my children will consider it so and folow the futsteps of their father and keep now [no] slaves longer than they pay for their raising and expenses." [30]

But conscience was a problem for many more Southerners than those who actually freed their slaves, as the proslavery philosophers were compelled to recognize. "I am perfectly aware that slavery is repugnant to the *natural* emotions of men," confessed William J. Grayson on the eve of the Civil War. James H. Hammond was one of many who sought to quiet the troublesome southern conscience by picturing slavery as an eleemosynary institution, maintained at considerable cost by generous slave-holders. Southerners must content themselves, said Hammond, with "the consoling reflection, that what is lost to us is gained to humanity." Grayson, on the other hand, despaired of quieting conscience and concluded grimly that conscience itself must be discredited. "I take the stand on the position that our natural feelings are unsafe guides for us to follow in the social relations." [31]

But a host of Southerners, perhaps including Grayson and Hammond, could neither satisfy nor ignore their consciences. One troubled master confided to his wife, "I sometimes think my feelings unfit me for a slaveholder." A North Carolina planter told his son that he could not discipline his slaves properly, believing that slavery was a violation of "the natural rights of a being who is as much entitled to the enjoyment of liberty as myself." In the rich Mississippi Delta country, where many of the largest slaveholders remained loyal to the Union in 1861, one man had long sought "some means . . . to rid us of slavery, because I never had any great fondness for the institution although I had been the owner of slaves from my youth up." Another Mississippi slaveholder was "always an abolitionist at heart," but "did not know how to set them free without wretchedness to them, and utter ruin to myself." Still another "owned slaves & concluded if I was merciful & humane to them I might just as well own them as other Persons . . . [but] I had an instinctive horror of the institution." How many masters held such opinions privately can never be known, but observers at the close of the Civil War noted a surprisingly general feeling of relief over the destruction of slavery. An upcountry South Carolinian certainly spoke for many Southerners when he said, "I am glad the thing is done away with; it was more plague than pleasure, more loss than profit." [32]

The nub of the Southerner's ambivalent attitude toward slavery was his inability to regard the slave consistently as either person or property. Slaves "were a species of property that differed from all others," James K. Polk declared as a freshman congressman, "they were rational; they were human beings." [33] The slave's indeterminate status was writ large in the ambiguity of the whole structure of southern society. A sociologist has analyzed the institutional features of slavery as lying along a "rationality-traditionalism range," whose polar points were mutually contradictory. At one pole lay the economic view. Since slavery was a labor system employed in a highly competitive market economy, a minimum of rational efficiency was necessarily

[30] Eaton, *Freedom of Thought*, 18–19; Stampp, *Peculiar Institution*, 235–36; England, "Free Negro," *Journal of Southern History*, IX, 43–44.

[31] Jenkins, *Pro-Slavery Thought*, 236; Stampp, *Peculiar Institution*, 383.

[32] Stampp, *Peculiar Institution*, 424; Eaton, *Freedom of Thought*, 19; Frank W. Klingberg, *The Southern Claims Commission* (Berkeley and Los Angeles, 1955), 11, 108; J. W. De Forest, "Chivalrous and Semi-Chivalrous Southrons," *Harper's New Monthly Magazine*, XXVIII (January, February, 1869), 200.

[33] *Register of Debates*, 19th Cong., 1st Sess., 1649.

prescribed for economic survival. This called for a "sheerly economic" view of slavery, one which regarded the slave as property, which gave the master unlimited control over the slave's person, which evaluated the treatment of slaves wholly in terms of economic efficiency, which structured the slave's situation so that his self-interest in escaping the lash became his sole motivation to obedience, which sanctioned the domestic slave trade and demanded resumption of the foreign slave trade as essential mechanisms for supplying and redistributing labor, and which dismissed moral considerations as both destructive of the labor supply and irrelevant. Though the plantation system tended during the latter part of the slavery period to approach the ideal type of a purely commercial economic organization, especially with the geographical shift to the new lands of the Southwest, few if any Southerners ever fully accepted this "sheerly economic" view of slavery.

At the other pole lay a "traditional" or "familial" view, which regarded the slave more as person than property and idealized "the patriarchal organization of plantation life and the maintenance of the family estate and family slaves at all costs." Both the "sheerly economic" and the "familial" views of slavery were sanctioned by southern society; economics and logic drove Southerners toward the former, while sentiment, liberalism, and Christianity dragged them in the other direction.[34]

This fundamental ambivalence was most clearly apparent in the law of slavery. Early colonial law had justified the enslavement of Negroes on the ground that they were heathens, so that the conversion of slaves to Christianity raised a serious problem. Though the Negro was continued in bondage, the older conviction that conversion and slave status were incompatible died hard, as was demonstrated by the successive enactments required to establish the new legal definition of slavery on the basis of the Negro's race rather than his heathenism. Even then problems remained. Not all Negroes were slaves, and the South could never bring itself to reduce free Negroes to bondage. Moreover the slave's admission to the privilege of salvation inevitably identified him as a person. But slavery could not be viewed as a legal relationship between legal persons; in strict logic it had to be a chattel arrangement that left the slave no legal personality.

Was the slave a person or merely property in the eyes of the law? This question southern legislatures and courts never settled. He could not legally marry, own property, sue or be sued, testify, or make contracts; yet he was legally responsible for crimes he committed, and others were responsible for crimes committed against him. The ambiguity was most striking in the case of a slave guilty of murder; as a person he was responsible and could be executed; but he was also property, and if the state took his life, his owner had to be compensated. "The slave is put on trial as a *human being*," declared a harassed court in one such case. "Is it not inconsistent, in the progress of the trial, to treat him as property, like . . . a horse, in the value of which the owner has a pecuniary interest which makes him incompetent as a witness?"[35]

The Southerner's resistance to the legal logic of making slavery a simple property arrangement is amply illustrated in court decisions. "A slave is not in the condition

[34] Wilbert E. Moore, "Slavery, Abolition, and the Ethical Valuation of the Individual: A Study of the Relations between Ideas and Institutions" (Ph.D. dissertation, Harvard University, 1940), 193–212.

[35] Wilbert E. Moore, "Slave Law and the Social Structure," *Journal of Negro History*, XXVI (April, 1941), 171–202.

of a horse," said a Tennessee judge. "He has mental capacities, and an immortal principle in his nature." The laws did not "extinguish his high-born nature nor deprive him of many rights which are inherent in men." Similarly a Mississippi court declared that it would be "a stigma upon the character of the State" if a slave could be murdered "without subjecting the offender to the highest penalty known to the criminal jurisprudence of the country. Has the slave no rights, because he is deprived of his freedom? He is still a human being, and possesses all those rights of which he is not deprived by the positive provision of the law." [36]

The anguish induced by the legal logic of slavery was expressed most clearly in a North Carolina decision. Recognizing the objectives of slavery to be "the profit of the master, his security and the public safety," and recognizing the slave to be "doomed in his own person, and his posterity, to live without knowledge, and without the capacity to make any thing his own, and to toil that another may reap the fruits," the court concluded that, "Such services can only be expected from one . . . who surrenders his will in implicit obedience to that of another. . . . The power of the master must be absolute." The judge felt "as deeply as any man can" the harshness of this proposition. "As a principle of moral rights, every person in his retirement must repudiate it. . . . It constitutes the curse of slavery to both the bond and the free portions of our population. But it is inherent in the relation of masters and slaves." [37]

The slave's indeterminate status was not just a legal problem, but a daily personal problem for every master. "It is difficult to handle simply as property, a creature possessing human passions and human feelings," observed Frederick Law Olmsted, "while, on the other hand, the absolute necessity of dealing with property as a thing, greatly embarrasses a man in any attempt to treat it as a person." Absentee owners and the masters of large, commercially rationalized plantations might regard their field hands as economic units, but few of them could avoid personalizing their relationships with house servants in a way that undercut the sheerly economic conception of the peculiar institution. The majority of slaveholders, moreover, were farmers who lived and worked closely with their slaves, and such masters, according to D. R. Hundley, "seem to exercise but few of the rights of ownership over their human chattels, making so little distinction between master and man, that their Negroes [are] . . . in all things treated more like equals than slaves." [38]

The personalized master-slave relationship was a direct threat to the peculiar institution, for slavery's stability as an economic institution depended upon the Negro's acceptance of the caste line between himself and the white man. Sociologists tell us that such caste systems as India's were stabilized by the fact that "those goals and value-attitudes which were legitimate for the dominant caste had no implications concerning their legitimacy for the subordinate caste." In the South, however, where the values of the dominant caste produced personalized master-slave relationships, and where Negroes could view manumission as the crucial product of personalization, members of the subordinate caste learned to regard the value system and goals of the dominant caste as at least partly valid for themselves. The presence of free Negroes in southern society meant that the caste line did not coincide

---

[36] Stampp, *Peculiar Institution*, 217; Helper, *Impending Crisis*, 223–24.

[37] Moore, "Slavery and Ethical Valuation," Ph.D. dissertation (Harvard), 187–88.

[38] Stampp, *Peculiar Institution*, 193; D. R. Hundley, *Social Relations in Our Southern States* (New York, 1860), 193.

completely with the color line, and the overlap made liberty a legitimate goal even for the slave. Thus the slave's passion for freedom, manifested in countless escapes and insurrection plots, was not "lit up in his soul by the hand of Deity," as a Virginia legislator thought, but was implanted by the white man's own inability to draw the caste line rigidly.[39]

Though Southerners could guard against the dangers of personalization in the abstract, as when legislatures prohibited manumission, the individual master, face to face with his human property, found it harder to behave in accordance with the sheerly economic view of slavery. Economic efficiency demanded "the painful exercise of undue and tyrannical authority," observed a North Carolina planter; and the famous ex-slave Frederick Douglass testified that kind treatment increased rather than diminished the slave's desire for freedom. Consequently humanity and the profit motive were forever struggling against each other in the master's mind. While the profit motive frequently won out, humanity had its victories too. "I would be content with much less . . . cotton if less cruelty was exercised," said a disturbed planter in Mississippi. "I fear I am near an abolition[i]st." Most often, perhaps, the master's humanitarian and economic impulses fought to a draw, leaving him continually troubled and frustrated in the management of his slaves. Slaveholding, concluded one master, subjected "the man of care and feeling to more dilemmas than any other vocation he could follow."[40]

Certainly southern opinion condemned thoroughgoing economic rationality in the treatment of slaves. This was most apparent in the low social status accorded to slave traders and overseers, when by normal southern canons of prestige their intimate relation with the peculiar institution and their control over large numbers of slaves should have given them a relatively high rank. Both groups were absolutely essential to the slavery system, and both bore a purely economic relation to it. The overseer, who was judged primarily by the profits he wrung out of slave labor, typified the sheerly exploitative aspects of slavery; while the slave trader, who presided over the forcible disruption of families and the distribution of slaves as marketable commodities, was the most conspicuous affront to the familial conception of the peculiar institution. These men certainly developed a cynical attitude toward the human property they controlled, but they did not uniformly exhibit the dishonesty, greed, vulgarity, and general immorality that southern opinion ascribed to them. By thus stereotyping these exemplars of the sheerly economic aspects of slavery, southern society created scapegoats on whom it could discharge the guilt feelings arising from the necessity of treating human beings as property.[41]

These guilt feelings seem to have increased during the final years of the antebellum period, as slavery approximated the sheerly economic pattern on more and more plantations. Never had Southerners regaled themselves and others so insistently with the myth of the happy slave. A European traveler met few slaveholders who could "openly and honestly look the thing in the face. They wind and turn about in all sorts of ways, and make use of every argument . . . to convince me that the

[39] Moore, "Slavery and Ethical Valuation," 233–35; Wilbert E. Moore and Robin M. Williams, "Stratification in the Ante-Bellum South," *American Sociological Review*, VII (June, 1942), 348–51; Robert, *Road from Monticello*, 103.

[40] Stampp, *Peculiar Institution*, 89–90, 141, 191.

[41] Moore, "Slavery and Ethical Valuation," 194–95; Moore and Williams, "Stratification," 345–46.

slaves are the happiest people in the world, and do not wish to be placed in any other condition." At the same time there developed a strong movement to extend and implement the paternalistic-personalistic pattern. Some states amended their slave codes to prescribe minimum standards of treatment, and there was agitation for more fundamental reforms—legalization of slave marriages, protection against disruption of slave families, and encouragement of Negro education.[42]

Especially significant was the crusade for religious instruction of slaves. "We feel that the souls of our slaves are a solemn trust, and we shall strive to present them faultless and complete before the presence of God," declared that high priest of southern Presbyterianism, Dr. James Henley Thornwell. The argument for religious instruction was also a justification of slavery, and the only one that effected any kind of real accommodation between the peculiar institution and the white Southerner's innate disposition to regard the slave as a human being. It was precisely for this reason that the religious interpretation of slavery quieted more southern qualms than any other facet of the proslavery argument. "However the world may judge us in connection with our institution of slavery," said Georgia's Bishop Stephen Elliott, "we conscientiously believe it to be a great missionary institution—one arranged by God, as he arranges all the moral and religious influences of the world so that the good may be brought out of the seeming evil, and a blessing wrung out of every form of the curse."

Yet the religious argument was ultimately subversive of slavery. By giving the slave's status as person precedence over his status as property, and by taking as its mission the elevation of the slave as a human being, the movement for religious instruction necessarily called into question the inherent beneficence and permanence of the institution. Dr. Thornwell resolutely argued that slavery could end only in heaven, because only there could the sin that produced it end; meanwhile the Christian's duty was to mitigate its evils. Bishop Elliott, on the other hand, believed that by giving the slaves religious instruction "we are elevating them in every generation" here on earth, and he spoke for many another southern churchman when he conceded that this implied ultimately some change in the slaves' worldly status. Thus, by the close of the slavery era, the religious defense of the institution was bringing the South back toward its old colonial doubts about the validity of continued bondage for converted men and women.[43]

Nowhere, in fact, was the South's painful inner conflict over slavery more evident than in the elaborate body of theory by which it tried to prove (mainly to itself) the beneficence of its peculiar social system. "It has not been more than . . . thirty years since the abolition of slavery was seriously debated in the legislature of Virginia," observed the *Southern Literary Messenger* on the eve of the Civil War. "Now, on the contrary . . . the whole Southern mind with an unparalleled unanimity regards the institution of slavery as righteous and just, ordained of God, and to be perpetuated by Man." Yet the stridency with which southern unanimity was ceaselessly proclaimed stands in suggestive contrast to the private views of many Southerners. "To expect men to agree that Slavery is a blessing, social, moral, and political," wrote a North Carolina congressman to his wife, "when many of those

[42] Stampp, *Peculiar Institution*, 423; Herbert Aptheker, *American Negro Slave Revolts* (New York, 1943), 59–60.
[43] Jenkins, *Pro-Slavery Thought*, 214–18.

who have all their lives been accustomed to it . . . believe exactly the reverse, is absurd." Even the fire-eaters confessed privately that outside South Carolina most slaveholders were "mere negro-drivers believing themselves wrong and only holding on to their negroes as something to make money out of." South Carolinians themselves had "retrograded," wrote Robert W. Barnwell in 1844, "and must soon fall into the same category." [44]

Close examination of the superficially impressive proslavery philosophy reveals, as Louis Hartz has brilliantly demonstrated, a "mass of agonies and contradictions in the dream world of southern thought." The peculiar institution could be squared theoretically with either the slave's humanity or democratic liberalism for whites, but not with both. Thus the necessity for justifying slavery, coupled with the white South's inability to escape its inherited liberalism or to deny the common humanity it shared with its Negro slaves, inspired "a mixture of pain and wild hyperbole." [45]

Recognizing that the religious argument by itself was a threat to the peculiar institution, one school of proslavery philosophers sought to preserve both slavery and the slave's humanity by sacrificing democratic liberalism and falling back to a neo-feudal insistence on the necessity of subordination and inequality in society. "Subordination rules supreme in heaven and must rule supreme on earth," asserted Bishop Elliott, and he did not attempt to disguise the repudiation of democratic liberalism that followed from this principle. Carried away by Revolutionary fervor, Southerners along with other Americans had "declared war against all authority and against all form"; they had pronounced all men equal and man capable of self-government. "Two greater falsehoods could not have been announced," Elliott insisted, "because the one struck at the whole constitution of civil society as it had ever existed, and because the other denied the fall and corruption of man." [46]

George Fitzhugh, the most logical and impressive of the proslavery philosophers and the leading exponent of southern neo-feudalism, would have preserved the humanity of the Negroes but denied freedom to the white masses by making both subject to the same serf-like subordination. Only thus could men be saved from the frightful corruption and turbulence of "free society." But southern planters were too much bourgeois capitalists and southern farmers were too much Jacksonian democrats to entertain the neo-feudalists' vituperation at "free society." "Soon counties, neighborhoods, or even individuals will be setting up castles," commented a sarcastic Alabamian.[47] Fitzhugh and his fellow intellectuals might talk all they pleased about reducing the masses, white and black, to serfdom, but practical politicians and publicists knew better than to fly so directly in the face of the South's liberal bias.

At the hands of men like James H. Hammond, therefore, neo-feudalism became a racial "mud-sill" theory, which divided society along the color line, relegating

[44] Jay B. Hubbell, "Literary Nationalism in the Old South," in David K. Jackson (ed.), *American Studies in Honor of William Kenneth Boyd* (Durham, 1940), 183n.; David Outlaw to Mrs. David Outlaw, July [28], 1848, David Outlaw Papers (Southern Historical Collection, University of North Carolina); Robert W. Barnwell to Robert Barnwell Rhett, November 1, 1844, Robert Barnwell Rhett Papers (Southern Historical Collection, University of North Carolina).

[45] Louis Hartz, *The Liberal Tradition in America: An Interpretation of American Political Thought since the Revolution* (New York, 1955), 145–200.

[46] Jenkins, *Pro-Slavery Thought,* 239–40.

[47] Ollinger Crenshaw, *The Slave States in the Presidential Election of 1860* (Baltimore, 1945), 253.

Negroes to bondage and reserving democratic liberalism for white men only. In the late forties a school of southern ethnologists arose to declare the Negro a distinct and permanently inferior species; and by 1854 Mississippi's Senator Albert G. Brown could invite Northerners to his state "to see the specimen of that equality spoken of by Jefferson in the Declaration of Independence." Nowhere else in the Union, said Brown, was there such an exemplification of Jefferson's beautiful sentiment. "In the South all men are equal. I mean of course, white men; negroes are not men, within the meaning of the Declaration." [48]

The racist argument was attacked with surprising vehemence by both religionists and feudalists. At least one Southerner went far beyond most northern abolitionists in asserting that "the African is endowed with faculties as lofty, with perceptions as quick, with sensibilities as acute, and with natures as susceptible of improvement, as we are, who boast a fairer skin." Indeed, said this Virginian, if Negroes were "operated upon by the same ennobling impulses, stimulated by the same generous motives, and favored by the same adventitious circumstances, they would, as a mass, reach as high an elevation in the scale of moral refinement, and attain as great distinction on the broad theatre of intellectual achievement, as ourselves." [49]

While few Southerners would go as far as this, the religionists did maintain stoutly "that the African race is capable of considerable advance." Religious instruction of slaves would have been pointless without some such assumption, but the churchmen objected more fundamentally to the racist argument because it robbed the slave of his essential humanity. The feudalists, too, rejected the idea of racial inferiority, with Fitzhugh arguing that "it encourages and incites brutal masters to treat negroes, not as weak, ignorant and dependent brethren, but as wicked beasts, without the pale of humanity." The Negro was essential to the web of reciprocal duties and affections between superiors and subordinates that was supposed to knit the idyllic neo-feudal world together. "The Southerner is the negro's friend, his only friend," said Fitzhugh. "Let no intermeddling abolitionist, no refined philosophy dissolve this friendship." [50]

The debate between the religionists and feudalists, on the one hand, and the racists, on the other, defined the Old South's central dilemma. The first two championed personalism and the familial view of the peculiar institution. The religionists were willing to question the beneficence and permanence of slavery in order to assert the slave's humanity; and the feudalists were willing to surrender democratic liberalism in order to retain a personalized system of servitude. The racists, on the other hand, denied the slave's full human status in order to reconcile slavery with democratic liberalism for whites. The South's ingrained liberalism and Christianity, in short, were continually thwarting the logic-impelled effort to develop a fully rationalized, sheerly economic conception of slavery, warranted by the racist argument.

It was this inner conflict which produced the South's belligerent dogmatism in the recurrent crises of the fifties. The whole massive proslavery polemic had the unreal ring of logic pushed far beyond conviction. "I assure you, Sir," Fitzhugh confessed in a private letter, "I see great evils in Slavery, but in a controversial work I

---

[48] *Congressional Globe*, 33rd Cong., 1st Sess., Appendix, 230.

[49] Goodloe, *Southern Platform*, 93.

[50] Jenkins, *Pro-Slavery Thought*, 281; Harvey Wish, *George Fitzhugh: Propagandist of the Old South* (Baton Rouge, 1943), 111.

ought not to admit them." [51] If the South's best minds resolutely quashed their doubts, it is small wonder that crisis-tossed editors and politicians took refuge in positive and extreme positions.

The final open collision between the two contradictory tendencies in the South's thinking about slavery came on the very eve of the Civil War, when some Southerners relentlessly pursued the logic of slavery's beneficence to the conclusion that the foreign slave trade should be reopened. "I would sweep from the statute-book every interference with slavery," shouted a fire-eating South Carolina congressman. "I would repeal the law declaring the slave trade piracy; I would withdraw our slave squadron from the coast of Africa; and I would leave slavery unintervened against, wherever the power of the country stretches." [52]

Despite the lip service paid to the "positive good" doctrine, majority southern opinion was deeply shocked by its logical extension to sanction the foreign slave trade. Few Southerners were willing "to roll back the tide of civilization and christianity of the nineteenth century, and restore the barbarism of the dark ages," declared a Georgia newspaper, and churchmen denounced the proposal with special vehemence. Even one of its original advocates turned against it when he witnessed the suffering of the Negroes aboard a captured slave ship. This "practical, fair evidence of its effects has cured me forever," confessed D. H. Hamilton. "I wish that everyone in South Carolina, who is in favor of re-opening of the Slave-trade, could have seen what I have been compelled to witness. . . . It seems to me that I can never forget it." [53] This was the agony of the proslavery South under the shadow of Civil War.

How, then, did the fundamentally liberal, Christian, American South ever become an "aggressive slavocracy"? * How did it bring itself to flaunt an aristocratic social philosophy? To break up the American Union? To wage war for the purpose of holding four million human beings in a bondage that violated their humanity? The answer is that Southerners did not and could not rationally and deliberately choose slavery and its fruits over the values it warred against. Rather it was the very conflict of values, rendered intolerable by constant criticism premised on values Southerners shared, which drove them to seek a violent resolution.

Social psychologists observe that such value conflicts—especially when they give rise to the kind of institutional instability revealed by the ambiguities of southern slavery—make a society "suggestible," or ready to follow the advocates of irrational

---

[51] Wish, Fitzhugh, 111.

[52] Harold S. Schultz, Nationalism and Sectionalism in South Carolina, 1852–1860: A Study of the Movement for Southern Independence (Durham, 1950), 182.

[53] Stampp, Peculiar Institution, 278; Schultz, Nationalism and Sectionalism, 158–59.

* The viewpoint of the present essay is not to be confused with the interpretation of the Civil War in terms of a "slave power conspiracy." Chauncey S. Boucher has demonstrated convincingly that the South was incapable of the kind of concerted action necessary for conspiracy. "In Re That Aggressive Slavocracy," Mississippi Valley Historical Review, VIII (June–September, 1921), 13–79. He is less persuasive, however, in demonstrating the equal inappropriateness of the designation "aggressive slavocracy." Boucher does admit (p. 30) that many Southerners "took a stand which may perhaps best be termed 'aggressively defensive.'" This is not too far from the attitude of the present essay, especially in view of Boucher's tantalizing suggestion (p. 70) that when Southerners talked of slavery as a divinely ordained institution, they were in the position of "saying a thing and being conscious while saying it that the thing is not true . . . but a position forced upon them by necessity of circumstances for their own immediate protection."

and aggressive action. † Thus it was fateful that the Old South developed an unusually able minority of fire-eating sectionalists, who labored zealously, from the 1830s on, to unite the South behind radical measures in defense of slavery. Though a majority of Southerners remained profoundly distrustful of these extremists throughout the antebellum period, their unceasing agitation steadily aggravated the South's tensions and heightened its underlying suggestibility. By egging the South on to ever more extreme demands, the Calhouns, Rhetts, and Yanceys provoked violent northern reactions, which could then be used to whip the South's passions still higher. At length, in 1860, capitalizing on intrigues for the Democratic presidential nomination, the fire-eaters managed to split the Democratic party, thus insuring the election of a Republican President and paving the way for secession.

Inflammatory agitation and revolutionary tactics succeeded only because Southerners had finally passed the point of rational self-control. The almost pathological violence of their reactions to northern criticism indicated that their misgivings about their moral position on slavery had become literally intolerable under the mounting abolitionist attack. "The South has been moved to resistance chiefly . . . by the popular dogma in the free states that slavery is a crime in the sight of GOD," said a New Orleans editor in the secession crisis. "The South, in the eyes of the North, is degraded and unworthy, because of the institution of servitude." [54]

Superimposed on this fundamental moral anxiety was another potent emotion, fear. John Brown's raid in October, 1859, created the most intense terror of slave insurrection that the South had ever experienced; and in this atmosphere of dread the final

---

† Hadley Cantril, *The Psychology of Social Movements* (New York, 1941), 61–64. The social sciences have much to contribute to southern historical scholarship; in fact, the essential key to understanding the Old South seems to lie in the area of social psychology. Though Harry Elmer Barnes asserted as much nearly 40 years ago, scholarly efforts in this direction have hardly moved beyond the naïve enthusiasm of Barnes' suggestion that "southern chivalry" was "a collective compensation for sexual looseness, racial intermixture, and the maltreatment of the Negro."—"Psychology and History: Some Reasons for Predicting Their More Active Cooperation in the Future," *American Journal of Psychology*, XXX (October, 1919), 374. A psychologist has interpreted southern behavior in terms of defense mechanism, rationalization, and projection.—D. A. Hartman, "The Psychological Point of View in History: Some Phases of the Slavery Struggle," *Journal of Abnormal Psychology and Social Psychology*, XVII (October–December, 1922), 261–73. A psychoanalyst has traced the white South's treatment of the Negro to the general insecurities of Western man uprooted by industrialism, and to an unconscious sexual fascination with the Negro as "a symbol which gives a secret gratification to those who are inhibited and crippled in their instinctual satisfaction."—Helen V. McLean, "Psychodynamic Factors in Racial Relations," *Annals of the American Academy of Political and Social Science*, CCLIV (March, 1946), 159–66. And a sociologist has sought to explain the South in terms of a concept of "social neurosis."—Read Bain, "Man Is the Measure," *Sociometry: A Journal of Inter-Personal Relations*, VI (November, 1943), 460–64.

These efforts, while suggestive, seem hardly more systematic and considerably less cautious than the historian's unsophisticated, commonsense way of trying to assess psychological factors. Yet Hadley Cantril's *Psychology of Social Movements* has demonstrated that the infant discipline of social psychology can, even in its present primitive state, furnish the historian with extremely useful concepts. Historians of the Old South have special reason for pressing their problems on their brethren in social psychology, while the social psychologists may find in historical data a challenging area for developing and testing hypotheses. Especially rewarding to both historians and social scientists would be a collaborative study of antebellum southern radicalism and its peculiar locus, South Carolina.

[54] Dwight L. Dumond (ed.), *Southern Editorials on Secession* (New York, 1931), 315–16.

crisis of 1860–61 occurred. The press warned that the South was "slumbering over a volcano, whose smoldering fires, may at any quiet starry midnight, blacken the social sky with the smoke of desolation and death." Southerners believed their land to be overrun by abolitionist emissaries, who were "tampering with our slaves, and furnishing them with arms and poisons to accomplish their hellish designs." Lynch law was proclaimed, and vigilance committees sprang up to deal with anyone suspected of abolitionist sentiments. A Mississippian reported the hanging of 23 such suspects in three weeks, while the British consul at Charleston described the situation as "a reign of terror." [55]

Under these circumstances a large part of the southern white population approached the crisis of the Union in a state of near-hysteria. One man thought that "the minds of the people are aroused to a pitch of excitement probably unparalleled in the history of our country." "The desire of some for change," reported a despairing Virginian, "the greed of many for excitement, and the longing of more for anarchy and confusion, seems to have unthroned the reason of men, and left them at the mercy of passion and madness." [56]

Just as important as the hysteria which affected some Southerners was the paralysis of will, the despair, the sense of helplessness, which the excitement created in their more conservative fellows. Denying that the southern people really wanted to dissolve the Union, a Georgia editor saw them as being "dragged on, blindfolded, to consummation of the horrid act." A "moral pestilence" had "swept over the South," said a prominent North Carolinian, "dethroning reason, & paralyzing the efforts of the best Union men of the country." But even some who decried the hysteria felt that "no community can exist & prosper when this sense of insecurity prevails," and concluded that almost any alternative was preferable to the strain of these recurrent crises. It was this conviction, more than anything else, which caused moderate men to give way to the bold and confident radicals. [57]

From the circumstances of the secession elections—the small turnouts, the revolutionary tactics of the fire-eaters, the disproportionate weighting of the results in favor of plantation areas, the coercive conditions under which the upper South voted, and the hysteria that prevailed everywhere—it can hardly be said that a majority of the South's white people deliberately chose to dissolve the Union in 1861. A member of South Carolina's secession convention frankly admitted that "the common people" did not understand what was at stake. "But whoever waited for the common people when a great movement was to be made?" he asked. "We must make the move and force them to follow. That is the way of all revolutions and all great achievements." [58]

The leaders made the move, and the people followed, but with what underlying misgivings the sequel only too plainly demonstrated. The first flush of enthusiasm was rapidly supplanted by an apathy and a growing disaffection which historians have identified as major factors in the Confederacy's failure. During the dark winter

---

[55] Crenshaw, *Slave States*, 100, 103, 106; Laura A. White, "The South in the 1850's as Seen by British Consuls," *Journal of Southern History*, I (February, 1935), 44.

[56] Crenshaw, *Slave States*, 111; Robert C. Gunderson, "William C. Rives and the 'Old Gentlemen's Convention,'" *Journal of Southern History*, XXII (November, 1956), 460.

[57] Crenshaw, *Slave States*, 111n., 237; Klingberg, *Southern Claims Commission*, 13. Cf. Cantril, *Psychology of Social Movements*, 61.

[58] White, *Rhett*, 177n.

of 1864–65, North Carolina's Governor Zebulon Vance commented on the supineness with which the southern population received the invading Sherman. It was evidence, said Vance, of what he had "always believed, that *the great popular heart is not now, and never has been in this war!* It was a revolution of the *Politicians, not the People.*" [59]

And when the cause was lost, Southerners abandoned it with an alacrity which underscored the reluctance of their original commitment. It was left for a leading ex-fire-eater to explain why they returned to the Union of their fathers with so little hesitation. Standing before the Joint Congressional Committee on Reconstruction in 1866, James D. B. De Bow attested in all sincerity the South's willingness to fight once again for the flag of the Union. "The southern people," he said, "are Americans, republicans." [60]

Yet it is idle to wonder whether secession represented the deliberate choice of a majority of white Southerners, or to speculate about the outcome of a hypothetical referendum, free from ambiguity, coercion, and hysteria. Decisions like the one that faced the South in 1860–61 are never reached in any such ideal way. And even had the South decided for the Union, its and the nation's problem would have remained unsolved, and a violent resolution would only have been postponed. Slavery was doomed by the march of history and by the nature of Southerners themselves, but so deeply had it involved them in its contradictions that they could neither deal with it rationally nor longer endure the tensions and anxieties it generated. Under these circumstances the Civil War or something very like it was unavoidable. It was also salutary, for only the transaction at Appomattox could have freed the South's people—both Negro and white—to move again toward the realization of their essential natures as Southerners, liberals, Christians, and Americans.

[59] Klingberg, *Southern Claims Commission,* 138.
[60] *Report of the Joint Committee on Reconstruction, at the First Session, Thirty-Ninth Congress* (Washington, 1866), 133.

Part III

THE FREE NORTH

8 / Romantic Reform in America, 1815–1865

John L. Thomas

At the very time the slave South was retiring behind a protective shell, the free North was responding ebulliently to the deep-running currents of the nineteenth-century world. It was a time of immense change and flux in the free states. Agriculture was giving way to industry as the factory system, especially in New England and the middle states, began to replace domestic industry and the small craft shop. Economic change in turn generated social change. Growing industry, and the enormous expanse of virgin land, drew millions from Europe with their alien languages, customs, religions, and ideas to the free states of the American West and the Northeast. Increasing population and industry stimulated rapid city growth almost entirely in the North.

Accompanying this social ferment was a remarkable restlessness of mind and spirit. The half-century preceding the Civil War saw more self-questioning, more intellectual and religious speculation, more social experimentation, and more impatience with the tried and tested, than any other period in our history. It was a time when it seemed that almost every man and woman, at least in New England, wanted to remake religion, society, the economy, the government, or the world as a whole. Describing the 1840 convention of the Friends of Universal Reform, Ralph Waldo Emerson noted that:

> Madmen, madwomen, men with beards, Dunkers, Muggletonians, Come-outers, Groaners, Agrarians, Seventh-Day Baptists, Quakers, Abolitionists, Calvinists, Unitarians, and Philosophers—all came successively to the top, and seized their moment, if not their hour, wherein to chide, or pray, or preach, or protest.

These schemes and movements differentiated the North from the South since the new ideas and currents bypassed the slave states. Moreover the greatest of the reform movements, the abolitionist crusade, threatened the South's basic interests and generated fierce sectional discord and resentment.

To what should we ascribe this great intellectual and social ferment in the ante-bellum North? Some historians see the reform movements as simple

American Quarterly, XVII, No. 4 (Winter 1965), 656–681. Copyright © 1965 by the Trustees of the University of Pennsylvania. Reprinted by permission.

responses to social evils. But why did people become crusaders against long-standing injustices at this particular moment? Slavery had been an inhumane and exploitive institution for two centuries, but few voices had been raised against it in America. Why did Americans find slavery increasingly intolerable after 1830, and how do we explain the sudden advent of William Lloyd Garrison, Wendell Phillips, Theodore Weld, and all of the other talented abolition leaders at that time?

In the following article, John L. Thomas sees the origin of the antebellum reform impulse in the intellectual history of the era. His essay is a thoughtful examination of the relation between ideas and action.

For further reading: * Alice Felt Tyler, *Freedom's Ferment: Phases of American Social History from the Colonial Period to the Outbreak of the Civil War* (Minneapolis, Minn.: University of Minnesota Press, 1944); Arthur E. Bestor, Jr., *Backwoods Utopias* (Philadelphia, Pa.: University of Pennsylvania Press, 1950); * Whitney R. Cross, *The Burned-Over District* (Ithaca, N. Y.: Cornell University Press, 1950); John R. Bodo, *The Protestant Clergy and Public Issues, 1812–1848* (Princeton: Princeton University Press, 1954); * George R. Taylor, *The Transportation Revolution, 1815–1860* (New York: Holt, Rinehart and Winston, Inc., 1951); * Paul Gates, *The Farmer's Age, 1815–1860* (New York: Holt, Rinehart and Winston, Inc., 1960).

Confronted by the bewildering variety of projects for regenerating American society, Emerson concluded his survey of humanitarian reform in 1844 with the observation that "the Church, or religious party, is falling away from the Church nominal, and . . . appearing in temperance and nonresistance societies; in movements of abolitionists and of socialists . . . of seekers, of all the soul of the soldiery of dissent." Common to all these planners and prophets, he noted, was the conviction of an "infinite worthiness" in man and the belief that reform simply meant removing "impediments" to natural perfection.[1]

Emerson was defining, both as participant and observer, a romantic revolution which T. E. Hulme once described as "spilt religion."[2] A romantic faith in perfectibility, originally confined by religious institutions, overflows these barriers and spreads across the surface of society, seeping into politics and culture. Perfectibility —the essentially religious notion of the individual as a "reservoir" of possibilities— fosters a revolutionary assurance "that if you can so rearrange society by the destruction of oppressive order then these possibilities will have a chance and you will get Progress." Hulme had in mind the destructive forces of the French Revolution, but his phrase is also a particularly accurate description of the surge of social reform which swept across Emerson's America in the three decades before the Civil War.

[1] Ralph Waldo Emerson, "The New England Reformers," *Works* (Centenary ed.), III, 251; "Man the Reformer," *Works*, I, 248–49.
[2] T. E. Hulme, "Romanticism and Classicism," *Speculations: Essays on Humanism and the Philosophy of Art,* ed. Herbert Read (London, 1924), reprinted in *Critiques and Essays in Criticism, 1920–1948,* ed. Robert Wooster Stallman (New York, 1949), pp. 3–16.

Out of a seemingly conservative religious revival there flowed a spate of perfectionist ideas for the improvement and rearrangement of American society. Rising rapidly in the years after 1830, the flood of social reform reached its crest at midcentury only to be checked by political crisis and the counterforces of the Civil War. Reform after the Civil War, though still concerned with individual perfectibility, proceeded from new and different assumptions as to the nature of individualism and its preservation in an urban industrial society. Romantic reform ended with the Civil War and an intellectual counterrevolution which discredited the concept of the irreducible self and eventually redirected reform energies.

Romantic reform in America traced its origins to a religious impulse which was both politically and socially conservative. With the consolidation of independence and the arrival of democratic politics the new nineteenth-century generation of American churchmen faced a seeming crisis. Egalitarianism and rising demands for church disestablishment suddenly appeared to threaten an inherited Christian order and along with it the preferred status of the clergy. Lyman Beecher spoke the fears of more than one of the clerical party when he warned that Americans were fast becoming "another people." When the attempted alliance between sound religion and correct politics failed to prevent disestablishment or improve waning Federalist fortunes at the polls, the evangelicals, assuming a defensive posture, organized voluntary benevolent associations to strengthen the Christian character of Americans and save the country from infidelity and ruin. Between 1815 and 1830 nearly a dozen moral reform societies were established to counter the threats to social equilibrium posed by irreligious democrats. Their intense religious concern could be read in the titles of the benevolent societies which the evangelicals founded: the American Bible Society, the American Sunday School Union, the American Home Missionary Society, the American Tract Society. By the time of the election of Andrew Jackson the benevolent associations formed a vast if loosely coordinated network of conservative reform enterprises staffed with clergy and wealthy laymen who served as self-appointed guardians of American morals.[3]

The clerical diagnosticians had little difficulty in identifying the symptoms of democratic disease. Infidelity flourished on the frontier and licentiousness bred openly in seaboard cities; intemperance sapped the strength of American working-men and the saving word was denied their children. Soon atheism would destroy the vital organs of the republic unless drastic moral therapy prevented. The evangelicals' prescription followed logically from their diagnosis: large doses of morality injected into the body politic under the supervision of Christian stewards. No more Sunday mails or pleasure excursions, no more grog-shops or profane pleasures, no family without a Bible and no community without a minister of the gospel. Accepting for the moment their political liabilities, the moral reformers relied on the homeopathic strategy of fighting democratic excess with democratic remedies. The Tract Society set up three separate printing presses which cranked out hundreds of thousands of pamphlets for mass distribution. The Home Missionary Society subsidized seminarians in carrying religion into the backcountry. The Temperance Union staged popular conventions; the Peace Society sponsored public debates; the Bible Society hired hundreds of agents to spread its propaganda.

[3] For discussions of evangelical reform see John R. Bodo, *The Protestant Clergy and Public Issues, 1812–1848* (Princeton, 1954) and Clifford S. Griffin, *Their Brothers' Keepers* (New Brunswick, N. J., 1960).

The initial thrust of religious reform, then, was moral rather than social, preventive rather than curative. Nominally rejecting politics and parties, the evangelicals looked to a general reformation of the American character achieved through a revival of piety and morals in the individual. By probing his conscience, by convincing him of his sinful ways and converting him to right conduct they hoped to engineer a Christian revolution which would leave the foundations of the social order undisturbed. The realization of their dream of a nonpolitical "Christian party" in America would ensure a one-party system open to moral talent and the natural superiority of Christian leadership. Until their work was completed, the evangelicals stood ready as servants of the Lord to manage their huge reformational apparatus in behalf of order and sobriety.

But the moral reformers inherited a theological revolution which in undermining their conservative defenses completely reversed their expectations for a Christian America. The transformation of American theology in the first quarter of the nineteenth century released the very forces of romantic perfectionism that conservatives most feared. This religious revolution advanced along three major fronts: first, the concentrated anti-theocratic assault of Robert Owen and his secular utopian followers, attacks purportedly atheistic and environmentalist but in reality Christian in spirit and perfectionist in method; second, the revolt of liberal theology beginning with Unitarianism and culminating in transcendentalism; third, the containment operation of the "new divinity" in adapting orthodoxy to the criticism of liberal dissent. The central fact in the romantic reorientation of American theology was the rejection of determinism. Salvation, however, variously defined, lay open to everyone. Sin was voluntary; men were not helpless and depraved by nature but free agents and potential powers for good. Sin could be reduced to the selfish preferences of individuals, and social evils, in turn, to collective sins which, once acknowledged, could be rooted out. Perfectionism spread rapidly across the whole spectrum of American Protestantism as different denominations and sects elaborated their own versions of salvation. If man was a truly free agent, then his improvement became a matter of immediate consequence. The progress of the country suddenly seemed to depend upon the regeneration of the individual and the contagion of example.

As it spread, perfectionism swept across denominational barriers and penetrated even secular thought. Perfection was presented as Christian striving for holiness in the "new heart" sermons of Charles Grandison Finney and as an immediately attainable goal in the come-outer prophecies of John Humphrey Noyes. It was described as an escape from outworn dogma by Robert Owen and as the final union of the soul with nature by Emerson. The important fact for most Americans in the first half of the nineteenth century was that it was readily available. A romantic religious faith had changed an Enlightenment doctrine of progress into a dynamic principle of reform.

For the Founding Fathers' belief in perfectibility had been wholly compatible with a pessimistic appraisal of the present state of mankind. Progress, in the view of John Adams or James Madison, resulted from the planned operation of mechanical checks within the framework of government which balanced conflicting selfish interests and neutralized private passions. Thus a properly constructed governmental machine might achieve by artifact what men, left to their own devices, could not— gradual improvement of social institutions and a measure of progress. Perfectionism, on the contrary, as an optative mood demanded total commitment and immediate action. A latent revolutionary force lay in its demand for immediate reform and its promise to release the new American from the restraints of institutions and precedent. In appealing to the liberated individual, perfectionism reinforced the Jacksonian attack on institutions, whether a "Monster Bank" or a secret Masonic order, entrenched monopolies or the Catholic Church. But in emphasizing the unfettered will as the proper vehicle for reform it provided a millenarian alternative to Jacksonian politics. Since social evils were simply individual acts of selfishness compounded, and since Americans could attempt the perfect society any time they were so inclined, it followed that the duty of the true reformer consisted in educating them and making them models of good behavior. As the sum of individual sins social wrong would disappear when enough people had been converted and rededicated to right conduct. Deep and lasting reform, therefore, meant an educational crusade based on the assumption that when a sufficient number of individual Americans had seen the light, they would automatically solve the country's social problems. Thus formulated, perfectionist reform offered a program of mass conversion achieved through educational rather than political means. In the opinion of the romantic reformers the regeneration of American society began, not in legislative enactments or political manipulation, but in a calculated appeal to the American urge for individual self-improvement.

Perfectionism radically altered the moral reform movement by shattering the benevolent societies themselves. Typical of these organizations was the American Peace Society founded in 1828 as a forum for clerical discussions of the gospel of peace. Its founders, hoping to turn American attention from the pursuit of wealth to the prevention of war, debated the question of defensive war, constructed hypothetical leagues of amity, and in a general way sought to direct American foreign policy into pacific channels. Perfectionism, however, soon split the Peace Society into warring factions as radical nonresistants, led by the Christian perfectionist Henry C. Wright, denounced all use of force and demanded the instant creation of an American society modeled on the precepts of Jesus. Not only war but all governmental coercion fell under the ban of the nonresistants who refused military service and political office along with the right to vote. After a series of skirmishes the nonresistants seceded in 1838 to form their own New England Non-Resistant Society; and by 1840 the institutional strength of the peace movement had been completely broken.

The same power of perfectionism disrupted the temperance movement. The founders of the temperance crusade had considered their reform an integral part of the program of moral stewardship and had directed their campaign against "ardent spirits" which could be banished "by a correct and efficient public sentiment." Until 1833 there was no general agreement on a pledge of total abstinence: some local societies required it, others did not. At the first national convention held in that year, however, the radical advocates of temperance, following their perfectionist proclivities, demanded a pledge of total abstinence and hurried on to denounce the liquor traffic as "morally wrong." Soon both the national society and local and state auxiliaries were split between moderates content to preach to the consumer and radicals bent on extending moral suasion to public pressure on the seller. After 1836 the national movement disintegrated into scattered local societies which attempted with no uniform program and no permanent success to establish a cold-water America.

By far the most profound change wrought by perfectionism was the sudden emergence of abolition. The American Colonization Society, founded in 1817 as another key agency in the moral reform complex, aimed at strengthening republican institutions by deporting an inferior and therefore undesirable Negro population. The cooperation of Southerners hoping to strengthen the institution of slavery gave Northern colonizationists pause, but they succeeded in repressing their doubts until a perfectionist ethic totally discredited their program. The abolitionist pioneers were former colonizationists who took sin and redemption seriously and insisted that slavery constituted a flat denial of perfectibility to both Negroes and whites. They found in immediate emancipation a perfectionist formula for casting off the guilt of slavery and bringing the Negro to Christian freedom. Destroying slavery, the abolitionists argued, depended first of all on recognizing it as sin; and to this recognition they bent their efforts. Their method was direct and intensely personal. Slaveholding they considered a deliberate flouting of the divine will for which there was no remedy but repentance. Since slavery was sustained by a system of interlocking personal sins, their task was to teach Americans to stop sinning. "We shall send forth agents to lift up the voice of remonstrance, of warning, of entreaty, and of rebuke," the Declaration of Sentiments of the American Anti-Slavery Society announced. Agents, tracts, petitions and conventions—all the techniques of the moral reformers —were brought to bear on the consciences of Americans to convince them of their sin.

From the beginning, then, the abolitionists mounted a moral crusade rather than an engine of limited reform. For seven years, from 1833 to 1840, their society functioned as a loosely coordinated enterprise—a national directory of antislavery opinion. Perfectionist individualism made effective organization difficult and often impossible. Antislavery delegates from state and local societies gathered at annual conventions to frame denunciatory resolutions, listen to endless rounds of speeches and go through the motions of electing officers. Nominal leadership but very little power was vested in a self-perpetuating executive committee. Until its disruption in 1840 the national society was riddled with controversy as moderates, disillusioned by the failure of moral suasion, gradually turned to politics, and ultras, equally disenchanted by public hostility, abandoned American institutions altogether. Faced with the resistance of Northern churches and state legislatures, the perfectionists, led by William Lloyd Garrison, deserted politics for the principle of secession. The come-outer abolitionists, who eventually took for their motto "No Union with Slaveholders," sought an alternative to politics in the command to cast off church and state for a holy fraternity which would convert the nation by the power of example. The American Anti-Slavery Society quickly succumbed to the strain of conflicting philosophies and warring personalities. In 1840 the Garrisonians seized control of the society and drove their moderate opponents out. Thereafter neither ultras nor moderates were able to maintain an effective national organization.

Thus romantic perfectionism altered the course of the reform enterprise by appealing directly to the individual conscience. Its power stemmed from a millennial expectation which proved too powerful a moral explosive for the reform agencies. In one way or another almost all of the benevolent societies felt the force of perfectionism. Moderates, attempting political solutions, scored temporary gains only to receive sharp setbacks. Local option laws passed one year were repealed the next. Despite repeated attempts the Sunday School Union failed to secure permanent adoption of its texts in the public schools. The Liberty Party succeeded only in electing a Democratic president in 1844. Generally, direct political action failed to furnish reformers with the moral leverage they believed necessary to perfect American society. The conviction spread accordingly that politicians and legislators, as Albert Brisbane put it, were engaged in "superficial controversies and quarrels, which lead to no practical results." [4] Political results, a growing number of social reformers were convinced, would be forthcoming only when the reformation of society at large had been accomplished through education and example.

The immediate effects of perfectionism, therefore, were felt outside politics in humanitarian reforms. With its confidence in the liberated individual perfectionism tended to be anti-institutional and exclusivist; but at the same time it posited an ideal society in which this same individual could discover his power for good and exploit it. Such a society would tolerate neither poverty nor suffering; it would contain no condemned classes or deprived citizens, no criminals or forgotten men. Impressed with the necessity for saving these neglected elements of American society, the humanitarian reformers in the years after 1830 undertook a huge rescue operation.

Almost to a man the humanitarians came from moral reform backgrounds. Samuel Gridley Howe was a product of Old Colony religious zeal and a Baptist education at Brown; Thomas Gallaudet, a graduate of Andover and an ordained minister; Dorothea Dix, a daughter of an itinerant Methodist minister, school mistress and Sunday school teacher-turned-reformer, E. M. P. Wells, founder of the reform school, a pastor of a Congregational church in Boston. Louis Dwight, the prison reformer, had been trained for the ministry at Yale and began his reform career as a traveling agent for the American Tract Society. Robert Hartley, for thirty years the secretary of the New York Association for Improving the Condition of the Poor, started as a tract distributor and temperance lecturer. Charles Loring Brace served as a missionary on Blackwell's Island before founding the Children's Aid Society.

In each of these cases of conversion to humanitarian reform there was a dramatic disclosure of deprivation and suffering which did not tally with preconceived notions of perfectibility—Dorothea Dix's discovery of the conditions in the Charlestown reformatory, Robert Hartley's inspection of contaminated milk in New York slums, Samuel Gridley Howe's chance conversation with Dr. Fisher in Boston. Something very much like a conversion experience seems to have forged the decisions of the humanitarians to take up their causes, a kind of revelation which furnished them with a ready-made role outside politics and opened a new career with which they could become completely identified. With the sudden transference of a vague perfectionist faith in self-improvement to urgent social problems there emerged a new type of professional reformer whose whole life became identified with the reform process.

Such, for example, was the conversion of Dorothea Dix from a lonely and afflicted schoolteacher who composed meditational studies of the life of Jesus into "D. L. Dix," the militant advocate of the helpless and forgotten. In a very real sense Miss Dix's crusade for better treatment of the insane and the criminal was one long self-imposed subjection to suffering. Her reports, which recorded cases of unbeliev-

[4] Albert Brisbane, *Social Destiny of Man: or, Association and Reorganization of Industry* (Philadelphia, 1840), introduction, p. vi.

able mistreatment, completed a kind of purgative rite in which she assumed the burden of innocent suffering and passed it on as guilt to the American people. The source of her extraordinary energy lay in just this repeated submission of herself to human misery until she felt qualified to speak out against it. Both an exhausting schedule and the almost daily renewal of scenes of suffering seemed to give her new energies for playing her romantic reform role in an effective and intensely personal way. Intense but not flexible: there was little room for exchange and growth in the mood of atonement with which she approached her work. Nor was her peculiarly personal identification with the victims of American indifference easily matched in reform circles. Where other reformers like the abolitionists often made abstract pleas for "bleeding humanity" and "suffering millions," hers was the real thing—a perfectionist fervor which strengthened her will at the cost of psychological isolation. Throughout her career she preferred to work alone, deploring the tendency to multiply reform agencies and ignoring those that existed either because she disagreed with their principles, as in the case of Louis Dwight's Boston Prison Discipline Society, or because she chose the more direct method of personal appeal. In all her work, even the unhappy and frustrating last years as superintendent of nurses in the Union Army, she saw herself as a solitary spokesman for the deprived and personal healer of the suffering.

Another reform role supplied by perfectionism was Bronson Alcott's educator-prophet, the "true reformer" who "studied man as he is from the hand of the Creator, and not as he is made by the errors of the world." Convinced that the self sprang from divine origins in nature, Alcott naturally concluded that children were more susceptible to good than people imagined and set out to develop a method for uncovering that goodness. With the power to shape personality the teacher, Alcott was sure, held the key to illimitable progress and the eventual regeneration of the world. The teacher might literally make society over by teaching men as children to discover their own divine natures. Thus true education for Alcott consisted of the process of self-discovery guided by the educator-prophet. He sharply criticized his contemporaries for their fatal mistake of imposing partial and therefore false standards on their charges. Shades of the prison house obscured the child's search for perfection, and character was lost forever. "Instead of following it in the path pointed out by its Maker, instead of learning by observation, and guiding it in that path; we unthinkingly attempt to shape its course to our particular wishes. . . ." [5]

To help children avoid the traps set by their elders Alcott based his whole system on the cultivation of self-awareness through self-examination. His pupils kept journals in which they scrutinized their behavior and analyzed their motives. Ethical problems were the subject of frequent and earnest debate at the Temple School as the children were urged to discover the hidden springs of perfectibility in themselves. No mechanical methods of rote learning could bring on the moment of revelation; each child was unique and would find himself in his own way. The real meaning of education as reform, Alcott realized, came with an increased social sense that resulted from individual self-discovery. As the creator of social personality Alcott's teacher was bound by no external rules of pedagogy: as the primary social reformer he had to cast off "the shackles of form, of mode, and ceremony" in order to play the required roles in the educational process.

[5] For a careful analysis of Alcott's educational theories see Dorothy McCuskey, *Bronson Alcott, Teacher* (New York, 1940), particularly pp. 25–40 from which these quotations are taken.

Alcott's modernity lay principally in his concept of the interchangeability of roles—both teacher and pupils acquired self-knowledge in an exciting give-and-take. Thus defined, education became a way of life, a continuing process through which individuals learned to obey the laws of their own natures and in so doing to discover the laws of the good society. This identification of individual development with true social unity was crucial for Alcott, as for the other perfectionist communitarians, because it provided the bridge over which they passed from self to society. The keystone in Alcott's construction was supplied by the individual conscience which connected with the "common conscience" of mankind. This fundamental identity, he was convinced, could be demonstrated by the learning process itself which he defined as "sympathy and imitation, the moral action of the teacher upon the children, of the children upon him, and each other." He saw in the school, therefore, a model of the good community where self-discovery led to a social exchange culminating in the recognition of universal dependency and brotherhood. The ideal society—the society he hoped to create—was one in which individuals could be totally free to follow their own natures because such pursuit would inevitably end in social harmony. For Alcott the community was the product rather than the creator of the good life.

Fruitlands, Alcott's attempt to apply the lessons of the Temple School on a larger scale, was designed to prove that perfectionist educational reform affected the "economies of life." In this realization lay the real import of Alcott's reform ideas; for education, seen as a way of life, meant the communitarian experiment as an educative model. Pushed to its limits, the perfectionist assault on institutions logically ended in the attempt to make new and better societies as examples for Americans to follow. Communitarianism, as Alcott envisioned it, was the social extension of his perfectionist belief in education as an alternative to politics.

In the case of other humanitarian reformers like Samuel Gridley Howe, perfectionism determined even more precisely both the role and intellectual content of their proposals. Howe's ideal of the good society seems to have derived from his experiences in Greece where, during his last year, he promoted a communitarian plan for resettling exiles on the Gulf of Corinth. With government support he established his colony, "Washingtonia," on two thousand acres of arable land, selected the colonists himself, bought cattle and tools, managed its business affairs, and supervised a Lancastrian school. By his own admission these were the happiest days of his life: "I laboured here day & night in season & out; & was governor, legislator, clerk, constable, & everything but patriarch."[6] When the government withdrew its support and brigands overran the colony, Howe was forced to abandon the project and return home. Still, the idea of an entire community under the care of a "patriarch" shouldering its collective burden and absorbing all its dependents in a cooperative life continued to dominate the "Doctor's" reform thinking and to determine his methods.

The ethical imperatives in Howe's philosophy of reform remained constant. "Humanity demands that every creature in human shape should command our respect; we should recognise as a brother every being upon whom God has stamped the human impress." Progress he likened to the American road. Christian individualism required that each man walk separately and at his own pace, but "the rear should

[6] Letter from Howe to Horace Mann, 1857, quoted in Harold Schwartz, *Samuel Gridley Howe* (Cambridge, 1956), p. 37.

not be left too far behind . . . none should be allowed to perish in their helplessness . . . the strong should help the weak, so that the whole should advance as a
band of brethren." It was the duty of society itself to care for its disabled or
mentally deficient members rather than to shut them up in asylums which were
"offsprings of a low order of feeling." "The more I reflect upon the subject the more
I see objections in principle and practice to asylums," he once wrote to a fellow-
reformer. "What right have we to pack off the poor, the old, the blind into asylums?
They are of us, our brothers, our sisters—they belong in families. . . ."[7]

In Howe's ideal society, then, the handicapped, criminals and defectives would
not be walled off but accepted as part of the community and perfected by constant
contact with it. Two years of experimenting with education for the feeble-minded
convinced him that even "idiots" could be redeemed from what he called spiritual
death. "How far they can be elevated, and to what extent they may be educated,
can only be shown by the experience of the future," he admitted in his report to the
Massachusetts legislature but predicted confidently that "each succeeding year will
show even more progress than any preceding one."[8] He always acted on his conviction that "we shall avail ourselves of special institutions less and the common
schools more" and never stopped hoping that eventually all blind children after
proper training might be returned to families and public schools for their real
education. He also opposed the establishment of reformatories with the argument
that they only collected the refractory and vicious and made them worse. Nature
mingled the defective in common families, he insisted, and any departure from her
standards stunted moral growth. He took as his model for reform the Belgian town
of Geel where mentally ill patients were boarded at public expense with private
families and allowed maximum freedom. As soon as the building funds were available he introduced the cottage system at Perkins, a plan he also wanted to apply
to reformatories. No artificial and unnatural institution could replace the family
which Howe considered the primary agency in the perfection of the individual.

Howe shared his bias against institutions and a preference for the family unit
with other humanitarian reformers like Robert Hartley and Charles Loring Brace.
Hartley's "friendly visitors" were dispatched to New York's poor with instructions
to bring the gospel of self-help home to every member of the family. Agents of the
AICP dispensed advice and improving literature along with the coal and groceries.
Only gradually did the organization incorporate "incidental labors"—legislative programs for housing reform, health regulations and child labor—into its system of
reform. Hartley's real hope for the new urban poor lay in their removal to the
country where a bootstrap operation might lift them to sufficiency and selfhood.
"Escape then from the city," he told them, "—for escape is your only recourse against
the terrible ills of beggary; and the further you go, the better."[9] In Hartley's formula the perfectionist doctrine of the salvation of the individual combined with the
conservative appeal of the safety-valve.

A pronounced hostility to cities also marked the program of Charles Loring Brace's

---

[7] Letter from Howe to William Chapin, 1857, quoted in Laura E. Richards, *Letters and
Journals of Samuel Gridley Howe* (2 vols.; New York, 1909), II, 48.

[8] Second Report of the Commissioners on Idiocy to the Massachusetts Legislature (1849),
quoted in Richards, *Howe*, II, 214.

[9] New York A.I.C.P., *The Mistake* (New York, 1850), p. 4, quoted in Robert H. Bremner,
From the Depths: the Discovery of Poverty in the United States (New York, 1956), p. 38.

Children's Aid Society, the central feature of which was the plan for relocating children of the "squalid poor" on upstate New York farms for "moral disinfection." The Society's placement service resettled thousands of slum children in the years before the Civil War in the belief that a proper family environment and a rural setting would release the naturally good tendencies in young people so that under the supervision of independent and hard-working farmers they would save themselves.[10]

There was thus a high nostalgic content in the plans of humanitarians who emphasized pastoral virtues and the perfectionist values inherent in country living. Their celebration of the restorative powers of nature followed logically from their assumption that the perfected individual—the truly free American—could be created only by the reunification of mental and physical labor. The rural life, it was assumed, could revive and sustain the unified sensibility threatened by the city. A second assumption concerned the importance of the family as the primary unit in the reconstruction of society. As the great debate among social reformers proceeded it centered on the question of the limits to which the natural family could be extended. Could an entire society, as the more radical communitarians argued, be reorganized as one huge family? Or were there natural boundaries necessary for preserving order and morality? On the whole, the more conservative humanitarians agreed with Howe in rejecting those communal plans which, like Fourier's, stemmed from too high an estimate of "the capacity of mankind for family affections."[11]

That intensive education held the key to illimitable progress, however, few humanitarian reformers denied. They were strengthened in their certainty by the absolutes inherited from moral reform. Thus Howe, for example, considered his work a "new field" of "practical religion." The mental defective, he was convinced, was the product of sin—both the sin of the parents and the sin of society in allowing the offspring to languish in mental and moral darkness. Yet the social evils incident to sin were not inevitable; they were not "inherent in the very constitution of man" but the "chastisements sent by a loving Father to bring his children to obedience to his beneficent laws."[12] These laws—infinite perfectibility and social responsibility—reinforced each other in the truly progressive society. The present condition of the dependent classes in America was proof of "the immense space through which society has yet to advance before it even approaches the perfection of civilization which is attainable."[13] Education, both the thorough training of the deprived and the larger education of American society to its obligations, would meet the moral challenge.

The perfectionist uses of education as an alternative to political reform were most thoroughly explored by Horace Mann. Mann's initial investment in public school education was dictated by his fear that American democracy, lacking institutional checks and restraints, was fast degenerating into "the spectacle of gladiatorial contests" conducted at the expense of the people. Could laws save American society? Mann thought not.

[10] Brace's views are set forth in his *The Dangerous Classes of New York and Twenty Years Among Them* (New York, 1872). For a brief treatment of his relation to the moral reform movement see Bremner, *From the Depths,* chap. iii.

[11] Letter from Howe to Charles Sumner, Apr. 8, 1847, quoted in Richards, *Howe,* II, 255–56.

[12] First Report of the Commissioners on Idiocy (1848), quoted in Richards, *Howe,* II, 210–11.

[13] *Ibid.,* pp. 210–11.

> With us, the very idea of legislation is reversed. Once, the law prescribed the actions and shaped the wills of the multitude; here the wills of the multitude prescribe and shape the law . . . now when the law is weak, the passions of the multitude have gathered irresistible strength, it is fallacious and insane to look for security in the moral force of law. Government and law . . . will here be moulded into the similitude of the public mind. . . .[14]

In offering public school education as the only effective countervailing force in a democracy Mann seemingly was giving vent to a conservative dread of unregulated change in a society where, as he admitted, the momentum of hereditary opinion was spent. Where there was no "surgical code of laws" reason, conscience and benevolence would have to be provided by education. "The whole mass of mind must be instructed in regard to its comprehensive and enduring interests." In a republican government, however, compulsion was theoretically undesirable and practically unavailable. People could not be driven up a "dark avenue" even though it were the right one. Mann, like his evangelical predecessors, found his solution in an educational crusade.

> Let the intelligent visit the ignorant, day by day, as the oculist visits the blind mind, and detaches the scales from his eyes, until the living sense leaps to light. . . . Let the love of beautiful reason, the admonitions of conscience, the sense of religious responsibility, be plied, in mingled tenderness and earnestness, until the obdurate and dark mass of avarice and ignorance and prejudice shall be dissipated by their blended light and heat.[15]

Here in Mann's rhetorical recasting was what appeared to be the old evangelical prescription for tempering democratic excess. The chief problem admittedly was avoiding the "disturbing forces of party and sect and faction and clan." To make sure that education remained nonpartisan the common schools should teach on the *"exhibitory"* method, "by an actual exhibition of the principle we would inculcate."

Insofar as the exhibitory method operated to regulate or direct public opinion, it was conservative. But implicit in Mann's theory was a commitment to perfectionism which gradually altered his aims until in the twelfth and final report education emerges as a near-utopian device for making American politics simple, clean and, eventually, superfluous. In the Twelfth Report Mann noted that although a public school system might someday guarantee "sufficiency, comfort, competence" to every American, as yet "imperfect practice" had not matched "perfect theory." Then in an extended analysis of social trends which foreshadowed Henry George's classification he singled out "poverty" and "profusion" as the two most disturbing facts in American development. "With every generation, fortunes increase on the one hand, and some new privation is added to poverty on the other. We are verging toward those extremes of opulence and penury, each of which unhumanizes the mind."[16] A new

---

[14] Horace Mann, "The Necessity of Education in a Republican Government," *Lectures on Education* (Boston, 1845), pp. 152, 158.

[15] "An Historical View of Education; Showing Its Dignity and Its Degradation," *Lectures on Education,* pp. 260, 262.

[16] This quotation and the ones from Mann that follow are taken from the central section of the *Twelfth Report* entitled "Intellectual Education as a Means of Removing Poverty, and Securing Abundance," Mary Peabody Mann, *Life of Horace Mann* (4 vols.; Boston, 1891), IV, 245–68. See also the perceptive comments on Mann in Rush Welter, *Popular Education and Democratic Thought in America* (New York, 1962), pp. 97–102, from which I have drawn.

feudalism threatened; and unless a drastic remedy was discovered, the "hideous evils" of unequal distribution of wealth would cause class war.

Mann's alternative to class conflict proved to be nothing less than universal education based on the exhibitory model of the common school. Diffusion of education, he pointed out, meant wiping out class lines and with them the possibility of conflict. As the great equalizer of condition it would supply the balance-wheel in the society of the future. Lest his readers confuse his suggestions with the fantasies of communitarians Mann hastened to point out that education would perfect society through the individual by creating new private resources. Given full play in a democracy, education gave each man the "independence and the means by which he can resist the selfishness of other men."

Once Mann had established education as an alternative to political action, it remained to uncover its utopian possibilities. By enlarging the "cultivated class" it would widen the area of social feelings—"if this education should be universal and complete, it would do more than all things else to obliterate factitious distinctions in society." Political reformers and revolutionaries based their schemes on the false assumption that the amount of wealth in America was fixed by fraud and force, and that the few were rich because the many were poor. By demanding a redistribution of wealth by legislative fiat they overlooked the power of education to obviate political action through the creation of new and immense sources of wealth.

Thus in Mann's theory as in the programs of the other humanitarians the perfection of the individual through education guaranteed illimitable progress. The constantly expanding powers of the free individual ensured the steady improvement of society until the educative process finally achieved a harmonious, self-regulating community. "And will not the community that gains its wealth in this way . . . be a model and a pattern for nations, a type of excellence to be admired and followed by the world?" The fate of free society, Mann concluded, depended upon the conversion of individuals from puppets and automatons to thinking men who were aware of the strength of the irreducible self and determined to foster it in others.

As romantic perfectionism spread across Jacksonian society it acquired an unofficial and only partly acceptable philosophy in the "systematic subjectivism" of transcendental theory.[17] Transcendentalism, as its official historian noted, claimed for all men what a more restrictive Christian perfectionism extended only to the redeemed. Seen in this light, self-culture—Emerson's "perfect unfolding of our individual nature" —appeared as a secular amplification of the doctrine of personal holiness. In the transcendentalist definition, true reform proceeded from the individual and worked outward through the family, the neighborhood and ultimately into the social and political life of the community. The transcendentalist, Frothingham noted in retrospect, "was less a reformer of human circumstances than a regenerator of the human spirit. . . . With movements that did not start from this primary assumption of individual dignity, and come back to that as their goal, he had nothing to do."[18] Emerson's followers, like the moral reformers and the humanitarians, looked to individuals rather than to institutions, to "high heroic example" rather than to political

[17] The phrase is Santayana's in "The Genteel Tradition in American Philosophy." For an analysis of the anti-institutional aspects of transcendentalism and reform see Stanley Elkins, *Slavery* (Chicago, 1959), chap. iii.

[18] Octavius Brooks Frothingham, *Transcendentalism in New England* (Harper Torchbooks ed.: New York, 1959), p. 155.

programs. The Brook-Farmer John Sullivan Dwight summed up their position when he protested that "men are anterior to systems. Great doctrines are not the origins, but the product of great lives." [19]

Accordingly the transcendentalists considered institutions—parties, churches, organizations—so many arbitrarily constructed barriers on the road to self-culture. They were lonely men, Emerson admitted, who repelled influences. "They are not good citizens; not good members of society. . . ." [20] A longing for solitude led them out of society, Emerson to the woods where he found no Jacksonian placards on the trees, Thoreau to his reclusive leadership of a majority of one. Accepting for the most part Emerson's dictum that one man was a counterpoise to a city, the transcendentalists turned inward to examine the divine self and find there the material with which to rebuild society. They wanted to avoid at all costs the mistake of their Jacksonian contemporaries who in order to be useful accommodated themselves to institutions without realizing the resultant loss of power and integrity.

The most immediate effect of perfectionism on the transcendentalists, as on the humanitarians, was the development of a set of concepts which, in stressing reform by example, opened up new roles for the alienated intellectual. In the first place, self-culture accounted for their ambivalence toward reform politics. It was not simply Emerson's reluctance to raise the siege on his hencoop that kept him apart, but a genuine confusion as to the proper role for the reformer. If government was simply a "job" and American society the senseless competition of the marketplace, how could the transcendentalist accept either as working premises? The transcendentalist difficulty in coming to terms with democratic politics could be read in Emerson's confused remark that of the two parties contending for the presidency in 1840 one had the better principles, the other the better men. Driven by their profound distaste for manipulation and chicanery, many of Emerson's followers took on the role of a prophet standing aloof from elections, campaigns and party caucuses and dispensing wisdom (often in oblique Emersonian terminology) out of the vast private resources of the self. In this sense transcendentalism, like Christian perfectionism, represented a distinct break with the prevailing Jacksonian views of democratic leadership and the politics of compromise and adjustment.

One of the more appealing versions of the transcendental role was the hero or genius to whom everything was permitted, as Emerson said, because "genius is the character of illimitable freedom." The heroes of the world, Margaret Fuller announced, were the true theocratic kings: "The hearts of men make music at their approach; the mind of the age is like the historian of their passing; and only men of destiny like themselves shall be permitted to write their eulogies, or fill their vacancies." [21] Margaret Fuller herself spent her transcendentalist years stalking the American hero, which she somehow confused with Emerson, before she joined the Roman Revolution in 1849 and discovered the authentic article in the mystic nationalist Mazzini.

Carlyle complained to Emerson of the "perilous altitudes" to which the transcendentalists' search for the hero led them. Despite his own penchant for hero-worship he came away from reading the *Dial* "with a kind of shudder." In their

---

[19] John Sullivan Dwight as quoted in Frothingham, *Transcendentalism*, p. 147.

[20] "The Transcendentalist," *Works*, I, 347–48.

[21] Such was her description of Lamennais and Beranger as quoted in Mason Wade, *Margaret Fuller* (New York, 1940), 195.

pursuit of the self-contained hero they seemed to separate themselves from "this same cotton-spinning, dollar-hunting, canting and shrieking, very wretched generation of ours." [22] The transcendentalists, however, were not trying to escape the Jacksonian world of fact, only to find a foothold for their perfectionist individualism in it. They sought a way of implementing their ideas of self-culture without corrupting them with the false values of materialism. They saw a day coming when parties and politicians would be obsolescent. By the 1850s Walt Whitman thought that day had already arrived and that America had outgrown parties.

> What right has any one political party, no matter which, to wield the American government? No right at all . . . and every American young man must have sense enough to comprehend this. I have said the old parties are defunct; but there remains of them empty flesh, putrid mouths, mumbling and speaking the tones of these conventions, the politicians standing back in shadow, telling lies, trying to delude and frighten the people. . . .[23]

Whitman's romantic alternative was a "love of comrades" cementing an American brotherhood and upholding a redeemer president.

A somewhat similar faith in the mystical fraternity informed Theodore Parker's plan for spiritual revolution. Like the other perfectionists, Parker began by reducing society to its basic components—individuals, the "monads" or "primitive atoms" of the social order—and judged it by its tendency to promote or inhibit individualism. "Destroy the individuality of those atoms, . . . all is gone. To mar the atoms is to mar the mass. To preserve itself, therefore, society is to preserve the individuality of the individual." [24] In Parker's theology perfectionist Christianity and transcendental method merged to form a loving brotherhood united by the capacity to apprehend primary truths directly. A shared sense of the divinity of individual man held society together; without it no true community was possible. Looking around him at ante-bellum America, Parker found only the wrong kind of individualism, the kind that said, "I am as good as you, so get out of my way." The right kind, the individualism whose motto was "You are as good as I, and let us help one another," [25] was to be the work of Parker's spiritual revolution. He explained the method of revolution as one of *"intellectual, moral* and *religious* education—everywhere and for all men." Until universal education had done its work Parker had little hope for political stability in the United States. He called instead for a new "party" to be formed in society at large, a party built on the idea that "God still inspires men as much as ever; that he is immanent in spirit as in space." Such a party required no church, tradition or scripture. "It believes God is near the soul as matter to the sense. . . . It calls God father and mother, not king; Jesus, brother, not redeemer, heaven home, religion nature." [26]

Parker believed that this "philosophical party in politics," as he called it, was already at work in the 1850s on a code of universal laws from which to deduce

[22] Quoted in Wade, *Margaret Fuller,* pp. 88–89.

[23] Walt Whitman, "The Eighteenth Presidency," an essay unpublished in Whitman's lifetime, in *Walt Whitman's Workshop,* ed. Clifton Joseph Furness (Cambridge, 1928), pp. 104–5.

[24] Quoted in Daniel Aaron, *Men of Good Hope* (Oxford paperback ed.: New York, 1961), p. 35.

[25] Theodore Parker, "The Political Destination of America and the Signs of the Times" (1848) excerpted in *The Transcendentalists,* ed. Perry Miller (Anchor ed.: Garden City, N. Y., 1957), p. 357.

[26] Quoted in R. W. B. Lewis, *The American Adam* (Chicago, 1955), p. 182.

specific legislation "so that each statute in the code shall represent a fact in the universe, a point of thought in God; so . . . that legislation shall be divine in the same sense that a true system of astronomy be divine." Parker's holy band represented the full fruition of the perfectionist idea of a "Christian party" in America, a party of no strict political or sectarian definition, but a true reform movement, apostolic in its beginnings but growing with the truths it preached until it encompassed all Americans in a huge brotherhood of divine average men. Party members, unlike time-serving Whigs and Democrats, followed ideas and intuitions rather than prejudice and precedent, and these ideas led them to question authority, oppose legal injustice and tear down rotten institutions. The philosophical party was not to be bound by accepted notions of political conduct or traditional attitudes toward law. When unjust laws interpose barriers to progress, reformers must demolish them.

So Parker himself reasoned when he organized the Vigilance Committee in Boston to defeat the Fugitive Slave Law. His reasoning epitomized perfectionist logic: every man may safely trust his conscience, properly informed, because it is the repository for divine truth. When men learn to trust their consciences and act on them, they naturally encourage others to do the same with the certainty that they will reach the same conclusions. Individual conscience thus creates a social conscience and a collective will to right action. Concerted right action means moral revolution. The fact that moral revolution, in its turn, might mean political revolt was a risk Parker and his perfectionist followers were willing to take.

Both transcendentalism and perfectionist moral reform, then, were marked by an individualist fervor that was disruptive of American institutions. Both made heavy moral demands on church and state; and when neither proved equal to the task of supporting their intensely personal demands, the transcendentalists and the moral reformers became increasingly alienated. The perfectionist temperament bred a comeouter spirit. An insistence on individual moral accountability and direct appeal to the irreducible self, the faith in self-reliance and distrust of compromise, and a substitution of universal education for partial reform measures, all meant that normal political and institutional reform channels were closed to the perfectionists. Alternate routes to the millennium had to be found. One of these was discovered by a new leadership which made reform a branch of prophecy. Another was opened by the idea of a universal reawakening of the great god self. But there was a third possibility, also deeply involved with the educational process, an attempt to build the experimental community as a reform model. With an increasing number of reformers after 1840 perfectionist anti-institutionalism led to heavy investments in the communitarian movement.

The attraction that drew the perfectionists to communitarianism came from their conviction that the good society should be simple. Since American society was both complicated and corrupt, it was necessary to come out from it; but at the same time the challenge of the simple life had to be met. Once the true principles of social life had been discovered they had to be applied, some way found to harness individual perfectibility to a social engine. This urge to form the good community, as John Humphrey Noyes experienced it himself and perceived it in other reformers, provided the connection between perfectionism and communitarianism, or, as Noyes put it, between "Revivalism" and "Socialism." Perfectionist energies directed initially against institutions were diverted to the creation of small self-contained communities as educational models. In New England two come-outer abolitionists, Adin Ballou and George Benson, founded cooperative societies at Hopedale and Northampton, while a third Garrisonian lieutenant, John Collins, settled his followers on a farm in Skaneateles, New York. Brook Farm, Fruitlands and the North American Phalanx at Redbank acquired notoriety in their own day; but equally significant, both in terms of origins and personnel, were the experiments at Raritan Bay under the guidance of Marcus Spring, the Marlboro Association in Ohio, the Prairie Home Community of former Hicksite Quakers, and the Swedenborgian Brocton Community. In these and other experimental communities could be seen the various guises of perfectionism.

Communitarianism promised drastic social reform without violence. Artificiality and corruption could not be wiped out by partial improvements and piecemeal measures but demanded a total change which, as Robert Owen once explained, "could make an immediate, and almost instantaneous, revolution in the minds and manners of society in which it shall be introduced." Communitarians agreed in rejecting class struggle which set interest against interest instead of uniting them through association. "Whoever will examine the question of social ameliorations," Albert Brisbane argued in support of Fourier, "must be convinced that *the gradual perfecting of Civilization* is useless as a remedy for present social evils, and that the only effectual means of doing away with indigence, idleness and the dislike for labor is to do away with civilization itself, and organize Association . . . in its place." [27] Like the redemptive moment in conversion or the experience of self-discovery in transcendentalist thought, the communitarian ideal pointed to a sharp break with existing society and a commitment to root-and-branch reform. On the other hand, the community was seen as a controlled experiment in which profound but peaceful change might be effected without disturbing the larger social order. Massive change, according to communitarian theory, could also be gradual and harmonious if determined by the model.

Perfectionist religious and moral reform shaded into communitarianism, in the case of a number of social reformers, with the recognition that the conversion of the individual was a necessary preparation for and logically required communal experimentation. Such was John Humphrey Noyes' observation that in the years after 1815 "the line of socialistic excitement lies parallel with the line of religious Revivals. . . . The Revivalists had for their one great idea the regeneration of the soul. The great idea of the Socialists was the regeneration of society, which is the soul's environment. These ideas belong together and are the complements of each other." [28] So it seemed to Noyes' colleagues in the communitarian movement. The course from extreme individualism to communitarianism can be traced in George Ripley's decision to found Brook Farm. Trying to win Emerson to his new cause, he explained that his own personal tastes and habits would have led him away from plans and projects. "I have a passion for being independent of the world, and of every man in it. This I could do easily on the estate which is now offered. . . . I

[27] Albert Brisbane, *Social Destiny of Man*, p. 286, quoted in Arthur Eugene Bestor, *Backwoods Utopias: The Sectarian and Owenite Phases of Communitarian Socialism in America: 1663–1829* (Philadelphia, 1950), p. 9.

[28] John Humphrey Noyes, *History of American Socialism* (Philadelphia, 1870), p. 26.

should have a city of God, on a small scale of my own. . . . But I feel bound to sacrifice this private feeling, in the hope of the great social good." That good Ripley had no difficulty in defining in perfectionist terms:

> . . . to insure a more natural union between intellectual and manual labor than now exists; to combine the thinker and the worker, as far as possible, in the same individual; to guarantee the highest mental freedom, by providing all with labor, adapted to their tastes and talents, and securing to them the fruits of their industry; to do away with the necessity of menial services, by opening the benefits of education and the profits of labor to all; and thus to prepare a society of liberal, intelligent, and cultivated persons, whose relations with each other would permit a more simple and wholesome life, than can be led amidst the pressure of our competitive institutions.[29]

However varied their actual experiences with social planning, all the communitarians echoed Ripley's call for translating perfectionism into concerted action and adapting the ethics of individualism to larger social units. Just as the moral reformers appealed to right conduct and conscience in individuals the communitarians sought to erect models of a collective conscience to educate Americans. Seen in this light, the communitarian faith in the model was simply an extension of the belief in individual perfectibility. Even the sense of urgency characterizing moral reform was carried over into the communities where a millennial expectation flourished. The time to launch their projects, the social planners believed, was the immediate present when habits and attitudes were still fluid, before entrenched institutions had hardened the American heart and closed the American mind. To wait for a full quota of useful members or an adequate supply of funds might be to miss the single chance to make the country perfect. The whole future of America seemed to them to hinge on the fate of their enterprises.

Some of the projects were joint-stock corporations betraying a middle-class origin; others were strictly communistic. Some, like the Shaker communities, were pietistic and rigid; others, like Oneida and Hopedale, open and frankly experimental. Communitarians took a lively interest in each others' projects and often joined one or another of them for a season before moving on to try utopia on their own. The division between religious and secular attempts was by no means absolute: both types of communities advertised an essentially religious brand of perfectionism. Nor was economic organization always an accurate means of distinguishing the various experiments, most of which were subjected to periodic constitutional overhauling and frequent readjustment, now in the direction of social controls and now toward relaxation of those controls in favor of individual initiative.

The most striking characteristic of the communitarian movement was not its apparent diversity but the fundamental similarity of educational purpose. The common denominator or "main idea" Noyes correctly identified as *the enlargement of home—the extension of family union beyond the little man-and-wife circle to large corporations.*[30] Communities as different as Fruitlands and Hopedale, Brook Farm and Northampton, Owenite villages and Fourier phalanstaeries were all, in one way or another, attempting to expand and apply self-culture to groups. Thus the problem

---

[29] Letter from Ripley to Ralph Waldo Emerson, Nov. 9, 1840, in *Autobiography of Brook Farm,* ed. Henry W. Sams (Englewood Cliffs, N. J., 1958), pp. 5–8.

[30] Noyes, *American Socialisms,* p. 23.

for radical communitarians was to solve the conflict between the family and society. In commenting on the failure of the Brook Farmers to achieve a real community, Charles Lane, Alcott's associate at Fruitlands, identified what he considered the basic social question of the day—"whether the existence of the marital family is compatible with that of the universal family, which the term 'Community' signifies." [31] A few of the communitarians, recognizing this conflict, attempted to solve it by changing or destroying the institution of marriage. For the most part, the perfectionist communitarians shied away from any such radical alteration of the family structure and instead sought a law of association by which the apparently antagonistic claims of private and universal love could be harmonized. Once this law was known and explained, they believed, then the perfect society was possible—a self-adjusting mechanism constructed in accordance with their recently discovered law of human nature.

Inevitably communitarianism developed a "science of society," either the elaborate social mathematics of Fourier or the constitutional mechanics of native American perfectionists. The appeal of the blueprint grew overwhelming: in one way or another almost all the communitarians succumbed to the myth of the mathematically precise arrangement, searching for the perfect number or the exact size, plotting the precise disposition of working forces and living space, and combining these estimates in a formula which would ensure perfect concord. The appeal of Fourierism stemmed from its promise to reconcile productive industry with "passional attractions." "Could this be done," John Sullivan Dwight announced, "the word 'necessity' would acquire an altogether new and pleasanter meaning; the outward necessity and the inward prompting for every human being would be one and identical, and his life a living harmony." [32] Association fostered true individuality which, in turn, guaranteed collective accord. In an intricate calculation involving ascending and descending wings and a central point of social balance where attractions equalled destinies the converts to Fourierism contrived a utopian alternative to politics. The phalanx represented a self-perpetuating system for neutralizing conflict and ensuring perfection. The power factor—politics—had been dropped out; attraction alone provided the stimulants necessary to production and progress. Here in the mathematical model was the culmination of the "peaceful revolution" which was to transform America.

The communitarian experiments in effect were anti-institutional institutions. In abandoning political and religious institutions the communitarians were driven to create perfect societies of their own which conformed to their perfectionist definition of the free individual. Their communities veered erratically between the poles of anarchism and collectivism as they hunted feverishly for a way of eliminating friction without employing coercion, sure that once they had found it, they could apply it in a federation of model societies throughout the country. In a limited sense, perhaps, their plans constituted an escape from urban complexity and the loneliness of alienation. But beneath the nostalgia there lay a vital reform impulse and a driving determination to make American society over through the power of education.

[31] Charles Lane, "Brook Farm," *Dial*, IV (Jan. 1844), 351–57, reprinted in Sams, *Brook Farm*, pp. 87–92.

[32] John Sullivan Dwight, "Association in its Connection with Education," a lecture delivered before the New England Fourier Society, in Boston, Feb. 29, 1844. Excerpted in Sams, *Brook Farm*, pp. 104–5.

The immediate causes of the collapse of the communities ranged from loss of funds and mismanagement to declining interest and disillusionment with imperfect human material. Behind these apparent reasons, however, stood the real cause in the person of the perfectionist self, Margaret Fuller's "mountainous me," that proved too powerful a disruptive force for even the anti-institutional institutions it had created. It was the perfectionist ego which allowed the communitarian reformers to be almost wholly nonselective in recruiting their membership and to put their trust in the operation of an atomistic general will. Constitution-making and paper bonds, as it turned out, were not enough to unite divine egoists in a satisfactory system for the free expression of the personality. Perfectionist individualism did not make the consociate family. The result by the 1850s was a profound disillusionment with the principle of association which, significantly, coincided with the political crisis over slavery. Adin Ballou, his experiment at Hopedale in shambles, summarized the perfectionist mood of despair when he added that "few people are near enough right in heart, head and habits to live in close social intimacy." [33] Another way would have to be found to carry divine principles into social arrangements, one that took proper account of the individual.

The collapse of the communitarian movement in the 1850s left a vacuum in social reform which was filled by the slavery crisis. At first their failure to consolidate alternative social and educational institutions threw the reformers back on their old perfectionist individualism for support. It was hardly fortuitous that Garrison, Mann, Thoreau, Howe, Parker, Channing, Ripley and Emerson himself responded to John Brown's raid with a defense of the liberated conscience. But slavery, as a denial of freedom and individual responsibility, had to be destroyed by institutional forces which could be made to sustain these values. The antislavery cause during the secession crisis and throughout the Civil War offered reformers an escape from alienation by providing a new identity with the very political institutions which they had so vigorously assailed.

The effects of the Civil War as an intellectual counterrevolution were felt both in a revival of institutions and a renewal of an organic theory of society. The war brought with it a widespread reaction against the seeming sentimentality and illusions of perfectionism. It saw the establishment of new organizations like the Sanitary and the Christian Commissions run on principles of efficiency and professionalism totally alien to perfectionist methods. Accompanying the wartime revival of institutions was a theological reorientation directed by Horace Bushnell and other conservative churchmen whose longstanding opposition to perfectionism seemed justified by the war. The extreme individualism of the ante-bellum reformers was swallowed up in a Northern war effort that made private conscience less important than saving the Union. Some of the abolitionists actually substituted national unity for freedom for the slave as the primary war aim. Those reformers who contributed to the war effort through the Sanitary Commission or the Christian Commission found a new sense of order and efficiency indispensable. Older perfectionists, like Dorothea Dix, unable to adjust to new demands, found their usefulness drastically confined. Young Emersonians returned from combat convinced that professionalism, discipline and subordination, dubious virtues by perfectionist standards, were essential in a healthy

---

[33] Letter from Ballou to Theodore Weld, Dec. 23, 1856, quoted in Benjamin P. Thomas, *Theodore Weld: Crusader for Freedom* (New Brunswick, N. J., 1950), p. 229.

society. A new emphasis on leadership and performance was replacing the benevolent amateurism of the perfectionists.

Popular education and ethical agitation continued to hold the post-war stage, but the setting for them had changed. The three principal theorists of social reform in post-war industrial America—Henry George, Henry Demarest Lloyd and Edward Bellamy—denounced class conflict, minimized the importance of purely political reform, and, like their perfectionist precursors, called for moral revolution. The moral revolution which they demanded, however, was not the work of individuals in whom social responsibility developed as a by-product of self-discovery but the ethical revival of an entire society made possible by the natural development of social forces. Their organic view of society required new theories of personality and new concepts of role-playing, definitions which appeared variously in George's law of integration, Lloyd's religion of love, and Bellamy's economy of happiness. And whereas Nemesis in the perfectionist imagination had assumed the shape of personal guilt and estrangement from a pre-established divine order, for the post-war reformers it took on the social dimensions of a terrifying relapse into barbarism. Finally, the attitudes of the reformers toward individualism itself began to change as Darwinism with the aid of a false analogy twisted the pre-war doctrine of self-reliance into a weapon against reform. It was to protest against a Darwinian psychology of individual isolation that Lloyd wrote his final chapter of *Wealth Against Commonwealth*, declaring that the regeneration of the individual was only a half-truth and that "the reorganization of the society which he makes and which makes him is the other half."

> We can become individual only by submitting to be bound to others. We extend our freedom only by finding new laws to obey. . . . The isolated man is a mere rudiment of an individual. But he who has become citizen, neighbor, friend, brother, son, husband, father, fellow-member, in one is just so many times individualized.[34]

Lloyd's plea for a new individualism could also be read as an obituary for perfectionist romantic reform.

[34] Henry Demarest Lloyd, *Wealth Against Commonwealth* (Spectrum paperback ed.: Englewood Cliffs, N. J., 1963), pp. 174, 178.

9 / Who Were the Abolitionists?

Betty Fladeland

Explanations of ante-bellum reform and abolitionism that emphasize ideas have seemed inadequate to some scholars. Why did the new intellectual forces convert so few people into antislavery men? The new currents of Enlightenment and Romanticism obviously transformed some and scarcely touched others. Was susceptibility to antislavery ideas a purely individual and fortuitous matter, or did certain broad social changes sensitize particular groups of men and women to the abolitionist appeal? One thing is clear: many abolitionists shared a heavy burden of race prejudice with their fellow Americans, and some special exemption from bigotry cannot explain why some men were willing to risk the ostracism and abuse that followed vigorous antislavery activities or even opinions in ante-bellum America.

In recent years we have become increasingly interested in the social and psychological characteristics of reformers and the movements they lead. Not in a spirit of censoriousness but for the purpose of understanding, social scientists and historians have detected in reformers social marginality and alienation from the predominant institutions and values of their day. One of the most interesting efforts in this genre is the controversial essay by David Donald entitled, "Toward a Reconsideration of Abolitionists," which identifies the abolitionist leadership of the 1830's as former patricians, particularly New Englanders, displaced by the new industrial leadership. According to Donald, these men and women found themselves an "elite without function," and turned to radical antislavery as a means of achieving the satisfactions and leadership otherwise denied them and of protesting "against a world they never made." The following essay by Betty Fladeland discusses Donald's interpretation of abolitionist origins as well as the hypotheses of other scholars and proposes an eclectic approach in place of various single-factor explanations of the abolitionist impulse.

For further reading: * David Donald, "Toward a Reconsideration of Abolitionists," in *Lincoln Reconsidered* (New York: Vintage Books, 1956); * Gilbert H. Barnes, *The Antislavery Impulse, 1830–1844* (New York: Appleton-Century-Crofts., 1933); * Louis Filler, *The Crusade Against*

Journal of Negro History, XLIX, No. 2 (April 1964), 99–115. Reprinted by permission.

Slavery, 1830–1860 (New York: Harper Torchbooks, 1960); *Dwight L. Dumond, *Anti-Slavery: The Crusade for Freedom in America* (Ann Arbor, Mich.: The University of Michigan Press, 1961); John L. Thomas, *The Liberator: William Lloyd Garrison* (Boston: Little, Brown and Company, 1963); *Benjamin Quarles, *Frederick Douglass* (Washington, D. C.: Associated Publishers, 1948); William H. Pease and Jane H. Pease, "Antislavery Ambivalence: Immediatism, Expediency, Race," *American Quarterly*, XVII (Winter 1965); Merton Dillon, "The Failure of American Abolitionists," *Journal of Southern History*, XXV (May 1959).

In surveying the historical writing on the abolitionists, one is struck by the fact that whether the writer was a contemporary or is a modern historian looking back at the anti-slavery movement, there runs throughout these writings the attempt to make psychological analyses of these people: what type of person would join such a movement? Did they have a common motivation, either selfish or unselfish? Does an explanation lie in individual psychoses? Implied in many of these analyses is the assumption that in one way or another the abolitionists were misfits, neurotics, or opportunists, and that rather than grouping them on the basis of a common conviction which dedicated them to a common cause, one must search for some ulterior or sub-conscious motive which furnished the mainspring of their activity.

It appears to me that each of these probings may suggest a grain of truth when applied to individual abolitionists, but that none of them is valid for the whole body of abolitionists; and the total result indicates such a multiplicity of labels, characteristics, and causative factors that one is left with still only one unifying factor: a common conviction in a common cause. If this is true, the key to understanding the abolitionist movement as a whole must lie in the social and economic ferments which produced it, not in the peculiarities of the individual leaders.

One would expect the epithets applied to the abolitionists in their own day to be more extreme than those of later generations. They were referred to as "rapacious . . . misguided fanatics," "Hellhounds of the North," "irresponsible revolutionaries," "reckless incendiaries," "designing demagogues," "nigger-thieves," "amalgamationists," and men whose "sole and avowed object was to sow the seed of discord, rapine and murder among the slaves of the South." Among the milder terms were "visionaries," and "dreamy philanthropists."[1]

In testing such labels, the first question arises: is there evidence that any abolitionist belonged in such extreme categories? The answer, I think, is yes; and the first person who comes to mind is John Brown, who perhaps exemplifies the visionary fanatic, willing to resort even to violence and bloodshed. Yet, although there were thousands of abolitionists in the United States by the time of the Harper's Ferry Raid, Brown could get less than ten men to make financial contribu-

---

[1] These terms may be found in numerous sources. I have taken them from the *Emancipator*, May 31, 1820; James G. Birney, "Vindication of Abolitionists," in *A Collection of Valuable Documents* [n.p., n.d.]; William Goodell, *Slavery and Antislavery* (New York, 1852); Ralph Korngold, *Two Friends of Man* (Boston, 1950); Russel B. Nye, *Fettered Freedom, Civil Liberties and the Slavery Controversy, 1830–1860* (East Lansing, 1949); and Alice Felt Tyler, *Freedom's Ferment* (Minneapolis, 1944).

tions to his cause, and a mere handful to actually fight with him. There are a few others who might be labeled incendiaries, such as the free Negro, David Walker, who issued an inflammatory *Appeal* advocating violence and insurrection; and a Reverend Moses Dickson who tried (unsuccessfully) to establish militant orders of knights.[2] For the most part, however, the incendiary language of emotional orators reached only Northern audiences, and second-handedly, white Southern audiences. The vast majority of abolitionists looked with abhorrence upon any suggestion that a slave insurrection should be incited in the South, and despite Southern fears to the contrary, abolitionist literature was not designed to reach the hands of the slaves. Had it been, language, phraseology and argument would have been pitched to a much simpler level. In their Declaration of Sentiments the members of the American Anti-Slavery Society contrasted their non-violent approach with that of the fathers of the American Revolution: "Their principles led them to wage war against their oppressors, and to spill human blood like water, in order to be free. Ours forbid the doing of evil that good may come, and lead us to reject and to entreat the oppressed to reject, the use of all carnal weapons for deliverance from bondage: . . . ."[3]

William Lloyd Garrison was certainly among those considered by his contemporaries to be an incendiary, and most modern historians seem to agree that he was of a radical nature. Clement Eaton calls him a "natural agitator;"[4] and Allan Nevins describes him as ". . . a man of intense convictions, of high moral elevation, of arid, colorless and narrow mind, and of a fanatical readiness to submit to any sacrifice."[5] His life would probably have been spent in protesting even if slavery had never existed. From childhood he had waged a bitter fight *against* obstacles and *for* a due recognition of his abilities," is the conclusion of Avery Craven.[6]

One may agree that Garrison fits the label of radical, and was reckless in his use of vituperative language; yet on the other hand, he was a pacifist who preached non-resistance even to mobs. "We justify no war," he wrote. "The victories of liberty should be bloodless, and effected solely through spiritual weapons."[7] Moreover, the very fact that Garrison was so frequently denounced by his own colleagues, who repeatedly expressed the opinion that he was doing more harm than good for the cause, indicates that he was not typical of the group. Theodore Weld termed some of Garrison's ideas "down-right fanaticism."[8] Several New England ministers published a "Clerical Appeal" severely castigating Garrison; and James G. Birney wrote to Lewis Tappan that ". . . his departure from us might be the best thing he could do for the cause of emancipations."[9] Birney, the Tappan brothers, and several others proposed the formation of a new anti-slavery society without Garrison which would

[2] See John Hope Franklin, *From Slavery to Freedom* (New York, 1956), p. 250; Herbert Aptheker, "Militant Abolitionism," *Journal of Negro History*, XXVI, No. 4 (October, 1941), 438–484.

[3] Wendell Phillips Garrison and Francis Jackson Garrison, *William Lloyd Garrison, 1805–1879* (New York, 1885), I, pp. 408–412.

[4] Clement Eaton, *A History of the Old South* (New York, 1949), p. 378.

[5] Allan Nevins, *Ordeal of the Union* (New York, 1947), I, p. 144.

[6] Avery Craven, *The Coming of the Civil War* (New York, 1942), p. 136.

[7] Benjamin Thomas, *Theodore Weld: Crusader for Freedom* (New Brunswick, 1950), p. 144.

[8] *Ibid.*, p. 147.

[9] Betty Fladeland, *James Gillespie Birney: Slaveholder to Abolitionist* (Ithaca, 1955), p. 162.

emphasize the moderate approach and thereby enlist the cooperation of even the slaveholders.[10]

The charges of "nigger-lover" and "amalgamationist" were intended to stir up antagonism against the abolitionists as promoters of social equality which would eventually lead to interracial marriages. On the first count, the American Anti-Slavery Society was proud to plead guilty. Their constitution stated: "This Society shall aim to elevate the character and conditions of the people of color, by encouraging their intellectual, moral and religious improvement, and by removing public prejudice, that thus they may, according to their intellectual and moral worth, share an equality with the whites of civil and religious privileges; . . ."[11]

Most of the abolitionists took this aim seriously, and worked well in harness with such Negro leaders as Frederick Douglass, Charles Remond, Dr. James McCune Smith, and Henry Garnet. In many communities there were active programs to promote social equality, especially through education. It was Theodore Weld's firm conviction that the only way to prove that the Negro was not inherently inferior was to help him advance along social and cultural lines. He urged that they everywhere establish day and night schools, debating societies, lyceums, and libraries.[12] The work of Lane Seminary students such as Augustus Wattles and Hiram Wilson is well known; as is the story of Prudence Crandall's school in Connecticut. The Massachusetts Anti-Slavery Society worked not only for bi-racial schools, but also for repeal of the state laws against mixed marriages.[13] "We have vowed unto the Lord," wrote Huntington Lyman, "to use our personal exertions and whatever influence we have or may acquire to raise up the free black population, and to persuade our fellow-men to love them as they do themselves."[14]

In addition to advocating integrated schools, the abolitionists waged a steady campaign for integrated churches. Pamphlets on the subject flooded the country. Among them was James G. Birney's attack on the churches as the "bulwarks" of slavery because of their refusal to take a stand on the issue. In 1846 when he helped to organize the First Congregational Church in Lower Saginaw, Michigan, he insisted that one of its Articles of Faith should attest to the equality of all men before God; and he steadily argued against treating the colored people—even in aiding them—as a class rather than as individuals.[15]

Yet, although social equality for the colored people was an avowed goal of the abolitionists, one must acknowledge that in this they failed of any widespread success.[16] In fact, one must admit that among some abolitionists there was prejudice. For some people it was one thing to favor the eradication of slavery, but quite beyond the call of duty to welcome the freedman to a position of social equality. The English painter, Benjamin Haydon, reported that when he made the painting of the delegates to the World Anti-Slavery Convention in London, there

[10] Gilbert Barnes, *The Anti-Slavery Impulse, 1830–1844* (New York, 1933), p. 61.

[11] Constitution of the American Anti-Slavery Society in Wendell P. Garrison and Francis J. Garrison, *op. cit.*, I, p. 414.

[12] Benjamin Thomas, *op. cit.*, pp. 117–118.

[13] Russel Nye, *op. cit.*, p. 15.

[14] Gilbert H. Barnes, *op. cit.*, pp. 68–69.

[15] Betty Fladeland, *op. cit.*, pp. 271, 281.

[16] Merton L. Dillon, "The Failure of the American Abolitionists," in *Journal of Southern History*, XXV (May, 1959), No. 2, pp. 159–177.

were some abolitionists who betrayed their prejudice by not wanting to be seated next to Charles Remond, a Negro delegate.[17]

For all the charges of "amalgamationist," I have yet to discover a record of an abolitionist marrying a Negro. Even though we should be able to establish evidence of such "amalgamation" between white abolitionists and Negroes, the presence of mulattoes in every area of the country and in every period of our history is silent testimony to the fact that racial mixing could never be considered characteristic of abolitionists alone. As for the charge of "nigger-thieves," it is common knowledge that forcible resistance to the fugitive slave laws was openly advocated and practiced by many Northerners. There were very few, however, who like the ex-slaves Harriet Tubman and Frederick Douglass, actually went into the South to encourage slaves to run away.

Another label applied by their contemporaries was that of "exaggerators." Robert Ludlum, in an article on Joshua Giddings,[18] claims that exaggeration is one of the characteristics of a radical reformer, and says that Giddings was typical in his "habitual use of violent, extravagant language." Ludlum even goes so far as to aver that radicals are more apt than other people to use pungent phrases. [By such a definition Winston Churchill, Adlai Stevenson, Theodore Roosevelt, and any number of backwoods mountaineers would be radicals.] On this count of exaggeration some of the abolitionists must again plead guilty, for they built up a stereotype of every Southern planter as a Simon Legree. To arouse people against slavery it was natural that they should publish all the accounts they could find of cruelty toward slaves, but as Professor Dwight Dumond has pointed out, the weakness in this sort of propaganda is the necessity for a constant increase in the enormity of the offenses charged lest the public become inured by familiarity.[19]

With many abolitionists exaggeration was a conscious tactic. James Freeman Clarke in his reminiscences recalled that some lecturers and pamphleteers thought that the only way to operate effectively was to make the opposition "mad," and took as their example Jesus, who minced no words in calling the Pharisees "hypocrites," "blind leaders of the blind," "children of hell," and "a generation of vipers." [20] Wendell Phillips was of that school of thought. "The scholar may sit in his study and take care that his language is not exaggerated," he wrote, "but the rude mass of men are not to be caught by balanced periods—they are caught by men whose words are half-battles. From Luther on down the charge against every reformer has been that his language is too rough. Be it so. Rough instruments are used for rough work . . ." [21] Professor Richard Hofstadter has remarked that "the same historians who have been indulgent with men who exaggerated because they wanted to be elected have been extremely severe with men who exaggerated because they wanted to free the slaves." [22]

The fact also remains that there were as many abolitionists who shunned violent, abusive language and exaggerated attacks as there were men who employed such

[17] Ralph Korngold, op. cit., p. 154.

[18] Robert P. Ludlum, "Joshua R. Giddings, Radical," in Mississippi Valley Historical Review, XXIII (June, 1936), No. 1, pp. 49–60.

[19] Dwight L. Dumond, Antislavery Origins of the Civil War in the United States (Ann Arbor, 1959 reprint), p. 38.

[20] James Freeman Clarke, Anti-Slavery Days (New York, 1883), pp. 77–78.

[21] Quoted in Korngold, op. cit., pp. 182–183.

[22] Richard Hofstadter, The American Political Tradition and the Men Who Made It (New York, 1954), p. 137.

weapons. One must remember that ministers constituted a large element in the group, as did the Quakers, whose mode of approach was that of gentle persuasion. While it is true that there was much abolitionist propaganda to arouse the emotions, one can find an equal amount which makes rather laborious, even tedious reading through a maze of religious, economic, and legal arguments. Even among the antislavery editors, proverbially thought to be a radical lot, one has to search for the sensational or inflammatory approach. Most of them are rather religious in tone. As usual the lecturers and editors who made the most noise received the most notice in history, but who can say whether they were more effective abolitionists than their quieter cohorts? For every Wendell Phillips one can find a Beriah Green; for every William Lloyd Garrison, a Benjamin Lundy.

In all eras of history it is customary for the conservatives who are trying to maintain the status quo to attempt to pin on the liberals or reformers guilt by association with eccentric, faddist, non-conformist or subversive groups. The abolitionists did not escape this form of attack. George Fitzhugh, in an open letter to the abolitionists asked, "Why have you Bloomer's and Women's Rights men, and strong-minded women, and Mormons, and anti-renters, and 'vote myself a farm' men, Millerites, and Spiritual Rappers, and Shakers, and Widow Wakemanites, and Agrarians, and Grahamites, and a thousand other superstitious and infidel isms at the North? . . . Why is all this, except that free society is a failure?" On another occasion Fitzhugh stated, "I do not believe there is a Liberty man, in the North who is not a socialist." [23]

A Northern paper, the Catholic Boston *Pilot,* charged that wherever you found an abolitionist you found " 'an anti-hanging man, woman's rights man, an infidel frequently, bigoted Protestant always, a socialist, a red republican, a fanatical teetotaler, a believer in Mesmerism, and Rochester Rappings.' " [24] The Richmond *Enquirer* felt that abolitionism fostered "lectures against marriage, licentious phalansteries, Oneida haunts of communism, agrarian doctrines and anti-rent practices, free love saloons, Mormon states and Quaker villages," which would soon displace the "moral, religious, and law-abiding" ideals of Southern Society. [25]

There is no denying that the abolition movement had its share of eccentrics. Charles Stuart, dressed in Scottish kilts, attracted attention wherever he went; Weld and the Grimké sisters dabbled in spiritualism; Beriah Green supported the Cold Water Society; Abby Kelley was something of a female Don Quixote, accused by her fellow workers of creating more smoke than fire; John Greenleaf Whittier was not only a Quaker pacifist but a poet; Garrison and a few of his followers called themselves Christian anarchists; several were vegetarians or Grahamites; and many of the women in the movement were "Bloomer Girls." But one must keep these people in the historical context, remembering that theirs was an age of individualism, of idealistic reform, of faddist panaceas, and of Utopian experimentation, and that these non-conformist tendencies were not the monopoly of the abolitionists. Here again is an example of how the personalities of some colorful individuals were assumed to be characteristic of the whole group.

Although a few of the abolitionists were Utopian socialists, or joined experimental communal settlements, the evidence that they were socialists or communists in the

[23] Harvey Wish, *George Fitzhugh, Conservative of the Old South* (Baton Rouge, 1938), pp. 15, 141.
[24] Nye, *op. cit.,* p. 13.
[25] *Ibid.,* p. 20.

generally applied political sense is, as far as I know, nil. And it is ironic that George Fitzhugh, who was truly a socialist in admitting the failure of free society, should have been using the term in an attempt to brand the abolitionists subversive. Judging from their political backgrounds, it seems apparent that a great many of the abolitionists were actually conservatives. Professor Dumond has pointed out that the Whig party, rather than the Democratic, was more rapidly infiltrated with antislavery doctrine.[26] David Donald emphasizes their Federalist origins prior to their Whig affiliation, and the opposition of so many antislavery leaders to Jackson's radical democracy.[27] Following this line of descent, we find that almost to a man they ended up in the Republican Party, supporting a platform which in its economic program was certainly conservative.

"Disunionist" was yet another indictment of the abolitionists, and the Garrisonians come first to mind as advocating separation of the sections, even going as far as to hold a disunion convention in Worcester, Massachusetts, in 1857. Although Garrison may have been the most extreme, he did not stand alone. "No union with slave-holders" is not an uncommon phrase in antislavery literature, especially in the last decade before the Civil War. Professor William Dodd implied that it was contempt of "church and State, of union and nationality," that laid the foundation for the sectional Republican Party.[28] Carter G. Woodson, on the other hand, has presented the thesis that the abolition agitation was an evidence of developing nationalism. Northerners, he argued, felt responsible for having helped establish slavery in the South, and therefore believed the federal government rather than the states should decide the issue.[29] Certainly this was an argument used over and over again in antislavery propaganda, more often and with more seriousness than the suggestion of separation. That some contemporaries took this point of view is illustrated by the resolution of a Democratic Party convention in Ohio in 1840 which declared that political abolitionism was but ancient federalism under a new guise.[30] Weld was convinced that although slavery was a regional institution, it was sustained by the commercial and financial power of the North.[31] Undoubtedly, many remarks such as Lincoln's that the Union could not endure half slave and half free, or that conflict "must" eventually separate the Union were interpreted as advocating rather than simply predicting such a consequence.

"Political opportunist" was and is another label to discredit the abolitionists, and there is no doubt that some men "came out" from their old parties when they saw a political bandwagon in the offing. Salmon P. Chase seems to fit this category. Although he had earned a reputation in the courts for defending fugitive slaves, he steadfastly refused to be called an Abolitionist. He maintained his Whig affiliation through the election of 1840, and as late as 1844 was making overtures to the Democrats. Old line Abolitionists such as Gerrit Smith and James G. Birney openly challenged his motives; ". . . he has appeared to me ambitious of individual preference and prominence," wrote Birney, ". . . not relying so much on the strength of

[26] Dumond, op. cit., p. 93.

[27] David Donald, Lincoln Reconsidered (New York, 1956), p. 27.

[28] William E. Dodd, Expansion and Conflict (Boston, 1915), p. 166.

[29] Carter G. Woodson, The Negro in Our History (Washington, D. C., 1922), p. 190.

[30] Theodore Clark Smith, The Liberty and Free Soil Parties in the Northwest (New York, 1897), p. 44.

[31] Barnes, op. cit., p. 61.

his principles as on the strength of the party by which he is supported."[32] Expediency rather than principle certainly dictated the transition from the Liberty Party to the Free Soil Party in 1848, with the nomination of Martin Van Buren and Charles Francis Adams. As late as 1840 Thomas Morris, a long time Abolitionist in the Democratic Party, denounced Van Buren; and at about the same time the Ohio Anti-Slavery Society tried to pass a resolution saying Van Buren's disregard for human rights made him unfit for the presidency.[33]

Theodore Clark Smith points out that not only Chase but Joshua Giddings, Benjamin and Edward Wade, Leicester King, and Samuel Lewis "followed the triumphal Whig car" in 1840, yet were later considered the "personification" of political Abolitionism. John P. Hale and Horace Greeley were other johnny-come-latelys.[34] Professor Hesseltine adds Wendell Phillips, Charles Sumner, and Henry Wilson to the list of "aspiring politicians;"[35] and Professor Craven agrees that anti-slavery politicians such as Giddings and Chase "quickly proved the value of the cause as a stepping-stone to public office."[36] The underlying assumption in all these charges of political opportunism seems to be that a man did not become an Abolitionist until he deserted the Whig or Democratic party to join one of the new parties; but certainly many Northern Whigs and some Northern Democrats were Abolitionist prior to their Free Soil or Republican affiliation. This was true of Giddings, Slade, Morris, Hale, Lewis, King, Sumner, and Phillips.

Merton Dillon concludes that "the work of the abolitionists as moral reformers had practically ended by 1844;"[37] and David Donald confines the abolition movement to the 1830's, excluding from his "reconsideration" all who joined after 1840,[38] implying that the later adherents were motivated by political rather than humanitarian considerations. While this may have been true of some of the leaders, surely many of the rank and file were brought into the crusade because of their reaction to the harshness of the new Fugitive Slave Law of 1850, or because they were pushed to an open stand by the controversy in the churches which culminated in the splits of the 1840's. Even if we confine our examination to the leaders, however, it seems to me we have been drawing too arbitrary and definite a line separating the abolitionists of the 1830's as moral reformers from those of the '40's and '50's who used political action, as if they were two completely different and distinct groups of people. While there were obviously many new recruits as time went on, and some fell by the wayside (several because of old age), it is still true that many of the "moral suasionists" of the '30's simply agreed to shift their strategy to political action. They were still Abolitionists. Old leaders continued to direct the petition campaign in Congress, and ended up voting not only the Liberty and Free Soil, but also the Republican ticket.[39] Such people must surely be absolved from the indictment of political opportunism. "Throughout the later agitation, from the forties to

[32] Fladeland, op. cit., p. 217 n.

[33] Smith, op. cit., pp. 40–42.

[34] Ibid., pp. 78, 88, 120.

[35] William B. Hesseltine, The South in American History (New York, 1943), p. 215.

[36] Craven, op. cit., p. 140.

[37] Dillon, op. cit.

[38] Donald, op. cit.

[39] William Goodell, a pioneer antislavery man himself, emphasizes this in his book, Slavery and Antislavery, cited above.

the sixties," concludes Gilbert Barnes, "the doctrine of the antislavery host thus continued in the moral tenets of the original antislavery creed." [40]

The ladies in the movement have come in for special criticism on the grounds of using the cause as a vehicle to promote their own selfish interests in women's rights. Arthur Young Lloyd is particularly critical in this respect.[41] Sarah and Angelina Grimké, Elizabeth Cady Stanton, Lydia Maria Child, Maria Weston Chapman, Abby Kelley Foster, and Lucretia Mott were all active workers in both causes, and boldly disregarded the social dictates of their day which decreed that women should not speak in public, especially if there were gentlemen in the gathering. Ralph Korngold states that some women refused to support the 15th Amendment without the addition of women's suffrage.[42] Admittedly, these women certainly capitalized on an opportunity to further two causes at once; but to say that none of them would have worked for the cause of the slave otherwise, is an untenable position. It disregards the countless wives who gave sincere and earnest support to their husbands without ever agitating for recognition for themselves. Furthermore, it disregards the fact that the two causes became inextricably intertwined. The right to speak in public had to be won before these women could speak for the slave.

In this day of the analyst's couch, it is not surprising that attempts have been made to prove that the Abolitionists must have been psychotics of one type or another. Hazel Wolf has characterized Weld, Garrison, Lovejoy, Birney, Prudence Crandall, George Thompson, Charles Torrey, John Brown, and several others less well known, as martyr complexes.[43] For each of these a case can be made. Each of them faced mobs, endured imprisonment, or accepted death rather than be silent; and from the writings of each one statements may be quoted to support the contention that he coveted martyrdom. Notwithstanding the array of evidence, it seems to me that historians must be wary of arguing teleologically, of assuming that because some Abolitionists experienced martyrdom, it was their goal and purpose. It must be remembered that it is one thing to be willing to face martyrdom if necessary, but quite another thing to seek it. The fact that some of the Abolitionists may have played up their persecutions and assigned to themselves the role of martyrs in order to gain public sympathy, may have contributed to this impression, and helped to distort the picture.

A contemporary of the Abolitionists who applied a Freudian analysis was J. H. Hammond, Governor of South Carolina. In a letter to the noted English Abolitionist, Thomas Clarkson, Hammond attacked antislavery propaganda which dwelt "with insatiable relish on licentious sexual relations between masters and slaves." Such an attitude, he declared, was especially true of the old maids. "Such rage without," he quoted, "betrays the fires within." The men who dwelt on this aspect of slavery, he went on, "Write, or with a rival's or an eunuch's spite." [44] There may have been a dose of truth in Hammond's analysis, but once more it must be pointed out that the use of such material in their propaganda was often conscious on the part of the

[40] Barnes, op. cit., p. 197.

[41] Arthur Young Lloyd, The Slavery Controversy (Chapel Hill, 1939), p. 58.

[42] Korngold, op. cit., p. 186.

[43] Hazel Wolf, On Freedom's Altar, the Martyr Complex in the Abolition Movement (Madison, 1952).

[44] J. H. Hammond, "Slavery in the Light of Political Science," in E. N. Elliott, ed., Cotton Is King (Augusta, Ga., 1860), p. 644.

pamphleteers. Such stories, more than any other type, could arouse emotional response against the degrading effects of slavery on both whites and Negroes. To just which old maids Hammond had reference is difficult to say, because of all the leading women writers and lecturers only Sarah Grimké remained unmarried.

There has been more attempt to classify the Abolitionists religiously than along any other line, but the characterizations run the gamut from labels of "atheist" and "infidel" to that of extreme religious zealots. Most of the charges of atheism and infidelism were hurled in conjunction with the cries of socialism and communism—any ism would do if it carried a subversive tinge. But the defenders of slavery knew that a good offense is the best defense. It was necessary, if slavery was to be justified as a Christian institution, to make the opposition appear not only un-Christian, but anti-Christian. Professor William Sumner Jenkins has pointed out[45] that the period of the 1830's was a time when many New England divines were greatly influenced by German rationalism. Transcendentalism and Unitarianism were growing. It was possible, consequently, for the Southerners to equate New England rationalism and Abolitionism, and label both as doctrines undermining the authority of the Bible and the church. Abolitionist attacks on the churches which refused to take a stand against slavery gave them fuel for the fire. We have mentioned Birney's pamphlet, *The American Churches the Bulwarks of American Slavery*. William Jay, son of the first Chief Justice, and a conservative Episcopalian, referred to the church as a "great buttress" of slavery;[46] and William Lloyd Garrison in his non-conservative fashion called the Methodist Church "a cage of unclean birds and a synagogue of Satan." [47]

Some of the Abolitionists were affiliated with religious groups which were considered unorthodox: the Unitarians, Swedenborgians, Hicksites, Mormons, and of course, Quakers. But it has been well established that the majority of abolitionists were Congregationalists, Presbyterians, Methodists, and Baptists, in addition to Quakers, with fewer Episcopalians and Catholics.[48] It is true also that the ministers of these churches dominated the leadership of the antislavery societies, and most of the local societies were formed in and as adjuncts to the local churches.

The Abolitionists' mirror image of themselves was that of earnest men led of God toward the accomplishment of good. In 1852 William Goodell concluded, "Thus does Divine Providence raise up and direct the voluntary instruments of his high design." [49] And Lewis Tappan in 1835 wrote, "The largest part of abolitionists are Christians, men devoutedly pious . . ." [50] James G. Birney, a Southerner and ex-slaveholder, went to his first antislavery conference not knowing quite what to expect, and in his report one can read between the lines he was somewhat relieved and surprised to find ". . . so much of sedate deliberation, of sober conclusion, of dignified moderation, sanctified by earnest prayer to God, not only for the oppressed, but for the oppressor of his fellowmen . . ." [51] But Charles Grandison Finney,

[45] William Sumner Jenkins, *Pro-Slavery Thought in the Old South* (Chapel Hill, 1935), pp. 237–238.

[46] Fladeland, *op. cit.*, pp. 202–203.

[47] Barnes, *op. cit.*, p. 93.

[48] *Ibid.*, p. 91; Dillon, *op. cit.*; Donald, *op. cit.*, p. 29.

[49] Goodell, *op. cit.*, p. 386.

[50] Thomas, *op. cit.*, p. 61.

[51] *A Collection of Valuable Documents, Being Birney's Vindication of Abolitionists—Protests of the American A. S. Society—To the People of the United States; or, To Such Americans As*

evangelist of the "Great Revival" is quoted as saying, "Our leading abolitionists are good men, but few are wise men;" [52] and Samuel J. May, in his rather piquant fashion agreed: "We abolitionists are what we are,—babes, sucklings, obscure men, silly women, publicans, sinners, and we shall manage this matter just as might be expected of such persons as we are"—and then added the rebuke: "It is unbecoming in abler men who stood by and would do nothing but to complain of us because we do no better." [53]

There is ample evidence that the religious impulse was a strong motivation in the antislavery crusade. Professor Barnes estimated that in a typical antislavery convention, two-thirds of the delegates were ministers.[54] Merton Dillon feels that it was their religious orientation that gave the Abolitionists most of their distinctive qualities, and that they felt a deep sense of obligation not only to help God in accomplishing his plans, but to save the nation from "immediate, temporal judgment." [55] Alice Felt Tyler points out that they were "heavily tinged with a Puritan's somewhat sanctimonious concern with the conduct of others." [56]

Dillon goes on to suggest that in its secular phase the antislavery movement was an effort to "reassert the declining influence of New England and the New England clergy," but believes the status motive remained recessive. Professor Donald finds in the status revolution of the old New England aristocracy the key to Abolitionist motivation: "In these plebeian days they could not be successful in politics; family tradition and education prohibited idleness; and agitation allowed the only chance for personal and social self-fulfillment." [57] Of course, all of us are handicapped by having to draw our evidence from what we know of the leaders in the movement, and this key applies only to the leadership. It seems apparent that the same key will not suffice as an explanation of why thousands of ordinary people from all walks of life joined the cause, particularly those from other sections than New England. Professor Barnes calculated, from his study of society records, that New Englanders comprised about one-fifth of the total antislavery membership.[58] And there still remains the task of accounting for the motivation of leaders who were not from New England.

The revisionist historians such as Professor Randall, in their attempts to de-emphasize the moral issue of slavery as a cause of the Civil War, tended to dismiss the Abolitionists as self-righteous, emotional fanatics; but among the current generation of historians there seems to be a rising tide of dissent. Before his death, Benjamin Thomas called for a new appraisal of the Abolitionists: "It has too long been the fashion to scoff at them, to write them off as humorless fanatics, to ignore their rich humanity, and to minimize the tremendous impact of the moral convictions

---

Value Their Rights—Letter from the Executive Committee of the N. Y. A. S. Society, to the Executive Committee of the Ohio State A. S. S. at Cincinnati—Outrage upon Southern Rights (Boston, 1836).

[52] Barnes, *op. cit.*, p. 275.
[53] Korngold, *op. cit.*, p. 81.
[54] Barnes, *op. cit.*, p. 98.
[55] Dillon, *op. cit.*
[56] Tyler, *op. cit.*, p. 490.
[57] Dillon, *op. cit.*; Donald, *op. cit.*, p. 34.
[58] Barnes, *op. cit.*, p. 88.

they avowed. And to misjudge the force of moral humanism invites distortion in history." [59]

One can make a good case for the Abolitionists as being the true conservatives of their time in seeking to preserve the basic American traditions of freedom of speech, of press, and of inquiry. The defense of freedom of the press by such men as Birney and Lovejoy, and of freedom of petition by John Quincy Adams brought thousands of people into the ranks who had hitherto been either apathetic or hostile. Among these recruits was William Ellery Channing, who wrote of the Abolitionists: "They are sufferers for the liberty of thought, speech, and the press; and in maintaining this liberty amidst insult and violence they deserve a place among its most honored defenders . . . Of such men I do not hesitate to say, that they have rendered to freedom a more essential service, than any body of men among us." [60] William Jay wrote, "We commenced the present struggle to obtain the freedom of the slave; we are compelled to continue it to preserve our own." [61] It is, of course, possible that there were some recruits who were exclusively concerned with their own rights and scarcely at all with those of the slave. Lord Charnwood, English biographer of Lincoln, felt that ". . . the North would have been depraved if it had not bred Abolitionists." [62]

The sheer number of Abolitionists, the thousands of unacknowledged and unsung, the myriad of personalities, and the vast diversity of exigencies which moulded each individual's decision to join the movement makes it impossible to label or categorize them. In my composite I find room for fanatics, reckless incendiaries, lawbreakers, sober "solid" citizens, natural agitators, natural conservatives, militant suffragettes, exaggerators, philanthropists, political and social eccentrics, political conservatives, visionaries, idealists ahead of their time, dedicated humanitarians, psychopaths, religious bigots, sincere Christians, atheists, political opportunists, and defenders of basic American liberties. In religion they ran the gamut from orthodox to unorthodox; in politics from militant nationalists to disunionists; socially, from those who believed in equality for all men to those who subscribed to *noblesse oblige* on the part of an aristocracy toward the lower classes; psychologically, from those who acted on sub-conscious and emotional impulses to those who were motivated by intellectual conviction. Geographically, they stretched from Maine to Texas; and people from all walks of life were enlisted.

They were called agitators because they stirred people to thought and to action. As William Ellery Channing once wrote, "There is a tendency in the laying bare of deep-rooted abuses to throw a community into a storm . . ." but "The progress of society depends on nothing more, than on the exposure of time-sanctioned abuses." [63]

[59] Thomas, *op. cit.*, vi.

[60] William Ellery Channing, *Letter of . . . to James G. Birney* (Boston, 1837), pp. 7–8.

[61] Tyler, *op. cit.*, p. 511.

[62] Lord Charnwood, *Abraham Lincoln* (New York, 1917), p. 126.

[63] Channing, *op. cit.*, p. 10.

Part IV

THE COURSE
TO WAR

10 / "The Cave of the Winds" and the Compromise of 1850

Holman Hamilton

Growing cultural and ideological differences may have magnified sectional antagonisms, but without the territorial question that emerged after 1846, there could have been no Civil War. At the opening of the Mexican War, the boundaries between slave and free territory had been clearly defined and settled. North of the Mason-Dixon Line and the Ohio River were the free states; south of it were the slave. To the west, the remaining area of the old Louisiana Purchase was divided along the line 36°30′ into future slave and free regions. In a word, on the eve of the Mexican struggle, the nation had been split into parts unequivocally either free or slave, present or prospective.

The war disrupted this arrangement by adding to the nation about 500,000 square miles of new land. The newly acquired territory immediately became a bone of sectional contention when Representative David Wilmot of Pennsylvania introduced a resolution excluding slavery from all land to be acquired from Mexico. The Wilmot Proviso failed to pass, but it was the opening gun of a long, disastrous struggle over the spread of slavery. What followed was a succession of legislative and constitutional crises that ended only with the secession of the South.

But at first, compromise, as in 1820, proved possible. In 1850 a group of Northern and border state leaders, most notably Henry Clay of Kentucky, Stephen A. Douglas of Illinois, and Daniel Webster of Massachusetts pieced together a sectional bargain that promised to end the growing dispute over the extension of slavery. Holman Hamilton's article describes how the accommodation was effected in the face of serious difficulties by a combination of political perspicacity and sheer good fortune.

For further reading: *Holman Hamilton, *Prologue to Conflict: The Crisis and Compromise of 1850* (New York: The Norton Library, 1966); Allan Nevins, *Ordeal of the Union* (New York: Charles Scribner's Sons, 1947), I; Robert R. Russel, "What Was the Compromise of 1850?" *Journal*

Journal of Southern History, XXIII, No. 3 (August 1957), 331–353. Copyright 1957 by the Southern Historical Association. Reprinted by permission of the Managing Editor.

of Southern History, XXII (August 1956); David D. Van Tassel, "Gentlemen of Property and Standing: Compromise Sentiment in Boston in 1850," *New England Quarterly,* XXIII (September 1950).

If Aeolus had forsaken his cave of the winds to visit Washington in late 1849, he would have felt thoroughly at home in the United States House of Representatives. Never before, in six decades under the Federal Constitution, had congressional chaos been more evident. Wordiness emanated from men who under normal conditions would have busied themselves with organization. For three hectic weeks the House could not organize because there was no Speaker on the dais, and none could be elected. House rules called for a majority decision, but there was no majority. And so, during most of December, orators tore passions to tatters and members voted ineffectually while the mere clerk of the previous session presided and sought a modicum of order. Often at night, when adjournment came, caucuses met in that same chamber—and southern, northern, western, and eastern partisan and factional storms continued as before. The House of December 1849 was truly a cave of political winds.

Capable men were members, people of past or future prominence. Horace Mann of Massachusetts and Henry W. Hilliard of Alabama were educators and men of literary skill. Thaddeus Stevens of Pennsylvania and Jacob Thompson of Mississippi represented extremist elements. The roster of able congressmen included Robert Ward Johnson of Arkansas, John A. McClernand and William A. Richardson of Illinois, Albert G. Brown of Mississippi, and James L. Orr of South Carolina. Thomas L. Clingman and David Outlaw of North Carolina rubbed elbows with Joshua R. Giddings of Ohio, James X. McLanahan of Pennsylvania, Frederick P. Stanton of Tennessee, and Volney E. Howard of Texas. In the large New York delegation were James Brooks, William Duer, and Preston King. Georgia had sent three gifted men in Howell Cobb, Alexander H. Stephens, and Robert Toombs. From Massachusetts came the scholarly Robert C. Winthrop, Speaker of the Thirtieth Congress; from Kentucky, the resourceful Linn Boyd who (like Orr) was a future Speaker; from New Jersey, the wealthy businessman James G. King; from Ohio, the irrepressible Free Soiler, Joseph M. Root; from Tennessee, a future president, Andrew Johnson of the Greeneville district; and from Virginia the devoted Richmond Democrat James A. Seddon.

Although these and other representatives measured up to standards of previous Congresses, they and their chamber soon would be overshadowed by a Senate of unusual brilliance. For the Thirty-first Congress was the one in which John C. Calhoun, Henry Clay, and Daniel Webster met for the final time. Thomas Hart Benton was a senator, too, and the tall Texan, Sam Houston of Huntsville, joined veterans like Alabama's William R. King and relative newcomers like Henry S. Foote in the senatorial drama. Leaders of the younger generation, Salmon P. Chase, Jefferson Davis, Stephen A. Douglas, William H. Seward, stood ready to challenge older senators' prominence.

At the start of the Thirty-first Congress, the contrast between the two houses seemed rooted less in personalities than in voting alignments. If the Senate Democracy's nationalistic and sectionalistic blocs were at odds on policy fundamentals, the large Democratic paper majority presented a united front for organizational purposes. Vice

President Millard Fillmore was a Whig, but Senate Democrats experienced no difficulty in dominating the committees.[1] Meeting and adjourning from day to day with no extensive debate, the Senate at the outset marked time while the House wrangled. Though some representatives like Meredith P. Gentry and George W. Julian reached Washington late, nearly all of the 231 House seats were occupied from the beginning. Of the members answering the roll call on the first ballot and the last, 108 were Democrats, 103 Whigs, and nine Free Soilers—while a single congressman (Lewis C. Levin) belonged to the Native American party. The principal candidates for Speaker usually were Cobb the Democrat and Winthrop the Whig. In the course of 62 ballots over the three-week span, the total vote ranged from a high of 226 to a low of 217, of which the Georgian's maximum was 103 and the Bostonian's 102. At various times, on their own responsibility or as a result of pressure, both Cobb and Winthrop withdrew their names to give ambitious colleagues a chance for preferment. But, with one exception, no other aspirant surpassed the Cobb-Winthrop crests. Not only was a House majority lacking, but a group of Southern Whigs refused to back Winthrop, some Southern Democrats declined to support Cobb, and the Free Soilers had their own candidate and with the dissident Southern Whigs held the balance of power.[2]

On the sixty-third ballot, the impasse ended. The winds in the cave spent themselves momentarily. Conflicting elements bowed to reason, finding a way out of their blind alley by resorting to a plurality decision.[3] When Howell Cobb thus won the speakership and named the committees' personnel, the Democratic party found itself in control of both House and Senate organizations.[4] Still, the fact that the lower chamber had to fall back on a plurality procedure suggested troubles that would develop as soon as the House tried to legislate.

Could House majorities ever be attained in the course of the 1850 debates? Sober onlookers were frankly pessimistic, for the speakership election reflected schisms within each of the major parties, not only in Washington but in the United States as a whole. According to many a Northerner and Whig, the annexation of Texas in 1845 had caused most of the problems now vexing Congress. Annexation had been followed swiftly by the Mexican War, the Wilmot Proviso, the acquisition from Mexico of a vast amount of western soil, and then the forty-niners' gold rush to the Sacramento Valley. Were Southerners entitled to own slave property in the new American West? Or should the Proviso be passed and slavery excluded from that area? Or was the popular sovereignty principle feasible and fair? Or did the solution lie in projecting to the Pacific Ocean the Missouri Compromise line of 36°30′, with slavery admitted below and forbidden above it? Intraparty Whig weaknesses and Whigs' want of accord on these questions had been symbolized in 1848 by General Zachary Taylor's presidential nomination. Taylor had been given no platform by the Whigs, and his personal statements on the issues of the hour invited conflicting views. His election, in

[1] *Cong. Globe,* 31 Cong., 1 Sess., 40–41, 44–45.

[2] *Ibid.,* 2–39, 41–44, 46–48, 51, 61–67; Holman Hamilton, *Zachary Taylor: Soldier in the White House* (Indianapolis, 1951), 247–52. Winthrop felt the Whigs erred in shifting votes from himself to other candidates. He believed that, if he had received 102 votes on the forty-first ballot, his supporters "would have made me Speaker." Robert C. Winthrop to John P. Kennedy, December 16, 1849, in Kennedy Papers (Peabody Institute, Baltimore).

[3] Frederick P. Stanton took credit for this, and stated that the solution was reached despite 48–28 opposition in the Democratic caucus. Stanton to James Buchanan, December 24, 1849, in Buchanan Papers (Historical Society of Pennsylvania, Philadelphia).

[4] *Cong. Globe,* 31 Cong., 1 Sess., 66–67, 88–89.

turn, had been due in great measure to a split in the northern Democracy with particular reference to New York. Thus the Taylor of the White House was a minority President, just as Cobb was a minority Speaker. The Whig Administration of 1849 and early 1850 lacked the mandate, experience, and cohesion essential to first-rate executive leadership.

The General in the Mansion, however, was not slow in making his influence felt. In the spring of 1849 Taylor had sent Representative Thomas Butler King of Georgia to the West Coast as his special agent. King in June informed the Californians of the "sincere desire of the Executive" to protect them "in the formation of any government, republican in its character, hereafter to be submitted to Congress, which shall be the result of their . . . deliberate choice." Before many months passed, California adopted a free-state constitution and applied for admission to the Union. In August at Mercer, Pennsylvania, Taylor asserted that "the people of the North need have no apprehension of the further extension of slavery." In November, an army officer left Washington for Santa Fe with a directive that "if the people of New Mexico desired to take . . . steps toward securing admission as a state, it would be his duty . . . 'not to thwart but to advance their wishes.'" The President's intent was unmistakable. If his hopes were realized, neither popular sovereignty nor projection of the 36°30' line could apply to California or New Mexico, and the free- and slave-state balance in the Senate would be permanently destroyed. Was the White House slaveholder a Wilmot Proviso man, an enemy of the South in Southern Whig clothing? The thought was appalling to many Southerners.[5]

With this as the background for the Thirty-first Congress, it might be supposed that Taylor would have drawn Northern accessions to his banner. His annual message in December ended on a ringing Union note, and a special message the third week in January underscored statehood in the West. The Free Soilers in the House, however, were not content with the Proviso's end-product; they demanded the letter of the law. Most Northern House Democrats, better disciplined than Whigs, maintained their records as party regulars. It is true that Northern Whigs were impressed, but, as subsequent trends unfolded, some veered away from the Administration to pursue a less drastic course. The unpopularity of Taylor's cabinet, inept distribution of federal patronage, and Whig losses in recent congressional races did not constitute the raw materials of which majorities are composed. Southerners, on the other hand, quickly sensed that Taylor personified danger to their interests. Southern Democrats favored popular sovereignty or the 36°30' plan. Such original Taylor-for-President boosters as Stephens, Toombs, and other Southern Whigs had turned thumbs down on Winthrop for Speaker and now would fight Taylor to the bitter end.

If the dilemma of December was not to be repeated during 1850, much would depend on Howell Cobb and his comrades of the Democratic high command. Chairman Boyd of the Committee on Territories proved to be the Speaker's right arm and presided over most of the debate as chairman of the Committee of the Whole. A third key figure was Douglas's lieutenant, chairman McClernand of the Committee on Foreign Affairs who, despite the title, would devote nearly all his energies to domestic problems. Still another was Virginia's Thomas H. Bayly, head of the Ways and Means Committee. The role of Cobb has been the subject of a scholarly monograph,[6] but

[5] Hamilton, *Zachary Taylor: Soldier in the White House, passim.*

[6] Robert P. Brooks, "Howell Cobb and the Crisis of 1850," in *Mississippi Valley Historical Review* (Cedar Rapids, 1914–), IV (December 1917), 279–98.

a statistical study of House speeches and votes can add a great deal to the story, and Boyd's, McClernand's, and Bayly's contributions certainly enter into the reckoning.

Most of the initiative for the Compromise of 1850 had its origin in the Senate. In the course of the next three-quarters of a century, almost every historian treating the topic gave a lion's share of credit to Clay and Webster.[7] In more recent times emphasis has been placed on Douglas and the Senate Democratic majority.[8] Latterly, too, a distinctive effort has been made to depart from vague or inaccurate remarks about the Compromise per se, and carefully to define the slavery provisions of the acts organizing New Mexico and Utah Territories.[9] In addition to establishing the two Western territories, with legislatures which could prohibit or establish or regulate slavery, the Compromise admitted California into the Union as a free state; settled the Texas-New Mexico boundary controversy; assured Texas that the United States would assume the Texas debt; included a fugitive slave law designed to plug loopholes in the old law of 1793, and abolished the slave trade in the District of Columbia.[10]

Bills incorporating the several parts of the Compromise were passed by Congress in July, August, and September. In the preceding December and January, outbursts of sectional pride and passion evoked general concern in and out of Congress. The New York Whig diarist, Philip Hone, compared representatives in Washington with the Jacobins of the French Revolution. The nation "trembles at its base," Hone brooded, and "for the first time in our history" men did not hesitate "openly to threaten a dissolution of the Union." Congressman McLanahan agreed that the slavery question had reached a dangerous crisis. "A lion is in the path of our Country's glory," the Pennsylvania Democrat reported privately. "May Heaven shield us from impending danger." "The issue between the South and the North is the all absorbing subject here," the sick but alert Senator Calhoun wrote his son from Washington. ". . . The Southern members are more determined and bold than I ever saw them. Many avow themselves to be disunionists." [11]

[7] James Ford Rhodes, *History of the United States from the Compromise of 1850* (7 vols., New York, 1893–1906), I, 120–95; James Schouler, *History of the United States under the Constitution* (6 vols., New York, 1880–99), V, 159–98; George P. Garrison, *Westward Extension, 1841–1850* (New York, 1906), 320–31. Of the older "standard" multi-volume histories, John B. McMaster, *A History of the People of the United States from the Revolution to the Civil War* (8 vols., New York, 1883–1913), VIII, 12–42, is in several ways the most satisfactory on the Compromise. In Edward Channing, *A History of the United States* (6 vols., New York, 1905–25), VI, 75–85, many of Rhodes's and Schouler's fundamental errors are avoided, but details are slighted, and the work is marred by numerous minor mistakes.

[8] Frank H. Hodder, "The Authorship of the Compromise of 1850," in *Mississippi Valley Historical Review*, XXII (March 1936), 525–36; George F. Milton, *The Eve of Conflict: Stephen A. Douglas and the Needless War* (Boston, 1934), 50–78; George D. Harmon, "Douglas and the Compromise of 1850," in *Journal of the Illinois State Historical Society* (Springfield, 1908–), XXI (January 1929), 453–99; Holman Hamilton, "Democratic Senate Leadership and the Compromise of 1850," in *Mississippi Valley Historical Review*, XLI (December 1954), 403–18.

[9] Robert R. Russel, "What Was the Compromise of 1850?", in *Journal of Southern History* (Baton Rouge, 1935–), XXII (August 1956), 292–309.

[10] 9 *U. S. Stat.* (69 vols., Boston, 1845–1955), 446–58, 462–68.

[11] Philip Hone, manuscript diary, December 15, 1849, and January 7, 1850 (New-York Historical Society, New York City); James X. McLanahan to Buchanan, December 2, 1849, in Buchanan Papers; J. Franklin Jameson (ed.), *Correspondence of John C. Calhoun*, American Historical Association *Annual Report . . . for the Year 1899* (2 vols., Washington, 1900), II, 780.

To William B. Ogden, who was soon to make a fortune in the city of Chicago, "the prospects ahead" were "not cheering in any way"; Calhoun was bent on the "dissolution of the Union," and "if a rupture does take place the North will have to unite" in rallying to Taylor and "aiding him to put it down." [12] The Whig Senator Webster and the Democratic Senator Lewis Cass later looked back on the situation as one of the most dangerous in American annals.[13] The junior senator from Illinois, a Democrat, saw "the extreme Southern men . . . in a state of excitement which prepares them for the most desperate resolves." A North Carolina Whig in the House feared that "armed men might be admitted into this Hall, and . . . this place might become a scene of bloodshed." Shortly before Christmas, one of the most conservative Northern Democrats found "more bad feeling" on Capitol Hill "than can be well conceived unless by those present." Over in Philadelphia an aristocratic Whig was pessimistic: "No one can say how soon we may be involved in the dangers & calamities of disunion. The house is not yet organized & parties are becoming inflamed." Slavery and related topics were being used "as the cloak of the ambitious designs of demagogues & to delude & excite the people—who . . . are victims & tools." An ex-congressman and ex-governor of the Bluegrass State warned a prominent Missourian: "You can hardly conceive of the irritation and bad feeling . . . excited in this northern border of Kentucky" by abolitionists and other Northern radicals. In mid-January, the Whig publisher of the Washington *National Intelligencer,* conversing with a Marylander when they met in the House, voiced alarm "in reference to the Southern movement on the Slave question, threatening a dissolution of the Union." [14]

Events in the House during most of January substantiated the forebodings. While in the Senate moves were being made for pacification, Clingman, Howard, Seddon, and Brown, irked by Free Soilers and also by the President, delivered fiery orations to their fellow representatives. Jeremiah Morton of Virginia and Samuel W. Inge of Alabama carried on in February the sharp Southern criticism of Taylor, King, the cabinet, the Proviso, statehood for California, and, in general, Northern attitudes toward the South. Stanton, though more moderate, joined in the attack. From January 22 through February 13, not a single Northern member made a set speech in the chamber. Seven Southern representatives delivered set speeches, each lasting approximately an hour, and one of these Southerners twice took the floor. All eight efforts, with the partial exception of Stanton's, were saturated with grievances and studded with threats. In mid-February, the balance began to be redressed by the calmer remarks of Hilliard the Alabama Whig and Marshall J. Wellborn the Georgia Democrat, the non-sectionalistic but intensely partisan observations of the Indiana Democrat, Graham N. Fitch, and the characteristic Wilmot Proviso slants of Root the Ohio Free Soiler and Mann the Massachusetts Whig. Of the forty-four formal, hour-long addresses heard in the House during the sixty-nine day period preceding April 1, nine-

[12] William B. Ogden to E. A. Russell, December 31, 1849, in Ogden Papers (Chicago Historical Society).

[13] Lexington *Kentucky Statesman,* October 30, November 23, 1850.

[14] James Shields to Buchanan, December 8, 1849, in Buchanan Papers; David Outlaw to Mrs. Outlaw, January 14, 1850, in Outlaw Papers (Southern Historical Collection, University of North Carolina, Chapel Hill); Daniel Sturgeon to Buchanan, December 22, 1849, in Buchanan Papers; Sidney G. Fisher, manuscript diary, December 16, 1849 (Historical Society of Pennsylvania); Thomas Metcalfe to David R. Atchison, December 26, 1849, in Atchison Papers (Western Historical Manuscripts Collection, University of Missouri, Columbia); John P. Kennedy, manuscript diary, January 19, 1850, in Kennedy Papers.

teen were Northern in origin and twenty-five Southern, despite the fact that Northerners constituted a three-fifths majority of the total membership.

The temper of the House in early 1850 could also be gauged by protracted corollaries of the battle between Winthrop and Cobb. Representatives voted twenty times before managing to elect a clerk. Three ballots were taken to choose a chaplain; eight were necessary for a sergeant-at-arms, and none of the fourteen candidates for doorkeeper could win that lofty office after fourteen trials.[15] Already Richard K. Meade of Virginia had rushed gesticulating at Duer of New York, when the latter branded Meade a liar. In February, an Illinoisan's comments in the House brought a challenge to a duel from Jefferson Davis. The first week in March, during a debate, Edward Stanly of North Carolina flung the charge of disgraceful rudeness at a fellow Whig from Alabama.[16] Moreover, the normal House routine, memorials, petitions, pensions, patent laws, the Seventh Census, the coastwise trade, and a contested election in Iowa, cluttered up the agenda and contributed to the delay. Concurrently, the Senate had its own moments of frustration and sectional wrath. But Foote, Cass, Douglas, Clay, and others were bent on achieving a compromise. And, six days after Clay introduced his resolutions in the Senate, there came the first of four important moves that helped somewhat to tranquilize the agitated House.

The first step involved the House's reaction to Root's resolution that the Proviso be applied to the region acquired from Mexico, with the exception of California. On February 4, the resolution was tabled 105–75—eighteen Northern Democrats and fourteen Northern Whigs siding with the South against the Proviso. Cobb did not vote; his vote was not needed. Especially significant was the presence of McClernand and Richardson in the majority, joining as they did Bayly and Boyd and other Southern Democrats like Baltimore's Robert M. McLane.

The following Sunday, February 10, an even more meaningful victory was scored for the compromise cause in a Washington hotel. Thomas Ritchie, now editor of the Washington *Union* and Nestor of the Democratic party, in his young manhood had been a warm friend of Henry Clay. Then for years they were opponents, Clay dominating the Whigs and running for president while Ritchie bossed the Virginia Democracy. Now, at last, they were reunited. After James W. Simenton of the New York *Courier & Enquirer* had taken part in the preliminary arrangements, Ritchie with Bayly at his side called on the Kentuckian at his quarters. No other Democratic journalist had more influence than white-haired "Father" Ritchie. No other Whig senator had more prestige than the venerable "Harry of the West." When the tall, fair, thirty-nine-year-old Bayly brought what Ritchie described as "ingenuity and learning" to the discussion, he was contributing "ways and means" of enormous value to House and Senate compromisers. Several days before, Ritchie criticized Clay in the columns of the *Union*. Henceforth, partisans would rub their eyes at the quantity and fervor of Democratic tributes to the Democratic party's traditional archfoe. That Clay-Ritchie handclasp at the National Hotel, as the shadows lengthened on a Sunday afternoon, symbolized the coalescing of compromise strength.

Then, on the 18th, there came the third test of the House leaders' control or in-

---

[15] *Cong. Globe*, 31 Cong., 1 Sess., *passim*. The speech of Oregon Delegate Samuel R. Thurston has been excluded from the statistical survey.

[16] *Ibid.*, 27, 467; Washington *National Intelligencer*, March 6, 1850; Outlaw to Mrs. Outlaw, February 24, 27, 28, 1850, in Outlaw Papers; Donald F. Tingley, "The Jefferson Davis-William H. Bissell Duel," in *Mid-America* (Chicago, 1918–   ), XXXVIII (July 1956), 146–55.

genuity. Five days before, Taylor had submitted a four-line message transmitting the California constitution, and James D. Doty of Wisconsin sought to capitalize upon it. A free-soil Democrat, Doty proposed that Boyd's Committee on Territories report a California statehood bill unconnected with other legislation. This, of course, was a red flag to Southerners, a signal for leaders to enter the fray. There were twenty-eight roll calls, and tactics of delay were dexterously employed, for it was clear that if Doty succeeded debate on California would be halted. With Bayly demanding resistance "at all hazards," Southerners and Northern Democrats stalled and dodged—their motions and maneuvers sustained by Cobb in the chair from early afternoon till midnight. Finally, Cobb decided that the day had expired; the resolution went over, and for the first time the full force of the speakership was unmistakably felt.[17]

The next night, Speaker Cobb's house on Third Street was the scene of a conference almost as significant as the one attended by Ritchie, Clay, and Bayly. With Douglas acting as a *deus ex machina*, McClernand invited Stephens and Toombs to join in a private discussion of objectives and methods with John K. Miller (an Ohio Democrat), Boyd, Cobb, Richardson, and McClernand himself. The four Southerners and three Northerners, five Democrats and two Whigs, agreed to a Douglas-McClernand plan of action. What McClernand proposed was that he should sponsor bills for the territorial organization of New Mexico and Utah on a popular sovereignty basis, with the understanding that California would be admitted as a free state and slavery retained in the District of Columbia. McClernand also promised that Douglas would follow a similar procedure in the Senate.[18] The fact that these Southern Whigs were willing to underwrite the Democrats' program of adjustment was encouraging not only to McClernand but to his Southern confreres, Cobb, Boyd, and Bayly.

Although each of these occurrences logically heartened the compromise men, three other facts were most discouraging. The first was the attitude of Calhoun, who set his face sternly against such adjustments. The second was President Taylor's opposition, for reasons diametrically opposed to Calhoun's. But even the combined influence of these two determined men, together with the votes of the Free Soilers, could never have prevented a compromise had it not been for a third consideration, a surprising tactical shift by Clay. It is ironic that Clay, who originally favored keeping all parts of a compromise separate and taking up bills one at a time, was persuaded by Foote and Ritchie in February and March that several of the measures ought to be combined.[19] While Clay was undergoing his fateful conversion congressional oratory continued and observers reacted variously to developments on the Hill.

Hone wished that Clay's February 5 speech would calm the "rage of contending factions," but concluded "I fear not." Senator James M. Mason of Virginia, on the other hand, believed in early February that "the danger of dissolution, once imminent, is diminishing every day."[20] On the 9th, Speaker Cobb looked "sanguinely to the period when all patriotic hearts will and can unite in saying 'all is well.'" Yet, four days later, Representative Stephens confessed: "I see very little prospect of future

---

[17] *Cong. Globe*, 31 Cong., 1 Sess., 276, 375–85; Henry S. Foote, *A Casket of Reminiscences* (Washington, 1874), 24; Charles H. Ambler, *Thomas Ritchie: A Study in Virginia Politics* (Richmond, 1913), 281–82; Richmond *Enquirer*, September 10, 1852.

[18] Alexander H. Stephens, *A Constitutional View of the Late War Between the States . . .* (2 vols., Philadelphia, 1868–70), II, 202–204.

[19] Foote, *A Casket of Reminiscences*, 24; *Cong. Globe*, 31 Cong., 1 Sess., 365–69.

[20] Hone, manuscript diary, February 8, 1850; James M. Mason to William C. Rives, February 4, 1850, in Rives Papers (Manuscripts Division, Library of Congress).

peace and quiet in the public mind." While Daniel Webster waxed optimistic ("The clamor about disunion rather abates"),[21] Calhoun declared: "The excitement . . . continues on the increase. I see no prospect of any satisfactory adjustment." Burgeoning confidence was mirrored in Representative James Gore King's report: "No reasons exist for any uneasiness on account of the angry discussions. . . . Of course some compromise will be found." A single violent speech from either side would ignite a flame, Outlaw felt on the first of March; still, the Whig congressman thought that "most of the steam is blown off by this time and that those who wish to speak, may be cool and temperate." Perhaps the best proof of growing moderation in both House and Senate is contained in one of Calhoun's letters. Writing on March 10 (six days after his own address had been read for him by Mason, and three days after Webster's Seventh of March Speech), the Carolinian considered it possible that the slavery question might be "patched up for the present, to brake [sic] out again in a few years." [22]

During March and April, the Senate was the setting for so much memorable political drama that there has been an understandable tendency to slight the House in most accounts. Not only Senators Calhoun and Webster but Thomas J. Rusk, Hannibal Hamlin, Seward, Douglas, and others reflected all shades of public opinion in their formal orations. Calhoun died the last morning in March and in mid-April the Senate created a Select Committee of Thirteen with Clay as chairman. In the latter part of April and the first week of May, while the committee's report was in the making and with numerous senators at home mending their fences, a greater share of attention was turned to recent and current trends in the House.

April's fifteen set speeches in the House were delivered by eight Southerners and seven Northerners, eight Democrats and seven Whigs. In May, two Free Soilers joined six Whigs and four Democrats, the sectional division of the orators being eight from the North and four from the South. Linn Boyd, as chairman of the Committee of the Whole, presided when most of the remarks were made. In June, one Southern Democrat complained that he had tried unsuccessfully for two months to win recognition from the dais. The fact that Southern Democrats controlled the machinery, and that Whigs and Democrats alternated in the spotlight, suggests that Boyd was exceedingly fair in recognizing the speakers. In June everyone who wished to speak had a chance, and the floor went begging more than once.[23] Each of forty-seven representatives was allotted his hour in the first June fortnight—26 Southerners, 21 Northerners, 29 Democrats, 12 Whigs, and six Free Soilers addressing themselves to the House and their constituents.

At times, the procedure verged on the ludicrous. In an effort to give each congressman his due, sessions often were held at night, so sparsely attended that on one occasion only twenty-eight members were present, and on another thirty-two. This was in June when, once again, senatorial jockeying had a greater appeal. Indeed it grew clear, as the late spring advanced, that many members of the House were more

[21] Ulrich B. Phillips (ed.), *The Correspondence of Robert Toombs, Alexander H. Stephens, and Howell Cobb,* American Historical Association *Annual Report . . . for the Year 1911* (2 vols., Washington, 1913), II, 183–84; Fletcher Webster (ed.), *The Private Correspondence of Daniel Webster* (2 vols., Boston, 1857), II, 355.

[22] Jameson, *Correspondence of John C. Calhoun,* 782–84; James G. King to Baring Brothers & Company, February 28, 1850, in Baring Papers (Public Archives of Canada, Ottawa); Outlaw to Mrs. Outlaw, March 1, 1850, in Outlaw Papers.

[23] *Cong. Globe,* 31 Cong., 1 Sess., 1110, 1123, 1171.

interested in defining their own stand for Buncombe or home appraisal than in debating colleagues' views or even determining what they were. One evening after the dinner recess, Cobb and Boyd were two of only eight men in the chamber when time came for the House to return to work, and no more than sixteen were on hand when at last the House did come to order and the orations were resumed.[24] Some of the speeches printed in the *Congressional Globe* never were delivered at all. Others were dressed up for the record, following informal "ad lib" remarks punctuated by laughter or boredom.

One hundred and eleven representatives held the floor between late January and mid-June. Forty-two were Southern Democrats, 17 Southern Whigs, 24 Northern Democrats, 20 Northern Whigs, and eight Northern Free Soilers. More significant ideologically is the breakdown which shows 10 Southerners in favor of an extension of 36°30′; 21 Northerners and Southerners backing Taylor's plan; 32 members from both sections preferring the popular sovereignty solution, and 11 speaking out clearly for the Wilmot Proviso. Some representatives did not say precisely what they were for, but stated pointedly what they were against. This was particularly true of South Carolinians Daniel Wallace and William F. Colcock. Williamson R. W. Cobb of Alabama lamented Congress' failure to create a joint Senate-House committee, with all sectional issues referred to it. Most atypical of their states were Meredith P. Gentry of Tennessee, Thomas S. Haymond of Virginia, and Edward Stanly of North Carolina (who followed President Taylor's lead) and Pennsylvania's Thomas Ross (who predicted "dissolution" of the Union, if "aggressions upon the domestic institutions of the South are persevered in").[25] Some representatives did not fully develop their positions. Others advocated California statehood, without identifying themselves either with Taylor or with the Proviso men. Still others apparently failed to hand in their speeches for publication in detail. Eight representatives spoke more than once. Over half the House membership sat silent or made the briefest comment, but the desire of almost 50 per cent to give utterance to their convictions or to awareness of expediency's benefits suggests the impact of the 1850 crisis.

So much for rank-and-filers' speeches. A few words of leaders at critical moments and parliamentary maneuvers later in the year would transcend most of them in importance. For many weeks, however, except on such matters as the Root and Doty moves heretofore mentioned, the pro-compromise chieftains made little headway. Back in March, the bills on which the conferees agreed at Cobb's house were reported in the Senate by Douglas. Still, it was noteworthy that the Senate chose to base its debate from May through July not on the methods favored by Douglas but on the "Omnibus Bill" and other parts of the report of Clay's Committee of Thirteen. The House, moreover, gave McClernand no opportunity from early spring well into the summer to go even as far as Douglas had gone. McClernand in April did announce a précis of the measures he stood ready to sponsor, if and when he got the chance.[26] But the long House debate was premised on Tayor's February 13 message and a bill of Doty's for California statehood. New Mexico, Utah, the Texas boundary, the Texas debt, fugitive slaves, and the slave trade in the District entered into the discussion only indirectly or inferentially. Wretched acoustics in the hall of the House brought

---

[24] *Ibid.*, 1123, 1151, 1167.
[25] *Ibid.*, Appendix, 336–45, 429–33, 459–64, 598–600, 646–49, 684–87, 832–36. Haymond hailed from the Wheeling district, part of the future state of West Virginia.
[26] *Cong. Globe,* 31 Cong., 1 Sess., 592, 628–29.

echo and confusion there, and the buzz of conversation in front of the dais resulted in frequent raps for order. Yet the verbosity persisted. Amendments were offered, and amendments to amendments, and provisos altering amendments' amendments. But, aside from the speechmaking, nothing substantial was done by the House, and no key legislation was passed, when, with little warning, on July 9 death came to President Zachary Taylor.

Millard Fillmore, the new President, looked with favor on compromise. But Taylor's death and Fillmore's accession met with less rapid political reaction in the House than in the Senate. Armed with Fillmore's co-operation, Clay pressed forward in the hope of gaining passage for the Omnibus Bill, the territorial part of which was successively amended by John Macpherson Berrien of Georgia, James W. Bradbury of Maine, and William C. Dawson of Georgia. The tinkering led on July 31 to the destruction of the New Mexico territorial provision in its entirety. The Texas dollars-for-acres arrangement was also cut out, as was California statehood. Nothing but Utah Territory remained, a tragic remnant, in Clay's eyes, of the bill on which he had set his heart.

After Clay's final defeat in the Senate, the tired old Kentucky Whig left the capital for a rest and young, dynamic Stephen A. Douglas came from the wings to the center of the stage. Taking up measures one at a time, Douglas within a fortnight rushed two bills through to Senate passage. In less than a month, the total was four. With Utah previously approved, all that remained when Clay returned from his seashore respite was the District slave trade's abolition. This last compromise provision met approval on September 19, under the personal guidance of Clay.[27] Meanwhile, all Washington and much of the nation turned from the Senate to the House to concentrate on developments there.

Wednesday, August 28, marked a striking change in the tone and tempo of the House of Representatives. No longer did California speeches virtually monopolize the members' time. No longer did discussion of land titles in Oregon, Revolutionary War pensions, Indian depredations, railroad rights of way, or even governmental appropriations delay action on the compromise. The General Appropriations Bill had been passed. California statehood had been shunted aside, and routine business for the most part postponed. Now, with the Senate example before them, Boyd and McClernand demanded decision as the Texas debt-and-boundary measure was taken up on the floor of the House. Straightway Boyd offered an amendment, combining this bill with the one providing for New Mexico's territorial organization. Granting doubt as to whether it was better to "consider the bills in a connected or in a separate form," Boyd hoped to test the sense of the House in relation to the establishment of territorial governments on the popular sovereignty principle. "We have . . . been listening to speeches for nine long months," the Democrat from western Kentucky exclaimed. ". . . I am astonished at the patience with which our constituents have borne our procrastination. I think we have talked enough—in God's name let us act."

Act the House did. On September 3, the combined bill or "little omnibus" became the special order of the day.[28] Immediately the question of Texas bonds, bondholders, and lobbyists cropped up. Senator Robert W. Barnwell believed that the "whole difficulty about the boundary of Texas was gotten up by . . . Clay . . . and others interested in the Bonds of Texas." Barnwell "never could at all understand the matter"

---

[27] Hamilton, "Democratic Senate Leadership and the Compromise of 1850," 407–12.
[28] *Cong. Globe,* 31 Cong., 1 Sess., 1696–97, 1727, 1736.

until the New England men, "almost in a body," voted for the Senate Texas bound-ary-and-debt bill. Similar suspicion was felt in the House concerning the "corruption of the 10,000,000" dollars,[29] with reference to Northern representatives and Northern holders of Texas securities. Congressman Giddings had already said that "the pay-ment of this ten millions" was intended "to raise Texan stocks from fifteen cents on the dollar to par value, to make splendid fortunes in little time. To take money from the pockets of the people and put it into the hands of stock-jobbers, and gamblers in Texas scrip." On September 4, Preston King likewise raised the issue of Texas bonds. Two days later, as the House neared a vote, Representative Jonathan D. Morris of Ohio, noting the lobbyists on the floor, demanded their expulsion and opined, "If there are any Texan bondholders in here, they can see and hear as well in the galleries."

Although Speaker Cobb replied to Morris that the seventeenth rule of the House (keeping lobbyists off the floor) "would be enforced," Brown of Mississippi later said it had "not been done." On that same September 6, the House approved the engrossment of the bill for a third reading—a highly consequential step which may be regarded as the pivot not only for the "little omnibus" but for the whole compromise in the House. The *Globe* for the 6th contains an unusual statement: "The announcement of the result was received with manifestations of applause of various kinds, the most peculiar and attractive of which was a sort of unpremeditated *allegro* whistle, which the Reporter does not remember to have heard before (certainly never in the House of Representatives). The other tokens of glorification were of a less musical order. It was evident that the greater portion of the applause, especially at the outset, was on the floor of the Hall itself." Cobb now interposed "vigorously" to check the noise. Cries of "Order!" were met with shouts of "Let them stamp! It is all right!" The chamber was "in an uproar."[30]

Passage of the "little omnibus" followed a few minutes later by a margin of 108 to 97. A debate of less than a single day was needed before the House officially approved of California's entrance into the Union. Here the vote was 150–56, and that on the Utah territorial bill 97–85, both on September 7. September 12 saw the fugitive slave measure triumph by 109–76. On September 9, by 31 to 10, the Senate ratified the House's union of the Texas and New Mexico bills, something that might have been impossible had Douglas first presented them there in combination. Aboli-tion of the slave trade in the District carried in the House, by 124–59, on September 17. On September 9, 18, and 20, President Fillmore's signature translated the com-ponent parts of the Compromise into law. Then, on the last day of the month, the first session of the Thirty-first Congress came to an end. The House and the Senate adjourned sine die, after Speaker Cobb and President Pro Tem William R. King spoke briefly and let their gavels fall. At last the Compromise of 1850 was an actuality.[31]

Reviewing the record in the House, it is instructive to discover that twenty-eight members cast their ballots for every one of the five measures. Twenty-five of these were Democrats, and three were Whigs. Twenty-five were Northerners, and three

[29] Robert W. Barnwell to James H. Hammond, August 14, 1850, in Hammond Papers (Manu-scripts Division, Library of Congress). On June 24, Barnwell of South Carolina succeeded Franklin H. Elmore, who had been appointed to Calhoun's Senate seat and died May 29, 1850.

[30] *Cong. Globe*, 31 Cong., 1 Sess., 1562, 1746, 1763–64.

[31] *Ibid.*, 1764, 1772, 1776, 1784, 1807, 1837, 2072, 2074; 9 *U. S. Stat.*, 447–58, 462–68.

Southerners. Only two were Southern Whigs. Only one was a Southern Democrat, and only one a Northern Whig. Such House statistics demonstrate that wholehearted backing of the Compromise was predominately Democratic and almost exclusively Northern. It was rooted principally in the Northwest, the extreme Northeast, and Pennsylvania.

A further analysis of the tallies shows how the Whigs came into the picture. Nine representatives supported the first four bills but conveniently absented themselves on the District slave trade test; all nine hailed from the slave states of Kentucky, Missouri, Tennessee, North Carolina, or Delaware—and two-thirds of them were Whigs. All eight who voted affirmatively four times but were not recorded on the Fugitive Slave Bill represented New York, Pennsylvania, or Ohio districts—four Whigs, three Democrats, and one Native American. Alexander W. Buel of Michigan failed to vote on the Utah bill, and William H. Bissell of Illinois on the Texas-New Mexico measure, but with these exceptions both stood with the majority. Sixteen members answered "yea" four times and "nay" once. Of all the thirty-five congressmen who cast affirmative ballots in four instances and either opposed or abstained in the fifth, 20 were Whigs, 14 Democrats, and one was a Native. Nineteen were Southerners, and sixteen Northerners. At this point, it becomes obvious that border-staters in general were willing to move along Compromise lines, provided they did not have to endorse abolition of the District slave trade; that a number of Compromise-minded Northerners could not see their way clear to underwriting the Fugitive Slave Bill, and that even some moderate representatives were absent when embarrassing showdowns came. Of the sixty-three men who backed at least four of the bills, 39 were Democrats, 23 Whigs, and one was a Native. Forty-one were Northerners, and twenty-two Southerners. The contrast between Democrats and Whigs on one hand, and between Northerners and Southerners on the other, is not as extreme in this larger category as where only the twenty-eight consistent yea-voters were involved. Still, the fact that the Compromise was primarily Democratic- and North-supported is borne out by both sets of figures.

Additional evidence respecting House sentiment may be obtained from the voting on particular measures. The Texas-New Mexico bill was supported by 59 Democrats, 48 Whigs, and one Native American; it was opposed by 42 Democrats, 45 Whigs, and 10 Free Soilers. Approval for California statehood came from 57 Democrats, 82 Whigs, 10 Free Soilers, and one Native American; opposition from 45 Democrats and 11 Whigs. The Utah bill passed thanks to 61 Democrats, 35 Whigs, and one Native; ranged against it were 28 Democrats, 47 Whigs, and 10 Free Soilers. Eighty-two Democrats and 27 Whigs voted in favor of the Fugitive Slave Bill, while 16 Democrats, 50 Whigs, and 10 Free Soilers composed the minority. When 50 Democrats, 66 Whigs, seven Free Soilers, and the single Native American supported the District of Columbia bill, 44 Democrats and 15 Whigs were opposed. Recapitulating, more House Democrats than Whigs gave aid to the Texas-New Mexico, Utah, and fugitive slave portions of the Compromise by margins of 11, 26, and 55 votes. Only 25 fewer Democrats than Whigs voted affirmatively on California, and only 16 fewer on the District bill. On all five of the measures taken together, there were 309 Democratic and 258 Whig "yea" votes, as against 175 Democratic and 168 Whig "nay" votes. Not only were Democrats chiefly responsible for the passage of a majority of the five bills, but also a larger proportion of Democrats than Whigs cast affirmative ballots in the aggregate. Projections on a percentage basis are even more impressive.

When the numerical superiority of the Democrats and the Whigs' greater inclination to duck or dodge are taken into consideration, the percentage analysis reinforces conclusions contained in this article.

In some ways, those figures may seem less significant than the study of ballots on the basis of sections. Fifty-six Northern representatives and 52 Southerners voted affirmatively on Texas; 123 Northerners and 27 Southerners on California; 41 Northerners and 56 Southerners on Utah; 31 Northerners and 78 Southerners on rendition of fugitives, and 120 Northerners and four Southerners on abolishing the District slave trade.[32] The 1850 North-South division and the nature of future sectional differences thus are mirrored. It is scarcely a surprise to anyone familiar with House speeches that Southern members provided most of the votes for the Fugitive Slave Bill, or that Northerners strongly favored a free California and the ending of the trade in the District. More interesting are the nearly equal South-North strength behind the touchy Texas-New Mexico plan and the slightly less even backing for Utah Territory. The District bill was extremely unpalatable to the South.

On the Sunday morning after the "little omnibus," California, and Utah bills were passed by the House, one of James Buchanan's intimate friends privately described the "almost universal rejoicing" in Washington on Saturday night. Bonfires, processions, serenades, speeches, suppers, drinking, and cannon salutes marked that delirious September weekend. Buchanan was informed that "Mr. Foote has diarrhea from 'fruit' he ate—Douglas has headache from 'cold' &c. No one is willing to attribute his illness to drinking or frolicking—Yet only last evg. all declared it was 'a night on which it was the duty of every patriot to get drunk.' I have never before known so much excitement upon the passage of any law. There were more than 1000 persons in the procession which in turn visited Cass, Webster, Foote, Clay (out of town)[,] Douglas[,] Cobb[,] Linn Boyd &c—each of whom, excepting Clay, gave a speech. Webster it was said 'was very happy and very eloquent because he was drunk' having had a dinner party."

On Monday, President Fillmore sighed his relief to Governor Hamilton Fish of New York: " 'The long agony is over.' . . . Though these several acts are not in all respects what I could have desired, yet, I am rejoiced at their passage, and trust they will restore harmony and peace to our distracted country." Charles Francis Adams disagreed. From Quincy, Massachusetts, he wrote an Indiana representative: "The consummation of the iniquities of this most disgraceful Session of Congress is now reached—I know not how much the people will bear. My faith in their *moral* sense is very much shaken. They have been so often debauched by profligate politicians that I know not whether a case of breach of promise will lie against their seducers." The future minister to Great Britain called for a "naked history of the events of the Session," leaving interpretation of them to the judgment of "honest people." [33]

Other Americans of 1850 shared Adams's reliance on the historical approach. "Over the main entrance to this Hall," declaimed Congressman David S. Kaufman of Texas in June, "we see represented Clio, the Muse of History, with pen in hand, mounted upon the chariot of Time, taking note of the events which daily transpire

---

[32] *Cong. Globe,* 31 Cong., 1 Sess., 1764, 1772, 1776, 1807, 1837.

[33] J. M. Foltz to Buchanan, September 8, 1850, in Buchanan Papers; Millard Fillmore to Hamilton Fish, September 9, 1850, in Fish Papers (Manuscripts Division, Library of Congress); Charles F. Adams to George W. Julian, September 14, 1850, in Giddings-Julian Papers (Manuscripts Division, Library of Congress).

here. She seems to be averting her face from the page of the present!—Oh! may it not be ominous of events, *unworthy of record,* about to transpire in this sacred hall of freedom! But may our action be such that she will be enabled, out of the events of this session, to fill the brightest page of human history—that which records the triumph of a free people over themselves, their passions, and their prejudices." The mordant Senator Benton of Missouri made this classical allusion: "Homer made a mistake when he thought he was writing history, and attributed to the pale-faced lady—about as pale as the moon, and about as cold—the labor of unraveling every night what she had woven during the day; and my opinion is, that instead of writing history, he had a vision, and saw the American Senate legislating on the compromise bill." [34]

What Benton said of the Senate was at least equally true of the House. According to Robert Toombs of Georgia, writing in March, "The present Congress furnishes the worst specimens of legislators I have ever seen here, especially from the North. . . . We can have but little hope of good legislation." In May, Webster observed: "It is a strange and a melancholy fact, that not one single national speech has been made in the House of Representatives this session. Every man speaks to defend himself, and to gratify his own constituents. That is all." Concurrently, a breakup of parties was seen by the discouraged Levi Woodbury: "I am heartily sick of staying here—. The democratic party seems quite disorganized & split into fragments & I look to no satisfactory settlement of their difficulties this session if ever." From Boston, in June, Charles Sumner wrote: "The old parties seem now, more than ever, in a state of dissolution. The cry will soon be

> Mingle, mingle,
> Ye that mingle may." [35]

Despite all the Cassandra-like prophecies, which continued to the very eve of September 6, somehow the necessary votes were mustered—somehow majorities were formed. How and why? Success can be fairly explained only in terms of multiple causation.

President Taylor's death was extremely important. On July 29, a New York congressman wrote that Fillmore's agents "are here every day in the Ho of Reprs & busy." Northern Whigs "caved in" and joined the Democrats, and Charles E. Clarke told of one who "laughs over his shame & admits it." The Texas bond lobby was hard at work. The sergeant-at-arms who failed to keep lobbyists off the floor of the House on the most critical day of the year was the same functionary to whom two of the wealthiest Texas bondholders loaned large sums; he, in turn, made a practice of loaning money to congressmen. The Free Soil Representative Julian charged that "slaveholding influences are . . . buying up one after another northern men, who are as mercenary in heart as they are bankrupt in moral principle." [36]

[34] *Cong. Globe,* 31 Cong., 1 Sess., Appendix, 940, 1484.

[35] Phillips, *The Correspondence of Robert Toombs,* II, p. 188; Webster (ed.), *The Private Correspondence of Daniel Webster,* II, 369–70; Levi Woodbury to Mrs. Montgomery Blair, May 1, 1850, in Woodbury Papers (Manuscripts Division, Library of Congress); Charles Sumner to Julian, June 6, 1850, in Giddings-Julian Papers.

[36] Charles E. Clarke to Thurlow Weed, July 29, 1850, in Weed Papers (University of Rochester); Adam J. Glossbrenner to Corcoran & Riggs, September 27, 1850, in Riggs Family Papers (Manuscripts Division, Library of Congress); *Cong. Globe,* 31 Cong., 1 Sess., Appendix, 578.

Sheer weariness certainly was a cause. "Let us at least try the strength of this bill," Representative George Ashmun urged, ". . . instead of longer trying the strength of our lungs and the patience of the House and the country." "Our debates . . . have degenerated into colloquies," said Benton; they "have run down to dialogues and catechisms." Clay and Webster probably were more influential in the country at large than on Capitol Hill. Foote, in his account of the crisis, stressed the big public meetings favorable to compromise which were held "in every part of the republic" and for which Clay was primarily responsible.[37] Thus the force of public opinion was brought to bear on the legislators.

That both major parties and numerous leaders shared in some degree the credit for the Compromise is readily demonstrable. That the achievement was more Democratic than Whig is substantiated not alone by the votes but by the source of the popular sovereignty emphasis. "We stand where we stood in 1848," Stephen A. Douglas proclaimed in the Senate, and Boyd, McClernand, and other Democrats echoed the rallying cry in the House. Whigs finally flocked to the Democrats' banner when a Higher Will aided human skill. And it was with relief that representatives journeyed home to their wives and children on those October days of 1850, released from what one congressman described as "not a Hall" but "a cavern —a mammoth cave, in which men might speak in all parts, and be understood in none." [38]

[37] *Cong. Globe,* 31 Cong., 1 Sess., 1664, 1698; Henry S. Foote, *War of the Rebellion; or, Scylla and Charybdis* (New York, 1866), 147; Henry Clay to Leslie Combs, December 22, 1849, in Louisville *Journal,* July 21, 1860.

[38] *Cong. Globe,* 31 Cong., 1 Sess., 1118, 1425.

11 / The Fugitive Slave Law: A Double Paradox

Larry Gara

Although "fire-eaters" in the South attempted to prevent the Southern states from accepting the settlement, the Compromise of 1850 did quiet sectional strife. At the very least, for the moment it ended the battle over slavery in the territories.

Unfortunately, as an adjustment of general sectional differences, it had one serious flaw. One of the constituent acts that made up the Compromise package was the Fugitive Slave Law. This measure represented a drastic tightening up of an earlier enactment of 1793 that had established federal machinery for apprehending and returning runaway slaves. Southerners maintained that the earlier measure had been ineffective largely owing to the obstructive tactics of Northern state legislatures and state and local officials. The new measure plugged the loopholes in the old law and provided an effective instrument for recovering slave property even in the face of local defiance and resistance.

But the law involved the South in a paradox, as Gara notes below. For the sake of what was largely a symbolic victory—since hardly more than a few hundred slaves escaped annually and most of these were from the border states—the South proved willing to strengthen national over local power and to offend Northern opinion out of all proportion to the possible gains. And offend Northern opinion it did. The measure seemed to suspend all rights of the accused, contrary to the most venerable traditions of Anglo-Saxon jurisprudence, and threatened to dragoon every citizen into the repellent task of helping to capture and return runaway slaves.

This contempt for personal freedom and freedom of conscience was bad enough, but as applied, the law was even more provocative. Beginning with the case of James Hamlet, barely a week after the passage of the law, until the final crisis of the Union, a month seldom passed without an incident involving a clash between an irate mob of Northerners and federal officials engaged in hot pursuit of a black fugitive. Actually most Northern communities acquiesced in the work of the slave-catchers, but at times, as in 1854, when Anthony Burns was apprehended in Boston, full-scale riots in which hundreds of citizens were pitted against federal marshals, threw entire

Civil War History, X, No. 3 (September 1964), 229–240. Reprinted by permission.

cities into an uproar and led states to pass "personal liberty" laws that sought to nullify the federal measure. These in turn deeply offended Southerners who felt cheated out of the chief concession to their side of the 1850 Compromise arrangement. Although it was an essential element in restoring sectional harmony in 1850, the Fugitive Slave Act in the long run did more harm to the Union than good.

For further reading: *Larry Gara, *The Liberty Line: The Legend of the Underground Railroad* (Lexington, Ky.: The University of Kentucky Press, 1961); *Henrietta Buckmaster, *Let My People Go* (Boston, Mass.: The Beacon Press, 1959); Wilbur H. Siebert, *The Underground Railroad from Slavery to Freedom* (New York: The Macmillan Company, 1898); Charles Sydnor, "Pursuing Fugitive Slaves," *South Atlantic Quarterly*, XXVIII (April 1929); Samuel Shapiro, "The Rendition of Anthony Burns," *Journal of Negro History*, XLIV (January 1959).

The Fugitive Slave Law of 1850, as one of the compromise measures of that year, was meant to help quiet the explosive slavery issue and to remove it from the realm of political discussion.[1] Instead, the law operated to keep the slavery question alive and to assure its inclusion in the political debates of the 1850's. This irony of political life was matched by another: that a measure which substantially increased the power of the general government was demanded by a section whose spokesmen consistently relied upon the arguments of state sovereignty for the protection of their interests.[2] The law was actually as much concerned with constitutional obligations as with the problem of returning fugitive slaves. Yet by its very nature it was a concession to nationalism, and a recognition by the South that when problems exceeded the ability of states to solve them the power of the national government should be brought into play.

The fugitive slave issue became an explosive one in the Southern states after the 1842 Supreme Court decision in *Prigg* v. *Pennsylvania*. In that decision the majority of the court declared unconstitutional a Pennsylvania personal liberty law because it interfered with the federal fugitive slave act of 1793. The court held that the constitutional obligation to return fugitive slaves was exclusively a federal responsibility, and this part of the decision opened the way for a new series of personal liberty laws which usually forbade state officials from participating in the arrest or return of runaways from slavery. Since the 1793 statute depended upon enforcement by state officials, the Northern state laws rendered it largely ineffective. Not surprisingly, a demand for new federal legislation followed from Southern spokesmen.[3]

[1] This article is based, in part, upon research made possible by a grant from the Penrose Fund of the American Philosophical Society. In slightly modified form the article was read at the annual meeting of the Mississippi Valley Historical Association in Cleveland, May 1, 1964.

[2] Arthur Bestor has pointed out the constitutional significance of the doctrine of state sovereignty and asserted that in its last analysis it was a doctrine of power rather than of rights and operated to make slavery a national rather than a local institution. See Bestor, "State Sovereignty and Slavery: A Reinterpretation of Pro-slavery Constitutional Doctrine, 1846–1860," *Journal of the Illinois State Historical Society*, LIV (1961), 117–180.

[3] Henry Steele Commager (ed.), *Documents of American History* (6th ed.; New York, 1958), pp. 292–295; Julius Yanuck, "The Fugitive Slave Law and the Constitution" (Ph.D. dissertation, Columbia University, 1953), p. 21.

The issues at stake were far more important than the monetary value of any slaves who might escape north.[4] A fugitive slave recaptured was worth little as a chattel and slave dealers found such "property" difficult to sell even at greatly reduced prices. In 1850 Virginia's Senator James Murray Mason opposed a clause in the proposed fugitive slave measure which provided a possible jury trial for a fugitive in the state from which he had fled. Mason's objection was that such a requirement would prevent the master from selling the runaway immediately after recapture. Such quick sale was usually advisable, said Senator Mason, "first, on account of the example, and, secondly, because by absconding he has forfeited the confidence of his owner."[5]

The example of a successful flight was indeed a serious problem for those who claimed title to slave property. Abolitionists and slaveowners alike recognized that the influence of escapes on those remaining in slavery was considerable. In 1857 J. Miller McKim, a Philadelphia abolitionist, reported an increased number of escapes and remarked that "the tenure by which slave property is held all along our borders, is greatly weakened by these multiplying flights. Human chattels, even when but partially enlightened, constitute a very uncertain sort of possession." Dr. Robert Collins, the owner of Ellen Craft, who had fled from slavery, expressed similar sentiments. "Every slave who gains his freedom by flight from the south, and by protection from the north," he said, "presents his fellow slaves the temptation to follow in his footsteps and find the same freedom."[6]

Although fears of a mass exodus from slavery, always uppermost in the minds of the slaveholders, proved largely unfounded, Southern political leaders could not afford to ignore them. Such apprehension often seemed justified in the border states where the majority of successful escapes from slavery originated. In arguing for passage of the 1850 Fugitive Slave Law, Kentucky's Henry Clay pointed out that with the possible exception of Virginia, his state suffered more than any other "by the escape of slaves to adjoining States." He charged further that it was "at the utmost hazard and insecurity of life itself" that a Kentuckian could cross the Ohio river "and go into the interior and take back the fugitive slave to the State from which he has fled."[7]

Slaveholders tended to blame abolitionist agitation and Northern interference for slave escapes and it was in relation to this phase of the problem that the very significant constitutional issues emerged. Article IV, Section Two, of the Constitution clearly implied that fugitives from labor who escaped into another state should be delivered to their masters, though the word "slave" was carefully avoided. In light of this constitutional obligation spokesmen for the South argued that the Northern states' personal liberty laws involved a breach of faith more serious than the mobs which attempted to rescue recaptured fugitives. In 1848 a committee of the Virginia legislature expressed the sentiments of many Southern groups when it proclaimed that "the south is wholly without the benefit of that solemn constitutional guaranty

---

[4] The number and actual value of slaves who escaped north is very difficult to determine. Southern spokesmen often exaggerated the monetary loss to the South, and official census figures undoubtedly underestimated the number when they indicated that about a thousand slaves a year escaped. For a discussion of this point see Larry Gara, *The Liberty Line: The Legend of the Underground Railroad* (Lexington, 1961), pp. 36–40.

[5] *Congressional Globe*, 31 Cong., 1 sess., Appendix, pt. 1, p. 649.

[6] J. Miller McKim, "The Slave's Ultima Ratio," in *The Liberty Bell. By Friends of Freedom* (Boston, 1858), pp. 326–327; Dr. Robert Collins to J. S. Hastings, Apr. 8, 1851, Theodore Parker Scrapbook, Boston Public Library.

[7] *Congressional Globe*, 31 Cong., 1 sess., pt. 1, p. 123.

which was so sacredly pledged to it at the formation of this Union." In his Seventh of March speech Daniel Webster agreed with many of his Southern colleagues that, in the matter of the return of fugitive slaves, "the South is right, and the North is wrong." [8]

To nineteenth-century Americans such constitutional questions were more than abstractions. They were truly vital issues—issues which, when added to such other divisive questions as economic interests, moral viewpoints and sectional pride, became highly explosive. Few questions were argued more heatedly than the nature of the government and the role of supposedly sovereign states within that government in the years before the Civil War. Furthermore, the debate took place at the same time that the industrial and transportation revolutions were raising new questions in the minds of many Americans concerning the nature of representative forms of government and the issues of central versus local self-government. It is in this light that the South's interest in a more stringent fugitive slave measure assumes importance far beyond that of the slaveholder's interest in returning individual fugitives. Even though the owner of an escaped slave might not particularly care to have him back in slavery he considered it his *right* to recapture him if he wished and the Northern states had an obligation guaranteed by the Constitution to assist him. The Fugitive Slave Law of 1850 was supposed to proffer the resources of the federal government towards that end.[9]

Even those who supported the new law admitted it was severe. The pro-compromise Cincinnati *Enquirer,* for example, deplored the absence of any provision for the alleged fugitive to testify on his own behalf.[10] The law created a new official, a commissioner, with special responsibility to enforce its provisions. Alleged fugitives could be arrested with or without warrants, were given only summary hearings, and could be returned on the sworn testimony of the masters or their agents. Any citizen could be summoned to aid in the capture of a fugitive slave and interference with the law was punishable by a fine of up to one thousand dollars and six months' imprisonment.[11] Opponents of the law correctly charged that the suspected fugitive was denied all semblance of due process of law, though this had also been a feature of the earlier statute. Years later Supreme Court Justice John M. Harlan noted that "Congress omitted from it nothing which the utmost ingenuity could suggest as essential to the successful enforcement of the master's claim to recover his fugitive slave." [12]

The law was the major concession to the South in the 1850 compromise measures. Southern moderates voiced the hope that it would be accepted in the North and enforced in such a way as to quiet the complaints of the more extremist spokesmen for Southern rights. "This law alone is worth far more to the slave-holders of the

---

[8] *Report of the Select Committee Appointed under a Resolution of the House to Enquire into the Existing Legislation of Congress upon the Subject of Fugitive Slaves, and to Suggest such Additional Legislation as may be Proper* ([Richmond, 1848], Virginia General Assembly, 1848–1849 [House of Delegates], Document No. 50), p. 11; *Congressional Globe,* 31 Cong., 1 sess., p. 481.

[9] Although some abolitionists denied that the North had any constitutional obligation to return fugitive slaves, the majority of them preferred to rely on the "higher law" doctrine to justify interference with the federal statute.

[10] Cincinnati *Enquirer,* Dec. 4, 29, 1850.

[11] Commager, *Documents,* pp. 321–323.

[12] Quoted from Justice Harlan's dissent in the Civil Rights Cases, 1883, in Yanuck, "Fugitive Slave Law and the Constitution," p. 64.

South than the running of the Missouri Compromise line through California, or anything of the kind could have been," commented a Kentucky newspaper. When the bill passed the Senate a Virginia editor voiced his belief "that a mob would respect the U.S. marshal, armed with all the power of the general government," and that the law "would be efficient in securing the constitutional rights of the slave power." [13]

Overlooked by many Southerners was the fact that the new Fugitive Slave Law involved a considerable expansion of federal power. Just as interest groups in other sections were looking to the federal government for such forms of aid as protective tariffs, internal improvement projects, and free homesteads, the South was demanding that federal power be used in order to protect its interests within the Union. Indeed, many Southern leaders insisted that strict enforcement of the Fugitive Slave Law should be a test of the North's sincerity in relation to its constitutional obligations. Missouri's Governor Austin A. King observed that "all assaults upon that law—all efforts to prevent its execution—all movements to deprive the South of its benefits, . . . are aimed directly at the constitution, and consequently at the perpetuity of the Union." A St. Louis editor asserted that

> If there be not the moral power in the free States to maintain that law—if there be not the moral and physical power in the General Government to enforce it, . . . then will the Southern States be compelled, in defence of their rights, . . . to dissolve all connection with the Union, and follow, alone, such destiny as their own courage, and genius, and trust in God, shall mark out for them.[14]

Nevertheless, at least a few Southern spokesmen were wary of the South's calling upon the physical power of the general government to protect its interests, and saw in the law a dangerous admission of national supremacy. "If Congress can legislate at all between the master and slave in a State, where can its power be stayed?" asked a group of delegates to a Southern convention. "It can abolish slavery in the States," they warned.[15] The extremist Charleston *Mercury* deplored the new power assumed by Congress in the law, and went so far as to support a Massachusetts statute which clashed directly with the federal measure. According to the *Mercury*, the Fugitive Slave Law demonstrated that in contesting an aggressive adversary "we lose the landmarks of principle—to obtain an illusive triumph, we press the Government to assume a power not confirmed by the instrument of its creation. . . ." The Charleston *Standard* maintained that the matter of returning fugitives involved a compact between sovereign states, and had nothing to do with Congress. "And instead of clinging to this provision of the compromise act as a compensation for its other most objectionable features," commented the editor, "it might be well for us to consider whether we have not, in fact, made a concession more fatal to our separate and distinct political existence, than even the founders of the Constitution themselves were prepared to make." [16]

Though some extremist politicians and writers may have been regarded as pur-

---

[13] Frankfort (Ky.) *Commonwealth*, Oct. 8, 1850; Richmond *Enquirer*, Aug. 30, 1850.

[14] St. Louis *Daily Union*, Jan. 4, 1851; St. Louis *Intelligencer*, Oct. 26, 1850.

[15] *Address to the People of Maryland, Virginia, North Carolina, South Carolina, Georgia, Florida, Alabama, Tennessee, Kentucky, Louisiana, Texas, Missouri, Mississippi, and Arkansas* (n.p., n.d.).

[16] New York *National Anti-Slavery Standard*, Oct. 6, 1855, quoting the Charleston *Mercury*; Salem (Ohio) *Anti-Slavery Bugle*, Dec. 24, 1853, quoting the Charleston *Standard*.

veyors of gloom by their contemporaries, they were nearer the truth than their more moderate countrymen. Ultimately, the Fugitive Slave Law, by recharging the highly emotional slavery debate, helped to bring on the Civil War with its eventual victory for national unification. It was a result not anticipated by the architects of the compromise whose Northern and Southern supporters hailed the statute as a triumph for moderation and pro-Union sentiments which would stifle extremism everywhere. When the measure passed the Senate the Richmond *Enquirer* commented that its passage by a strong vote "should naturally have the effect of inducing a better feeling and aiding the adjustment of the alarming difficulty." In the spring of 1851 a Buffalo newspaper noted that opposition had nearly subsided "except in purely Abolition quarters, and we shall soon see the Adjustment Measures, as a whole, not merely acquiesced in, but heartily sustained all over the country." A year after the law went into effect Senator Stephen A. Douglas asserted that "the whole country is acquiescing in the compromise measures—everywhere, North and South. Nobody proposes to repeal or disturb them." [17]

Those who made such sanguine predictions had to overlook many signs which indicated quite a different future from that prophesied by Senator Douglas. Regarded in the abstract, and considering the terrible alternatives of disruption or civil conflict, the compromise as a whole undoubtedly received the support of a majority of the people. But the Fugitive Slave Law was another matter. It enabled the abolitionists once again to link their cause with that of civil liberties and to reach large numbers of people untouched by the purer antislavery arguments. Southerners considered it their inalienable right to have runaway slaves returned, but Northerners viewed the demand as an affront to their pride. Returning men to slavery was nasty business and a measure which attempted to require it was very much out of step with public opinion in the states where slavery itself did not exist. Some Southern leaders recognized the problem. Early in 1850, before the passage of the law, Senator Jefferson Davis commented, "I feel that the law will be a dead letter in any State where the popular opinion is opposed to such rendition." Mississippi's Congressman Jacob Thompson also believed that the new statute would "prove a mere mockery." He thought the older law was "full and strong enough, if the States of the North would comply, or were disposed to comply with their constitutional obligations." [18]

A segment of Northern press reaction to the law confirmed Congressman Thompson's fears. An Ohio editor lamented that "We are all Slave-Catchers," pointing out that all were now compelled by law to render aid to the *"legal* kidnappers." A Massachusetts paper could find no language strong enough "to express the contempt with which we regard the miserable-tools, sycophants and traitors whose votes have brought about this result." Even the moderate New York *Courier and Enquirer* predicted that the measure "will not substantially aid the recovery of fugitive slaves, while it will deepen and strengthen the prevalent feeling upon that subject." [19]

The abolitionists capitalized upon and widened the already strong Northern sentiment against returning fugitives to slavery. In countless meetings they passed resolutions promising resistance to the law and solemnly vowed that as individuals, as Mil-

[17] Richmond *Enquirer,* Aug. 30, 1850; Wilmington *Delaware State Journal,* Mar. 25, 1851, quoting the Buffalo *Commercial Advertiser;* Stephen A. Douglas, *Remarks of Mr. Douglas of Illinois . . . Delivered in the Senate of the United States, December 23, 1851* (Washington, 1851), pp. 14–15.

[18] *Congressional Globe,* 31 Cong., 1 sess., Appendix, pt. 1, pp. 150, 660.

[19] Press comments quoted in Salem *Anti-Slavery Bugle,* Oct. 5, 1850.

waukee's Sherman M. Booth expressed it, they would "trample this law under foot, at the first opportunity." [20] They made certain that any fugitive slave incident was widely publicized through demonstrations, special meetings, and publications. They petitioned for the law's repeal and organized special vigilance committees to prevent its successful enforcement. They usually referred to the law in such terms as "the bloodhound bill," "the infamous law," the "slave-catching bill," or the "enactment of hell."

The abolitionists quickly recognized that the "infamous law" had a significance far greater than the relatively small number of fugitive slaves it was designed to return. In 1853 the Massachusetts Anti-Slavery Society reported that events of the previous year had confirmed that the fugitive slave act "was but an electioneering trick, not designed nor expected to be of material advantage to the Slaveholders." It was a bid for Southern votes and "was meant rather as a homage to the Slave Power than as a Remedy from which intelligent Slaveholders hoped for much relief from the flight to which this form of riches was peculiarly exposed." The report noted that though the number of escapes from slavery had increased, there had been few arrests. William Jay pointed out that in a period of two years and nine months, not fifty slaves had been recovered under the act, an average of less than eighteen slaves a year. "Poor compensation this to the slaveholders," he concluded, "for making themselves a bye-word, a proverb, a reproach to Christendom—for giving a new and mighty impulse for abolition. . . ." [21]

In light of the number of fugitive slaves remanded under the law, it was indeed poor compensation for the slaveholders. In a decade of enforcement only about two hundred escaped slaves were returned south. Despite the lack of procedural legal protection for the fugitives, most government officials were scrupulous in preventing the use of the law to enslave Negroes not actually named in the warrants. About thirty persons were arrested as alleged fugitives and later released on the basis of mistaken identity.[22] Nevertheless, one abolition newspaper charged that the only ones to benefit from the law were the professional slave-catchers who, after 1850, were able "to do openly, what they were before compelled to do in the dark." Abolitionists also contended that the law encouraged the kidnaping of free Negroes and "built up a regular NORTHERN SLAVE TRADE" which threatened "to victimize every person in whom a suspicion of African blood" existed, and would assuredly not stop with them.[23]

Pride in Northern concepts of civil liberties, along with a justified concern for protecting free Negroes from being taken into slavery, led a number of Northern states to enact a new series of personal liberty laws. On the surface the laws provided legal protection for free Negroes but they were also designed to impede the enforcement of the federal statute. Many lengthy legal disputes resulted when state officials, concerned with the enforcement of the personal liberty laws, clashed with federal officials trying to enforce the Fugitive Slave Law. In 1854 Wisconsin's supreme court went so far as to declare the federal law unconstitutional. The personal liberty laws were based upon the same concept of state sovereignty which Southern spokesmen were

[20] Milwaukee *Daily Free Democrat*, Oct. 5, 1850.

[21] *Twenty-first Annual Report Presented to the Massachusetts Anti-Slavery Society, by Its Board of Managers, January 26, 1853* (Boston, 1853), p. 43; William Jay, "The Fugitive Slave Act," in Julia Griffiths (ed.), *Autographs for Freedom* (Auburn and Rochester, 1854), p. 39.

[22] Samuel May, Jr., *The Fugitive Slave Law and Its Victims* (Anti-Slavery Tracts, n.s. no. 15, rev. and enlarged ed.; New York, 1861).

[23] Chicago *Western Citizen*, Jan. 7, 1851; May, *Fugitive Slave Law*, p. 55.

using for other purposes. When discussing such a proposed bill in the New York assembly, Gerrit Smith argued that the time had come "for New York, in her sovereign capacity, to assert her independence as a sovereign State, and, by positive enactment, pass such laws as shall protect all persons coming within her jurisdiction."[24]

The new personal liberty laws were political manifestations of growing anti-Southern sentiment in the Northern states. They were a reaction to a measure which a group of abolitionists characterized as "a reproduction, on the soil of Massachusetts, New York, and Ohio, of the most diabolical features of the slave code, and that, too under the Federal authority." Although very few people actually were called upon to help send fugitives back into slavery, the law brought the issue home in a way that nothing else had done. Numerous ministers used it to further antislavery doctrine. The Reverend B. M. Hall told his congregation that "it is the duty of every Christian citizen to obey God rather than man," and to resist peacefully the execution of "this unjust and unconstitutional law." A New England minister likened closing one's door to the fugitive slave to shutting out "your Saviour himself." He told his congregation that were a fugitive to come to him he would defy the authorities and render assistance, urging them to do the same, "and trust God with the result." After his sermon one Sunday a minister in Painesville, Ohio, announced that five fugitive slaves, including two infants, had just arrived and needed money for their journey to Canada. Anyone contributing to the fund, he warned dramatically, would be liable to the penalties of the Fugitive Slave Law. The congregation promptly gave thirty dollars. The local newspaper commented: "Heartless politicians and 'lower law' priests will soon learn that there is a higher law than man-enslaving, woman-whipping, baby-stealing and God-defying enactments."[25]

Such strong reactions were typical. No other issue related to slavery stirred people in quite the same way. From time to time abolitionists had aroused a certain amount of popular support for their cause by associating it with the right of petition or some other issue. Yet for the most part the slavery question remained an abstraction until fugitive slave incidents brought it into the realm of the emotions. A frightened, shivering fugitive aroused a sympathetic response even from those who theoretically accepted the compromise measures. Some of the abolitionists were well aware of the significance of the fugitive issue. "There are only a few, unfortunately," said J. Miller McKim, "who can understand an abstract idea or comprehend a general principle. . . . To make our anti-slavery idea fully understood we must put legs on it."[26]

Abolitionists called attention to arrests under the law, and special vigilance committees worked overtime to prevent rendition when possible, and to publicize those that could not be prevented. They sometimes arranged for the purchase of fugitives who had been captured and returned to slavery. Anthony Burns and other former slaves frequently spoke to antislavery audiences and attracted large numbers of listeners from outside the ranks of the dedicated abolitionists. Such incidents as the rescue in 1851 of William Henry, or "Jerry," from his captors in Syracuse provided the occasion for special protest meetings. The complicated legal struggle growing out

[24] New York *National Anti-Slavery Standard*, Apr. 7, 1860.

[25] "Address of the Convention of Radical Political Abolitionists," in *Proceedings of the Convention . . . Held at Syracuse, New York, June 26th, 27th, and 28th, 1855* (New York, 1856), pp. 31–32; B. M. Hall, *The Fugitive Slave Law. A Sermon* (Schenectady, 1850), pp. 18–19; Kazlitt Arvine, *Our Duty to the Fugitive Slave* (Boston, 1850), pp. 20–21; New York *National Anti-Slavery Standard*, Oct. 15, 1852.

[26] J. Miller McKim to Mrs. Chapman, Dec. 11, 1857, Weston Papers, Boston Public Library.

of the government's unsuccessful attempt to punish the rescuers aroused additional interest. Following a large anti-Fugitive Slave Law convention, and while the legal cases were still pending, Samuel J. May reported that

> The sentiment of our City and County is nobly right on the question which the rescue has raised. Men that I supposed cared not at all for the enslavement of our colored countrymen, have taken pains to express to me their detestation of the attempt to rob Jerry of his liberty.

To keep the issue alive in Syracuse abolitionists annually celebrated the Jerry rescue with as much fanfare as they could muster.[27]

Rescues of fugitive slaves provided exciting moments, and those who participated in one or two such affairs or assisted only a few fugitive slaves along their way to Canada added their emotional experiences to an already widespread antislavery commitment in the North. Levi Coffin and other abolitionist veterans recalled in later years the effectiveness of the presence of a fugitive slave in arousing a sympathetic response. Oftentimes the humanitarian reaction was not consciously antislavery but rather another example of practical behavior overriding abstract principles.

Uncle Tom's Cabin also helped "put legs" on the antislavery principles. The novel was a reaction to the Fugitive Slave Law and, according to a contemporary commentator, it "served its purpose. What truth could not accomplish, fiction did, and Harriet Beecher Stowe has had the satisfaction of throwing a firebrand into the world, which has kept up a furious blaze ever since." The demand for the novel seemed unlimited and its sales quickly broke all previous records for fiction. By personifying various aspects of slavery and creating stereotyped characters, Mrs. Stowe touched the emotions of millions of readers. Numerous artists found it profitable to make pictorial reproductions and statues of the novel's characters. In 1853 the *Liberator* commented that in Boston and the larger towns, people had become "accustomed to see Uncle Toms, Evas and Topseys without number, in engravings of various degrees of merit and price." [28]

Numerous dramatic troups added *Uncle Tom's Cabin* to their repertoires and thus brought the message to many who had not read the book. One of these productions was playing in Milwaukee at the time that Sherman M. Booth was being held by United States authorities for rescuing Joshua Glover, a fugitive slave. Booth's newspaper, the *Daily Free Democrat,* called attention to the fact that the drama was "preaching up the old Patrick Henry Doctrine of Liberty or Death—the very doctrine carried out by the people at the Court-House in rescuing Glover." It noted that the play justified a fugitive's shooting down slave-catchers rather than return to slavery, and suggested that the approving audience should be arrested at once and tried for riot. "They are in the same category with us," continued the editorial, "and when the Judge has disposed of them he should get up an indictment against Human Nature, which is a Great Incendiary—always taking the part of the oppressed." [29]

The Booth case succeeded in calling attention to the harsh law and gave new

[27] Samuel J. May to Charlotte G. Coffin, Oct. 15, 1851, William Lloyd Garrison Papers, Boston Public Library; New York *National Anti-Slavery Standard,* Sept. 16, 1852.

[28] F. G. de Fontaine, *American Abolitionism, from 1787 to 1861. A Compendium of Historical Facts, Embracing Legislation in Congress and Agitation without* (New York, 1861); John Herbert Nelson, *The Negro Character in American Literature* (Bulletin of the University of Kansas Humanistic Studies, vol. IV, no. 1; Lawrence, 1926); Boston *Liberator,* Dec. 23, 1853.

[29] Milwaukee *Daily Free Democrat,* Mar. 16, 1854.

weight to the abolitionist view of events. "The object of this prosecution is to establish the law of Slavery and kidnapping on the free soil of Wisconsin," commented Booth's paper, "and to make this a Slave State. . . . The people of this State are to be taught that they are the slaves of the Slave Power." Although the government prosecuted only about a dozen cases under the Fugitive Slave Law, each of them contributed to a growing popular reaction against enforcement. The court cases also inspired protest demonstrations, special publications, and countless petitions. According to an antislavery society report, the Oberlin-Wellington rescue and the prosecutions growing out of it "stimulated discussion, roused popular feeling, extended and deepened the abhorrence felt toward Slave-Catching . . . and called forth many an emphatic utterance of that sentiment from pulpit, and press, and public meeting." [30]

The renditions, rescues of arrested fugitives, and prosecutions played a major role in bringing the whole slavery question home to the people of the free states. When combined with such other related issues as the Nebraska Bill and slavery in the territories, the Brooks-Sumner affair, and the troubles in Kansas, the Fugitive Slave Law added fuel to a fire which was burning the remaining ties between the sections. Many moderates in the North who had supported the 1850 compromise measures found themselves unable to support the law and what it came to mean. It became the abolitionists' most powerful propaganda weapon and reopened the whole slavery question with an intensity previously unknown.

For those Southerners who had demanded the law with its enlarged concept of national power, nothing was gained. Instead of strengthening it weakened the position of the southern Unionists who had supported it. Few slaves were returned and often those few renditions required considerable outlays of time and money. The return of Anthony Burns cost a total of more than $20,000, which caused a Virginia editor to comment that "under the Massachusetts style of doing business, it is a law without a sanction, and, except for the mere principle which it asserts, it is not worth a copper to the South." [31] By 1860 it was clear that the principle it asserted was also worthless.

---

[30] Ibid.; The Anti-Slavery History of the John Brown Year; Being the Twenty-Seventh Annual Report of the American Anti-Slavery Society (New York, 1861), p. 71.

[31] New York National Anti-Slavery Standard, July 21, 1855, quoting the Petersburg (Va.) Intelligencer.

12 / The Kansas-Nebraska Act: A Century of Historiography

Roy F. Nichols

Whatever the failings of the Fugitive Slave Act, until 1854 the territorial question seemed settled. Then Senator Stephen Douglas blundered. Driven by a combination of presidential fever, a desire to strengthen the Democratic Party, and concern for Chicago real estate and for Western development, the "Little Giant" introduced a bill in January 1854 to organize the Platte country, to the west of Missouri and Iowa, into a territory. In the new region the slavery issue would be decided by "the decision of the people residing therein, through their appropriate representatives." This was "popular sovereignty," a principle that was to become increasingly identified with Douglas' effort to find a compromise formula to decide whether new territories would be free or slave. The scheme not only seemed like a reasonable adjustment of sectional differences, it also appealed to American respect for grass-roots democracy. Moreover, it had already been successfully applied to a part of the Mexican Cession under the 1850 Compromise. But whatever its merits, it suspended the Missouri Compromise in the Platte country, effectively opening that region to the possible intrusion of slavery.

In the following selection, Roy F. Nichols discusses how the Kansas-Nebraska Bill evolved and how events, particularly party necessities and circumstances, pushed Douglas and its other partisans along a course they had not intended. He also gives us a fine, brief summary of the voluminous literature of the bill's origin and of Douglas' motives.

For further reading: Frank Hodder, "The Railroad Background of the Kansas-Nebraska Act," *Mississippi Valley Historical Review*, XII (June 1925); James C. Malin, *The Nebraska Question, 1852–1854* (Lawrence, Kansas, 1953); *Paul W. Gates, *Fifty Million Acres: Conflicts Over Kansas Land Policy, 1854–1890* (Ithaca, N. Y.: Cornell University Press, 1954); Alice Nichols, *Bleeding Kansas* (New York: Oxford University Press, 1954); Robert R. Russel, "The Issues in the Congressional Struggle Over the Kansas-Nebraska Bill, 1854," *Journal of Southern History*, XXIX (May 1963).

Mississippi Valley Historical Review, XLIII, No. 2 (September 1956), 187–212. Reprinted by permission.

The process of federal lawmaking can be very intricate, and correspondingly baffling to the historian. Few acts of Congress have had a passage more difficult to trace accurately than that of Kansas-Nebraska fame, and few have received more attention from historians. The historiography of the measure has been the more difficult because of the sectional conflict in which it was a significant episode. Historical thinking about it has been colored by the emotional overtones produced by the historians, conditioned by their several geographical and cultural backgrounds. Despite the hundred years which have elapsed since the episode occurred, historians are still of several minds about it and there is cause to doubt whether the full story has yet been told. A century of historiography has produced an extensive bibliography, a variety of interpretations, much argument, and certain questions yet unanswered.[1]

Historical thinking and writing about the bill began very shortly after its enactment. The subsequent struggle to make the territory of Kansas into a state, and the political fortunes of Senator Stephen A. Douglas, the sponsor of the bill, called forth frequent reference to the circumstances of its passage in various famous political campaigns involving his senatorial and presidential ambitions.[2] Two very divergent views concerning the nature of the bill and the motivation of its supporters became current almost immediately. The friends of Douglas described the bill in terms of his own committee report as designed to advance "certain great principles, which would not only furnish adequate remedies for existing evils, but, in all time to come, avoid the perils of similar agitation, by withdrawing the question of slavery from the halls of Congress and the political arena, committing it to the arbitration of those who were immediately interested in, and alone responsible for, its consequences." [3] Another and much more numerous company, including Douglas' foes, found something akin to their views in "An Appeal of the Independent Democrats in Congress," which appeared twenty days after Douglas presented his own statement. These opponents of the measure thundered forth in print: "We arraign this bill as a gross violation of a sacred pledge; as a criminal betrayal of precious rights; as part and parcel of an atrocious plot." [4]

These views, so wide apart in their implications, provided the ideas basic to the two schools of thought which have been dominant ever since, and much of what has been written on the subject has been conditioned either by one of these ideas or by the other. The second view was almost the only one prevalent in the historical literature which appeared during the Civil War. This writing was highly colored by the conflict and when the popular authors who were chronicling the battles and campaigns alluded to the Act they generally characterized it as a move of southern aggression, part of the plot, a thing which was evil, and by statement or implication Douglas was an evildoer.[5]

---

[1] This article is a revised version of a paper which was presented at a luncheon session of the annual meeting of the Mississippi Valley Historical Association in St. Louis on April 29, 1955.

[2] The Douglas campaign biographies of 1860 made some of the earliest contributions to the historiography of the bill. A Member of the Western Bar [Henry M. Flint], *Life and Speeches of Stephen A. Douglas* (New York, 1860); James W. Sheahan, *Life of Stephen A. Douglas* (New York, 1860).

[3] *Senate Reports,* 33 Cong., 1 Sess., No. 15.

[4] *Cong. Globe,* 33 Cong., 1 Sess., 281.

[5] Thomas J. Pressly, *Americans Interpret Their Civil War* (Princeton, 1954), *passim* and bibliography. See particularly 142 n., 263–64, 298, 315.

The next phase of the historiography of the bill was supplied by writers of reminiscences, such as Joshua R. Giddings, Ohio congressman, Horace Greeley, famous editor of the New York *Tribune,* and Henry S. Foote, sometime senator from Mississippi. They supplied some scattered details designed to belittle Douglas and to demonstrate the idea of a southern conspiracy. Practically all of this writing was northern in origin and sympathy.[6] This disparagement of Douglas was soon followed by an effort on the part of his brother-in-law to glorify his leadership in the matter. In a book consisting of a series of statements which he said had been dictated to him by the Senator, J. Madison Cutts presented an extended account of Douglas' efforts to open Nebraska, pointing out the pressure of the population on the frontier and the absolute necessity of making concessions to southern legislators who had the power of blocking the measure indefinitely. Douglas was said to have boasted: "I passed the Kansas-Nebraska Act myself. I had the authority and power of a dictator throughout the whole controversy in both houses. The speeches were nothing. It was the marshaling and directing of men and guarding from attacks, and with a ceaseless vigilance preventing surprise."[7]

The climax of this phase of the bill's historiography came with the publication, beginning in 1872, of the *History of the Rise and Fall of the Slave Power in America,* written by Henry Wilson, vice-president under Grant and formerly a leading Free-Soiler. Wilson made an extensive effort to gather facts by consulting his contemporaries. His own viewpoint was well illustrated by the title of his work and by the following quotation:

> No event in the progress of the great conflict stands out more prominently than the abrogation of the Compromise of 1820. As both effect and cause it defies competition and almost comparison with any single measure of the long series of aggressions of the Slave Power. . . . No single act of the Slave Power ever spread greater consternation, produced more lasting results upon the popular mind, or did so much to arouse the North and to convince the people of its desperate character.[8]

Thus the verdict of these participants—practically all of them pro-Union and antislavery—as they penned their memoirs was largely in agreement with the theory that there had been a conspiracy against the best interests of the nation, though there was no clear outline of who had conspired or how. And there was no agreement as to the part Douglas had played or about his motivation. Was he a statesman, a conspirator, or a tool?[9]

---

[6] Joshua R. Giddings, *History of the Rebellion, Its Authors and Causes* (New York, 1864), 364; Horace Greeley, *The American Conflict* (2 vols., Hartford, 1864–1866), I, 224; Henry S. Foote, *War of the Rebellion* (New York, 1866), 182–84, and *Casket of Reminiscences* (Washington, 1874), 93. Of the very slight amount produced by southern writers, only Alexander H. Stephens, *A Constitutional View of the Late War between the States* (2 vols., Philadelphia, 1868–1870), was much noticed by historians. Stephens accepted Douglas' interpretation of his work and motives. The foes of the Compromise of 1850 were the aggressors. *Ibid.,* II, 241–57.

[7] J. Madison Cutts, *A Brief Treatise upon Constitutional and Party Questions* (New York, 1866), 122.

[8] Henry Wilson, *History of the Rise and Fall of the Slave Power in America* (3 vols., Boston, 1872–1877), II, 378.

[9] Other accounts by participants continued to appear: Jefferson Davis, *The Rise and Fall of the Confederate Government* (2 vols., New York, 1881); William Cullen Bryant and Sydney H. Gay, *Popular History of the United States* (4 vols., New York, 1876–1881); James G. Blaine,

At this point a new element entered into the historiography of the bill. This was provided by men who had not participated in the scenes of conflict, but who were now coming forward to examine the records and write from them in a fashion which began to be called scientific. The first of these was a trained German historian, Professor Hermann E. von Holst of the University of Freiburg. During political exile in the United States he had begun thinking about its history and when he returned to Germany he wrote a multi-volume work. That which included the Kansas-Nebraska episode appeared in English in 1885 and in it he devoted some two hundred pages to a very detailed account of the Act.[10] He had read little but the official documents, yet he was the only writer so far to grasp the influence of the complexities of American politics upon the shaping of the bill. Nevertheless, he was content with the simple conclusion natural to a liberal who hated slavery, that the rivalry of Douglas and Pierce for southern support for the presidency was the prime motivation.[11] At the same time, he effectively destroyed the constitutional pretensions of Douglas' arguments,[12] though he failed to grasp the realistic value of the Senator's planning. His work did much to strengthen the current northern or Republican theory of an evil thing done at the behest of the slave power.

While von Holst's volumes were appearing, two wealthy men, turned historians, were engrossed in similarly extensive works. In 1891, the fifth volume of James Schouler's *History of the United States under the Constitution* appeared,[13] and in the next year James Ford Rhodes began the publication of his *History of the United States from the Compromise of 1850*. Both used much more source material than did von Holst but they reached much the same conclusion. The Kansas-Nebraska bill was the reprehensible creation of Douglas, the demagogic aspirant for the presidency.[14]

Hardly had this canon of Republican interpretation been "scientifically" established by this trio of historians when a measure of reaction set in and efforts were made in the direction of the rehabilitation of Douglas. In 1897, Professor John W. Burgess of Columbia University published a volume entitled *The Middle Period*, which covered the Kansas-Nebraska situation. Professor Burgess was a Tennessee Unionist, veteran of the Civil War. He had the prevailing German concepts of scientific history and was a nationalistic liberal. He was closely associated with his most brilliant student, William A. Dunning, whose father had been a war Democrat. Burgess pictured Douglas as a sincere representative of the West sharing with his

---

Twenty Years of Congress (2 vols., Norwich, Conn., 1884–1886); John A. Logan, *The Great Conspiracy* (New York, 1885); Samuel S. Cox, *Three Decades of Federal Legislation* (Providence, 1885); John G. Nicolay and John Hay, *Abraham Lincoln: A History* (10 vols., New York, 1890); Varina H. Davis, *Jefferson Davis: A Memoir* (2 vols., New York, 1890); Mrs. Archibald Dixon, *True History of the Missouri Compromise and Its Repeal* (Cincinnati, 1898).

[10] Hermann E. von Holst, *Constitutional and Political History of the United States* (7 vols., Chicago, 1876–1892), IV, 256–461.

[11] *Ibid.*, 314.

[12] *Ibid.*, 375–402.

[13] James Schouler, *History of the United States of America under the Constitution* (7 vols., Boston, 1880–1913), VI, 285.

[14] James Ford Rhodes, *History of the United States from the Compromise of 1850* (7 vols., New York, 1892–1906), I, 420–98. For Rhodes's motivation see Frank H. Hodder, "Propaganda as a Source of American History," *Mississippi Valley Historical Review* (Cedar Rapids), IX (June, 1922), 3–18.

fellow citizens a keen sense of the importance of local autonomy. He defended him for declaring his principles and pointed out that men often identify themselves and their ambitions with principles which they believe essential for the peace and welfare of their country.[15]

At the turn of the century, younger scholars, products of the burgeoning graduate schools, began to take up the problem. A young Columbia graduate student, Allen Johnson, had been within the range of Burgess's influence although taking his doctorate in European history. When he settled down to teach in Grinnell College, Iowa, he chose as his next work a study of Stephen A. Douglas, who had been waiting forty years for a scholarly and comprehensive biographer. Johnson explored vigorously, turned up a certain amount of new source material including what few fragments the Douglas family then seemed to have preserved, and produced a scholarly, well-written biography which appeared in 1908.

His was a well-rounded account of Douglas and the bill. He had a more comprehensive grasp of the part which the needs of the West played in creating this measure. He discounted the immediate presidential ambitions of Douglas and pictured him as a sincere believer in popular sovereignty as the solution of the problem of the peaceable opening up of new territories. His effort to maintain a judicial attitude is illustrated by his verdict that the effort of the Senator to repeal the Missouri Compromise by "subtle" indirection was the "device of a shifty politician." Douglas, nevertheless, was the dominant figure, the resourceful statesman to whom the responsibility for the measure was due.[16]

In the next year after the publication of Johnson's *Douglas*, P. Orman Ray's Cornell doctoral dissertation, *The Repeal of the Missouri Compromise*, was published.[17] This work represented an intensive, unprejudiced recanvass of the evidence and the discovery of significant new material. Ray challenged the theory of Douglas' exclusive agency and emphasized the idea suggested by the memoir writers and von Holst that various political situations, particularly the bitterness of Missouri local politics, were the controlling factors.[18] As some reviewers of this book pointed out, probably Ray claimed too much, the evidence which he marshaled was not altogether conclusive, the Missouri question was only one of a series of factors in a complex situation.[19]

One of the reviewers was Professor Frank H. Hodder of the University of Kansas. He had been long at work on the history of the bill, in fact as early as 1899 he had published an almost unnoticed article defending Douglas as a sincere statesman

---

[15] John W. Burgess, *The Middle Period, 1817–1858* (New York, 1897).

[16] Allen Johnson, *Stephen A. Douglas* (New York, 1908).

[17] P. Orman Ray, *The Repeal of the Missouri Compromise* (Cleveland, 1909).

[18] John A. Parker, "The Secret History of the Kansas-Nebraska Bill," *National Quarterly Review* (New York), XLI (July, 1880), 105–18, and reprinted as a pamphlet under the title, *The Missing Link. . . . What Led to the War, or the Secret History of the Kansas-Nebraska Act*, with an introductory note by Waldorf H. Phillips (Washington, 1886). John A. Parker to Lyon G. Tyler, June 1, 1889, Tyler Papers (Division of Manuscripts, Library of Congress). Parker was clerk to the House Judiciary Committee in 1854. Parker to James Buchanan, March 29, 1854, Buchanan Papers (Historical Society of Pennsylvania). See also *A Statement of Facts and a Few Suggestions in Review of Political Action in Missouri* (n. p., 1856).

[19] The principal reviews of Ray's book were by Allen Johnson, *American Historical Review* (New York), XIV (July, 1909), 835; by Frank H. Hodder, *Dial* (Chicago), XLVII (September 1, 1909), 120; and by William A. Dunning, *Political Science Quarterly* (New York), XXIV (September, 1909), 527.

laboring for western development. Hodder was developing a theory regarding the bill, which he presented before the State Historical Society of Wisconsin in 1912.[20]

Hodder's perspective was much broader than Ray's and he played up an idea which he had not advanced in his earlier article. He was impressed by the part played in western development by railroad promoters, particularly those seeking to construct a line to the Pacific.[21] It was Hodder's conclusion that the chief interest at work in opening up Nebraska was the promoters' desire to secure a right of way for this transcontinental line. He saw Douglas as the railroad promoter motivated by this role rather than by his political ambitions. Though he had some complimentary things to say about Ray's work, he brusquely dismissed his main thesis as "untenable."

Ray replied at the annual meeting of the American Historical Association in 1914 by describing Hodder's thesis as unproven and untenable.[22] Some years later, Hodder devoted his presidential address before the Mississippi Valley Historical Association, in 1925, to providing further evidence of Douglas' railroad interest.[23]

While we applaud the zeal of these protagonists we may also comment on the inflexibility which controversy develops. The truth probably would have been more nearly attained had each recognized that the other had made a contribution and had they united their points of view. This, in fact, was done by Albert J. Beveridge in his *Abraham Lincoln* in 1928. In this fragment in which interestingly enough Douglas was the hero, Beveridge, in an elaborate account of the Kansas-Nebraska bill, re-canvassed all the evidence and brought back Douglas as the glamorous leader dealing with and influenced by the combination of forces developed by Hodder and Ray.[24]

The 1930's produced at least two additions to the growing corpus of analysis and interpretation. The author of this essay and George Fort Milton re-examined the roles of two of the prominent figures in the action, Franklin Pierce and Stephen A. Douglas. Since the work of Henry Wilson, various allusions had been made to the part played by the President under pressure either of ambition or of expediency. Not until the publication of *Franklin Pierce* in 1931 had any comprehensive attempt been made to explain the President's situation and the practical motivation which led him to make the bill an administration measure. The factional strife in the Democratic party was explored, and with it the President's need of regaining the support of important elements in his party, particularly in the Senate. The success of his administration depended upon congressional endorsement of his patronage program, his domestic legislative plans, and particularly of his ambitious foreign policy. Without the support of the Senate leaders he would be helpless and discredited. Therefore, when the leading bloc of senators demanded his endorsement of the measure, he felt he must acquiesce.[25]

[20] Frank H. Hodder, "Stephen A. Douglas," *Chautauquan* (Meadville, N. Y.), XXIX (August, 1899), 432–37, reprinted in *Kansas Historical Quarterly* (Topeka), VIII (August, 1939), 227–37; Hodder, "The Genesis of the Kansas-Nebraska Act," State Historical Society of Wisconsin, *Proceedings*, 1912 (Madison), 69–86. See also James C. Malin, "Frank Heywood Hodder, 1860–1935," *Kansas Historical Quarterly*, V (May, 1936), 115–21.

[21] This idea had been discussed and discarded by Ray. See *Repeal of the Missouri Compromise*, 237–42.

[22] Ray, "The Genesis of the Kansas-Nebraska Act," American Historical Association, *Annual Report*, 1914 (2 vols., Washington, 1916), I, 259–80.

[23] Hodder, "The Railroad Background of the Kansas-Nebraska Act," *Mississippi Valley Historical Review*, XII (June, 1925), 3–22.

[24] Albert J. Beveridge, *Abraham Lincoln, 1809–1858* (4 vols., Boston, 1928), III, 165–217.

[25] Roy F. Nichols, *Franklin Pierce* (Philadelphia, 1931); Wilson, *Rise and Fall of the Slave*

George Fort Milton, in the meantime, had conceived of a comprehensive trilogy of volumes to embrace the whole period from 1850 to 1869. He had finished the last one, *The Age of Hate*, and he then turned to the first. As in the last he had chosen a central figure, Andrew Johnson, so in the first he would concentrate on Douglas. He turned to the problem with great ingenuity and enterprise and shortly discovered what had always been thought to be lost, namely, the papers of Douglas in great quantity. Mining this great treasure and working indefatigably in repositories all over the land he produced a very comprehensive biography. In his consideration of the Kansas-Nebraska bill, he recognized the inadequacy of simple explanations of complex phenomena and brought together in a comprehensive synthesis the fruits of his own labors and of those of his many predecessors. He showed calm judgment and capacity to evaluate many of the controversial factors in the situation. For much of Douglas' career, his work will be definitive. But he did not deal with the chief historiographical problem connected with Kansas-Nebraska, namely, the influences, external and internal, which produced the various drafts of the bill; nor did he provide a systematic reconstruction of what Douglas personally went through in his connection with the legislative process which produced the law. To Milton, Douglas more than ever was the dominant courageous statesman, the master of the situation. Milton's work, published in 1934, placed the capstone on the structure of Douglas' rehabilitation; von Holst, Rhodes, *et id genus omne* had been revised.[26]

But revision does not stay put and there is ever a yearning for new and more satisfying synthesis and interpretation. Allan Nevins of Columbia determined to rewrite Rhodes completely and in the course of this work made a thorough recanvass of the circumstances attending the enactment of the Kansas-Nebraska bill. In 1947 his first volumes appeared containing his findings.[27] He was impressed by the inadequacy of the various specialized interpretations and prepared an inclusive and complicated narrative designed to retell and resynthesize the story. While he still maintained Douglas in the central position, he took much of the heroic statesman away from him. He showed him as a powerful and ruthless opportunist, playing by ear, with little respect for logic or truth, determined above all things to carry his bill and demonstrate his leadership. Despite his exhaustive studies, Nevins found enigma and mystery in the framing of the bill.[28] Why did a man of Douglas' experience behave in such a curious, complex, and heedless fashion?

Six years later, another thoughtful historian, Avery Craven, published the results of his mature judgment. He had given some of his findings in *The Coming of the Civil War* in 1942,[29] but his further thought was presented in *The Growth of Southern Nationalism*, published in 1953.[30] His special contribution was a pene-

---

Power, II, 382–83; Jefferson Davis, *Rise and Fall of the Confederate Government*, I, 27–28; Varina H. Davis, *Jefferson Davis*, I, 669; Nicolay and Hay, *Abraham Lincoln*, I, 349–50; Charles E. Hamlin, *Hannibal Hamlin* (Cambridge, 1899), 270; Sidney Webster, "Responsibility for the War of Secession," *Political Science Quarterly*, VIII (June, 1893), 276; John Bach McMaster, *History of the People of the United States* (8 vols., New York, 1883–1913), VIII, 195–96 n.; Henry B. Learned, "Relation of Philip Phillips to the Repeal of the Missouri Compromise in 1854," *Mississippi Valley Historical Review*, VIII (March, 1922), 303–15.

[26] George Fort Milton, *Eve of Conflict: Stephen A. Douglas and the Needless War* (New York, 1934).

[27] Allan Nevins, *Ordeal of the Union* (2 vols., New York, 1947), II, 43–159.

[28] *Ibid.*, 91, 107.

[29] Avery Craven, *The Coming of the Civil War* (New York, 1942).

[30] Craven, *The Growth of Southern Nationalism, 1848–1861* (Baton Rouge, 1953), 172–205.

trating analysis of public opinion in the South, tracing in enlightening detail the way in which northern attack changed indifference into united support on the part of the South. This change of opinion in turn gave birth to the northern idea of southern aggression which did so much to furnish the stereotype of an aggressive and wicked South. He painted a most realistic picture of Douglas and showed how his turgid character made him either loved or feared and made him so easy to hate. Like Nevins, Craven alluded to an elusive element. On the question of the motivation for the peculiar metamorphosis of the bill, he wrote, "Who and what were responsible for this remains a mystery." [31]

Finally, the latest in the chapters of the historiography of the bill, written by James C. Malin, *The Nebraska Question, 1852–1854,* likewise appeared in 1953.[32] Malin, a disciple of Hodder, returned to the theme of Douglas the great statesman. Douglas, in his opinion, was fighting the tendency toward centralization which the mechanical revolution was advancing. His doctrine of popular sovereignty or local self-government was designed to restore the balance and preserve democracy. Malin has made a minute analysis of as much of public opinion as he could find recorded in western Missouri to show that Douglas was but reflecting ideas current on the Missouri-Kansas frontier. However, as he has not yet fully investigated the problem of the congressional action on the bill, he has not penetrated the depths of its "mysteries."

The fact that both Craven and Nevins made mention of unsolved problems in the historiography of the Kansas-Nebraska bill presents a convenient opportunity to join with them in expressing the belief that something is still lacking in the complete history of the bill. Despite all this great labor and highly intelligent consideration, historians have been studying Hamlet with Hamlet either left out or incorrectly identified. For Stephen A. Douglas was not Hamlet. This situation has arisen because of what appears to be the historian's principal intellectual difficulty. He is, speaking generally, an excellent reporter but he frequently leaves something to be desired as an interpreter. This does not mean that he does not sense the working of the forces that shape events but rather that the nature of the process by which these forces influence human behavior eludes him. He fails to trace adequately the connections between antecedent situations and accomplished fact, the process of becoming.

This is the difficulty with the historiography of the Kansas-Nebraska bill. We now very clearly understand the various forces making it inevitable but we have contented ourselves with thinking of Douglas as the agency through which they worked to shape the bill. This is not an adequate consideration of the extremely complex process by which the bill took its peculiar shape and was enacted into law. This process of becoming is the Hamlet which has been left out.

This key to the whole matter, this process of becoming, can only be discovered by exploring some of the intricate processes of American political behavior connected with our party system and law-making mechanism. Such an exploration may help to clear up the mystery, to identify Hamlet.

The growth of the nation and the expansion of its population had reached a point

---

[31] *Ibid.,* 180.

[32] James C. Malin, *The Nebraska Question, 1852–1854* (Lawrence, Kan., 1953). See also Robert W. Johannsen, "The Kansas-Nebraska Act and the Pacific Northwest Frontier," *Pacific Historical Review* (Berkeley), XXII (May, 1953), 129–41.

in the early 1850's when the passage of a bill opening up the Nebraska territory had become inevitable, and whether Douglas was interested in it or not probably in the end did not much matter. As far as the achievement of the object of the bill was concerned, states were going to be organized between the Missouri and the Rockies regardless of any man or men. In the short session of the Thirty-second Congress, a simple bill organizing a territory called Nebraska had passed the House. The territory was given limits approximately those of the present state of Kansas and no reference was made to slavery. It had failed in the Senate in its last hours for lack of four southern votes.

True understanding of what happened next can be best secured by reference to the disorganized state of American politics of that particular time. In 1853–1854 there was prevalent a feeling of political uneasiness, probably symptomatic of the process of disintegration going on within existing political combinations, an uneasiness which ordinarily precedes the reintegration of a series of political elements into a new party. In the United States in the nineteenth century there were such periods of disintegration and reintegration in politics every twenty years or thereabouts just as there were financial panics. Democrats and Whigs had crystallized about 1834–1836 and now a new combination was about to form as the Republican party in 1854–1856.

The chief indication of this disintegration-reintegration process was the prevalence of a factionalism in both major parties which was producing a growing sense of insecurity among the leaders. This insecurity produced a tendency among politicians to grasp any possible advantage which might arise from current interests and to push it to extreme length. It was above all else a period of political expediency and sometimes of desperate expedients.

The factionalism current at the close of the 1840's seemed to have very dangerous implications. A split in the ranks of the Jacksonians had lost them the presidency in 1848. In the fight over the organization of the Mexican Cession both Democrats and Whigs had been so fragmentized in 1850 that it had been extremely difficult to reorganize them for the campaign of 1852. The force of traditional combat and the lure of spoils and power, however, had temporarily restored an uneasy unity within each party. In an election which careful analysis showed to be very close, the Democrats won by only a small margin in the popular vote.[33] They had won only to fall into a more complex factionalism which bore the promise of even greater demoralization than that of 1848, and their executive leadership showed itself incompetent to deal with the situation.

The Whig party, which the election returns showed to have a great political voting strength, was plagued by the fact that in combatting the usually victorious Democrats on the state level its two wings had supported policies that nationally were irreconcilable. In the South the Whigs had become very southern, in the North, very northern; so extreme had been their expressions that it was more than ever difficult to get them together on any platform of national agreement. How could they escape this dilemma?

Two other developments added to the disorganized state of politics. During the turmoil over Texas, the Mexican War, and the Compromise of 1850, three resourceful men, John P. Hale of New Hampshire, Salmon P. Chase of Ohio, and Charles Sumner of Massachusetts, had gained places in the Senate by skillful maneuvering

[33] Nichols, *Franklin Pierce*, 216.

in badly divided state legislatures. But without regular party support, these Free-Soilers were now faced with private life. They were men of desperate fortunes and likely to undertake disruptive policies. And a final disturbing force in the politics of the time was a revival of antagonism to foreigners and to Catholicism.

Politics, it can be seen, were thus in such confusion that a maximum number of politicos were disturbed and disorientated by it. An unusual number were uncertain of their proper roles and were confusedly groping for new alignments which would insure some greater security and more certain prospect of victory. Under such circumstances, any legislation which offered opportunity for political controversy and advantage would be seized upon. For this purpose the Nebraska question was ideal. It was obvious that some bill must be passed and soon, therefore, each faction and individual was alert to gain the greatest possible advantage from the inevitable.

Most observers, including probably Douglas, thought that the chief reason why the Nebraska bill had failed in March, 1853, was because the arbitrary limits of the short session did not give enough time to complete the measure. And there is reason to believe that Douglas thought that in the next session it would go through with little trouble. Certainly no one seems to have foreseen the terrific explosion which developed. The reasons why these unforeseen developments were precipitated in the disturbing fashion which so aroused the nation can be better understood if we examine a series of situations which were cumulating during the summer of 1853 and which had little to do with the ostensible purpose of this legislation, with territorial organization, railroad projects, or anything else but politics.

The first of these were the personal difficulties of Douglas, which were many. In 1852, as a relatively young man, not yet forty, he had challenged his elders and made a strenuous effort to secure the Democratic nomination for the presidency. In doing so, he had stepped out of line and had, therefore, gained the ill will of many of his party associates, particularly those of more advanced years. The friends of Lewis Cass were particularly ill-disposed toward him. Largely as a result of this precocity, Pierce had given him no part or influence in the new administration, a snub which was all too obvious. Added to these political difficulties, he had suffered great personal sorrow in the death of his wife.

Thus beset, Douglas literally fled from the scene of his griefs and disappointments and spent some six months between sessions in Europe. From the middle of May until the end of October he was out of the country and largely out of touch with American politics. He traveled widely and talked with monarchs and statesmen. There were indications that he was planning to take up foreign affairs and to seek a new role in the Senate as a leader in shaping foreign policy.[34] It might enable him to recover lost ground and give him a new means of forging ahead in popular esteem for, as the Democrats had discovered, foreign affairs were sometimes more effective politically than domestic affairs—and safer.

But while Douglas was far away that summer of 1853, the game of politics in the Democratic party was becoming intense and bitter. The Pierce administration had realized that the Democrats were in power only because the Barnburners, the bolters of 1848, had returned to the fold; and the returning group had been admitted to the patronage. But many party members were not forgiving and bitterly opposed their readmission to good standing. One group in New York who were called Hard-shells, a current term for believers in closed communion, fought this policy of Pierce so

[34] Milton, *Eve of Conflict*, 12–14. New York *Herald*, November 18, 19, 1853.

hard that the Democrats lost the state in 1853.[35] In the South, radical followers of Calhoun displayed equal bitterness as they battled to regain control of the Democratic party in their section. In several southern states "soft" men had accepted the Compromise of 1850 and had come to power on coalition Union tickets dedicated to sectional peace, a policy endorsed by Pierce in his distribution of patronage.[36] The heirs of Calhoun and the Hard-shells were likely to make trouble when the Senate took up the confirmation of Pierce's Barnburner and "Soft-shell" appointees.

A final issue which created dissension within the party had appeared during the summer, when the President and members of his cabinet made a ceremonial excursion to New York City to open the Crystal Palace Exhibition. On the journey, James Guthrie, secretary of the treasury, and Jefferson Davis, secretary of war, had spoken in support of federal aid for a transcontinental railroad to the Pacific. There were important elements in the Democratic party, notably in Virginia, who were opposed to the exercise of such powers by the federal government as well as to the appropriation of such sums of money.[37] So there was dissatisfaction on this count.

All these tangled relationships increased distrust of Pierce as a political chief. His policies were considered demoralizing, his platform inadequate. The party was thought to be falling apart under his incompetent leadership. Certain influential people became convinced that it had been a mistake to choose a leader so young and untried. Some more experienced party tacticians, it was believed, must come forward to repair the damage before it was too late. They must provide some new platform on which the party might once again unite.

A move in this direction appears to have started rather early that summer in an obscure way in Virginia. The so-called national party organ, the Washington *Union*, had been supporting Pierce's patronage recognition of the rebels of 1848. Its editor, Robert Armstrong of Tennessee, who never wrote a line, had reorganized his staff and had fired a Virginian, Roger A. Pryor, replacing him with John W. Forney of Pennsylvania. This act may not have been unrelated to the next journalistic development. In September, a new Democratic newspaper, *The Sentinel*, appeared in Washington. This sheet was edited by a Virginian, Beverley Tucker, who undertook to combat the "free-soil" tendencies of the Pierce administration.[38]

Whether this journalistic venture was a part of a wider plan for supplying the leadership which Pierce had failed to produce is not altogether clear. But it is obvious that as Congress was assembling there was a movement in that direction in the Senate under leadership very definitely southern. The chairmen of the three principal committees—foreign relations, finance, and judiciary—Senators James M. Mason and Robert M. T. Hunter of Virginia and Andrew P. Butler of South Carolina,

[35] Roy F. Nichols, *Democratic Machine, 1850–1854* (New York, 1923), *passim*, and *Franklin Pierce*, 241–58, 276–93; Craven, *Growth of Southern Nationalism*, 172–77; Nevins, *Ordeal of the Union*, II, 69–77.

[36] This southern political complex has never been given adequate attention. We are in particular need of a closer analysis of Virginia politics during the 1850's. See New York *Herald*, November 25, 29, 30, 1853; Philadelphia *Ledger*, January 2, 1854; Francis P. Blair to Martin Van Buren, March 4, 1854, Van Buren Papers (Division of Manuscripts, Library of Congress); von Holst, *Constitutional and Political History of the United States*, IV, 314–15 and notes, 318 n.

[37] Nichols, *Franklin Pierce*, 279–80.

[38] *Ibid.*, 279; New York *Herald*, November 12, December 9, 1853; Diary of Edward Everett, December 6–7, 1853 (Massachusetts Historical Society); Washington *Union*, August 19, September 25, 1853.

together with David R. Atchison of Missouri, president pro tempore and acting vice-president, were congenial spirits who kept house together on F Street near the Patent Office. Politically they were the heirs of Calhoun and they were among those who were distressed at Pierce's "weakness" and the seeming disintegration of their party. They liked Pierce personally but they realized that he needed help. They could hardly have been said to approve of his patronage recognition of Barnburners, but they did not want to revolt against him this early by refusing to confirm his "free-soil" appointees. They were the most powerful men in the Senate, but they were burdened by a sense of responsibility and they were looking for a way out.[39]

Atchison's political situation in Missouri may have given them a suggestion as to the means, particularly as events in the early days of the new session were especially irritating to them. When Congress assembled in December, 1853, Forney, of the *Union,* was elected clerk of the House. Hardly had he entered office than he dismissed a Virginian, John A. Parker, the librarian of the House. The clannish and powerful Virginians liked this no better than the dismissal of Pryor. They did not find it difficult, therefore, to join with the Whigs and some Hard-shell Democrats in arranging an obvious snub to the President. They joined in defeating the plan of the administration to assign the Senate printing to Armstrong of the *Union,* and instead chose Beverley Tucker for the contract.[40]

At the same time the members of the F Street Mess were planning a more aggressive step in the direction of taking over party leadership. They seem to have determined to reinterpret the party platform and to prescribe it as a test which the Barnburners must accept before the Senate would approve certain of the President's principal New York appointees. The Hard-shell press mentioned this possibility with enthusiasm.

In the shaping of this new test Atchison's needs could be used as a convenient instrument. The Senate was about to resume consideration of the Nebraska bill which had so nearly passed during the last session. In a bitter campaign which Atchison had been fighting with Thomas H. Benton that summer in Missouri for re-election to the Senate, he had promised to secure the organization of the new territory without the exclusion of slavery or else withdraw. These messmates seemed now to have become convinced that they could use the Nebraska question as a means to prescribe a new test, and incidentally to help their colleague retain his seat in the face of Benton's onslaught. The basic tenet in Pierce's political creed was acceptance of the Compromise of 1850, which prescribed self-government in the territories and popular sovereignty, particularly regarding the existence of slavery. To this general creed the Barnburners had subscribed. But if popular sovereignty was good for some territories, it must be good for all. Therefore, the logical implication of this policy was that it should be extended to all territories, even those dedicated to freedom by the Missouri Compromise. The party must now recognize this logic by extending popular sovereignty to Nebraska, and the Barnburners must demonstrate their sincerity by accepting it.

Behind this brief for consistency was southern feeling, particularly among those

[39] Ray, *Repeal of the Missouri Compromise,* 229–33; Blair to Van Buren, August 24, 1854, Van Buren Papers.

[40] New York *Herald,* December 10, 1853; John A. Parker to J. F. H. Claiborne, December 23, 1853, Claiborne Papers (Division of Manuscripts, Library of Congress); *Cong. Globe,* 33 Cong., 1 Sess., Appendix, 44–45; Washington *Union,* December 8, 13, 17, 24, 1853; Everett Diary, December 12, 16, 1853; Washington *Star,* December 13, 14, 17, 1853; St. Louis *Missouri Republican,* December 20, 1853.

with speculative interests, that if great railroad and real estate operations were to be undertaken, the South must be allowed to participate; its leaders would no longer submit to the humiliation of exclusion.[41] Some among the southern leadership appear to have become convinced that if they could produce a measure which would organize Nebraska along the lines of the Compromise of 1850 and "requiring a distinct vote now either for or against . . . this would compel honorable gentlemen to show their hands and let the country know what they understand by the administration phrase 'acquiesce in the compromise measures.'"[42] They were in truth the heirs of Calhoun.

Douglas, as chairman of the committee on territories, must of course be dealt with. There was no political love lost between the Calhounites and the opportunistic and pushing young Illinoisan. He might be described as a boon companion of Atchison and his name might be coupled with Hunter's in political and business enterprises, but they did not think of him as one of them and his power was frequently a threat to theirs. The Senate managers, who included Jesse D. Bright of Indiana, lieutenant of Cass and Douglas' rival for the dominant role in the Northwest, were busy with a plan to enlarge the membership of the Senate committees by adding another Democrat to each of the major groups. Whether they were ready to deprive Douglas of his cherished post if he proved recalcitrant is not known, though they did take it from him five years later. Bright was busy with this reshuffling and Atchison perhaps found it an opportune time to approach Douglas, who could not fail to recognize him as a member of the Mess.

Atchison, according to his own testimony, which Douglas never categorically and unequivocally denied, reminded Douglas that he needed at least four southern votes for the Nebraska bill. These he could not have unless some way were found to permit slaveholders to go with their property into the new territory at its opening. The bill of the previous session, which ignored this question, would not do. Atchison further told Douglas that if he did not want to father this new bill, he, Atchison, would resign as vice-president de facto and assume the chairmanship of the committee on territories. Douglas realized he must heed Atchison's "suggestions"; he was helpless and he knew it. Without the votes of the Mess he could secure no bill, and the pressures for its enactment were mounting.[43]

But he would do it in his own way, for he knew he had taken on no easy assignment. He had canvassed the possibility of abandoning the Missouri Compromise a year before this but had discarded it as too hazardous and had nearly succeeded in getting through a bill which ignored the issue. Now he must face the slavery question in some fashion, but under real difficulties. Contrary to the accepted belief, Douglas did not have comfortable control of his own committee. It had been recon-

---

[41] See notes 18 and 39; also New York *Herald*, January 2, 4, 11, 25, 1854; Baltimore *Sun*, December 21, 1853, January 9, 1854; Philadelphia *Ledger*, January 9, 1854; Washington *National Intelligencer*, February 6, 1854; Washington *Union*, February 18, 1854.

[42] New York *Herald*, January 4, 1854.

[43] Everett Diary, December 10, 1853; New York *Herald*, December 10, 1853; Washington *Star*, March 4, 1854; Blair to William Allen, February 10, 1854, William Allen Papers (Division of Manuscripts, Library of Congress). See Ray, *Repeal of the Missouri Compromise, passim*, particularly 274 n. and 276–88. Senator Andrew P. Butler declared on the floor of the Senate: "General Atchison . . . had perhaps more to do with the bill than any other Senator." *Cong. Globe*, 34 Cong., 1 Sess., Appendix, 103. Senator James M. Mason also discussed the subject. *Cong. Globe*, 35 Cong., 2 Sess., 1248.

structed by some of his senatorial enemies, either by accident or design, in a way embarrassing to him. He was associated with three Democrats and two Whigs; but one of the Democrats was Sam Houston. The Texas senator had his own ideas about Nebraska, and in the last session he had voted against the simple bill then under discussion. Now he delayed coming to Washington for a month and upon arriving would not attend committee meetings. Douglas could do nothing until Houston agreed, and it turned out that Houston would accept nothing outside the framework of the Compromise of 1850. So in the end Douglas copied the phraseology of the act organizing Utah with an explanatory stipulation that the design of the Nebraska bill was to leave all question pertaining to slavery in this new territory "to the decision of the people residing therein, through their appropriate representatives." Nothing was said about the Missouri restriction; it was just ignored. The new bill embraced not the small area of the previous bill but all the remainder of the Louisiana Purchase.[44]

The presentation of Douglas' revision of the 1853 bill on January 4, 1854, gave other interests ideas about political uses to which they might put the measure. Senator William H. Seward, a leader of the Whig party, shrewdly grasped some rather intricate possibilities. He urged some of his northern Whig associates to lead in attacks upon Democrats by encouraging public meetings of protest and sponsoring legislative resolutions demanding that northern senators and congressmen oppose the bill. In after years he described the more Machiavellian role he played. He suggested that southern Whigs place their Democratic opponents at a disadvantage by assailing them for dodging repeal, and at the same time to proclaim the Whigs as true friends of the South by opposing the dodge or by offering a repeal amendment to the act. Beyond this, Seward had an even more subtle intent. He wished to make the bill as obnoxious as possible to northern voters, for this would help northern Whigs discredit the Democrats. Although Whig Senator Archibald Dixon of Kentucky offered the repeal amendment, he claimed many years later that he could not remember Seward's influence.[45]

Dixon's move gave the cue to a third group to engage in the politics of the bill. The Free-Soil senators and representatives moved much more directly than the subtle Seward. Sumner offered an amendment reaffirming the Missouri exclusion and the Ohio men, led by Giddings and Chase, drafted the "Appeal of the Independent Democrats," arraigning the bill as "a gross violation of a sacred pledge." This manifesto was designed to and did set off a chain reaction which gave northern leaders their desired opportunity to mobilize the anti-southern voting strength of the more populous North.[46]

While the Whigs and Free-Soilers were planning these moves, elements in the Democratic party had become increasingly dissatisfied with Douglas' dodge. Some

[44] *Private Letters of Parmenas Taylor Turnley* (London, 1863), 104–106. Rhodes, *History of the United States from the Compromise of 1850*, I, 425 n., says Douglas was the Committee on Territories, but this is questionable. Everett Diary, January 4, 1854.

[45] William H. Seward to Thurlow Weed, January 7, 8, 1854, Thurlow Weed Papers (University of Rochester Library); Dixon, *Missouri Compromise and Its Repeal*, 457, 591; Nicolay and Hay, *Abraham Lincoln*, I, 345–50; Member of Western Bar [Flint], *Life and Speeches of Douglas*, 171–74; James T. Du Bois and Gertrude S. Mathews, *Galusha A. Grow* (Boston, 1917), 144–45; Thomas L. Clingman, *Speeches and Writings* (Raleigh, 1877), 335.

[46] Malin, *Nebraska Question*, 300–302. Chase had been affronted only a few days before when Atchison had excluded him from a select committee on the Pacific Railroad appointed on Chase's motion.

Calhounite lawyers thought it would not admit slavery to Nebraska. Then, too, the repeal amendment of Dixon further embarrassed southern Democrats because it served to expose them to a charge that they were acquiescing in a subterfuge and so gave advantage to their Whig opponents. Simultaneously, doubts were rising in the minds of certain northern Democrats like Cass and members of the administration, none too friendly with Douglas, that the matter was being badly handled in a fashion that might easily split the party again. Therefore, various Democrats, including Pierce and his cabinet, began seeking a new formula which might insure united Democratic support and the passing of the much desired bill.[47]

The Calhounites, Douglas, and the President finally achieved a formula to which they got the rather unstable Pierce committed in writing. They would open Nebraska to slavery by declaring that the Missouri Compromise had been "superseded" by the Compromise of 1850 and "declared inoperative." Also, two territories were created instead of one, one west of a slave state and the other west of a free state. This division, reminiscent of the arrangement of 1820, gave the measure more of an air of compromise, and Pierce agreed to give the bill his support.[48]

The second revision of the bill and the "Appeal" were launched almost simultaneously on January 23 and 24 and they brought immediate results. Such a wave of indignation swept through the North at this blow to liberty that the possibility of support from northern Democrats was threatened; and if there were to be a serious revolt among them, the seemingly overwhelming majorities in the Senate and House might disappear, for in both bodies there were more Democrats from the North than from the South.

A further matter for concern was the discovery by the Calhounites of a great and seemingly unexpected indifference to the measure in the South. Many in that region just did not believe that climate would permit any more slave states, and they were not interested in efforts to open territories that would only create more free states. Furthermore, they did not trust Douglas' popular sovereignty. To many it implied that a host of free state people unhampered by any slave property might move right in and elect a territorial legislature which would immediately exclude slavery. Such a proposition was a tricky device to get more free states with no possible advantage to the South. Many so-called Compromise or Union Democrats in the South held these views.

Thus the Democratic strength seemed to be melting away, north and south. The fate of the bill, therefore, hung on selling the idea to the South, particularly by appealing to the southern Whigs, and on whipping northern Democrats into line behind an administration bill. For these purposes, the second revision—the January 23 bill—was proving unsatisfactory, so a series of partisan and bipartisan senatorial

[47] Notes of Philip Phillips, left for his children, Philip Phillips Papers (Division of Manuscripts, Library of Congress); John Wentworth, Congressional Reminiscences (Chicago, 1882), 54–55; John Moses, Illinois, Historical and Statistical (2 vols., Chicago, 1892), II, 588–89; George M. McConnell, "Recollections of Stephen A. Douglas," Illinois State Historical Society, Transactions, 1900 (Springfield), 48–49; Philadelphia Ledger, January 13, 14, 1854; George W. Jones to Howell Cobb, February 16, 1854, Robert P. Brooks (ed.), "Howell Cobb Papers," Georgia Historical Quarterly (Savannah), VI (June, 1922), 149.

[48] See note 20, and Everett Diary, January 23, 1854; Joseph Robinson to John H. George, January 24, 25, 1854, John H. George Papers (New Hampshire Historical Society); Jefferson Davis to John A. Parker, June 13, 1888, Dunbar Rowland (ed.), Jefferson Davis, Constitutionalist (10 vols., Jackson, Miss., 1923), IX, 459; John Bigelow, Retrospections of an Active Life (5 vols., New York, 1909–1913), I, 171.

caucuses was organized to hammer out another formula which would really insure repeal without using the word and which would overcome southern suspicions of popular sovereignty.

In this series of caucuses in which the leadership was now definitely southern and bipartisan, and in which Douglas by the nature of things could have only a restricted part, a new formula was achieved. The Missouri Compromise was at last specifically declared "void." Recent immigrants were excluded from voting in the territorial elections, an idea attractive to the revived nativism which was becoming popular among southern Whigs. The question of the legality of slave property in the territories was by peculiar language assigned to the Supreme Court. By these caucus actions southern Democrats and southern Whigs were brought to agreement and persuaded to present an almost completely united front. The force behind the caucus procedure was not Douglas but the increasing violence of the attacks against the bill as an act of aggression on the part of the slave power. This insult roused the latent southern nationalism which had been slowly taking shape and for the first time the South presented a united front. Such a combination had a leadership which included not only Douglas, but the members of the Mess and the fiery Whig, Robert Toombs of Georgia. Douglas had the spectacular floor leadership but these others dominated the caucuses that supplied the votes. The bill in this shape finally secured a very comfortable margin in the Senate—37 to 14. But it still had to pass the House.[49]

The heated contest in the Senate had been simple compared with the complex situation that was developing among the representatives. The historian finds that little critical attention has been given over the century to this phase of the struggle and, what is more damaging to the cause of truth, little evidence regarding the contest remains beyond the official record and scattered partisan newspaper comment. Personal correspondence, diary, and memoir material seems not to have survived in any significant quantity. Most historians, absorbed in Douglas and the Senate contest, have expended their pages liberally on that phase of the problem, and have then passed quickly over the struggle in the House. Von Holst, who treated it most extensively, failed to grasp the principal problems of strategy.

The bill ran into trouble in the House from the start. The principal reason was the political hazard which it provided for so many of the representatives. Most members were concerned by the fact that they were in the midst of or on the eve of their re-election campaigns. The rising tide of indignation in the North was frightening to many Democrats who would have to face angry voters, indignant at contrivers or supporters of this measure. Furthermore, the nature of the Democratic majority in the House provided a problem. On paper it was so huge, 159 to 75, that there might seem to have been no conceivable trouble. But the difficult hurdle was that 92 of the 159 Democrats, by far the greater part, came from northern constituencies. So

---

[49] New York *Herald*, February 3, 4, 8, 1854; Washington *Star*, February 6, 1854; Baltimore *Sun*, February 7, 1854; Philadelphia *Ledger*, February 8, 1854; Robert Toombs to W. W. Burwell, February 3, 1854, Ulrich B. Phillips (ed.), *The Correspondence of Robert Toombs, Alexander H. Stephens, and Howell Cobb*, American Historical Association, *Annual Report*, 1911 (2 vols., Washington, 1913), II, 342–43; Arthur C. Cole, *The Whig Party in the South* (Washington, 1913), 286; St. Louis *Missouri Republican*, February 23, 1854. The final draft of the bill, written in a clerk's hand, is in the Senate Files (National Archives). That its wording received close attention up to the last minute is illustrated by the fact that in a sentence concerning "The principle of non-intervention by Congress with slavery in the States and Territories, as established by the legislation of 1850 . . ." the word "established" was crossed out and "recognized," written in another hand, substituted.

there was trouble, even in the House Committee on the Territories. The chairman of this group was one of Douglas' most loyal associates, William A. Richardson of Illinois, who presided over a committee made up of four southern Democrats, another from Missouri, a second Democrat from a free state—William H. English of Indiana—and two Whigs. The original plan had been to report out a duplicate of Douglas' January 23 version on that day, but English and the Whigs objected and delayed the report until January 31, and with it English then filed a minority pronouncement.[50]

The discussion in the House committee defined the strategy of the contest which was to ensue. English represented a large proportion of the ninety-two northern Democrats. These men resented the semantic gymnastics used to deal with the slavery question. They wanted a forthright statement of the doctrine of popular sovereignty, of self-government in the territories, acknowledging the complete control of the slave question by the territorial governments. They felt they would have a chance in the coming election if they were fighting a positive battle to extend democracy, whereas if they were forced on the defensive by charges of destroying the Missouri Compromise they were in grave danger.

The final version of the bill as it came from the Senate put them at the greatest disadvantage. This version—the revision of the January 23 bill—not only declared the Missouri Compromise void, but it gave no specific authority to the territorial governments over the admission of slavery. To make matters worse for some of the congressmen, the bill excluded unnaturalized foreign immigrants from political participation in the organization of the territories. Not only did this provision exclude numerous potential free state voters but it aroused foreign-born voters against the Democrats in various districts.

A group of northern Democrats, therefore, planned some embarrassing strategy which, if successful, would for the time being at least take the bill out of the control of the administration leaders. Sixty-six of the ninety-two northern Democrats revolted and successfully completed this maneuver. The administration was defeated, 110 to 95. Of the thirteen delegations which the northern Democrats "controlled," only Pennsylvania, Illinois, and California showed any real loyalty. New England, New York, and New Jersey failed utterly. Even Michigan and Indiana, bailiwicks of Cass and Bright, fell away. Ohio and Wisconsin would have little of the measure.

This defeat was a blow which challenged all the ingenuity which the administration, Douglas, and the bipartisan southern coalition could muster. Probably few of the sixty-six wanted to prevent the organization of the territories but many either wanted a different bill or hoped to get something for themselves out of the measure's passage. In fact the revolting northern Democrats were fighting not so much to defeat the bill as to change it. They wanted a return to Douglas' first bill of January 4 or else to have English's popular sovereignty amendment or something like it inserted. Furthermore, they wanted to strike out the immigrant-exclusion amendment.

So three forces girded themselves for final efforts. The opposition sought to enlist the revolting sixty-six Democrats in the final defeat of the bill. The administration and the congressional managers were trying to get them to return to regularity. The revolters themselves were battling to get their terms accepted. Here history draws the curtain. The evidence of what went on in the minds and emotions of these sixty-six still remains hidden, if it exists. What experiences these sixty-six had, what pressures

[50] English's minority report is in *House Reports*, 33 Cong., 1 Sess., No. 80.

were exerted on them, how they reacted, what they wanted and either got or did not get, whether some reasoned it out or reacted to pressure from home, how many were moved by moral indignation or were swayed by party loyalty, remains hidden. Answers to these questions would supply the real history of this phase of the bill's passage, yet these answers are not known.

It was, of course, obvious that the President and his cabinet made some efforts with patronage promises, offers of administrative favors, and persuasive arguments, but they were handicapped by the fact that much of their patronage had been used up. Furthermore, the unstable President and the administration newspaper, the Washington *Union,* blew hot and cold. Some effort was made to re-form the ranks by appeals to party loyalty, and Douglas sought to persuade, to order, to overawe; in fact he used all the tactics his ingenious mind and dynamic personality could contrive. Who was promised what, and why shifts were made is still almost wholly unknown. We have only the bare results. No change was made in the bill save the restoring of political privilege to unnaturalized settlers and the bill passed.[51]

On one occasion before final passage of the bill, some eighteen Democrats were persuaded to return to the ranks of regularity and on one other strategic roll-call, when a two-thirds vote was required, a second eighteen, who on no other occasion supported the bill, contributed their votes. Even then the final victory was won, not by Douglas and his Democratic cohorts, but by a bipartisan coalition marshaled by the Georgia Whig, Alexander H. Stephens, who devised the slick maneuver which in the end put the bill over. The eighteen Democratic rebels who had been persuaded to change and vote "aye" were not enough. Had it not been for the support of thirteen southern Whigs, the now impotent Democratic majority could not have carried the bill.[52]

Thus the act came into being. It bore little resemblance to the bill for which Douglas had struggled in the short session of the preceding Congress. The Calhoun faction, southern and northern Whigs, Free-Soilers, the administration, and certain Hard-shell Democrats had all made use of this measure in one way or another and the final bill was the work of many hands and the fruit of much strategic planning. Its real history is the analysis of how a bill ostensibly to organize a territory had been made an instrument of the fundamental political reorganization that the disintegration of the old parties had made inevitable. The story of these political maneuvers is the neglected element in the history of the bill; it is the so-called mystery, the Hamlet which has been hitherto either omitted or only very sketchily treated.

In this fateful legislative session a new plank had been added to the Democratic

[51] *Cong. Globe,* 33 Cong., 2 Sess., Appendix, 31, 35, 47, 64; Sidney Webster to George, June 5, 1854, George Papers.

[52] Richard M. Johnston and William A. Browne, *Alexander H. Stephens* (Philadelphia, 1878), 277. The final affirmative vote was 113 to 100, with only 100 of the 159 Democrats voting aye. Of the northern Democrats who voted, forty-four were favorable and forty-three opposed. Eight southern Democrats and five northern Democrats did not vote; from their own statements and previous votes the last five seem certainly to have been opposed to the measure. Full Democratic support for the bill can be reckoned as 108, which was not enough to carry it. Of the eighteen rebels who finally voted for the bill, eight came from New York, three from Pennsylvania, two from New Jersey, three from Indiana, one from Ohio, and one from Michigan. The other eighteen who "obliged" just once were mostly from New England, Ohio, and Indiana. They supplied the only substantial help the administration got from New England and Ohio in this struggle. Of the thirteen state delegations controlled by the Democrats, only four—Pennsylvania, Indiana, Illinois, and California—remained anywhere near loyal to the party leadership.

platform, the President and the principal Barnburner and Soft-shell officeholders had accepted it, the appointments had been confirmed. Douglas himself had lost an essential portion of his northern support without improving his position in the South. A significant segment of the northern Democracy had left the party. Likewise, a real anti-southern coalition which could capitalize the voting superiority of the more populous North was insured; the seed of the Republican party had been planted. Finally, and not usually noted, was the fact that in this winter of political discontent, the southern members of Congress for the first time organized and presented a well-nigh solid political front and among them traditional party divisions were largely laid aside. It was but a few steps onward to secession, the Confederacy, and the Solid South.

The great volcano of American politics was in a state of eruption. In the midst of the cataclysm, one sees Douglas crashing and hurtling about, caught like a rock in a gush of lava. When the flow subsided, old landmarks were found to be either greatly altered or obliterated. Two new masses were prominent on the political landscape, the Republican party and the Solid South. Douglas had disappeared.

13 / Lincoln, Douglas, and the "Freeport Question"

Don E. Fehrenbacher

The Kansas-Nebraska Act set loose all the explosive forces of sectional acrimony and strife. The following few years saw "bleeding Kansas" wracked by violence, fraud, and civil disorder as both North and South sought to capture the territory for their own social systems. The Kansas struggle also nurtured violence and incivility in the rest of the nation. In Congress, men began carrying weapons, and in 1856 Senator Charles Sumner of Massachusetts was beaten insensible by South Carolina Congressman Preston Brooks for delivering a militantly anti-Southern speech on Kansas. The party system also felt the impact of growing sectional antagonism. With gathering momentum "anti-Nebraska" men, or "Fusionists," drawn from among Whigs, Democrats, and Know-Nothings alike, began to coalesce into a new sectional party dedicated to stopping the spread of slavery. In 1856 the new Republican Party ran explorer John C. Frémont for President, and although it was beaten by the Democrats under James Buchanan, it came within five states of sweeping the North.

In 1857 the Supreme Court under Chief Justice Roger Taney added fuel to the divisive fires. In March of that year the Chief Justice announced the Court's decision in the case of Dred Scott *v.* Sandford, a legal tangle involving a slave's suit for his freedom that incidentally raised many questions concerning the spread of slavery into the territories. In a pronouncement that dismayed many Northerners, Taney declared that neither Congress nor a territorial legislature had the power to prohibit slavery. Voting for or against slavery was the exclusive prerogative of state legislatures, and hence the Missouri Compromise was unconstitutional.

In one stroke, Taney opened all the federal territories to slavery. The decision clearly was a great victory for the South and for Southern militants who denied that the federal government had any control over slavery. At the same time it undermined both the Republican principle that Congress could exclude slavery from the newer regions and Douglas' doctrine that the people of the territories could decide the question of slavery for themselves. The Republican response to this conundrum was to insist that the Court could change its mind. Douglas's reply came at Freeport during the

The American Historical Review, LXVI, No. 3 (April 1961), 599–617. Reprinted by permission of the author.

famous Lincoln-Douglas debate in the Illinois Senatorial campaign of 1858.

Much mythology surrounds this encounter and Douglas' "Freeport Doctrine." As D. E. Fehrenbacher notes in the following selection, Lincoln is supposed to have trapped Douglas in a dilemma: if the "little giant" successfully salvaged the popular sovereignty principle, he would win reelection to the Senate, but he would alienate the South and diminish his chances for the Presidency; if he surrendered popular sovereignty, he might keep his Southern support but only at the expense of antagonizing his Illinois constituents and losing the Senate race to Lincoln. In the end, according to legend, he chose the second course and ruined his chances to become President. Fehrenbacher's article exposes the myths surrounding the Freeport debate and places the "Freeport Question" in perspective.

For further reading: * Vincent C. Hopkins, *Dred Scott's Case* (New York: Russell and Russell, 1967); Harry V. Jaffa, *Crisis of the House Divided* (Garden City, N. Y.: Doubleday & Co. 1959); William E. Baringer, *Lincoln's Rise to Power* (Boston, Mass.: Little, Brown and Company, 1937); Robert W. Johannsen, "Stephen A. Douglas, 'Harper's Magazine,' and Popular Sovereignty," *Mississippi Valley Historical Review*, XLV (March 1959); George F. Milton, *The Eve of Conflict: Stephen A Douglas and the Needless War* (Boston, Mass.: Houghton Mifflin Company, 1934).

One of the fascinations of the Lincoln-Douglas debates is the pattern of paradox that can be traced in their consequences. Lincoln, the loser, did not sink back into the obscurity which ordinarily awaits a twice-defeated candidate for the Senate, but emerged instead as a serious presidential contender. Douglas' victory, on the other hand, is generally thought to have been gained at a ruinous cost, primarily because of what he was compelled to say in response to Lincoln's second question at Freeport. Few tableaux of American history are more familiar or striking than this famous exchange of August 27, 1858. The tall, awkward prairie lawyer cleverly pins his distinguished opponent upon the horns of a dilemma; the pugnacious Little Giant, his back to the wall, unhesitatingly chooses to risk the displeasure of slaveholders rather than that of his constituents:

> LINCOLN: Can the people of a United States Territory, in any lawful way, against the wish of any citizen of the United States, exclude slavery from its limits prior to the formation of a State Constitution?
>
> DOUGLAS: It matters not what way the Supreme Court may hereafter decide as to the abstract question whether slavery may or may not go into a territory under the constitution, the people have the lawful means to introduce it or exclude it as they please, for the reason that slavery cannot exist a day or an hour anywhere unless it is supported by local police regulations. Those police regulations can only be established by the local legislature, and if the people are opposed to slavery they will elect representatives to that body who will by unfriendly legislation effectually prevent the introduction of it into their midst.[1]

[1] *The Collected Works of Abraham Lincoln*, ed. Roy P. Basler *et al.* (8 vols. plus index, New Brunswick, N.J., 1953–55), III, 43, 51–52.

Momentous results are customarily attributed to this "Freeport doctrine," which retained the husk of the Dred Scott decision while saving the core of popular sovereignty. To put the matter in its bluntest terms, the Douglas pronouncement is said to have secured his re-election to the Senate while destroying much of his support in the South and to have divided the Democratic party, thus contributing decisively to Lincoln's victory in 1860. The various qualifications and refinements that careful scholars usually add to this primitive causal analysis have not materially altered its effect. In the mainstream of American history-as-record, the Freeport question has become one of those pivots upon which great events turn. Lincoln, by one brilliant maneuver, "outgeneraled Douglas and split the Democrats." [2]

The skeptical investigator must deal not only with a sturdy folklore tradition but also with a certain amount of undeniable fact. The unfriendly legislation doctrine did indeed grate upon southern ears and contribute to the disruption of the Democratic party. Determining the weight of that contribution is the real historical problem and the aim of this essay. In so far as a dissent is registered in the pages that follow, it is to the undue emphasis commonly put on the Freeport question and to the inflated estimate of its influence. Such emphasis tends to throw the debates themselves out of focus and to magnify the importance of finespun doctrinal differences in the breakup of the Democrats.

Before studying Douglas' reply, it will be well to take some notice of the legend that has grown up around the question. At Freeport, Lincoln began by answering seven questions previously posed by his adversary at Ottawa and then countered with four of his own. The story goes that when he submitted the latter to the scrutiny of certain advisers, they shook their heads at number two. It would give Douglas a chance to increase his popularity in antislavery circles, they warned. It might easily cost Lincoln the election. But Lincoln, we are told, waved the protests aside and declared, "I am after bigger game. The battle of 1860 is worth a hundred of this."

Although the more extravagant aspects of this tale have won only partial acceptance, the tradition that Lincoln asked his question against the advice of several leading Republicans has never been seriously challenged.[3] At the very least he is made to appear wiser and bolder than those around him, with the result that one more colorful thread is woven into the fabric of the Lincoln myth. Yet no part of the story can be substantiated by contemporary testimony. It turned up first as an undocumented assertion in one of the 1860 campaign biographies and was retold many times during the years that followed.[4] In 1892 Horace White published his

---

[2] Nathaniel W. Stephenson, "Abraham Lincoln," *Encylopedia Britannica* (23 vols., Chicago, 1959), XIV, 141. Similar statements can be found by the score in writings about Lincoln over the past hundred years. Examples in recent publications are Jay Monaghan, *The Man Who Elected Lincoln* (Indianapolis, 1956), 117; Harry V. Jaffa, " 'Value Consensus' in Democracy: The Issue in the Lincoln-Douglas Debates," *American Political Science Review*, LII (Sept. 1958), 746, 753; *Created Equal? The Complete Lincoln-Douglas Debates of 1858*, ed. Paul M. Angle (Chicago, 1958), v, xxx.

[3] Two writers who express doubt about Lincoln's "bigger game" remark, but otherwise accept the story that he asked the Freeport question over the protests of various advisers, are Albert J. Beveridge, *Abraham Lincoln, 1809–1858* (2 vols., Boston, 1928), II, 656, and William Baringer, *Lincoln's Rise to Power* (Boston, 1937), 24.

[4] John L. Scripps, *Life of Abraham Lincoln* (Chicago, 1860), 28; Henry J. Raymond, *The Life and Public Services of Abraham Lincoln* (New York, 1865), 66; J. G. Holland, *The Life of Abraham Lincoln* (Springfield, Mass., 1866), 188–89; Isaac N. Arnold, *The History of Abraham Lincoln and the Overthrow of American Slavery* (Chicago, 1866), 133; Ward H. Lamon, *The Life of Abraham Lincoln* (Boston, 1872), 415–16; John G. Nicolay and John Hay,

version, adding that he had learned all the details from one of the men involved in the attempt to dissuade Lincoln. This was Charles H. Ray, long since dead, but in 1858 the chief editor of the Chicago *Tribune*.[5] White chose the wrong witness, however, for there is clear proof that Ray was on a business trip to New York at the time of the alleged conference. He was, furthermore, in no mood to preach caution. On the eve of his departure, he wrote as follows to Congressman Elihu Washburne: "When you see Abe at Freeport, for God's sake tell him to 'Charge Chester! charge!' Do not let him keep on the defensive. . . . We must not be parrying all the while. We want the deadliest thrusts. Let us see blood follow any time he closes a sentence."[6] And so White's evidence is not even good hearsay.

Finally, in 1895, an eyewitness offered his belated corroboration. Joseph Medill's account of the Freeport episode, first published in his own Chicago *Tribune*, requires special attention because it was reprinted in the Edwin Erle Sparks edition of the debates and has been relied upon by scholars of the first rank like Albert J. Beveridge and Allan Nevins.[7] Medill's recollection was that Lincoln showed him the questions on the train to Freeport and that he objected to the second one because it would enable the Little Giant to escape from a "tight place." Lincoln stubbornly insisted, however, that he would "spear it at Douglas" that afternoon. Before the debate, other prominent Republicans, at Medill's urging, argued the point with Lincoln, but to no avail. Two years later, just after the presidential election, Lincoln reminded Medill of their disagreement and asked, "Now don't you think I was right in putting that question to him?" "Yes Mr. Lincoln," Medill responded, "you were, and we were both right. Douglas' reply . . . undoubtedly hurt him badly for the Presidency but it re-elected him to the Senate . . . as I feared it would." Then Lincoln with a broad smile said, "Now I have won the place that he was playing for."

Medill had safely outlived all the men who might have contradicted his little fable, but in the end he contradicted himself. The Robert Todd Lincoln collection, opened in 1947, contains a letter which he wrote on the morning of the Freeport debate and probably handed personally to Lincoln. The letter summarized conclusions reached the night before by a conference of Chicago Republicans, whose primary concern, it is clear, was to help Lincoln with his answers to Douglas' seven questions.[8]

Abraham Lincoln, A History (10 vols., New York, 1890), II, 160; Lord Charnwood, *Abraham Lincoln* (New York, 1917), 148–49; Carl Sandburg, *Abraham Lincoln: The Prairie Years* (2 vols., New York, 1926), II, 154–55.

[5] Horace White's account is in a chapter on the debates that he wrote for the second edition of William H. Herndon and Jesse W. Weik, *Abraham Lincoln: The True Story of a Great Life* (2 vols., New York, 1892), II, 109. Herndon wrote out approximately the same story in a letter to Weik on October 2, 1890. Herndon-Weik collection, Manuscript Division, Library of Congress. He identified his informant as Norman B. Judd, but since Judd helped formulate the advice in the Joseph Medill letter, discussed below, Herndon's hearsay evidence is also unreliable.

[6] Charles H. Ray to Elihu B. Washburne [Aug. 23, 1858], Elihu B. Washburne Papers, Manuscript Division, Library of Congress. See also Monaghan, *The Man Who Elected Lincoln*, 115–20. Monaghan's effort to make Ray the real author of the Freeport question is, however, unpersuasive.

[7] *The Lincoln-Douglas Debates of 1858*, ed. Edwin Erle Sparks (Springfield, Ill., 1908), 203–206; Beveridge, *Lincoln*, II, 656; Allan Nevins, *The Emergence of Lincoln* (2 vols., New York, 1950), I, 381–82.

[8] A recently discovered letter from Lincoln to Ebenezer Peck, Aug. 23, 1858 (photostat in Illinois State Library, Springfield), furnishes additional proof that Lincoln and his advisers were chiefly concerned with phrasing answers rather than preparing questions.

Along with their advice on this subject, Medill transmitted the recommendation that Lincoln "put a few ugly questions" of his own. He went on to list some examples, one of which has a very familiar ring: "What becomes of your vaunted popular sovereignty in [the] Territories since the Dred Scott decision?" Medill also echoed Ray's plea for more aggressiveness. "Employ your best hour in pitching into Dug," he exhorted. "Make your assertions dogmaticall and unqualified. Be saucy . . . [in] other words give him h--l." [9]

The story of all the apprehensive talk about the dangerousness of the second Freeport question lacks both proof and credibility. The fact is that Lincoln did not decide to ask *the* question, but to ask *questions*—partly as a matter of *quid pro quo*,[10] and partly as a way of taking the offensive. Many of his friends thought that he had done too much backpedaling in the Ottawa debate.[11] Far from advocating restraint, they were, like the managers of a sluggish prizefighter, imploring him to "open up" in the next round, to "Charge Chester! charge!"

Once Lincoln made up his mind to fire a return volley of questions, it was hardly a display of "uncanny skill" to select one that was already being asked on all sides. He himself had raised the point in an earlier speech,[12] and Republican newspapers had been hammering away for many months at the incompatibility of popular sovereignty and the Dred Scott decision. To cite an example, the Bloomington (Illinois) *Pantagraph* of July 15, 1858, printed eight questions directed at Douglas, and the first one read: "Do you believe that the people of a Territory, whilst a Territory, and before the formation of a State constitution, have the right to exclude slavery?" Shortly before the Freeport debate, Lincoln received from a Chicago editor a newspaper clipping containing this same query.[13] It had also been suggested to him a few weeks earlier by a Quincy lawyer.[14] And Medill, as we know, included the substance of it in his list of last-minute instructions. Lincoln's final phrasing was an improvement, but otherwise it might be said that the celebrated question was virtually shoved into his hands as he stepped onto the platform. Since the celebrated reply had also been enunciated by Douglas on several previous occasions, not much was really new or surprising in the exchange at Freeport.

Not only evidence but logic is against the view that Lincoln deliberately courted defeat in order to deprive Douglas of southern support for the presidency. Well before the debates began, Douglas' fight against the Lecompton Constitution had alienated large numbers of slaveholders, so many, in fact, that Lincoln wrote late in July: "He cares nothing for the South—he knows he is already dead there." [15] Why,

[9] Medill to Lincoln [Aug. 27, 1858], Robert Todd Lincoln collection, Manuscript Division, Library of Congress.

[10] Before answering the seven questions put to him, Lincoln tried to extract from Douglas a promise that he would answer as many in return. *Collected Works of Lincoln*, ed. Basler *et al.*, III, 15, 39.

[11] J. Jordan to Lincoln, Aug. 24, 1858; Henry C. Whitney to Lincoln, Aug. 26, 1858, Robert Todd Lincoln collection. For the opinion of Theodore Parker that Douglas "had the best of it" at Ottawa, see his letter to Herndon of Sept. 9, 1858, in Joseph Fort Newton, *Lincoln and Herndon* (Cedar Rapids, Iowa, 1910), 208.

[12] *Collected Works of Lincoln*, ed. Basler *et al.*, II, 487.

[13] Charles L. Wilson (editor of the Chicago *Journal*) to Lincoln, undated, but obviously written between Aug. 21 and Aug. 27, 1858, Robert Todd Lincoln collection. See also *Illinois State Journal* (Springfield), July 30, 1858; Chicago *Press and Tribune*, Aug. 4, 1858.

[14] Henry Asbury to Lincoln, July 28, 1858, Robert Todd Lincoln collection.

[15] Lincoln to Henry Asbury, July 31, 1858, *Collected Works of Lincoln*, ed. Basler *et al.*, II, 530–31.

then, would this man who wanted so badly to become senator jeopardize his chances in order to kill something he considered "already dead"? Besides, if Lincoln did propose to knock Douglas out of the presidential race, there was scarcely a better way of doing it than by ousting him from the Senate, for such a defeat on his home grounds would have been a staggering blow to the Little Giant's prestige. It must be remembered also that whatever course southern politicians took, the Republican party could capture the presidency in 1860 only by sweeping the North, and in Illinois, which was one of the most doubtful states, any strategy that hurt or helped Lincoln in 1858 would have been expected to exert a similar influence upon Republican prospects two years later. There was, in short, no observable conflict between Lincoln's personal ambition and the welfare of his party, hence no reason for the sacrifice often attributed to him.

Although Lincoln and his advisers apparently did not anticipate any ill effects from the asking of the Freeport question, one must still consider the possibility that such effects did in fact ensue. Numerous historians have joined Medill in asserting that Douglas' reply at Freeport procured his re-election to the Senate.[16] Close examination reveals, however, that the assertion is demonstrably true only to the extent that it is pointless. By his anti-Lecompton heroics, Douglas had projected a new and attractive image of himself upon the public consciousness in the free states. Had he chosen at Freeport to smash that image, then the day would indeed have marked a turning point. Yet such a decision was beyond the realm of possibility because Douglas fully realized that any attempt to crawl back into the good graces of the slaveholders and the Buchanan administration would invite almost certain defeat. In other words, no one is likely to deny that Lincoln would have profited immensely if his opponent had elected to commit political suicide, but historical consequences are not ordinarily ascribed to improbable events that never happened.

The pertinent question, surely, is whether the things that *did* happen at Freeport actually changed enough votes to cause the defeat of no less than four Republican candidates for the state legislature. Since lack of data rules out an answer based on empirical investigation,[17] one can only rummage through the possibilities and take his choice. If the Freeport doctrine won some uncommitted voters to Douglas' side, it may also have alienated others, especially Democrats still on friendly terms with the administration.[18] Perhaps there was a net balance in his favor, and perhaps it was large enough to be important. But even then, in an election so close that a switch of a few hundred votes in the right places would have reversed the outcome,[19] any

[16] For example, Nathaniel W. Stephenson, *Lincoln* (Indianapolis, 1922), 89; Samuel E. Morison and Henry S. Commager, *The Growth of the American Republic* (4th ed., 2 vols., New York, 1950), I, 629.

[17] For an interesting, but, in my opinion, less than satisfactory effort to measure the effect of the campaign as a whole upon the voters, see Forest L. Whan, "Stephen A. Douglas," in *A History and Criticism of American Public Address*, ed. William Norwood Brigance (2 vols., New York, 1943), II, 821–24.

[18] Some leading scholars believe that this was the main purpose of Lincoln's question. See Benjamin P. Thomas, *Abraham Lincoln* (New York, 1952), 189; Baringer, *Lincoln's Rise to Power*, 24.

[19] A study of the election abstract for 1858 (MS, Illinois State Archives, Springfield) reveals that a shift of less than 150 votes from the Democratic to the Republican columns in each of three counties (Fulton, Tazewell, and Madison), a total of 357, to be precise, would have given Lincoln a fifty-one to forty-nine majority in the legislature, which re-elected Douglas, fifty-four to forty-six. In several other counties the Democratic victory was similarly narrow.

one among scores of factors can be made decisive by definition. Republicans blamed their narrow defeat upon such things as the inequitable apportionment, the editorial antics of Horace Greeley, the influence of Senator John J. Crittenden, the inclement weather on election day, and illegal voting by peripatetic Irishmen.[20] Nobody at the time ventured to add the Freeport question to the list.

But now the more significant problem claims attention. What part did the Freeport doctrine play in the disruption of the Democratic party and the election of Lincoln? Beginning at the far end of the subject, it must be pointed out that the connection between the two latter events is by no means clear. That a united Democratic party could have retained the presidency in 1860 is possible, but hardly probable. The election figures lend support to the conclusion that the division of Lincoln's opposition did not give him the victory, but merely increased his electoral majority.[21] Yet there are good reasons for studying the Democratic split at Charleston. It severed one of the strongest bonds of union and helped prepare the South emotionally for secession. In the words of Roy F. Nichols, it was like "the bursting of a dike which unloosed an engulfing flood." [22] And there is no denying that the subject of bitterest dispute in the final hour of crisis was the issue raised by Lincoln at Freeport.

The dispute had roots that went much deeper than Lincoln's question, however, for the Freeport doctrine was of course the post-Dred Scott remnant of popular sovereignty. Throughout the previous decade, Democrats had been discussing the power of a territorial government to prohibit slavery, with no more definite results than some periodic agreements to camouflage their disagreement. What needs to be explained is why the issue should have become a matter of such deadly concern after 1858, when it was of less practical importance than ever before.

Although Douglas became its greatest champion, popular sovereignty had been broached in 1847 by Lewis Cass as a middle way between the Wilmot Proviso and the Calhoun-inspired proposition that slaveholders possessed an indefeasible right to take their property into any territory.[23] At first the principle was more commonly called "nonintervention." The two terms, while roughly equivalent, were in a sense also complementary. Nonintervention meant that Congress, whether as a matter of policy or because of constitutional inability, should not interfere with the "domestic institutions" of a territory.[24] Popular sovereignty lodged the control of

[20] Illinois State Journal, Nov. 8, 9, 1858; Ebenezer Peck to Lyman Trumbull, Nov. 22, 1858, Lyman Trumbull Papers, Manuscript Division, Library of Congress; Clinton Central Transcript, Dec. 17, 1858; Central Illinois Gazette (Champaign), May 11, 1859; Weekly Chicago Democrat, Nov. 13, 1858; L. H. Waters to Ozias M. Hatch, Nov. 3, 1858, Ozias M. Hatch Papers, Illinois State Historical Library; Lincoln to Crittenden, Nov. 4, 1858, in Collected Works of Lincoln, ed. Basler et al., III, 335–36; David Donald, Lincoln's Herndon (New York, 1948), 125; D. E. Fehrenbacher, "The Historical Significance of the Lincoln-Douglas Debates," Wisconsin Magazine of History, XLII (Spring 1959), 196–97.

[21] W. Dean Burnham, Presidential Ballots, 1836–1892 (Baltimore, 1955), 86; Fehrenbacher, "Lincoln-Douglas Debates," 196.

[22] Roy Franklin Nichols, The Disruption of American Democracy (New York, 1948), 513.

[23] Lewis Cass drew upon the ideas of other men in formulating his doctrine, but for practical purposes it may be said to have originated with his Nicholson letter of December 24, 1847. See Milo M. Quaife, The Doctrine of Non-Intervention with Slavery in the Territories (Chicago, 1910), 51–59.

[24] Cass based his doctrine upon a strict construction of the Constitution which limited Congress to merely establishing territories and ordering their forms of government. See his statement in

those institutions with the territorial populations and their authorized governments.[25] The practical result, it was thought, would be to banish the most dangerous of political issues from the halls of Congress in the name of local democracy. Introduced first as a piece of campaign strategy for the election of 1848, this formula was incorporated (in its nonintervention sense, at least) in the Compromise of 1850, established as official territorial policy by the Kansas-Nebraska Act, and acknowledged in the Democratic platform of 1856. In all of these applications, however, the principle retained a basic ambiguity which proved to be its most viable characteristic.

The Cass-Douglas doctrine, which northern Democrats assumed to mean territorial home rule on the slavery question, was imprecise enough to allow the shaping of a southern interpretation that differed little from the views of Calhoun. Specifically, the principle of nonintervention implied congressional passivity and repudiated restrictive measures like the Missouri Compromise, but it in no way impaired the assertion of a southern right under the Constitution to take slave property into the territories. And as long as the right was asserted, only a truncated version of popular sovereignty could be admitted into the southern scheme of things; that is, a territory might establish or prohibit slavery when it framed a constitution in preparation for statehood, but not before. To construe the doctrine in this way was obviously to eviscerate it. Yet northern Democrats, realizing the practical advantage of having different constructions under a cover of verbal accord, prudently avoided forcing the issue and even cooperated in the perpetuation of the ambiguity. Thus when Cass was confronted with an equivalent of the Freeport question in 1848, he flatly refused to clarify his Nicholson letter.[26] Two presidential elections later, Buchanan talked out of both sides of his mouth as he interpreted the popular sovereignty plank in the Democratic platform.[27] And in a committee report the same year, Douglas made a remarkable attempt to run with both hares and hounds on this subject which was supposedly dear to his heart.[28]

But if the double meaning of popular sovereignty enabled northern and southern Democrats to keep up a thin pretense of unity on a divisive issue, it also served as a ready target for political opponents. Before Lincoln took up the Freeport question, it had been asked and answered many times, especially during the year 1856. Lyman Trumbull of Illinois, for example, challenged Douglas on the Senate floor to say whether the territorial legislature of Kansas had a right to exclude slavery.[29] In the House, Humphrey Marshall of Kentucky chided the Democrats for peddling two contradictory explanations of the Kansas-Nebraska Act, and Galusha Grow of Pennsylvania demanded to know whether the Democratic platform meant that "previous to the formation of a State constitution the people of a Territory could

---

Congressional Globe, 34 Cong., 1 sess., Appendix, 519–20, but his fullest exposition of popular sovereignty is in *ibid.*, 31 Cong., 1 sess., Appendix, 58–74. Douglas' views, while similar in many respects to those of Cass, were less clear and consistent.

[25] The phrase "squatter sovereignty" was often used interchangeably with "popular sovereignty," but it sometimes had other meanings: the assumption of governing powers by settlers before they were authorized to do so, and, in the South, the unacceptable northern interpretation of popular sovereignty.

[26] Quaife, *Doctrine of Non-Intervention*, 67–69.

[27] Nichols, *Disruption of American Democracy*, 49–50.

[28] *Senate Reports*, 34 Cong., 1 sess., No. 34 (Ser. 836), 1–5, 39.

[29] *Congressional Globe*, 34 Cong., 1 sess., 1369–75.

prohibit or permit slavery." [30] In Georgia, meanwhile, an American candidate for presidential elector named Cincinnatus Peeples was badgering his Democratic opponent, Junius Hillyer, with the very same query. [31]

Douglas' reply to Trumbull was the standard one being offered by Democrats in 1856. The Kansas-Nebraska Act, he said, had conferred upon the territorial governments all the control over their domestic institutions that the Constitution allowed. But whether that included the power to deal with slavery was strictly a legal question and had been left to the judiciary. Douglas, in other words, plainly conceded that his brand of popular sovereignty might be unconstitutional and agreed to accept a decision of the Supreme Court in the matter. [32] This idea of dumping the whole problem into the lap of the Court, which can be traced back to the abortive Clayton compromise of 1848, was about as far removed as possible from the idea of leaving it to the people of a territory. Yet the two solutions had been more or less wrapped up together in the Utah and New Mexico Acts of 1850 and in the Kansas-Nebraska Act. [33] Thus the Democratic party, under pressure to enunciate a coherent territorial policy and incapable of doing so, could evade the consequences of its internal disunity by proposing to convert a political issue into a courtroom case. But of course if the Supreme Court ever rendered a definitive decision, this escape valve would cease to function.

There were some Democrats, however, who, instead of evading the issue, sought to minimize its seriousness. Buchanan, for instance, took note in his inaugural address of the difference between northern and southern versions of popular sovereignty and then pronounced it "a matter of but little practical importance." [34] It was as a contribution to this strategy of depreciation that the Freeport doctrine first appeared on the scene. Junius Hillyer in Georgia and James L. Orr of South Carolina, responding to Humphrey Marshall's taunts in Congress, were among those who anticipated Douglas' reply to Lincoln. So was Samuel A. Smith of Tennessee, who answered Galusha Grow as follows:

> I regard this as a question of no practicability. I have held that in a territorial capacity they had not the right to exclude slavery. Yet the majority of the people in the Territory will decide this question after all. In a Territory we must have laws, not to establish, but to *protect* the institution of slavery; and if a majority of the people of a Territory are opposed to the institution, they will refuse to pass laws for its protection. [35]

And what was the remedy if protection were refused? "None, sir," declared Orr, adding that slavery would then be "as well excluded as if the power was invested in the Territorial legislature, and exercised by them, to prohibit it." [36]

[30] *Ibid.*, 3 sess., 67, 103–104.

[31] Horace Montgomery, "A Georgia Precedent for the Freeport Question," *Journal of Southern History*, X (May 1944), 205–206.

[32] *Congressional Globe*, 34 Cong., 1 sess., 1371, 1374; Appendix, 797.

[33] The words "consistent with the Constitution" in the 1850 acts and "subject only to the Constitution" in the Kansas-Nebraska Act, together with special provisions for carrying slavery cases to the Supreme Court, furnished the statutory basis for the subsequent assertion that the matter had been left to the judiciary. See especially the remarks of Judah P. Benjamin in 1856, 1858, and 1860 in *ibid.*, 1093; 35 Cong., 1 sess., 615; 36 Cong., 1 sess., 1969.

[34] *A Compilation of the Messages and Papers of the Presidents*, ed. James D. Richardson (11 vols., [New York,] 1913), IV, 2962.

[35] *Congressional Globe*, 34 Cong., 3 sess., 67.

[36] *Ibid.*, 103–104. Orr was especially close to the position of Douglas at Freeport in that he

These statements were not entirely new. Upon other occasions, southerners had conceded that even a full confirmation of their constitutional rights could accomplish only so much and that a certain residue of popular sovereignty would always survive as one of the extralegal facts of life.[37] Orr and Smith resorted to the Freeport doctrine in the hope of quieting controversy and mollifying the opponents of slavery. They soothingly implied that the North could safely yield the South its theoretical rights because in practice slavery would never go where it was not wanted. Later, when Douglas appropriated it, this unguent became an irritant, but the effects were still primarily cutaneous.

Before March 6, 1857, then, northern and southern Democrats were substantially united upon a negative principle of congressional nonintervention in the territories and had implemented it by repealing the Missouri Compromise. At the same time they differed sharply over what positive principle should operate in the vacuum thereby created, but this disagreement was muted by the obscurity of party pronouncements and an informal understanding that the whole problem was deposited with the Supreme Court. The Dred Scott decision put an end to the period of dissimulation, however, and compelled a redefinition of the Democratic party's position on the subject of slavery in the territories.

Southerners could see no room for further argument. Slavery had won its case in court, and Democrats of both sections were pledged to accept the verdict. The northern wing of the party must therefore abandon popular sovereignty, except in its innocuous southern version. This is precisely what James Buchanan proceeded to do. Yet for Douglas and others like him who were already hard pressed by Republicans at home, an abject surrender to the doctrines of Calhoun would mean disaster. Somehow the old face-saving ambiguity must be restored. If party loyalty dictated a formal assent to the Dred Scott decision, political necessity required that its teeth be drawn in the process of interpretation.

Actually, the Court had ruled only that Congress was without constitutional authority to bar slavery from the territories. The Chief Justice, to be sure, had implied that territorial governments were similarly inhibited, and there was logic in the southern argument that a power denied to Congress could not be delegated by it to a subordinate legislative body.[38] Nevertheless, Douglas was prepared to insist that the decision itself had no direct bearing upon territorial regulation of slavery; thus he could treat the Freeport question, when it came, as purely hypothetical.[39] His major

---

asserted the finality of territorial nonprotection. His statement that there was no remedy for the latter amounted to a repudiation of congressional intervention in the form of a territorial slave code.

[37] For example, the New Orleans *Courier*, Apr. 2, 1854 (quoted in Washington *National Intelligencer*, Apr. 11, 1854), declared that a southerner had the right to carry his slaves anywhere, "provided the local authority of State or Territory permitted him to locate his habitation within their limits."

[38] The pertinent passage in Roger B. Taney's opinion is as follows: "And if Congress itself cannot do this—if it is beyond the powers conferred on the Federal Government—it will be admitted, we presume, that it could not authorize a Territorial Government to exercise them. It could confer no power on any local Government established by its authority, to violate the provisions of the Constitution." 19 Howard 451. But see the statement of a concurring justice, John A. Campbell, *ibid.*, 514, which reflects a different view.

[39] This is why Douglas used the word "hereafter" in his reply to Lincoln at Freeport, a point that seems to have puzzled Andrew C. McLaughlin. See his *A Constitutional History of the United States* (New York, 1935), 584.

resource, however, was bound to be the Smith-Orr doctrine of residual popular sovereignty. Speaking at Springfield on June 12, 1857, he delivered a powerful defense of the Buchanan administration, white supremacy, and the Dred Scott decision, but then added:

> While the right [to carry slaves into a territory] continues in full force under the guarantees of the Constitution, and cannot be divested or alienated by an act of Congress, it necessarily remains a barren and worthless right, unless sustained, protected and enforced by appropriate police regulations and local legislation prescribing adequate remedies for its violation. These regulations and remedies must necessarily depend entirely upon the will and wishes of the people of the Territory, as they can only be prescribed by the local Legislatures. Hence the great principle of popular sovereignty and self-government is sustained and firmly established by the authority of this decision.[40]

This speech received national attention, and, far from provoking a storm or splitting the party, it was highly praised in the Democratic press North and South. The Washington *Union,* which would lead the attack upon the Freeport doctrine in 1858, printed the address in full and said that it deserved "unqualified commendation."[41] Consequently there is reason to suspect that as long as Douglas remained loyal in other ways, southerners were willing to view with tolerance his use of the Freeport doctrine as a sop to public opinion in Illinois.

The storm broke when Douglas took his stand against the admission of Kansas with the Lecompton Constitution, for here he was levying open war against the President and the South on a concrete issue of major importance—something that could not be tolerated. It was bad enough that he should bring about the defeat of the Lecompton measure and refuse to approve even the English compromise, but the Little Giant's worst offense in southern eyes was his intimate collaboration with the Republican enemy throughout the legislative struggle. The man who had given aid and comfort to the Sewards, Wilsons, and Wades, who had become a special favorite of Horace Greeley, could never again command the full trust of the slaveholding states. In the volume and intensity of recrimination heaped upon him by the southern press during the early months of 1858 there is adequate proof that Douglas had already sacrificed much of his standing in the South before he entered upon the contest with Lincoln. With scarcely an exception, the newspapers that denounced the Freeport doctrine had been denouncing its author for the better part of a year, while southern editors who defended or tolerated Douglas before the Freeport debate maintained the same attitude afterward.[42]

[40] New York *Times,* June 23, 1857. This was not Douglas' first use of the argument that the will of the people in a given locality would always triumph over an unpopular restraint imposed by outside authority. Previously, however, he had used it to demonstrate the ineffectiveness of federal laws prohibiting slavery in the territories. See his statement during the Compromise debates of 1850 in *Congressional Globe,* 31 Cong., 1 sess., Appendix, 369–70.

[41] Washington *Union,* June 23, 1857.

[42] Consulting numerous files of southern newspapers for 1858, I found that Douglas' Chicago speech had a much greater effect upon editorial opinion than did the Freeport doctrine. Denunciation of the latter was confined almost entirely to newspapers already bitterly inimical toward him like the Washington *Union, North Carolina Standard,* Charleston *Mercury,* Mobile *Register,* and Jackson *Mississippian.* A few journals which had either condoned or only mildly reproved Douglas' anti-Lecompton stand actually defended the Freeport doctrine. Among them were the Louisville *Democrat,* Richmond *Enquirer,* and Augusta *Constitutionalist.* A surprising number of southern newspapers, furthermore, took little or no notice of the doctrine in the weeks

During the Lecompton battle in Congress from December 1857 to May 1858, Douglas betrayed a curious reluctance to defend the constitutionality of popular sovereignty in the light of the Dred Scott decision. Trumbull, in effect, raised the Freeport question on the Senate floor in February, but Douglas brushed it aside.[43] At one point he even seemed on the verge of retreating to the sterile southern definition of his cardinal principle.[44] He obviously wanted to avoid giving administration leaders additional grounds for charging him with apostasy. Not until his return to Illinois in the summer did he resume use of the Freeport doctrine, and then it was more the progress of events than pressure from Lincoln that induced him to do so.

Douglas came home to a hero's welcome in Chicago on July 9, 1858, and made a speech that carried him past the point of no return in his relations with the Buchanan administration. During the final weeks of the congressional session, with the thorny Kansas problem temporarily resolved, the breach in the Democratic party had begun to heal. Douglas had left Washington in a conciliatory mood, knowing that his friends were negotiating a truce with the administration. But as he traveled westward, Nichols says, the Illinois Senator realized that the temper of the people would not permit the slightest backward step.[45] At Chicago, therefore, he renewed his attack upon the "Lecompton fraud" and the "arrogant" attempt to force it through Congress.[46] That ended all hope of reconciliation. The administration continued its patronage reprisals, and pro-Lecompton newspapers redoubled their abuse of the party "traitor." Douglas, with the last bridge burned behind him, now had little reason to suppress his extenuating corollary to the Dred Scott decision. He gave the subject a prominent place in his very next speech, but not, it must be added, without some prompting from Abraham Lincoln.

It has escaped general notice that Lincoln actually posed the Freeport question when he spoke in reply to Douglas at Chicago on July 10, six weeks before the debates began. What was left of popular sovereignty since the Dred Scott decision, he demanded. "Can you get anybody to tell you now that the people of a territory have any authority to govern themselves in regard to this mooted question of Slavery, before they form a State Constitution?"[47] Douglas, although under no formal obligation to respond, was evidently eager to speak his mind. In speeches at Bloomington and Springfield, he not only reaffirmed the doctrine that he had enunciated the year before, but made it more aggressive by introducing the words "unfriendly legislation."[48] This went beyond the Smith-Orr version, which contemplated only a refusal to pass friendly laws, and bore a striking resemblance (as Lincoln later pointed out) to the principle of nullification.[49]

---

after its enunciation, and some, like the Memphis *Appeal* and Montgomery *Confederation*, even became more friendly toward Douglas after the debates began. Thus southern press opinion concerning Douglas in 1858 was both varied and variable, but one conclusion appears to be sound: The Freeport doctrine produced no significant change.

[43] *Congressional Globe*, 35 Cong., 1 sess., 524.

[44] *Ibid.*, 616.

[45] Nichols, *Disruption of American Democracy*, 212–15.

[46] *Created Equal?* ed. Angle, 12–17.

[47] *Collected Works of Lincoln*, ed. Basler *et al.*, II, 487.

[48] *Political Speeches and Debates of Abraham Lincoln and Stephen A. Douglas, 1854–1861*, ed. Alonzo T. Jones (Battle Creek, Mich., 1895), 110; *Created Equal?* ed. Angle, 58–60.

[49] *Collected Works of Lincoln*, ed. Basler *et al.*, III, 316–18. This was Lincoln's final point in the final debate at Alton.

At Freeport, then, Douglas merely followed the course that he had already marked out for himself in adjusting to political circumstances which Lincoln exploited, but in no way produced. The latter did tighten the screws a little when he attached the phrase "in any lawful way" to his famous question. But Douglas, if he had wished, could have skirted the legal issue by confining his attention to the inevitable fact of ultimate popular control.[50] Instead, he boldly declared that the people of a territory had the "lawful means" to exclude slavery. To legalistic southerners the difference between means and lawful means was important, and such a statement could not fail to bring added censure upon its author. Only in this very restricted sense, however, is there any substance to the legend that Douglas walked into a trap at Freeport.

The Freeport doctrine, which had originated in offhand remarks of various southerners, thus became more formidable in the hands of Douglas and was at last angrily repudiated by the South. It is usually said that the doctrine made Douglas obnoxious in southern eyes. Yet the reverse was perhaps equally true; that is, the doctrine was to some extent rendered repulsive by its association with Douglas. A case in point is the strange behavior of Jefferson Davis.

Fifteen days after the Freeport debate, the Mississippi Senator, who had been vacationing in New England, addressed a Democratic meeting at Portland. Anxious to disclaim his reputation as a narrow sectionalist, and apparently not yet aware of Douglas' reply to Lincoln, he offered the following observations on the territorial problem:

> If the inhabitants of any territory should refuse to enact such laws and police regulations as would give security to their property . . . it would be rendered more or less valueless, in proportion to the difficulty of holding it without such protection. In the case of . . . slave property, the insecurity would be so great that the owner could not ordinarily retain it. Therefore, though the right would remain, the remedy being withheld, it would follow that the owner would be practically debarred . . . from taking slave property into a territory where the sense of the inhabitants was opposed to its introduction. So much for the oft-repeated fallacy of forcing slavery upon any community.[51]

Here Davis was unmistakably subscribing to the Smith-Orr version of the Freeport doctrine, using it in the customary way as a formula of reassurance to those who feared the aggressiveness of the slave power. Later, however, when he found himself quoted in support of Douglas and fiercely criticized at home, he hastened to belie the clear meaning of his words. Territorial governments, he told a Mississippi audience, had the naked power but not the legal authority to exclude slavery. The dependence of the institution upon local law conferred no "right to destroy," but rather created "an obligation to protect." [52] With this explanation, which was a brazen transposition of his Portland utterance, Davis sought to purge himself of doctrinal affiliation with the renegade from Illinois. And during the next two years he continued to atone for his slip by leading the southern assaults upon Douglas in the Senate.

[50] Lincoln expected him to do just that. See *ibid.*, II, 530.

[51] Portland *Eastern Argus*, Sept. 13, 1858.

[52] *Jefferson Davis, Constitutionalist: His Letters, Papers and Speeches,* ed. Dunbar Rowland (10 vols., Jackson, Miss., 1923), III, 344–48. For a good discussion, see Nevins, *Emergence of Lincoln,* I, 416–18. The difference between Davis in Maine and Davis in Mississippi is essentially the difference between Douglas and his southern critics. In each case the legal right of the slaveholder is contrasted with the effective power of the territorial population, and one's final judgment depends upon which is given primacy.

The distinction between power and right was the key to the next phase of the controversy. There were really two parts to the Freeport doctrine: a statement of fact (that slavery could not survive without local protection) and an inference (that it therefore could not be forced upon an unwilling people). But the southern leadership now proceeded to stand the doctrine on its head by conceding the fact and then drawing an entirely different conclusion. The Richmond *Enquirer* pointed the way in what purported to be a defense of Douglas. With an irony that may or may not have been intended, it characterized him as an honest observer who had done the South the distinct service of demonstrating a need for federal protection of slavery in the territories.[53] Thus the Freeport doctrine was to be converted into an argument for a territorial slave code.

This handful of dust obscured no one's vision, however, for it was obvious that the *Enquirer* had misrepresented Douglas' position. At Jonesboro, on September 15, Lincoln cleared the air when he propounded what might be called the second half of the Freeport question:

> If the slaveholding citizens of a United States Territory should need and demand Congressional legislation for the protection of their slave property in such territory, would you, as a member of Congress, vote for or against such legislation? [54]

Douglas responded rather vaguely by reaffirming the principle of nonintervention, but in a subsequent debate he explicitly declared his opposition to a congressional slave code for the territories.[55]

And so northern and southern Democrats were at last brought face to face over the paltry remnant of an issue that had long been troublesome but never a sufficient reason for breaking up the party. Back in the Senate, Douglas was greeted with hostility by many of his colleagues and removed from the chairmanship of the Committee on Territories. Then, in February of 1859, Albert G. Brown of Mississippi issued a demand for the protection of slavery in the territories and set off a bitter debate which ended with Davis and Douglas snarling defiance at one another. The embattled Illinoisan continued the controversy in his provocative *Harper's* article later that year, and Davis renewed the southern attack with a series of resolutions early in 1860. The running battle finally carried over into the Charleston Convention, where the rejection of a slave code plank was used by southern delegates as the excuse for their withdrawal.[56]

[53] Richmond *Enquirer*, Sept. 10, 17, 30, Oct. 15, Nov. 12 (semiweekly), 1858. The *Enquirer* angrily denied the suggestion of the Washington *Union* (Sept. 14) that its defense of Douglas had been written "ironically," but it conveniently ignored his subsequent repudiation of a territorial slave code.

[54] *Collected Works of Lincoln*, ed. Basler *et al.*, III, 132. See O. M. Dickerson, "Stephen A. Douglas and the Split in the Democratic Party," in *Proceedings of the Mississippi Valley Historical Association*, VII (1913–14), 204.

[55] *Collected Works of Lincoln*, ed. Basler *et al.*, III, 141–42, 270. There is no need here to enter into a detailed description of Lincoln's powerful assaults upon the Freeport doctrine. For an enlightening discussion of his views, see Harry V. Jaffa, *Crisis of the House Divided: An Interpretation of the Issues in the Lincoln-Douglas Debates* (Garden City, N. Y., 1959), 352–59.

[56] *Congressional Globe*, 35 Cong., 2 sess., 1241–59; 36 Cong., 1 sess., 658; Nichols, *Disruption of American Democracy*, 296–305; Robert W. Johannsen, "Stephen A. Douglas, 'Harper's Magazine,' and Popular Sovereignty," *Mississippi Valley Historical Review*, XLV (Mar. 1959), 606–31. The decision of the Charleston Convention to write a platform before choosing a candidate has inflated the part played by doctrinal controversy in the breakup of the party. The

In retrospect, the whole quarrel seems utterly senseless because nothing of practical value was at stake. Douglas and his southern adversaries were agreed that a slaveholder had the legal right to take slaves into any territory. They agreed also that such a right would be barren without the protection of local laws. They disagreed as to whether unfriendly local legislation should be offset by federal intervention. But on the other hand, it was more or less agreed that a test case for the issue could not be produced. Although challenged to put their demands in the form of specific bills, the southerners refused to go beyond hollow generalities. "We want a recognition of our right, because it is denied," said Judah P. Benjamin of Louisiana, "but we do not want to exercise it now, because there is no occasion for exercising it now." Asked about Kansas, where the territorial legislature had passed a law prohibiting slavery, Benjamin replied that he was not interested because there was no hope of its becoming a slave state.[57] Thus he frankly admitted that congressional intervention would be futile in the one place where it was needed.

The obtrusion of the slave code question makes sense only in the way that a chip on the shoulder makes sense—as a pretext for fighting, as the symbol of deep-seated antagonisms. The conduct of the Douglas Democrats is easy enough to understand. Losing ground steadily to Republicans at home, they simply could not yield another inch to the slaveholders. But why did the South press its hopeless pursuit of an almost useless prize? A satisfactory answer is difficult to find. While certain southern leaders may have desired to break up the Democratic party as a step toward secession, the motives of the majority were too complex and variable to be explained by the convenient word "conspiracy." Among the influences at work, there was a feeling that it would be humiliating to be cheated of the Dred Scott victory, however little it might actually be worth; a bitter aftertaste of anger and frustration from the Lecompton struggle; a knowledge that the presidential nomination would be wide open if Douglas could be sidetracked; and, of course, a fierce personal animosity toward the recreant Illinois Senator.

The most fundamental factor of all, however, was a vague and perhaps unreasoning sense of apprehension which was something more than the specific fear of abolitionism. Southerners could see the walls closing in upon them, and the defection of Douglas vividly dramatized the growing isolation of slave society. Above everything else, the South wanted security for the future. It was fighting dangers that had not yet fully materialized, and the battlefields available for such phantom warfare were neither numerous nor spacious. In the end, as Nichols says, southern leaders "sought refuge in a formula."[58] They drew an arbitrary line on the ground and took their stand behind it. But there was much more on either side of that line than an interpretation of the Dred Scott decision, for the rending of the great Democratic party was caused by the same massive, complex, and persistent forces

---

southern demand for a slave code plank was an attack not so much upon the mild and reasonable platform of the Douglas delegates as upon their distasteful candidate.

[57] *Congressional Globe,* 36 Cong., 1 sess., 1970.

[58] Nichols, *Disruption of American Democracy,* 321. Two prominent historians who differ widely in their interpretations of the Civil War, but substantially agree in asserting the superficial nature of the slave code controversy that grew out of the Freeport question, are Nevins, *Emergence of Lincoln,* I, 418, and Avery O. Craven, *Civil War in the Making, 1815–1860* (Baton Rouge, La., 1959), 86.

that were dividing the nation itself. In the total picture, the Freeport question appears as one of the rivulets contributing to a mighty stream.

Furthermore, emphasis upon the Freeport episode has tended to obscure the real significance of the Lincoln-Douglas debates. In 1860 there were actually two presidential elections, and the one in the South between John Bell and John Breckinridge proved to be irrelevant. It was the decision of the free states (well nigh unanimous in terms of electoral votes) that determined the subsequent course of events. And every element of that fateful choice was embodied in the Illinois contest of 1858, as the same candidates and the same opposing principles competed for supremacy in one of the most critical states. It is in the representative appeals of both men to the northern voter, not in any side maneuvers directed toward southern opinion, that one finds the main themes of the debates. The results of this Illinois election in 1858, revealing that the most powerful northern Democrat, in spite of his praiseworthy stand against the Lecompton Constitution, could not command a majority of the popular vote in his own state, foreshadowed the political revolution of two years later.[59]

In summary, it seems reasonable to suggest that the famous exchange at Freeport is not the key to the historical significance of the great debates; that no great amount of cleverness or originality was required to draft the question; that Lincoln included it among his queries at the urging of his friends, rather than against their advice; that there was nothing very decisive about Douglas' reply at Freeport because he had already fully committed himself on the subject, and his earlier pronouncements were easily available to southern critics; that the Freeport doctrine was elicited more by the logic of circumstances than by Lincoln's questioning; that Douglas' opposition to the Lecompton Constitution was the principal reason for his loss of standing in the South; and that the Freeport doctrine, for all the talk about it, was only a superficial factor in the disruption of the Democratic party.

[59] In the election, Douglas Democrats polled approximately 48 per cent of the total vote; Republicans, very nearly 50 per cent; Buchanan Democrats, 2 per cent. Douglas was nevertheless re-elected because the southern counties were somewhat overrepresented in the legislature and because a majority of the holdovers in the upper house were Democrats.

14 / The Secession of the Lower South: An Examination of Changing Interpretations

Ralph A. Wooster

Following the Dred Scott decision, the Union moved closer to its final rupture. Meanwhile, bit by bit, the emotional and institutional bonds that united the sections were rent. In 1859, John Brown undertook his mad scheme to seize the federal arsenal at Harpers Ferry, arm the slaves of the upper South, and provoke a general slave insurrection. Already a perpetrator of atrocities in Kansas in the name of freedom, Brown and his followers were quickly captured, and hanged.

Under chronic sectional stress, the party system that had helped keep the nation together collapsed. On the eve of the 1860 campaign, the Democratic Party represented one of the last remaining institutions binding North and South. The Democratic Convention in Charleston, South Carolina, in April 1860, was to be the occasion for the destruction of this last link. No sooner had the delegates assembled than they became engaged in a platform fight over slavery in the territories. The Douglas wing opposed federal intervention in the territorial slavery question. The intransigent Southerners led by William Yancey of Alabama demanded federal protection for slavery except where the "peculiar institution" had been prohibited by state law. The Douglas forces triumphed, and Yancey and the Alabama delegation, joined by most of the delegates from the lower South, walked out. Unable now to get the necessary two-thirds majority for any candidate, the convention adjourned to Baltimore at a later time.

At Baltimore, Douglas was finally nominated, but again the Southerners walked out and in separate Southern conventions nominated John C. Breckinridge of Kentucky. Meanwhile the Republicans had assembled at Chicago and selected Lincoln as a compromise candidate on a platform pledging to uphold freedom in the territories, and to support a protective tariff, a transcontinental railroad, a homestead bill, and federal funds for improving river and harbor facilities. A fourth party composed of former Whigs and Know-Nothings also entered the race with John Bell as its candidate on a platform that attempted to evade the slavery issue completely.

Civil War History, VII, No. 2 (June 1961), 117–127. Reprinted by permission.

Long before the fall elections, Southerners were threatening to withdraw from the Union if Lincoln won. Following the Republican electoral sweep in November, they were as good as their word. As Ralph A. Wooster notes in the following essay, on December 20, 1860, a South Carolina Convention, called for the purpose of considering secession, declared the state out of the Union. By February 1861, seven states of the lower South had seceded and had organized the Confederate States of America. Wooster's article seeks to discover whether secession of the lower South was a genuinely popular movement or the work of a small minority of intransigent men. The issue is not only interesting in itself but has important implications for understanding Civil War origins. Widespread, grass-roots support for secession implies deep-seated Southern disaffection from the Union and points to fundamental, long-standing factors at the root of sectional conflict. Limited support for secession necessarily directs our attention to the machinations of small, strategically located groups and would, indeed, tend to confirm contemporary unionist claims of a "slave-power" conspiracy to ruin the nation for selfish ends. Wooster's work does much to resolve the problem.

For further reading: Dwight L. Dumond, *The Secession Movement, 1860–1861* (New York: The Macmillan Company, 1931); Avery Craven, *The Growth of Southern Nationalism, 1848–1861* (Baton Rouge, La.: Louisiana State University Press, 1953); Percy L. Rainwater, *Mississippi: Storm Center of Secession, 1859–1861* (Baton Rouge, La.: Louisiana State University Press, 1938); Ralph A. Wooster, *The Secession Conventions of the South* (Princeton, N. J.: Princeton University Press, 1962).

On December 20, 1860, the Convention of the People of South Carolina by a vote of 169–0 adopted an ordinance dissolving "the Union between the State of South Carolina and other States United with her under the Compact Entitled 'The Constitution of the United States of America.'"[1] During the next six weeks the other states of the lower South also held state conventions, and one by one they too severed their ties with the Union. By early February, 1861, the tier of states from South Carolina through Texas had withdrawn from the Union and formed a new nation, the Confederate States of America.

From the moment South Carolina first took the road to disunion historians have discussed the nature of the secession movement in the states of the lower South. Much of the early discussion focused on the question of whether or not the secession of these states was the result of a conspiracy on the part of a few Southern office-holders and slaveholders, who succeeded by a skillful combination of demagoguery and deception in overriding the wishes of the people and carrying their states out of the Union. This belief that Southern leaders conspired to divide the Union was popular in the North throughout the Civil War. It became, as Thomas J. Pressly has said, the "well-nigh universal theme in the Unionist histories."[2] Popular writers such as Joel T. Headley, John Smith Dye, and John S. Cabot Abbott were quick

[1] *Journal of the Convention of the People of South Carolina* (Columbia, 1862), pp. 43–45.
[2] Thomas J. Pressly, *Americans Interpret Their Civil War* (Princeton, 1954), p. 21.

to place all guilt upon Southern leaders for causing the destruction of the Union and the subsequent devastation of the bloody Civil War.[3] The image was created of Southern slaveholders and political leaders plotting the destruction of the Union long before the presidential election of 1860. The breakup of the Democratic party and the subsequent election of a Republican administration were the work of these conspirators, who thus assured the secession of the slaveholding states.

The publication in 1864 of the first volume of Horace Greeley's *The American Conflict* gave impetus to this image being created by popular writers. Greeley placed full blame upon the South. He gave special attention to the role of the Southern governors and officeholders in this "conspiracy," commenting that "four-fifths of all those in office in the slave states . . . were ardent secessionists."[4] In Greeley's view these officeholders banded together to take the South out of the Union and into the Confederacy. Upon them he placed full guilt for the Civil War.

In the years immediately following the war several works appeared which paralleled in philosophy that of Greeley. *The Great Rebellion,* written by a Virginia unionist and former congressman, pictured the secession movement as unpopular among the great majority of Southern non-slaveholders and the work of a group of Southern slaveholders and officeholders who conspired to take their states from the Union.[5] The next year the first volume of the extremely popular *History of the American Civil War,* written by John W. Draper, also expressed the conspiracy thesis of secession.[6] This theme was echoed several years later in *The History of the Rise and Fall of the Slave Power in America* by Vice President Henry Wilson; in *The Outbreak of Rebellion* by former secretary to President Lincoln, John Nicolay; and in *The Great Conspiracy* by the popular military and political leader, John A. Logan.[7] The conspiracy thesis thus seemed fairly well established as a part of Northern philosophy and belief.

Although the historians of the nationalistic school of the late nineteenth century were convinced that slavery was the basic cause for secession, they were divided over the question of the "conspiracy" thesis. The distinguished German liberal, Hermann von Holst, felt that the Union had been destroyed by a slaveholders' conspiracy. In his *Constitutional and Political History of the United States,* von Holst emphasized that the secessionists were only a minority of the Southern population but were able to succeed in their task of destroying the Union by use of trickery and deceit.[8] Another nationalistic historian, James Schouler, however, offered more moderate views regarding the secession movement. While hinting that the success of the movement owed much to the "class and oligarchical political methods" of the area and sharply

[3] Joel T. Headley, *The Great Rebellion* (Hartford, 1863–66); John Smith Dye, *The Adder's Den* (New York, 1864); John S. Cabot Abbott, *The History of the Civil War in America* (Springfield, Mass., 1862–65).

[4] Horace Greeley, *The American Conflict: A History of the Great Rebellion in the United States of America, 1860–1865* (Hartford, 1864–66), I, 341.

[5] John Minor Botts, *The Great Rebellion: Its Secret History, Rise, Progress and Disastrous Failure* (New York, 1866).

[6] John W. Draper, *History of the American Civil War* (New York, 1867–70), I, 513–14; II, iii.

[7] Henry Wilson, *History of the Rise and Fall of the Slave Power in America* (Boston, 1872–77); John G. Nicolay, *The Outbreak of the Rebellion* (New York, 1881); John A. Logan, *The Great Conspiracy: Its Origin and History* (New York, 1886).

[8] Hermann von Holst, *The Constitutional and Political History of the United States* (Chicago, 1892), VII, 254–55.

criticizing Southern leadership, Schouler believed that by the 1860's secession was a popular cause in the lower South and could not simply be attributed to a conspiracy of the leaders.

> We must divest ourselves of the false impression that the crimes of a few Southern leaders produced the real mischief. Plunderers, treacherous abusers, like Floyd, Thompson, and Twiggs, of the power confided in them must ever be execrated by all who respect honor and principle; but they who led the cotton States into rebellion felt a strong public opinion behind them, and led in what among their constituents was a popular cause. . . .[9]

In his comprehensive *History of the United States from the Compromise of 1850*, James Ford Rhodes was willing to go even further than Schouler. While agreeing with Schouler that secession had the support of the populace, Rhodes was not as critical of Southern leadership as was Schouler. Rejecting the conspiracy theme in its entirety, Rhodes testified to the high character of the Southern leaders and expressed the view that if Davis, Toombs, or Benjamin had not headed the secession movement the people would have found other leaders.[10] There was opposition to secession in the Southern states, but the extent of such opposition he felt had been exaggerated. The failure of the conventions to submit their work to a popular vote did not bother Rhodes as it had earlier writers; Rhodes believed the conventions had the best of precedents for their action—the Constitutional Convention of 1787.

The rejection of the conspiracy theme by Rhodes marked a turning point in interpretation of the secession movement. While no longer attributing the secession movement exclusively to slavery as did Rhodes and the other nationalistic historians of the late nineteenth century, most contemporary historians have followed Rhodes in rejecting the conspiracy thesis on secession. Carl Russell Fish, for example, . . . expressed the belief that the decision of the South for good or ill was one of conviction, not one based upon trickery or force.[11] Clement Eaton in 1949 agreed that the conspiracy theme could not be accepted. "In surveying the secession movement of the lower South," he wrote, "the evidence points to the conclusion that it was not a conspiracy of a few leaders but a genuinely popular movement." [12] In another work published five years later, Eaton expressed the view that the desire of the Southern people to leave the Union developed rapidly in the two months following Lincoln's election. Such an accentuation Eaton attributed not to a conspiracy of a few leaders but to emotionalism, the failure to obtain a reasonable compromise, and the contagious example of the more extreme states such as South Carolina and Mississippi.[13] Avery O. Craven also refuted the idea that aggressive leaders tricked Southerners into secession. He noted that although there were politicians working early for secession they did not lead until the very end, when the pressure of events in the

[9] James Schouler, *History of the United States under the Constitution* (New York, 1894–99), V, 509.

[10] James Ford Rhodes, *History of the United States from the Compromise of 1850 to the End of the Roosevelt Administration* (New York, 1928), III, 167. For an appraisal of Rhodes's contribution in rejecting the conspiracy thesis, see Charles W. Ramsdell, "The Changing Interpretation of the Civil War," *Journal of Southern History*, III (1937), 10.

[11] Carl Russell Fish, *The American Civil War: An Interpretation* (New York, 1937), p. 57.

[12] Clement Eaton, *A History of the Old South* (New York, 1949), p. 591.

[13] Clement Eaton, *A History of the Southern Confederacy* (New York, 1954), p. 15.

1850's had forced the majority of Southerners to accept secession as the only way out.[14]

Specialized studies of the secession movement within the individual states of the lower South have tended either to reject the conspiracy thesis or to ignore it completely. Charles E. Cauthen, for example, in his study of South Carolina wrote that there could be no doubt that secession in South Carolina was essentially an act of the people.[15] Percy Lee Rainwater in his scholarly *Mississippi: Storm Center of Secession, 1859–1861*, stated his belief that by 1860 the majority of the unionist masses in Mississippi had lost their former faith and confidence in the Union.[16] In a study of neighboring Alabama, Clarence P. Denman treated the separation of that state as a popular movement rather than a conspiracy of officeholders and slaveholders.[17] And in an article on the secession movement in Florida, Dorothy Dodd, while emphasizing that conservative strength in that state was greater than is usually assumed, placed blame for secession not on the large slaveholders and congressional leaders organized in a statewide conspiracy, but on local political and social differences.[18] Although U. B. Phillips in his earlier study of *Georgia and State Rights* stressed the influence of strong personalities such as Alexander H. Stephens, Herschel V. Johnson, Joseph E. Brown, Robert Toombs, and Howell Cobb in the secession movement in that state, he noted that these leaders were pretty well divided and exercised as much influence to stay in the Union as to withdraw.[19] In his study of the secession movement in Louisiana, Willie M. Caskey observed that, although there existed a widespread impression that a conspiracy carried Louisiana out of the Union, a close examination of the evidence does not seem to substantiate such a conclusion.[20] Roger Shugg, another scholar who studied the Louisiana movement, was more critical of the procedure of the convention than was Caskey. The convention acted like a slaveholders' junto, he wrote, and rode over all opposition without parliamentary decorum. But even Shugg hastened to note that the secession of Louisiana was not a slaveholders' conspiracy.[21] And, finally, the late Charles W. Ramsdell, who placed particular stress upon the problem of frontier defense as a factor for Texas' dissatisfaction with the Union, pictured the secession of that state as a popular movement of the people rather than a slaveholder-officeholder conspiracy.[22]

The trend started by Rhodes in rejecting the conspiracy thesis has thus received the support of numerous twentieth-century scholars who have surveyed the secession movement of the lower South from both a regional and state standpoint. The con-

---

[14] Avery O. Craven, *The Growth of Southern Nationalism, 1848–1861* (Baton Rouge, 1953), pp. 399–401.

[15] Charles E. Cauthen, *South Carolina Goes to War, 1860–1865* (Chapel Hill, 1950), p. 32.

[16] Percy Lee Rainwater, *Mississippi: Storm Center of Secession, 1859–1861* (Baton Rouge, 1938), p. 218.

[17] Clarence P. Denman, *The Secession Movement in Alabama* (Montgomery, 1933), p. 122.

[18] Dorothy Dodd, "The Secession Movement in Florida, 1850–1861," *Florida Historical Quarterly*, pt. 1, XII (1933), 65.

[19] Ulrich B. Phillips, *Georgia and State Rights*, American Historical Association *Annual Report*, 1901 (Washington, 1902), II, 209–10.

[20] Willie M. Caskey, *Secession and Restoration of Louisiana* (Baton Rouge, 1938), p. 35.

[21] Roger Shugg, *Origins of Class Struggle in Louisiana: A Social History of White Farmers and Laborers during Slavery and after, 1840–1875* (Baton Rouge, 1939), p. 168.

[22] Charles W. Ramsdell, "The Frontier and Secession," in *Studies in Southern History and Politics Inscribed to William Archibald Dunning* (New York, 1914), pp. 61–79.

spiracy thesis, however, refuses to play completely dead, and has won acceptance in the new multi-volume narrative of the Civil War period being written by Allan Nevins. In the earlier volumes of this series Nevins seemed to reject the conspiracy thesis when he wrote that the "conspiracy theory of secession furnishes no illumination of events," and noted that "a large body of people in the cotton States had lost their old attachment to the Union." [23] But in a more recent volume, Nevins has accepted the conspiracy theme. "A group of leaders, in a carefully planned conspiracy," he wrote, "took steps which first split the Democratic Party and so ensured Lincoln's election, and which then used his election to inspire Southern secession.[24] Nevins does seem to feel that the leaders were supported by a large mass of the Southern people rather than the handful as described by earlier proponents of the conspiracy theme, but otherwise the Nevins interpretation differs little from that of Greeley, Logan, and Nicolay.

Whether the Nevins resurrection of the conspiracy interpretation will be accepted by the majority of scholars remains to be seen. Professor Roy F. Nichols, reviewing Nevins' *War for the Union*, has already taken issue with Nevins on this point, stating that any planning on the part of Southern leaders to form a confederacy did not develop until well after the breakup of the Democratic convention at Charleston.[25] In an earlier volume Nichols expressed the view that the sentiment for action was strongest not among the slaveholders and political leaders but among the Southern poor and non-slaveholders, the classes which would suffer most from the economic and social struggle with the freed slaves.[26] If Nichols' position concerning the support for secession among the non-slaveholding groups is correct, the conspiracy theory would not seem valid.

This question of *who* supported secession is quite important to an understanding of the movement in the lower South. Was it only a minority group as maintained by the early unionist writers, or was it actually a majority of the people in the lower South? In refuting the conspiracy thesis James Ford Rhodes treated secession as a popular movement of the Southern people, a position that has won wide acceptance among twentieth-century scholars, including Dwight L. Dumond, Clement Eaton, and E. Merton Coulter. Dumond, who wrote the most scholarly general treatment of the secession movement, felt that the secessionists had a working majority in all the states of the lower South and that the opposition to secession in the winter of 1860–61 was principally over the methods of separation.[27] Eaton, author of two widely used textbooks of Southern history, noted that emotionalism encouraged by agitators helped to sweep the people along; he added that the wave of rejoicing which followed the passage of the secession ordinances indicated a deep popular approval.[28] And Professor Coulter observed that outside of a few very wealthy and a few extremely poor all sections of the lower South favored separate state action in 1861.[29]

[23] Allan Nevins, *The Emergence of Lincoln* (New York, 1950), II, 329.

[24] Allan Nevins, *The War for the Union* (New York, 1959–60), I, 10.

[25] See Nichols' review in *American Historical Review*, LXV (1960), 627–29. See also Nichols' "1461–1861: The American Civil War in Perspective," *Journal of Southern History*, XVI (1950), 158.

[26] Roy F. Nichols, *The Disruption of American Democracy* (New York, 1948), pp. 415–16.

[27] Dwight L. Dumond, *The Secession Movement, 1860–1861* (New York, 1931), p. 145.

[28] Eaton, *History of the Southern Confederacy*, p. 16.

[29] E. Merton Coulter, *The Confederate States of America, 1861–1865* (Baton Rouge, 1950), p. 16.

The above views have not been accepted by all contemporary scholars. Outstanding in his opposition to these views is David M. Potter. While not advocating the old conspiracy thesis of secession, Potter does express the view that secession was unpopular not only in the upper and border slaveholding states but in the lower South as well. He stated:

> Furthermore secession was not basically desired even by a majority in the lower South, and the secessionists succeeded less because of the intrinsic popularity of their program than because of the extreme skill with which they utilized an emergency psychology, the promptness with which they invoked unilateral action by individual states, and the firmness with which they refused to submit the question of secession to popular referenda.[30]

As evidence of his contention, Professor Potter pointed out that there was an appreciable decline in the number of voters participating in the election for convention delegates from the number voting in the presidential election of November, 1860. Not only did the foes of immediate secession poll at least 42 percent of the vote in each state election except in South Carolina, but in every case the secessionists failed to secure "a vote large enough to have constituted a majority of the votes cast by the state in the presidential election of a few weeks earlier."[31]

Within the work of the conventions themselves, Potter found other evidence to illustrate opposition to secession. In the Alabama, Georgia, Louisiana, and Florida gatherings the vote on several key issues was extremely close. Potter believed that this opposition within the convention, plus that which refused to participate in the election for convention delegates, constituted a majority of the Southern people. The failure of the conventions to submit their work to a popular referendum indicated a belief that a majority of people would vote against secession.[32]

The contention of Potter that the majority of people in the lower South did not support secession is thus based upon four main points: (1) the appreciable decline in number of people participating in the election for convention delegates compared to the total vote in the November presidential vote; (2) the shortness of the period for canvassing and campaigning; (3) the strength of the opposition to secession in all conventions with the exception of South Carolina, Mississippi, and Texas; and (4) except in the case of Texas, the non-submission of the work of the conventions to popular referendum.

A study of the secession movement in the individual states of the lower South reveals a number of weaknesses in the above contentions. The decline in the number of votes between the presidential election and the elections for convention delegates,

[30] David M. Potter, *Lincoln and His Party in the Secession Crisis* (New Haven, 1942), p. 208. On the state level, Roger Shugg, *Origins of Class Struggle in Louisiana*, agreed with Potter that a minority group pushed through secession. Charles G. Sellers, Jr., in *The Southerner as American* (Chapel Hill, 1960), pp. 67–71, while treating the South as a whole, rather than making a distinction between upper and lower South, emphasized some of the points made by Potter. Noting the small turnouts, the revolutionary tactics of the fire-eaters, the disproportionate weighting of the results in favor of plantation areas, and the coercive conditions under which the upper South voted, Sellers stressed the moral anxieties, fears, and near-hysteria that prevailed during the secession crisis.

[31] Potter, *Lincoln and His Party in the Secession Crisis*, p. 214.

[32] Potter's central thesis in regard to the secession movement is that leadership on both sides failed to heed the danger in the crisis of 1860–61.

for example, cannot be attributed simply to opposition to separate state action. To many Southerners in 1860–61, secession was an accomplished fact even before the election of convention delegates; some of them therefore did not bother to participate in what they regarded to be a *fait accompli*. In his *Secession Movement in Alabama*, Clarence P. Denman noted that eighteen counties in that state were carried by a vote of 90 percent or more of the total and that, since the vote in most of these counties was very small in comparison with that cast in the presidential election, it can only be inferred that a considerable number of people had not troubled themselves to vote because they were confident of the outcome.[33] Many counties in Georgia, South Carolina, and Mississippi returned a light vote because the separate state action ticket was unopposed and its supporters were under no pressure to go to the polls. Too, in Georgia an extremely bad storm on election day reduced the vote cast for convention delegates. Obviously, to consider all the voters who failed to participate in the elections as antisecessionists is an oversimplification.

The criticism of the shortness of the period for canvassing and campaigning, the second point in Potter's argument, fails to take account of the exigencies of the situation in the winter and spring of 1860–61. Whether the South should remain in the Union upon certain conditions, or secede at once, was a decision that had to be made before Lincoln was inaugurated. Although some Southerners feared an overt act from the new administration, many more feared a subtle campaign to divide the South and to array non-slaveholders against slaveholders. Even conservative Southerners admitted the necessity of agreement upon some type of policy before that time. Moreover, the states of the lower South had previously given warnings that conventions would be called should Lincoln be elected. It is therefore difficult to sustain a charge that the convention elections were unduly hurried when four or five additional weeks were allowed for debating issues that had already been under discussion for a decade.[34]

The contention that there was strong opposition to secession in nearly all of the conventions would not stand alone, nor do its proponents intend it to do so. Instead, they maintain that such a powerful opposition within the conventions despite threats and intimidation if reinforced by the opposition which refused to participate in the elections, amounted to a majority of the inhabitants of the various Southern states. A principal fallacy in this line of argument is the assumption that the organized opposition in the conventions of the cotton states was predominantly unionist. Such an assumption is in many cases erroneous. With the exception of the Texas convention, where only eight members voted against secession, the opposition to separate state secession in the lower South was mainly centered on the principle of "cooperation," which to part of its supporters meant cooperative action by the slave states to secure their rights either in or out of the Union as events might dictate. To others it meant simply secession from the Union, but *en masse*, and by concurrent action rather than by separate state action.[35]

[33] Denman, *Secession Movement in Alabama*, p. 122.

[34] Eaton, *History of Southern Confederacy*, and Charles E. Cauthen, "South Carolina's Decision To Lead the Secession Movement," *North Carolina Historical Review*, XVIII (1941), 369, both stressed the importance of public opinion in causing the South Carolina legislature to call an early convention. One state study, that by Rainwater, is sharply critical of the hurried election campaign, and states that thousands stayed away from the polls because they were confused over the issues.

[35] Dumond, *Secession Movement*, pp. 121–23, divided this second group of cooperationists into

In two states, Mississippi and Louisiana, a majority of cooperationists belonged to this second class; they were genuine secessionists who disagreed with the separate state actionists not over the need for but over the question of time and method of withdrawal.[36] In Florida the cooperationists were a badly divided group, some favoring secession if Alabama or Georgia acted first, some favoring secession if approved by a vote of the people, and a few opposing any form of separation. Even in Alabama and Georgia many of the cooperationists were actually secessionists, but felt that a last united effort should be made to compromise. Comparatively few Alabamians and Georgians of 1861 were unconditional unionists desiring to stay in the Union at all costs. Nor were a majority of the "conditional unionists" present in the conventions "submissionists." Certainly the conditional unionists were opposed to immediate separation from the Union, and in that respect were more conservative than the cooperationists proper; but only a few favored remaining in the Union at any cost.[37] Even if we consider all conditional unionists as opposed to secession at any time—though in fact a majority of this group favored secession should guarantees from the North not be forthcoming—their strength was slight.[38]

The failure of the conventions to submit their work to a popular referendum may be explained by the fact that the delegates regarded such a procedure as not only costly and time-consuming, but also as entirely unnecessary. The delegates were fresh from the people, having been chosen only a few weeks before, and knew the will of the people. As James G. Randall has pointed out, the referendum was not part of the Southerner's time-honored theories on secession; the only instrument in the secession procedure was the constituent convention such as was elected in each state of the lower South.[39]

Thus the aforementioned contentions that a minority group carried secession seem open to question. That there was opposition to immediate separation both within and without the conventions is true; that this opposition was equal to the secessionist strength is not. And once the conventions had acted in favor of immediate secession the public generally accorded its approval. The bulk of contemporary accounts from both secessionist and unionist sources testify to the joyful reception accorded the news that the conventions had acted for secession. Insofar as public display of enthusiasm

---

two factions: one would secede by concurrent action before the inauguration of Lincoln; the other faction would wait until some overt act of aggression by the Lincoln administration was committed before secession by concurrent action would be employed.

[36] Rainwater, *Mississippi: Storm Center of Secession*, pp. 177–79, 207–8; James B. Ranck, *Albert Gallatin Brown, Radical Southern Nationalist* (New York, 1937), p. 204; Caskey, *Secession and Restoration of Louisiana*, p. 40.

[37] Some writers have mistakenly labeled all conservatives as "unionists" and thus present a much stronger picture of Southern unionism in the secession crisis than actually existed. See Lillian A. Kibler, "Unionist Sentiment in South Carolina," *Journal of Southern History*, IV (1938), 346–66.

[38] In the Georgia, Alabama, and Florida conventions there were no factions that could be labeled "conditional unionists"; the opposition to secession centered upon the principle of "cooperation" and the few conditional unionists present voted with that group. In the Mississippi convention twenty-one members could be labeled conditional unionists, twenty-four could be so labeled in the Louisiana convention, and eight in the Texas convention. See *Journal of the Mississippi State Convention and Ordinances and Resolutions Adopted in January, 1861* (Jackson, Miss., 1861), pp. 14–15; *Proceedings of the Louisiana State Convention . . .* (New Orleans, 1861), pp. 15–16; *Journal of the Secession Convention of Texas, 1861* (Austin, 1912), p. 49.

[39] James G. Randall, *The Civil War and Reconstruction* (New York, 1937), p. 192.

and zeal can be taken as a true measure of the feelings of a people, Southerners in 1860–61 favored the ordinances of separation. Rightly or wrongly, the majority of people in the lower South were convinced that their hopes lay not within but without the Union. From South Carolina on the Atlantic to Texas on the Gulf, party ties and labels were forgotten; the lower South was at last united.

15 / Lincoln and the Strategy of Defense in the Crisis of 1861

Kenneth M. Stampp

The weeks and months following the secession of the lower South were tumultuous. Buchanan, the lame-duck President until March, 1861, was a weak man at best and was slow to defend federal rights in the newly organized Confederacy. Federal forts, post offices, customs houses, and other property were taken over piecemeal by Confederate or Southern state officials. At the same time the federal army virtually disintegrated since many officers went with the South. In the upper South, where unionist sentiment remained strong, confusion and painful uncertainty prevailed as most men adopted a wait-and-see attitude, opposed both to secession and to federal coercion of the secessionists.

Meanwhile moderate men both in Congress and the states sought to devise a compromise. Most proposals emphasized protection of slavery at least within the states and division of the remaining unorganized territory between slave and free. But all of the many plans devised came to naught, wrecked on the intransigence either of uncompromising secessionists or of equally stubborn Republicans, the latter insisting that to concede any part of the territories to the South was to surrender the results of the electoral victory. Thus, by Inauguration Day, March 4, 1861, nothing was settled and the new President faced a set of unresolved dilemmas.

The most pressing of these was how to protect the remaining federal property within the seceded states. In microcosm this was the issue of whether to attempt enforcing federal law within the Confederacy. The alternatives seemed to be coercion, with the likelihood that much Northern opinion would be outraged and the upper South driven to secede, or acquiescence, and the inevitable dissolution of the Union. The crisis occurred over supplying Fort Sumter in Charleston harbor where Major Robert Anderson and his troops were besieged by Southern forces.

An immense amount of historical energy has gone into unraveling the details of Lincoln's resolution to enforce the laws and supply Fort Sumter.

Journal of Southern History, XI, No. 3 (August 1945), 297–323. Copyright 1945 by the Southern Historical Association. Reprinted by permission of the Managing Editor.

Knowing the impatience of the South with the federal forces still within its borders, and recognizing the reluctance of many Northerners and Southern unionists to condone coercion, did the wily Lincoln maneuver the South into firing the first shot? Or did the troubled President have no alternative but to send supplies to Major Anderson in order to reassert federal authority and stop further disintegration of the Union? At times the historical argument over these issues has become acerbic. Lincoln has been accused of duplicity, not for the sake of the Union but for partisan Republican purposes. Other historians, under the spell of the Lincoln *mystique*, have insisted that there was no guile in the President's actions. Kenneth Stampp in the following article gives us both a realistic and a sympathetic assessment of Lincoln's dilemma and the way the untried, but perceptive President sought to resolve it.

For further reading: *Kenneth M. Stampp, *And the War Came: The North and the Secession Crisis, 1860–1861* (Baton Rouge, La: Louisiana State University Press, 1950); *David Potter, *Lincoln and His Party in the Secession Crisis* (New Haven, Conn.: *Yale University Press*, 1942); Charles W. Ramsdell, "Lincoln and Fort Sumter," *Journal of Southern History*, III (August 1937); George H. Knoles (ed.), *The Crisis of the Union 1860–1861* (Baton Rouge, La.: Louisiana State University Press, 1965); William E. Baringer, *A House Dividing: Lincoln as President Elect* (Springfield, Ill.: Abraham Lincoln Association, 1945); John S. Tilley, *Lincoln Takes Command* (Chapel Hill, N. C.: University of North Carolina Press, 1941).

"Lincoln never poured out his soul to any mortal creature at any time. . . . He was the most secretive—reticent—shut-mouthed man that ever existed." [1] This, the studied opinion of William H. Herndon who knew his subject as well as any contemporary, defined the perplexing quality in the character of Abraham Lincoln which caused him to be assigned to the trite category of enigmas. This is why his acts frequently permit antithetical explanations; perhaps too why forthright motives often appear devious. Through the unwarranted assumption that "shut-mouthed" men are necessarily complex, his reticence always seemed to belie his self-professed simplicity.

As President-elect during the months of the secession crisis, Lincoln kept his own counsel even more completely than usual. The confessions of close associates like Herndon and Judge David Davis that they knew nothing of his plans [2] gave partial validity to the remark of a newspaper correspondent that "Mr. Lincoln keeps all people, his friends included, in the dark. . . . Mr. Lincoln promises nothing, but only listens." [3] Hence it is not difficult to understand why the available evidence could at the same time fortify the conclusion that Lincoln deliberately maneuvered

[1] Paul M. Angle (ed.), *Herndon's Life of Lincoln* (New York, 1930), xxxix.
[2] *Ibid.*, 387, 408. Herndon quoted Davis as saying in 1866: "I know it was the general impression in Washington that I knew all about Lincoln's plans and ideas, but the truth is, I knew nothing. He never confided to me anything of his purposes."
[3] New York *Herald*, February 27, 1861.

the Confederates into firing upon Fort Sumter to save his party from disintegration,[4] and, conversely, bolster the contention that the Sumter episode was precisely what Lincoln hoped to avoid—that it was in effect a defeat for his whole policy.[5] The same scanty evidence, however, suggests still another interpretation.

Happily the President-elect left the record unmistakably clear on two points. First, there can be no doubt that Lincoln was an intense nationalist and that he regarded the Union as indestructible. Having sprung from the party of Webster and Clay, he repeatedly expressed pride in his political origins[6] and scoffed at the dogmas of the state rights school. In his inaugural address Lincoln took pains to prove that "the Union of these States is perpetual." While he added little to the classical nationalist argument, he showed that the thought of acquiescing in disunion never entered his mind:

> It follows from these views that no State upon its own mere motion can lawfully get out of the Union; that resolves and ordinances to that effect are legally void; and that acts of violence, within any State or States, against the authority of the United States, are insurrectionary or revolutionary, according to circumstances.
>
> I therefore consider that, in view of the Constitution and the laws, the Union is unbroken.[7]

At the same time, through private and confidential letters to political friends in Congress, Lincoln expressed inflexible opposition to any compromise on the issue of slavery expansion. His past speeches, he contended, made it clear that he assumed no right to interfere with slavery where it existed, that he had no desire to menace the rights of the South, and that he would enforce the fugitive slave law.[8] But concerning slavery in the territories he cautioned his friends to "hold firm, as with a chain of steel." [9]

Any explanation of Lincoln's opposition to compromise must be speculative, for his words are subject to varying interpretations. He objected to the restoration of the

[4] Charles W. Ramsdell, "Lincoln and Fort Sumter," in *Journal of Southern History* (Baton Rouge, 1935–   ), III (1937), 259–88; John S. Tilley, *Lincoln Takes Command* (Chapel Hill, 1941).

[5] James G. Randall, "When War Came in 1861," in *Abraham Lincoln Quarterly* (Springfield, 1940–   ), I (1940), 3–42; David M. Potter, *Lincoln and His Party in the Secession Crisis* (New Haven, 1942).

[6] See, for example, Lincoln's speech at Ottawa, Illinois, during his debates with Douglas in 1858, in John G. Nicolay and John Hay (eds.), *Works of Abraham Lincoln*, 12 vols. (New York, 1905), III, 223–57. One of Lincoln's biographers contends that part of his dislike of the abolitionists arose from their lack of national feeling. Nathaniel W. Stephenson, *Lincoln; An Account of His Personal Life* (Indianapolis, 1922), 142–43, 145.

[7] Nicolay and Hay (eds.), *Works of Abraham Lincoln*, VI, 169–85. See also Lincoln's reply to the mayor of New York, February 20, 1861, *ibid.*, VI, 149–50; John G. Nicolay and John Hay, *Abraham Lincoln: A History*, 10 vols. (New York, 1890), III, 247–48.

[8] Nicolay and Hay (eds.), *Works of Abraham Lincoln*, VI, 63–64, 66–67, 68–69, 70–71, 74–75, 79–82, 85–86, 87–89, 119–21. On February 1 Lincoln wrote Seward of his intention to protect the rights of the South, and even hinted that he might accept the admission of New Mexico as a slave state. "As to fugitive slaves, District of Columbia, slave-trade among the slave States, and whatever springs of necessity from the fact that the institution is amongst us, I care but little, so that what is done be comely and not altogether outrageous. Nor do I care much about New Mexico, if further extension were hedged against." *Ibid.*, VI, 102–104.

[9] *Ibid.*, VI, 77–78, 78–79, 82, 93–94, 102–104; Gilbert A. Tracy (ed.), *Uncollected Letters of Abraham Lincoln* (Boston, 1917), 171.

Missouri Compromise line with the assertion that this would settle nothing, that it would simply stimulate "filibustering for all South of us and making slave States of it." [10] Simultaneously he expressed a distaste for the personal humiliation involved in proposals to "buy or beg a peaceful inauguration" through concessions. [11] Considerations of prestige and "face-saving" clearly were involved. Lincoln may also have decided that the time had come for a final settlement of the questions of secession and slavery expansion. "The tug has to come," he wrote to Senator Lyman Trumbull, "& better now than any time hereafter." [12] If this was the case, Lincoln expressed an opinion widely held among his Republican contemporaries. "If we must have civil war," wrote Edward Bates, "perhaps it is better now than at a future date." [13] A western Republican paper asserted that "we are heartily tired of having this [secession] threat stare us in the face evermore. . . . We never have been better prepared for such a crisis than now. We most ardently desire that it may come." [14] Indeed, throughout the secession crisis, it is remarkable how often Lincoln shared, or merely reflected, popular views.

In these same letters the President-elect made intriguingly vague remarks to the effect that as soon as compromise was accepted, "they have us under again: all our labor is lost, and sooner or later must be done over." [15] Compromise "would lose us everything we gain by the election," he added, and it would be "the end of us." [16] Here, perhaps, Lincoln indicated primary concern for the well-being of the Republican party and a fear that compromise would mean its ruin. [17] Certainly his party friends and advisers were acutely aware that concession would menace their organization and that the radical wing might bolt the new administration. Ever before them was the fate of the Whig party, which, one Republican insisted, had "died

[10] Nicolay and Hay (eds.), *Works of Abraham Lincoln*, VI, 78–79, 82; Emanuel Hertz, *Abraham Lincoln; A New Portrait*, 2 vols. (New York, 1931), II, 795.

[11] Horace White, *Life of Lyman Trumbull* (New York, 1913), 111. During the month of February the New York *Tribune* headed its editorial columns with an alleged statement of Lincoln to Dr. C. H. Ray of the Chicago *Tribune*: "I will suffer death before I will consent to any concession or compromise which looks like buying the privilege of taking possession of the Government to which we have a constitutional right."

[12] Lincoln to Trumbull, December 10, 1860, in Tracy (ed.), *Uncollected Letters of Lincoln*, 171. See also, Lincoln to William Kellogg, December 11, 1860, in Nicolay and Hay (eds.), *Works of Abraham Lincoln*, VI, 77–78; Lincoln to J. T. Hale, January 11, 1861, *ibid.*, VI, 93–94.

[13] Howard K. Beale (ed.), *The Diary of Edward Bates, 1859–1866*, in American Historical Association, *Annual Report*, 1930, IV (Washington, 1933), 157–58.

[14] Indianapolis *Indiana American*, November 21, 1860. For similar views see Centreville *Indiana True Republican*, January 31, 1861; New York *Courier and Enquirer*, November 2, 5, 6, 1860; New York *Tribune*, December 19, 20, 1860; January 4, 1861; Conneautville (Penn.) *Record*, quoted in New York *Tribune*, February 19, 1861; Worcester *Spy*, December 4, 1860; Boston *Daily Advertiser*, December 20, 1860; Charles R. Williams (ed.), *Diary and Letters of Rutherford Birchard Hayes*, 4 vols. (Columbus, 1922–1925), I, 566; Trumbull to E. C. Larned, January 16, 1861, in White, *Life of Lyman Trumbull*, 113–14.

[15] Nicolay and Hay (eds.), *Works of Abraham Lincoln*, VI, 77–79; Tracy (ed.), *Uncollected Letters of Lincoln*, 171; Stephenson, *Lincoln*, 114–15.

[16] Lincoln to Thurlow Weed, December 17, 1860, in Nicolay and Hay (eds.), *Works of Abraham Lincoln*, VI, 82.

[17] In a speech delivered in Kansas in December, 1859, Lincoln insisted that to yield on the issue of slavery expansion would wreck the party: "Simultaneously with such letting down the Republican organization would go to pieces, and half its elements would go in a different direction, leaving an easy victory to the common enemy." *Ibid.*, V, 274–75.

of compromises." [18] Thurlow Weed, on a visit to Washington, found the Republicans overwhelmed by this fear. [19] Open the territories to slavery, admonished one of the faithful, and "Republicanism is a 'dead dog.' " [20]

Yet the fact remains that there was little in these sentiments to invalidate the possibility that Lincoln, in opposing compromise, was thinking less of party than of what he regarded as the best interests of the North, perhaps of the whole nation. More likely the two concepts were fused in Lincoln's mind. Professional politicians have a happy facility for identifying personal and party interests with broad national interests, and Lincoln may have believed sincerely that what helped the Republican party would help everyone.

Having flatly rejected both compromise and acquiescence in disunion, Lincoln could have hoped to solve the secession crisis in only two other ways. Either loyal Southerners might have been encouraged to overthrow the secessionists, voluntarily to renew their allegiance to the federal government, and thus to secure a peaceful reconstruction of the Union, [21] or Lincoln might have used force to protect federal property and maintain national authority in the South. In other words, the secessionists could have been coerced, defining coercion broadly as any attempt to enforce federal laws against the wishes of state authorities or large bodies of disaffected citizens.

Probably Lincoln regarded neither the device of peaceful reconstruction nor coercion as a basic policy. These were mere stratagems to be used according to circumstances. From the viewpoint of practical statesmanship the preservation of peace or the launching of war are never the supreme objects of policy. They are means to an end; the more fundamental aim is to preserve, defend, and advance primary national interests. Such interests are guarded by peaceful means when possible, but the use of force is never ruled out as a last resort. "National defense" has ever been a prime concern of the statesmen.

When Lincoln's problem is placed in this context his words and acts during the secession crisis take on a semblance of rational consistency. Because the President-elect opposed compromise and peaceful secession it does not follow that his basic purpose was either peace or war. Rather, his chief concern was the maintenance of the Union, a national interest which he regarded as vital enough to have precedence

---

[18] Letter of "J. W." in Worcester *Spy*, December 29, 1860.

[19] Thurlow Weed Barnes (ed.), *Memoir of Thurlow Weed* (Boston, 1884), 312–13.

[20] Indianapolis *Daily Journal*, December 25, 1860. See also, Boston Correspondence in New York *Evening Post*, January 11, 1861; New York *Herald*, November 24, 1860; January 12, 1861; Washington Correspondence in New York *Courier and Enquirer*, January 10, 1861; New York *Tribune*, November 29, 1860; January 26, February 8, 14, 1861; Burlington (Vt.) *Times*, quoted in New York *Tribune*, February 16, 1861; Th. Heilscher to George W. Julian, November 30, 1860, in George W. Julian Papers (Indiana State Library, Indianapolis); Trumbull to Lincoln, December 4, 1860, in Nicolay and Hay, *Lincoln*, III, 254.

[21] This plan was discussed considerably in the northern press, especially in the early weeks when there was a tendency to treat the crisis lightly. See, for example, Boston *Daily Evening Traveller*, November 10, 12, 19, 1860; Boston *Journal*, November 10, 12, 19, 1860; Boston *Evening Transcript*, November 13, 1860; Boston *Daily Advertiser*, November 12, 17, 22, December 3, 1860. The idea was still being advanced by the Springfield (Mass.) *Republican* as late as February 26, 28, and March 23. The New York *Tribune* presented the plan, but did not endorse it, on March 27. The Washington Correspondent of the Boston *Daily Advertiser*, December 10, 1860, asserted that peaceful reconstruction was Seward's basic formula. See also, Potter, *Lincoln and His Party in the Secession Crisis*, 219 ff.

over all other considerations. And the integrity of the Union continued to be his paramount objective throughout the ensuing conflict.[22] There is no reason to doubt that Lincoln would have accepted peaceful and voluntary reconstruction as a satisfactory solution within the time limits fixed by expediency.[23] But there is abundant evidence that the possible necessity of coercion entered Lincoln's calculations as soon as he understood the seriousness of the crisis.[24] Lincoln was not a pacifist,[25] and, as a practical statesman, he looked upon disunion as sufficiently menacing to northern interests to justify resistance by force if necessary.

"The most distinctive element of Mr. Lincoln's moral composition," wrote Henry Villard, the shrewd and observant correspondent of the New York *Herald*, "is his keen sense and comprehensive consciousness of duty. Upon taking his oath of office he will not be guided so much by his party predilections as by the federal constitution and laws. . . . That he will endeavor to fulfill the obligations thus imposed upon him faithfully and fearlessly may be expected with the utmost certainty."[26] Making due allowances for inconsistencies and spells of irresolution, Villard was essentially correct in his surmise that Lincoln was strongly impressed with his obligation to "enforce the laws" under all conditions, and whatever the consequences. "I see the duty devolving upon me," he told a friend in early January, adding bitterly that he was "in the garden of Gethsemane now."[27] Lincoln was perhaps as frank and blunt on this point before his inauguration as he could have been under the circumstances. Certainly he had no desire to provoke a conflict before the fourth of March; the peaceful organization of his administration was essential before decisive action could be taken.

Nevertheless, it requires no unwarranted assumptions or tortured meanings to read coercion implications into Lincoln's public and private utterances before his inaugural address. On December 13 John G. Nicolay recorded Lincoln's current views on the matter: "The very existence of a general and national government implies the legal power, right, and duty of maintaining its own integrity. . . . It is the duty of the President to execute the laws and maintain the existing government."[28] One of the earliest acts of the President-elect was to establish contact with General Winfield Scott, whom he urged "to be as well prepared as he can to either hold or retake the forts, as the case may require, at and after the inauguration."[29] At least twice Lincoln

[22] See, for example, Lincoln's reply to Horace Greeley's "Prayer of Twenty Millions," in Nicolay and Hay (eds.), *Works of Abraham Lincoln*, VIII, 15–16.

[23] For the evidence that this was Lincoln's formula for saving the Union, see Potter, *Lincoln and His Party in the Secession Crisis*, 219 ff.

[24] Herndon noted that in November Lincoln, like most of the northern people, was reluctant to believe that the South was in earnest. This attitude soon changed, and before his departure for Washington, "Mr. Lincoln had on several occasions referred in my presence to the gravity of the national questions that stared him in the face." Angle (ed.), *Herndon's Lincoln*, 382, 408.

[25] Apparently another reason for Lincoln's hostility to the abolitionists was the pacifism which pervaded their ranks. Stephenson, *Lincoln*, 142–43.

[26] New York *Herald*, February 1, 1861.

[27] Interview with Judge Gillespie, in Ida M. Tarbell, *Life of Abraham Lincoln*, 4 vols. (New York, 1900), I, 405–407. For biographers of Lincoln who concluded that he contemplated coercion from the start, see *ibid.*, I, 395–97, and Stephenson, *Lincoln*, 145.

[28] John G. Nicolay Personal Memorandum, in Nicolay and Hay, *Lincoln*, III, 247–48. See also, Lincoln to Weed, December 17, 1860, in Nicolay and Hay (eds.), *Works of Abraham Lincoln*, VI, 82.

[29] Nicolay and Hay (eds.), *Works of Abraham Lincoln*, VI, 84–85. See also, Nicolay and Hay, *Lincoln*, III, 249–51.

assured friends that if the southern forts were occupied by secessionists, "my judgement is that they are to be retaken." [30] The resolutions adopted by the Illinois legislature, demanding the preservation of the Union and pledging "the whole resources of the State . . . to the Federal authorities," were drawn by Lincoln's own hand.[31] His response to the request of Pennsylvania's governor-elect, Andrew G. Curtin, for advice regarding his inaugural address was equally clear:

> I think of nothing proper for me to suggest except a word about this secession and disunion movement. On that subject, I think you would do well to express, without passion, threat, or appearance of boasting, but nevertheless, with firmness, the purpose of yourself, and your state to maintain the Union at all hazards. Also, if you can, procure the Legislature to pass resolutions to that effect.[32]

More than once during his trip to Washington in February, Lincoln gave additional evidence of his coercionist views. His remarks to an Indianapolis audience on February 11 were aptly defined as his "keynote." [33] By the simple process of putting suggestive questions to his listeners, he implied an intention to "hold and retake . . . [the] forts and other property, and collect the duties on foreign importations." [34] From this the Washington correspondent of the New York *Tribune* concluded that Lincoln believed "that he has a right to use force against the seceding States to the extent of recovering United States property, collecting the revenues and enforcing the laws generally." [35] To the New York *Herald* the speech was "the signal for massacre and bloodshed by the incoming administration." [36] Thereafter, perhaps alarmed by the sensational response, Lincoln spoke with greater caution.[37] Yet he told the New Jersey state assembly, on February 21, that "it may be necessary to put the foot down firmly." [38]

Meanwhile the President-elect had been revising and polishing his inaugural address.[39] The original document had contained a blunt coercion threat. "All the power at my disposal," it stated, "will be used to reclaim the public property and places which have fallen." While rejecting Seward's proposal to substitute a meaningless vagary, he accepted the advice of Orville H. Browning and omitted this phrase. But this deletion does not necessarily imply a change in Lincoln's original plans. Indeed Browning had defended his suggestion purely on the grounds of expediency. "The

[30] Lincoln to Major David Hunter, December 22, 1860, in Nicolay and Hay (eds.), *Works of Abraham Lincoln,* VI, 86; Lincoln to Trumbull, December 24, 1860, in Tracy (ed.), *Uncollected Letters of Lincoln,* 173.

[31] Hertz, *Abraham Lincoln,* II, 809.

[32] Lincoln to Andrew G. Curtin, December 21, 1860, in Paul M. Angle (ed.), *New Letters and Papers of Lincoln* (Boston, 1930), 260.

[33] John G. Nicolay, *The Outbreak of Rebellion* (New York, 1881), 48.

[34] Nicolay and Hay (eds.), *Works of Abraham Lincoln,* VI, 111–12; Indianapolis *Daily Journal,* February 12, 1861.

[35] New York *Tribune,* February 18, 1861. See also, New York *Evening Post,* February 12, 13, 1861.

[36] New York *Herald,* February 13, 14, 1861.

[37] Tarbell, *Life of Lincoln,* I, 417.

[38] Nicolay and Hay (eds.), *Works of Abraham Lincoln,* VI, 152–54.

[39] According to Herndon, Lincoln used only four references in the preparation of his inaugural: a copy of the Constitution, Jackson's proclamation on nullification, Clay's speech in the Senate in February, 1850, and Webster's reply to Hayne, which he admired as the "grandest specimen of American oratory." Angle (ed.), *Herndon's Lincoln,* 386.

fallen places ought to be reclaimed," he wrote. "But cannot that be accomplished as well or even better without announcing the purpose in your inaugural?" [40] Even after this change, the address still indicated that the new President might feel constrained under certain conditions to resort to the use of force. Besides referring to contingencies which could produce civil war, Lincoln announced his intention to see "that the laws of the Union be faithfully executed in all the States," to "hold, occupy, and possess the property and places belonging to the government, and to collect the duties and imposts." [41]

To one northern Democratic paper the inaugural was "a tiger's claw concealed under the fur of Sewardism." [42] Secessionists agreed almost unanimously that it threatened coercion.[43] The Republican Boston *Daily Advertiser* penetrated its meaning with uncommon acumen. The President, it believed, had implied that he would be discreet and conciliatory, but that he recognized "the natural limits of that discretion."

> . . . The address itself [it concluded] contemplates the possibility of an interruption of the peace. We understand the President to disclaim the intention of doing many things which he thinks himself authorized to do, but which he can forbear doing without detriment to the claims of the government. . . . But there is obviously a limit to this forbearance, and a limit to the concessions which the government should make for the preservation of peace. . . . Such powers as are confided to him . . . the President will use, with a due regard to practical policy, but with no thought of foregoing the exercise of a right essential to the existence of the government, because resistance to it is threatened.[44]

The fact that Lincoln intimated the possible use of force does not necessarily imply that he visualized, as an inevitable consequence, a long civil war, or the need for any war at all. Like many others, he may have felt that "a little show of force," entailing a minimum of bloodshed, would suffice to crush the southern rebellion.[45] The South might submit to the first military or naval demonstration, or soon thereafter. The consequence of coercive measures, however, was really out of the President's hands. It would depend upon the secessionists. And it was from this critical fact that Lincoln formulated his basic stratagem.

From the outset the new President had three clear advantages in dealing with the disunion crisis. First, the northern people, with few exceptions, agreed with him in denying the right of secession. However many may have favored compromise and hoped to avoid war, the masses of Republicans and Democrats alike shared the belief that the Union was perpetual.[46] It was not difficult, or even necessary, to convince

[40] Nicolay and Hay, *Lincoln*, III, 333–34.

[41] Nicolay and Hay (eds.), *Works of Abraham Lincoln*, VI, 169–85.

[42] Philadelphia *Pennsylvanian*, quoted in New York *Evening Post*, March 5, 1861.

[43] New York *Evening Post*, March 8, 9, 1861; New York *Tribune*, March 5, 1861.

[44] Boston *Daily Advertiser*, March 9, 1861.

[45] The Washington Correspondent of the New York *Tribune*, December 18, 1860, wrote: "The national government may have to *show* its teeth, but it is not at all likely that it will have to *use* them." See also, Philadelphia Correspondence in *ibid.*, January 21, 1861; Boston *Evening Transcript*, November 30, 1860; Laura A. White, "Charles Sumner and the Crisis of 1860–61," in Avery Craven (ed.), *Essays in Honor of William E. Dodd* (Chicago, 1935), 152–55.

[46] In his last message to Congress in December, 1860, President Buchanan not only denied the right of secession, but asserted that it would be his duty to enforce the laws in the South. James D. Richardson (ed.), *A Compilation of the Messages and Papers of the Presidents, 1789–*

them that the preservation of the Union was a vital national interest. A second advantage grew out of the fact that the burden of direct action rested with the seceding states which, after all, were seeking to disturb the political *status quo*. They felt it necessary, in order to make their independence a reality, to seize government forts and other property, and to destroy the symbols of federal authority. As a result, the Union government could easily pretend to forego aggressive action and simulate a defensive pose. In other words, the exigencies of the situation dictated to a practical statesman the strategy of defense, of throwing the initiative to the South.

And here is where Lincoln's third great advantage found its usefulness. Given the general northern belief that the Union was not and could not be dissolved, the government was free to make a number of "defensive" moves. These seemingly non-aggressive acts could include such things as collecting the revenues, holding federal property, perhaps even reinforcing the forts or recovering those that might be seized. Such action, it was widely felt, would be far different from marching a hostile army into the South to overawe and coerce it.[47] Of course secessionists, who regarded the dissolution of the Union as an accomplished fact, brushed aside these fine distinctions and branded any federal intervention in the South as coercion. But, although abstract logic was doubtless on their side, to Lincoln this was irrelevant. Always holding the Union above peace, he exploited his three strategic advantages in order to cast coercion in the mold of "defense," and to shift the responsibility for consequences to his "dissatisfied fellow-countrymen."

1897, 10 vols. (Washington, 1896–1899), V, 626–37. See also, Buchanan's letter to the South Carolina Commissioners, December 31, 1860, in *War of the Rebellion: A Compilation of the Official Records of the Union and Confederate Armies,* 129 vols. and index (Washington, 1880–1901), Ser. I, Vol. I, pp. 115–18. Senator Stephen A. Douglas repeatedly denied the right of secession. See his letter to the Memphis *Appeal,* quoted in New York *Evening Post,* February 5, 1861; Washington Correspondent of New York *Herald,* December 8, 1860; George Fort Milton, *The Eve of Conflict: Stephen A. Douglas and the Needless War* (Boston, 1934), 520–21. For expressions of this opinion in the Democratic press, see New York *Herald,* November 13, 21, December 12, 27, 30, 1860; New York *Leader,* January 5, 1861; Boston *Post,* November 10, December 6, 1860; New York *Journal of Commerce,* November 8, December 6, 1860; Albany *Atlas and Argus,* quoted in New York *Evening Post,* January 2, 1861. For a similar view in a Bell-Everett paper, see Boston *Daily Courier,* March 23, 25, 1861.

Significantly the Republican papers which allegedly favored permitting the South to secede in peace almost invariably placed such qualifications on the process as to make it meaningless. See, for example, New York *Tribune,* November 2, 9, 16, 26, December 3, 1860; January 14, 1861; New York *World,* December 8, 15, 1860; Springfield *Republican,* November 10, 15, 22, December 3, 1860; Indianapolis *Daily Journal,* December 24, 1860; January 19, 1861. See also, David M. Potter, "Horace Greeley and Peaceable Secession," in *Journal of Southern History,* VII (1941), 145–59.

[47] The Boston *Daily Advertiser,* December 24, 1860, said: "There is no form in which coercion . . . can be applied. The general government can do no more than see that its laws are carried out." See also, New York *Evening Post,* December 20, 1860; January 30, February 16, March 6, 1861; New York *Tribune,* November 24, 1860; Hartford *Courant,* quoted in New York *Tribune,* February 15, 1861; Springfield *Republican,* November 24, December 8, 1860; Indianapolis *Daily Journal,* December 6, 21, 1860. This is the precise distinction which Buchanan made when he denied the right of coercion but proclaimed it to be his duty to enforce the laws. Richardson (ed.), *Messages and Papers of the Presidents,* V, 626–37. Lincoln made the same distinction in his Indianapolis address on February 11. Nicolay and Hay (eds.), *Works of Abraham Lincoln,* VI, 112–15. Yet, whatever constitutional distinction exists between coercing a sovereign state and using force to maintain federal authority, the practical result is the same.

In no sense was this defensive concept an original contribution to the crisis on Lincoln's part. From the outset the Republican press expressed the formula with remarkable spontaneity. "The Republican policy," asserted the Springfield (Massachusetts) *Republican*, "will be to make no war upon the seceding states, to reject all propositions for secession, to hold them to the discharge of their constitutional duties, to collect the revenues as usual in southern ports, and calmly await the result. There can be no war unless the seceders make war upon the general government." [48] The New York *Evening Post* suggested that if South Carolina should make it impossible to collect duties at Charleston, Congress could simply close it as a port of entry. "Here then we have a peaceful antidote for that 'peaceful remedy' which is called secession. It is no act of war, nor hostility, to revoke the permission given to any town to be opened as a port of entry; but when that permission is revoked it would be an act of hostility . . . to disregard the injunction." [49] A northern clergyman summed up the strategy neatly in advising the South: "Secede on paper as much as you please. We will not make war upon you for that. But we will maintain the supremacy of the constitution and laws. If you make war on the Union, we will defend it at all cost, and the guilt of blood be on your heads." [50] Thus the strategy, occasionally defined as one of "masterly inactivity," [51] had been outlined in advance; Lincoln had only to read the newspapers to discover its value.

From the time the President-elect left Springfield in February until the firing upon Fort Sumter, the central theme of his public utterances was the further development and clarification of the strategy of defense. Holding inflexibly to the view that his fundamental purpose must be the preservation of the Union, he chose his words carefully and shrewdly to absolve himself from any charge of aggression. Appreciating the possibility that hostilities might ensue, Lincoln seemed preoccupied with an intense desire to leave the record clear, to make it evident to the northern people that war, if it came, would be started by the South. His words were not those of a man confused about the true situation, about what his policy should be, or about possible consequences. The coercive intimations were nearly always of a sort that could be perceived only by southern secessionists, seldom by northern Unionists.

During his first stop, at Indianapolis, Lincoln began at once to expound his defensive strategy. In a speech from the balcony of the Bates House he denied any intention to invade the South with a hostile army, and implied that the government would only defend itself and its property. [52] On February 21 he assured the New Jersey legislature that he would do everything possible to secure a peaceful

[48] Springfield *Republican*, December 19, 1860.

[49] New York *Evening Post*, December 10, 1860.

[50] Rev. C. S. Henry to Senator ——, *ibid.*, January 30, 1861. For additional expressions of the strategy of defense, see *ibid.*, January 18, February 16, 18, 1861; New York *Tribune*, January 24, 1861; New York *Courier and Enquirer*, December 10, 29, 1860; New York *World*, February 1, 1861; Boston *Journal*, January 16, 1861; Springfield *Republican*, January 2, 12, February 4, 9, 19, 1861; Worcester *Spy*, February 6, 1861; Indianapolis *Daily Journal*, December 27, 1860; January 8, 1861.

[51] New York *Times*, March 21, 1861; Boston *Daily Advertiser*, November 12, 16, 17, 22, December 3, 1860.

[52] Nicolay and Hay (eds.), *Works of Abraham Lincoln*, VI, 112–15; Indianapolis *Daily Journal*, February 12, 1861.

settlement. "The man does not live who is more devoted to peace than I am." [53] The next day, before the Pennsylvania legislature, he expressed regret "that a necessity may arise in this country for the use of the military arm. . . . I promise that so far as I may have wisdom to direct, if so painful result shall in any wise be brought about, it shall be through no fault of mine." [54] A few hours later, shortly before his secret trip to Washington, Lincoln spoke with unusual clarity. "Now in my view of the present aspect of affairs," he said, "there is no need of bloodshed and war. There is no necessity for it. I am not in favor of such a course; and I may say in advance that there will be no bloodshed unless it is forced upon the government. The government will not use force, unless force is used against it." [55]

The strategy was rounded out with additional assurances to the South that its rights would be protected, thereby denying the necessity of secession in self-defense.[56] Hence he could insist innocently that "there is no crisis but an artificial one," that "there is nothing that really hurts anybody." [57] Always embarrassed by the popular election returns, Lincoln also sought to convey the impression that a major issue was the right of the majority to rule.[58] Finally, he placed the question of the Union squarely in the hands of the American people. He was but their servant, elected to do their wishes. Without their support he was helpless; with it the Union must triumph. Summing up, he said:

> In all trying positions in which I shall be placed, and doubtless I shall be placed in many such, my reliance will be upon . . . the people of the United States; and I wish you to remember, now and forever, that it is your business, and not mine; that if the Union of these States and the liberties of this people shall be lost, it is but little to any one man of fifty-two years of age, but a great deal to the thirty millions of people who inhabit these United States, and to their posterity in all coming time. It is your business to rise up and preserve the Union and liberty for yourselves, and not for me. I appeal to you again to constantly bear in mind that not with politicians, not with Presidents, not with office-seekers, but with you, is the question: shall the Union and shall the liberties of this country be preserved to the latest generations.[59]

Since there were few aspects of the strategy of defense that had not already been discussed, Lincoln's inaugural address presented little more than a final clear exposition of the formula. He again insisted that in maintaining the authority of the government "there needs be no bloodshed or violence; and there shall be none, unless it be forced upon the national authority." He would abstain from doing many things which he had a right to do, but which could be foregone without injury to the prestige of the government. He desired a peaceful solution, but contended that the matter was really beyond his control. "In your hands, my dissatisfied fellow-countrymen," he declared, "and not in mine, is the momentous issue of civil war. The government will not assail you. You can have no conflict without being your-

[53] Nicolay and Hay (eds.), *Works of Abraham Lincoln*, VI, 152–54.
[54] *Ibid.*, VI, 162–65.
[55] *Ibid.*, VI, 156–58.
[56] See especially Lincoln's address to the mayor and citizens of Cincinnati, *ibid.*, VI, 119.
[57] *Ibid.*, VI, 121–22, 124–29.
[58] *Ibid.*, VI, 122–23.
[59] *Ibid.*, VI, 111–12, 142–44, 145, 160–62.

selves the aggressors. You have no oath registered in heaven to destroy the government, while I shall have the most solemn one to 'preserve, protect, and defend it.'" [60]

Thus by the time of his inauguration Lincoln had made it clear enough that his policy would be the preservation of the Union through a defensive strategy. With consummate skill he had at once hamstrung the South, satisfied the mass of the northern people that he contemplated no aggression, and yet conveyed his determination to defend the authority of the federal government. The Republican press glowed with appreciation. "No party can be formed against the administration on the issue presented by the inaugural," observed one friendly editor.[61] Another noted that "the fiat of peace or war is in the hands of Mr. Davis rather than of Mr. Lincoln." [62] Samuel Bowles of the Springfield *Republican* believed that the inaugural had put "the secession conspirators manifestly in the wrong, and hedges them in so that they cannot take a single step without making treasonable war upon the government, which will only defend itself." [63] By the fourth of March Lincoln had already cornered the disunionists.

It should be evident, then, that Lincoln's reaction to the problem of supplying Fort Sumter, which faced him as soon as he came into office, was in perfect harmony with his strategy of defense. His decision to sustain the Sumter garrison involved no change of plans or sudden determination to provoke the war.[64] It was a logical consequence of the President's fixed determination to defend the Union even at the risk of hostilities. Had the Sumter crisis not arisen, or had Lincoln been convinced ultimately that military necessity dictated evacuation,[65] his strategy inevitably would have led to some comparable result. In fact, while the new administration prepared to supply Major Robert Anderson, it also sought other means of developing its defensive formula. On March 9, for example, Lincoln instructed General Scott "to exercise all possible vigilance for the maintenance of all the places within the military

[60] *Ibid.*, VI, 169–85. In the first draft the following words concluded the paragraph quoted above: "You can forbear the assault upon it, I cannot shrink from the defense of it. With you, and not with me, is the solemn question of 'Shall it be peace or a sword.'" Nicolay and Hay, *Lincoln*, III, 343.

[61] Springfield *Republican*, March 6, 1861.

[62] Boston *Journal*, March 12, 1861.

[63] Springfield *Republican*, March 6, 1861.

[64] Lincoln finally decided on March 29 to prepare the Sumter expedition. Nicolay and Hay (eds.), *Works of Abraham Lincoln*, VI, 226–27. For alleged evidence that the Sumter garrison was not short of supplies, and that Anderson never reported such a shortage, see Tilley, *Lincoln Takes Command, passim.* For evidence that Anderson did report the approaching exhaustion of his supplies in a letter (since lost) dated February 27, see Potter, *Lincoln and His Party in the Secession Crisis,* 333–35. For additional evidence that the garrison had nearly exhausted its supply of pork, flour, beans, coffee, sugar, and salt, see Anderson to Colonel L. Thomas, April 1, 1861, in *Official Records,* Ser. I, Vol. 1, pp. 230–31. In another letter to Thomas, dated April 4, Anderson actually referred to his letter of February 27 reporting the exhaustion of his supplies. *Ibid.*, Ser. I, Vol. 1, pp. 236–37.

[65] For the testimony of army men that military necessity required the evacuation of Sumter, see Secretary of War Simon Cameron to Lincoln, March 16, 1861, in Nicolay and Hay (eds.), *Works of Abraham Lincoln,* VI, 202–207. There is evidence that Lincoln proposed the abandonment of Fort Sumter to a delegation of Virginia Unionists if they "would break up their convention, without any row or nonsense." But the offer was rejected. See Potter, *Lincoln and His Party in the Secession Crisis,* 353–58. Whether Lincoln seriously expected the Virginians to accept the offer cannot be ascertained. In any event, the President still would have been free to develop his strategy of defense in other directions.

department of the United States, and to promptly call upon all the departments of the government for the means necessary to that end." [66] A few days later when he learned that Texas secessionists had deposed Governor Sam Houston, Lincoln offered him military and naval support if he would put himself at the head of a Union party.[67] Simultaneously the President considered the collection of duties from naval vessels off southern ports, or even a blockade of the Confederacy.[68]

But Lincoln's most important action, aside from the move to supply Sumter, had reference to Fort Pickens. In January, President Buchanan had sent reinforcements on the U.S.S. *Brooklyn* to Pensacola Harbor, but they were not landed when he agreed to a truce with certain secessionist leaders. On March 11, Lincoln ordered Scott to instruct the commander to land these troops at once.[69] On April 6, however, a special messenger arrived from Pickens with the news that the reinforcements had not disembarked, for Captain H. A. Adams of the *Brooklyn* denied that Scott's orders could supersede those of the former Secretary of the Navy. The President dispatched new instructions immediately, and the troops landed on April 12 while Anderson was still in possession of Sumter.[70]

Yet, in his message to the special session of Congress which assembled on July 4, Lincoln suggested that he might have ordered the evacuation of Sumter if Pickens could have been reinforced before Anderson exhausted his supplies. He could have avoided injuring the national cause, he said, by thus demonstrating that he was yielding only to military necessity. Apparently still seeking to impress the nation with his peaceful intentions, Lincoln declared that the April 6 report on the failure to reinforce Fort Pickens had prompted him to send the relief expedition to Anderson. This decision was motivated, he added, by the desire to prevent "our national destruction" and to give "bread to the few brave and hungry men of the garrison." [71]

In stating that the voluntary surrender of Sumter hinged upon the successful reinforcement of Pickens, Lincoln gave evidence of confusion, for it is difficult to harmonize this interpretation with the known facts. No member of the cabinet, at any time, revealed the knowledge that this was Lincoln's plan. Indeed, on April 1, the President informed Seward categorically that he did "not propose to abandon Fort Sumter." [72] Moreover, the debate on supplying Sumter went on in the cabinet and in Lincoln's mind *after* the order to reinforce Pickens had been sent, an order which the President had no reason to believe would not be executed at once. Most important was the fact that Captain Gustavus Vasa Fox, who commanded the relief expedition to Sumter, received his final instructions to go forward on April 4, the same day that a letter was written to Anderson notifying him that supplies were

[66] Nicolay and Hay (eds.), *Works of Abraham Lincoln*, VI, 188.

[67] For Houston's rejection of this offer, see Houston to Charles A. Waite, March 29, 1861, in Amelia W. Williams and Eugene C. Barker (eds.), *The Writings of Sam Houston*, 8 vols. (Austin, 1938–1943), VIII, 294. See also, Nicolay, *Outbreak of Rebellion*, 14, and Tarbell, *Life of Lincoln*, II, 20–22.

[68] Nicolay and Hay (eds.), *Works of Abraham Lincoln*, VI, 224–25.

[69] Montgomery C. Meigs, Diary, entry of March 31, 1861 (Division of Manuscripts, Library of Congress); Nicolay and Hay, *Lincoln*, III, 393–94; *Official Records*, Ser. I, Vol. I, p. 360.

[70] *The Diary of Gideon Welles*, 3 vols. (Boston, 1911), I, 29–32; Nicolay and Hay, *Lincoln*, IV, 7–9, 11–13; Nicolay, *Outbreak of Rebellion*, 53.

[71] Nicolay and Hay (eds.), *Works of Abraham Lincoln*, VI, 297–325. In a sense, Lincoln thereby confessed that he held the prevention of "our national destruction" above peace.

[72] *Ibid.*, VI, 236–37.

being sent.[73] Since the expedition did not start for several days, there was still time to countermand Fox's orders. But the letter to Sumter must have been dispatched before the arrival of the messenger from Pickens on April 6, for Anderson received it the following day.[74] A letter could not have reached Anderson in less than twenty-four hours. And finally, since reinforcements actually entered Pickens on April 12, Lincoln *did* achieve that objective before Anderson's capitulation. That a second body of troops under Captain Montgomery C. Meigs did not reach Fort Pickens until April 17 was, therefore, irrelevant.[75] Lincoln had approached Sumter and Pickens as separate problems, although his action in each case was part of a unified program.

Thus it was not the Sumter plan alone, but all these activities combined, which illustrated the rapid development of Lincoln's strategy of defense. Step by step he was quietly moving to assert and vindicate federal authority in the South. Before each advance the secessionists would have had to retreat, until they found themselves discredited before their own people and, for all practical purposes, back in the Union. Their only alternative was resistance, but always the burden of aggression would be upon them. Lincoln's record would remain clear in the eyes of the northern people.

If Lincoln ever seriously believed that his problem could be solved by voluntary reconstruction—and there is nothing to indicate that he had completely ruled out this solution in the early stages of the crisis—his mind must have been disabused of this notion long before the guns of Sumter began to speak. The transparent hostility of the leading secessionists to plans for adjustment,[76] the rapid organization of a Confederate government, and the military preparations in the South would have hardly encouraged confidence in this formula. Besides, the Republican press had confidently predicted that Lincoln would pursue a "vigorous policy." Amid the abuse directed at Buchanan for his "weakness" and "submission to treason" came assertions that the new President would soon demonstrate that "we still have a government." The following comment in the New York *Courier and Enquirer* was typical:

> Mr. Buchanan may strive to get rid of his obligations to the Constitution and the Union, imposed by his oath of office and "the Supreme law of the land;" but Mr. Lincoln . . . is not the man to shrink from the performance of any duty. Like Jackson he may regret the necessity of shedding blood in the faithful discharge of his duties; but having accepted the Presidency, and solemnly sworn to sustain the Constitution, preserve the Union, and execute the laws, he will not be wanting in the hour of trial.[77]

[73] *Ibid.,* VI, 239–40; Nicolay and Hay, *Lincoln,* IV, 27–29. See also, Ramsdell, "Lincoln and Fort Sumter," *loc. cit.,* 279, and Randall, "When War Came in 1861," *loc. cit.,* 18–25.

[74] Anderson reported receiving the message "by yesterday's mail" in a letter to Colonel Thomas, dated April 8. *Official Records,* Ser. I, Vol. I, p. 294. Lincoln's private secretaries insisted that the letter to Anderson of April 4 "was immediately sent by mail to Sumter." Nicolay and Hay, *Lincoln,* IV, 27–29.

[75] Nicolay and Hay, *Lincoln,* IV, 3–7, 16–17. Quite relevant, however, was the fact that the Meigs expedition to Fort Pickens was instructed to stop en route at Key West. Meigs brought commissions for new federal officers to replace the secessionist, and authority for the commanding officer at Fort Taylor to proclaim martial law. *Ibid.,* IV, 14–15.

[76] Alda Gregory, "The Southern Congressional Delegation and Compromise, 1860–1861" (M.A. thesis, University of Maryland, 1944).

[77] New York *Courier and Enquirer,* December 14, 1860. For similar expressions see *ibid.,* January 8, 9, 15, 16, 23, 1861; New York *Evening Post,* November 6, 13, 1860; January 21,

These earlier prognostications, combined with the secrecy which covered the development of Lincoln's strategy, threatened to discredit his administration unless there was immediate and vigorous action. The widespread rumors in March that Sumter was to be evacuated gave the anti-Republican press an opportunity to jibe at the new President. "This administration," mocked the Democratic Cleveland *Plain Dealer*, "after all its blustering about 'enforcing the laws in all the states,' not only surrenders Sumter but South Carolina and the whole South." [78] The opposition insisted that Lincoln was merely continuing Buchanan's "weak" policy.[79]

Even before Lincoln's inauguration there were abundant signs that the general uncertainty was becoming intolerable.[80] More and more it appeared that time was not on the side of the Union, that the secession movement was actually gaining in strength. After March 4, Republican leaders bombarded Lincoln with advice favoring a decisive move, and with warnings that the people would not tolerate the abandonment of Sumter.[81] Simultaneously the differences between northern and southern tariff schedules frightened many conservative merchants into a mood for drastic remedies.[82] By the end of March numerous businessmen had reached the point where they felt that anything—even war—was better than the existing indecision which was so fatal to trade. "It is a singular fact," wrote one observer, "that merchants who, two months ago, were fiercely shouting 'no coercion,' now ask for anything rather than *inaction*." [83] Even anti-Republican and anti-coercion papers

1861; New York *World*, February 14, 25, 1861; New York *Tribune*, December 15, 16, 20, 1860; January 19, February 8, 19, 1861; Bangor *Whig and Courier*, quoted in New York *Tribune*, February 19, 1861; Bridgeport *Standard*, quoted in *ibid.*, February 25, 1861; Chicago *Journal*, quoted in *ibid.*, February 26, 1861; Springfield *Republican*, November 15, 1860; January 9, 1861; Indianapolis *Daily Journal*, February 12, 1861.

[78] Cleveland *Plain Dealer*, quoted in New York *World*, March 22, 1861. See also New York *Herald*, March 12, 1861; Boston *Post*, March 16, 21, 1861.

[79] New York *Herald*, March 16, 25, 1861; New York *Morning Express*, April 1, 1861; Boston *Daily Courier*, March 11, 16, 1861; Buffalo *Courier*, quoted in Springfield *Republican*, March 29, 1861. On April 8, the Republican New York *Evening Post* confessed: "Since Mr. Lincoln came into power there has been with some a disposition to censure his seeming inactivity, and to complain that his Administration, thus far, has been only a continuation of the disgraceful policy of his predecessor."

[80] See, for example, New York *Herald*, January 21, 1861; New York *World*, February 23, 27, 1861; letter from "One," in New York *Evening Post*, February 25, 1861; Washington Correspondence in Springfield *Republican*, February 22, 1861.

[81] New York *Evening Post*, March 11, 13, 23, 1861; Washington Correspondence in New York *Herald*, March 14, 28, 1861; New York *Courier and Enquirer*, March 26, April 4, 1861; New York *World*, March 9, April 4, 1861; New York *Times*, April 3, 1861; New York *Tribune*, March 12, 14, 16, 18, 25, April 2, 3, 1861; Boston *Evening Transcript*, March 20, April 6, 1861; Boston *Daily Advertiser*, March 13, 1861; Boston Correspondence in Springfield *Republican*, March 16, 1861; William D. Foulke, *Life of Oliver P. Morton*, 2 vols. (Indianapolis, 1899), I, 113–14; Samuel W. Crawford, *The Genesis of the Civil War: The Story of Sumter* (New York, 1887), 364.

[82] New York *Evening Post*, March 7, 12, 21, 22, 26, 1861; New York *Herald*, March 16, 23, 1861; New York *Courier and Enquirer*, March 14, 15 (Commercial Column), 1861; Boston *Daily Advertiser*, March 14, 1861; Boston *Daily Evening Traveller*, April 6, 1861. For a brilliant analysis of the influence of the tariff issue on the New York merchants, see Philip S. Foner, *Business and Slavery: The New York Merchants and the Irrepressible Conflict* (Chapel Hill, 1941), 275 ff.

[83] Washington Correspondence in New York *Evening Post*, March 29, 1861. See also, Commercial Columns of New York *Herald*, March 20, 26, April 5, 1861; of New York *Courier and Enquirer*, March 16, 18, 19, 25, 1861; and of New York *Tribune*, March 23, 1861.

could bear the suspense no longer and urged that something be done.[84] Lincoln might well have desired a little more time to organize his administration before dealing with the secessionists. But the general unrest in the North, as well as the Sumter crisis, forced his hand at once. The time for delay had passed.

It was in this atmosphere that Lincoln dispatched the relief expedition to Fort Sumter.[85] Every circumstance combined to make this a satisfactory culmination of his defensive strategy. Popular attention long had been focused upon this point. A southern attack was almost certain to consolidate northern opinion behind the new administration, and submission would seriously damage Confederate prestige. Having authorized Seward to promise the southern commissioners that relief would not be sent without due notice,[86] the President could be doubly sure that this step would be decisive. Above all, the fact that he could force the issue by merely sending supplies served to underscore the defensive nature of his move.[87] Whether the Confederates attacked or submitted, Lincoln would triumph.

The President himself pointed to the Sumter expedition as the fulfillment of the strategy he had outlined in the past. He did it first in his reply to Seward's memorandum of April 1, in which the Secretary of State proposed, for all practical purposes, a strategy of defense, except that he favored the evacuation of Sumter.[88] Professing surprise at this, Lincoln reminded Seward that his inaugural embraced "the exact domestic policy you now urge, with the single exception that it does not propose to abandon Fort Sumter." [89] Even more emphatic was his response, on April 13, to the delegation sent by the Virginia Convention to inquire about his policy. "Not having as yet seen the occasion to change," he said, "it is now my purpose to pursue the course marked out in the inaugural address." He would still hold federal property in the South. If it proved true, however, that "an unprovoked assault has been made upon Fort Sumter," he would then feel free to "repossess" the places seized before his inauguration. It was at this point, if he had not done so before, that Lincoln expressed a clear and unqualified decision in favor of coercion. Yet he still took pains to give it a defensive cloak, for he added that he would simply "repel force by force." [90]

The Confederate attack upon Fort Sumter was, in effect, a striking victory for Lincoln's strategy of defense. And just as Republican editors had first presented the formula, their appreciation of its success was immediate and spontaneous. In one

[84] New York *Herald*, March 9, 1861; New York *Morning Express*, April 5, 1861; New York *Leader*, March 30, 1861; Boston *Post*, March 23, April 6, 1861. A Washington dispatch to the New York *Tribune*, April 8, 1861, reported that there was as much pressure for decisive action from Democrats as from Republicans.

[85] Nicolay and Hay (eds.), *Works of Abraham Lincoln*, VI, 239–40; Nicolay and Hay, *Lincoln*, IV, 27–29. For details of the preparations and last minute negotiations, see Tarbell, *Life of Lincoln*, II, 17–19; Ramsdell, "Lincoln and Fort Sumter," *loc. cit.*, 273–82; and Potter, *Lincoln and His Party in the Secession Crisis*, 336 ff.

[86] Nicolay and Hay, *Lincoln*, IV, 33–35; Nicolay, *Outbreak of Rebellion*, 55.

[87] See Lincoln's instructions to R. S. Chew, his messenger to Governor Francis W. Pickens of South Carolina, in Nicolay and Hay (eds.), *Works of Abraham Lincoln*, VI, 241.

[88] Seward advocated the defense and reinforcement of all the Gulf ports, and the establishment of a blockade. "This will raise distinctly the question of union or disunion," he wrote. "I would maintain every fort or possession in the South." Nicolay and Hay (eds.), *Works of Abraham Lincoln*, VI, 234–36.

[89] *Ibid.*, VI, 236–37.

[90] *Ibid.*, VI, 243–45.

great chorus they united in denouncing the secessionists as the aggressors. "It was," wrote one, "an audacious and insulting aggression upon the authority of the Republic, without provocation or excuse." [91] A Boston paper piously regarded the event as one which furnished "precisely the stimulus which . . . a good Providence sends to arouse the latent patriotism of the people." [92] "*Let it be remembered*," cried the Providence *Journal*, "*that the Southern government has put itself wholly in the wrong, and is the aggressor*. On its head must be the responsibility for the consequences." [93] These, of course, were mere reflections of the opinions of an indignant northern people.

Only a few cynical editors survived in those exciting days. Early in April the Albany *Argus* hinted "that the administration of Mr. Lincoln is disposed to secretly provoke a fight; and that it looks to some collision at the South, commenced on that side, to arouse Northern feeling." [94] Another critic believed that the Sumter expedition was designed "*to provoke and draw the first fire, from the Montgomery government*." [95] "By this cunningly contrived plan," added a Democratic editor, "it is hoped the responsibility of commencing hostilities will be thrown upon the South." [96] The reason: "Nothing but a war can keep together the Republican party." [97] Within a few days, however, the doubters were either converted or silent.

That Lincoln calculated the danger of Confederate resistance at Charleston is beyond a reasonable doubt. The messengers sent to Sumter in March gave him abundant opportunities to know the state of feeling in South Carolina. During the period of preparation the President strove to organize the defenses of Washington. [98] On April 9 he warned Governor Curtin of "the necessity of being ready," and urged him to prepare for an emergency. [99] John G. Nicolay and John Hay, Lincoln's private secretaries, believed that it was "reasonably certain" that he expected hostilities to ensue. [100] And when the news arrived of the attack upon Sumter, they noted that Lincoln was neither surprised nor excited. [101] Most conclusive was the fact that if the President believed that Sumter could be supplied peacefully, there was no reason why he should ever have considered evacuation as a possible military necessity.

There is no evidence that Lincoln regarded the result of his strategy with anything but satisfaction. Having founded his policy upon the desire to preserve the Union at all costs, he had reason to congratulate himself, for with a united North

[91] New Haven *Journal and Courier*, quoted in New York *Tribune*, April 15, 1861.

[92] Boston *Daily Advertiser*, April 15, 1861.

[93] Providence *Journal*, quoted in Boston *Evening Transcript*, April 13, 1861. See also New York *Tribune*, April 5, 9, 11, 1861; New York *World*, April 6, 8, 13, 16, 1861; New York *Courier and Enquirer*, April 10, 1861; New York *Commercial Advertiser*, April 9, 1861; Springfield *Republican*, April 13, 1861; Boston *Journal*, April 11, 1861; Indianapolis *Daily Journal*, April 11, 13, 1861.

[94] Albany *Argus*, quoted in Boston *Post*, April 6, 1861.

[95] New York *Morning Express*, April 11, 1861.

[96] Utica *Observer*, quoted in New York *Tribune*, April 13, 1861. See also, New York *Herald*, March 9, 11, 19, April 5, 9, 1861.

[97] Washington Correspondence of New York *Journal of Commerce*, quoted in New York *Morning Express*, April 15, 1861.

[98] Nicolay and Hay, *Lincoln*, IV, 64–68.

[99] Angle (ed.), *New Letters and Papers of Lincoln*, 266. See also, Lincoln to Cameron, April 10, 1861, in Nicolay and Hay (eds.), *Works of Abraham Lincoln*, VI, 242.

[100] Nicolay and Hay, *Lincoln*, IV, 44–45.

[101] *Ibid.*, IV, 70.

behind him that achievement was inevitable. "You and I both anticipated," he wrote to Captain Fox, "that the cause of the country would be advanced by making the attempt to provision Fort Sumter, even if it should fail; and it is no small consolation now to feel that our anticipation is justified by the result." [102] A few months later, when he had gained greater perspective, Lincoln again expressed this opinion to Senator Browning, but added the belief that the fall of the fort, in the long run, was more useful than a successful effort to supply.[103]

Nicolay and Hay also believed that Lincoln regarded the success or failure of the Sumter expedition as "a question of minor importance." More significant was his determination that "the rebellion should be put in the wrong," that the Confederates "would not be able to convince the world that he had begun civil war." [104] Indeed Nicolay was certain that it was Lincoln's "carefully matured purpose to force rebellion to put itself flagrantly and fatally in the wrong by attacking Fort Sumter." [105] The transparent admiration of Lincoln by his secretaries did not prevent their reaching an accurate conclusion:

> When he finally gave the order that the fleet should sail he was master of the situation; master of his Cabinet; master of the moral attitude and issues of the struggle; master of the public opinion which must arise out of the impending conflict; master if the rebels hesitate or repent, because they would thereby forfeit their prestige with the South; master if they persisted, for he would then command a united North.[106]

With the fall of Sumter the strategy of defense lost its usefulness, and instantly Lincoln changed his ground. In his proclamation of April 15 calling for 75,000 volunteers there was no reference to the defensive strategy of "holding" or "possessing" federal property. Instead he summoned the militia to suppress an insurrection, "to cause the laws to be duly executed," to preserve the Union, and "to redress wrongs already long enough endured." [107] Thus, again, as in his reply to the Virginia delegation, the President endorsed the use of coercive force. A few days later, while addressing the Frontier Guards in Washington, Lincoln gave additional evidence that he had always preferred coercion to disunion. While professing peaceful intentions, he added the opinion that "if the alternative is presented, whether the Union is to be broken in fragments, . . . or blood be shed, you will probably make the choice, with which I shall not be dissatisfied." [108] Having calculated this contingency almost from the start, Lincoln was now ready to maintain a basic national interest by force, the last resort of all practical statesmen.

Although Lincoln accepted the possibility of war, which, in retrospect at least, was the inevitable consequence of his strategy of defense, the indictment—if such it be—can be softened by surrounding circumstances. Clearly the burden rested not on Lincoln alone, but on the universal standards of statesmanship and on the whole concept of "national interest." This was a thing worth fighting for! If Lincoln was

---

[102] Nicolay and Hay (eds.), *Works of Abraham Lincoln*, VI, 261–62.

[103] Theodore C. Pease and James G. Randall (eds.), *The Diary of Orville H. Browning*, 2 vols. (Springfield, 1927), I, 475–76.

[104] Nicolay and Hay, *Lincoln*, IV, 33, 44–45.

[105] Nicolay, *Outbreak of Rebellion*, 55, 74.

[106] Nicolay and Hay, *Lincoln*, IV, 62.

[107] Nicolay and Hay (eds.), *Works of Abraham Lincoln*, VI, 246–48.

[108] Hertz, *Abraham Lincoln*, II, 830.

no pacifist, neither were his contemporaries. The growing impatience in the North and the widespread demand for action must have contributed something toward shaping his final decision. And it is still a moot question whether it is the function of politicians in a democracy to yield to popular pressures or to resist them. Moreover, without quibbling over who was guilty of the first act of aggression, the fact remains that southern leaders shared with Lincoln the responsibility for a resort to force. They too preferred war to submission.

Nor was it certain that acquiescence in disunion was necessarily a peace formula. Many Northerners believed sincerely that the clash of interests in a divided Union would lead, sooner or later, to armed conflict. Lincoln contended "that far less evil & bloodshed would result from an effort to maintain the Union and the Constitution, than from disruption and the formation of two confederacies." [109] That this was more than a Republican rationalization was attested by the fact that some conservative Democrats held the same opinion. Thus the pro-Breckinridge Boston *Post* declared: "We have no faith, if the States separate, that there can be a peaceable issue of the vast interests, and the public property, at stake." [110] Certainly Lincoln had no way of knowing positively that his decision to risk hostilities through the Sumter expedition would pave the way to four years of bloody war. He doubtless shared the common belief that the contest would be short. [111]

Finally, it may well have been true that the outbreak of war saved the Republican party from disintegration, and that a practical politician like Lincoln could not have overlooked that possibility. [112] But its Machiavellian implication is based on sheer speculation. The evidence makes equally valid the conclusion that Lincoln considered only "the cause of the country." Or, again, he may have had a comprehensive understanding of what both the country and political expediency demanded. Perhaps it was simply Lincoln's good fortune that personal, party, and national interests could be served with such favorable coincidence as they were by his strategy of defense.

[109] Pease and Randall (eds.), *Browning Diary*, I, 453.

[110] Boston *Post*, December 5, 1860. See also, New York *Herald*, November 19, 30 (Commercial Column), December 3 (Commercial Column), 1860; Washington Correspondence of New York *Tribune*, January 15, 1861; Washington Correspondence of New York *Journal of Commerce*, November 3, December 10, 1860; New York *Courier and Enquirer*, January 8, 1861; New York *Leader*, December 29, 1861; Buffalo *Express*, quoted in New York *World*, March 28, 1861; Boston Correspondence in Springfield *Republican*, March 22, 1861; Boston *Daily Courier*, November 13, 1860.

[111] Thus the Springfield *Republican*, April 17, 1861, said: "There will be no prolonged and doubtful struggle. The country is coming down like an avalanche upon the conspiracy, and it will be annihilated at one fell swoop."

[112] Ramsdell, "Lincoln and Fort Sumter," *loc. cit.*, 271–72.

Part V

THE WAR
FOR THE UNION

16 / Civil War Dissidence in the North: The Perspective of a Century

William G. Carleton

The South's attack on Fort Sumter rallied most Northerners to the Union cause. Lincoln's call for 75,000 volunteers was oversubscribed as men flocked to defend their nation and their government against attack. Even the political opposition rallied to the old flag. Douglas immediately offered his help to the President, and other Northern Democrats followed his example.

But the pro-Union enthusiasms of April were neither universal nor lasting. Not all Democrats were Unionists, and many of those who were at the outset lost their enthusiasm as the conflict dragged on and the sacrifices grew. But many other factors in addition to partisan politics contributed to the growing resistance to the war. As the months passed, East-West conflict, hitherto largely submerged under the more intense and dangerous North-South battle, came to the surface and posed a threat to federal unity. Ethnic tensions, especially those directed against the Negro, also turned men away from the Union cause. And there were social and economic ingredients in the disunionist mixture as described by William G. Carleton in the following article. In the end the Union cause was triumphant. There would be occasions, however, when it seemed likely that the Confederacy would win its independence not on the battlefields of the South but on the political hustings of the North.

For further reading: Wood Gray, *The Hidden Civil War: The Story of the Copperheads* (New York: The Viking Press, Inc., 1942); Frank Klement, *The Copperheads in the Middle West* (Chicago, Ill.: University of Chicago Press, 1960); Frank Klement, "Middle Western Copperheadism and the Genesis of the Granger Movement," *Mississippi Valley Historical Review*, XXXVIII (March 1952); George F. Milton, *Abraham Lincoln and the Fifth Column* (New York: Vanguard Press Inc., 1942); Richard O. Curry, "The Union as it was: A Critique of Recent Interpretations of the 'Copperheads,'" *Civil War History*, XIII (March 1967).

South Atlantic Quarterly, LXV, No. 3 (Summer 1966), 390–402. Reprinted by permission.

I

At first sight it seems paradoxical that during our Civil War the Union, which was the repository of traditional American nationalism, should have suffered as much serious internal dissent as the Confederacy, which represented a newer nationalism. This, however, should not really be surprising, for the North, even after the secession of the eleven Southern states, was territorially much vaster than the South; it was economically and socially more diversified; its society was less class-structured and less closely knit; it had far more new European immigrants; it contained sizable areas where the people were mainly of Southern origin; its population was pervasively affected by what today is called racism, which produced grave doubts about changing the status of the Negro; and its tradition of constitutional government gave rise to qualms about maintaining by force a Union originally conceived in consent.

Obviously, the most widespread disaffection within the Union was in the border states of Delaware, Maryland, Kentucky, and Missouri, where slavery and a considerable plantation system existed. It was difficult to keep these states in the Union at all; in part they were kept there by military and other high-handed measures of the Federal government. All of them furnished large numbers of men to the Confederate armies, and frequently these men fought in Confederate regiments which bore the flags and names of their states. Rump governments in Kentucky and Missouri were formally admitted to the Confederacy, and these sent representatives to the Congress at Richmond. There were at all times partisan undergrounds and guerrilla wars in these two states. Some territories in Kentucky and Missouri ultimately became as much conquered provinces of the Union as did the Confederate states themselves.

There was trouble in the new Pacific states of Oregon and California, where for a time some leading politicians flirted with a movement to take these states out of the Union and form an independent Pacific Confederation.

There was some disaffection in the powerful Eastern states. The Peace Democrats there found their chief support in the foreign-born laboring populations of the large cities, particularly the Irish. These people feared that the war would result in the emancipation of the Negro, his migration North, and the consequent competition of unskilled white labor with Negro labor.

However, the Peace Movement and the Peace Democrats were never as strong in the East as in the Middle West. The Eastern states contained fewer people of Southern origin; their agrarian elements were weaker; the war was largely financed in the East; the East got the lion's share of government war contracts; and Eastern businessmen, responding to a trend which had begun earlier, were increasingly shifting their investments from trade to manufacturing, from shipping to railroads. Republicans made great gains among businessmen of the East, but even the Democratic party there was affected by the changing interests of the business community. It was the Eastern delegations to the Democratic national convention of 1864 which checked the Midwestern peace forces of Ohio's Vallandigham and compelled the presidential nomination of General George B. McClellan.

In the Middle West, however, it was a different story. In wide parts of Ohio, Indiana, and Illinois, the people were transplanted Southerners. When one reads the speeches and press of this period, he is struck by the prevalent emotional dislike in these areas for "New England Yankees." The Middle West was still largely agrarian, and there was much suspicion of Eastern business interests. Many communities in the Middle West were still dependent on river traffic, and the rivers flowed to the Mississippi, which flowed to the South. There was a widespread feeling that the people of the Mississippi Valley, north and south, were culturally and economically bound together.

In short, during the Civil War, the Middle West continued to play the role it had played during the prior four decades; it held the balance of power between the South and the Northeast; the rivers tugged in one direction, the canals and railroads in the other. Ohio, Indiana, and Illinois were historically the oldest and at that time the most populous of the Midwestern states. These states would determine the balance of power in the Middle West, which would determine the balance of power in the nation.

All through the war, in Ohio, Indiana, and Illinois, the Democratic party remained strong in most of the poor and the undeveloped counties. It remained strong, too, in the counties along the Ohio, the Wabash, and the Mississippi rivers. The notable concentration of Democratic support in downstate Indiana and Illinois was produced by a combination of three factors: most of the downstate counties were poor counties, many were river counties, and a large part of the population was of Southern origin.

Paradoxically, in proportion to its population, the Middle West, including Ohio, Indiana, and Illinois, did far better in furnishing recruits to the Union armies than did the East. Some of the Democratic counties were among the banner recruiting counties. Because they filled their volunteer quotas repeatedly, numerous communities in the Middle West did not become subject to the draft until 1864, near the close of the war. Why this rush to volunteer? The volunteers were chiefly poor farm boys, members of families with a tradition of mobility, families less rooted than the farm families of the East. They were mainly attracted to the cash bounties proffered volunteers.

II

The most massive criticism of the war came from the Democrats, and during the war the Democratic party was roughly divided into three factions: the War Democrats, the Majority Democrats, and the Peace Democrats. The War Democrats supported the war measures as vigorously as the Republicans, and many of them, such as John A. Logan in Illinois, John Brough in Ohio, and General Grant himself, passed over to the Republican party. The Majority Democrats were committed to winning the war and bringing the seceded states back into the Union, by force if necessary. Unlike the War Democrats, they never for an instant adjourned partisan politics for the sake of the war, and they kept up a running fire of sharp criticism of the Lincoln administration. Typical Majority Democrats in the Middle West were Allen G. Thurman in Ohio and Thomas A. Hendricks in Indiana. Majority Democrats kept alive the traditional party conflict of agrarians against Hamiltonians. They charged that the Republicans were taking advantage of the war to foist on the country a Hamilton-Clay program—a protective tariff, a hard-money banking system, and federally subsidized railroads. Much was made of the high freight rates of the railroads, and it was held that the roads were taking unfair advantage of the monopoly which had come to them with the closing of the Mississippi River.

Republicans were denounced for seeking a "military dictatorship." This had a broad popular appeal, for the American political creed was simple and made small allowance for crisis. There were only two kinds of government (and no in-between)—a centralized autocracy and a decentralized republicanism which touched the individual very little in his everyday activities. America, of course, was the shining example of the latter. Many Americans were deeply disturbed by the war censorship, the muzzling of editors, the suspension of the writ of habeas corpus, the military arrests of civilians and trials of civilians by military commissions, and the military draft, which invaded personal liberty in unprecedented fashion, contained the undemocratic feature of allowing purchase of a substitute, and went so far as to require all those subject to conscription to get a pass before they could travel beyond the confines of their home counties.

The most explosive issue exploited by the Democrats was the Negro question. Democrats charged that beginning with the preliminary Emancipation Proclamation in the autumn of 1862 the objective of the war had been drastically shifted from saving the Union to freeing the slaves. This was a telling argument, for contemporary accounts leave no doubt that among the people of the Ohio Valley there was a deep folk aversion to the Negro as "a creature apart." In the summer of 1862, in a state referendum in Illinois, voters approved by a majority of over 100,000 a state constitutional amendment barring the entry of free Negroes into the state. When Secretary of War Stanton sent some "contraband" Negroes to Illinois with orders that military officers find them civilian employment, there was a furor in the state. Undoubtedly the Emancipation Proclamation damaged war morale in Ohio, Indiana, and Illinois. It was attacked not only by the Democrats but by some non-Democrats. Many Democrats made no allowance for it as a war measure. Some Democrats said publicly that it had so changed the character of the war as to absolve army volunteers from the terms of their enlistment.

Sheer political partisanship was doubtless one of the motives of the Democratic opposition. During the nineteenth century, party warfare in the United States had the flavor of a fanatical sectarianism. The coming of the war could not long dampen such intense party feelings. In the rural America of that time, cash was scarce, and government jobs and the public printing fed to partisan newspapers meant much financially to politicians and editors. Partisanship was traditionally expressed in an exaggerated, bombastic manner, and it would have been impossible to change the political style overnight. Americans have not had the custom of coalition government in time of war; during all of America's foreign wars, even those of the twentieth century, there has been more or less of partisan opposition and criticism; and the Civil War touched the traditional issues of domestic politics far more than have America's foreign wars.

III

The third Democratic faction, the Peace Democrats, like the Majority Democrats, were agrarians, civil-libertarians, and anti-abolitionists. However, in their opposition they went far beyond these issues. They claimed that Lincoln and the Republicans had balked all attempts to settle the differences with the South by sabotaging the Crittenden Compromise and other conciliatory measures. They called the war "Mr. Lincoln's War," a "Republican War." They insisted that the American Union was based on consent, that to keep the South in the Union without its consent and by force would turn the whole Union into a despotism and make the South "another Poland, another Hungary, another Ireland." They called on the government in Washington to explore all possibilities to restore "the Union as it was and the Constitution as it is." With or without a cease-fire or an armistice, the North should set in motion negotiations with the South looking to the assembling of a national convention to work out a grand compromise.

Who were the leading Peace Democrats? In Ohio, they were Congressmen Clement L. Vallandigham, Chilton A. White, Alexander Long, George H. Pendleton, "Sunset" Cox, and Samuel Medary, the slashing editor of the *Crisis*. In Illinois, they were Congressmen William J. Allen, William A. Richardson, and James C. Robinson. Robinson, as the Democratic candidate for governor in 1864, is now known to have accepted a large campaign contribution from Jacob Thompson, the Confederate representative in Canada. In Indiana, the Peace Democrats were Jesse D. Bright (until he lost his influence when he was expelled from the United States Senate for "pro-Southern" sympathy); J. J. Bingham, editor of the Democratic party's leading newspaper in that state; Horace Heffren, Democratic leader in the Indiana legislature; and to a considerable degree Congressman Daniel W. Voorhees, destined for a long career in the United States Senate, and Michael C. Kerr, who in the post-war period was to serve a term as Speaker of the national House of Representatives. After the Emancipation Proclamation, Senator David Turpie leaned to the Peace Democrats.

Vallandigham finally emerged as the most brilliant and daring of the Peace Democrats. He was no mere opportunist. He had sincere and deep convictions about the nature of constitutional government. He abhorred the giant wartime strides to centralized and consolidated federal government, which he regarded as permanent threats to liberty, a trend to tyranny. Indeed, his views on constitutional government and civil liberty were almost identical with those of Alexander H. Stephens of Georgia, whose extreme libertarian positions were a problem to Jefferson Davis. But because Vallandigham's public career was cast in a different environment from that of Stephens, Vallandigham has gone down as odious, one of "the damaged souls" of American history, whereas Stephens was repeatedly honored by his people during and after the war and is a respected figure in our history. The place of the articulate "impossibilist" in history has yet to be adequately explored by the historian and the philosopher.

Now, what were the Peace Democrats prepared to do if their program proved impractical? What if the Union refused to enter into negotiations with the Confederacy? What if the Confederacy spurned such negotiations? What if a national convention called to find a compromise failed to reach an agreement? Most Peace Democrats refused to face these questions. But some faced them squarely, and these men talked of a Northwestern or Western Confederacy that would establish friendly relations with the Southern Confederacy and reach accords that would keep open the Mississippi River.

By 1864, with victory eluding the North time after time and perceptible war-weariness setting in, the Peace Democrats became more extremist in their talk and their plans. The various "temples" and "castles" of the Knights of the Golden Circle, which had originally operated as local clubs to protect Democrats from the taunts and attacks of Unionist patrioteers and Republican extremists (although some of their individual members had without doubt carried on various and sundry subversive activities), were absorbed in the more centralized Order of American Knights, which in turn became the even more centralized Sons of Liberty, with Vallandigham, then in exile in Canada, its "Supreme Commander." As membership fell and the Peace Democrats came to dominate the Sons of Liberty, secret military sections of the order were formed. There were plans here and there in Indiana and Illinois to obstruct the draft by force. Federal troops from New York were sent to Indiana to administer the draft in the most dissident counties. In the summer of 1864 a conspiracy was afoot which involved the crossing over into the United States of escaped Confederate prisoners of war, then refugees in Canada, and their joining the military sections of the Sons of Liberty in an armed uprising. The plans called for capturing the Federal arsenals, liberating the Confederate prisoners in the big prison camps in the Northwest, seizing the state governments of Ohio, Indiana, Illinois, Kentucky, and Missouri, and proclaiming a Western Confederacy. This grandiose scheme miscarried for a number of reasons: Federal officials got wind of it and took measures to insure its failure; most Democratic politicians who heard of it vehemently opposed it and many resigned from the Sons of Liberty; and by August, 1864, Vallandigham was convinced that the Democrats had a chance to win the presidency on a peace platform and that nothing should jeopardize that chance.

About this same time, Indiana's indefatigable Governor Oliver P. Morton ferreted out evidence which seemed to link several leading Indiana Democrats, all members of the Sons of Liberty, to the conspiracy. A famous treason trial before a military commission in Indianapolis followed. One of those accused escaped and fled to Canada; two were allowed to turn state's evidence; the others were sentenced to death or life imprisonment. All of those convicted subsequently escaped punishment when a celebrated decision of the United States Supreme Court, in the aftermath of the war, held illegal the trial of civilians before a military commission. But the trial had served the purpose for which it was intended: in the public mind it linked Copperheads, Vallandigham, and Democrats to overt treason, and it furnished the Republicans with sensational ammunition for the presidential election of 1864.

IV

What was the impact on our history of the barrage of criticism by the Majority Democrats and the Peace Democrats? It provided the Democrats with their share of election victories during the war. It slowed down the movement to abolition, and the attitudes it fostered would later do much to scuttle Radical Reconstruction and measures designed to give the Negro first-class citizenship. It checked an overzealous military intervention into civilian affairs. The device of the Democrats of nominating for Congress and the state legislatures popular "martyrs" of military arrest and often electing them proved effective. This and other spectacular forms of protest frequently stayed the hand of local military commanders.

The issues of the Civil War also cast their long shadows over the fortunes of the political parties in the three decades following the war. So accurately did the Democrats of the war period reflect attitudes of large segments of voters in Ohio, Indiana, and Illinois that these states became classic examples of two-party states, razor-edge "swing" states, decisive determiners of the outcomes of national elections. Most of the Copperhead leaders did not suffer for their views, and even many of those who represented the rump governments of Kentucky and Missouri in the Confederate Congress later had long careers in the United States Congress. Wood Gray, author of that little classic on Civil War dissidence, *The Hidden Civil War,* observed that "the Copperhead leaders lived on, for the most part in careers that seemed strangely unaffected by their wartime activities." But there is nothing strange about this, and Professor Gray's comment is an ex post facto judgment. The generation which lived through the Civil War was not as pervasively impressed by the Union-Lincoln mystique as were succeeding generations. Later, when Democrats became more affected by this mystique, they had a way of keeping the mystique and their practical political behavior in two separate compartments.

As to the long-range major trends to industrialism and centralization, the Democratic opposition made little impact. To be effective in this area, the Peace Democrats would have had to be powerful enough to force a compromise before the Union victory or prevent a Union victory by successfully organizing a Western Confederation. (Even then it is probable that industrialism would not have been permanently stayed but only temporarily slowed, and that industrialism in turn would ultimately have reunited the country and increasingly centralized government and society.) Actually, the Peace Democrats were never as strong as they sometimes appeared to be. Concentration on a single aspect of a given historical situation always runs the risk of unduly magnifying that aspect. Despite Professor Gray's scholarly restraint and warning, the impression on the general reader left by his book is that Midwestern disaffection was more overtly dangerous to the Union than it really was.

After all, membership in the Copperhead organizations was never as large as rumor had it, and membership fell after Gettysburg and Vicksburg. Only a portion were full members; the rest were mere "vestibule" members deemed unworthy of initiation into the inner circle. Those who belonged to the secret military sections were fewer still. Most of those connected with the Copperhead organizations never knew the extremist intentions of a few daring leaders. Alarms about a forcible resistance to the draft proved to be without much substance. Conspiracies for organizing a Western Confederation fizzled. Unlike Kentucky and Missouri, partisan undergrounds and guerrilla wars never developed in Ohio, Indiana, and Illinois. Even when Captain Thomas H. Hines in June, 1863, and General John Morgan the following month led Confederate raids deep into Democratic sections of southern Indiana, there were not enough active Southern sympathizers there to seize these opportunities for operating a real underground, much less a guerrilla war.

The real threat to the Union in Ohio, Indiana, and Illinois was less spectacular. The vast majority in those states wanted to preserve the Union, but among that majority there were segments with nagging doubts about building up the element inimical to the agrarian interest, about abolition and the freed Negro, about whether a union maintained through coercion would be a Union compatible with liberty. As the war dragged on, these doubts increased. The Democratic party expressed those doubts; it exploited them; it contributed to a weakening of the will to victory. With a little more war-weariness and defeatism, the victory might have gone to the Confederacy.

V

We must beware of "inevitability," of what Herbert Butterfield has called "the Whig theory of history." This disposition to treat history as though no outcome were possible except that which actually prevailed is especially strong in the case of our Civil War because of the vast superiority of the North in technology, wealth, and manpower. Yet when one studies the concrete narrative of the war, he is struck by the narrowness of the Union victory. Indeed that victory was just in the nick of time. By 1864 war-weariness was almost as much in evidence in the North, particularly in the Midwestern states, which had contributed so handsomely in military manpower, as it was in the South. The military levies were becoming increasingly difficult. How much longer could the Union armies have been sustained?

One is struck, too, with the significance of the fortuitous. For instance, in 1862, the year the Democratic party swept the congressional and local elections in Ohio, Indiana, and Illinois, it so happened that in none of these states was a governor scheduled to be elected. If gubernatorial elections had been held in these states that year, as they were in many other states, Democratic governors would have been elected in all of them. With Morton and Yates out of the governorships of Indiana and Illinois, with Democratic governors installed in Columbus, Indianapolis, and Springfield, how well would Unionist sentiment have stood up in those states during the months of despair which followed Fredericksburg and Chancellorsville? True, the same doubts were expressed about Horatio Seymour in New York, and he turned out to be an acceptable war governor. But the New York Democracy did not contain nearly so many Peace Democrats as did the Democracy in Ohio, Indiana, and Illinois.

Again, in 1863, what if the Union victory at Gettysburg had been postponed just several months, until after the autumn elections—would Vallandigham have been elected governor of Ohio, and if so, what then? And again, the years 1862 and 1863 saw bumper crops in the Middle West and poor harvests in Europe, increasing Britain's dependence on Northern wheat and bringing prosperity to Northern farmers. But what if this happenstance had been reversed—poor crops in the North and bumper crops in Europe? Still again, in 1864, with Grant bogged down before Petersburg, what if the fall of Atlanta had been postponed for just two months, until after the election (which might well have been the case had President Davis not supplanted Joseph E. Johnston with Hood)—would McClellan then have capitalized on Northern war-weariness and defeatism and been elected president; and what would have been the consequences of that?

VI

Lincoln may have been the decisive element in the Union victory. Here the reference is not to the Union-Lincoln mystique, which Edmund Wilson has brilliantly delineated as being mostly authored by Lincoln himself, even to the extent of anticipating his own tragic death as an apocalyptic climax of a passion play, but to the mundane Lincoln, with his phenomenal dexterity in practical politics. Lincoln was extremely sensitive to every nuance of opinion; he circumspectly mediated between the conflicting groups and factions within the Union and the parties; he cautiously found at any given time the widest common denominator of opinion which would allow for effective action. To have prematurely or permanently alienated any sizable group in the Union coalition would have been fatal.

No doubt Lincoln possessed the seismographic instincts naturally, but the fact that he had lived his life in Kentucky, southern Indiana, and downstate Illinois, where opinion on slavery and the Negro was most divided and where war dissidence and potential dissidence were rife, made him acutely aware of the various shades of public opinion. During the 1850's, Douglas often charged that in northern Illinois, Lincoln was black; in central Illinois, mulatto; and in southern Illinois, lily white. There is some truth in this statement, but Lincoln's very resilience was a source of his effectiveness as a national leader.

It was Lincoln's flexibility which confounded his critics. Were the Democrats suspicious that the war would be waged to the glory of the Republicans? Lincoln responded by giving the Democrats their fair share of the military officerships and commands. Were the people of the Ohio and Mississippi valleys exasperated by the cutting off of Southern trade? Lincoln reacted by winking at the intersectional trade which persisted in spite of the war, by acquiescing in halfhearted enforcement of the rules designed to stop it. Was there an outcry against military arrests of civilians? Lincoln often quietly overruled the more zealous decisions of department commanders; and Vallandigham was allowed to return to Ohio with impunity, resume his political career, and play a conspicuous role at the Democratic national convention in 1864. Was there fear of abolition and a freed Negro? Lincoln moved slowly and guardedly, and made each step toward abolition appear a reluctant, belated, but necessary measure to win the war.

Behind the Lincolnian "procrastination," "temporizing," "opportunism," "deviousness," and "slovenliness," there was a calculated shrewdness which parried dissidence and even greater potential dissidence, particularly in Lincoln's home country. Had that dissidence ever reached the point of overt resistance or even spread further as paralyzing defeatism, the Civil War would probably have had a different outcome. And had the North been forced to yield, there is little doubt that leading Peace Democrats would then have been brought forward to negotiate the settlement with the South—another example of that thin line which not infrequently in history, and in politics, separates the blessed from the damned.

VII

Yet in the deeper sense, distinguished from the externalities of the narrative, there may be "irresistible" forces in history, or at a certain stage forces may become irresistible. Would a Tory "settlement" in 1689 and 1714 have checked the commercial revolution in Britain? Would a Confederate victory have stayed industrialism, its attendant erosion of slavery, its accompanying centralization in government and society? Were not De Bow, Fitzhugh, and some other representatives of the Southern conservative enlightenment of the 1850's already urging, with considerable internal inconsistency, the industrialization of the South? In this view, Stephens and Vallandigham could never have become wise prophets of the future; nor could Davis. Nor can Lincoln. For if we pursue this line of thought, the Civil War itself becomes a tragic irrelevance, and Lincoln's name stands associated with one of the most gigantically wasteful interludes in all history. We would then have to look elsewhere for the more insightful exemplars of the age—perhaps to the Clays and Websters of 1850, the Crittendens and Douglases of 1860.

17 / The Republican Party and the Emancipation Proclamation

Mark Krug

In addition to opposition from Copperheads and peace Democrats, Lincoln encountered schisms within his own party that limited his freedom of action. Few Republicans disagreed with the President that the chief purpose of the war was to suppress the rebellion and restore the Union, but there were deep divisions over the men and the means to be employed.

Most important was the disagreement over the future of slavery. Although a Westerner with Southern roots, Lincoln was relatively free from racial bias. However, he shared the views of all but a few white Americans that color prejudice was ineradicable and that the black man could not live comfortably side by side with whites in freedom. He wished the Negro well, but he was scarcely an abolitionist, and in the months following Sumter he was far more concerned with the fate of the Union than with the future of the slaves. He particularly feared that any move against slavery would drive the border states into the arms of the rebels.

To the "Radicals" in the Republican Party, the President's willingness to sacrifice the slave to the Union seemed outrageous and shortsighted. Some were willing to risk the Union in order to free the slave. Most believed that freeing the slave would preserve the Union and strike a blow against the Confederacy.

Gradually the strong antislavery wing of the Republican Party increased its pressure, forcing Lincoln to adopt a scheme for compensated emancipation in the border states and to accept a Congressional measure abolishing slavery in the District of Columbia. The logic of events also bore down on Lincoln. As Union forces advanced into the South, hundreds and then thousands of blacks fled to the Union lines. It was difficult to decide what policy to adopt toward these refugees. Why not use these ex-slaves to defend the Union? Here was a large pool of potential recruits for the Northern armies, and although the fighting qualities of blacks were as yet untested,

Journal of Negro History, XLVIII, No. 2 (April 1963), 98–114. Reprinted by permission.

This paper was read at the American Historical Association meeting in Chicago, Ill., December 1962.

it seemed sensible to grant freedom to them and their families and to use them as Union soldiers.

World opinion, particularly that in France and England, also influenced Lincoln. Enlightened men in Europe deplored slavery. At the same time many English and French conservatives disliked the Yankees and admired the spunk of the South. From the outset of the war, the French and British governments had taken what Northerners considered to be unneutral actions, and British shipyards had built and equipped the Confederate raiders that cut a wide swath through Northern shipping. Lincoln and the Radicals both believed that diplomatic intervention by the major European powers on the side of the South—an event that the North feared and the South eagerly anticipated—could be prevented if the war were converted into a battle to destroy slavery.

But the military events of 1862 were decisive. The war, especially in the East, had not been going well for Union arms. A series of defeats during the summer of 1862 created a profound sense of discouragement. Seemingly the rebellion was being won in spite of the nation's utmost military efforts. Lincoln now thought that the time had come to use whatever political weapons against secession he could command. As early as mid-July, the President had determined to announce general emancipation as a war measure. He stayed his hand at this point only because he wished the move to come from apparent strength rather than from desperation. Lee's repulse at Antietam on September 18, while an equivocal Union victory at best, was sufficient to brighten the gloomy military picture, and in late September the President issued the preliminary Emancipation Proclamation announcing that after January 1, 1863, slavery was ended in all regions still in rebellion. On the first day of the new year, as scheduled, the President issued the definitive Proclamation.

The Emancipation Proclamation actually did little to change the status of the vast majority of slaves. It applied only to the regions still in rebellion, or, in other words, only to those parts of the Confederate States where the federal government had no power to abolish anything. Because of its limited application, because it seemed to be extracted from a reluctant administration, and because of its laconic tone and language, the Proclamation has often been disparaged and its author's role as the Great Emancipator belittled. In line with other interpretations that muffle the idealistic, antislavery components of the war, the Proclamation has been reduced to little more than a gesture motivated by expediency and imposed on a reluctant President by his Radical antagonists. In the article that follows, Mark Krug defends Lincoln and reiterates the older view of the central significance of the Proclamation.

For further reading: Benjamin Quarles, *The Negro in the Civil War* (Boston, Mass.: Little, Brown and Company, 1953); *Dudley T. Cornish, *The Sable Arm: Negro Troops in the Union Army, 1861–1865* (New York: W. W. Norton & Company, Inc., 1966); Fred A. Shannon, "The Federal Government and the Negro Soldier," *Journal of Negro History*, XI (October 1926); *David Donald, "The Radicals and Lincoln," in *Lincoln Recon-*

sidered (New York: Vintage Books, 1956); David Donald, "Devils Facing Zionwards," in Grady McWhiney (ed.), *Grant, Lee, Lincoln and the Radicals* (Evanston, Illinois: Northwestern University Press, 1964); T. Harry Williams, *Lincoln and the Radicals* (Madison, Wisc.: University of Wisconsin Press, 1941); Hans Trefousse, *The Radical Republicans, Lincoln's Vanguard for Racial Justice* (New York: Alfred A. Knopf, 1969).

It might be of interest to contemplate the different ways in which history and historians have dealt with the Gettysburg Address and with the Emancipation Proclamation. The Address received a little more than polite applause from those who heard it, few favorable, and mostly critical or contemptuous newspaper notices, but was later hailed and still continues to be hailed by historians as one of the greatest speeches in the history of men, as a most eloquent expression of moral and ethical fervor and as a clear and resounding call for self-government by a free people.

How different was the fate of the Emancipation Proclamation. When issued it was, as the evidence will show, hailed as an epoch-making revolutionary document, as a clarion call for human freedom, but as the years went by, historians became, in an increasing measure, disenchanted with it. It is now the accepted thing for historians to treat the Proclamation as one of Lincoln's war measures which was dictated only by military necessity. A distinguished historian, in a book published a few years ago did not hesitate to state: "The Emancipation Proclamation of January 1, 1863 had all the moral grandeur of a bill of lading." [1] There is something mystifying and perturbing in this strange fate of the Proclamation. How was it possible for millions of Americans in the North and yes, in the South, for shrewd and knowledgeable newspaper editors, Republicans and Democrats alike, to be so blind and so naive in their evaluation of the motives of Lincoln and of the importance of the Proclamation? How did it happen that the nation, North and South, white and black alike, was convinced that the Proclamation was an important turning point in the history of the war when in fact, as historians so often assert, the Proclamation was nothing of the sort?

It would seem indeed worth-while to examine this paradox. It might also be of importance to examine critically some of the commonly held assumptions concerning the Proclamation. I would list among these the following:

1. That Lincoln issued the Proclamation primarily from military necessity and that he was influenced little, if at all, by considerations of justice, freedom and morality;
2. That Lincoln issued the Proclamation with a great deal of reluctance and that his decision came mainly in response to the unbearable pressure exerted on him by the Radicals;
3. That Lincoln neither wished nor realized that the Emancipation Proclamation would make the abolition of slavery a central issue of the Civil War;
4. That the Republication Party was lukewarm and split in its reaction to the Proclamation;
5. And finally, that the issuance of the Proclamation was the major cause of the Republican defeats in the November, 1862 elections.

[1] Richard Hofstadter, *The American Political Tradition* (New York, 1957), p. 132.

The assessment of Lincoln's convictions on slavery is of decisive importance in evaluating his motive in the issuance of the Proclamation. If it is true, as so many historians have asserted, that Lincoln was lukewarm and vacillating on the issue of slavery, that there actually was little difference between his views on slavery and those of Stephen Douglas, then obviously the popular assertion that Lincoln issued the Proclamation reluctantly and as a military necessity seems quite plausible. On the other hand, if it should be possible to prove that Lincoln detested slavery and desired its prompt abolition, his motives in issuing the Proclamation must have been more complex.

One historian, in a letter of comment on the recent article of Fawn Brodie entitled "Who Won the Civil War Anyway"? which appeared in the *New York Times* wrote: "Presumably she [Mrs. Brodie] would not deny that Lincoln in his debates with Douglas . . . was in favor of white supremacy." [2] Mrs. Brodie will undoubtedly reply in due time, but it seems to me, on the basis of evidence, that in 1858 Lincoln did not endorse Douglas' concept of white supremacy.

In fact, Lincoln rejected Douglas' views on the subject. Douglas stated in Jonesboro: "I hold that this government was made on the white basis, by white men, for the benefit of white men and none others! I do not believe that the Almighty made the Negro capable of self-government . . . I say to you . . . that the signers of the Declaration had no reference to the Negro when they declared all men to be created equal." [3]

In his answer, Lincoln said that the Declaration of Independence *did* pertain to the Negroes as far as their right to life, liberty, and the pursuit of happiness was concerned. He rejected any attempt to exclude Negroes from the benefits and privileges implicit in the Declaration. He added: "I should like to know, if taking this old Declaration of Independence, which declares that men are equal upon principle and making exception to it, where will it stop. If one man says it does not mean a Negro, why not another say it does not mean some other man"? [4]

The frequently made claim that there was no central issue in the Debates must be squared with Lincoln's own evaluation of the major disagreement between himself and Douglas. "The real issue in this controversy," Lincoln declared in Alton, "the one pressing upon every mind is the sentiment on the part of one class that looks upon the institution of slavery as a wrong and of another class that does not look upon slavery as a wrong." [5]

It has often been suggested that Lincoln was a moderate on the issue of slavery because he said during the Debates in Charleston that he did not favor the social and political equality of the white and black races. The fact is that social and political equality of Negroes was not an issue in 1858. Few, if any, abolitionists advocated social and political equality of the Negroes at that time. The only relevant question to our subject concerns an analysis of Abraham Lincoln's convictions on slavery and the assessment of the role that these convictions played in the issuance of the Emancipation Proclamation.

[2] Ludwell H. Johnson in a letter to the Editor, *New York Times*, (September 23, 1962).

[3] Edwin Earle Sparks, (editor), *The Lincoln-Douglas Debates of 1858* (Springfield, Illinois, 1908), p. 225.

[4] Paul M. Angle and Earl Schenck Miers, (eds.), *The Living Lincoln* (New Brunswick, New Jersey, 1955), p. 189.

[5] *The Lincoln-Douglas Debates*, p. 482.

Let us look at the record. In the early 1830's Lincoln, a young and poor lawyer undertook, at his own expense, together with Lyman Trumbull and Gustave Koerner, to destroy the legal basis of the Negro indenture system which amounted to a de-facto slavery in Illinois. In 1839 Lincoln, in the case of *Cromwell vs. Bailey* won a decision in the Illinois Supreme Court on behalf of an indentured Negro slave girl Nancy. The court ruled, in an historic decision, that in Illinois the presumption was that a Negro was free and not subject to sale. It took, in those early days of Illinois, great courage for a young lawyer and budding politician to fight for Negro freedom. In 1836, Lincoln, a Representative in the Illinois House of Representatives, inserted a protest in the *Journal of the House* where he castigated pro-slavery resolutions passed by the Illinois General Assembly. In 1846, when in the U. S. House of Representatives, Lincoln fought for the abolition of slavery in the District of Columbia.

Lincoln's condemnation of slavery in the 1858 Debates was clear and unequivocal. In his opening speech of his Senatorial campaign in Chicago, he said on July 10, "I have always hated slavery, I think as much as any abolitionist." [6] On October 7, in Galesburg Lincoln stated, "Now, I confess myself as belonging to that class in the country who contemplate slavery as a moral, social, and political evil [and] . . . desire a policy that looks to the prevention of it as a wrong. . . ." [7] In Ottawa on August 21, Lincoln castigated slavery as a source of perpetual friction in the nation.[8] And in Freeport on August 27, he said, "I should be exceedingly glad to see slavery abolished in the District of Columbia." [9]

Lincoln was not indifferent to the fate of three and a half million Negro slaves. In a letter to George Robertson of Kentucky dated August 15, 1855, he wrote, "the condition of the Negro slave in America, scarcely less terrible to the contemplation of a free mind, is now as fixed and hopeless of change for the better, as that of the lost souls of the finally impenitent." [10]

In view of his long record of hatred of slavery and his long expressed desire to see it abolished, it seems reasonable to assume that Lincoln, as he told Chase, issued the Emancipation Proclamation to help the military situation of the Union and to right a moral wrong. Chase recalled that Lincoln told him: "When the rebel army was at Frederick, I determined, as soon as it should be driven out of Maryland, to issue a Proclamation of Emancipation . . . I said nothing to anyone, but I made the promise to myself, and (hesitating a little) to my Maker." [11] Chase's testimony seems to me to refute the theory that Lincoln issued the Proclamation with reluctance. It might also be well to give weight to the testimony of the editors of the *Chicago Tribune* who knew Lincoln well and who wrote on December 3, 1861, "the cautious language of the President on slavery does not hide from us, who know the deep moral conviction of the man, the purpose that he has in view. He comes to an advanced position—we make progress, we foresee the end, perhaps a long way off, a Republic without a traitor or a slave." [12]

What of the assertion of some historians that Lincoln issued the Emancipation Proclamation in response to an unbearable pressure put on him by the Radicals? One

[6] *The Living Lincoln,* p. 224.
[7] *The Lincoln-Douglas Debates,* p. 353.
[8] *Ibid.,* p. 104.
[9] *Ibid.,* p. 151.
[10] *The Living Lincoln,* p. 188.
[11] Quote from Chase's Diary in *The Lincoln Reader* (New York: 1959), p. 447.
[12] *Chicago Tribune,* December 3, 1861.

of our colleagues has suggested that "the wily Lincoln surrendered to the conquering Jacobins in every controversy before they could publicly inflict upon him a damaging reverse." [13] One wonders how this sweeping statement of Lincoln's abject surrender to the so-called Jacobins could be squared with his rescinding of Frémont's and Hunter's proclamations, his refusal to fire Seward, his taking the decision to dismiss McClellan only after he himself became convinced of the necessity for the step.

Those who insist on portraying Lincoln as patiently suffering the wrath, the vilification, and the pressure from the Radical extremists must find an answer to a number of perplexing questions. Is it not a fact that President Lincoln received from the 37th Congress, which was supposedly dominated by the so-called Jacobins, excellent cooperation? Is it not a fact that the 37th Congress, in its short session between December 4, 1861 to July 17, 1862, passed a very impressive list of legislative acts which included appropriation bills for the army and navy, an income tax law, a new tariff law, the Homestead Act, the College Land Grant Act, the act abolishing slavery in the District of Columbia? Is it not a fact that Lincoln received excellent cooperation from such Radical leaders as Charles Sumner, Chairman of the Senate Committee on Foreign Relations; Henry Wilson, Chairman of the Senate Committee on Military Services and the Militia; John P. Hale, Chairman of the Senate Committee on Naval Affairs; and from Zachariah Chandler, Chairman of the Senate Committee on Commerce, not to mention his close relations with men who are still mistakenly classed as Radicals like William Pitt Fessenden, Chairman of the Senate Committee on Finance, and Lyman Trumbull, Chairman of the Senate Committee on the Judiciary? Even Thaddeus Stevens, as Chairman of the powerful House Ways and Means Committee, gave Lincoln full support on the measures sought by the Administration for the prosecution of the war in spite of the private misgivings he had about Lincoln's caution in emancipating the slaves.

This impressive legislative record, of which every President would be very proud, could not have been accomplished without the active cooperation of this band of so-called Jacobins. The pages of the *Congressional Globe* do not bear out the contention that the Radicals badgered Lincoln and obstructed his program. On the contrary, these pages provide proof that Sumner, Wilson, Hale and Chandler, and of course, Fessenden and Trumbull, had a deep and abiding affection for the President and gave him their faithful and unstinted cooperation. Carl Schurz, an astute observer and himself no admirer of Sumner, wrote later in his autobiography: "Lincoln regarded and esteemed Sumner as the outspoken conscience of the advanced, antislavery element, the confidence and hearty cooperation of which was to him of highest moment. . . . While it required all his fortitude to bear Sumner's intractable insistence, Lincoln did not deprecate Sumner's public agitation for an immediate emancipation policy. . . . On the contrary, he rather welcomed everything that would prepare the public mind for the approaching development." [14]

In addition to Stevens, there was in the House another abolitionist Congressman, Owen Lovejoy of Illinois, the brother of Reverend Elijah Lovejoy, who was murdered by the pro-slavery mob in Alton. Owen Lovejoy was a faithful friend and supporter of the President. On May 30, 1864 Lincoln wrote to John H. Bryant, chairman of the committee on the erection of a monument to Lovejoy, who had died a month earlier, that during the ten years of their close relationship "every step in it has been

[13] T. Harry Williams, *Lincoln and the Radicals*, (Madison, Wisconsin: 1960), p. 18.

[14] *The Autobiography of Carl Schurz* (New York: 1961), p. 190.

one of increasing respect and esteem, in ending with his life, in no less than affection on my part. . . ." On Lovejoy's record in Congress Lincoln wrote: "Throughout my heavy and perplexing responsibilities here, to the day of his death, it would scarcely wrong any other to say, he was my most generous friend. Let him have the marble monument, along with the well-assured and more enduring one in the hearts of those who love liberty, unselfishly, for all men." [15]

It might be helpful to consider a remarkable statement made by Lincoln which contains *his* appraisal of his relationship to the Radicals and to the Conservatives. The statement is found in a letter to Charles Drake of Missouri which dealt with the constant strife between the Radicals and the Conservatives in Missouri and was dated October 5, 1863. The letter to Drake reads in part, "I do not feel justified to enter upon the broad field you present in regard to the political differences between Radicals and Conservatives. From time to time, I have done and said what appeared to me proper. . . . The public knows it well. It obliges nobody to follow me, and I trust it obliges me to follow nobody. The Radicals and the Conservatives each agree with each other, and would be too strong for any foe. . . . They, however, choose to do otherwise, and I do not question their right. I, too, shall do what seems to me my duty. . . . It is my duty to hear all; but, at last, I must, within my sphere, judge what to do and what to forbear." [16] This statement clearly indicates that Lincoln not only did not resent, but actually welcomed the pressures and the attacks on his policies by the Radicals on one hand and the Conservatives on the other. These attacks and these pressures gave him a free hand to act according to his own judgment and actually preserved his freedom of action.

It has often been stated that Lincoln's hand on the Emancipation Proclamation was forced by the projected Conference of War Governors which was scheduled to open in Altoona, Pennsylvania on September 24, 1862. A strong supporter of this theory wrote that "In Lincoln's desk the Emancipation Proclamation would probably have remained had it not been for the increased activities of the Radicals and a new move from the governors." [17] The argument continues that Lincoln became very apprehensive about what the governors might decide at their meeting on the 24th and therefore issued the Proclamation on the 22nd to avoid the wrath of the governors. This theory which has been used to destroy the supposedly naive notion of Lincoln as the Great Emancipator is ingenious, but is woefully lacking in evidence to support it. Who were those wild-eyed, irresponsible war governors who threw such a scare at Lincoln? Is it not a fact that Governor John Andrew of Massachusetts, Andrew Curtin of Pennsylvania, Richard Yates of Illinois and Austin Blair of Michigan, to name but a few, while often critical of the admitted inefficiency of Lincoln's Administration and his caution on the matter of slavery, were his staunch and loyal friends and supporters? After all, their patriotism, their devotion to the Union and their heroic effort to send troops to Washington in April and May of 1861, saved the Union and Lincoln from utter defeat and disaster. It should not be forgotten that in those bleak days of April, 1861, the Sixth Massachusetts, sent by John Andrew, was the first to brave the wrath of the pro-slavery mob in Baltimore and to arrive at Washington to reinforce the feeble garrison of the capital.

[15] *The Living Lincoln*, p. 606.

[16] Henry J. Raymond, *The Life and Public Services of Abraham Lincoln, Together with His State Papers* (New York, 1865), p. 436.

[17] William B. Hesseltine, *Lincoln and the War Governors* (New York, 1955), p. 244.

The papers of Richard Yates of Illinois and of John Andrew do not provide evidence of animosity or of an intended break with Lincoln at the Altoona Conference. Yates was too busy to attend the conference and sent Lieutenant Governor Gustave Koerner, a close friend of Lincoln, to represent him. He did send on July 11, 1862, a telegram to Lincoln stating that "blows must be struck at the vital parts of the rebellion." Calmly, Lincoln answered his friend, "Dick, hold still and see the salvation of God." [18] The theory of the sinister plot of the Radical governors cannot be reconciled with the fact that Governors Andrew and Curtin went to see Lincoln before the scheduled conference to consult with the President. Lincoln told them that he intended to issue the Proclamation and asked them whether they wished him to defer his action until after the Altoona Conference and thus make it appear that the Proclamation was issued in response to the call of the Governors' Conference.[19] Andrew and Curtin requested Lincoln to issue the Proclamation on the 22nd. The Conference, which met a day later, issued an Address, drafted by Governor Andrew, commending the action of the President.[20] So much for the Altoona plot.

There seems to be overwhelming evidence that the Emancipation Proclamation met with approval of all the factions in the Republican Party. The applause was not limited to the Radical Wing. There is also sufficient evidence to suggest that most Republican leaders were convinced that the Proclamation, cautious and limited in scope as it was, represented a turning point in the war because it made the issue of slavery a central issue of the Civil War.[21] The Democrats in the North and the leaders of public opinion in the Confederacy shared this view. Few, if any, contemporaries looked upon the Proclamation as a simple war measure taken by the Union's Commander in Chief.

The proclamation was received with warmth and enthusiasm by the Republican newspapers in the country. Significantly, newspapers which represented the Radical Republican point of view found nothing to criticize in the Emancipation Proclamation. Horace Greeley's *New York Tribune* wrote on September 24th that Lincoln

[18] Allan Nevins, *War for the Union*, Vol. 1 (New York, 1960), p. 147.

[19] Governor Austin Blair wrote sometime later in a memorandum summarizing the Conference: "Some ill-informed persons have asserted that the call for the Conference had occasioned the issue of the Emancipation Proclamation, though the Proclamation itself was issued and published to the country two days before the Conference assembled. That assertion was certainly not true. It was well understood by all men, at all conversant with the views of President Lincoln, that he had for a long time contemplated the Proclamation and only waited for a favorable occasion to put it forth." From a 24-page manuscript by Austin Blair entitled, "The Conference of Loyal Governors at Altoona, Pennsylvania in 1862," pp. 20–21, *Austin Blair Collection*, the Detroit Public Library.

[20] The Address stated, in part: "The decision of the President to strike at the root of the rebellion will lend new vigor to the efforts and new life and hope to the hearts of the people cordially tendering to the President our respectful assurance and personal and official confidence. We trust and believe that the policy now inaugurated will be crowned with success, will give speedy and triumphant victories over our enemies and secure to this nation and this people the blessing and power of the Almighty God." Copy of the Address in the *John Andrew Papers*, Massachusetts Historical Society, Boston.

[21] Lincoln told a group of Negro leaders who visited him at the White House on August 14, 1862, "But for your race among us there could not be war . . . without the institution of slavery, and the colored race as a basis, the war could not have an existence." *The Life and Public Services of Abraham Lincoln, Together with His State Papers*, pp. 505–506. See also the unequivocal statement by Pieter Geyl in his *Debates With Historians* (New York: 1958), p. 244: "The quarrel which broke up the Union in 1860–1861 was about slavery."

had not only pledged in the Proclamation the freedom of the four million blacks but had also freed twenty million whites from the curse of slavery.[22] The *Chicago Tribune* which advocated the unconditional and uncompensated abolition of slavery from the beginning of the war, declared, "The President has set his hand and affixed the great seal to the grandest proclamation ever issued by man. . . . So splendid a vision has hardly shone upon the world since the day of Messiah. From this proclamation begins the history of the Republic, as our Fathers designed to have it. . . . Let no one think to stay the glorious reformation. . . ."[23]

The moderate *New York Times* stated that the President's Proclamation was "the most far-reaching document ever issued by the Government and its wisdom and necessity indisputable."[24] The influential Springfield *Republican* praised the Proclamation as timely, just and magnanimous. It predicted that the President's action will have the support of the mass of the loyal people, North and South. It concluded with this statement: "Thus, by the courage and prudence of the President, the greatest social and political revolution of the age will be triumphantly carried through in the midst of the Civil War."[25] The *Philadelphia Press* wrote that "The President has done a good deed, at a good time. The rebellion is at an end!"[26] The Democratic *Chicago Times* denounced Lincoln's action and concluded that by the issuance of the Proclamation, "the war is reduced to a contest of subjugation. It has assumed that character that abolitionism has designed from the outset it should assume."[27]

How are we to square these enthusiastic appraisals of the importance of the Proclamation by the leading Republican newspapers with the views of so many contemporary historians who find that evidence suggests that the document was neither very important nor very exciting? Are we to suppose that editors and politicians of the caliber of Horace Greeley, Henry J. Raymond, Joseph Medill, and Wilbur F. Storey were wrong and naive when they wrote their appraisals of the Proclamation?

Governor John Andrew said that the Proclamation was "a mighty act."[28] He wrote to a friend, "Our Republicans must make it their business to sustain this act of Lincoln."[29] Austin Blair, the Governor of Michigan, exclaimed, "I can now with my whole heart, support the administration and the President of the United States."[30] Judge David Davis reported on the reaction in Illinois in a letter to a friend, "The Proclamation seems to take well. . . ."[31] The *Chicago Tribune* reported on September 27 that a mass meeting attended by two thousand Republicans acclaimed the Proclamation as "the greatest event in modern history."[32]

The Negroes in the North hailed the Proclamation with unbridled joy and enthusiasm. Frederick Douglass wrote that the war was now "invested with sanctity,"[33]

[22] *New York Tribune,* September 24, 1862.
[23] *Chicago Tribune,* September 24, 1862.
[24] *New York Times,* September 23, 1862.
[25] *Chicago Tribune,* September 24, 1862.
[26] *Philadelphia Press,* September 23, 1862.
[27] *The Chicago Times,* September 23, 1862.
[28] John G. Nicolay and John Hay, *Abraham Lincoln, Complete Works: Comprising his Speeches, Letters, State Papers, and Miscellaneous Writings,* Vol. 1 (New York: 1894), p. 160.
[29] *Lincoln and the War Governors,* p. 256.
[30] *Ibid.,* p. 267.
[31] Willard King, *David Davis, Lincoln's Manager* (Cambridge, Mass.: 1960), p. 198.
[32] *Chicago Tribune,* September 27, 1862.
[33] Benjamin Quarles, *Lincoln and the Negro* (New York: 1962), p. 131.

and large mass meetings of Negroes were held throughout the North to hail the President's action.

Republicans in Congress, radicals, moderates and conservatives, ranging from the conservative Jacob Collamer of Vermont to Zachariah Chandler and Jacob Howard of Michigan, endorsed the Proclamation. Even those Senators, including Lyman Trumbull of Illinois and John Sherman of Ohio, who had doubts whether the President had the right, under the Constitution, to issue the Proclamation in his capacity as Commander in Chief, publicly supported the President.

Charles Sumner expected that the Proclamation would encourage Negro uprisings in the South.[34] Indeed, there is sufficient evidence to suggest that through the grapevine and smuggled Northern newspapers, the news of the Proclamation reached the Southern Negroes. The *Chicago Tribune* reported on October 21st that a refugee from Amesville, Virginia related that "the white people of that region are in great terror of a slave revolt. Seventeen Negroes, most of them free, have been arrested on suspicion of being engaged in plotting an uprising of the entire Negro population. *Copies of newspapers that printed President Lincoln's Emancipation Proclamation were found in their possession. All the Negroes know that such a proclamation has been made, and this terrorizes the whites.* The seventeen Negroes have been taken to Amesville and lynched." [35]

On December 11, 1862, Congressman George Yeaman of Kentucky introduced the following joint resolution in the House: "Resolved by the House of Representatives (the Senate concurring) that the proclamation of the President of the United States of the 22nd of September, 1862, is not warranted by the Constitution." Congressman Owen Lovejoy immediately moved to table the motion. The vote to table was 94 to 45. It was a strictly party line vote, the Republicans voting to kill the motion and the Democrats voting for it.[36]

There was, however, an important debate on the Proclamation in the House when the President's message to Congress was discussed. Two major speeches were delivered, one by a Republican and one by a Democrat. It is of interest to our discussion to note that while the Republican spokesman vigorously hailed the Proclamation and the Democrat had bitterly denounced it, they both agreed on one crucial point. Both accepted the fact that the Emancipation Proclamation was a document of lasting historic importance and that it marked a turning point in the Civil War by making slavery a central issue of the war.

Republican Congressman John Hutchins of Ohio said: "The President's Proclamation, whatever may be the issue of it, marks a new era in our politics, and marks a new epoch in history. . . . I have watched too long and carefully the growth of anti-slavery sentiment, and have too much faith in the teachings of the war, in the ways of Providence, to doubt the final success of this grand scheme, which, in the termination of the war, will strike the chains of cruel bondage from three million human beings, restore freedom to a race, secure peace to a continent, and nobly save the last, best hope on earth—the Republic of the United States." [37]

The Democrat, John W. Menzies of Kentucky, maintained that Lincoln's Emancipation Proclamation was the decisive step which proved that the President was

---

[34] *Cong. Globe,* 37th Congress, 3rd Session (December 16, 1862), p. 6.
[35] *Chicago Tribune,* October 21, 1862. (Italics mine.)
[36] *Cong. Globe,* 37th Congress, 3rd Session (December 11, 1862), p. 76.
[37] *Ibid.,* pp. 78–79.

determined to abolish slavery, even if it meant violating the Constitution. "[The Proclamation] made," said Menzies, "all of the slaves in the South free, and promised that in one hundred days the President would let them know who were the recipients of the blessing. And then the Army and the Navy of the United States— he did not exactly say that they would help, but the intimation was that they would help the slaves to assert the claim to freedom which was given by the Proclamation." Congressman Menzies concluded with this warning of disaster: "Whenever the people of the North sustain these proclamations, the southern rebellion will be a success and our popular representative government a failure." [38] It seems clear that both Republicans and Democrats in Congress did not regard the Proclamation merely as a war measure caused by military necessity but recognized the great moral and political issues involved in it.

There is evidence to suggest that the Northern army overwhelmingly approved and fully recognized the import of the Proclamation. General John M. Palmer wrote to Senator Lyman Trumbull from his command post in Nashville, Tennessee saying that the army "is beginning to understand the real character of this controversy. The war has become a *revolution* which is widening and deepening." [39]

What remains to be examined is the oft-repeated assertion that the issuance of the preliminary Emancipation Proclamation on September 22, 1862, was a major cause of the Republican defeats suffered in the November election of that year. "The verdict of the polls clearly showed," writes an historian of the period, "that the people of the North were opposed to the Emancipation Proclamation. . . ." [40] In support of this view the following evidence is usually cited: Democrats won the gubernatorial races in New York and in New Jersey and scored victories in Congressional elections in Ohio, Pennsylvania, Illinois and Indiana. This is impressive evidence, but I should like to suggest that it is not impressive enough to cancel out other evidence concerning the election results. That evidence has been largely overlooked or ignored.

First, Abraham Lincoln who, as even his detractors have to admit, was a shrewd politician, did not think that the Emancipation Proclamation had an adverse effect on the Republican fortunes at the polls. Lincoln's analysis of the election is contained in his letter to Carl Schurz who previously wrote to the President obliquely accusing him of causing the Republican defeats by appointing Democrats to high military positions. In his letter of November 10, 1862, Lincoln refuted Schurz's position and stated that Republican reverses can be accounted for by the fact that his Administration came into power by the support of a minority of the popular vote. He also pointed to the absence of many Republicans from their states because of service in the army and to the vitriolic attacks on the Administration by the Republican newspapers which were exploited by the opposition.[41]

An appraisal of the November elections must include the point that it was an off-year election and that such elections usually result in losses for the party in power. The Republicans suffered their most important defeat in New York where Democrat Horatio Seymour was elected governor. Several important points should, however, be kept in mind in connection with this election. First, General James Wadsworth, com-

---

[38] *Ibid.*, pp. 80–81.

[39] John M. Palmer to Lyman Trumbull (December 19, 1862), Lyman Trumbull Papers, Library of Congress. (Italics mine.)

[40] *Lincoln and the War Governors*, p. 265.

[41] *The Living Lincoln*, p. 509.

manding general of the District of Columbia and a militant anti-slavery man, accepted the Republican nomination for governor with great reluctance. He did not get to New York, after his nomination, until October 30 and showed a great distaste for campaigning. Second, Thurlow Weed, the most influential Republican politician in New York State, and William Seward gave Wadsworth little or no support because they opposed his abolitionist views and were angered that their proposal to nominate General John A. Dix as a bi-partisan candidate was rejected. Weed refused to make the support of the Emancipation Proclamation an issue in the campaign in spite of strong indications that the Proclamation had popular support.[42] An influential New York Republican, John Bigelow, told Weed that unless he would make "an issue with Seymour on the President's Proclamation . . . the Republican party is ruined." [43]

There is evidence to suggest that the Emancipation Proclamation was the decisive factor in the re-election of John Andrew and Austin Blair as governors of Massachusetts and Michigan, respectively.[44] The victory of Andrew, the alleged chief plotter of the Altoona Conference, was overwhelming. He defeated his Democratic opponent by a vote of 79,835 to 52,587.

The Proclamation undoubtedly proved a great boon to Michigan Republicans. Austin Blair was re-elected Governor and the two arch-radicals Zachariah Chandler and Jacob Howard were elected to the Senate. Chandler wrote to Lyman Trumbull around the middle of September and urgently asked him to come to Michigan to help in the election campaign. On September 28, Trumbull sent his reply that he was ready to come but thought his help unnecessary. He wrote: "Do not believe there is the least danger in Michigan. Lincoln's Proclamation should do the trick to swing the election in Michigan." [45]

The *Missouri Democrat* stated editorially that the Proclamation helped the Republican party in the November election,[46] and Senator James W. Grimes asserted that the Proclamation helped to assure Republican victories in Iowa.[47]

In describing the harmful effects of the Proclamation on the Republican fortunes in the November election, a great deal has been written about the defeat of the Republican candidate Leonard Swett who lost the race for a seat in Congress from Lincoln's own district in Illinois. The defeat of Orville Browning in a Senate race in Illinois has also repeatedly been cited as proof of the unfortunate effects of the Proclamation.[48] This piece of evidence is of doubtful validity.

Leonard Swett lost because he was a small-time politician, who was opposed by a close friend and law partner of Lincoln, a respected Judge and former Congressman John Todd Stuart, a cousin of Mary Lincoln. The election proved the validity of

[42] On Thurlow Weed's opposition to the Proclamation, see *Harper's Weekly*, January 10, 1863.

[43] John Bigelow to Thurlow Weed (October 7, 1862), The Thurlow Weed Collection, University of Rochester Library.

[44] *Lincoln and the War Governors*, p. 266.

[45] Lyman Trumbull to Zachariah Chandler (September 28, 1862). Copy in Lyman Trumbull's handwriting in the Lyman Trumbull Papers, Library of Congress.

[46] *Missouri Democrat*, November 7, 1862.

[47] James W. Grimes to Lyman Trumbull (October 6, 1862), Lyman Trumbull Papers, Library of Congress. Grimes added, "We must build up . . . our President with sturdy rods in the shape of Cabinet ministers."

[48] See Reinhard H. Luthin, *The Real Abraham Lincoln* (Englewood Cliffs, New Jersey: 1960), pp. 349–351.

the boxing adage that "you can't beat a somebody with a nobody." Furthermore, Swett, like his mentor, Judge David Davis, was bitterly opposed to the Proclamation and thus it could well be argued that his known hatred of abolitionism had caused his defeat.

Similarly, Orville H. Browning became *persona non grata* with the Illinois Republicans a long time before the election. As long as he thought that Lincoln would appoint him to the Supreme Court, Browning was the President's staunch supporter, but when Lincoln appointed Judge Davis in his stead, the haughty Browning became a biting critic of the Administration and reverted to his original conservative convictions. He made no secret of this opposition to the Proclamation.[49] The two most powerful Republican newspapers in Illinois, the *Chicago Tribune* and the *Illinois State Journal,* hardly mentioned Browning's name during the election campaign. The issuance of the Emancipation Proclamation surely did not contribute to the defeat of Orville H. Browning. As a matter of fact, it might be more plausible to argue that Browning could have won had he come out strongly in support of the Proclamation.

The ceremony of the signing of the Proclamation was a solemn one. It is significant that the President gave the pen with which he slowly wrote his name to Charles Sumner. If the Emancipation Proclamation, as it has been said, is as exciting as a bill of lading, then one can only conclude that it constitutes the most exciting bill of lading in the history of modern man. In the eyes of the Civil War generation, the Emancipation Proclamation was a clarion call for human freedom and Lincoln was the Great Emancipator. The evidence indicates that this was a valid judgment.

[49] Orville Hickman Browning, *The Diary of Orville Hickman Browning,* Vol. 1, Theodore Pease and James G. Randall, eds. (Springfield, Illinois: 1925–1933), p. 601.

18 / The Confederacy and the American Tradition

Frank E. Vandiver

Americans have been far more interested in the history of the Union than of the Confederacy. It is not difficult to think of reasons for this attitude. The charismatic Lincoln had no equivalent on the other side. Equally important is that the Confederacy lost. Finally, most Americans identify closely with the twin issues of Union and freedom that rode on federal victory, and even most Southerners find it difficult to endorse the Confederate cause of separatism and slavery.

And yet the experience of the South during the war is an inextricable and important part of the nation's history. These were tumultuous and agonizing years for the 11 states that made up the Confederate States of America. Under massive attack almost from the moment of its birth, the Confederacy was never allowed a normal existence. Three months after establishing a provisional government at Montgomery, the new, self-declared nation was at war with its powerful neighbor, and for much of its remaining brief life large sections of its territory were occupied by hostile military forces.

Here was a young nation in crisis and its story is not unlike that of the United States itself some 80 years previously. In both cases the government had to function while violent, disruptive battles were being fought on its territory. In both cases the attitudes of European powers were important for success. In both cases popular commitment and loyalty had not yet fully hardened into a solid structure sufficient for national existence. Add to these problems the difficulties shared with the mature Union—mobilizing armies, finding competent leaders, raising money—and it becomes clear that the Confederacy required almost superhuman effort to remain afloat.

In the face of these tremendous difficulties, as Frank Vandiver shows in the following article, the Confederate leadership performed creditably. More important, the people of the South rallied to their new nation. There was dissension within the Confederacy, especially among the restless unionists. Governors such as Joseph E. Brown of Georgia and Zebulon Vance of North

Journal of Southern History, XXVIII, No. 3 (August 1962), 277–286. Copyright 1962 by the Southern Historical Association. Reprinted by permission of the Managing Editor.

Carolina jeopardized the Southern cause by their exaggerated concern for the narrow prerogative of their own states and their own citizens. Yet the Confederacy engaged men's affections and loyalties. Thousands fought—and died—bravely and honorably for what they believed to be a worthy cause. The war was also democratizing and educational. Thousands of provincial young men were brought together and learned something about the world outside, and about themselves. In the end, as Vandiver suggests, "the lost cause" was probably worth a tear, after all.

For further reading: Clement Eaton, *A History of the Southern Confederacy* (New York: The Free Press, 1965); E. Merton Coulter, *The Confederate States of America, 1861–1865* (Baton Rouge, La.: Louisiana State University Press, 1950); Charles P. Roland, *The Confederacy* (Chicago, Ill.: University of Chicago Press, 1960); Frank Owsley, *States Rights in the Confederacy* (Gloucester, Mass.: Peter Smith, 1961); Rembert Patrick, *Jefferson Davis and His Cabinet* (Baton Rouge, La.: Louisiana State University Press, 1944); Burton J. Hendrick, *Statesmen of the Lost Cause: Jefferson Davis and His Cabinet* (Boston, Mass.: Little, Brown and Company, 1939).

Currently the tide of historical interpretation is running against the Confederacy. And this is hardly surprising, for the Confederates fought a losing fight, apparently in defense of such unprogressive anachronisms as slavery and local sovereignty. Not only did nineteenth-century experience point against these relics of feudalism, but especially has the American progressive urge in the twentieth century tended to make the South in the Civil War a regressive and sterile topic. Historians will give credit to the South's bravery but damn its leaders, its mores, and its un-Americanism. As a result, although Civil War history enjoys an unparalleled popular following, it appears historiographically important only as it gave freedom to the black man, cleared the way for railways west, and marked a certain technical proficiency in warfare. The Confederate side is studied, by Southerners usually, to find flaws in an agrarian economy and in Jefferson Davis' executive leadership, to show the greatness of Robert E. Lee and Stonewall Jackson. But even Southern historians have shied away from a positive approach to the Confederate years in Southern history.

In 1955 Francis Butler Simkins, speaking ex cathedra as president of the Southern Historical Association, chided his fellow factitioners to give up looking backward in twentieth-century anger, give up deploring the South's past. Instead, he called for an acceptance of Southern history, for an honest admission of slavery, of class consciousness, of racism, even of commonality.[1]

But the summons had little effect. Scarcely a historical voice can be heard raised in defense of the Americanness of the South. A few novelists have worked to keep the Southern experience within reach of the nation. William Faulkner, Eudora Welty, and others, like Joel Chandler Harris and Ellen Glasgow before them, have tried to show the Southerner as much an American as a Southron. But until recently

[1] Francis B. Simkins, "Tolerating the South's Past," *Journal of Southern History*, XXI (February 1955), 3–16.

they were deserted by academe. Historians have abandoned the possibly fertile vine-yard of nationalism for a vision of rectitude. They write of Southern things with a kind of hang-dog tone, half apologizing for so iniquitous a section. Simkins thinks this is because most modern historians have accepted the egalitarian philosophy of the North, have a sense of guilt lingering from slavery and race prejudice. He may be correct. Certainly there is either a deprecatory tinge to present historical study in the South or a ringing demand for fulfillment of the promises of the Declaration of Independence. Southern historiography has continued in the pattern of Frank L. Owsley's agrarian-state rights concept, Charles Ramsdell's view of Confederate in-sulation, or has taken up the "special burdens" theory of C. Vann Woodward.[2] So common is this impression of the nonparticipation of the South in the stream of American history that standard textbooks dealing with national affairs tend to treat the South as a kind of vestigial appendage which gradually became partly absorbed in the early twentieth century.

In the welter of introspection and the avalanche of progressive rejection of the Southern past in recent decades, Simkins has not stood completely alone in his rebuttal. Robert S. Cotterill, in "The Old South to the New," dared wonder if the New South began long before 1861 and sees the origins of the modern South in the decade of the 1850's. Wilbur J. Cash found consistent patterns of Southern thought that survived "the War," and Thomas P. Govan suggested that the old South dif-fered not much from the new when he boldly asserted in 1955 that the South's rejoining the Union following the war "was not an abandonment of its ancient tradition, but a return to it, and the subsequent changes, including industrialization, were a continuation of movements already well developed in the Southern states before the outbreak of the war."[3]

But there is still no claim that the Confederacy stands as anything but a terrible anachronism, even in Southern life. Whether neo-Confederate, anti-Confederate, or simply a-Confederate, all Southern historians have agreed on one ultimate truth: The South's experience from 1861 to 1865 was different from the experience of the rest of America. There seems a sort of desperate drive among these scholars to show why the difference. Things that happened in Dixie, ideas which germinated there, men who guided the section's destinies and who suffered its thwarts were not in the mold of the American dream.

If historians are to heed Simkins' call, are to tolerate the South's past, and to see it without present-tinted glasses, they should take a long look at the Confederate South. And especially should those concerned with basic American traditions look at the years of the Confederacy. For much that happened within the beleaguered Southland was peculiarly American, and many Confederate ideals were rooted deep in the history of the Republic.

Take first the problem of revolution, or rebellion. Many students point to secession

[2] Frank L. Owsley, *State Rights in the Confederacy* (Chicago, 1925; Gloucester, Mass., 1961); Charles W. Ramsdell, *Behind the Lines in the Southern Confederacy*, Wendell H. Stephenson, ed. (Baton Rouge, 1944); C. Vann Woodward, *The Burden of Southern History* (Baton Rouge, 1960). Some views in defense of the South's Americanness are presented in Charles Grier Sellers, Jr. (ed.), *The Southerner As American* (Chapel Hill, 1960).

[3] Robert S. Cotterill, "The Old South to the New," *Journal of Southern History*, XV (February 1949), 3–8; Wilbur J. Cash, *The Mind of the South* (New York, 1941), viii–xi; Thomas P. Govan, "Was the Old South Different?" *Journal of Southern History*, XXI (November 1955), 447–55.

as the ultimate rejection of American traditions and argue that this act alone is sufficient to shut the South away from the central theme of national unity. Without pressing the point of revolution as one of the fundamentals of the American system, the question of the unity of the United States in the ante bellum years is open to serious debate. Roy F. Nichols, in *The Disruption of American Democracy*, pointed out the upheaval wrought in the body politic by the crises of the 1850's and 1860's, and David Donald, in a lecture delivered before the University of Oxford in May 1960, titled *An Excess of Democracy*, stated that "American society in the 1850's was singularly ill equipped to meet any shocks, however weak. It was a society so new and so disorganized that its nerves were rawly exposed." [4]

There is much to be said for the idea that this lack of national cement made for strong sectionalism. It did, and it certainly helped to foster the sectional interests of the South. But sectionalism, of course, can not be historically consigned to the South alone. Western advocates had touted the greatness of the lands beyond the Ohio for years, and New England oligarchs were hardly behindhand in proffering the wants of their states when threatened with social or economic pressure. If sectionalism and lack of a spirit of unity were evils, then the whole country was tainted.

The Federal Union had been much talked about in the prewar South, and many Southerners were as strong for the Union as were citizens of New England and the Midwest—more so, some of them. These Southern nationalists, men like Alexander H. Stephens and Sam Houston, were as concerned to build a strong nation as were men in the North. They recognized, as did such men as Daniel Webster and Henry Clay, that the edifice of the nation, though growing and expanding with amazing zest, lacked a good deal of cement; that cohesion dwindled in direct ratio to size; that, without some binding element, the Union might simply outgrow itself.

A sense of common destiny, of common goal, came hard to the South. More than any other part of the former United States, the South had been a rural area—not so much the legendary land of untrammeled agrarianism as one of fragmented localism, of provincialism so entrenched as to be best described by an upcountry South Carolinian in the 1850's: "I'll give you my notions of things; I go first for Greenville, then for Greenville District, then for the upcountry, then for South Carolina, then for the South, then for the United States; and after that I don't go for anything. I've no use for Englishmen, Turks and Chinese." [5] Many Southerners, at the outbreak of the war, were still close enough to the frontier to feel the pull of individualism, and many had the assertive independence of the rustic. Most of them knew something of the tangible fancy called the "Southern way of life" but felt content in an easy isolation.

Even city folk shared this sense of separation. Although there apparently was a larger middle class flourishing in the South than historians have been willing to allow, these merchants, lawyers, factors, professional men were under the political yoke of the planter class, since their economic future was closely linked to that of the landed gentry. About the most common purpose felt in the South of the prewar years was that of the planters, and they were subject to the shifting fortunes of cotton and slaves. Cotton was the center of things. There was an active industrial

[4] David Donald, *An Excess of Democracy: The American Civil War and the Social Process* (Oxford, 1960), 22; Roy F. Nichols, *The Disruption of American Democracy* (New York, 1948).

[5] Donald, *Excess of Democracy*, 20–21.

interest in various parts of the section, along with some concern for diversified planting, but as long as cotton ruled, all paid homage to the King. For this reason, then, despite the contacts Southern businessmen had with Northern counterparts, they remained essentially isolated and inward looking. They worried about slavery and threats to it, but always in the planter context. And their worries were diffuse, coalescing occasionally over some violent editorial or some apt Southron speech. In general, though, they had no truly sectional viewpoint.

Actually it seems that few Southerners thought much about the whole South. Some talked of it, recited the catechism of cotton, chivalry, and courage, but usually saw the South in terms of their own locality.

While evidence can be paraded to show that a group of fanatics rushed the South into secession and that the secessionists were attempting a counterrevolution against the growth of a leviathan state, something ought to be said on another side. Fanatics always have the loudest voices in moments of crisis, at least for a time, and so it was in the South through the critical winter of 1860–1861. Men of the William L. Yancey and Robert Barnwell Rhett stripe, who wanted immediate withdrawal from the Union and soul-searching later, had the plan and hence won their point. But in the election of delegates from the various seceded states to the Montgomery Convention and in the deliberations of that body, once it was organized, moderation held sway. Some straight-outs were there, some die-hard secessionists who frothed and fumed of dire plottings by Lincoln and his henchmen. But present in greater numbers were calm and mild men, who came to prevent excesses like those of the French Revolution.

The interesting thing about these moderates is their political and economic heritage. Many of them were displaced Whigs who still cherished the American System ideals of Clay and hence stood for good money and law and order. Others were of the conservative Democratic fold, who accepted the general principles of democracy without going so far left as to join the disunionists. A look at the work of the Montgomery Convention—the men picked for leadership, the Provisional and Permanent constitutions, the early economic, social and military legislation—shows that the secessionists found themselves dispossessed of their own revolution. And the same look will also show that the revolution was a conservative one right enough, but conservative in an unusual sense: Southern moderates worked to preserve old American principles of nationalism, not to foster radical sectionalism. And as their government took shape, they could console themselves with the thought that the war really represented an evolutionary move rather than a revolutionary one. American principles of democracy and nationalism were expanding and flourishing in Southern hands.

Since most of these Whiggish conservatives had long held nationalist views, it is not surprising that many simply transferred their nationalism to the South. Striving to prevent the awful possibilities of an unbridled upheaval of society, they stuck to their ideas of strong government, usually supported Jefferson Davis—their choice for President of the Confederacy—in his efforts to construct a nation and an administration adequate to a huge war. They began by drawing up a constitution which gave the President more power than Lincoln had, and they continued by supporting, with occasional lapses, most of the war program laid down by Davis.

In finding Davis these moderates were singularly fortunate, for he proved almost exactly the type of man suited to the time and to Confederate circumstance. Most of his active political life had been spent in defending Southern and state rights, and in this service he had gained invaluable military, legislative, and administrative experience. He, too, became a Confederate nationalist, and as he moved increasingly in this direction he learned to use executive power. As he developed skills as a modern executive—skills not unlike those of his counterpart across the Potomac—he led the nation more and more down the road being traveled by the United States.

Naturally the first task facing the new administration was the construction of a country and the projection of a cause. With single-minded dedication Davis and the Congress preached the virtue of unity, girded in old Southern myths of chivalry and martial prowess, and brandished the buckler of King Cotton. Unity came to the South, as to the North, with the attack on Fort Sumter. Uncertainty ended: There would be war.

War works its own changes in a nation, but it wrought especially significant ones in the Confederacy. In the North it opened new revenues, lent power to the central government, developed latent energies and resources, and evoked a sense of purpose never before present. It did all these things in the South, and others as well.

New revenues were found in expanded and in previously unknown types of taxation, including a personal income levy; they were found, too, in special produce loans and in reliance on cotton for credit. Power came to the Confederate government not only from tax authority, but also from commercial legislation, from military control of transportation and internal improvements, and from management of manpower under the conscription laws. New sources of minerals and other sinews of war were developed by dire necessity, and untapped springs of human resourcefulness came full-blown into being with workable substitutes for silks, for medicines, for coffee, for leather, steel, and copper.

The greatest alteration came with the Confederate army. With the formation of the army everything about the South changed. To the extent that war made the army necessary, it is correct to say that war changed the South. But the greatest changes were wrought by the army as a social institution.

For the first time in their lives, Southern boys came from the hills, from the remotest farms, from lonesome and lavish plantations, from hamlets, villages, towns, and cities, from shanties, hovels—they came not just to the local general store, the post office, the saloon, but to far away and dimly known places like New Orleans, Montgomery, Atlanta, Savannah, Charleston, Jacksonville, Raleigh, Richmond, San Antonio, and Little Rock. They congregated to create a national army, one forged to defend the whole South, to carry a country's banner in battle. The enemy now was no hostile family in some lost feud, no gang of street plug-uglies, no gentleman on a field of honor; the enemy counted in thousands, wore blue, and had a hated generic name—Yankee.

The transformation can hardly be exaggerated. Provincialism lifted from the limits of a county now to take in all of the Confederate States, lifted to the level of real nationalism. A cause came into the lives of the soldiers, a cause to take their hearts, steel their nerves and become the greatest thing that ever happened to them. Never would they be the same local boys—they would, if they lived, be veterans, companions in one of the largest armies ever collected together; they would be men of a wider, wiser world. After it had all ended they would go home, some of them maimed in body, take up old pursuits—but with a different eye and spirit. These

Rebels learned of the outside, learned that not all strangers were hostile, not all "furriners" despicable. Their brothers from all parts of the South taught the lesson of comradeship, and their sturdy blue enemies, the lesson of respect.

Confederate soldiers were remarkable. They exasperated their officers with their independence, their easy discipline, but they fought with fury and surpassing heroism. And the rigors of the camp and field, the tempering of rules and regulations made an important alteration in them, made them readier than perhaps anything else could have for the future of the United States.

Obviously the Confederate army functioned as a nationalizing agent, and continued to do so, even after the war. It also served to bring about no small amount of democratization in the Southern social structure. At first the prominent families expected and received the better ranks and assignments, and usually won officer elections handily. But as the war settled into hard dying, into combat of the fiercest, where sheer ability counted for everything, men rose in rank whether or not they had the pedigree. In time the administrative hierarchy of the War Department recognized this important fact and began conducting officer candidate examinations in the field. Anyone was eligible to earn a commission through these tests, and many qualified as officers who would never have had a chance in the prewar elite units. The leadership lessons of the field were not entirely forgotten in the postwar South.

The existence of the army fostered democracy all across the Confederacy. The army became an incredibly voracious consumer; to feed it, clothe it, and move it took the whole energy of the Southern people. Logistical necessities made bond agents of bankers, nurses of grand dames, quartermasters of businessmen, tax collectors of farmers, industrialists of ironmongers. War became such a big business that it brought about a managerial revolution in the South. Techniques of management previously used only by Yankees—and some new ones unknown to anyone before—became essential to running the Confederate war effort. The civil service list of the central government grew to amazing proportions, and the tentacles of Davis' administration reached everywhere. Minor officials appeared in every town and increased public irritation in direct ratio to their numbers. Especially did this happen as the government relied more heavily on impressment of private property to sustain the field forces. A large staff was required to reach the farms in the interior and to get at their produce and livestock—and it appeared to the angered farmers that this corps of official scavengers was made up mostly of men shirking front line duty.

With the growth of civil and military administration there developed, as a natural consequence, a status revolution in Southern society. A new class of manager appeared —the bureaucrat—who sought not only economic security through a war job, but also social advancement as well.

Hand in glove with the managerial and status changes in the South went a ruthless shift in the spirit of government. Although President Davis showed more respect for the Confederate Constitution than did Lincoln for that of the North, the Rebel Chief Executive found it increasingly necessary to impose harsh war measures. Conscription he supported firmly; impressment, too, and he worked even to control transportation networks and communication systems. At the last he urged using slaves in Rebel ranks and thought they should be given freedom for service. He went so far as to advocate a deal with England which was proposed in March 1865: Emancipation for independence—the cornerstone for the edifice.

And although the Confederate Congress paid due obeisance to ideas of *laissez faire,* it went along with Davis in most of his program for centralizing the government. Resistance from the states grew apace, and such state rights fulminators as Governors Joseph E. Brown of Georgia and Zebulon Vance of North Carolina harangued their legislatures constantly about growing dictatorship from Richmond. But in order to retard the encroachment of the Confederate government, the states had to resort to the same tactics of centralization and tight administration. The managerial and status revolutions reached even to local levels in some parts of the South, and parties and politics were surely affected.

Although he never received the co-operation of all the Southern governors and sometimes had to curb the power of his administration because of political pressure, Davis did become a strong executive who learned new ways of running a burgeoning power state. His lessons were harder than Lincoln's, for the strength of the Confederacy dwindled steadily, and deepening crisis spawned fiercer frenzy. The lessons were harder, too, because Davis had neither the will nor the wile to be a constitutional dictator. That he made himself fill the role sufficiently to run the Confederacy to the end of its strength is no small accomplishment.

Some historians argue that the South ought to have managed its war more ably, ought to have husbanded its resources with larger wisdom, fought its armies to better effect. Had these things been done, they prophesy the South might have won or at least gained something tangible from the war.

To the extent that it spent all its money, fought out its armies, drained its economy, the South's administration was a success. As for something tangible from the war?

The Southern states went into the war disunited, disorganized, localistic, and politically amorphous. They entered the fray to fight for their conception of the American dream of liberty and independence, endured the same nationalizing experience as the North, underwent a social upheaval so basic as to change their class and racial structure, experienced the beginnings of bureaucracy, and sustained a total war for four years. By the end of the fighting, the South had been unified, turned into a small, modern power state, and had been defeated—but much of the change lingered. What had been learned in war was not entirely forgotten in peace, even in the turbulent peace of Reconstruction.

So the wartime experience of the South should not be regarded as entirely negative, as outside the stream of the nineteenth century. The section's new-found cohesion, greater democracy, its new techniques of management, were all in the best American tradition and paved the way for "the emergence of modern America," for a true unification of the United States.

19 / The Confederate as a Fighting Man

David Donald

If Confederate survival owed much to competent leaders, it owed still more to the magnificent performance of the "Johnny Rebs"—the boys in gray who suffered and died for their new country. For many years after Appomattox, Southern myth-makers, as if to assuage the deep pain of defeat, insisted on turning these men into unblemished heroes. The myth reached its apogee in the image of Robert E. Lee, a truly great military leader and a man of unusual integrity and aristocratic grace. But it also encompassed the ordinary Confederate soldier, and here it passed well beyond the limit of credibility. The boys in gray were not merely brave, high-spirited young men, they were spotless innocents, utterly devoted to their cause, who loved and obeyed their commanders, felt no malice toward their enemies, and died with a sentimental or patriotic slogan on their lips.

The definitive social history of the Civil War soldier by Bell I. Wiley of Emory University makes it clear that this portrait bears little resemblance to the truth. Johnny Reb, like Billy Yank, and every other soldier for that matter, was an imperfect human being. He was brave, no doubt, but he was also at times cowardly; he was chivalrous, but he was also sometimes brutal and vindictive; he was a dedicated patriot, but he was also frequently disobedient and mutinous.

As David Donald suggests in the following article, the Confederate Army reflected the society it was defending. This was a class society which, in spite of the forms of democracy and the lip service given to popular rule, was still permeated by aristocratic values. Donald notes that the prestige of the Southern planter elite carried over to the army. Its ranks full of unruly natural democrats, that organization was commanded by men of high standing and status in civilian life. Although an advantage at first, the class system in the end hurt the Confederate cause and contributed to the South's final defeat.

For further reading: *Bell I. Wiley, *The Life of Johnny Reb* (Indianapolis, Ind.: The Bobbs-Merrill Company, 1943); Frank E. Vandiver, *Rebel Brass*

Journal of Southern History, XXV, No. 2 (May 1959), 178–193. Copyright 1959 by the Southern Historical Association. Reprinted by permission of the Managing Editor.

A paper delivered at the First Annual Civil War Conference at Gettysburg College in November 1957.

(Baton Rouge, La.: Louisiana State University Press, 1956); Douglas S. Freeman, *R. E. Lee: A Biography* (New York: Charles Scribner's Sons, 1934–1935); Douglas S. Freeman, *Lee's Lieutenants: A Study in Command* (New York: Charles Scribner's Sons, 1942–1944).

The Confederate soldier was, in most important respects, not materially different from one of Xenophon's hoplites or Caesar's legionnaires. He enlisted for a variety of reasons; he was brave or he was cowardly; he fought till the end of the war or he was killed, wounded, or captured. If it is hard to generalize about him, it is even more difficult to think of him as unique. His story is that of all soldiers in all wars.

In basic attitudes he was very much like World War II GIs. The recent study of *The American Soldier* would puzzle him by its sociological lingo, but, if translated into layman's language, it would not surprise him by its conclusions. Like his GI descendants, the Confederate soldier agreed that the infantry was the most dangerous and difficult branch of service, and he preferred his own equivalent of the air force —the cavalry. Depending upon what the psychologists call his "personal esprit," his "personal commitment," and his "satisfaction with status and job," he would have expressed varying opinions when asked how well the Confederate army was run. He did not have any very clear idea as to what caused the Civil War, but, if questioned, he would very probably have responded as did ninety-one percent of World War II soldiers who felt "whatever our wishes in the matter, we have to fight now if we are to survive." [1]

Johnny Reb was even more similar to Billy Yank, his opponent in the Union forces. In two fascinating and learned studies of the everyday life of Civil War soldiers Bell I. Wiley has amply proved that "the similarities of Billy Yank and Johnny Reb far outweighed their differences. They were both American, by birth or by adoption, and they both had the weaknesses and the virtues of the people of their nation and time." [2]

Yet contemporaries with opportunities to observe soldiers in both the opposing armies found the Southern fighting man subtly and indefinably different. He looked "the genuine rebel." That astute British diarist, Colonel Fremantle, found that "in spite of his bare feet, his ragged clothes, his old rug, and tooth-brush stuck like a rose in his button-hole," the Confederate warrior had "a sort of devil-may-care, reckless, self-confident look, which is decidedly taking." [3]

Most impartial observers found a want of discipline among Confederate troops, a peculiar indifference to "their obligations as soldiers." [4] At the outset of the war, one participant later wrote, "The Southern army . . . was simply a vast mob of rather ill-armed young gentlemen from the country." [5] Six months before Appomattox the

---

[1] Samuel A. Stouffer and others, *The American Soldier: Adjustment during Army Life* (Princeton, 1949), I, *passim*, especially 102, 432.

[2] Bell Irvin Wiley, *The Life of Billy Yank: The Common Soldier of the Union* (Indianapolis, 1951), 361. My indebtedness in these pages to Professor Wiley's massive researches is very great. His studies provide a vivid detailed portrait of the Southern soldier.

[3] Arthur J. L. Fremantle, *Three Months in the Southern States: April, June, 1863* (Mobile, 1864), 293.

[4] *Ibid.*, 123.

[5] George Cary Eggleston, *A Rebel's Recollections* (Indianapolis, 1959), 69.

inspector-general of the Army of Northern Virginia concluded that things had not greatly changed: ". . . the source of almost every evil existing in the army is due to the difficulty of having orders properly and promptly executed. There is not that spirit of respect for and obedience to general orders which should pervade a military organization . . . ." [6]

The Southerners' want of military discipline is not surprising. Confederate soldiers were mostly recruited from the independent small farmers who composed the vast majority of the ante bellum Southern population.[7] They came from a society that was not merely rural but, in many areas, still frontier, and isolation of settlements, absence of established traditions, and opportunities for rapid social mobility encouraged a distinctive Southern type of self-reliance.[8] In the years before the Civil War political democracy triumphed in the South,[9] and demagogues repeatedly capitalized upon Southerners' resentments against the planter aristocrats. Even slavery was defended in terms of equalitarian ideals. "With us," said Calhoun, "the two great divisions of society are not the rich and poor, but white and black; and all the former, the poor as well as the rich, belong to the upper classes, and are respected and treated as equals . . . ." [10]

Southerners were citizens before they were soldiers, and they did not take kindly to military discipline. At the outbreak of the war they rushed to enlist, fearing the fighting would be over before they could get to the front. Instead of "fun and frolic," [11] they soon learned that being a soldier meant drill, spit-and-polish, military discipline, and more drill. An Alabama enlisted man became disillusioned: "A soldier is worse than any negro on Chatahooche [sic] river. He has no privileges whatever. He is under worse taskmasters than any negro. He is not treated with any respect whatever. His officers may insult him and he has no right to open his mouth and dare not do it." [12]

Such a reaction was, of course, perfectly normal; it has happened in all American wars. Fifty-one per cent of our soldiers in World War II felt that discipline was "too strict about petty things" and seventy-one per cent thought they had "too much 'chicken' to put up with." [13] But the distinctive thing about the Confederate army is that Southern soldiers never truly accepted the idea that discipline is necessary to the effective functioning of a fighting force. They were "not used to control of any sort, and were not disposed to obey anybody except for good and sufficient reason given. While actually on drill they obeyed the word of command, not so much by reason of its being proper to obey a command, as because obedience was in that case necessary to the successful issue of a pretty performance in which they were

[6] *The War of the Rebellion: A Compilation of the Official Records of the Union and Confederate Armies* (Washington, 1880–1901), series 1, XLII, part 2, 1276–77. Hereafter cited as *Official Records*.

[7] Frank L. Owsley, *Plain Folk of the Old South* (Baton Rouge, 1949), *passim*.

[8] W. J. Cash, *The Mind of the South* (New York, 1941), 4 ff.

[9] Fletcher M. Green, "Democracy in the Old South," *Journal of Southern History*, XII (1946), 3–23.

[10] Allan Nevins, *Ordeal of the Union* (4 vols., New York, 1947–1950), I, 419.

[11] Wiley, *The Life of Johnny Reb: The Common Soldier of the Confederacy* (Indianapolis, 1943), 27.

[12] Edmund Cody Burnett (ed.), "Letters of Three Lightfoot Brothers, 1861–1864," *Georgia Historical Quarterly*, XXV (1941), 389.

[13] Stouffer *et al.*, *American Soldier*, I, 396.

interested. Off drill they did as they pleased, holding themselves gentlemen, and as such bound to consult only their own wills." [14]

They found routine training assignments tedious, and they shirked them. A Mississippi sergeant reported that his men objected to being put on details "because they said they did not enlist to do guard duty but to fight the Yankees . . . ." [15] When they did serve, they behaved with characteristic independence. Colonel Fremantle at first thought Confederate sentries "quite as strict as, and ten times more polite than, regular soldiers" when they challenged him as he entered Longstreet's camp. But when he complimented the Confederate commander, Longstreet "replied, laughing, that a sentry, after refusing you leave to enter a camp, might very likely, if properly asked, show you another way in, by which you might avoid meeting a sentry at all." [16]

On the march Southern troops were seldom orderly. Even Stonewall Jackson had trouble with stragglers,[17] and Lee's men moved "at a slow dragging pace" and were "evidently not good marchers naturally." In spite of repeated orders from headquarters, Confederates could never see the need for carrying heavy packs, and they were "constantly in the habit of throwing away their knapsacks and blankets on a long march." Particularly in the early years of the war, Southern soldiers found victory nearly as demoralizing as defeat, and after a battle "many would coolly walk off home, under the impression that they had performed their share." [18]

Toward their officers, and particularly toward their immediate superiors, they exhibited a typical democratic disrespect for authority. The whole highly stratified system of military organization, "in which hierarchies of deference were formally and minutely established by official regulation," [19] was a denial of the principle of equality. Confederates disliked "the restrictions placed on the privates," when the officers were permitted to "go to town at option, stay as long as they please, and get gloriously drunk in and out of camp when it suits them to do so." Like one peevish Texan they felt that officers "are living better and wear better clothes than they did before the war." Officers had, another private echoed hungrily, "bacon to eat, Sugar to put in their coffee and all luxuries of this kind," while the common soldier had "the hardships to under go." Another Texan wrote home: ". . . I will stay and tuff it out with Col Young and then he can go to Hell . . . he has acted the dam dog and I cant tell him so if I do they will put me in the Guard House . . . but I can tell him what I think of him when this war ends . . . I will come [home] when my time is out or die I wont be run over no longer not to please no officers they have acted the rascal with me . . . ." [20] Clearly most Confederates would have agreed with the American soldier in World War II who grumbled: "Too many officers have that superior feeling toward their men. Treat them as if they were way below them . . . What's the matter with us enlisted men, are we dogs?" [21]

[14] Eggleston, *Rebel's Recollections*, 70–71.
[15] Quoted in Wiley, *Johnny Reb*, 27.
[16] Fremantle, *Three Months*, 247.
[17] Douglas Southall Freeman, *Lee's Lieutenants: A Study in Command* (3 vols., New York, 1942–1944), I, 367.
[18] Fremantle, *Three Months*, 226, 123.
[19] Stouffer *et al.*, *American Soldier*, I, 55.
[20] Quoted in Wiley, *Johnny Reb*, 236, 140.
[21] Stouffer *et al.*, *American Soldier*, I, 372.

Such resentments against a caste system are normal among democratic citizen-soldiers. But where American troops in World Wars I and II had to vent their aggressions in grumbling and goldbricking, Confederates more often took direct action against their superiors. Confederate court martial records are full of such cases as that of Private George Bedell of Georgia, who called his commanding officer "a damned son of a bitch, a damned tyrant, a damned puppy, a damned rascal." If an officer persisted in acting like a martinet, his men might ride him on a rail until he promised "better behavior," [22] or they might petition for his resignation.[23]

In fact, to an extent almost unparalleled in any other major war, the Confederate common soldier was the master of his officers. Southern armies were organized upon the principle that the men might voluntarily choose their commanders. The system grew up without much planning. The peacetime militia, a quasi-social, quasi-political organization, had always elected officers, and the Confederate army was constituted on the same basis. When volunteers enlisted, they chose from among themselves noncommissioned officers, lieutenants, and captains; in general the man who organized and helped outfit a company was elected its captain. "The theory was," as George Cary Eggleston noted, "that the officers were the creatures of the men, chosen by election to represent their constituency in the performance of certain duties, and that only during good behavior." [24] Only the high ranking field officers were appointed by Richmond.

A wartime emergency compelled the Confederate government to continue the inefficient elective system. At first Southerners had thought the war would be short, and most original Confederate volunteers enrolled for only twelve months' service. In December 1861 the Confederate Congress abruptly awoke to the fact that these troops, the mainstay of the Southern army, would be mustered out in the spring. To oppose McClellan's magnificently equipped Northern troops the South would have only a skeleton army. Hurriedly the Southern Congress passed a law to encourage reenlistment by granting furloughs and bounties to veterans who promised once more to volunteer. As a special inducement the measure provided that all troops who reenlisted should have the power to reorganize themselves into companies and elect new company officers; these companies, in turn, should "have the power to organize themselves into battalions or regiments and to elect their field officers." The law, as General Upton tersely remarked, should have borne the title, "An act to disorganize and dissolve the . . . Army." [25]

In the spring of 1862, while McClellan's army pushed up the Peninsula and Halleck's troops moved on Corinth, Southern forces were "in the agony of reorganization." [26] In some few cases, company officers managed the elections with a high hand. A North Carolina officer, for example, had his men fall in with arms, read the official order for the election of a second lieutenant, and said: "Men, there are but two candidates for the office, and there is but one of them worth a damn. I nominate him. All who are in favor of electing Sergeant Blank, come to a shoulder. Company,

[22] Quoted in Wiley, *Johnny Reb*, 49, 242.

[23] John Q. Anderson (ed.), *Brokenburn: The Journal of Kate Stone, 1861–1868* (Baton Rouge, 1955), 162–63.

[24] Eggleston, *Rebel's Recollections*, 71.

[25] Emory Upton, *The Military Policy of the United States* (Washington, 1917), 460–61.

[26] Susan Leigh Blackford (ed.), *Letters from Lee's Army: Or Memoirs of Life in and out of the Army in Virginia* . . . (New York, 1947), 81.

Shoulder arms . . . . Sergeant, take charge of the company and dismiss them." [27]

But in most companies there was an orgy of electioneering. Candidates were "interested and busy." "I could start out here now," a Georgia private reported, "and eat myself dead on 'election cake,' be hugged into a perfect 'sqush' by most particular, eternal, disinterested, affectionate friends. A man is perfectly bewildered by the intensity of the affection that is lavished upon him. I never dreamed before that I was half as popular, fine looking, and talented as I found out I am during the past few days." [28] The demoralization did not end with the voting. After a typical election, a Mississippi volunteer recorded, "The new Lt. Col. celebrated his election by 'treating' the men of each company to a gallon or two of whiskey, consequently there is considerable noise in the air." [29]

The painful process of reorganization had a disastrous effect on military efficiency. The Confederate common soldier sharply reacted against discipline and order. The "men have defeated almost every good officer," T. R. R. Cobb lamented, "and elected privates and corporals to their places." [30] General E. P. Alexander agreed that ". . . the whole effect was very prejudicial to the discipline of the army." [31] General Beauregard in the West and General Joseph E. Johnston in the East united in reporting that their troops were "demoralized" by the elections.[32]

Though professional military men unanimously disapproved of the elective system, subsequent Confederate legislation retained it without material alteration. Until almost the end of the war Confederate companies were repeatedly disorganized by these political campaigns for military office. In September 1862 a Mississippi company saw "Great electioneering" with "Party lines . . . sharply drawn, two tickets . . . in the field, and the adherents of each . . . manfully working for success." [33] The following April the proud First Virginia Infantry was almost wrecked when recently added conscripts threatened to elect one of themselves lieutenant. That calamity was averted only when the colonel "told the Company in case any *raw recruit was elected* that he would instantly have him *examined* before the board," which weeded out incompetent officers.[34] As late as January 1864 Texas troops prepared to choose new commanders. "There is great wire-pulling among the officers just at this time," one Confederate wrote his wife. "Some that I know of will not *reign* again unless I am much mistaken." [35]

Time after time Confederate military authorities demanded that the election of officers be stopped. "This system has almost utterly destroyed the efficiency of non-commissioned officers, whose services in the work of discipline are incalculably important," the assistant adjutant-general reported in November 1863, "while it per-

[27] Freeman, *Lee's Lieutenants*, I, 173.

[28] Quoted in Wiley, *Johnny Reb*, 20.

[29] William Pitt Chambers, "My Journal: The Story of a Soldier's Life. . . ," *Mississippi Historical Society Publications: Centenary Series* (1925), V, 234.

[30] T. R. R. Cobb, "Extracts from Letters to His Wife, February 3, 1861–December 10, 1862," *Southern Historical Society Papers*, XXVIII (1900), 292.

[31] E. P. Alexander, "Sketch of Longstreet's Division," *ibid.*, X (1882), 37.

[32] *Official Records*, series 1, X, part 1, 779, and XI, part 3, 503.

[33] Chambers, "My Journal," 248.

[34] Joseph T. Durkin (ed.), *John Dooley: Confederate Soldier, His War Journal* (Georgetown, 1948), 89.

[35] Frank E. Vandiver (ed.), "Letters from the Confederate Medical Service, 1863–65," *Southwestern Historical Quarterly*, LV (1952), 390.

petuates day after day all the derelictions of duty winked at by successful aspirants." Secretary of War James A. Seddon agreed: ". . . the policy of elections . . . may be well questioned, since inseparable from it [arise] an undue regard to popularity, especially among the non-commissioned officers, and a spirit of electioneering subversive of subordination and discipline." [36]

Though militarily indefensible, the system was politically necessary, and it was retained until the closing months of the war. Confederate soldiers, liberty-loving citizens from a democratic society, cherished the right to elect their officers, and the politicians defended them. Soldiers "are not automatons," a Confederate congressman insisted, "dancing to the turning of some official organ grinder. The best *mind* and the best *blood* in the country are in the army, and much of both are found in the ranks. They have not lost the identity of the citizen in the soldier." [37] Even President Jefferson Davis justified the system: "The citizens of the several States volunteered to defend their homes and inherited rights . . . the troops were drawn from the pursuits of civil life. Who so capable to judge of fitness to command a company, a battalion or a regiment as the men composing it?" [38]

The election of officers unquestionably contributed to the chronic lack of discipline in Confederate forces, but it was also a reflection of the fact that Southern soldiers were unwilling to obey orders which struck them as onerous or commanders who seemed to them unreasonable. Like a tedious refrain, the theme of poor discipline runs through the official reports of all Confederate commanders. Even the Army of Northern Virginia, for all its intense devotion to Lee, was poorly controlled. When Lee took command in 1862, his troops were described as "an 'Armed mob' . . . magnificent material, of *undisciplined individuality*, and, as such, correspondingly unreliable and disorganized." [39] Three more years of fighting saw some improvement, yet in November 1864 Lee sorrowfully announced: "The great want in our army is firm discipline." [40]

Few Southern soldiers showed deference to the officers whom they themselves had elected, but some felt that there was another sort of rank which should be maintained and respected, namely, that of social position. "The man of good family felt himself superior, as in most cases he unquestionably was, to his fellow-soldier of less excellent birth; and this distinction was sufficient, during the early years of the war, to override everything like military rank." [41]

These upper-class Southerners belonged to that small group of planter, merchant, and professional families who still dominated the social and economic, if no longer the political, life of the region. Membership in this Southern aristocracy depended not merely upon wealth but upon family, education, good breeding, and intelligence. Nineteenth century equalitarian currents had eroded the political power once held by the Southern gentry, but they had left the plantation ideal untouched as the goal of social aspiration.[42]

[36] *Official Records,* series 4, II, 948, 1001.

[37] Quoted in E. Merton Coulter, *The Confederate States of America, 1861–1865* (Baton Rouge, 1950), 329.

[38] Dunbar Rowland (ed.), *Jefferson Davis, Constitutionalist: His Letters, Papers and Speeches* (10 vols., Jackson, 1923), IX, 543.

[39] *Ibid.,* VII, 410.

[40] *Official Records,* series 1, XLII, part 3, 1213.

[41] Eggleston, *Rebel's Recollections,* 72.

[42] For the power and prestige still retained by the planter aristocracy see Nevins, *Ordeal of the*

The members of this upper class were dedicated Southerners, but they saw no reason why war should seriously alter their pattern of life. Some brought along slaves to serve as their personal attendants while in the army. Such was Tom, who cared for Richard Taylor, son of a former President of the United States, throughout the war. A "mirror of truth and honesty," Tom "could light a fire in a minute under the most unfavorable conditions and with the most unpromising material, made the best coffee to be tasted outside of a creole kitchen, was a 'dab' at camp stews and roasts, groomed . . . horses . . . , washed . . . linen, and was never behind time." [43]

George Cary Eggleston has left a classic, if exaggerated, account of the life these young aristocrats under arms led during the opening months of the war at one camp: ". . . it was a very common thing indeed for men who grew tired of camp fare to take their meals at the hotel, and one or two of them rented cottages and brought their families there, excusing themselves from attendance upon unreasonably early roll calls, by pleading the distance from their cottages to the parade-ground. Whenever a detail was made for the purpose of cleaning the camp-ground, the men detailed regarded themselves as responsible for the proper performance of the task by their servants, and uncomplainingly took upon themselves the duty of sitting on the fence and superintending the work. The two or three men of the overseer class who were to be found in nearly every company turned some nimble quarters by standing other men's turns of guard-duty at twenty-five cents an hour; and one young gentleman of my own company, finding himself assigned to a picket rope post, where his only duty was to guard the horses and prevent them . . . from becoming entangled in each other's heels and halters, coolly called his servant and turned the matter over to him, with a rather informal but decidedly pointed injunction not to let those horses get themselves into trouble if he valued his hide." [44]

Such young bloods might not be numerous, but they contributed to the want of discipline in the Confederate forces. They resented having to take orders. When one well-to-do private could not take "a dozen face and a smaller number of foot or bath towels" on campaign with him, he "actually wrote and sent in to the captain an elegant note resigning his 'position'." [45] "It is," wrote another of these snobs, "galling for a gentleman to be absolutely and entirely subject to the orders of men who in private life were so far his inferiors, & who when they met him felt rather like taking off their hats to him than giving him law and gospel." [46] When the gentleman-soldier found army regulations unduly restrictive, he was likely to defy them, and if he had good family connections, he was fairly certain not to suffer for his insubordination. A Mississippi judge complained that it was "but a mockery of form" to "convict a soldier of any offense, who has social position, friends, and influence." [47]

These Southern aristocrats were, of course, at a great disadvantage in competing

---

Union, I, 416–19; Clement Eaton, *A History of the Old South* (New York, 1949), 444–54; and Roger W. Shugg, *Origins of Class Struggle in Louisiana* . . . (University, La., 1939), *passim.*

[43] Richard Taylor, *Destruction and Reconstruction: Personal Experiences of the Late War* (New York, 1879), 63.

[44] Eggleston, *Rebel's Recollections,* 73.

[45] Robert Stiles, *Four Years under Marse Robert* (New York, 1903), 46–47.

[46] Quoted in Wiley, *Johnny Reb,* 344.

[47] *Official Records,* series 4, III, 709.

in company elections. A planter's son had to be habile in concealing his social superiority and skilful in the arts of mass persuasion if he hoped to rise from the ranks
through popular choice. All the class tensions and prejudices felt against him in
civilian life carried over into military service, and the poorer soldiers were suspicious
of "the genteel men," who "think all you are fit for is to stop bullets for them,
your betters, who call you poor white trash." [48] A high Confederate administrator
concisely summarized the social consequences of having elected officers: ". . . in
our armies . . . to be an officer is not necessarily to be a gentleman . . . ." [49]

If he was handicapped at the lower levels of advancement in the Confederate
army, the Southern aristocrat found that the upper command posts were reserved
almost exclusively for men of his class. Far more than the Confederate civilian
administration, which had few claims to social distinction and included among
the cabinet members a plantation overseer, the son of a keeper of a dried-fish shop,
and a penniless German orphan immigrant,[50] the Southern army leadership was
recruited from the most exclusive elements of ante bellum society.

A list of Southern generals reads like a roster of the South's best and oldest
families. During the four years of war, 103 men were given commissions as generals,
lieutenant-generals, and major-generals in the Confederate army.[51] Senators, congressmen, governors, state legislators, and wealthy planters clustered thickly upon
their family trees.[52] The fathers of these ranking Confederate officers included one
President of the United States, two Senators, two Congressmen, three governors,
one French nobleman, ten officers of the regular United States army, eleven physicians, and six lawyers. Their remote relatives were even more distinguished. One
was a grandnephew of Patrick Henry, another of James Robertson, and yet another
of Andrew Jackson. There were nephews of Matthew F. Maury, the oceanographer,
A. B. Longstreet, the author and college president, and A. P. Butler, the South
Carolina Senator. These generals had the kind of education only wealth and breeding
could procure. Most, naturally, had been to the United States Military Academy,
but others were graduates of Virginia Military Institute, South Carolina College,
Harvard, Yale, Princeton, and assorted smaller Southern schools.

It was natural that the Confederacy should turn to this trained leadership when
hostilities broke out. But it is significant that as the war wore on and deaths and
resignations made new promotions possible, the South continued to recruit its military
leaders from the same small aristocratic social stratum. Southerners appointed to
high military rank in 1864 were, to be sure, much younger than the commanders

[48] Bessie Martin, *Desertion of Alabama Troops from the Confederate Army: A Study in Sectionalism* (New York, 1932), 122; Hugh C. Bailey, "Disloyalty in Early Confederate Alabama,"
Journal of Southern History, XXIII (1957), 525.

[49] *Official Records*, series 4, II, 949.

[50] Burton J. Hendrick, *Statesmen of the Lost Cause: Jefferson Davis and His Cabinet* (Boston,
1939), 9.

[51] Charles C. Jones, Jr., "A Roster of General Officers, Heads of Departments, Senators, Representatives, Military Organizations, &c., &c., in Confederate Service during the War between the
States," *Southern Historical Society Papers*, I (1876), 467 ff.

[52] For biographical data about these commanders I have relied chiefly upon Allen Johnson and
Dumas Malone (eds.), *Dictionary of American Biography* (22 vols., New York, 1928–1958);
National Cyclopedia of American Biography (42 vols., New York, 1892–1958); and Francis B.
Heitman, *Historical Register and Dictionary of the United States Army*. . . (2 vols., Washington,
1903). To prevent duplication, I have counted each general only once in my statistics, listing him
under the date of his highest ranking appointment.

chosen in 1861, and a significantly smaller proportion of them had been trained at West Point.[53] But in family background, wealth, and social position there was no real change. At the end of the war as at its beginning the Confederacy recruited its military chiefs from its finest families.

Though the Southern armies in the West were mostly raised from the rough, semi-frontier Gulf states, their commanders also came from the upper-class planter aristocracy. In the west as in the east, field officers were drawn almost exclusively from wealthy families, usually associated with planting, which had a long tradition of social leadership and military activity. Both groups of generals were well educated, though a somewhat higher proportion of those in the Eastern theater had attended the United States Military Academy.[54] From the point of view of social position, the two groups were virtually interchangeable.

The class line which separated field commanders from lower, elective officers was not completely impassable, but it was virtually so. The few who crossed it were made to feel conspicuous as social misfits. Nathan B. Forrest, the West's most daring cavalry leader, was never allowed to forget that he was "wholly without formal education" and that he had been in civilian life a trader in horses and slaves.[55] A Mississippi gentleman placed under Forrest indignantly expressed his "distaste to being commanded by a man having no pretension to gentility—a negro trader, gambler,—an ambitious man, careless of the lives of his men so long as preferment be *en prospectu*." "Forrest may be . . . the best Cav officer in the west," he added, "but I object to a tyrannical, hotheaded vulgarian's commanding me." [56] Forrests in the Confederacy were few; the Southern army offered only limited opportunities for social mobility.

The Confederate army was, thus, at the same time an extraordinarily democratic military organization and an extraordinarily aristocratic one. The paradox was the reflection of the basic ambivalence of Southern society itself, which believed in the equality of all white men and simultaneously recognized sharp gradations between the social classes.

At the outbreak of the war this ambiguous Southern attitude toward democracy proved a major asset to the Confederate cause. There was little time to convert civilians into proper soldiers, and it was an advantage that Southern recruits were sturdy, independent-minded individualists. Their subaltern officers often lacked training and knew "nothing of details or how to look after the thousand wants which arise and must be met." [57] Even the West Pointers at first needed experience in handling

---

[53] The median age of generals, lieutenant-generals, and major-generals commissioned in 1861 was 51 years; the median age of those appointed in 1864 was 37. Of the 12 men commissioned at these ranks in 1861, 10 had attended the United States Military Academy; of the 29 commissioned in 1864, only 14 had been at West Point.

[54] Of the 38 generals, lieutenant-generals, and major-generals clearly identified with the Western theater of operations, 57 percent had attended the United States Military Academy; their mean age at the date of appointment to their highest rank was 40.7 years. Of the 50 top commanders identified with Eastern operations, 64 percent had been at West Point; their mean age at achieving highest rank was 39.8 years. Generals like Samuel Cooper, who were identified with neither theater of action, and those like Joseph E. Johnston, who fought for long periods in both, have been omitted from these computations.

[55] Thomas M. Spaulding in Johnson and Malone (eds.), *Dictionary of American Biography*, VI, 533.

[56] Quoted in Wiley, *Johnny Reb*, 338.

[57] Blackford (ed.), *Letters from Lee's Army*, 9.

large numbers of men. In 1861 when General R. S. Ewell, who had previously commanded a company of dragoons on the Indian frontier, was told that the country-side around Manassas was bare of supplies for his men, he sallied forth on a cattle hunt himself. Late in the day he returned to camp triumphantly leading one bull to the slaughter. When one of his fellow officers "observed that the bull was a most respectable animal, but would hardly afford much subsistence to eight thousand men," the general ruefully exclaimed, "Ah! I was thinking of my fifty dragoons." [58] In the circumstances it was just as well that Southern recruits were not army regulars.

At the same time it was a decided asset to have in the South recognized, trained leaders who merely required time and experience to develop into expert army commanders. There was some grumbling at times against the upper-class professional officers who preempted the high positions, particularly the staff officers, "young sprouts with bobtailed coats and vast importance, . . . who obviously thought the war was gotten up that they might dazzle the world by their talents." [59] Occasionally President Davis had to yield to popular prejudices and appoint political generals of no very great military knowledge or aptitude, such as "Extra Billy" Smith, former governor of Virginia, who "was equally distinguished for personal intrepidity and contempt for what he called 'tactics' and for educated and trained soldiers, whom he was wont to speak of as 'those West P'int fellows.'" [60] But the Confederacy never saw an organized attempt to oust the military experts comparable to the Northern Radical Republicans' campaign against the West Pointers in the Union army. In the South training, tradition, and social position kept qualified officers in control.

But what was an advantage in the opening days of the war became a serious handicap later. When both opposing armies were little more than armed mobs, the Confederate soldier, fighting on his own terrain, could ignore orders, rely on his wits, and still achieve victory. But as gigantic and highly disciplined Northern armies pressed forward, the Confederate, though still a magnificent individual fighter, was put at a disadvantage by his indifference to discipline. These differences must not be exaggerated; Northern armies too were shockingly undisciplined by modern standards. But the Confederacy, with its shortages of men and material, could scarcely afford the high price of individualism. In February 1865 General Lee sadly concluded: "Many opportunities have been lost and hundreds of valuable lives have been uselessly sacrificed for want of a strict observance of discipline." [61]

The rigidity of social structure which had provided the Confederacy with a secure, trained top command at the outbreak of the war also became a disadvantage as the conflict continued. The Confederate high command showed a remarkable continuity through the four years of war. While the Northern army was led successively by McDowell, McClellan, Pope, Burnside, Hooker, and Meade, the Southern forces in Northern Virginia had only two generals-in-chief—Joseph E. Johnston and Robert E. Lee. As the war progressed and death or incapacity made room for fresh leaders there were, of course, new faces in the Confederate high command, but these were from the same social class, with the same kind of training and the same social outlook as their predecessors. Had the art of war remained unchanged, this continuity in Confederate leadership would have been only an advantage, but the Civil War,

[58] Taylor, *Destruction and Reconstruction*, 38.
[59] Blackford (ed.), *Letters from Lee's Army*, 12.
[60] Stiles, *Four Years under Marse Robert*, 110.
[61] Quoted in Wiley, *Johnny Reb*, 243.

the first truly modern war, witnessed technological changes of an unprecedented nature—new kinds of rifles, new uses for artillery, new possibilities for railroad warfare. The Northern winning team of Lincoln, Grant, and Sherman came from a more openly structured society and was trained to improvise and adapt. Confederate leadership had an aristocratic hostility toward change.[62]

The Southerner as a fighting man, then, was a product of the paradoxical world that was the ante bellum South, devoted to the principles of democracy and the practice of aristocracy. And to compound the paradox, the Southerner's assets at the outbreak of the war became his liabilities by its conclusion. Historians in seeking the reasons for the collapse of the Confederacy have correctly pointed to inadequate Southern resources, poor transportation, unimaginative political leadership, and state rights. All these, and more, deserve to be taken into account, yet perhaps more basic to the Confederate failure was the fundamental ambivalence in the Southern attitude toward democracy. Because of that weakness the Southerner made an admirable fighting man but a poor soldier.

[62] I have developed this theme in more detail in my *Lincoln Reconsidered: Essays on the Civil War Era* (New York, 1956), 82–102.

20 / Who Whipped Whom? Confederate Defeat Re-examined

Grady McWhiney

Professional historians often see the diplomatic, political, economic, or constitutional events of the Civil War as more important and interesting than the military confrontations. But to the average American it is the agony and the glory of battle that make the struggle endlessly engrossing. Today Civil war buffs frequently know more about the battles of Shiloh and Gettysburg than they do about the World War II Battle of the Bulge or the Vietnam Tet Offensive.

Unfortunately, much of the military history that the enthusiasts read is superficial, the work of amateurs interested in milking sentiment or pathos from the events of 1861–1865. Alternately, Civil War military history consists of pedantic, inch-by-inch examinations of individual leaders, battles, fighting units, and campaigns. The Civil War centennial generated hundreds of special studies, most of which were paralyzingly detailed, overblown, and pretentious epics.

Happily there are exceptions to this generalization. General accounts such as Allan Nevins' as yet unfinished work, *The War for the Union*, and biographies such as Douglas Southall Freeman's magisterial *Robert E. Lee* have both depth and sweep. There are some excellent, brief histories of regiments and campaigns, and special monographic studies, such as Donald's essay, that throw vivid light on larger issues of the war or are filled with intense human drama. The following essay by Grady McWhiney is a model of compressed synthesis. In a few pages McWhiney takes up the central military problem of the war and advances some thought-provoking hypotheses.

For further reading: * Bruce Catton, *Mr. Lincoln's Army* (Garden City, N.Y.: Doubleday & Co., Inc., 1951); * *Glory Road* (Garden City, N.Y.: Doubleday & Co., Inc., 1952); * *A Stillness at Appomattox* (Garden City: Doubleday & Co., Inc., 1953); * David Donald (ed.), *Why the North Won the Civil War* (Baton Rouge, La.: Louisiana State University Press, 1960);

Civil War History, XI, No. 1 (March 1965), 5–26. Reprinted by permission.

Kenneth P. Williams, *Lincoln Finds a General—A Military Study of the Civil War* (New York: The Macmillan Company, 1949–1959); John B. Walters, "General William T. Sherman and Total War," *Journal of Southern History*, XIV (November 1948).

Sometime after the Civil War an unreconstructed rebel, Robert Toombs, was arguing with a Federal army officer over the relative fighting qualities of Union and Confederate soldiers.

"Well, we whipped you," the exasperated officer finally told Toombs.

"No," Toombs retorted, "we just wore ourselves out whipping you." [1]

Although as a general Toombs left a great deal to be desired, he was a perceptive military analyst. His statement that the Confederacy beat itself may have been intended as a joke, but as an appraisal of how the South lost the Civil War it was surprisingly accurate.

More than 600,000 Americans died in the Civil War—a greater American mortality than in the two World Wars and the Korean Conflict combined. The charge of the British Light Brigade at Balaclava (almost 40 percent of its men were shot in the "Valley of Death") has symbolized needless sacrifice, but heavier losses were common during the Civil War. Some sixty Union regiments lost more than half their men in a single engagement, and at least 120 Union regiments sustained losses equal to the Light Brigade's. In eleven different campaigns the Union suffered ten thousand casualties; over a thousand men were killed or wounded in fifty-six different actions. At Gettysburg one out of every five Federal soldiers present was hit, and a Minnesota regiment was decimated—it lost 82 percent of its men.

Proportionally, Confederate losses were even greater. More than eighty thousand Confederate soldiers fell in just five battles. At Gettysburg three out of every ten southerners present were hit; one North Carolina regiment lost 85 percent of its strength, and every man in one company was killed or wounded. In the first twenty-seven months of combat the South lost 175,000 men.[2] This number exceeded the entire Confederate military service in July, 1861, and the strength of any army Robert E. Lee ever commanded.

Losses were so staggering because officers on both sides fought by the books, and the books were wrong. Every treatise on tactics available in the 1860's was outdated. All the official and unofficial tactical manuals insisted that bayonets would decide the outcome of battles and that troops should assault either in long lines or in massed columns.[3] Such assumptions were tragically in error, for by 1861 bayonets were obsolete weapons and played no significant role in the outcome of the Civil War. During the Virginia campaign of 1864, when there was more close combat

---

[1] Pleasant A. Stovall, *Robert Toombs* (New York, 1892), p. 322.

[2] William F. Fox, *Regimental Losses in the American Civil War, 1861–1865* (Albany, 1889), pp. 47, 554, 22; Thomas L. Livermore, *Numbers and Losses in the Civil War in America: 1861–65* (Bloomington, 1957), pp. 63–64, 140–141.

[3] See Winfield Scott, *Infantry Tactics* (New York, 1861); William J. Hardee, *Rifle and Light Infantry Tactics* (Philadelphia, 1861); Silas Casey, *Infantry Tactics* (New York, 1862); George B. McClellan, *Manual of Bayonet Exercise: Prepared for the Use of the Army of the United States* (Philadelphia, 1862); John H. Richardson, *Infantry Tactics, or, Rules for the Exercise and Manoeuvres of the Confederate States Infantry* (Richmond, 1862).

than usual, 33,292 Federal soldiers were treated for bullet wounds but only thirty-seven for bayonet wounds.[4]

Before the Civil War bayonet attacks had been justifiable because the basic infantry firearm—the smoothbore musket—was highly inaccurate. A soldier might fire a smoothbore musket at a man all day from a distance of a few hundred yards and never hit him.[5] Nevertheless, field commanders of the early 1800's favored smoothbores over rifles for general infantry use. Rifles required too much time and effort to load because each bullet had to be slightly larger than the bore; otherwise, when the weapon was fired, the bullet would fail to spin through the barrel along the rifled grooves. These rifled grooves gave the rifle both its name and its superiority in range and accuracy over the smoothbore. Usually only special units such as the British sharpshooters at Waterloo were equipped with rifles, and then the men were also issued ramrods and mallets with which to hammer in their shots. Loading took two minutes.[6]

Tactics during the first half of the nineteenth century were designed to compensate for the smoothbore's inaccuracy and short range. Armies learned to perform series of stylized maneuvers, and sometimes prepared for battle within a few hundred yards of each other. Soldiers fought in tight formations and fired in volleys. The usual battle alignment was two or three lines of infantry, armed with smoothbores and long bayonets, supported in the rear by artillery and on the flanks by cavalry. After the infantrymen had fired a volley, they advanced, elbow to elbow, at a trot. The defenders, who had time to fire only one or two volleys before the attackers reached their line, either repulsed the assault or retreated to reform and counterattack. Success in battle usually depended upon strict discipline and precise movements. If the infantrymen on either side broke, enemy cavalry dashed in from the flanks to slash at the retreaters with sabers. Most infantry attacks were checked by artillery firing scattershot. Although an army might advance and retreat several times during a battle, it rarely suffered heavy losses.

Americans had used these conventional tactics successfully in the Mexican War. At Palo Alto in 1846 Zachary Taylor formed his three-thousand-man army in one long line. "The Mexicans immediately opened fire upon us, first with artillery and then with infantry," wrote an American officer.

[4] Among the works which explain how new weapons outdated Civil War tactics, I have found most useful: J. F. C. Fuller, *The Generalship of Ulysses S. Grant* (New York, 1929), pp. 57–62, and "The Place of the American Civil War in the Evolution of War," *Army Quarterly*, XXVI (1933), 316–325; G. F. R. Henderson, *The Civil War: A Soldier's View*, ed. Jay Luvaas (Chicago, 1958), pp. 197–224; Bruce Catton, *America Goes to War* (New York, 1958), pp. 14–20; John K. Mahon, "Civil War Infantry Assault Tactics," *Military Affairs*, XXV (1961), 57–68.

Moreover, though I disagree with some of their conclusions, a number of authors have influenced my thought on the relationship of tactics and weapons to strategy and command. I am particularly indebted to: Bruce Catton, "The Generalship of Ulysses S. Grant," *Grant, Lee, Lincoln and the Radicals: Essays on Civil War Leadership*, ed. Grady McWhiney (Evanston, Ill., 1964), pp. 3–30; David Donald, *Lincoln Reconsidered* (New York, 1956), especially chap. v; Douglas S. Freeman, *R. E. Lee* (New York, 1935), and *Lee's Lieutenants* (New York, 1942–44); Archer Jones, *Confederate Strategy from Shiloh to Vicksburg* (Baton Rouge, 1961); Charles P. Roland, "The Generalship of Robert E. Lee," *Grant, Lee, Lincoln and the Radicals*, ed. McWhiney, pp. 31–71; Kenneth P. Williams, *Lincoln Finds a General* (New York, 1949–59); T. Harry Williams, *Lincoln and His Generals* (New York, 1952), and *Americans at War* (Baton Rouge, 1960); Frank E. Vandiver, *Rebel Brass* (Baton Rouge, 1956).

[5] Ulysses S. Grant, *Personal Memoirs* (New York, 1885), I, 95.

[6] T. H. McGuffie, "Musket and Rifle," *History Today*, VII (1957), 475.

At first their shots did not reach us, and the advance . . . continued. As we got nearer, the cannon balls commenced going through the ranks. They hurt no one, however, . . . because they would strike the ground long before they reached our line, and ricochetted through the tall grass so slowly that the men would see them and open ranks to let them pass. When we got to a point where the artillery could be used with effect, a halt was called, and the battle opened on both sides.

The Americans attacked; the Mexicans retreated, and by nightfall Taylor's men occupied the Mexican position. American losses were only nine killed and forty-seven wounded.[7]

Bayonet assaults in the 1860's were far more costly than ever before because the smoothbore musket had been replaced by a better weapon. The technological innovation that finished the smoothbore as the standard infantry arm was the development in the 1850's of the Minié "ball." Neither Captain Minié's invention nor a ball, the projectile actually was an elongated bullet with a hollow base which was small enough to fit easily into the rifle's bore, but would expand automatically when fired and fit snugly into the rifled grooves. The Minié bullet made the rifled muzzleloader a practical military weapon.

Both sides used a variety of small arms during the Civil War, but the basic infantry weapon was the single-shot rifled muzzleloader, either the Springfield caliber .58, or the British Enfield caliber .577. The Springfield rifle was fifty-six inches long and weighed nearly ten pounds when fitted with its eighteen-inch triangular bayonet. All parts were interchangeable. Between 1861 and 1865 over 1,600,000 of these rifles were produced in the United States at a cost of $14.93 each. The Enfields, which were more popular in the South, varied considerably in length and bayonet type, but they all fired the same ammunition. Moreover, they were the equal of any Union rifle—so good, in fact, that after the fall of Vicksburg General U. S. Grant rearmed some of his Union regiments with captured Enfields.[8]

Compared with pre-Civil War shoulder weapons, the rifled muzzleloader was a firearm of deadly accuracy. It could be fired two or three times a minute, it could stop an attack at up to four hundred yards, and it could kill at a distance of one thousand yards. In October, 1861, a Union soldier wrote his parents: "We went out the other day to try [our rifles]. We fired [from a distance of] 600 yards and we put 360 balls into a mark the size of old Jeff [Davis]." In contrast, some Illinois soldiers armed with smoothbore muskets fired 160 shots at a flour barrel 180 yards away. It was hit only four times.[9]

The rifle became the great killer of the Civil War. It inflicted 80 percent of all wounds and revolutionized tactics. Because of the rifle's range and accuracy, Civil War infantry assaults were always bloody. They were sometimes suicidal. For the first time in over a century defenders had the advantage in warfare. "One rifle in the trench was worth five in front of it," wrote General J. D. Cox. Perhaps Cox

[7] Grant, *Personal Memoirs*, I, 94–95.

[8] Arcadi Gluckman, *United States Muskets, Rifles and Carbines* (Harrisburg, 1959), pp. 229–244; Francis A. Lord, "Strong Right Arm of the Infantry: The '61 Springfield Rifle Musket," *Civil War Times Illustrated*, I (1962), 43; Jac Weller, "Imported Confederate Shoulder Weapons," *Civil War History*, V (1959), 170–171, 180, 158.

[9] Quoted in Bell I. Wiley, *The Life of Billy Yank* (Indianapolis, 1951), p. 63; Fritz Haskell (ed.), "Diary of Colonel William Camm," *Journal of the Illinois State Historical Society*, XVIII (1926), 813.

exaggerated a bit, but a few entrenched men armed with rifles *could* hold a position against great odds. The rifle and the spade had made defense at least three times as strong as offense.[10]

But no one knew this at the time. Shortly before the Civil War the army had decided to modify infantry tactics, because officers believed they could offset the rifle's range and accuracy simply by teaching soldiers to move more quickly in battle. "They are introducing the light infantry tactics this spring, a new thing," wrote Cadet Henry A. du Pont from West Point on March 28, 1857.

> There are a great many very rapid movements in it, and many of them are performed in double quick time, that is running. Within the last week [Colonel William J.] Hardee [author of the new tactics book and Commandant of Cadets] has had the whole battalion going at double quick with the band. . . . It will take time for everyone to learn to keep step. I expect that they will almost run us to death when the board of visitors come.

Two months later du Pont admitted that the new tactics were

> no doubt better in some respects, that is to say that troops drilled to them would be more efficient, but they do not look so well, for it is impossible to attain . . . the same precision and accuracy with all this running and quick movements, as was possible under the old system, and besides it is much harder work.[11]

If the new tactics could have stressed dispersal as well as speed then attackers might have had a chance to overcome the advantage rifles had given defenders, but dispersal of forces was impracticable in the 1860's. In some ways the Civil War was a modern struggle: in minutes generals communicated with each other by telegraph over thousands of miles; trains quickly carried large armies great distances, and piled mountains of supplies at railheads. But, in other ways, the war was strikingly antiquated: men walked or rode horses into battle, and their supplies followed in wagons. No telegraph or telephone lines connected combat units with each other or with field headquarters; all messages went by courier on horseback. This traditional system of battlefield communication bound Civil War generals to close order formations. They had no choice; the dispersal of forces to avoid the rifle's firepower and accuracy would have made communication even more difficult, and further weakened a commander's control of his men in battle. Even though they usually kept their troops in tight formations, Civil War commanders never completely solved the problems of battlefield communication and control. In the Wilderness in 1864 both Lee and Grant lost effective control of their armies after the action began. To relieve his frustration, Grant sat on a stump and started to whittle, but forgot to remove his new gloves and soon they were snagged and ruined.[12]

Except for the quicker movements required of troops, the new tactics were much like the old ones. Both emphasized close order formations, and taught men to rely on the shock effect of bayonet assaults. A Prussian officer who visited the South in 1863 recalled that

[10] Jacob D. Cox, *Atlanta* (New York, 1909), p. 129; Fuller, *Generalship of Ulysses S. Grant,* pp. 361, 367.

[11] Stephen A. Ambrose (ed.) "West Point in the Fifties: The Letters of Henry A. du Pont," *Civil War History,* X (1964), 306–307.

[12] Bruce Catton, *A Stillness at Appomattox* (New York, 1955), pp. 64–65.

There was diligent drilling in the camps according to an old French drill manual that had been revised by Hardee, and I observed on the drill field only linear formations, wheeling out into open columns, wheeling in and marching up into line, marching in line, open column marching, marching by sections, and marching in file. . . . The tactical unit in battle seemed to be the brigade. The drilling, according to my observation, seemed to be somewhat awkward. The cavalry drilled in a manner similar to ours, and the main emphasis was on a good jog, with loud yelling and shouting. The infantry also used this sound, the famous rebel yell, in bayonet attacks.[13]

The Confederate yell was intended to help control fear. As one soldier explained: "I always said if I ever went into a charge, I wouldn't holler! But the very first time I fired off my gun I hollered as loud as I could, and I hollered every breath till we stopped." Jubal Early once told some troops who hesitated to charge because they were out of ammunition: "Damn it, holler them across." [14]

Union soldiers studied the same manuals and practiced the same drills as the Confederates. "Every night I recite with the other 1st Sergts and 2nd Lieutenants," wrote a Union sergeant in 1862. "We shall finish Hardee's Tactics and then study the 'Army Regulations.' Theory as well as practice are necessary to make the perfect soldier." In 1863 a Union corporal explained that the noncommissioned officers of his company "have lessons in tactics every night at the Captain's quarters to fit them to drill the privates in squads according to the book." Union General Marsena R. Patrick, a graduate of West Point, wrote on March 30, 1862, that "Although this is the Sabbath, I have been obliged to look over Tactics, Regulations etc. etc." The next day he described how he drilled his troops for combat: "Formed [them] in Mass—then in Column—then deployed by Battalion—in 4 lines, . . . and then handled them in masses almost exclusively. . . ." On April 1 he drilled his men "in Mass Movements some 2 or 3 hours," and on July 18 he wrote: "The Drills, for some time back, have been very interesting, as the men are beginning to see the value of them. . . ." [15]

After the war Union General William B. Hazen admitted that most Civil War battles were merely the formation of troops into lines to attack or to repel attacks. Almost any battle can serve as an example. "I saw our infantry make a charge [at Murfreesboro]," wrote a Confederate; "they got [with]in fifty yards of the yanks [before the Federals] fired a shot, when they poured the heaviest volley into them that I ever saw or heard." A Louisiana soldier wrote of the fight at Perryville: "The men stood right straight up on the open field, loaded and fired, charged and fell back as deliberately as if on drill." [16] At Shiloh the Confederates attacked by corps in four lines across a three-mile front. Such an arrangement of forces could only result in disorder and confusion, and within a few minutes after their first contact with the enemy the southerners became hopelessly tangled, with corps, divisions,

---

[13] Captain Justus Scheibert, *Seven Months in the Rebel States During the North American War, 1863,* ed. William Stanley Hoole (Tuscaloosa, Ala., 1958), pp. 37–38.

[14] Quoted in Bell I. Wiley, *The Life of Johnny Reb* (Indianapolis, 1943), pp. 71–72.

[15] Quoted in Wiley, *Life of Billy Yank,* p. 50; David S. Sparks (ed.), *Inside Lincoln's Army: The Diary of Marsena Rudolph Patrick* (New York, 1964), pp. 62–63, 108.

[16] Henderson, *The Civil War,* p. 207; Robert W. Williams, Jr., and Ralph A. Wooster (eds.), "With Terry's Texas Rangers: The Letters of Dunbar Affleck," *Civil War History,* IX (1963), 311–312; E. John Ellis to his mother, Oct. 21, 1862, E. John, Thomas C. W. Ellis and Family Papers, Louisiana State University, Baton Rouge.

and brigades pell-mell in one battle line.[17] At Winchester in 1862 Richard Taylor's brigade attacked in long lines with the men elbow to elbow. As they advanced many fell and others wavered. "What the hell are you dodging for?" screamed Taylor. "If there is any more of it, you will be halted under fire for an hour." With Taylor leading the way, the brigade marched to within fifty yards of the enemy "in perfect order, not firing a shot." Taylor proudly reported that his men closed "the many gaps made by the [enemy's] fierce fire," and preserved "an alignment that would have been creditable on parade." [18] Two weeks later Taylor used a similar attack formation at Port Republic. These two battles cost him five hundred casualties and taught him nothing.

Many generals besides Taylor favored traditional weapons and tactics. Stonewall Jackson, often praised as a military innovator, was partial to bayonet assaults. General Alexander R. Lawton claimed Jackson "did not value human life. . . . He could order men to their death as a matter of course. Napoleon's French conscription could not have kept him supplied with men, he used up his command so rapidly." In little less than six months in 1862 Jackson's tactics cost the South over twenty thousand casualties—the equivalent of one entire army corps—or almost twice the number of men under Jackson's command when the campaign began.[19] Jackson was so committed to conventional offensive tactics that he once actually requested that some of his troops be equipped with pikes instead of muskets. Pikes, he explained, should be "6 or more inches longer than the musket with the bayonet on, so that when we teach our troops to rely upon the bayonet they may feel that they have the superiority of arm resulting from its length." Apparently Lee saw nothing wrong with such a request; he approved it and ordered Josiah Gorgas, Chief of Ordnance, to send pikes to Jackson. Gorgas sent muskets instead.[20]

One Confederate general even considered the bayonet too modern, and "inferior to the *knife*," because southerners "would require long drilling to become expert with the [bayonet] . . . , but they instinctively know how to wield the bowie-knife." General Henry Wise, a former governor of Virginia, scoffed at both new weapons and new tactics. He insisted "it was not the improved *arm*, but the improved *man*, which would win the day. Let brave men advance with flint locks and old-fashioned bayonets, . . . reckless of the slain, and he would answer for it with his life, that the Yankees would break and run." [21]

Wise's views were extreme, but even the highest ranking officers failed to recognize the limitations of traditional arms, formations and services. Winfield Scott predicted at the outset that the war would be won by artillery. He was wrong, of course;

[17] U. S. War Dept. (comp.), *The War of the Rebellion: A Compilation of the Official Records of the Union and Confederate Armies* (Washington, 1880–1901), Ser. I, X, pt. 1, 392–395, 463–466, pt. 2, 387. (Hereafter cited as *OR*, and unless otherwise indicated all references are to Ser. I.)

[18] Richard Taylor, *Destruction and Reconstruction* (New York, 1879), p. 58; John H. Worsham, *One of Jackson's Foot Cavalry* (New York, 1912), p. 87.

[19] Mary Boykin Chesnut, *A Diary From Dixie*, ed. Ben Ames Williams (Cambridge, Mass., 1949), p. 330. The campaigns and Jackson's losses were: 2,095 in the Valley; 6,700 during the Seven Days; 1,365 at Cedar Mountain; 4,629 at Second Bull Run; and 6,095 in the Maryland campaign. Robert Underwood Johnson and Clarence Clough Buel (eds.), *Battles and Leaders of the Civil War* (New York, 1887–1889), II, 300–301, 315–316, 496, 500, 601–602.

[20] *OR*, XII, pt. 3, 842.

[21] John B. Jones, *A Rebel War Clerk's Diary*, ed. Earl Schenck Miers (New York, 1958), p. 3.

only about 10 percent of all Civil War casualties were caused by artillery fire.[22] In February, 1862, Joseph E. Johnston, commander of Confederate forces in Virginia, wrote Adjutant General Samuel Cooper that "We should have a much larger cavalry force. The greatest . . . difficulty, in increasing it, is said to be the want of proper arms. This can be easily removed by equipping a large body of lancers." Johnston claimed lances "would be formidable . . . in the hands of new troops, especially against the enemy's . . . artillery." [23] Cooper wisely ignored Johnston's suggestion; cavalry armed with sabers or lances were no match for artillery or infantry in the 1860's.

No one guessed just how much the rifled musket had diminished the importance of cavalry and artillery. At first cavalry officers trained their troopers to charge infantry and artillery. A Union private recalled a drill in December, 1861, where infantry regiments fired blank shots at each other and "a squadron of cavalry dashed around . . . and charged down on them with the wildest yells." Another Union infantryman wrote in 1862: "We had our first Brigade drill day before yesterday. . . . The Cavalry charged down on us and for the first time I saw something that looked like fighting. . . . It was a beautiful sight, and our officers expressed themselves well satisfied with the drill." One soldier described how his regiment formed a hollow square to repel cavalry charges:

> When they charge us with wild yells (some of them get awfully excited, so do the horses), it takes some nerve to stand against them, although it is all a sham. But we have found out one thing—horses cannot be driven onto fixed bayonets and I dont believe we shall be as afraid of the real charge if we ever have to meet one in the future. We are learning a good deal, so are the Cavalry.[24]

But cavalry generals on both sides learned their lessons slowly. "Not until the closing days of the war did we wake up to what our experience . . . ought to have taught us," confessed James H. Wilson. When Philip H. Sheridan took command of the Army of the Potomac's cavalry in 1864 he proposed to concentrate it to fight the enemy's cavalry, but George Meade objected. Sheridan recalled that "my proposition seemed to stagger General Meade," who "would hardly listen . . . , for he was filled with the prejudices that, from the beginning of the war, had pervaded the army regarding the cavalry. . . ." Until his death J. E. B. Stuart held the archaic and romantic view that the

> duty of the cavalry after battle is joined is to cover the flanks to prevent the enemy from turning them. If victorious, it improves the victory by rapid pursuit —if defeated it covers the rear and makes charges to delay the advance of the enemy—or in the supreme moment in the crisis of battle . . . the cavalry comes down like an avalanche upon the . . . troops already engaged and with splendid effect.[25]

[22] Philip H. Sheridan, *Personal Memoirs* (New York, 1888), I, 355; L. Van Loan Naisawald, *Grape and Canister . . . the Field Artillery of the Army of the Potomac* (New York, 1960), p. 535.

[23] Johnston still thought enough of lances after the war to include a copy of his proposal in the appendix of his *Narrative of Military Operations* (Bloomington, 1959), p. 479.

[24] Quoted in Wiley, *Life of Billy Yank*, pp. 51–52.

[25] James H. Wilson, "The Cavalry of the Army of the Potomac," *Papers of the Military Historical Society of Massachusetts*, XIII (1913), 85; Sheridan, *Personal Memoirs*, I, 354–356; William W. Blackford, *The War Years With Jeb Stuart* (New York, 1945), p. 26.

A number of bloody failures occurred before even the more astute cavalry commander learned he could no longer use pre-Civil War tactics successfully. The charge of the 5th U. S. Cavalry at Gaines's Mill in June, 1862, was an excellent example of the frequent misuse of horsemen. This regiment lost 60 percent of its troopers in a saber attack on Confederate infantry and artillery. One of the attackers, Private W. H. Hitchcock, recalled the action: "We dashed forward with a wild cheer, in solid column of squadron front; but our formation was almost instantly broken. . . . I closed in to re-form the line, but could find no one at my left, so completely had our line been shattered by the musketry fire in front. . . ." At this point Hitchcock's horse veered off to the rear. "I dropped my saber," Hitchcock admitted, "and so fiercely tugged at my horse's bit as to cause the blood to flow from her mouth, yet could not check her." Finally he gained control of his mount, "turned about and started back. . . . The firing of artillery and infantry . . . was terrific," he remembered. "None but the dead and wounded were around me. It hardly seemed that I could drive Lee's . . . veterans alone, so I rode . . . off the field." Nearly 250 men had galloped into action; only about a hundred returned.[26]

After such tragic experiences many horsemen and their commanders became so gun shy that General John A. Logan allegedly offered a reward for a dead cavalryman, Federal or Confederate; and one of Sherman's soldiers wrote in 1863: "We have considerable cavalry with us, but they are the laughing stock of the army and the boys poke all kinds of fun at them. I really have as yet to see or hear of their doing anything of much credit to them." [27] Despite such derision, cavalrymen performed many creditable services: they were excellent couriers, scouts, and raiders; when necessary, they dismounted and fought as infantry. But Civil War horsemen were no longer effective as a shock force in assaults. They were too vulnerable to accurate rifle fire.

Unlike the modifications in cavalry tactics, changes in Civil War artillery tactics were less marked. Artillery remained primarily a defensive weapon throughout the war, for it lacked the range, precision, or elevation needed to cover assault troops in that critical area just in front of the enemy's line. Civil War guns were usually incapable of providing what is now called effective preparation, or softening up the enemy, for an assault.

Nevertheless, some generals attempted to use artillery as an offensive weapon, and almost invariably they failed. Before Pickett's charge at Gettysburg 150 Confederate guns pounded the Union line without doing much damage. The Federals merely dug in and waited for the bombardment to end; they suffered very few casualties from artillery fire. In his assault on the Federal left at Murfreesboro, John C. Breckinridge placed his batteries between two lines of infantry and ordered them to join the attack. He ignored a young artillery officer's warning that such an arrangement of guns would cause confusion and misdirection of fire. As the Confederate gunners advanced, sandwiched between the infantry lines and unable to find clear fields of fire, they hit some of the southern infantrymen. Federal shells disabled several Confederate guns and three were captured when the attack failed.[28]

[26] W. H. Hitchcock, "Recollections of a Participant in the Charge," *Battles and Leaders*, II, 346.

[27] Quoted in Wiley, *Life of Billy Yank*, p. 327.

[28] Henry J. Hunt, "The Third Day at Gettysburg," *Battles and Leaders*, III, 372–374; E. Porter Alexander, "The Great Charge and Artillery Fighting at Gettysburg," *ibid.*, 363–365; *OR*, XX, pt. 1, 759–761.

Though relatively ineffective as an offensive weapon, artillery was a most important adjunct to the infantry on defense. At Malvern Hill the Federals massed over two hundred guns to stop what could have been a breakthrough; at Gettysburg twenty-five cannon along Plum Run held the Union line without infantry support; at Atlanta only twenty-nine guns checked twelve thousand Confederates; and at Murfreesboro fifty-eight pieces of artillery helped disrupt Breckinridge's assault. Used on defense, artillery was deadliest in precisely those areas offensive artillery could not reach. When infantry assault columns got within four hundred yards, the defenders loaded their guns with scattershot which decimated closely bunched infantry.[29]

Attacks on strongly posted batteries rarely succeeded, and nearly always penalized the attackers heavily. A Confederate diarist wrote of his brigade's attempt to take some Federal guns at Spotsylvania in 1864: ". . . After being subjected to a heavy artillery fire for some time we were ordered . . . to charge the enemy. We charged them. . . . Our loss [was] heavy. We fell back. . . ." Perhaps General D. H. Hill left the best description of the Confederate attack on the Union line at Malvern Hill. "I never saw anything more grandly heroic," he wrote.

> As each brigade emerged from the woods, from fifty to one hundred guns opened upon it, tearing great gaps in its ranks. . . . Most of them had an open field half a mile wide to cross, under the fire of field-artillery . . . and . . . heavy ordnance. . . . It was not war—it was murder.[30]

When the struggle began neither the North nor the South was prepared for war, much less for murder. There were no strategic plans ready; indeed, it was uncertain which side, if either, would be the invader. President Lincoln and Secretary of War Simon Cameron, who had no military experience, gladly relegated the awesome responsibility of strategic planning to Winfield Scott, hero of two previous wars. "General Scott seems to have carte-blanche," noted an observer in May, 1861. "He is, in fact, the Government. . . ."[31]

Yet Scott failed to inspire confidence. He was seventy-five years old and a semi-invalid. State Senator Alexander K. McClure and Governor Andrew Curtin of Pennsylvania, who saw Scott the morning after Fort Sumter fell, concluded "that the old chieftain had outlived his . . . usefulness, and that he was utterly unequal to the appalling task he had accepted." After the Pennsylvanians had left Scott's office Curtin threw up his hands and exclaimed: "My God, the country is at the mercy of a dotard." A few days later, when the governor of Iowa called, Scott dodged any discussion of strategy, reminisced instead about his service in the War of 1812, and then fell asleep in his chair. But Scott may have put on a senile act to disarm nosey politicians, for President Lincoln only half jokingly told a visitor: "Scott will not let us outsiders know anything of his plans."[32]

[29] Mahon, "Civil War Infantry Assault Tactics," pp. 66–67; Williams, *Lincoln Finds a General,* IV, 278, 281.

[30] Entry of May 12, 1864, Charles M. Walsh Diary, owned by Mr. and Mrs. John K. Read, Norfolk, Va.; Daniel H. Hill, "McClellan's Change of Base and Malvern Hill," *Battles and Leaders,* II, 391–395.

[31] Edwin M. Stanton quoted in George Ticknor Curtis, *The Life of James Buchanan* (New York, 1883), II, 548.

[32] Alexander K. McClure, *Recollections of Half a Century* (Salem, Mass., 1902), pp. 205–206; Charles Winslow Elliott, *Winfield Scott: The Soldier and the Man* (New York, 1937), p. 724;

Scott revealed his scheme in May. He told the President the best way to defeat the Confederacy was to encircle it, and then divide it by means of a naval blockade and a drive down the Mississippi River. Such action, Scott believed, would make it possible "to envelop the insurgent States and bring them to terms with less bloodshed than by any other plan." Cut off from the outside world, the Confederacy would slowly strangle and die as if caught in the grip of a giant anaconda.[33]

The "Anaconda" plan proved that Scott could still view military problems realistically, but that he misunderstood the nation's temper. He knew the Union was unprepared for an immediate offensive, and that no major action should be taken until a large army of regulars and three-year volunteers had been assembled and trained. His mistake was in assuming that the people would wait. William T. Sherman recalled: "Congress and the people would not permit the slow and methodical preparation desired by General Scott." Northerners demanded action; Scott's policy was too conservative, too cautious. Sherman observed in late June how Scott "seemed vexed with the clamors of the press for immediate action, and the continued interference in [military] details by the President, Secretary of War, and Congress." Secretary of the Navy Gideon Welles admitted that he disapproved of Scott's plan as "purely defensive." Welles wrote in his diary that "Instead of halting on the borders, building intrenchments, . . . we should penetrate their territory." [34] The cry "On to Richmond!" soon became too insistent for Lincoln to ignore. He realized that, whatever its military merits, Scott's plan was politically inexpedient. So on June 29, 1861, the President and his cabinet overruled the old general's objections to an immediate offensive. Thence the Union would follow an offensive strategy aimed at the occupation and conquest of the South.[35]

At first the Confederacy planned to fight a defensive war. President Jefferson Davis explained that "the Confederate Government is waging this war solely for self-defense, . . . it has no design of conquest or any other purpose than to secure peace and the abandonment by the United States of its pretensions to govern a people who have never been their subjects and who prefer self-government to a Union with them." [36]

The South's decision to fight a defensive war was sound; in fact, it was the only tenable military policy the government could have followed. The North had greater resources and a three-to-two military manpower advantage over the South. An offensive strategy would almost certainly exhaust the Confederacy more quickly than the Union because an invasion takes more men and resources than a defense. As a rule, defense is the most economical form of warfare. As explained above, Civil War defenders enjoyed even greater advantages than usual because tactics lagged behind military technology. The rifled muzzleloader gave the defense at least three times the strength of the offense; theoretically the Confederates could have stayed in en-

George William Curtis (ed.), *The Correspondence of John Lothrop Motley* (New York, 1889), II, 143.

[33] OR, Ser. III, I, 148–149, 177–178, 250.

[34] Elliott, *Winfield Scott*, pp. 722–723; William T. Sherman, *Memoirs* (Bloomington, 1957), I, 178, 179; Howard K. Beale (ed.), *Diary of Gideon Welles* (New York, 1960), I, 84, 242.

[35] John G. Nicolay and John Hay, *Abraham Lincoln: A History* (New York, 1904), IV, 323.

[36] Dunbar Rowland (ed.), *Jefferson Davis, Constitutionalist: His Letters, Papers and Speeches* (Jackson, Miss., 1923), V, 338.

trenchments and killed every man in the Union Army before the South exhausted its own human resources.[37]

But the Confederacy flung away its great advantage because southern sentiment overwhelmingly favored an invasion of the North. Confederate Secretary of State Robert Toombs announced in May, 1861, that he was for "taking the initiative, and carrying the war into the enemy's country." He opposed any delay. "We must invade or be invaded," he said. In June, 1861, the famous Confederate war clerk, John Jones, wrote in his diary: "Our policy is to be defensive, and it will be severely criticized, for a vast majority of our people are for 'carrying the war into Africa' without a moment's delay. The sequel will show which is right, the government or the people. At all events, the government will rule."

Jones was wrong; the government did not rule. Just after First Manassas in July, 1861, Davis indicated in a public speech that he was ready to abandon his defensive strategy. "Never heard I more hearty cheering," recorded Jones.

> Every one believed our banners would wave in the streets of Washington in a few days; . . . that peace would be consummated on the banks of the Sus-quehanna or the Schuylkill. The President had pledged himself . . . to carry the war into the enemy's country. . . . Now . . . the people were well pleased with their President.

Although Davis called his new policy defensive-offensive, it was in fact an offensive strategy, for the President held a view best described by one of today's clichés: the best defense is a good offense. In September, 1862, Davis wrote the commanders of the South's two largest armies that "we [must] . . . protect our own country by transferring the seat of war to that of [the] . . . enemy . . . the sacred right of self defence demands that if such a war is to continue its consequences shall fall on those who persist in their refusal to make peace." Davis concluded his instructions with an order that Confederate armies "occupy the territory of their enemies and . . . make it the theatre of hostilities." [38]

The substitution of an offensive for a defensive strategy early in the war probably doomed the Confederacy. Southern leaders could have enjoyed all the moral and military advantages of defenders. Instead they chose to be aggressors. Confederate forces attacked in eight of the first twelve big battles of the war, and in these eight assaults 97,000 Confederates fell—20,000 more men than the Federals lost in these same battles.[39] President Davis's cult of the military offense bled the South's armies to death in the first three years of combat. After 1863 the Confederates attacked less

---

[37] Over two million men enlisted in the Union Army, but Thomas Livermore (*Numbers and Losses*, p. 63) estimated that only about 1,556,000 Northerners and about 1,082,000 Southerners actually served as long as three years in either army.

[38] Jones, *A Rebel War Clerk's Diary*, pp. 18, 27, 36; Rowland (ed.), *Jefferson Davis*, V, 339.

[39] The first twelve major campaigns of the war, those in which the total casualties exceeded six thousand men, were: Shiloh, Fair Oaks, the Seven Days, Second Bull Run, Antietam, Perry-ville, Fredericksburg, Stone's River, Chancellorsville, Vicksburg, Gettysburg, and Chickamauga. The Confederates clearly assumed the tactical offensive in all these battles except Antietam, Fredericksburg, and Vicksburg. Both sides attacked for a time at Shiloh and Second Bull Run, so one is counted here as a Confederate attack and the other as a Union attack. Livermore, *Numbers and Losses*, pp. 140–141.

often. Attrition forced them to defend; they had spent too much of their limited manpower in unsuccessful offensives. Even so, Confederate generals attacked in three of the last ten major campaigns of the war.[40]

A close examination of two battles indicates in some detail how so many men were lost. Both Stone's River and Chickamauga are examples of sustained Confederate attacks, and an analysis of regimental losses in each battle reveals a high degree of correlation between assaults and casualties. Because the Federals were on the defense in both battles they suffered relatively fewer casualties, except for those units which were outflanked or surrounded. It is significant that half of the most battered Union regiments incurred their highest casualties when they attacked or counterattacked.[41] At Stone's River, for example, the 15th Indiana lost 130 of its 440 men in a single bayonet charge, and the 34th Illinois and the 39th Indiana each sustained 50 percent casualties in a counterattack. In still another attempt to check the Confederate advance a brigade of regulars charged into a dense cedar grove and lost five hundred men in about twenty minutes. The 16th and 18th U. S. Infantry regiments, which formed the center of this assault group, lost 456 men from a combined total of 910.[42] At Chickamauga the 87th Indiana suffered over 50 percent casualties in one charge across an open field, and three Illinois regiments—the 25th, 35th, and 38th—together with the 26th Ohio, tried to dislodge part of Bushrod Johnson's Confederate division from the crest of a hill. The attack failed, and cost the Federal regiments 791 of their 1,296 men.[43]

Confederate losses were even more exceptional. Of the eighty-eight Confederate regiments present at Stone's River, twenty-three suffered over 40 percent casualties. Moreover, 40 percent of the infantry regimental commanders were killed or wounded, and in several regiments every field officer was lost. Eight of the twenty Confederate brigades which fought at Stone's River sustained more than 35 percent casualties, and 25 percent of the infantry brigade commanders were killed or wounded.[44]

Reckless assaults accounted for most Confederate casualties. At Stone's River the 1st Louisiana charged across an open field. "Our loss was very severe at this place," wrote the commander. The regiment lost seven of its twenty-one officers and nearly a hundred of its 231 men.[45] Attacks made by other Confederate units were just as costly. Colonel J. J. Scales, commander of the 30th Mississippi, was ordered to charge

[40] The last ten campaigns in which the total casualties in each exceeded six thousand men were: Chattanooga, the Wilderness and Spotsylvania, Johnston's Atlanta campaign (which included the battles of Buzzard's Roost, Snake Creek Gap, New Hope Church, and Kenesaw Mountain), Hood's Atlanta campaign (which included the battles of Peach Tree Creek, Atlanta, July 22 and 28, and Jonesborough, Aug. 31 and Sept. 1), Cold Harbor, Petersburg, Winchester, Cedar Creek, Franklin, and the Appomattox campaign. The Federals took the tactical offensive in all of these actions except Hood's Atlanta campaign, Cedar Creek, and Franklin. Livermore, *Numbers and Losses*, pp. 140–141.

[41] I am grateful to Thomas M. Baumann, one of my former graduate students, who helped me to establish regimental numbers and losses at Stone's River and Chickamauga.

[42] *OR*, XX, pt. 1, 495–496, 305–306, 314–315, 319–321, 325–326, 394–395, 401–403.

[43] *Ibid.*, XXX, pt. 1, 1058–1059, 427–430, 529–531, 521–522, 654–658, 590, 839–840, 173, 174.

[44] *Ibid.*, XX, pt. 1, 676–681, 693, 758, 780, 852, 855, 875, 900; unpublished reports in the William P. Palmer Collection of Braxton Bragg Papers, Western Reserve Historical Society, Cleveland.

[45] Report of Capt. Taylor Beatty, 1st Louisiana Infantry, *ibid.*

and capture several Federal batteries. Five hundred yards of open ground "lay between us and those . . . batteries," wrote Scales.

> As we entered [this field] a large body of [Union] infantry in addition to the Batteries on my flanks and front rained their leaden hail upon us. Men fell around on every side like autumn leaves and every foot of soil over which we passed seemed dyed with the life blood of some one or more of [my] gallant [men]. . . . Still no one faltered, but the whole line advanced boldly and swiftly to within seventy-five yds. of the battery when the storm of death increased to such fury that the regt. as if by instinct fell to the ground.

This single charge cost the 30th Mississippi half of its four hundred men.[46] A young soldier in the 24th Alabama recalled how his regiment made three desperate charges at Stone's River and that each time thirty or forty of his comrades fell.[47] The commander of the 26th Alabama reported the Federal fire so heavy that thirty-eight of his men defected during the first thrust.[48]

It takes courage to charge at any time, but it is almost unbelievable what some units endured. General James R. Chalmers' brigade of Mississippians hit the strongest part of the Union line at Stone's River. This in itself was in no way remarkable, but half the men in the 44th Mississippi Regiment went into battle armed only with sticks, and most of the 9th Mississippi's rifles were still too wet from the previous night's rain to fire. Nevertheless the men charged.[49]

As the Mississippians faltered, General Daniel S. Donelson's brigade of Tennesseeans came up. No unit on either side fought any harder than this brigade; it dashed itself to bits against the Union center in the Round Forest. One of Donelson's regiments lost half its officers and 68 percent of its men; another lost 42 percent of its officers and over half its men. The 8th and 16th Tennessee regiments spent several hours and 513 of their combined total of 821 men in brave but unsuccessful efforts to break the Federal line.[50]

Sometime in the early afternoon two fresh Confederate brigades tried where Chalmers' and Donelson's men had failed. Generals John K. Jackson and Daniel W. Adams led their men across a field thick with bodies. Both of Jackson's two furious assaults aborted. In an hour of combat he lost more than a third of his men, including all his regimental commanders. One of his regiments, the 8th Mississippi, lost 133 of its 282 men. Adams had no more success than Jackson, though his men made what one Federal called "the most daring, courageous, and best-executed attack . . . on our line." Adams was wounded and his brigade, caught in a cross fire, retreated. One

[46] Report of Lt. Col. J. J. Scales, 30th Mississippi Infantry, *ibid*.

[47] Charles T. Jones, Jr., "Five Confederates: The Sons of Bolling Hall in the Civil War," *Alabama Historical Quarterly*, XXIV (1962), 167.

[48] Report of Lt. Col. N. N. Clements, 26th Alabama Infantry, Palmer Collection.

[49] Reports of Maj. J. O. Thompson, 44th (Blythe's) Mississippi Infantry, and Lt. Col. T. H. Lyman, 9th Mississippi Infantry, *ibid*. Thompson reported: "During the night of Friday [Dec.] 26 all guns in the hands of Blythe's Regiment were taken from them and distributed among the regiments of Chalmers' Brigade. The Sunday morning following we were furnished with refuse guns that had been turned over to the Brigade ordnance officer. Many of these guns were worthless. . . . Even of these poor arms there was not a sufficiency and after every exertion on my part to procure arms, one half of the Regt. moved out with no other resemblance to a gun than such sticks as they could gather."

[50] OR, XX, pt. 1, 710–712, 714–718, 543–546.

of his units, the 13th and 20th Consolidated Louisiana Infantry, entering the fight with 620 men, lost 187 on the afternoon of December 31, and another 129 in an attack two days later.[51]

Confederate losses at Chickamauga were even more severe than at Stone's River. At least twenty-five of the thirty-three Confederate brigades present lost more than a third of their men, and incomplete returns indicate that at least forty-two infantry regiments suffered over 40 percent casualties. Nearly half of all regimental commanders and 25 percent of all brigade commanders were killed or wounded.[52]

Just as at Stone's River the heaviest losses at Chickamauga occurred when units assaulted strong Union positions. General Lucius E. Polk's brigade of about fourteen hundred men attacked Kelly's field salient twice on September 20. The first attack, checked by heavy guns and musket fire, cost the Confederates 350 casualties in about ninety minutes. In the second attack the brigade lost two hundred men. In an assault against the Federal position on Horseshoe Ridge the 22nd Alabama lost 55 percent of its men, and two battalions of Hilliard's Legion lost nearly 60 percent of their effectives in an attack on Snodgrass Hill, where the Federals had thrown up breastworks.[53]

Bloody battles like Stone's River and Chickamauga took the lives of the bravest southern officers and men. Relatively few combat officers went through the conflict without a single wound, and most of those who did could claim, as did General Reuben L. Walker—who participated in no less than sixty-three battles—that "it was not my fault." Only three of the eight men who commanded the famous Stonewall Brigade survived the war. What happened to the commanders of one regiment is told in a bare sketch penned by semiliterate Bartlett Yancey Malone, who

> was attached to the 6th N. C. Regiment . . . which was commanded by Colonel Fisher who got kild in the first Manassas Battel. . . . And then was commanded by Colonel W. D. Pender untell [his promotion; he was subsequently killed in battle]. . . . And then Captain I. E. Av[e]ry . . . was promoted to Colonel and . . . in command untell . . . the day the fite was at Gettysburg whar he was kild. And then Lieut. Colonel Webb taken command.[54]

Casualty lists prove that generals often led their men into action. Fifty-five percent of all Confederate generals (235 of 425) were killed or wounded in battle.[55] Thirty-one generals were hurt twice, eighteen were wounded three times, and a dozen were hit four or more times. Clement A. Evans, William ("Extra Billy") Smith, and William H. Young were wounded five times. Young was hit in the shoulder and had two horses shot from under him at Murfreesboro; he was hit in the leg at Jackson, in the chest at Chickamauga, in the neck and jaw at Kenesaw Mountain, and again in the leg at Allatoona, where another horse was shot from under him and he was captured. John R. Cooke, William R. Terry, and Thomas F. Toon were

[51] Ibid., 838–839, 841–842, 795–799; Alexander F. Stevenson, The Battle of Stone's River (Boston, 1884), p. 113.

[52] OR, XXX, pt. 2, 11–532.

[53] Ibid., 176–178, 336–337, 424–429.

[54] James I. Robertson, Jr., The Stonewall Brigade (Baton Rouge, 1963), p. 243; William Whatley Pierson, Jr. (ed.), Whipt 'Em Everytime: The Diary of Bartlett Yancey Malone (Jackson, Tenn., 1960), p. 28.

[55] These figures are based upon data taken from Ezra J. Warner, Generals in Gray (Baton Rouge, 1959), and Mark Mayo Boatner, III, The Civil War Dictionary (New York, 1959).

wounded seven times, but the record seems to have been set by William Ruffin Cox, who joined the 2nd North Carolina Infantry as major in 1861 and fought through the war with the Army of Northern Virginia. He was wounded eleven times.

Twenty-one of the seventy-seven Confederate generals who were killed or mortally wounded in battle had been shot at least once before they received their fatal injuries. Some of them had been hit two or more times. William D. Pender survived three wounds before a shattered leg killed him at Gettysburg. Stephen D. Ramseur recovered from wounds received at Malvern Hill, Chancellorsville, and Spotsylvania, only to die at Cedar Creek.

More generals lost their lives leading attacks than any other way. Seventy percent of the Confederate generals killed or mortally wounded in action fell in offensives.[56] In a single charge against Federal fortifications at Franklin in 1864, six Confederate generals were killed or mortally wounded—John Adams, John C. Carter, Patrick R. Cleburne, States Rights Gist, Hiram B. Granbury, and Otho F. Strahl.

Precisely why the Confederates attacked so often is unclear. Professors David Donald and T. Harry Williams think Jomini's theories of war contributed to Confederate defeat.[57] At first both Union and Confederate generals followed the strategic and tactical concepts of this famous European military writer which they had learned at West Point. Southerners continued to fight as Jomini suggested, argues Donald, because they were unlucky enough to win most of the first battles and saw no reason to change their outdated methods of warfare until it was too late. Northerners began to abandon Jomini's concepts and to innovate after they were defeated in the early campaigns.

Perhaps southerners attacked more frequently at first because of what Thomas Livermore called "the greater impetuosity of the Southern temperament." Union General Winfield Scott, himself a Virginian, understood this temperament. He predicted that southerners were too undisciplined to fight a defensive war. They "will not take care of things, or husband [their] . . . resources," said Scott. "If it could all be done by one wild desperate dash [then southerners] . . . would do it, but [they cannot] . . . stand the long . . . months between the acts, the waiting." Livermore pointed out that "Southern leaders were, at least up to 1864, bolder in taking risks than their opponents, but also that they pushed their forces under fire very nearly to the limit of endurance." [58]

Whatever the reason, Confederate leaders ignored the casualty lists and continually mutilated their armies. Throughout the war Jefferson Davis favored offensive operations, and five of the six men who at one time or another commanded the South's two largest armies were as devoted to aggressive warfare as was Davis. Albert Sidney Johnston, P. G. T. Beauregard, Braxton Bragg, John B. Hood, and Robert E. Lee all preferred to be on the offensive; of the major field commanders, only Joseph E. Johnston really enjoyed defense. "What we have got to do must be done quickly," said Sidney Johnston. "The longer we leave them to fight the more difficult will they

[56] Only 23 percent of these seventy-seven generals were killed while on defense. Seven percent died in ways which can be classified neither as offense nor defense. Stonewall Jackson and Micah Jenkins, for example, were accidentally killed by their own men, and John H. Morgan was killed by Union cavalrymen after he was surprised while asleep in a private home.

[57] Donald, *Lincoln Reconsidered*, pp. 82–102; T. Harry Williams, "The Military Leadership of North and South," *Why the North Won the Civil War*, ed. David Donald (Baton Rouge, 1960), pp. 23–47.

[58] Chesnut, *A Diary From Dixie*, p. 245; Livermore, *Numbers and Losses*, p. 71.

be to defeat." Beauregard, who helped Sidney Johnston plan the bloody assault at Shiloh, favored a Confederate invasion of Maryland in 1861, and in 1862 he wrote: "I desire to . . . retake the offensive as soon as our forces . . . have been sufficiently reorganized." [59] Bragg, who objected to trenches because he believed they destroyed an army's aggressiveness, attacked in three of the four major battles he directed.[60]

Hood, who took command of the Army of Tennessee after Joe Johnston's removal, was the general most committed to assault tactics. In fact, his only qualification for army command was his reputation as the hardest hitter in the Confederacy. Everyone knew Hood would attack Sherman's army; that was why he had been given command. To prevent defeat at this time the Confederacy certainly needed a military miracle. Johnston did not believe in military miracles, but Davis and Hood did. So Davis appointed Hood to high command, and Hood—a gambler and a visionary, a man unaware of just how little he knew—wagered the lives of his men that he could beat the Federals by repeated attacks. Johnston's defense of Atlanta in May and June, 1864, cost the Federals five thousand more men than the Confederates lost. Hood lost eleven thousand more men than Sherman in operations around Atlanta from late July to early September, 1864.[61]

Lee, too, liked to attack. He often suggested offensives to the President and urged other generals to be aggressive. In May, 1862, a month after what Lee called the Confederate "victory of Shiloh," he advised Beauregard to invade Tennessee.[62] When Lee assumed command of Confederate forces in Virginia in June, 1862, he promptly abandoned a defensive strategy and launched two offensives—one by Jackson in the Valley and Lee's own Seven Days campaign against McClellan. The President's wife recalled: "General Lee was not given to indecision, and they have mistaken his character who supposed caution was his vice. He was prone to attack. . . ." [63] At Gettysburg, when James Longstreet advised Lee to move his army around the Federal left flank, select a strong position, and wait for Meade to attack, Lee announced that "If he is there to-morrow I will attack him." To which Longstreet replied, "If he is there to-morrow it will be because he wants you to attack." [64]

Though Lee was at his best on defense, he adopted a defensive strategy only after attrition had deprived him of the power to attack. His brilliant defensive campaign against Grant in 1864 made the Union pay in manpower as it had never paid before. But the Confederates adopted defensive tactics too late; Lee started the campaign with too few men, nor could he replace his losses as could Grant.[65]

Even after the Wilderness campaign Lee still wanted to launch another offensive.

[59] Confederate Veteran, III (1895), 83; Jones, A Rebel War Clerk's Diary, p. 54; OR, XVII, pt. 2, 599.

[60] In April, 1863, Pres. Davis's military aide wrote (OR, XXIII, pt. 2, 761): "General Bragg says heavy intrenchments demoralize our troops." And a member of Bragg's staff wrote in his diary about the same time (J. Stoddard Johnston Diary, April 13, 1863, Palmer Collection): "The Engineers are busy in strengthening the field works around Tullahoma. Gen. Bragg has never shown much confidence in them—Murfreesboro for example."

[61] Livermore, Numbers and Losses, pp. 119–121, 122–126.

[62] OR, X, pt. 2,546.

[63] Varina H. Davis, Jefferson Davis . . . A Memoir (New York, 1890), II, 318–319.

[64] James Longstreet, From Manassas to Appomattox, ed. James I. Robertson, Jr. (Bloomington, 1960), p. 358.

[65] A recent study estimates that Grant lost about fifty thousand men between the Wilderness and Cold Harbor, about the number Lee started the campaign with. Clifford Dowdey, Lee's Last Campaign (Boston, 1960), p. 299.

He continued to hope that he could maneuver Grant out into the open and attack him. In May, 1864, Lee wrote Davis: "[Grant's] position is strongly entrenched, and we cannot attack it with any prospect of success without great loss of men which I wish to avoid if possible . . . my object has been to engage him when [his army is] in motion and . . . I shall continue to strike him whenever opportunity presents itself." Just two weeks before he surrendered, Lee lost 3,500 men in an assault on the Federal fortifications at Petersburg. "I was induced to assume the offensive," Lee explained to Davis, "from the belief that the point assailed could be carried without much loss." [66] As it happened, Lee's push failed to break the Union line, and the Confederates lost three times as many men as the defenders.

Perhaps the best way to illustrate the advantage defenders enjoyed over attackers is by a comparison of casualties. In half the twenty-two major battles of the Civil War the Federals attacked. They lost 119,000 men when they assaulted and 88,000 when they defended—a difference of 31,000 men. The Confederates lost 117,000 men when they attacked, but only 61,000 when they defended—a difference of 56,000 men, or enough to have given the South another large army. Every time the Confederates attacked they lost an average of ten more men out of every hundred engaged than the Federal defenders, but when the Confederates defended, they lost seven fewer men out of every hundred than the Union attackers.[67]

Bismarck is reputed to have said that fools learn from their own mistakes, but that he preferred to learn from the mistakes of others. The Confederacy failed because its leaders made the same mistakes time and again. "The rebls," observed a Union private in 1863, "fight as though a mans life was not worth one sent or in other words with desperation; or like Gen. Lafeyet said to Washington, there is more *dogs* where them came from." [68] By 1865 southern military leaders had exhausted their human resources. In attacking when they should have defended, they had, in Toombs' apt phrase, simply worn themselves out trying to whip the Yankees.

[66] Douglas Southall Freeman and Grady McWhiney (eds.), *Lee's Dispatches to Jefferson Davis* (New York, 1957), pp. 183–184, 341–342.

[67] These computations are based upon figures given in Livermore, *Numbers and Losses*, pp. 140–141.

[68] Quoted in Naisawald, *Grape and Canister*, p. 536.

21 / A Major Result of the Civil War

Allan Nevins

The original goal of most Unionists was the preservation of the nation. Circumstances, however, sometimes forced men to go beyond their initial intentions. Northerners may have only wished to restore the Union, but to do so, they discovered that they had to destroy slavery first.

And there were other important instances of unforeseen changes, accidental by-products of the war. The departure from Congress of Southern Senators and Representatives in the winter of 1860–1861 shifted the *sectional* balance of power and hence, to some degree, the *economic* balance of power as well. The Thirty-seventh and Thirty-eighth Congresses enacted not only necessary military legislation but also a Homestead Act, a new National Banking System, a Pacific Railroad bill, and a high protective tariff. Clearly the war eliminated Southern opposition that had obstructed these measures in the 1850's, but it does not follow that the Republicans somehow contrived the struggle to achieve their ends or even welcomed it when it came.

Another supposed by-product of the war was an accelerated economic growth. Since Emerson Fite's 1910 volume, *Social and Industrial Conditions in the North During the Civil War,* many historians have believed that the conflict gave an enormous fillip to the national economy. One student, Louis Hacker, has even asserted that without the massive government outlays of 1861–1865, the American economy would have remained indefinitely limited to a commercial agricultural base.

More recently, economic historians, employing a more rigorous statistical approach, have expressed doubts that the war was an industrial accelerator. On the contrary, they believe that it was a decelerator. Almost every index of industrial production during the war years was below the period preceding and the period following the conflict. Nor is Hacker's notion that the war moved the economy to a higher stage valid. The Civil War did not generate the Industrial Revolution in the United States, because that event was well under way before the firing on Fort Sumter.

The "econometric" historians, according to some scholars, have manipulated their data to suit their purposes. The figures, they say, yield very different conclusions when looked at differently or when supplemented with other data. Other historians have raised more fundamental objections. They

Civil War History, V, No. 3 (September 1959), 237–250. Reprinted by permission.

insist that it was the shift of *power* from one class to another that made the war a boon to business and the economy. It was, above all, a *political* event with economic effects, and no amount of statistical analysis, they claim, can deal effectively with such a change.

The following selection by the eminent historian Allan Nevins re-examines the economic and social consequences of the Civil War and reasserts its role as one of the great "watersheds" of our national development.

For further reading: Emerson D. Fite, *Social and Industrial Conditions in the North During the Civil War* (New York: The Macmillan Company, 1910); *Ralph Andreano (ed.), *The Economic Impact of the American Civil War* (Cambridge, Mass.: Schenkman Publishing Co., 1962); *David T. Gilchrist and W. David Lewis (eds.), *Economic Change in the Civil War Era* (Greenville, Del.: Eleutherian Mills-Hagley Foundation, 1965); *Louis Hacker, *The Triumph of American Capitalism* (New York: Columbia University Press, 1947); Harry Scheiber, "Economic Change in the Civil War Era: An Analysis of Some Recent Studies," *Civil War History*, XI (December 1965).

Thomas Carlyle shrank in horror from our Civil War. The fact that multitudes of Americans should take to butchering one another seemed to him an indictment of our democracy; the issue of the Negroes' status struck him as far from justifying such a holocaust of lives and property. His remark that the war was a fire in a dirty chimney, and his little fable called "Ilias Americana in Nuce" deeply offended the North.

Among the Northern soldiers who gave their lives were two gallant young men, Robert Gould Shaw and Charles Russell Lowell, who had warmly admired Carlyle. Shaw, leader of Massachusetts colored troops, died in trying to capture Fort Wagner; Lowell, who had married Shaw's sister Josephine, was slain at Cedar Creek. Both were graduates of Harvard. Three years after the war short biographies of them, and of ninety-five others who had been killed, appeared in the *Harvard Memorial Biographies,* edited by Thomas Wentworth Higginson. Thereupon Charles Lowell's young widow, Mrs. Josephine Shaw Lowell, sent the volumes to Carlyle, with a note describing their admiration of him, and a request that he read their lives, and reconsider his views on the war. Carlyle replied, in a letter here published for the first time:

CHELSEA—10 March, 1870

DEAR MADAM

I rec'd your gentle, kind and beautiful message, and in obedience to so touching a command, soft to me as sunlight or moonlight, but imperative as few cld be, I have read those lives you marked for me; with several of the others and intend to read the whole before I finish. Many thanks to you for these Volumes and that note. It would need a heart much harder than mine not to recognize the high and noble spirit that dwelt in these young men, their heroic readiness, complete devotedness, their patience, diligence, shining valour & virtue in the cause they saw to be the highest—while alas any difference

I may feel on that latter point, only deepens to me the sorrowful and noble tragedy [that] each of their brief lives is. You may believe me, Madam, I would strew flowers on their graves along with you, and piously bid them rest in Hope. It is not doubtful to me that they also have added their mite to what is the eternal cause of God and man; or that, in circuitous but sure ways, all men, Black & White, will infallibly get their profit out of the same.

With many thanks & regards, dear Madam, I remain

Yrs sincerely T. CARLYLE.

They "added their mite" to the "eternal cause of God and man." So Francis Parkman had earlier written Mrs. Robert Gould Shaw, saying that he envied her husband his death, so eloquent of the highest consecration.

Many of the gains and losses of any great war are intangible and incomputable. No one can say whether the gain to society of the work two such rare spirits as Robert Gould Shaw and Charles R. Lowell would have done, had they lived, was greater than the gain from the heroic example they set. Other gains and losses, some material, some moral, can partly be appraised. But in looking at the effects of the war, it is safe to lay down two generalizations at the outset: The tremendous magnitude of the change it wrought was not anticipated in its early phases, and the nature of the change was not and could not be accurately analyzed when it closed in 1865.

To be sure, some of its consequences *were* foreseen. Shrewd men perceived in 1861 that if the war was protracted and ended in Northern victory, it would strengthen not only the Union and the federal government, but the spirit of national unity. They perceived that it would result in the destruction of slavery. John Quincy Adams, indeed, had predicted a generation earlier that if civil conflict began, the government would use its war powers to extinguish slavery. Shrewd men also foresaw in 1861 that a long civil war, and the arming of the United States, would profoundly alter the world position of the republic and augment its authority in world affairs. Other changes were anticipated, and men did not hesitate to predict that their total effect would be revolutionary. In fact, as early as the autumn of 1861 the *New York Herald* prophesied (November 24) just this in a column editorial headed "The Great Rebellion: A Great Revolution." The war, said the *Herald,* was not only a great revolution in itself, but was causing many minor revolutions. It went on:

> All sorts of old fogy ideas, manners, and customs have gone under, and all sorts of new ideas, modes, and practises have risen to the surface and become popular. We begin to discover, and we shall find it truer by and by, that a revolution is sometimes a very good thing, and that our changes have been for the better. We have had a revolution in commerce, but it has diminished our imports and increased our exports. . . . We have had a revolution in business, but it has resulted in the smashing up of rotten old firms, in a healthier vitality in those which remain, and in greater prudence, economy, and industry all round. Our manufactories have been revolutionized, but the war and its necessaries keep them busy now. . . . Our manner of living has been changed, but there is now less sham and more comfort than formerly. . . . Everything the war touches is revolutionized.

Verily, in its effects the Civil War did constitute a revolution. In politics, for example, the old domination of the government by an alliance of agrarian interests of the South and West was overturned by a new alliance of the industrial East and grain-growing Northwest. But some of the predictions of change which men made most confidently in 1861 were utterly erroneous, while the most important single change flowing from the war was not grasped at the time, and is not fully comprehended even today.

To understand the effects of the conflict we must venture certain generalizations —very broad generalizations. The first is that the results of a victorious war lie in the main in the positive sphere, those of defeat in the negative sphere. Success arouses a spirit of confidence, optimism, and enterprise not seen in a defeated society. For evidence of this assertion we may point to the exuberant spirit of Elizabethan England after the defeat of the Great Armada; the exuberant and even arrogant spirit of Germany after the Franco-Prussian War. The effects of the Civil War were positive in the North, negative in the embittered and depressed South. The second broad generalization is this: that no effect of war, no matter how marked it may appear to be for a time, will last if it runs counter to a long-continued and deeply felt national tradition. The third generalization is the converse of the second: That effect is greatest which harmonizes with and carries forward some tendency in national life already partly developed and growing, though it may still lie beneath the surface. For example, the Revolution, in the currents it set flowing, chimed with the belief of Americans that they had a plastic society which they could and should change to fit their ideals, with their confidence that they alone knew the secret of true liberty, and with their conviction that they were the predestined teachers of this liberty to the whole of mankind. The strength which the victorious Revolution gave these exuberant beliefs raised in America a galaxy of great statesmen, and truly made the United States of Washington, Adams, Hamilton, Jefferson, and Madison an example to the entire world.

One false prediction of 1861 illustrates the second of our generalizations. A favorite assertion was that the United States would become militarized. "Whether this war shall be long or short," said the *Springfield Republican* of June 4, 1861, "it is evident that hereafter we shall be a more military people." Some even prophesied that militarism would infect our politics, "Mexicanizing them" as the phrase then went—introducing the military dictator. Such ideas proved absurd. Our huge armies in 1865 melted almost overnight into civil life; military expenditures sank almost to zero, and the standing army to only 25,000 men; and the one President, Grant, who was elected primarily because of his military exploits became an object of strong public condemnation. Why did we not become militarized? Partly because no *continuing* peril existed. Wavers of the bloody shirt after the war sometimes tried to conjure up a continued peril from rebel brigadiers, but sensible men laughed at them. In the second place, and more importantly, militarization went completely against the long national tradition—indeed, against an Anglo-American tradition of five centuries; the same tradition which discarded all militarist tendencies after the first world war, and effected rapid disarmament just after the second.

What was the most important effect of the Civil War upon the character of the American people and the texture of society? Nobody would venture to say; but certainly one of the most important effects was, in an essentially inadequate phrase, the conversion of an unorganized nation into an organized nation, with an irresistible impetus toward greater and greater organization.

The United States in 1860 stood in almost as primitive a state of organization, socially and economically, as China in 1940. It was an agricultural country with a long historic belief in individualism; far more attached to the principle of self-reliance than to that of association. The shrewd French observer, Auguste Laugel, who wrote a book on the United States during the war, correctly stated, "There is a horror of all trammels, system, and uniformity." The population still lived close to the soil. Of the 8,200,000 whose occupations were noted by the census of 1860, 3,300,000 were farmers, planters, farm laborers, or stockmen, while as many more were indirectly connected with agriculture.

A few facts are significant of the lack of organization: The country as yet had no standard time—Boston, New York, Philadelphia, and Washington each had its own time. It had no accepted gauge for railroads; the eight or more gauges ranged from three to six feet. The postal system was so wretched that in New York in 1856, ten million letters were delivered privately in contrast to one million carried by the government. In 1860 the American population slightly exceeded that of Great Britain; but that year Americans posted 184 million letters, while Great Britain posted 564 million. It had no national labor union worthy of the name; the typographers, iron molders, and hat-makers possessed unions, but they were shadowy bodies which did little more than meet and pass resolutions. The panic of 1857, indeed, had paralyzed the infant movement toward labor organization. It had few other organizations. Not one state bar association had been formed. Only two American cities in 1865 had paid fire departments. In all of New England in 1860 there were only three hospitals; in the entire South, four or five. The American Medical Association was twelve years old, but when the hour struck to establish medical and surgical services for the war, it was so feeble that nobody thought of using it. Three trunk-line railways had been established, for the Pennsylvania, the New York Central, and the Baltimore & Ohio could be termed interstate railroads. But ninety-five percent of such manufacturing as existed was on a local basis and managed in small units. In fact, state laws of the time generally forbade corporations to hold property outside their own states except by special charter. Most business firms were managed as family affairs. Another significant detail is that in a country where whole libraries now groan with books on business organization and management, down to 1860 not one book—not one pamphlet—had been published on these subjects.

Modern organization, apart from politics, education, and religion, is built mainly on the machine, which is effective only with and through it. A mechanized country is of necessity an organized country; a land without machines is unorganized. Great Britain in 1860, with approximately the same population as the United States, was much better equipped with machine industry, and in consequence far better organized. With us, the industrial revolution was hardly beyond its beginnings. The partially mechanized area extending from Boston to Philadelphia was learning what organization meant, but learning slowly.

In just one broad field can the nation be said to have developed a considerable degree of organization before 1860: the field of westward expansion. Since the main fact in American life was the movement of population toward the setting sun, the major energies of the nation were channeled into its promotion. The building of highways, canals, steamboats, and railroads to carry people west; the manufacture of plows, axes, drills, and harvesters to maintain them there; the production of arms to help them deal with Indians and wild beasts; the extension of churches, schools, and post offices to keep them linked with the older communities—all this was fairly well organized. Yet westward expansion was itself to some extent a disorganizing process, spreading civilization thin and straining the bonds of society.

This sprawling, inchoate country, much of it a veritable jellyfish, suddenly had to pull itself together; raise armies which (for the North alone) numbered 2,300,000 individuals before the war ended; clothe, arm, transport, and feed them; hospitalize many of them; obtain more than four billion dollars in taxes and loans; and, in short, make an effort then almost unprecedented in human history. To describe this effort in administrative outline would require a volume. To translate it into statistical tables would rob it of meaning. To suggest its scope, complexity, and impact, we can perhaps best deal with it in terms of a single individual—Montgomery C. Meigs, one of the key figures of the momentous change, for as quartermaster general he had charge of the spending of one and one-half billion dollars, half of the direct cost of the war to the North.

In any just view of the Civil War record, Quartermaster General Meigs ought to stand in relief as a central personage. He had charge of the spending of a vast amount of money, which he directed into channels that largely remade America. But what are the facts? In James Ford Rhodes's history of the war, so generally well proportioned and broad of view, Meigs is thrice just barely mentioned. Not once is he characterized or appraised. Though his last two reports are praised, his work is never described. In Carl Russell Fish's book on the war, again large minded and well planned, Meigs is given one line of praise, and his initials are misstated. In James G. Randall's admirable *Civil War and Reconstruction*, Meigs is mentioned once in a footnote, and once in a dry list of civil officers. McMaster and Channing do not mention him at all.

To say that Meigs was quartermaster general is to say little, for few people have any idea of that functionary's duties. To say that he, with the chief of ordnance and commissary general, divided the entire work of equipping the two million Union soldiers for camp and field, drill and battle, is to do little better. Of the three, Meigs bore by far the heaviest responsibility. His duties included the procurement and distribution of uniforms, tents, horses, harness, wagons, ambulances, shoes, blankets, knapsacks, forage and a vast miscellany of other articles. His authority covered three-quarters of Northern industry. The Northern government in July 1861, issued a call for 500,000 men. These men wore out shoes in two months and uniforms in four. They therefore needed 3,000,000 pairs of shoes and 1,500,000 uniforms a year. They needed mountains of arms, a hundred miles of wagons, great base hospitals, and an incredible amount of miscellaneous supplies.

The national government, be it remembered, had no War Production Board, no Priorities and Allocations Board, no possibility of any of the great administrative agencies developed in the two world wars; it had no basis for them. It had no organized partnership with industry, with labor, with agriculture, or with transportation, for they were all unorganized. Meigs had to create organization where none existed. In shaping government contract policy, he shaped much of the future economy of the United States. What share of contracts should go to small manufacturers, what to large? How much should go to New England, and how much to the West? What part of the arms contracts, with dire necessity pressing the government, should go to slow American makers, and what part to Europeans who could make quick deliveries? Meigs rose magnificently to the initial crisis of supplying the hundreds of thousands who rushed to the colors in 1861. He wrote just after Bull Run:

> The nation is in extremity. Troops, thousands, wait for clothes to take the field. Regiments have been ordered here [to Washington] without clothes.

> Men go on guard in drawers for want of pantaloons. The necessity is far greater than I imagined when I saw you. I had no idea of this destitution, this want of preparation of this [War] Department, when I took charge of it. . . . The plan of general supply should go on and as soon as possible be brought into operation and furnish the great stock [needed]. We must bear the clamor of fools who would pick flaws in a pin while the country hangs in the balance [July 24, 1861].

It was Meigs who set new standards for American shoe manufacture, finished early in the war almost wholly by hand, and hence in small lots, but before the end of the war by machinery in carload lots. Uniforms were lifted to the same quantity plane. It was Meigs who insisted that the army abandon for field use the large Adams and Sibley tents, which had to be transported by wagon, and use the little shelter tent portable on a soldier's back. It was Meigs who adapted French mess equipment for American use. He decided that the Northern armies were heavily overwagoned, and helped reshape their transport equipment. He read lectures to McClellan and other generals on the cruel and wasteful destruction of horses by undisciplined troops. He built temporary barracks; he even bought coal for army steamers. He had command of Grant's supply base at Fredericksburg and Belle Plain in 1864; and he took personal charge of the refitting of Sherman's worn army at Savannah in January, 1865.

By the close of 1862 the North had more than 1000 regiments, full or incomplete; each had its regimental quartermaster, who was required to send a monthly report to Washington with accounts; thus 12,000 accounts a year had to be settled.

Meigs's reward for all this is casual mention in James Ford Rhodes, a misspelling of his name by Carl Russell Fish, and almost total silence by other historians. So far as this neglect means the overlooking merely of one talented and devoted individual, it is of no great importance. But it is very important indeed as a symptom of the neglect of one key aspect of the war, its organizational side. Meigs was one of the organizers not merely of the war effort but of the modern America about to emerge, for he helped stimulate industry, systematize its efforts, and bring it into efficient operation for victory and for larger services after victory. His labors helped change the American character.

For the formless, protoplasmic United States of 1861 emerged from the war in 1865 at least half-organized and clearly conscious of the paths it would take forward. Under the forcing blast provided by government contracts, protective tariffs, and inflation a thousand businesses trebled or quadrupled in size. Government offices swelled to what would previously have seemed incredible proportions. A national banking system was created. More trunk-line railroads began to take form. Truly national industries, reaching out for national as distinguished from local markets, appeared in flour milling, meat packing, clothing and shoe manufacture, and the making of machinery. Sir Morton Peto, coming to the United States in 1865 and finding the nation in the happy throes of a great boom, was struck with the evidences that not only capital but organizing ability was being invested in business as never before. The colonel of every regiment had learned a great deal about organization; and Peto walked into large industrial offices to hear the manager pointing out executives with the words, "That man was a colonel—the one at that desk yonder a major." The one fault he discerned was that they were all eager for too quick results.

Of great significance in this growth of organization was the instruction which

Americans had received in the principles of capital formation and in the use of credit. While the national banking system was being organized, the government was floating its large bond issues. Jay Cooke, when the normal market was exhausted, undertook selling them in every street and hamlet. His canvassers sought far and wide for buyers; never before had so many men purchased securities. The greenbacks, the national bank notes based on bonds, and the ready extension of bank credit gave a powerful impetus to the industrial revolution and helped change the whole outlook of Americans.

The acceleration of investment and industrial expansion lasted until 1873, producing a remarkable array of new business captains, and accustoming the people to broader and bolder concepts of affairs. Not hitherto a nation, as Langel said, of "joiners," they had learned much from association in regiment and armies, in Union League Clubs and relief societies. They began to develop a spirit of voluntary combination which within a few years ran the gamut from the trusts and the grange to the GAR. By 1885 one of the most powerful organizers of modern times, John D. Rockefeller, was able to make his momentous pronouncement, "The age of individualism has gone, never to return."

This effort to organize the energies of the nation harmonized with a tendency in national life already partly formed in 1860 and, underneath the surface of affairs, vigorously growing; a tendency necessitated by the increase of population and other basic factors, and simply given extraordinary impetus by the war. Through this effort, as it was carried on after the war, ran a vibrant self-confidence: the exuberance of victory, the pride of a record of service. S. Weir Mitchell, the doctor-novelist, for example, strikes this note of elation when, after recalling how the physicians had built great wartime hospitals, admirably equipped, without the help of architects, he describes what the conflict did for his calling:

> Among the many permanent marks which the great war left upon the life of the nation . . . none were more deep and more alterative than those with which it stamped the profession of medicine. In all other lands medicine had places of trust and even power, in some way related with government; but with us . . . [the] physician . . . lived unnoted by the great public, and for all the larger uses he should have had for the commonwealth quite unemployed. The war changed the relations of the profession to the state and to the national life, and hardly less remarkably altered its standards of what it should and must demand of itself in the future. Our great struggle found it, as a calling, with little of the national regard. It found it more or less humble, with reason enough to be so. It left it with a pride justified by conduct which blazoned its scutcheon with endless sacrifice and great intellectual achievements, as well as with professional conscience educated by the patient performance of every . . . duty which the . . . calls of a hard-pressed country could make upon its mental and moral life.

Tens of thousands of Union veterans came back from the hard lessons of war with this self-confidence born of success, and this pride born of duty done. Tens of thousands of civilians who had built machine shops, run arms factories, filled contracts for shovels, canned foods, and blankets, or managed recruiting, income tax collection, or home relief, felt the same combination of experience, confidence, and pride. Men thought in larger terms. The day of small affairs began to pass; the family firm gave way to the joint stock corporation; visions of great undertakings became common. Improvisation yielded to hardheaded planning and individualism to disciplined action. In the eight years before the postwar boom spent itself, the continent was spanned by the rails of the Union Pacific; Carnegie and Abram S. Hewitt respectively founded the Bessemer and open-hearth steel industries; the first big industrial pools were formed; two specially chaotic businesses, oil and tobacco, were taken in hand by Rockefeller and Duke. Labor organized the National Union; farmers organized the National Grange. Research and invention began to be organized.

Of all the changes effected by the war, this replacement of an amorphous, spineless society by a national life organized for efficient action—organized first to win the conflict, and after that for peace—was one of the greatest. The first two years of the Civil War might be called "the improvised war"; the second two years, "the organized war." The transition from one to the other was a transition from the old America to the new. It was accompanied with a corresponding alteration in the national psychology. Men's ideas were thrown into new patterns. Americans still detested regimentation; but they had learned the power—the necessity—of voluntary combination for definite objects, leaving themselves perfectly free in all other relations.

This emergence of a society organized on national lines reinforced the political nationalism generated by the conflict. It was a war for the nation as a unit; for centripetal as opposed to centrifugal impulses. We are all aware of the strength of state attachments in the prewar South. Robert E. Lee and Joseph E. Johnston, for example, fought with the Confederacy not because they approved of slavery, or endorsed secession, but because they loved Virginia. An intransigent State Rights spirit gravely crippled the Southern effort. But while we all know this, few comprehend the strength of state and regional feeling in the prewar North. General John Pope gravely proposed, early in the conflict, that all Illinois troops be used in a separate Illinois army, to be kept intact under Illinois commanders, and some Indiana officers made the same proposal for Indiana troops. The early distrust of Lincoln by such Easterners as Charles Francis Adams was founded on sectional feeling. What good leadership could come out of the raw West? Our literature before the war was not truly national; in sentiment as in the geographic distribution of authors and publishers, it was a literature of New England and New York.

Out of the furnace heat of war, in the North, came a true national passion. It would be erroneous to say that the East learned that the Westerner Grant was the Union's greatest soldier, and wept for the Westerner Lincoln as the West wept. In great degree, men simply ceased to think of themselves as Vermonters or Ohioans, Easterners or Westerners; they were Americans, and Grant and Lincoln were American leaders. I do not find the great Northern upsurge of excitement and patriotic fervor just after Fort Sumter impressive; it reflected too much cheap, frothy excitement and too little earnest, thoughtful planning. But it was at least an upsurge of national feeling, which grew stronger as the conflict went on. The long succession of disasters did as much for Northern unity as final Northern victory. It is obvious that the new spirit of nationalism profoundly reinforced the new spirit of organization.

From the world point of view, also, the replacement of a formless, amoebic America by a nation sturdily pursuing the path of organized growth was one of the most important results of the war. As we know, the abolition of slavery and the triumph of the North were telling blows for the cause of liberalism throughout the world.

They constituted a vindication of democracy. The Englishman A. V. Dicey, talking with an emigrant Irishwoman in the States during the war, heard her say, "This is a blessed country, sir. I think God made it for the poor." No longer could conservative Europe respond to such statements with the jeer, "What about your slaves?" Lincoln in his Gettysburg Address placed the war in its world setting as a war to keep the hope of government of, by, and for the people alive for all mankind. John Bright, in the most famous of his many wartime defenses of America, put the conflict in the same setting. Old world privilege, he said, had a great stake in the defeat and frustration of the American democracy:

> And every morning, with blatant voice, it comes into your streets and curses the American republic. Privilege has beheld an efflicting [sic] spectacle for many years past. It has beheld thirty millions of men, happy and prosperous, without emperor, without king, without the surroundings of a court, without nobles, except such as are made by eminence in intellect and virtue, without State bishops and State priests . . . without great armies and great navies, without great debts and great taxes. Privilege has shuddered at what might happen to old Europe if the great experiment should succeed.

Bright had been sure, even while the war was most doubtful, that the Union would succeed. He did not believe that disunion and slavery could triumph. "I have another and a far brighter vision before my gaze," he said. "I see one vast confederation, stretching from the frozen North in unbroken line to the glowing South, and from the wild billows of the Atlantic westward to the calmer waters of the Pacific main—and I see one people, and one language, and one law, and one faith, and over all that wide continent, the home of freedom, and a refuge for the oppressed of every race and of every clime."

It is impossible to deny the value to the world of the vindication of American democracy embodied in the Emancipation Proclamation and the restoration of the Union on a foundation at last built for the ages. No one would underestimate the importance of these results in contributing to the advance of British democracy shortly registered in the second Reform Act [1867], to the unification of Italy and Germany, and to the stimulation of democratic currents in France, where such haters of Napoleon III as Laboulaye had been staunch wartime defenders of the Northern cause. The victorious emergence of the nation from its trial seemed a victory for world liberalism—for the ideas of Bright and Cobden, Mazzini and Gambetta. The belief of Americans that the Civil War had given the republic that "new birth of freedom" of which Lincoln had spoken, and that America had greater lessons of liberty than ever to teach other lands, was expressed with emphasis by the most idealistic voices in our midst—by Whittier in his poem on the first autumn of peace, for example, and by Lowell in his ode for the Fourth of July, 1876, and by Emerson in his address on "The Fortunes of the Republic" in 1878, the last address he made.

Nevertheless, without underrating this impetus to liberalism, we can say that in the long run the greatest consequence of the war for the globe was the replacement of the awkward, unformed, immature nation of 1860 by the confident, purposeful, systematized nation of 1870. What had been gristle, in Burke's phrase, became bone. Once economic and social organization had gained momentum, it achieved new goals every year. We might instance a thousand men, trained in the war, who carried the change forward. One son of the Union, Francis A. Walker, would be as good an example as any. He began his career learning lessons of organization as a private in the Second Corps of the Army of the Potomac; he continued it by organizing a Federal Bureau of Statistics and a Census Bureau which became models for other lands; and he ended it by organizing at the Massachusetts Institute of Technology, of which he was the true maker, a system for training engineers admired and imitated both abroad and at home. The United States strode forward, applying greater and greater system to its natural wealth, until by 1900 it was the most powerful and in many ways the best-organized industrial nation in the world.

Its great rival was Germany, which had been given a similar access of energy and self-confidence by the War of 1870, and which with its compact population and sharp economic necessities displayed an even greater bent toward organization. The two came into collision in 1917—the great exemplar of military and autocratic organization, and the great exemplar of peaceful and democratic organization. Well it was that the United States had received an impulse toward disciplining and systematizing its energies as early as it did. While the first world war was still raging, the genius of technology gave birth on American soil to a great new world force—mass production, a new method of applying half a dozen components—system, speed, precision, continuous motion, uniformity, economy—to the quantity manufacture of complex engines of wealth and war. Only a highly organized nation could have brought forth this revolutionary implement called mass production, which has done so much to revolutionize the modern world, and only a nation armed with it could have won World War II.

As the United States became an organized nation, much that was ugly crept into American life. Insofar as discipline is antithetical to individual freedom, it is unpleasant, even repellent. Organization undeniably raised the standards of welfare in our society, enabling more people decade by decade to live in greater comfort and well-being. At the same time, however, it increased the strain of materialism in the United States, making people all too intent upon mere wealth and comfort. Our civilization seemed coarser, greedier, and more aggressive, than in the quiet prewar days. The country that men had died for in the 1860's seemed hardly worth the sacrifice in the 1870's and 1880's. But this was a temporary phase, which by the last decade of the century was being forgotten as new currents of radicalism and idealism made themselves felt. The nation needed the iron strength forged in the war for the great tasks that lay ahead of it. It needed the lessons of organization and association it had learned if it was to play a powerful part in world affairs, and improve its national life at home. Walt Whitman struck the right note when he called upon it to forget the errors of the past and face the challenge of the future. He wrote:

> The Four Years War is over, and in the peaceful, strong, exciting, fresh occasions of today, and of the future, that strange sad war is hurrying even now to be forgotten. The camp, the drill, the lines of sentries, the persons, the hospitals (ah, the hospitals)—all have passed away, all seem now like a dream. A new race, a young and lusty generation, already sweeps in with oceanic currents, obliterating the war, and all its scars, its mounded graves, all its reminiscences of hatred, conflict, death. So let it be obliterated. I say the life of the present and the future makes undeniable demands upon us each and all, south, north, east, west. To help put the United States hand in hand, in one unbroken circle in a chant—to rouse them to the unprecedented grandeur of the

part they are to play, and are even now playing—to the thought of their great future, and the attitude conformed to it—especially their great aesthetic, moral, and scientific future.

Even in the generation after the war, however, many remembered its truer lessons. No inconsiderable body of veterans could say what Captain Oliver Wendell Holmes, Jr.—the wounded captain whom the Autocrat of the Breakfast Table sought on the field of Antietam—said: "In our youth our hearts were touched with fire. It was given us to learn at the outset that life is a profound and passionate thing. While we are permitted to scorn nothing but indifference, and do not undervalue the worldly rewards of ambition, we have seen with our own eyes, above and beyond the gold fields, the snowy heights of honor, and it is for us to bear the report to those who come after us."

We come after, and we can hear the report; by taking it to heart our generation can redress the balance a little. Let us not cease to regard the war as proof of a breakdown of American statesmanship, and let us conceal nothing of its cruel, ignoble side. But we should make the most of its inspirations. Charles Eliot Norton said that on the whole he thought the character of Lincoln the greatest single gain of the nation from the war. Lincoln's ability to awaken the North to the moral issues bound up in the conflict; his conviction that the struggle must be fought through for the sake of man's vast future; his patience in adversity; his fortitude in defeat, his magnanimity in victory, can never be staled or lost. Beside him stands Lee; not Lee the warrior, but Lee the man—the Christian gentleman who lived a life of stainless purity, whose innate modesty never failed him, who like Grant was free from any trace of vainglory, whose consecration to duty never flagged—who, in a word, set an unsurpassable example of character. Behind these figures we have the humble soldiers from South and North alike who fought on one red field after another with unyielding courage, always ready to give up their young lives for what they deemed threatened principle and imperiled liberty.

A freshened remembrance of these inspiring elements can contribute an idealism counteractive of the materialism that accompanied the necessary work of national organization. It will justify for all the dead the statement that Carlyle made of Charles Lowell and Robert Gould Shaw, that they added each his "mite to the eternal cause of God and man."

Part VI

RECONSTRUCTION

22 / Negroes in the First and Second Reconstructions of the South

August Meier

In April 1865, after four destructive years, the nation faced the problems of returning to a normal existence. Some Americans thought the readjustment would be easy. Many Democrats, certainly, took seriously their party's 1864 campaign slogan, "The Constitution as it is, the Union as it was," and concluded that merely readmitting duly-elected Southern representatives to Congress would be all the "reconstruction" necessary.

But most Northerners realized that rebuilding would not be so easily accomplished. The most pressing problem from our modern perspective was how to reintegrate the four million freedmen into Southern life and work. The blacks were now free, or at least no longer slaves, but what did freedom mean? Before the war a half million free Negroes had lived in the United States, half of them in the slave states. Almost nowhere did they enjoy the full rights of citizenship. Only in parts of New England were they allowed to vote on the same basis as whites. In several states they could not testify in court against white men, and socially and economically they were degraded. A few Negroes were respected and prosperous, but the vast majority of free blacks worked at the most menial tasks and occupied the lowest rungs of the American social ladder. Everywhere they were ostracized and segregated.

Most Southerners expected that with slavery officially ended, a similar fate would now befall the four million freedmen. The new provisional governments elected in the South under President Johnson's reconstruction proclamations acknowledged the end of slavery by ratifying the new thirteenth amendment to the federal constitution, and conferred on the blacks certain minimal rights. The freedman could own and convey property and move about freely. His marriage was given legal sanction, if only to make him responsible for the care of his own family, and his legal status before the courts was improved. The black man now could sue or be sued, and could testify against white men.

Negroes and their white friends complained that these gains were not enough. No states gave blacks political rights, even though President Johnson had recommended giving the vote to well-qualified Negroes. More important,

Civil War History, XIII, No. 2 (June 1967), 114–130. Reprinted by permission.

the South refused to surrender full social control over its black population. In a series of measures—the "black codes"—most Southern states imposed severe restrictions on the Negro population. The so-called vagrancy laws made idleness a misdemeanor and allowed county sheriffs to hire out unemployed Negroes if they could not pay a fine. The scheme was motivated by Southern fears that the blacks would not work now that they were legally free, but Northerners regarded the law as a covert way of re-establishing a system of virtual bondage. In addition to the vagrancy measures, the codes excluded blacks from certain occupations and certain areas, prohibited interracial marriages, segregated public facilities along racial lines, barred Negroes from jury service, and prescribed a number of criminal penalties harsher for blacks than for whites. The over-all purpose of the black codes, as Kenneth Stampp has written, "was to keep the Negro, as long as possible, exactly what he was: a propertyless rural laborer under strict controls, without political rights, and with inferior legal rights." *

The black codes clearly represented the racial views of a majority of Southern whites through most of Reconstruction. But the white majority was not to have its own way entirely, at least not for a decade. When Congress took away control of Reconstruction from the President, the Johnson governments were replaced by new regimes.

The new Radical governments sought to provide education for the ex-slaves and their children, and to guarantee them equal protection of the law. Reinforced by the fourteenth and fifteenth amendments, the Radical state governments gave the Negro the vote and the right to hold both local and federal offices. In these posts he often served with distinction.

To the liberal historians of the last generation, the Reconstruction era was a period of unique achievement and progress for the black man. It was a bright early dawn prematurely darkened by revived white oppression. The following selection by August Meier of Kent State University, reflecting the skepticism of recent militant thought regarding the past racial performance of America, holds that even the Reconstruction era was a time of racial darkness in most parts of the South and in most areas of American life. In measuring the experience of black men from 1865 to 1877 against the ideal of the present, Meier may be providing us with a valuable perspective; he may also be ahistorical, for we must not forget how degrading slavery was, and how difficult it always is for any society to throw over the attitudes and institutions of centuries. Surely, during Reconstruction, enormous advances were made. If we look at where the black man had been, the changes between 1865 and 1877 were substantial, although clearly there was also a very long way to go.

For further reading: George R. Bentley, *A History of the Freedmen's Bureau* (Philadelphia, Pa.: University of Pennsylvania Press, 1955); Henderson H. Donald, *The Negro Freedman* (New York: Abelard-Schuman Ltd., 1952); Theodore B. Wilson, *The Black Codes of the South* (Birmingham, Ala.: University of Alabama Press, 1965); LaWanda Cox, "The Prom-

---

* Kenneth M. Stampp, *The Era of Reconstruction, 1865–1877* (New York: Alfred A. Knopf, Inc., 1965), p. 79.

ise of Land for the Freedmen," *Mississippi Valley Historical Review*, XLV (December 1958); * James M. McPherson, *The Struggle for Equality: Abolitionists and the Negro in the Civil War and Reconstruction* (Princeton, N. J.: Princeton University Press, 1964); *Joel Williamson, *After Slavery: The Negro in South Carolina During Reconstruction, 1861–1877* (Chapel Hill, N. C.: University of North Carolina Press, 1965); C. Vann Woodward, "Seeds of Failure in Radical Race Policy," in Harold Hyman (ed.), *New Frontiers of the American Reconstruction* (Urbana, Ill.: University of Illinois Press, 1966); Vernon Wharton, *The Negro in Mississippi, 1865–1890* (Chapel Hill, N. C.: University of North Carolina Press, 1947).

"Revolutions never go backwards": so declared the editors of the first Negro daily newspaper, the New Orleans *Tribune*, late in 1864.[1] Northern troops had occupied the city and much of Louisiana as early as 1862, and the *Tribune* insisted that the logical second step, after crushing the slaveholders' rebellion, was that the national government divide their plantations among the freedmen. Washington failed to act upon this proposal, and seventy years later W. E. B. DuBois, in assessing the reconstruction experience, perceived it as a revolution that had indeed gone backwards. It had gone backwards, he held, mainly because Congress had failed to press forward to the logical corollary of its reconstruction program; the distribution of the former slaveowners' lands among the Negroes.[2] More recently, Willie Lee Rose, though starting from a different philosophy of history, arrived at rather similar conclusions. In her volume on the South Carolina Sea Island Negroes during the Civil War she describes how the military authorities divided many of the Sea Island plantations among the freedmen. President Andrew Johnson, however, returned the lands to the former owners, and Congress failed to intervene. Mrs. Rose pithily sums up this sequence of events by entitling the last chapter of her book "Revolutions May Go Backwards." [3] Nevertheless, in the face of such distinguished scholarly opinion, I would like to suggest that what occurred during reconstruction was really not a genuine revolution, not even an abortive one.

Consider the following example. In Georgia, in April, 1868, slightly a year after the passage of the Reconstruction Act of 1867, a constitution drawn up under the procedures required by Congress was ratified by the voters, and new officials were elected. The process of reconstruction was supposedly completed when, in July, the legislature ratified the Fourteenth Amendment, and military authority was withdrawn. The new state government, however, was no genuinely "radical" regime. Just six weeks later the legislature expelled its Negro members, on the grounds that Negroes, though guaranteed the right to vote, had not been specifically made eligible for office.[4]

[1] New Orleans *Tribune*, Nov. 29, 1864. This paper was one of a series read at Roosevelt University in the fall of 1965, marking the centennial of reconstruction.

[2] W. E. B. DuBois, *Black Reconstruction* (New York, 1935).

[3] Willie Lee Rose, *Rehearsal for Reconstruction: The Port Royal Experiment* (Indianapolis, 1964).

[4] Ethel Maude Christler, "The Participation of Negroes in the Government of Georgia, 1867–1870" (M.A. thesis, Atlanta University, 1932), *passim*, is the best general treatment. See also C. Mildred Thompson, *Reconstruction in Georgia, Economic, Political and Social* (New York, 1915), chaps. vii, viii, and x.

Before they departed, one of the Negro representatives, Henry M. Turner, a minister of the African Methodist Episcopal Church, and formerly a Civil War chaplain and Freedmen's Bureau agent, delivered a ringing, sarcastic speech, defiantly expressing his vision of a democratic America. He would not, he said, behave as some of his thirty-one colored colleagues had, and attempt to retain his seat by appealing to the magnanimity of the white legislators. He would not, "fawn or cringe before any party nor stoop to beg them for my rights," like "slaves begging under the lash. I am here to defend my rights, and to hurl thunderbolts at the men who would dare to cross the threshold of my manhood. . . . I was not aware that there was in the character of the [Anglo-Saxon] race so much cowardice, . . . pusillanimity . . . [and] treachery." It was the Negroes who had "set the ball of loyalty rolling in the State of Georgia . . . and [yet] there are persons in this legislature, today, who are ready to spit their poison in my face, while they themselves . . . opposed the ratification of the Constitution. *They* question my right to a seat in this body."

Then, in rhetoric typical of the era, Turner stated the Negro's claims.

> The great question is this. Am I a man? If I am such, I claim the rights of a man. Am I not a man because I happen to be of darker hue than honorable gentlemen around me? . . . Why, sir, though we are not white, we have accomplished much. We have pioneered civilization here; we have built up your country; we have worked in your fields, and garnered your harvest, for two hundred and fifty years. And what do we ask of you in return . . .? Do we ask retaliation? We ask it not. . . . but we ask you now for our RIGHTS. It is extraordinary that a race such as yours, professing gallantry, and chivalry, and education and superiority, living in a land where ringing chimes call child and sire to the Church of God—a land . . . where courts of justice are presumed to exist . . . can make war upon the poor defenseless black man. . . .
>
> You may expel us, gentlemen, but I firmly believe that you will someday repent it. The black man cannot protect a country, if the country doesn't protect him; and if, tomorrow, a war should arise, I would not raise a musket to defend a country where my manhood is denied . . . . You may expel us . . .; but while you do it remember that there is a just God in Heaven, whose All-Seeing Eye beholds alike the acts of the oppressor and the oppressed, and who, despite the machinations of the wicked, never fails to vindicate the cause of justice.[5]

The events just described epitomize two things: the aspirations and hopes of Negroes on the one hand; and the superficial character of the reconstruction process on the other. Pressure from Congress and the state supreme court did later secure a reversal of the ban on Negro legislators, and one Georgia Negro, Jefferson Long, sat in Congress for a term. Nevertheless, southern whites actually dominated the state's government, and by 1872 the Redeemers, or Democrats, had returned to power. Thus the period of so-called Radical or Black reconstruction can scarcely be said to have existed in Georgia; and what happened in that state can hardly be called a revolution, even a revolution that later went backwards. Most writers on the history of Negroes during reconstruction have dwelt upon developments in South Carolina, Louisiana, and Mississippi, where Negroes formed a majority of the population and therefore held more high offices than elsewhere. What happened in Georgia was, however, a

[5] Henry M. Turner, *Speech on the Eligibility of Colored Men to Seats in the Georgia Legislature . . . September 3, 1868* (Augusta, 1868), *passim.*

good deal more typical of what happened in most of the southern states during reconstruction.

The failure of congressional reconstruction, the return of the southern states to white hegemony, and the subordination and oppression of the black man were due not only to southern white recalcitrance, but equally as much to northern indifference and to the limitations in congressional policy. Northern indifference to the Negro's welfare and the consequent inadequacies of Congress' program were deeply rooted in the historical racism of the American public. They were thus fundamentally a continuation of a cultural tradition that had not only permitted the existence of slavery in the South, but had relegated free Negroes to second-class citizenship in the North.

In the opening months of the Civil War, for example, Negroes and the small band of white abolitionists had been far in advance of northern opinion in regarding the war as fundamentally a struggle for the emancipation of the slaves. From the day of the firing on Fort Sumter, Negroes had envisioned the situation as an irrepressible moral conflict between slavery and liberty, and a war for the rights of man in fulfillment of the genius of the American democratic faith. However, the President, the Congress and most of the nation at first regarded the war simply as a campaign to preserve the Union, and only slowly and reluctantly, and as a result of the exigencies of a prolonged and difficult military conflict, did the Federal government come to emancipate the slaves and enlist Negroes in the armed forces.[6] Moreover, the vast majority of northerners continued to resist the idea that Negroes should be accorded the rights of citizens. In 1863, at the thirtieth anniversary convention of the founding of the American Anti-Slavery Society, Frederick Douglass excoriated those abolitionists who felt that their work was accomplished when the slaves were freed. Negroes, along with a handful of white abolitionists, formed the vanguard of those who insisted that with emancipation the struggle for Negro freedom had only begun. To Negroes the issues were moral ones, based upon the promise of American life, upon the assumptions of the American faith that were rooted in the Declaration of Independence and the ethics of Christianity. As a conclave of Pennsylvania leaders declared in 1868: "It is America that you have to civilize, to Christianize, and compel to accept and practically apply to all men, without distinctions of color or race, the glorious principles and precepts laid down in her immortal Declaration of Independence." [7]

Long before the war had ended, northern Negro leaders had spelled out the specific program they deemed essential for the creation of a truly democratic America. In October, 1864, the race's most prominent men met in Syracuse, New York, to organize an Equal Rights League that would agitate for citizenship rights and racial equality. At that time the slaves had not yet been freed in the loyal Border States, and most of the northern states prohibited Negroes from voting, from testifying against whites in court, from serving on juries, and in some cases from attending public schools (even segregated schools). The convention delegates were critical of the fact that most

[6] James M. McPherson, *The Negro's Civil War* (New York, 1965), chaps. ii and iii; McPherson, *The Struggle for Equality: Abolitionists and the Negro in Civil War and Reconstruction* (Princeton, 1964), chap. iii.

[7] *Proceedings of the American Anti-Slavery Society at Its Third Decade . . . December 3, 4, 5, 1863* (New York, 1864), pp. 110–118; *Proceedings of the Fourth Annual Meeting of the Pennsylvania State Equal Rights League . . . 1868* (Philadelphia, 1868), p. 35.

northern states still refused to accord Negroes the ballot, and they even denounced the Republican party for being arrayed with the proslavery Democratic party in its support of racial prejudice. Their two chief demands were abolition and political equality. As Douglass pointed out in an address before the Massachusetts Anti-Slavery Society a few months later, Negroes wanted the suffrage . . .

> because it is our *right*, first of all. No class of men can, without insulting their own nature, be content with any deprivation of their rights. Again, I want the elective franchise . . . because ours is a peculiar government, based upon a peculiar idea, and that idea is universal suffrage. If I were in a monarchical . . . or aristocratic government, where the few ruled and the many were subject, there would be no special stigma resting upon me because I did not exercise the elective franchise . . ., but here, where universal suffrage . . . is the fundamental idea of the Government, to rule us out is to make us an exception, to brand us with the stigma of inferiority, and to invite to our heads the missiles of those about us. . . .[8]

Douglass and other Negro leaders, while addressing the nation on matters of abolition and citizenship, advocated also a program of economic and moral improvement to be undertaken by Negroes themselves. The Syracuse convention exhorted the freedmen "to shape their course toward frugality, the accumulation of property, and above all, to leave untried no amount of effort and self-denial to acquire knowledge, and to secure a vigorous moral and religious growth." To men of the nineteenth century thrift and industry and the acquisition of property—especially land—were essential parts of the good life, along with citizenship rights. Moreover, a common school education was almost a *sine qua non* for securing a comfortable livelihood. It cannot be overemphasized that along with agitation for political and civil rights, Negro leaders stressed the cultivation of middle-class morality, the pursuit of education, and the acquisition of property. To use the phraseology of the time, these things, like the ballot, were regarded as essential for elevating the race and securing its inclusion in the "body politic."

Southern Negroes espoused the same program, and in some respects were more radical than the northern ministers, editors and artisan-businessmen who predominated at Negro conventions. Representative of the point of view of articulate southern Negroes was the New Orleans *Tribune*, which in 1864 and 1865 prefigured the outlook of most Negro spokesmen during the decade after the war. This journal denounced Lincoln's plan of reconstruction and endorsed that of the congressional Radicals. Only through congressional reconstruction would Negroes "secure the full enjoyment of our rights—not as a matter of gratuitous or benevolent grant, revocable at will—but as an embodiment of the principles set forth in the Declaration of Independence." [9] Highest among these rights was that of the franchise, for it was the only means by which Negroes could protect themselves from civil and economic discrimination.[10] To those who argued that a time of preparation should elapse before the ex-slaves were enfranchised, the *Tribune* replied: "We do not know of a single reform, in the whole course of history, that was brought about by gradual and systematic

---

[8] *Proceedings of the National Convention of Colored Men . . . 1864* (Boston, 1864); Frederick Douglass, "What the Black Man Wants," in William D. Kelley, Wendell Phillips and Frederick Douglass, *The Equality of all Men Before the Law* (Boston, 1865), pp. 36–37.

[9] New Orleans *Tribune,* Jan. 3, 1865.

[10] *Ibid.,* Aug. 5, 1865; Sept. 13, 1864.

preparation. In fact, how is preparation practicable without the free exercise of the right contended for . . . ? Could the white man of America be prepared to the general exercise of the franchise, unless by going to the polls and voting?" Given the opportunity, the freedmen would show a comprehension of "their own interests" and a "Devotion to the Union" that should justify their immediate enfranchisement.[11]

The *Tribune* also gave pointed attention to the question of segregation. It opposed a bill introduced in the legislature, providing for separate schools,[12] and it continually protested against the system of "star cars" for Negroes in the city until the military authorities ordered the provisional governor to end this example of discrimination.[13] The editors regarded segregation as silly, since it was due to the white man's lust that miscegenation had proceeded to the point where "it would be a pretty hard thing to find a pure . . . Negro in the whole city of New Orleans, where seventy thousand persons of African descent are now residing." [14]

The journal devoted much space to economic matters, especially to the conditions under which the former slaves labored on the plantations. On this subject the *Tribune* went far beyond the thinking of most northern Negro leaders at this time, and beyond the thinking of many southern leaders as well. The editors boldly advocated what only the most radical of the Republicans and abolitionists were thinking of—the destruction of the plantation system. It criticized the United States government for not immediately confiscating and dividing the lands of the rebellious planters into five-acre lots, to be assigned to the "tillers of the soil" at a nominal price, so that the freedmen would be "thoroughly imbued with that . . . praiseworthy 'Yankee' idea, *that every man should own the land he tills, and head and hands he works with.*" [15] In calling for these steps the editors hoped to accomplish a democratic revolution in the South against the power of the antebellum slaveowning aristocracy: "The division of the lands is the only means by which a new, industrious and loyal population may be made to settle in the South. Large estates will always be in the hands of an aristocracy. Small estates are the real element of democracy." [16]

Broadly speaking, the Negro elite stressed above all the importance of the franchise and civil rights. Next in order of importance, in the thinking of most of them, was the value of at least a common school education for the masses of the race. Finally, they were concerned with the economic problems of the freedmen. Most of them urged the masses to work hard, save their money, and acquire property; but some at least advocated a radical expropriation of the slaveowners' plantations and the creation, under Federal benevolence, of a numerous landowning yeoman peasantry. Such a policy would not only provide Negroes with an economic opportunity, but would supply the foundation for loyal and democratic governments in the southern states.

On the other hand, the evidence indicates that the masses had a scale of priorities that was precisely the opposite of that of the elite. Their primary interest was in land ownership. Close to this in importance for them was education. Though politics was of somewhat lesser value in their thinking, enfranchisement did initiate enthusiastic political participation on the part of the freedmen. Like the elite Negroes they dis-

[11] *Ibid.*, May 4, 1865.
[12] *Ibid.*, July 26, Dec. 24, 1864; Feb. 17, 1865.
[13] *Ibid.*, Feb. 28, May 21, Aug. 10, 1865.
[14] *Ibid.*, Aug. 15, 1865.
[15] *Ibid.*, Sept. 10, Sept. 24, 1864.
[16] *Ibid.*, Sept. 15, 1865.

played a profound awareness of the importance of political activity in American culture. The same is true of their interest in education. Old and young flocked to the schools opened by the northern missionaries and the Freedmen's Bureau. Especially notable were the freedmen's own efforts at self-help in education, establishing schools, hiring teachers, and erecting buildings.

Most of all, like oppressed peasants the world over, the freedmen wanted land. As Vernon Lane Wharton put it in his study of Negroes in Mississippi after the Civil War: "Their very lives were entwined with the land and its cultivation; they lived in a society where respectability was based on ownership of the soil; and to them to be free was to farm their own ground." [17] When President Andrew Johnson restored the Sea Island plantations to their former owners, he sent General O. O. Howard, head of the Freedmen's Bureau, to Edisto Island to inform the freedmen of his decision. The Negroes who crowded the church at which Howard spoke were disappointed and angry, and shouted "No, no!" to his remarks. Howard later recorded in his autobiography that one man called out from the gallery: "Why, General Howard, why do you take away our lands? You take them from us who have always been true, always true to the Government! You give them to our all-time enemies! That is not right!" The committee selected by the freedmen to meet with the representatives of the planters in order to arrange the details of the transfer of property informed Howard that they would not work for their old masters under overseers, though they were willing to *rent* the land if ownership was ruled out. The planters, however, were not interested in this kind of arrangement and after a series of indignation meetings the freedmen wrote a final appeal to the President. They insisted that it was "very oppressing . . . [that] wee freemen should work for wages for our former oners." They felt it was unfair for the President to expect the freedmen to ask "for bread or shelter or Comfortable for his wife and children" from men whom they had fought against "upon the feal of battle." They had, they said, no confidence in their former masters, one of whom had declared he would refuse to sell land to freedmen, even at $100 an acre. Johnson, of course, remained unmoved, and in the end the Negroes had to capitulate.[18]

A significant number of the freedmen attempted to buy their own farms, even in the face of white reluctance to sell land to them. Travelers from the North, Freedmen's Bureau agents and missionaries reported enthusiastically upon evidence of progress in this direction. A New England cotton planter on the Sea Islands reported the case of "a black Yankee . . . [with] the energy" and eye "for his own advantage of a born New Englander." His industry and sharp dealing had put him ahead of the others on the plantation, though half of them had fenced in their own gardens and were raising vegetables for the Hilton Head market.

> Linus in his half-acre has quite a little farmyard besides. With poultry-houses, pig-pens, and corn-houses, the array is very imposing. He has even a stable, for he made out some title to a horse, which was allowed; and then he begged a pair of wheels and makes a cart for his work; and not to leave the luxuries behind, he next rigs up a kind of sulky and bows to the white men from his carriage. As he keeps his table in corresponding style . . . the establishment is rather expensive. So, to provide the means, he has three permanent irons in the fire, his cotton, his Hilton Head express, and his seines. . . . While other families

[17] Vernon Lane Wharton, *The Negro in Mississippi, 1865–1890* (Chapel Hill, 1947), p. 59.
[18] Rose, *Rehearsal for Reconstruction*, pp. 353–355.

"carry" from three to seven acres of cotton, Linus says he must have fourteen. . . . With a large boat which he owns, he usually makes weekly trips to Hilton Head, twenty miles distant, carrying passengers, produce and fish. . . . I presume his savings since . . . the capture of the island amount to four or five hundred dollars. He is all ready to buy land, and I expect to see him in ten years a tolerably rich man.[19]

Only a few with exceptional ability or luck were able to become permanent and substantial landowners. The plantation system remained intact. In fact, it may even have increased in extent. It simply changed its form. Instead of slavery, the characteristic labor arrangement became that known as sharecropping.

By the last quarter of the nineteenth century sharecropping, in combination with the crop-lien system, had become a system of gross exploitation, which reached its most extreme form in debt peonage. Here was a system in which the Negro tenant was almost at the complete mercy of the white planter. Yet, in its origins at least the share-cropping system was not something that was simply forced upon Negroes, but was in part a result of the freedmen's desire for independence, freedom and economic advancement. Much research on this subject remains to be done before the origins of sharecropping during the reconstruction period will be fully understood but recent studies suggest that what likely happened followed the general pattern outlined below.[20]

After the emancipation of the slaves and the close of the Civil War, planters generally attempted to employ Negroes as wage laborers with annual contracts. Under these contracts the freedmen were worked in gangs as they had been under slavery. In order to enforce the contractual obligation, it was common for planters to hold back part of the pay until the end of the cotton harvest. Such a system, characterized by gang labor and with its powers of coercion lodged in the planter's hands, smacked altogether too much of slavery and Negroes resisted working under it. Universally the freedmen wanted to own their own land; where this was not possible they preferred to rent land for cash if they could. But, as in the case of the Sea Islands, planters resisted such an arrangement because it did not give them as much control over the labor force as they desired. The sharecropping system thus seems to have emerged, in large part, as a sort of compromise. Under it, the tenants had their own plots, organized their own time, and were not subject to the *direct* discipline of the planters. On the other hand the system was beneficial to the planter in that it encouraged the tenant to stay on the land until the crop was harvested, and encouraged him to work hard since he kept a share of the crop. Nevertheless, as late as the 1880's it was common for planters in certain areas to complain about the sharecropping system.

Rudimentary sharecropping arrangements had appeared even before the close of the Civil War, but they received considerable impetus from the encouragement of the Freedmen's Bureau during the late 1860's. Negroes were never satisfied with the system; they always aspired to become cash renters or landowners. Moreover, what started out as a concession to the freedmen's desire for independence, quite rapidly became a system of racial repression.

[19] Elizabeth Ware Pearson (ed.), *Letters from Port Royal* (Boston, 1906), p. 37.

[20] The ideas developed in the following discussion owe a good deal to material in Martin Abbott, "Free Land, Free Labor, and the Freedmen's Bureau," *Agricultural History*, XXX (1956), pp. 150–156; and Joel Williamson, *After Slavery: The Negro in South Carolina During Reconstruction, 1861–1877*, chaps. iii and v.

The responsibility for the unsatisfactory resolution of the land question did not rest entirely with the southern whites. In large part it rested upon the actions of the northern whites. Despite the talk of confiscation, most political leaders—even many of the Radical Republicans and abolitionists—had too strong a sense of the importance of property rights to espouse confiscation of anyone's estates—even those of the rebels. In the end it was Congress and the Republicans as much as President Johnson who betrayed the freedmen on this crucial matter. The proposal was entirely too revolutionary for nineteenth-century America. The Republican leaders and the upper- and middle-class white abolitionists were for the most part simply too conservative to accept confiscation with equanimity. In fact, in their thinking, the right of an individual to his personal freedom and to his property were two closely interrelated rights, both of them founded in the values of individualism. For a similar reason there was a lack of unity among the friends of the freedmen regarding the degree to which the government should practice a paternalistic benevolence in uplifting the ex-slaves. Many thought that government assistance to the freedmen in the form of granting them land would discourage the individual initiative and independence which they hoped the freedmen, crushed down under slavery, would quickly develop.[21]

In some ways the land issue was the central or crucial issue in reconstruction as far as Negroes were concerned. As the New Orleans *Tribune* suggested, and as students as diverse as W. E. B. DuBois and Gunnar Myrdal have maintained more recently,[22] it can be argued that the failure to confiscate the large estates and redistribute them in small plots among the freedmen, doomed Congress' plans for political reconstruction to failure and the black men to generations of oppression. Viewed more broadly, the North's failure to grapple seriously with the land question was simply part and parcel of the whole pattern of northern indifference to the status of Negroes in American society. To put the matter baldly, most of the people in a position of political influence were not really interested in the Negroes' welfare. Only a handful of Radical Republicans had any sincere desire to make Negroes full citizens. Citizenship rights and the franchise were provided almost as a by-product of political squabbling in Washington. The civil rights bills and the Fourteenth and Fifteenth Amendments were passed reluctantly, and only as the result of long battles and many compromises. Recent research suggests that they would not have been passed at all if President Johnson and the Democrats had acted skillfully instead of pushing the moderate Republicans into accepting the proposals of the Radicals. Negro suffrage resulted mainly from the desire to protect southern white unionists and from northern fears about the disloyalty of the ex-rebels.[23]

Moreover, as noted above, at the end of the Civil War Negroes did not enjoy equal rights, even in a legal sense, in most of the North. The states of the Old Northwest rejected efforts to enfranchise Negroes within their borders, and outside of New England and New York Negroes did not obtain the franchise until after the passage of the Fifteenth Amendment. And because the Fifteenth Amendment was rejected

[21] For a suggestive discussion see Kenneth Stampp, *The Era of Reconstruction* (New York, 1965), pp. 28–30.

[22] DuBois, *Black Reconstruction, passim*; Gunnar Myrdal, *An American Dilemma* (New York, 1944), I, 224–227.

[23] I have been greatly stimulated by Eric L. McKitrick, *Andrew Johnson and Reconstruction* (Chicago, 1960); LaWanda and John H. Cox, *Politics, Principle, and Prejudice, 1865–1866* (New York, 1963), and Stampp, *The Era of Reconstruction*, though none of these authors would necessarily fully agree with conclusions stated here and elsewhere in this paper.

by a number of northern states, it was ratified only with the votes of the reconstructed southern states. Jim Crow practices existed in most of the Old Northwest and the Middle Atlantic states. In Pennsylvania, for example, only a long fight led by Negro abolitionists finally secured a state law against segregation in public conveyances in 1867; and not until 1881 was school segregation abolished in that state.[24] The Fourteenth Amendment, now interpreted as making segregation unconstitutional, was actually extremely vague on the matter of Negro rights. For most congressmen, even the Radicals, granting protection to life, liberty and property, and equality before the law, meant nothing more than the right to own and dispose of property, to sue and be sued, and to testify in courts. It apparently did not imply desegregation of transportation and public accommodations—a lack rectified only with the passage, after several years' arduous agitation, of Sumner's Supplementary Civil Rights Act in 1875. This law, unfortunately, for the most part went unenforced. The Fourteenth Amendment certainly did not encompass the idea of school desegregation. All these things, however, have been read into the amendment by the Supreme Court during the last twenty years.

Whether one accepts the older view that politicians and capitalists desirous of continued Republican ascendancy brought about Negro enfranchisement in order to protect their interests, or whether one accepts the newer view that Negroes received suffrage and citizenship rights as a sort of by-product of the political factionalism in Washington and the self-defeating tactics of Johnson and the northern Democrats, one thing emerges quite clearly—responsible whites in positions of influence were simply not listening to the Negroes. Negroes received their rights in the South for a few brief years during reconstruction not because of the brilliantly worded resolutions, addresses and petitions of the Negro conventions and orators, or because of the deep-rooted desires of the mass of freedmen for economic independence and dignity, but because of the activities of the northern whites, to whom the welfare of the Negroes was usually an incidental or secondary issue. What was true for the Republicans was also true in modified form for the abolitionists. James McPherson, in his recent volume, *The Struggle for Equality*, makes a good case for attributing at least a part of the development of congressional sentiment for Negro rights to the agitation of some of the old abolitionists who felt that their work was not done with the emancipation of the slaves. Yet even the abolitionists were divided, many of them asserting that once emancipated the southern freedmen should be left to help themselves. Others, like the great orator, Wendell Phillips, and certain of the northern school teachers who went south after the war and made the education of the freedmen their life work, were sincerely interested in bringing citizenship rights and real equality for the Negroes. Even these idealists often had an unconscious paternalism about them. They sincerely believed in racial equality, but they also believed that they knew what was best for the Negroes. Willie Lee Rose records the shock that some of the white missionaries on the Sea Islands received when Negroes wanted to make their own decisions.[25]

There is little evidence that such people listened, at least very much, to what the Negroes were saying. Rather, their views in favor of citizenship rights and, in some

[24] Leslie H. Fishel, Jr., "Northern Prejudice and Negro Suffrage, 1865–1870," *Journal of Negro History*, XXXIX (1954), 8–26; McPherson, *Negro's Civil War*, pp. 255–261; McPherson, *Struggle for Equality*, chap. x.

[25] McPherson, *Struggle for Equality, passim*; Rose, *Rehearsal for Reconstruction*, p. 369.

cases, of land for the Negroes, were not a response to Negro demands, but grew out of their own philanthropic ideals. McPherson carefully records the influence of Negro abolitionists upon the white abolitionists during the Civil War and reconstruction. But from reading his book it is clear that the only Negro whom the white abolitionists really listened to in this period was Frederick Douglass, a figure so Olympian that he commanded respect; and it does not appear that they listened even to him very much.

The granting of citizenship rights and the vote to Negroes came about not because of what the Negroes were articulating, but because of what whites, for their own various reasons, decided to do about the Negroes. Even the most advanced and liberal journals did not deem it worth their while to report what Negroes themselves were thinking and doing about their status and their future. Since the white abolitionists and Radical Republicans were not, for the most part, genuinely committed to a belief in the essential human dignity of Negroes—much as many of them verbally protested that they did—it was easy for many of them to become disillusioned with reconstruction, to accept the southern viewpoint about corruption and black power and to wash their hands of the whole problem. This was even true of many who had once been enthusiastic about guaranteeing Negroes their citizenship rights.

It is thus clear how it was that Turner and his colored colleagues were so easily expelled from the Georgia legislature, and how it was that even though they were readmitted the following year, Georgia returned to the hands of the white supremacists in 1872. It also should be clear why Congress was really ineffective in dealing with the violence perpetrated by the Ku Klux Klan and other terrorist organizations, and why it was that, one after the other, the southern states were all permitted to return to white supremacy. The fact is that neither the North as a whole, nor Congress, nor even the majority of the white abolitionists were sufficiently concerned about Negroes to protect the citizenship rights which they had guaranteed them.

These attitudes, characteristic even of the Negroes' friends, afford some insight into the role which Negroes played in southern politics during the era of congressional or black reconstruction. We can spell out the numbers and names of prominent Negro officeholders, and at first glance the list is impressive. Two Negroes, Alonzo J. Ransier and Richard H. Gleaves, served as lieutenant-governor in South Carolina; three, Oscar J. Dunn, C. C. Antoine, and P. B. S. Pinchback, held this office in Louisiana, and Pinchback served briefly as acting governor; and one, A. K. Davis, was lieutenant-governor in Mississippi. South Carolina and Mississippi had Negro speakers of the house—Robert B. Elliott and Samuel J. Lee in South Carolina, and John R. Lynch in Mississippi. William J. Whipper was an associate justice of the supreme court of South Carolina. James J. Hill served as secretary of state in Mississippi; Francis L. Cardozo held both that post and that of state treasurer in South Carolina; and Jonathan C. Gibbs was first secretary of state and superintendent of education in Florida. Three other states also had Negro superintendents of education; Mississippi, Louisiana, and Arkansas. On the national level Mississippi sent two Negroes to the Senate—Blanche K. Bruce and Hiram R. Revels; and seven states elected Negroes to the House of Representatives during reconstruction.

No one has really yet investigated the question: exactly how did the Negro politicians function in the southern reconstruction governments? [26] Probably, just as their

---

[26] For a thoughtful discussion of the Negro political leaders during reconstruction see John Hope Franklin, *Reconstruction: After the Civil War* (Chicago, 1961), pp. 86–92, 133–138.

numbers were small in proportion to the number of Negroes in the southern states, so their influence was less than their abilities or numbers warranted. After all, even the white abolitionists, the most equalitarian group in American society, did not permit their Negro colleagues in the movement to play a significant leadership role. Douglass, the only Negro of real influence in the movement, had to establish himself as an independent force outside of the two major antislavery societies. It is therefore most unlikely that the mixed bag of northerners and southerners, idealists, opportunists and adventurers that composed the southern Republican party were willing to accord Negroes a vital role.

Only three states, South Carolina, Louisiana, and Alabama, sent more than one Negro to the national House of Representatives; four others—Georgia, Mississippi, Florida, and Louisiana—were represented by one each; while three southern states— Virginia, Arkansas, and Texas—sent no Negroes at all to Congress during reconstruction. Moreover, outside of Florida, where Gibbs was superintendent of education, only Arkansas and the three states with a Negro majority in their population selected Negroes for prominent state-wide office. Even taking these three states— Mississippi, Louisiana, and South Carolina—we find that never was a Negro elected governor; that Negroes were unable to send one of their number to the United States Senate from either Louisiana or South Carolina, despite efforts to do so; and that only one of the states, South Carolina, had a Negro on its supreme court. And only in South Carolina did Negroes form a majority in the constitutional convention or even for a brief period in one house of the state legislature.

We know practically nothing of the interaction among the Negro and white politicians, but it would appear that to a remarkable extent officeholding at the highest levels tended to be a symbolic function. Each of the three states with a Negro majority had Negro lieutenant-governors—a purely honorific post. The two Negroes who served in the United States Senate were both moderates. Revels, the first one, voted Democratic consistently after reconstruction, while the other, Bruce, became a large plantation owner. In post-reconstruction Mississippi, the Bruce-Hill-Lynch triumvirate, which dominated the state's Republican party, cooperated closely with the Democrats, making a deal known as fusion, whereby a few posts would go to Negroes in those sections of the state where they were in a heavy majority, though most of the posts and all the important ones remained in white hands. A similar arrangement obtained in the black counties of coastal South Carolina.[27]

The power of the Negro politicians in these states is revealed by what happened to the school system. A nonsegregated school system was an important issue raised in a number of the state constitutional conventions. But only South Carolina and Louisiana provided for mixed schools in their constitutions. Even in these two states, in fact, the schools were administered so that there was practically no integration. Only the New Orleans school system and the University of South Carolina were integrated.[28] Neither on this issue nor on land reform were the Negro politicians able to deliver— any more than they were able to control a fair proportion of the offices.

The foregoing should not be taken as suggesting that Negro politicians were power-

[27] Wharton, *Negro in Mississippi*, pp. 202–203; George B. Tindall, *South Carolina Negroes, 1877–1900* (Columbia, S.C., 1952), pp. 62–64.

[28] Louis R. Harlan, "Segregation in New Orleans Public Schools During Reconstruction," *American Historical Review*, LXVII (1962), pp. 663–675; Williamson, *After Slavery*, pp. 219– 223, 232.

less. They were not. In Florida, for example, Negroes exercised a balance of power between two white factions, and under the astute leadership of the state superintendent of education, Jonathan C. Gibbs, were able to obtain certain concessions and keep Florida in the ranks of the Radical states until 1877. In Louisiana and South Carolina the Negro majorities among the voters did exercise some power, and certain individuals, such as Robert Brown Elliott and Francis L. Cardozo, seem to have been men with a measure of influence. But not only was their influence far less than the pro-southern historians have insisted, but it was also considerably less than their numbers, education, and ability warranted. Neither southern white opportunists, nor paternalistically benevolent northern whites, were inclined to accord positions of real power to Negroes.[29]

If the states with Negro majorities experienced a relative lack of political power on the part of Negroes, it is clear why in other states Negro officeholders had even less of a role, beyond the symbolic one. Effective power stayed in the hands of the whites in all the southern states. Much of the responsibility for this situation rests with the Republicans in Congress.

As the North, the Republicans, and many of the abolitionists deserted and betrayed the southern Negroes, the visions of the equal rights conventions of the 1860's and the hopes of the rural black masses remained only hopes. Sharecropping and peonage, mob violence and disfranchisement became the order of the day. By 1877 southern Negroes were left with only the shreds of their status during the apogee of congressional reconstruction. And even these shreds were destroyed in the wave of proscriptive legislation passed at the turn of the century. Meanwhile, the Supreme Court turned the Fourteenth Amendment upside down. In 1883 it held the Civil Rights Act of 1875 unconstitutional, and thirteen years later, in 1896, it enunciated the separate-but-equal doctrine, justifying state laws requiring segregation. And two years after that, in 1898, it sustained the provisions of the Mississippi constitution of 1890 with its subterfuges that effectively emasculated the Fifteenth Amendment.

Yet these two amendments, passed during the first reconstruction, are the constitutional basis of the new or second reconstruction of the present decade. First of all they were the foundation for the NAACP court victories which, starting in 1915, had by the 1950's so undermined the legal underpinnings of the southern race system that they produced a revolution of expectations among Negroes. And that revolution in expectations is at the bottom of the civil rights revolution of the 1960's. Secondly, it is largely in these reconstruction amendments that the legislative and executive branches have found constitutional sanction for increasing federal intervention in the South.

Although tactics differ markedly from those employed during the first reconstruction, Negro demands today are remarkably similar to those made a hundred years ago —civil rights, the franchise, and economic opportunity. Like prominent Negroes then, civil rights leaders today are concerned with more than constitutional rights; and, quite remarkably, in both cases there is the conviction that the Federal government should undertake the responsibility of providing special assistance to the Negro to compensate for the past. Yet there is a striking difference in the dynamics of the two situations. A hundred years ago whites were not listening to what Negroes were saying. But in the 1960's Negroes, rather than whites, furnished the impetus for social change.

[29] For a sharply contrasting view see Williamson, *After Slavery*, chaps. xii and xiii.

A century ago, as in our own day, something of a moral revolution was going on in the conscience of white America, a revolution forced by the slavery question. It is true that the causes behind that moral revolution were not themselves entirely moral. For one thing they were largely military. Northerners who expected a short war were shocked by military defeat into advocating the destruction of the slave system; and this very practical and *amoral* consideration blended inextricably with, and gave enormous stimulus to fervently moral antislavery doctrines. For the first time white northerners generally became convinced that slavery was a moral evil that had to be swept away; that the Civil War was God's punishment upon a transgressing nation that had condoned slavery for so long. But few came to believe that Negroes were inherently equal to whites.

In the 1960's again military exigencies have played their role in changing the moral climate—the country's leading role in world affairs, the Cold War, and the crucial position of colored nations in the international power system. Yet unquestionably more and more white Americans have become aware that Negroes have aspirations that should be respected. This new awareness has been manifested not only in the increasing concern for equal rights but also in the way in which whites have been paying attention to what Negroes are saying and doing.

Will the new reconstruction prove as temporary and evanescent as the old? The history of the first reconstruction suggests that revolutions—if indeed there was a revolution—can go backwards; that the white majority may grow disillusioned or just weary of idealism.[30] On the other hand, the recent changes in the attitudes of white Americans appear more deeply rooted than those of a hundred years ago. For one thing changing racial views are part of a long-term trend rooted in the New Deal period, in the moral sensitivities aroused as a result of the struggle with racist Nazi Germany, and the postwar international pressures. Moreover for the past couple of decades the northern Negro vote has been a decisive factor in many elections, and the weight of increasing numbers of registered Negro voters in the South will be felt, the current "white backlash" notwithstanding.[31]

Reforms can be reversed; revolutions may indeed go backwards. It is conceivable that the new reconstruction will be undone as was the old. Certainly, at best it will be accomplished in a halting and spasmodic manner, and every advance will be the fruit of costly and hard-fought struggles, involving compromises and even reverses along the way. Nevertheless, if one may hazard a prediction, the increasing sensitivity of whites to the Negroes' needs and demands—a growing concern for Negroes as *persons* as contrasted to concern about the *institution* of slavery—suggests that the new reconstruction is more likely to prove to be a permanent one.

[30] For sensitive discussion of such trends see C. Vann Woodward, "What Happened to the Civil Rights Movement?" *Harper's Magazine* (Jan., 1967), pp. 29–37.

[31] See, for example, Reese Cleghorn and Pat Watters, "The Impact of Negro Votes on Southern Politics," *The Reporter* (Jan. 26, 1967), pp. 24–25, 31–32.

23 / Carpetbagger Constitutional Reform in the South Atlantic States, 1867-1868

Jack B. Scroggs

One of the myths of Reconstruction is the supposed "descent into barbarism" of Southern state governments under Radical and Negro rule. As stated by contemporary journalists such as James S. Pike, or later by historians such as William A. Dunning and his students, the racially mixed governments of the former Confederacy were a mockery of free government. The Radical state regimes were composed of ignorant, illiterate blacks, of renegade Southern whites, and of Northern adventurers and profit-seekers who badly mismanaged public affairs and abused their authority. They raised taxes and stole public funds. They piled up gigantic debts for the purpose of financing foolish and extravagant projects. They harassed white men of good family whose only crime was loyalty to the cause of Southern independence.

In recent years, historians have rejected this harsh picture. The Reconstruction governments, it now appears, were remarkably progressive. They spent money for internal improvements and public services such as schools, hospitals, and prisons—facilities that the Southern states had badly neglected before the war. Conservatives complained bitterly, largely because they were unaccustomed to the tax burden necessary to a modern society and because for the first time they were being forced to pay their fair share.

Corruption surely existed, but not everywhere. Mississippi, for example, was governed by a markedly honest regime, although Conservatives still condemned it. South Carolina, however, was notoriously bilked and cheated by its public officials. The legislature gave itself funds to pay for lunches and whiskey, and to provide gifts to the members' girlfriends. Extravagant amounts were spent for services and for facilities that were often worth far less than the state paid.

Still, in condemning this performance, we must not lose our perspective. In the North, at the same time, long-established state and local governments, with white electorates, were also making a mockery of democracy. In New York City, the notorious Tweed Ring stole millions from the taxpayers. In private business life these years witnessed the notorious business machina-

Journal of Southern History, XXVI, No. 4 (November 1961), 475–493. Copyright 1961 by the Southern Historical Association. Reprinted by permission of the Managing Editor.

tions of Daniel Drew, Jay Gould, and Jim Fisk. In Washington, corruption reached into high places, with scandals touching both President Grant's official and personal family.

Southern Reconstruction governments, moreover, compiled a record of considerable accomplishment, and all three elements of these regimes contributed to that record. Scalawags were not a small group of Southern renegades, but included substantial numbers of native Southern whites. As much as 25 percent of native white voters in Mississippi, for example, joined the Republicans. These men were often ex-Whig planters and commercial men who had deplored disunion. Although the make-up of the Scalawag element varied from region to region and from state to state, they were scarcely the ne'er-do-wells and crude opportunists depicted in the older accounts.

There are also many misconceptions regarding the black man's role in the Radical state governments. No doubt there were instances of incompetence and malfeasance among black officials and legislators, but considering the stultifying effects of slavery, the public performance of many black men was quite impressive. Few occupied the leading positions in state governments, although many served well in the legislatures and in local offices, and about a score of black men went to Congress from Southern states during the Reconstruction era.

The most talented of the Radical elements, however, were the Carpetbaggers, who played a major role in writing new state constitutions. As the following article by Jack B. Scroggs demonstrates, these immigrants to the South were often men of fine education and considerable political sophistication, and their work as applied political philosophers bears comparison with that of almost any other group in our history.

For further reading: Thomas B. Alexander, *Political Reconstruction in Tennessee* (Nashville, Tenn.: Vanderbilt University Press, 1950); Francis B. Simkins and Robert H. Woody, *South Carolina During Reconstruction* (Chapel Hill, N. C.: University of North Carolina Press, 1932); David Donald, "The Scalawag in Mississippi Reconstruction," *Journal of Southern History*, X (November 1944); Allen W. Trelease, "Who Were the Scalawags?" *Journal of Southern History*, XXIX (November 1963); Jack B. Scroggs, "Southern Reconstruction: A Radical View," *Journal of Southern History*, XXIV (November 1958).

The Reconstruction Period brought to the South fundamental changes in state politics and in political theory, climaxing a strong ante bellum movement in this direction. Among the many changes produced by the social-political revolution of the postwar era were lasting constitutional reforms of a progressive and democratic nature. Not least responsible for this development were the newly arrived Northerners —the carpetbaggers, who, along with the Southern scalawags, have long borne the major blame for all Reconstruction ills in the South. Accused by contemporaries of every conceivable crime, both political and civil, the term *carpetbagger* even among recent writers has carried with it the taint of ineptness, fraud, and corruption. This has tended to obscure the basic contributions made by the Northern immigrants who engaged in politics and to distort the role of the new Republican organizations in the South.

Only of local importance during the early stages of Reconstruction, these Northern "adventurers" achieved a commanding position in state politics with the advent of Radical control of the Reconstruction program early in 1867. The triumph of the Radicals in Congress brought about in the South a corresponding emergence of state Radicals, both white and Negro, and the Republican party developed as a formidable force in the new Southern political orientation. The strength of these new political organizations was clearly demonstrated in the results of the constitutional convention elections of 1867 in the five South Atlantic states—Virginia, North Carolina, South Carolina, Georgia, and Florida. The delegates to these conventions were largely representatives of the Negroes and lower class whites, who, as it happens, composed the two segments of society most eager to secure constitutional reform. Although the carpetbaggers were never in a majority in these delegations, their influence on Southern politics reached its high point in the framing of the new constitutions.

The degree of carpetbagger leadership and influence in the constitutional conventions varied from state to state. In Virginia, North Carolina, and South Carolina, convention debates and proceedings were dominated by recently arrived Northerners.[1] The same was true of the Florida convention, but internal party schism brought ultimate defeat to the Radical Republican element there.[2] Georgia alone of the South Atlantic states was relatively free from carpetbagger influence in the formation of her new constitution.[3]

[1] Of the nineteen standing committees appointed to draw up the constitution of North Carolina, ten were headed by carpetbaggers, while in Virginia half of the standing committees were filled by Northerners. *Journal of the Constitutional Convention of the State of North-Carolina at Its Session, 1868* (Raleigh, 1868), 43–44; *Journal of the Constitutional Convention of the State of Virginia, Convened in the City of Richmond December 3, 1867 . . .* (Richmond, 1867), 28–29. See also *Proceedings of the Constitutional Convention of South Carolina, Held at Charleston, S. C., Beginning January 14th . . . 1868* (Charleston, 1868), 37; and Raleigh *Daily Sentinel*, January 22–23, 1868.

[2] The regular Radical Republicans, under the leadership of Daniel Richards from Illinois, Liberty Billings from New Hampshire, William U. Saunders from Maryland and Jonathan C. Gibbs from Pennsylvania, reflected the opinion of the Republican National Committee, of which they were the agents in Florida. A more conservative group, led by Harrison Reed and Edward M. Randall, was closely tied with President Andrew Johnson. A third group, of less power and significance, was led by Thomas W. Osborn of Massachusetts. Ultimately, the more conservative Reed faction, in co-operation with Conservative leaders and the military, ousted the more numerous Radical group and seized complete control of the convention. L. D. Strickney to Elihu B. Washburne, May 21, 1868, and Daniel Richards to Washburne, February 2, 11, 12, 1868, in Elihu B. Washburne Papers (Division of Manuscripts, Library of Congress); William Watson Davis, *The Civil War and Reconstruction in Florida* (New York, 1913), 470, 509–16; John Wallace, *Carpet Bag Rule in Florida; the Inside Workings of the Reconstruction of Civil Government in Florida After the Close of the Civil War* (Jacksonville, 1888), 55, 64–68; "Report of the Secretary of War," *House Ex. Docs.*, 40 Cong., 3 Sess., Vol. III, Pt. 1 (Serial 1367), 77, 86–88.

[3] Clara Mildred Thompson, *Reconstruction in Georgia, Economic, Social, Political, 1865–1872* (New York, 1915), 193; Isaac Wheeler Avery, *The History of the State of Georgia from 1850 to 1881 . . .* (New York, 1881), 377. Only two carpetbaggers received committee chairmanships in Georgia. *Journal of the Proceedings of the Constitutional Convention of the People of*

An appraisal of the motives of the carpetbagger leaders in the state conventions is difficult except in terms of the final products of their deliberations. Political and economic self-interest doubtless dictated the moves of many of the key Republican leaders, but in the drafting of new constitutions instances of attempts to limit the political freedom of any segment of the population were rare. Indeed, the primary aim of the carpetbagger group was the extension of political democracy, the assumption being that with complete political equality for all men Republican principles would prevail and the Southern Republican party would capture and retain control of the state governments. Demonstrating a lack of understanding of Southern society and politics, a great many of these leaders were struggling to impose constitutional changes on a reluctant South simply because they considered the changes long overdue.

With control of three of the South Atlantic state conventions firmly lodged in the carpetbagger element, it was evident that fundamental changes would appear in the new constitutions of these states. Even in Florida and Georgia, where a certain amount of co-operation with native white Conservatives tended to alleviate the revolutionary nature of constitutional innovations, it was clear that a return to the *status quo ante bellum* would not suffice. Unlike the conventions of 1865 which had primarily aimed at making only required amendments to old constitutions, the conventions of 1867–1868 were to embark on a program of basic constitutional reform.

Liberal constitutional provisions embodying the ideal of democratic equalitarianism which had developed during the past half century formed the framework of the new instruments of government. Many of these provisions were copied from constitutions of Northern states, and the carpetbaggers, as one would expect, were generally foremost in their advocacy. The states with the most able carpetbagger leadership emerged with the most democratic and progressive constitutions, and, as able Northern leadership decreased, the liberality of the documents tended to decrease proportionally. The Southern Republicans of course understood that democratizing of government would serve to strengthen the voting elements upon which they depended while at the same time weakening the former Democratic leaders who, standing to gain nothing from constitutional change, were on record as favoring no further change, and were declaring the whole process of Reconstruction an unconstitutional abridgement of the South's rights.[4]

When the constitutional conventions met in late 1867 and early 1868, they initially faced problems outside the realm of pure constitution-drafting. While the standing committees were preparing their reports, the convention sessions were taken up with the pressing matter of the people's destitute condition. The results of their deliberations were the passage of ordinances of relief, or stay laws, measures which the Radicals had freely promised in their campaign for control of the conventions.[5] These

---

Georgia, Held in the City of Atlanta in the Months of December, 1867, and January, February and March, 1868 . . . (Augusta, 1868), 40–41.

[4] See statement of Benjamin H. Hill in Americus, Ga., *Tri-Weekly Republican*, July 13, 1867; address of John Pool, of North Carolina, in Raleigh, N. C., *Tri-Weekly Standard*, April 9, 1868; Governor Charles J. Jenkins' letter to the people of Georgia in Americus *Tri-Weekly Republican*, April 16, 1867; Raleigh *Daily Sentinel*, October 16, 1867.

[5] See circular in Americus *Tri-Weekly Republican*, September 21, 1867; Raleigh *Daily Standard*, March 6, 1868.

ordinances intended to alleviate financial suffering were to remain in force only until adequate provisions could be inserted in the new constitutions.

The debate over a relief ordinance in the South Carolina convention disclosed a division in carpetbagger ranks in that state.[6] Carpetbaggers William J. Whipper and Niles G. Parker were the principal supporters of a temporary relief measure, basing their argument on the assumption that the legislation they favored would not only protect debtors but also those laborers who were dependent upon property owners for wages. In opposition, Negro carpetbaggers Richard H. Cain and Francis L. Cardozo maintained that by refraining from passing a relief act the convention would force the large plantation owners to sell their holdings and thereby permit the poor people of the state to purchase small farms. Whipper's answer to this was that "it would be perfect folly to entertain the opinion that in the present miserable destitution of the South the poor people will become the owners of the vast tracts of land if thrown into the market." He alleged that another consideration prompted the opponents of the ordinance when he joined native Negro R. C. De Large in asserting that a great part of the opposition was initiated by Northern and local investors who would be able to buy up the estates and become "large land monopolists." The dispute was resolved when General E. R. S. Canby issued a general relief order for the Carolinas, but the South Carolina convention carried relief further by declaring all contracts and liabilities for the purchase of slaves null and void.[7]

In North Carolina the question of relief initiated a vigorous debate over the constitutional status of the state itself, with the carpetbagger leaders displaying a considerable divergence of opinion. Albion W. Tourgée maintained the "old North Carolina was dead and buried in the tomb of the Confederacy." From a territorial status she must be brought back to statehood with adequate homestead provisions to protect the mass of people. Tourgée's constitutional position led naturally to his support of repudiation of the old state debt, but the convention refused to back him in this.[8]

In all of the South Atlantic states the conventions incorporated into the new constitutions permanent relief measures under the provisions protecting homesteads, which had the advantage of avoiding the odium attached to the term "stay laws." These liberal homestead provisions assured the citizen of retaining in his possession a minimum amount of property by exempting it from attachment for debts. Although an innovation in these states, homestead provisions provoked little opposition from any quarter, the only controversy developing over the amount of the exemption. The Radicals wished to make the exemption large enough to protect the small owners but not so large as to give protection to owners of large landholdings. North Carolina and

---

[6] South Carolina carpetbaggers were again split over the question of petitioning the national government for a million-dollar loan to purchase land for the freedmen. Despite carpetbagger C. P. Leslie's accusation that his fellow Radicals were acting solely from political considerations, knowing full well that Congress would not consider such a proposal, most of the carpetbaggers supported the petition, which was adopted by a large majority. *Proceedings of the Constitutional Convention of South Carolina, 1868,* 196–97, 376–439.

[7] *Ibid.,* 104–25, 214–32. This provision was later declared unconstitutional as it impaired obligation of contracts. Francis Butler Simkins and Robert Hilliard Woody, *South Carolina During Reconstruction* (Chapel Hill, 1932), 100.

[8] Raleigh *Daily Standard,* February 5, 1868; Raleigh *Daily Sentinel,* February 17–18, 1868; Wilmington, N. C., *Daily Journal,* February 18, 1868.

South Carolina, following the leadership of the carpetbaggers, limited their homestead exemption to a moderate $1,500, while Florida provided for the exemption of $1,000 in personal property and one hundred and sixty acres in land, or one acre within the limits of an incorporated town.[9] Virginia gave a larger exemption, real and personal property to the value of $2,000;[10] and the Georgia convention under the sway of conservative business men and planters led by Joseph E. Brown and Rufus Bullock, gave the largest exemption, real and personal property to the value of $3,000. Other relief provisions were put into the new constitutions. In Georgia, for instance, a sweeping relief ordinance was included in the constitution over the protests of the Democrats who questioned its constitutionality and charged that the forces of Brown and Bullock designed it as a snare to catch the ignorant debtor.[11]

In view of subsequent developments, of particular interest is the movement which developed in the conventions for specific provisions for the payment of the state debts and for limitation of state aid to companies and corporations. All of the conventions acknowledged responsibility for the old state debts, excepting war debts. Tourgée, the Ohio carpetbagger in North Carolina, opposed the payment of the state debt, arguing that since the war had left North Carolina in a territorial status, the old state debt had already ceased to exist, despite the demand of Northern speculators that it be paid. For his stand in favor of repudiation Tourgée was vigorously attacked by fellow Northerners in the convention, as well as by the Conservative press. With the entire carpetbagger element opposing him Tourgée lost his fight on the repudiation issue. He subsequently led in the movement for prompt payment of the state debt, and the convention passed an ordinance which provided for the payment of the interest due on state bonds and for the funding of the debt in new six percent state bonds.[12]

All five conventions set limitations upon the use of public credit. In South Carolina carpetbagger Niles G. Parker, chairman of the finance committee, presented a report which called for limiting the state debt to $500,000 and for prohibiting the legislature from extending the state credit to the aid of any private company. The North Carolina convention forbade the legislature to contract new debts except to supply a casual deficit or to suppress invasion or insurrection, unless the same bill included a tax to cover the deficit. Virginia went further in declaring the credit of the state would

[9] Francis Newton Thorpe (ed.), *The Federal and State Constitutions, Colonial Charters, and Other Organized Laws of the States, Territories, and Colonies Now or Heretofore Forming the United States of America* (7 vols., Washington, 1909), II, 717 (Fla., Art. X), V, 2818–19 (N. C., Art. X); *Proceedings of the Convention of South Carolina, 1868*, 888–89.

[10] Thorpe (ed.), *Federal and State Constitutions*, VII, 3896 (Va., Art. XI, Sec. 1).

[11] *Ibid.*, II, 836*n*–37*n* (Ga., Art. V, Sec. 17, Pt. 3, deleted by Congress), 838 (Ga., Art. VII, Sec. 1).

[12] Joseph C. Abbott, carpetbagger from New England, led the attack on Tourgée, declaring that his remarks were "infamous." Raleigh *Daily Sentinel*, January 23, February 15, 17–18, 1868; Raleigh *Daily Standard*, February 5, 1868; see also Wilmington *Daily Journal*, February 18, 1868. Subsequent investigations revealed that Tourgée was essentially right in his contention that bondholders were the driving force in the fight against repudiation. General Abbott, L. G. Estes, carpetbagger lobbyist Milton Littlefield, and G. Z. French, all carpetbagger opponents of Tourgée, were involved in heavy bond speculations with a New York group, and repudiation would have meant financial ruin to them. *Report of the Commission to Investigate Charges of Fraud and Corruption, Under Act of Assembly, Session 1871–'72* . . . (Raleigh, 1872), 397–98, 522–24; *Journal of the Constitutional Convention of North Carolina, 1868*, 308, 454–55.

not "be granted to, or in aid of, any person, association, or corporation." Both the Georgia and Florida conventions provided that the state credit could be used in support only of internal improvements and in no other cases.[13]

The debates on the bills of rights in the conventions disclosed the determination of the carpetbaggers to incorporate in the new constitutions basic principles of equalitarianism despite the bitter opposition which greeted their attempts to eradicate the legal distinctions between the races. Only after a vicious parliamentary struggle did the carpetbaggers of North Carolina, in league with the Negro members, secure the adoption of a provision in the bill of rights stating that "all men are created equal." The South Carolina convention accepted an amendment offered by Negro carpetbagger B. F. Randolph which specifically forbade any distinction on account of race or color and provided that all citizens "enjoy all common, public, legal, and political privileges." [14] The Florida and Georgia constitutions contained no specific guarantee of equal civil and political rights.

All of the bills of rights reaffirmed the right to *habeas corpus* and provided that henceforth no one was to be imprisoned for debt except in cases of fraud; and in North Carolina Tourgée secured the adoption of a section stating that no man would be "compelled to pay costs or jail fees, or necessary witness fees of the defense, unless found guilty." The bills of rights in the Virginia, North Carolina, and South Carolina constitutions had sections designed to prevent in the future the imposition of property qualifications for voting or for holding office, and carpetbagger S. S. Ashley secured the adoption of a section guaranteeing all people in North Carolina the right to a public education. Finally, the bill of rights adopted in each of the state conventions except in Georgia declared that all rights not delegated by the constitutions were reserved to the people.[15]

An important progressive measure sponsored by each convention was the establishment of a state controlled system of public education. It was generally conceded that improvements in public education were needed, but carpetbagger leaders were particularly active in fostering plans for raising the educational level of the South. Although there was no serious opposition in Virginia to a public school system, a bitter controversy developed over segregation of whites and blacks in a dual system. Extremists on both sides were silenced when the convention accepted a compromise offered by C. H. Porter from New York which evaded the issue by making no specific reference to either mixed or separate schools.[16] In North Carolina liberal provisions

[13] *Proceedings of the Constitutional Convention of South Carolina, 1868*, 362–63; *Journal of the Constitutional Convention of North Carolina, 1868*, 304; Thorpe (ed.), *Federal and State Constitutions*, II, 719 (Fla., Art. XIII, Secs. 7–8), 830 (Ga., Art. III, Sec. 5, No. 5, Sec. 6), V, 2814 (N. C., Art. V, Sec. 5), VII, 3895 (Va., Art. X, Sec. 12).

[14] *Journal of the Constitutional Convention of North Carolina, 1868*, 169–70; Raleigh *Daily Standard*, February 13, 1868; *Proceedings of the Constitutional Convention of South Carolina, 1868*, 353–56; Thorpe (ed.), *Federal and State Constitutions*, VI, 3284 (S. C., Art. I, Sec. 39).

[15] Thorpe (ed.), *Federal and State Constitutions*, II, 704–706 (Fla., Art. I, Secs. 1–2, 6, 16), 823 (Ga., Art. I, Secs. 13, 18), V, 2801–2803 (N. C., Art. I, Secs. 11, 16, 21–22, 27, 37), VI, 3283–85 (S. C., Art. I, Secs. 17, 20, 32, 41), VII, 3874–75 (Va., Art. I, Secs. 8, 10, 21); *Journal of the Constitutional Convention of North Carolina, 1868*, 214–15; Raleigh *Daily Sentinel*, January 22, February 17, 1868.

[16] Alrutheus A. Taylor, "The Negro in the Reconstruction of Virginia," *Journal of Negro History*, XI (April 1926), 481. Porter was a lawyer and later a member of Congress from Virginia. Lyon Gardiner Tyler (ed.), *Encyclopedia of Virginia Biography* (5 vols., New York, 1915), III, 125.

for public education were sponsored by Ashley, chairman of the committee on education. Tourgée gave him valuable aid, at one time unsuccessfully trying to amend the finance section so as to allocate to educational purposes all funds received from the poll tax. In North Carolina, as in Virginia, Conservatives attempted to insert provisions for the establishment of separate schools for the two races, but no stipulation was made in the section on segregation as adopted.[17] South Carolina carried the principle of equality even further by declaring that all public schools, colleges, and universities of the state would be open to all children and youths "without regard to race or color." Disagreement in South Carolina came over the issue of compulsory attendance in the public schools, with C. P. Leslie opposing the greater part of the carpetbagger leadership in their promotion of compulsory education. Leslie took the occasion to deliver a denunciation of the Massachusetts members of the convention, but his fulminations failed to prevent the passage of the section requiring all children from six to sixteen to attend school for at least twenty-four months.[18] Georgia and Florida followed the trend and adopted provisions calling for the establishment of a system of public schools and with no specific statement as to segregation of the races.[19]

The conventions achieved other significant reforms. There was a general revision of the state penal systems with a lowering of the number of crimes punishable by death. Tourgée expressed the attitude of the Northern immigrants on penal reform when he said,

> Not only is punishment to satisfy justice but to reform the offender. That . . . is the key-note of civilization. Now as we are laying slavery and all its concomitants . . . a higher and nobler penal system should be devised.

North Carolina, South Carolina, and Florida also made specific provisions for state penitentiaries.[20] The constitutions of Virginia, North Carolina, and South Carolina included elaborate sections outlining the form of a new county-township government, and in all of the South Atlantic states except Florida provisions were made for the popular election of county officers.[21] Local control of civil affairs was avowedly de-

[17] *Journal of the Constitutional Convention of North Carolina, 1868*, 304–307, 342–43; Raleigh *Daily Sentinel*, March 5, 7, 1868; Thorpe (ed.), *Federal and State Constitutions*, V, 2817–18 (N. C., Art. IX).

[18] Thorpe (ed.), *Federal and State Constitutions*, VI, 3300 (S. C., Art. X). For the debate on the issue see *Proceedings of the Constitutional Convention of South Carolina, 1868*, 685–709.

[19] *Journal of the Constitutional Convention of Georgia, 1868*, 482–83; Thorpe (ed.), *Federal and State Constitutions*, II, 716 (Fla., Art. IX, Sec. 1), 838 (Ga., Art. VI). Conservatives in Georgia attempted to preserve something of the stigma formerly attached to "poor" schools in the South by adoption of a provision levying taxes for "a general school fund for the indigent," but carpetbaggers secured the withdrawal of the objectionable word "indigent." Augusta *Tri-Weekly Constitutionalist*, January 29, 1868.

[20] Raleigh *Daily Standard*, March 4, 1868; Thorpe (ed.), *Federal and State Constitutions*, II, 718 (Fla., Art. XI, Sec. 2), V, 2820 (N. C., Art. XI). Despite their apparent concern for penal reform, however, the new Radical state governments continued the convict lease system which became notorious in the postwar South. Fletcher Melvin Green, "Some Aspects of the Convict Lease System in the Southern States," in Green (ed.), *Essays in Southern History* . . . (Chapel Hill, 1949), 116.

[21] The division of Virginia counties into townships was vigorously condemned by Conservatives, who maintained that the new arrangement was cumbersome and overly expensive. Hamilton James Eckenrode, *The Political History of Virginia During the Reconstruction* (Baltimore, 1904), 102. In North Carolina this change resulted in a transfer of power from the county courts to

signed to stimulate the interest of the masses of people in government. Tax reforms provided for by the new constitutions tended to shift the burden of taxation from individuals to the owners of property, and made taxes uniform throughout each state.[22] Property rights of women were extended by providing that property in the possession of a woman at the time of marriage or acquired by her thereafter was not liable in payment of the debts of her husband.

In all five states, the new constitutions altered to a greater or lesser degree the structure of the three traditional branches of state government. The executive branch underwent drastic changes in two of the states, while the remaining three states retained vestiges of ante bellum centralization. In North Carolina the convention eliminated the old Executive Council, heretofore elected by the General Assembly, and over the protests of the Conservatives created four new elective positions: lieutenant governor, superintendent of public works, auditor, and superintendent of public instruction. The election of these officials, along with that of the secretary of state and attorney general, was placed in the hands of the voters. The tendency to make the officers of the executive department directly responsible to the people was evident in the constitution of South Carolina, but Georgia and Florida, under more Conservative influence, made all executive officers except the governor, and in the case of Florida, the lieutenant governor, either appointive by the governor or elective by the General Assembly. Virginia also reserved to the General Assembly the right to elect all executive officers except the governor and lieutenant governor. The period of required residence for election to the governorship was generally made low in order to assure the eligibility of the Northern newcomers, and each state abolished property requirements of candidates for the governorship. North Carolina Conservatives made determined efforts to retain a section requiring a freehold to qualify for governor, but in vain. The Conservative press was loud in its condemnation of the changes in the executive branch:

> The whole tenor of the report . . . [the Raleigh *Sentinel* declared], smacks of Yankee manipulations, and ignores the safe and staid temper of the Old North State, which has always eschewed inducements to experiment, at the sacrifice of her conservatism and well-earned integrity.[23]

The judicial branch of the new state governments reflected the extent of the tide of democratic thought. In North Carolina Tourgée, unable to persuade the judiciary committee to approve his proposals to have the people elect the judges and to abolish the distinction between suits at law and suits in equity, carried his fight to the convention floor and secured the adoption of both proposals. The North Carolina convention appointed Tourgée, Victor C. Barringer, and W. B. Rodman as commissioners to prepare rules of judicial procedure and to codify the laws under the changes adopted by the convention. The *Sentinel* branded the popular election of judges as

---

the voters. South Carolina previously had been divided into judicial districts rather than counties. Recent scholars conclude that reform of local government was the South Carolina convention's greatest permanent achievement. Simkins and Woody, *South Carolina During Reconstruction*, 101.

[22] There existed a belief among some Negroes and carpetbaggers that increased taxes on landed property would force the aristocratic landlords of the South to break up their holdings and sell small parcels to freedmen and poor whites. For an example of this attitude, see *Proceedings of the Constitutional Convention of South Carolina, 1868*, 104–25.

[23] Raleigh *Daily Sentinel*, January 29, 1868.

"the most dangerous stride towards mobocracy yet made by the destructives"; and North Carolina was, in fact, the only state in the South Atlantic area to take so democratic a stand. South Carolina provided that the General Assembly elect judges; and, although definite terms of office were fixed for each of the court judges, the carpetbagger leaders were not completely satisfied. D. H. Chamberlain declared that the "doctrine that the people are not to be trusted with the selection of those who are to administer justice to them, I believe to be wholly unfounded." Division among the carpetbagger leaders in South Carolina, however, prevented approval of popular election of judges even though one of their strongest leaders insisted in this connection that "the whole program of the age is in favor of removing power from the hands of the few, and bestowing it on the many." [24] Virginia, like South Carolina, provided that the General Assembly elect her judges, but both Georgia and Florida eliminated any vestiges of local control of the judiciary by permitting the governor, with the consent of the senate, to appoint them. In fact the Georgia constitution, insofar as the judiciary was concerned, was less democratic than the constitution of 1865, which had provided for the election of supreme court judges by the General Assembly and lesser judicial officials by the voters. Carpetbagger A. L. Harris recognizing this retrogression protested against the enormous appointive power being concentrated in the chief executive.[25] North and South Carolina abolished county and district courts, and all five states fixed the tenure of office for judges at a specific number of years.

There were far-reaching reforms incorporated in the provisions of the new constitutions dealing with the legislative branches and with the suffrage. After replacing North Carolina's ancient title of House of Commons with the more common House of Representatives, the North Carolina convention abolished property qualifications for membership in either house.[26] The other four South Atlantic states continued to require no property qualifications for membership in either house. Virginia Radicals, however, inserted a section imposing the same disabilities for officeholding as were imposed by the Fourteenth Amendment,[27] and the native whites in the Georgia convention, when considering a section of the report of the committee on franchise providing that "all qualified electors" should be eligible to hold office, persuaded the Negroes that they were eligible for office without this clause, and that its inclusion would only serve to make it more difficult to secure ratification of the constitution.

[24] *Journal of the Constitutional Convention of North Carolina, 1868,* 180–86; Thorpe (ed.), *Federal and State Constitutions,* V, 2812 (N. C., Art. IV, Sec. 26); Raleigh *Daily Sentinel,* February 12, 1868. Before the Civil War, Georgia and Virginia had provided for popular election of judges. Fletcher Melvin Green, *Constitutional Development in the South Atlantic States, 1776–1860* . . . (Chapel Hill, 1930), 240, 196. See also Thorpe (ed.), *Federal and State Constitutions,* II, 802–804 (Ga., 1812 Amendment), VI, 3292–93 (S. C., Art. IV, Secs. 2, 13), VII, 3847 (Va., 1850, Art. VI, Secs. 6, 10); *Proceedings of the Constitutional Convention of South Carolina, 1868,* 601–602, 621.

[25] Thorpe (ed.), *Federal and State Constitutions,* II, 712–14 (Fla., 1868, Art. VII, Secs. 3, 7, 9), 818–20, 835 (Ga., 1865, Art. VII, 1868, Art. V, Sec. 9), VII (Va., Art. VI., Secs. 5., 11, 13); Ethel Kime Ware, *A Constitutional History of Georgia* (New York, 1947), 123n; Thorpe, *Federal and State Constitutions,* II, 818–20; *Journal of the Constitutional Convention of Georgia, 1868,* 112.

[26] Thorpe (ed.), *Federal and State Constitutions,* V, 2802, 2805 (N. C., Art. I, Sec. 22, Art. II, Secs. 9–10).

[27] Thorpe (ed.), *Federal and State Constitutions,* VII, 3876–77 (Va., Art. III, Secs. 6–7). Florida had never imposed a property qualification for such membership, and Virginia and Georgia had abolished property qualifications for legislators in the ante bellum period. See Green, *Constitutional Development,* 239, 294.

The political trick worked; by a vote of 126 to 12 the section was dropped, and the only specific guarantee of the right of the Negro to hold office in Georgia was lost.[28]

The liberalization of the qualifications for membership in the various general assemblies was effected with little difficulty, but on the long-standing question of the basis of apportionment the Conservatives waged a bitter battle. In North Carolina Conservative John W. Graham contended that unless the amount of taxes paid by a district were to be used in apportioning seats in the upper house in the time-honored manner, property would be left defenseless before the weight of sheer numbers. Carpetbagger John R. French gave voice to the more democratic view:

> Our fathers wrought according to the light of their day, and have entered upon the reward of their honest toil. Another future opens before us. Not property, not a few families, however old, or however respectable, are to rule the North-Carolina of the hereafter—but the free and mighty people . . . these are to be her voters and her legislators.[29]

The old rivalry between the Charleston area and the upcountry of South Carolina was revived in that state convention with the upcountry delegates expressing fear of continued low-country domination. In the three upper South Atlantic states the demands of the western areas were met by specific constitutional provisions of future apportionment of senators and representatives on the basis of population. Florida limited the number of representatives to four from any one county, and Georgia devised a complex system by which the state was divided into districts of three counties each for the purpose of electing senators; and in the apportionment of representatives the six largest counties were allowed three each, the thirty-one next largest, two each, and the remaining ninety-five, one each.[30]

In the case of Florida the initial apportionment, and the limitation of representation from any one county to a maximum of four, meant that control would be assured for the whites, inasmuch as the Negroes were concentrated in the few populous counties. The Radicals tried to persuade Congress to disallow the second Florida constitution on the grounds that its legislature was unrepresentative, but their efforts

---

[28] Augusta, Ga., *Tri-Weekly Constitutionalist*, February 16, 1868; *Americus Tri-Weekly Republican*, February 18, 1868; *Journal of the Constitutional Convention of Georgia, 1868,* 148–50, 311–12. A competent historian of Reconstruction in Georgia gives former Governor Joseph E. Brown the credit for this political maneuver which allowed the Republicans to appeal to the whites of Cherokee Georgia by saying the Negro was given no right to hold office by the constitution and, on the other hand, to appeal to the masses of Negroes by saying they had that right as it was not specifically forbidden. Thompson, *Reconstruction in Georgia,* 196–97.

[29] Raleigh *Daily Sentinel,* February 14, 1868; *Journal of the Constitutional Convention of North Carolina, 1868,* 196–97. This long-standing argument over opportionment had been compromised in 1835 by making population the basis of representation in the lower house and taxation the basis in the upper house. *The Constitutions of the Several States of the Union . . .* (New York, 1854), 260–61. For an account of this intrastate sectional controversy, see Green, *Constitutional Development,* 228–29, 270–71.

[30] Thorpe (ed.), *Federal and State Constitutions,* II, 726–27 (Fla., Art. XVII, Sec. 29), 827–28 (Ga., Art. III, Secs. 3–4), V, 2804–2805 (N. C., Art. II, Secs. 5–7), VI, 3285–86 (S. C., Art. II, Secs. 3–4, 6, 8), VII, 3880–83 (Va., Art. V, Secs. 2–3); *Proceedings of the Constitutional Convention of South Carolina, 1868,* 527–37; Davis, *Civil War and Reconstruction in Florida,* 511–12. For the Radical protest in Florida, see *House Misc. Docs.,* 40 Cong., 2 Sess., Vol. II (Serial 1350), No. 109. Only eight counties in Florida, heavily populated counties, had a Negro majority. White dominated counties with small populations were given representation out of all proportion to population figures. *A Compendium of the Ninth Census (June 1, 1870) Compiled Pursuant to a Concurrent Resolution of Congress* (Washington, 1872), 32–33.

were in vain.[31] Similarly, the Georgia constitution achieved white control of the legislature by its system of geographic apportionment.[32] Thus, the issue of representation was not entirely a continuation of the old struggle between democrats and aristocrats; Negro suffrage brought a new facet to the problem. As was true in Georgia and Florida, apportionment of seats in the legislature could be used as a means of maintaining white political supremacy.

The question of suffrage caused great apprehension among the Conservatives, and one reactionary organ predicted that once the Republicans decreed suffrage to be an "inherent right" there would remain "no security for the rights of property, and every man will hold whatever property he does hold at the mercy of the rabble." But there was never any real doubt in any of the states about the inevitability of Negro voting, and Negro suffrage was generally accepted by Conservatives in all of the states except North Carolina as a necessity forced upon the states by an overbearing conqueror. In the Old North State young Plato Durham and William A. Graham resolutely opposed the universal manhood suffrage movement. Durham went so far as to press the issue by early presenting resolutions which stated that any attempt to abolish or abridge the natural distinction between the white and black race would be a crime against civilization and God. The resolutions were immediately tabled, but the able young Confederate veterans, who continued to harass the exponents of universal manhood suffrage for the remainder of the session, were able to define the position of the Conservatives in a minority report of the committee on suffrage. "We do not regard the right to vote as natural or inherent, but constitutional merely—to be regulated in such way as will best promote the welfare of the whole community." Durham and Graham condemned the whole scheme of universal manhood suffrage

> as intended to advance party purposes, in the expectation that the States of the South being Africanized and Radicalized may more than counterbalance the loss of electoral votes . . . in other sections of the Union.[33]

Attempts to limit Negro suffrage in this manner proved futile, and the sections of the new constitutions dealing with the franchise all embodied the principle of universal manhood suffrage. Radicals in the Virginia, North Carolina, and Georgia conventions sought to restrict the franchise of former rebels, but only Virginia placed restrictions on former Southern leaders, and this was done over the bitter opposition of some of the leading carpetbaggers and against the advice of General John M.

[31] *House Misc. Docs.*, 40 Cong., 2 Sess., No. 109; Daniel Richards to Washburne, May 25, 1868, in Washburne Papers; Davis, *Civil War and Reconstruction in Florida*, 511–12. Before the Civil War, the Florida constitution had been more democratic in respect to representation than the other South Atlantic states. The constitution of 1838 had provided for apportionment in both houses on the basis of federal enumeration. Thorpe (ed.), *Federal and State Constitutions*, II, 676.

[32] *Ibid.*, 826–28. C. C. Richardson, a Georgia carpetbagger, severely condemned the apportionment devised by the convention as "the superstructure of an aristocracy . . . which has so riveted the shackles of legislation upon the mass of the people as to keep them bound in the almost hopeless chains of poverty, degradation, and ruin, and who now tenaciously cling to their Bourbon idea, and refuse to release their unscrupulous grasp upon the rights of the people." *Journal of the Constitutional Convention of Georgia, 1868*, 130.

[33] Salisbury *Old North State*, February 8, 1868; *Journal of the Constitutional Convention of North Carolina, 1868*, 32–33, 233–38. The principle of Negro suffrage was the only issue involved; all of the South Atlantic states had adopted white manhood suffrage before the Civil War.

Schofield.[34] Several of the South Carolina carpetbaggers favored the imposition of a poll tax as a requirement for voting in order to "instill into the minds and hearts of the people the sacredness of the ballot-box," and one South Carolina report on suffrage would have required after 1875 an ability to read and write as a requirement for voting. But the ideal of universal manhood suffrage exercised too great a hold on the minds of the delegates to allow any limitation on the right to vote.[35] With the exception of Virginia, all of the South Atlantic states extended the ballot to all males over twenty-one, born or naturalized in the United States, who had resided in their state for one year (six months in the case of Georgia); and all the constitutions except those of Georgia and Florida guaranteed qualified electors the right to hold a state office.[36]

Conservative delegates in the three conventions securely under carpetbagger domination were powerless to stop the changes instituted by the Northern "adventurers," but they persisted in offering amendments supporting the "white supremacy" position and used the debates on the convention floors to appeal to native whites and arouse their fear of Negro supremacy. William A. Graham, for instance, attempted to secure passage of an amendment to the section on militia providing that no white North Carolinian would have to serve with a Negro or ever obey an order from a Negro. Young Plato Durham was more extreme in his demands that no Negro or anyone with Negro blood ever be eligible for the office of governor, lieutenant governor, or any other executive office, and that intermarriage between the "Caucasian and African races" be prohibited.[37]

As has been seen, in the two states of Georgia and Florida where carpetbagger influence proved less effective and native white Conservatives or groups co-operating with them controlled the conventions, the resulting constitutions were relatively conservative. The apportionment of seats in the legislature assured continued white domination of the General Assembly, and the broad appointive power of the governor and legislature in each state, even on the local level, made for centralization of

[34] J. E. Bryant, Georgia carpetbagger, advocated that those persons disqualified by the Fourteenth Amendment or by the Reconstruction Acts be disfranchised, with the added provision that these disabilities not extend beyond January 1, 1869, *i.e.*, that they apply only for the first elections a provision already incorporated in the second Reconstruction Act. *Journal of the Constitutional Convention of Georgia, 1868,* 148–50. Virginia carpetbagger Edgar Allen warned the convention that it was being misled; and Negro carpetbag leader Thomas Bayne offered a resolution exempting all persons who were disfranchised from the payment of taxes. John C. Underwood also supported the move to give the franchise to all citizens of the state. Other Radicals, however, were conferring with congressional Republicans as to the advisability of further disfranchisement of rebels. Richmond *Whig,* April 18, 1868; Richard Lee Morton, *The Negro in Virginia Politics, 1865–1902* (1919), 58; *Journal of the Constitutional Convention of Virginia, 1868,* 40, 90; J. W. D. Bland to Washburne, March 15, 1868, in Washburne Papers.

[35] *Proceedings of the Constitutional Convention of South Carolina, 1868,* 724–26.

[36] North Carolina excepted from office those electors who denied the existence of God, those convicted of treason, felony, perjury, or an infamous crime (unless pardoned) or of corruption or malpractice in office. Thorpe (ed.), *Federal and State Constitutions,* V, 2814–15 (N. C., 1868, Art. VI, Sec. 5).

[37] *Journal of the Constitutional Convention of North Carolina, 1868,* 162–63, 175, 216; Raleigh *Daily Sentinel,* February 17, 1868. Although these amendments called forth the scorn of the Republicans, on the day before adjournment the convention accepted a Negro delegate's resolution declaring it to be the sense of the convention that intermarriage and illicit intercourse between the races should be discountenanced and that separate schools should be established for whites and Negroes. *Journal of the Constitutional Convention of North Carolina, 1868,* 473.

power.[38] As long as the whites held the office of governor, they could effectively deprive the Negroes of any real share in state government. The constitutions of Georgia and Florida attest to the considerable confidence of the Conservatives in their ability to carry the forthcoming elections inasmuch as the technique could work in reverse if the Radicals captured control of the executive. The Florida constitution, even more clearly than that of Georgia, bears the stamp of Conservative influence. Some liberal constitutional reform was desired by Conservatives or Democrats in both states, but the Negro issue brought about a coalition of Conservative Republicans and former Democrats and Whigs dedicated to the maintenance of white supremacy at all costs.

Even so, constitutional changes adopted by the Reconstruction conventions of 1867–1868 made a sweeping extension of political democracy in the South Atlantic states. Except for the changed status of the Negro, the innovations represented reforms long sought and so designed to capture the support of a large number of Southern whites as well as the large new bloc of Negro voters. During the course of the ante bellum period the poorer classes of Southern whites had successfully fought for an extension of the franchise to all white adult males and, with less success, for equal opportunities of officeholding. The imposition of Congressional Reconstruction extended the sphere of democracy still further by according the franchise, and generally the right to hold office, to all adult men, including the Negro,[39] and by retaining and enlarging the principles of earlier bills of rights. The constitutional conventions of Virginia, North and South Carolina based apportionment of representation upon population for the first time, extended popular control of local government, and made most offices, both state and local, elective rather than appointive.

The carpetbagger who successfully championed political democracy revealed no such enthusiasm for extending economic democracy. The Northern settlers in the South, whose respect for property rights precluded an extensive program of debt repudiation or property confiscation, seemed to have been convinced that the same industry and commerce which had transformed the North would revolutionize the South. One carpetbagger expressed his confidence that "the plaster of profit laid upon the sores of war would work a miraculous cure." [40] Whenever Negro spokesmen did display a desire for radical economic measures, property-conscious Northerners and Southerners combined to block them.

The success of the Republicans in the South depended upon the adoption of major political changes, for without guarantees of continued political democracy the basis of Radical strength would be undermined; and Northern immigrants, the carpetbaggers, took the lead in providing for the South a democratic political structure. But time demonstrated that democratic institutions, too, were capable of manipulation.

[38] *Journal of the Constitutional Convention of Georgia, 1868,* 551, 554, 556; Thorpe (ed.), *Federal and State Constitutions,* II, 712 (Fla., Art. VI, Secs. 17–19). The only county position made elective was that of constable. *Ibid.,* 709 (Fla., Art. V, Sec. 26).

[39] The Virginia provision limiting the vote was eliminated from the constitution in the ratification election which allowed a separate vote on this issue.

[40] Albion W. Tourgée, *An Appeal to Caesar* (New York, 1884), 58.

24 / The President Declares War

LaWanda and John H. Cox

Negro aspirations, white prejudice and idealism, interest-group pressures, party needs—all of these "forces" and others shaped the course of Reconstruction. But so did the personalities and idiosyncrasies of strategically placed men. The Radical leaders, Senator Charles Sumner, Representative Thaddeus Stevens, Senator Benjamin Wade, Zachariah Chandler, and others, were influential figures in the sectional readjustment. But it was the personality of Andrew Johnson, President of the United States by the grace of John Wilkes Booth, that most emphatically affected Reconstruction politics.

An older view of Johnson absolved him of blame for the political turmoil that occurred after 1865. According to this interpretation, the vindictive, short-sighted, ambitious, and intensely partisan Radicals successfully defied the wise and compassionate President and defeated every one of his measures to restore the Union as quickly and as amicably as possible. In this view, Johnson was a tragic hero who did his duty but was powerless to avoid national catastrophe. A worthy successor to the Great Emancipator, he wished nothing but good for his country, but proved unable to defeat the selfish and narrow aims of the "vindictives."

According to recent historians, the President was neither innocent nor the blameless victim of unprovoked attack. He failed because of his own ineptitude, irascibility, and stubbornness, and his own foolish and unrealistic ambitions. Johnson, according to Eric McKitrick, threw away the opportunity to lead the country in Reconstruction by his failure to understand legitimate Northern demands on the South, and by his fatuous susceptibility to flattery by Southern aristocrats who won his favor. Added to this was an obstinacy, a defensiveness, and at the same time a self-righteousness that irritated, confused, and offended others. McKitrick concedes that Johnson was a competent administrator and a courageous and well-meaning man; but he was also, he insists, a leader of monumental political ineptitude and insensitivity who helped create intransigence and "extremism" in his opponents.

The portrait of Johnson that emerges from the work of John and LaWanda Cox is still more astringent. In their book *Politics, Principle and Prejudice*, Johnson is not only inept and difficult; he is also bigoted and self-seeking. A

Politics, Principle and Prejudice, 1865–1866: Dilemma of Reconstruction America (New York: The Free Press of Glencoe, 1963). Reprinted by permission.

man of the yeoman South, the President possessed all of the racial prejudices of his class. White racism was pervasive in nineteenth-century America, but according to the Coxes, Johnson as President expressed his views with brutal frankness and, more important, allowed his attitudes to cloud his judgment of the political realities and to deny the black man's claims of common humanity.

In addition to Johnson's bigotry there was his political ambition. The Coxes argue that Johnson was intent on reviving the Democratic Party, the party he had joined at the outset of his public career, by uniting conservative Republicans and Unionists behind his leadership. The Radicals could not ignore such a challenge and fought Johnson in order to survive. In the end, the "sustained and open warfare" between the President and the Republican majority in Congress was Johnson's own doing, they insist, and he deserves little sympathy from us.

For further reading: *Eric McKitrick, *Andrew Johnson and Reconstruction* (Chicago, Ill.: University of Chicago Press); *W. R. Brock, *An American Crisis: Congress and Reconstruction, 1865–1867* (New York: Harper Torchbooks, 1966); *Fawn M. Brodie, *Thaddeus Stevens: Scourge of the South* (New York: The Norton Library, 1966); Howard K. Beale, *The Critical Year: A Study of Andrew Johnson and Reconstruction* (New York: Harcourt, Brace & World, Inc., 1930); George F. Milton, *The Age of Hate: Andrew Johnson and the Radicals* (New York: Coward-McCann, Inc., 1930); *William A. Dunning, *Reconstruction, Political and Economic, 1865–1877* (New York: Harper & Row, Publishers, 1907).

"The fight is on!" This was the jubilant announcement sent by Samuel S. Cox, Democratic leader in the House of Representatives, to Manton Marble on the day following Johnson's veto of the Freedmen's Bureau Bill. "He [Johnson] is in great earnest. I am sure," Cox further advised the editor of the most influential Democratic paper in the nation, "that you cannot say too much now tho I have been very wary." [1] North and South and West, the Democracy rejoiced and prepared for battle under Johnson's banner. Moderate men in the Union-Republican ranks were confused and dismayed. "We had . . . a veto yesterday," the conciliatory Henry L. Dawes of Massachusetts wrote home to his wife. "Everything looks very dark and what is before us cannot well be seen." [2] And two days later he added, "The veto has made Congress very furious—and the war has begun which *can* end only in general ruin of the party." [3] Those who could not, or would not, recognize a second Sumter were soon shaken by the reverberation of further blasts—Johnson's February 22 speech and his March veto of the Civil Rights Bill. The second veto, the *Herald* trumpeted, "is in fact an emphatic declaration of war against the radicals. . . . The veto of the Freedmen's Bureau bill was but the distant thunder announcing the approaching storm. This veto is the storm itself. . . . It is a declaration of war

[1] Cox to Marble, Feb. 20, 1866, Marble MSS.
[2] Dawes to wife, Feb. 20, 1866, Henry L. Dawes MSS, Library of Congress.
[3] *Ibid.*, Feb. 22, 1866.

against the radicals and their impracticable schemes, and Andrew Johnson, as in the rebellion, is the man to fight it through on his platform of the Union and the Constitution." [4] One Democratic paper greeted the Freedmen's veto as: [5]

GLORIOUS NEWS   PRESIDENT JOHNSON
THROWS HOT SHELL IN THE ABOLITION CAMP! !
THE FIRST GUN! !   LET HER BLAZE!

The war which President Johnson declared in February and March of 1866 brought to a climax the long-standing design to force the Radicals out of the Union-Republican party and inaugurate a reorganization of national parties. Much of the pressure for an assault upon the Radicals came from the Democrats, both the "regulars," who had opposed the war, and the War Democrats who had wholeheartedly supported the national effort. It is difficult to determine the exact expectation of the former group in their support of Johnson and their attack upon the Radicals. Some of their number clearly welcomed the prospect of a new Johnson party which would purge them of any guilt of association with the peace plank of the wartime Democracy. For them, the issue was the extent to which they would be able to control the new party. Others sought merely to split the Union-Republican ranks into an ineffectual opposition, regain political ascendancy with the support of a restored South, and use the presidential influence for their own party advantage. This use of Johnson's prestige and power might, or might not, include a tacit understanding that he would be offered the Democratic nomination for the Presidency in 1868. Others hedged, waiting upon events to decide whether they would transfer allegiance to a new Union party or gather up dissident Republicans into the old organization of the Democracy. Individual Democrats shifted from one expectation to another with the changing currents of the political scene. Both "regulars" and War Democrats, and Conservative Republicans as well, sought for themselves a central role of power in postwar politics.

The drive to isolate the Radicals had gained momentum since the convening of Congress. Even as that body assembled for its first session since victory, Democrats were scheming to "precipitate the fight with the Radicals." An intimate was informing Marble, the World's editor, that "I have inspired Cox to set things in train (if he can do it so covertly as not to seem officious) for launching some sort of thunderbolt immediately on the reading of the message to set the Radicals on fire and kindle a conflagration. . . . I hope a fight may be brought on in such a way that only the Radicals may take part against us. If the President will give us a good pretext for fighting the Radicals under *his* banner, we can get them wild, widen the breach by an exciting debate, and all will come out right." [6] The wartime Democratic governor of New York, Horatio Seymour, was soon advising Montgomery Blair that the "President must strike" at the Radicals. [7] Through the correspondence and comment respecting the long, sharp contest over the appointment to the vacant New York collectorship there flowed a pervasive expectation of impending political realignments

[4] New York *Herald*, March 28, 1866.

[5] Columbia [Penna.] Democrat, clippings on Freedmen's Bureau veto, Scrapbook, Johnson MSS.

[6] "J. C." to Marble, Dec. 2, 1865, Marble MSS.

[7] Seymour to Blair, Jan. 3, 1866, Blair MSS.

in which the winner of that patronage plum would be expected to play a key role.[8]

As the weeks passed, Democrats, and even some Union men ready to join forces with them under Johnson's leadership, grew restive. "Action is what the Democratic party requires from the President before putting its entire faith in him," read an editorial of the Newton, New Jersey, *Herald and Democrat,* "and any new party got up to sustain him, must show that his *actions* sustain his sentiments. A veto on any of the unconstitutional acts of the present congress would be vastly more effectual than all the addresses he has ever made since he became President." [9] Lewis D. Campbell, Johnson's Whig-Republican political lieutenant, wrote from Ohio that "the sooner you cut yourself loose from them [the Radicals] the better for you and for the country." [10] What was needed, in Campbell's view, was the organization of a party on the basis of the President's policy. "The *Union party* as an organization is rapidly going under. *Burnt brandy* won't save it. . . . He [Johnson] must sooner or later accept the *fact* that the great Union party has fulfilled its mission." [11] By the end of January, the Springfield *Republican*'s Washington correspondent was reporting that the President and Senator Dixon of Connecticut "have gone into a scheme to smash up the radicals . . . and to prepare the way for the great Johnson party which (according to Doolittle, Cowan and others) is to grow out of the ruins of the present two political organizations." [12] The *National Intelligencer,* which was already beginning to be recognized as spokesman for the Administration,[13] commented four days before the veto that the day was "not now distant" when a spontaneous movement of the people in behalf of the President might lead to "A JOHNSON PARTY." [14] The *World*'s position was more ambiguous, but left the door open for such a development. While ridiculing Bennett's call for a new Johnson party and joyfully citing past election figures to support the contention that the Democracy, the "Party of the Past," would be the "Party of the Future," the *World*'s editor also praised Johnson's fitness "for the double work of a disintegrator and a reorganizer." The President was "the nucleus around which the party of the future is to crystallize," since he enjoyed "contact and sympathy with all that is sound and healthy in every considerable party." [15]

Two days before the final passage of the Freedmen's Bureau Bill, John Cochrane, War Democrat of New York, wrote the President that the Democratic masses were "restlessly expectant of the period when an overt act by you, in resistance of systematic Congressional encroachment, shall enable them to muster into your service." [16] Two days after the passage of the bill, Edward Bates, Lincoln's conservative Attorney General, sent off a long letter denouncing the intended extension of the Freedmen's Bureau jurisdiction and reassuring the President that in a split between the Administration and the Radicals the latter would be "trodden out like so many sparks on the floor." [17] A Democratic leader in Pennsylvania, eager to secure an endorsement

[8] *See above,* Chapter 4.
[9] Enclosed in M. Ryerson to Seward, Feb. 15, 1866, Seward MSS.
[10] Campbell to Johnson, Jan. 19, 1866, Johnson MSS.
[11] Campbell to D. L. Patterson, Jan. 22, 1866, *ibid.*
[12] Springfield *Republican,* Feb. 2, 1866.
[13] Chicago *Tribune,* Feb. 13, 1866; S. S. Cox to Marble, Feb. 20, 1866, Marble MSS.
[14] Washington *National Intelligencer,* Feb. 15, 1866.
[15] New York *World,* Feb. 12, 1866, Jan. 25, 1866.
[16] Cochrane to Johnson, Feb. 4, 1866, Johnson MSS.
[17] Bates to Johnson, Feb. 10, 1866, *ibid.*

of the President at the approaching state Democratic convention, damned the Freedmen's Bureau Bill and sent word that "Considerations of this kind weigh with our
Delegates. . . . I hope you will veto that Freedmans Bill." [18]

John Cochrane may not have anticipated that the "signal" so eagerly awaited
would be the veto of the Freedmen's measure, for he had counseled that in any
conflict there should be not "even the colour of an inference that your line of policy
is unfriendly to the negro." [19] All was in readiness, however, whatever might be the
"overt act," particularly in the key political state of New York. There Cochrane was
ardently engaged in consultations with Dean Richmond, the upstate Democratic
boss, with Bennett of the *Herald,* and with General J. B. Steedman of Ohio, one of
Johnson's most trusted military politicos. Dean Richmond, Cochrane reported, was
awaiting developments in Washington and wanted the President to know that whenever he was in a position to accept the cooperation of his Democratic friends, support
would "not be delayed." Bennett was urging the feasibility and importance of "a
coalition between the moderate Republicans and the loyal Democrats." General Steedman had promised to confer with the President "upon the propriety of holding a
large meeting here in behalf of your policy and to write me the result. Whenever
you think it seasonable you must be aware that a formidable demonstration can be
made." [20] Cochrane and Bennett held that pro-Johnson voters, rank-and-file Democrats,
and Union men—mostly former Democrats—would have a preponderance of 50,000
in New York and a proportional majority in the central and northwestern states, and
that the "logical sequence" of their organization would be the "reproduction of your
power in 1868." [21]

The anticipated "signal" may have been the ousting of Secretary Stanton from
the Cabinet and his replacement by General Steedman as Secretary of War. Within a
week, at the end of January and the beginning of February, letters of recommendation
for General Steedman reached the President from Dean Richmond, Samuel J. Tilden,
George H. Pendleton of Ohio, Horace Greeley, and Augustus Schell, the affluent
and influential brother of Seward's friend Richard Schell.[22] A change in the post of
Secretary of War could have signaled a new direction not only in respect to personalities and patronage but also in regard to the role of the army and the Freedmen's
Bureau in the still-occupied South; for the Secretary's office held a large measure of
influence over the conduct of those arms of the national government. Rumors of
Stanton's exit from the Cabinet, however, proved premature, probably in large part
because he had powerful support from the Seward-Weed forces.[23] Another possibility
to which some Johnson men looked hopefully as the cleaver by which the Radicals
could be severed from the Union ranks was the bill passed by the House, but later
buried in the Senate, to extend suffrage to Negroes in the District of Columbia.[24]
The issue of Negro suffrage would have afforded to Conservatives a tactical advan-

---

[18] J. H. Brinton to Johnson, enclosed in Brinton to T. B. Florence, Feb. 14, 1866, *ibid.*

[19] Cochrane to Johnson, Jan. 23, 1866, *ibid.*

[20] *Ibid.*

[21] Cochrane to Johnson, Feb. 4, 1866, Bennett to Johnson, Feb. 1, 1866, *ibid.*

[22] Letters to Johnson from Greeley, Jan. 28, 1866, Pendleton, Jan. 28, 1866, Richmond, Jan. 31,
1866, Tilden, Feb. 1, 1866, Schell, Feb. 2, 1866, *ibid.*

[23] New York *Times,* Feb. 6, 1866.

[24] B. Rush to Johnson, Jan. 20, 1866; Cochrane to Johnson, Jan. 23, 1866; Memorial from
Hamilton, Ohio, Jan. 23, 1866; W. Patton to Johnson, Jan. 30, 1866, Johnson MSS.

tage. Johnson was ready to veto the District of Columbia bill had it passed the Senate.[25]

In contrast, a veto of the Freedmen's Bureau Bill held certain disadvantages. The bill was identified not with the Radicals, but with the moderate leadership in Congress, and it enjoyed overwhelming support among Republicans in and out of Congress. Rumors of an impending veto alarmed Republicans friendly to the President. They feared such action would be received as an indication that the Administration was not determined to protect the Negro, and they saw in it a potential rupture between the President and the Union party which would disastrously shatter the latter.[26] On the other hand, unlike the question of suffrage in an area clearly under congressional jurisdiction, the freedmen's bill afforded an opportunity for a direct statement on Reconstruction policy. In addition, a veto of the measure would allay the bitter resentment of the Bureau in the South and the stock Democratic complaint in the North against the "unconstitutional" interference of the military in civil affairs. The leading Democratic organ, the *World*, had denounced the Bureau bill in a comprehensive indictment; and not one Democrat had voted for the measure in either the Senate or the House.[27] The veto also gave Johnson an opportunity to flatter James Gordon Bennett, whose editorials were belaboring the bill and calling for a Presidential veto.[28] When the President's message was released, a telegram went from the White House to James Gordon Bennett, Jr.: "Your Saturday's article in reference to the Freedmen's Bureau Bill is highly approved. Veto message has just gone in." [29]

The Tennessee President was particularly sensitive to opinion and pressures from the border states, and letters that reached his desk during January and February made their demands articulate and unmistakable. They wanted an end to the Freedmen's Bureau, to military jurisdiction, and to the suspension of *habeas corpus*. The governor of Kentucky threatened that unless the Bureau "be taken away" he himself would take the lead in compelling the Negro to leave Kentucky or starve. His threat was to convene the state assembly and procure an act making it a crime for any white person to lease or rent lands or houses or to employ in any way any Negro or mulatto.[30] Johnson undoubtedly knew, without waiting to be told, that his support in the border states would be in jeopardy unless he took some step toward removing the Freedmen's Bureau and restoring *habeas corpus*. "I say to you frankly if that is not done," wrote a Kentucky state senator, "you will not get a cordial endorsement from Kentucky." [31] A few days later his belligerent admonisher hailed the veto message "with infinite satisfaction and approval." [32]

[25] P. Ripley to Marble, Feb. 8, 1866, Marble MSS.

[26] T. T. Davis to Johnson, Feb. 17, 1866, Johnson MSS; M. Ryerson to Seward, Feb. 15, 1866, Seward MSS.

[27] New York *World*, Jan. 29, 1866.

[28] New York *Herald*, Feb. 17, 1866.

[29] W. Rives (of the President's staff) to J. G. Bennett, Jr., Feb. 19, 1866, Johnson MSS.

[30] T. E. Bramlette to Johnson, Feb. 12, 1866; *see also* letters to Johnson from J. Hughes, Jan. 17, 1866, L. H. Rousseau, Jan. 17, 1866, A. G. Hodges, Jan. 20, 1866, J. W. Graham, Feb. 6, 1866, C. O. Faxon, Feb. 17, 1866, and Johnson to Hughes, Jan. 19, 1866, *ibid.*

[31] J. L. Helm to Johnson, Feb. 17, 1866; *see also* W. Dudley to M. Blair, Feb. 19, 1866, *ibid.*

[32] J. L. Helm to Johnson, Feb. 20, 1866, *ibid.* For an examination of charges against the Bureau and of the reasons for southern hostility, see John and LaWanda Cox, "General O. O. Howard and the 'Misrepresented Bureau,'" *Journal of Southern History*, XIX (Nov., 1953), pp. 427–56.

The President was well aware that the Bureau was as unpopular in the deep South as in the border states. He had been for some time under much pressure from leading men of South Carolina who were hostile to the Bureau and the provisions of the new bill, particularly those in respect to the Sea Island lands.[33] Benjamin F. Perry, Johnson's provisional governor and now senator-elect from South Carolina, made clear the Southern position toward the Bureau bill in a letter to the *National Intelligencer*. Trumbull's bill was "a monstrous injustice to the planter," a "demoralizing influence on the freedman," "ruinous" to the culture of Sea Island cotton, a startling extravagance that would tax the poor white men of the North "to support the vicious and vagrant Southern negro." Perry returned from Washington with confidence that Southern representatives would soon be admitted and that "the radicals will be utterly defeated and routed." [34] Just prior to the veto, Southerners were cheered by a series of reports that the President was holding firm against any congressional requirements preliminary to admission of their representatives; and they were anticipating "an approaching crisis." [35]

Despite much speculation by contemporaries and historians, it is extremely unlikely that Johnson experienced any real indecision as to his course once the Freedmen's Bureau Bill had reached his desk. Two days after the passage of the measure, and eleven days before the veto message, "the clerks & so on, down in the Executive office" were "unanimous . . . in declaring that Johnson will veto the Freedmen's Bureau Bill." [36] Among the Presidential manuscripts there have been preserved six working papers for the message. All are arguments *against* the bill, apparently solicited by the President.[37] There exists in the Johnson Papers not one such brief in support of the measure. The contention that the veto was a last-minute decision dependent upon the action of the Joint Committee on Reconstruction in respect to Tennessee has been convincingly refuted by Eric McKitrick.[38] Johnson's action has also been attributed to irate reaction to Radical provocation, such as the remarks of Stevens, Sumner, and Wendell Phillips. Such a hypothesis ignores too many aspects of the contemporary scene—the plans for party reorganization, the pressures upon Johnson for some such action as the veto, the moderate rather than Radical sponsorship of the bill, and the large measure of deference and concession which most Republicans in and out of Congress still offered the President. Sumner and Stevens, let alone Wendell Phillips—with their sharp words and their desires for Negro suffrage, confiscation, and prolonged territorial status for the South—did not speak for the congressional majority. And it was the congressional majority that had spoken for the freedmen's bill. Clearly, Presidential hostility to the extreme Radicals cannot alone explain the veto. Neither can it be attributed solely to Johnson's constitutional principles, for they were not so consistent and sharply defined as to constitute a compelling necessity for so sweeping a rejection of the bill.[39] The weight of evidence, including a comparison of the final message with the drafts from which it was prepared, indicates

[33] Columbus [Ga.] *Sun*, Feb. 9, 1866, quoting letter of Governor J. L. Orr of South Carolina to the President, Jan. 19, 1866.

[34] Columbia [S.C.] *Phoenix*, Feb. 25, 1866, with letter of Perry, Feb. 16, 1866.

[35] Columbus [Ga.] *Sun*, Jan. 10, 1866, Feb. 1, 2, 11, 1866, with quotations from Chicago *Tribune*, Cincinnati *Gazette*, Macon *Telegram*, and Philadelphia *Ledger*, respectively.

[36] P. Ripley to Marble, Feb. 8, 1866, Marble MSS.

[37] Cox, "Andrew Johnson and His Ghost Writers," pp. 462–65.

[38] *Andrew Johnson and Reconstruction*, pp. 285–87.

[39] *See above*, Chapter 5, footnotes 55 and 56.

that Johnson's first veto represented a considered decision. In view of the letters that had crossed his desk and the comments of the press, it was a decision Johnson could not possibly have made without giving thought to its political impact. It would strengthen his ties with the Northern Democracy and the South, force an issue with those of the Republicans whom he considered his opponents, and signal the beginning of a major political realignment under his leadership.

William H. Seward's role in the veto message is of particular interest in view of his pre-eminent position in Johnson's official family, his early identification with a generous policy toward the South, and his long-standing interest in a reorganization of parties. The Secretary's policy of refraining from political comment in his personal letters[40] sorely handicaps the inquiring historian. We know that Seward supported the veto in Cabinet meeting,[41] and that he later defended it skillfully in an effective public appearance in New York City. These facts reveal little. Fortunately, there is another source of information—Seward's own draft for the veto message. This paper, and other Seward draft messages, have long been available in the Johnson manuscripts at the Library of Congress, but their authorship was unknown. The type of paper used and the characteristic manner of writing on alternate lines were the identifying clues.[42] It is unlikely that Seward composed his draft for the veto, which is written in the presidential first person, without prior consultation with the President; hence we cannot be certain whether Seward advised that the measure be rejected, or simply acquiesced in Johnson's decision. There is much, however, that Seward's version does reveal.

Seward's central argument was that the enlargement and extension of the Bureau at that time was unnecessary, although he acknowledged that future developments might require additional legislation to prolong the Bureau. He interpreted the existing law as maintaining the Bureau in force until a full year after a formal declaration of peace, an announcement which had not yet been made, and expressed hope that by the end of that year the necessity for the Bureau would have ceased. Seward made little use of any other argument against the bill, though in passing he gently criticized its extension of the Bureau both as to time, which he considered indefinite, and as to jurisdiction, which included all parts of the United States containing refugees and freedmen. He also pointed out that martial law and military tribunals should be used only on occasion of absolute necessity and that the fiscal condition of the country required "so far as possible" severe retrenchment. He had kind words for the Bureau, making reference to its "beneficent operations" and the "care and fidelity" with which it had been administered.

Seward also raised the general problem of restoration. His draft expressed pleasure that the bill contemplated a full restoration of the several states. Here his reference was to the bill's provision for terminating Bureau jurisdiction over freedmen's civil rights in any state fully restored "in all its constitutional relations to the United States," and enjoying the unobstructed functioning of the civil courts. He added, however, that the bill was "vague and uncertain in defining the conditions which will be accepted as evidences of that full restoration," and continued:

[40] *See above,* Chapter 2, footnotes 17 and 18.

[41] *Diary of Gideon Welles,* II, p. 435.

[42] Cox, "Andrew Johnson and His Ghost Writers." Three of the other four drafts for the veto were identified as those of Secretary Welles, Senator Doolittle, and Senator Cowan.

It is hardly necessary for me to inform the Congress that in my own judgment most of those states so far at least as depends upon themselves have already been thus fully restored and are to be deemed as entitled to enjoy their constitutional rights as members of the Union. Since Congress now proposes to make so important a proceeding as the prolongation of the Freedmen's Bureau dependent upon a restoration in some sense which differs from the one entertained by the Executive Department it would seem to be important that Congress and the President should first agree upon what actually constitutes such restoration.

He ended the draft on a similar note:

Without trenching upon the province of Congress I may be permitted in explaining my own course on the present occasion to say that when a state at some previous time comes not only in an attitude of loyalty and harmony but in the persons of representatives whose loyalty cannot be questioned under any existing constitutional or legal test that in this case they have a claim to be heard in Congress especially in regard to projected laws which bear especially upon themselves.

In short, Seward's draft of the veto message both in referring to the bill itself and in stating the Presidential theory of restoration was gentle and conciliatory. Unlike the official message, it did not make a slashing indictment of the military jurisdiction through which the Bureau was to operate in the future, as it had in the past, to protect the civil rights of freedmen whenever they were discriminated against by "local law, custom, or prejudice." Unlike the official message, it did not criticize the bill for providing relief for destitute freedmen and lands for the building of asylums and schools and for rental to those who could not find employment. Neither did it object to the provision that freedmen holding lands under Sherman's order on the Sea Islands be confirmed in their possession for three years, with the proviso that any such land could earlier be restored to its original owner if the Bureaus' commissioner procured for the freedmen occupants, with their written consent, other lands for rental or purchase. Nor did Seward's draft imply, as did the President's official message, that special protection for the newly freed Negro was in effect discrimination against white men.

A comparable divergence between Seward's approach and that of the President is apparent in the references to Congress and the restoration process. That part of the official message incorporated much of Seward's wording but changed the order and emphasis, omitted phrases, and added comments. The result was a virtual Presidential fiat to Congress. The right of each house to judge the qualifications of its members, read a critically important sentence, "cannot be construed as including the right to shut out, in time of peace, any State from the representation to which it is entitled by the Constitution." [43] Because the President was chosen by all the states, Johnson asserted that he as President stood in a different relationship to the country than did any member of Congress; it was his duty to present the "just claims" of the eleven states not represented in either House of Congress. He closed the message with what was in effect a challenge to Congress to submit the issues he had raised to the "enlightened public judgment" of the people.

Seward's draft for the veto was a statement to which the moderates of the Republican party, and even many men known as Radicals, might have accommodated

[43] McPherson, *Political Manual for 1866*, p. 71.

without too much strain. Johnson's veto included a few passages that could be interpreted as conciliatory if taken out of the context of the message as a whole, but in essence it did not invite Congress to negotiate but defied Congress to act. The message still held a measure of that ambiguity so characteristic of Johnson's actions and statements during the previous months, but only a small measure.[44] To most Democrats and Radicals who were his contemporaries, and to historians who look back upon the course of events, the ambiguity was resolved. Only Republicans who were moderate and trusting, timid or self-interested, or more Democrat than Republican in their view of race and their attitude toward states' rights and Federal power —only such men clung to the illusions with which the President's December message had been so generally and hopefully received. The surprising fact is that their number was considerable. Seward's influence was in part responsible, for he publicly interpreted the President's veto in the spirit of the one which he had written and would doubtless have preferred.

It is evident from Seward's draft that the Secretary had some share of responsibility for the veto of the Freedmen's Bureau Bill. Also, this document confirms what would seem apparent from his earlier and later public statements and action: namely, that Seward wished the rebellious states to be promptly readmitted to their old seats in Congress in keeping with his wartime contention that the government had no intent to "subjugate" them, but only to restore the Union.[45] In this essential commitment to a policy of speedy reunion and reconciliation, Seward's position coincided with that of the Democracy. In other respects, however, his arguments in the draft message conceded little to Democratic contentions and attitudes. We can be certain, in view of the political activities of Thurlow Weed, that Seward and his political manager were still planning a reorganization of parties; we cannot be equally certain that they welcomed a veto of the freedmen's bill as the starting signal for realignment. If such were the case, Seward clearly did not wish that signal to carry the boom and destruction of cannon fire in defense of the entrenched positions of the old Democracy.

Andrew Johnson, in contrast, went far toward accepting and defending the position of the Democrats. He did not, it is true, go so far as to voice the Democratic argument that any federal action on behalf of the freedmen by the Federal Government was an invasion of state and local rights. The common ground which he, but not Seward, held with the Democracy was of considerable extent. It is evident in the following aspects of the official message: the sweeping nature of the condemnation of the bill and by implication of the Bureau itself; the omission of any kindly word for the Bureau or of any assurance of its continuation; the emphasis upon violation of the constitutional rights of white men by the Bureaus' jurisdiction over cases involving discrimination to Negroes; the argument that a federal "system of support of indigent persons" was contrary to the Constitution; the contention that the message would keep the freedmen in a state of expectant restlessness; the assurance that the Negro could protect himself because his labor was necessary to the Southern economy; the censure of the Sea Island provisions as a violation of the property rights of Southern owners; the stress upon the immense Federal patronage and expense that

---

[44] Johnson's treatment of the civil rights-states' rights issue was evasive. See Cox, "Andrew Johnson and His Ghost Writers," pp. 466–67.

[45] After military defeat, Seward expected that in reponse to a judicious policy of mingled pressure and persuasion the rebel states would return to a genuine allegiance to the Union. *Mr. Seward at Auburn in 1865,* p. 7.

the bill allegedly would make mandatory; and lastly, the oblique appeal to race prejudice.

The President's veto was greeted by a series of "spontaneous" demonstrations, mass meetings, and resolutions of support and approval. The 22nd of February, Washington's birthday and a holiday, resounded with the firing of cannon and the oratory of prominent public figures celebrating the "patriotic and statesmanlike act of the present chief executive." [46] The largest, noisiest, and most successful of these meetings was held in New York's Cooper Institute, and it was Secretary Seward's show. Thousands were reportedly unable to find room within the hall, and minor orators were hurriedly enlisted to entertain the crowds outside the building. Within, the hall was gay with patriotic decorations, music, and a huge portrait of Andrew Johnson. Making his first public appearance in New York since the assassination attempt upon his life, Seward in his entrance upon the stage was "greeted with the most rapturous applause, the whole house rising and cheering vociferously." [47] The "eloquent scar" across his cheek, the "broken voice," added to the drama of the old Republican's appearance to explain and support Johnson's action. He spoke leaning with his left arm and his body against the rostrum, yet his delivery was reported as reaching at times as high a "pitch of animation and vigor" as ever it had shown in the prewar years.[48]

Seward assumed a light touch in his oratory, evoking laughter by his sallies, reassuring his audience that "There are no dangers, there are no perils, there is no occasion for alarm." The country was safe, the difference between Congress and the President was only a "dispute between the pilots," all honest, all well meaning, all seeking the same port. President and Congress agreed that the freedmen could not be abandoned during the transition from war to peace. The President thinks the transition period is nearly ended, that there is no necessity for an indefinite extension of the Bureau; "for that reason" he vetoed the bill. Seward explained that the Bureau would continue under the original law for another year; if Congress then found it still needed, Congress could take "the necessary steps." The President ought not to be denounced, in the absence of any necessity, "for refusing to retain and exercise powers greater than those of any imperial magistrate in the world!" [49]

The meeting was page one news in the New York press, and most of the editorial comment was an enthusiastic endorsement. The chief voice of dissent came from the columns of Greeley's *Tribune*. It conceded that Seward's speech was "ingenious, and in some points able" but objected that Seward like the other speakers ignored the real questions in the controversy. These were two: whether the late rebel states had shown such signs of returning loyalty as to make it prudent to restore all their suspended rights; and whether the nation ought not to interpose "a fixed, absolute and impassable barrier" between the freed Negroes and "the few Southern Whites who seek to oppress them." [50] The *Herald*'s Friday treatment was warm, including pleasant references to the "distinguished" Secretary of State; its Saturday comments became critical of Seward's optimism, his "incapacity to practically comprehend the vital ques-

---

[46] New York *Daily News*, Feb. 23, 1866.

[47] *Ibid.*

[48] New York *Herald*, Feb. 23, 1866.

[49] *Mass Meeting of the Citizens of New York Held at the Cooper Institute, February 22d, 1866, to Approve the Principles Announced in the Message of Andrew Johnson, President of the United States* (pamphlet, New York, 1866), pp. 12–21.

[50] New York *Tribune*, Feb. 23, 1866.

tions which agitate the country." [51] The first reaction of the *World* to the triumphant performance of the man so long and bitterly assailed in its columns was caustic:[52]

> Secretary Seward's speech to the repentant Republicans at the Cooper Institute last night was pitched in the key of his famous ninety day prophecies.
>
> The Ship of State has out-breasted the storm and is now in the haven of rest. There is no cloud in the future; the Union is fully restored; it does not much matter whether Congress or the President prevail—all will come right in the end. In short, according to the Secretary—
>
> > Everything is lovely
> > And the goose hangs high
>
> The query is, if everything is so serene, why was the meeting held? and why did Mr. Seward come all the way from Washington to give it his countenance?

Seward was a "rose-water statesman"; "the greater affairs of the world are moved by the passions; but Mr. Seward is passionless, and therefore blind." Yet his speech would do great good, "not as he intends by uniting and reconciling, but by hastening the division and disintegration of the doomed Republican party." [53] On second thought, however, the *World* softened its tone and joined the general chorus of acclaim for the meeting. Seward had been speaking for readers in Europe, which was quite within his province; the point of the meeting was that the "respectable Republican gentlemen" who ran it "have *indorsed* [sic] Mr. Johnson in his fight with the Radicals in Congress . . . have proclaimed the present Congress to be a Rump Congress, and the Radicals . . . to be *Disunionists.*" The *World* would accept them, presumably even Seward, as "new recruits" and after their fortitude had been tested, even advance them "to the post of honor." [54]

Seward and Weed clearly had no intention of playing the role of penitent sinners turned novitiates under the rule of the *World*. They recognized, as Weed wrote Senator Morgan a few days after the meeting, that "We are in a crisis." [55] Both Weed and Wakeman, the Seward politico who held the office of surveyor of the port, had sent Seward urgent appeals to address the meeting. "It is deemed important that you should be present," wired Wakeman on the 19th.[56] "Can you come to our meeting," read Weed's telegram of the 20th; "I have reflected well and hope you can come." [57] "Our meeting" was designed not just to rally support for the President, but in the discreet words of the official call "to promote harmony in the public Councils of the Country." [58] It was Weed and Seward's most important public move to keep the pro-Johnson movement under their control; to do this, not only did they need to maintain some good Democratic contacts, but most importantly they also needed to retain a substantial following among *Republicans*. With Democrats pledging unqualified allegiance to the President, their leaders were in a position to assert authority as commanding generals. Seward and

[51] Compare New York *Herald* of Feb. 23, 1866, and Feb. 24, 1866.
[52] New York *World,* Feb. 23, 1866.
[53] *Ibid.,* Feb. 24, 1866.
[54] *Ibid.,* Feb. 26, 1866.
[55] Weed to Morgan, Feb. 26, 1866, Morgan MSS.
[56] Wakeman to Seward, Feb. 19, 1866, Seward MSS.
[57] Weed to Seward, Feb. 20, 1866, *ibid.*
[58] *Mass Meeting at Cooper Institute,* p. 3. An elaborately prepared copy of the call and the resolutions is also in the Johnson MSS under date of Feb. 28, 1866.

Weed had to assemble all the political strength they could rally to counter this danger and particularly "to promote harmony" in the Republican ranks.

The roster of vice presidents, officers, and speakers for the Cooper Institute meeting included not only Seward's faithful among the New York Republicans but also such leaders of the dissident faction as William C. Bryant, editor of the *Evening Post,* David Dudley Field, and George Opdyke. James Gordon Bennett was there also. Democrats were not excluded; Daniel S. Dickinson, prominent War Democrat, sent a letter which was read from the platform, and Francis B. Cutting, a prewar ultra-Southern Democrat who had supported Lincoln and the war effort, was permanent chairman of the meeting. Although there appeared nowhere in the proceedings the name either of Fernando Wood or of his brother Ben, editor of the *Daily News,* the enthusiastically warm response of the *News* to the meeting suggests that this extreme wing of the New York Democracy had not been overlooked by Weed and Wakeman in their preparations for the meeting. The roster, however, did not include the most prominent War Democrats such as Dix and Cochrane, nor did it contain the names of leaders among the regular Democrats such as Tilden and Barlow.

Preserved among the Seward papers is an anonymous printed lampoon of the meeting.[59] This opens with a scene in a back room at Washington, just before the veto, where Seward, Weed, and Richard Schell were planning the New York meeting. Weed urged the need to obtain strength from the Union War Democrats; Seward was made to reply:

> Yes, and they are ready to help us on; but you must remember that they may impress the President *too* strongly and claim our places. This point must not be lost sight of. Will not lesser lights answer our purpose and make us stronger, rather than jeopardize our future!

We have no evidence to indicate whether Weed asked Dix to participate and he refused, as the skit implied, or whether the most prominent War Democrat of the state was deliberately omitted from the list of sponsors. As for Tilden and other close associates of the *World*'s editor, the ungracious attitude of that paper toward the meeting suggests that they were not among the especially invited.

Contemporaries variously assessed the political complexion of the Cooper Institute meeting. The hostile *Tribune* thought the meeting "bore the unmistakable marks of a good old-fashioned Democratic gathering." [60] The *World* jibed that the crowd consisted of repentant rank-and-file Republicans and "the entire corp of anxious officeholders in the city of New York." [61] Bryant's *Evening Post* reported that it was a respectable gathering composed of men of all parties, "old democrats, old whigs, old free-soilers, and old conservatives." [62] Bennett's *Herald* agreed that the meeting was composed of "our most respectable classes," although "we believe that they all belong to one political party." [63] Seward's organ, the New York *Times,* characterized the occasion as one "for the suppression of everything like mere party and

[59] *Before the Meeting; or Behind the Scenes: A Political Extravaganza; Characters by Wm. H. Seward, Thurlow Weed, Richard Schell & Co.*

[60] New York *Tribune,* Feb. 23, 1866.

[61] New York *World,* Feb. 23, 1866.

[62] New York *Evening Post,* Feb. 23, 1866.

[63] New York *Herald,* Feb. 24, 1866.

partisan feeling." [64] The urbane George Templeton Strong commented in his diary that it was a " 'Conservative' meeting. . . . got up by men of weight, political purity, and unquestioned loyalty, Republicans and War Democrats." [65] Despite these conflicting opinions—indeed, in view of the particular political orientation of each—it is evident that the meeting was largely Republican in complexion.

This was clearly shown in the formal resolutions and accompanying address which were presented by David Dudley Field. Although unqualified in approval of Johnson's position, they emphasized that the participants in the meeting, and also both Congress and the President, were agreed that the freedmen must have "all the civil rights of any other class of citizens . . . they must have equality *before the law.*" Field stated that the only dividing question was whether the freedmen should have the suffrage. He summarized with remarkable equity and lack of rancor the arguments on each side of this question, and then took his stand against suffrage. Those who argue that the Negro could not be protected in his rights without the franchise, Field pointed out, forget the power given to Congress by the enforcement clause of the Thirteenth Amendment and also forget that the men and women of the South have a sense of justice.[66] The emphasis upon the Negro's civil rights had a distinctively Republican flavor.

Seward and Weed had scored a local victory at the Cooper Institute. Their support from Greeley's former allies within the Union-Republican party, however, could be retained only so long as there was confidence in Johnson's readiness to protect the freedman as a citizen. Nor did their success on February 22, any more than their triumph in the election of the previous November, bring a capitulation from Democratic rivals among the friends of the President. After the meeting, Seward wired his son, the President, and Senator Morgan an almost identical message: "ALL RIGHT AND SAFE THE WORK IS DONE THE TROUBLE IS ENDED." [67] But all was not safe and the work had not ended. John Dix sent off an emissary to Johnson;[68] Tilden utilized the influence of Montgomery Blair to warn the President that he could not succeed if he placed "an *exclusive reliance on the republican machine.*" [69] Pressure mounted from the Democrats in respect to the New York collectorship, and it was directed primarily against the Seward-Weed forces.[70] Weed reassured Seward that he was "in frequent communication with leading Democrats (not Copperheads) who are preparing the way for political reconstruction." For success, however, "the new organization" must be "based on the Conservative Plan in the Union Platform." [71]

Other than in New York City, it was the Democracy which dominated the movement to celebrate and endorse the President's veto. Democrats showered the President with individual letters and joint resolutions of approval, some direct from

[64] New York *Times,* Feb. 24, 1866.

[65] *The Diary of George Templeton Strong,* IV: *Post-War Years, 1865–1875* (ed., Allan Nevins and M. H. Thomas, New York, 1952), p. 70.

[66] *Mass Meeting at Cooper Institute,* pp. 7–12.

[67] Seward to Morgan, Feb. 23, 1866, Morgan MSS; Seward to F. W. Seward, Feb. 23, 1866, Seward to Johnson, Feb. 23, 1866, Johnson MSS.

[68] Dix to Johnson, March 2, 1866, Johnson MSS.

[69] Tilden to Blair, March 10, 1866, Blair MSS.

[70] *See above,* Chapter 6, footnotes 29, 33, 34, 47, 51, 75, 77, 78.

[71] Weed to Seward, March 21, 1866; *see also* Weed to Seward March 17, 1866, Seward MSS.

party conventions. In meetings "irrespective of party," they sought to place Conservative Republicans, and especially Republican officeholders, conspicuously on the front rows, while keeping direction of the proceedings in their own hands. Often Republicans balked at the prospect of appearing on programs which to them seemed calculated merely to reinvigorate their old foes—the Copperheads and Peace Democracy.[72] The most persuasive argument against such meetings came from the conciliatory but principled John A. Andrew, former governor of Massachusetts, in reply to the elder Frank Blair, who had asked Andrew's support of a Johnson meeting:[73]

> Seeing so clearly as I do, the duty of us all, of endeavoring to meet the present and coming emergencies, in the spirit, and in the manner of calm, patriotic, liberal minded statesmanship, I am opposed to public meetings, called in support of, or the interest of, any man, leader or party. All the men whose names are made prominent in a controversial way, will have to yield something of what they may have said. . . . And in this remark, I include President Johnson. . . .
> Now, if one set of men get up meetings for Paul, another set will get up meetings for Apollo. The result will be antagonism, not patriotism.

The calm approach that Andrew desired to the problem of the freedmen and of restoration had been made more difficult by Johnson's own speech of February 22, in which he had named Sumner, Stevens, and Wendell Phillips as traitors and intimated that the Radicals were bent upon his assassination. Democrats hailed the performance. General George McClellan, the Democrats' 1864 presidential candidate who was vacationing in Europe, was so pleased with the speech that he came to the conclusion that "the least the country can do for him [Johnson] is to make him the next President," and encouraged his political friends in the States to initiate such a movement.[74] Conciliatory Republicans attempted to explain it away as an intemperate emotional outburst under provocation. Both Seward and Weed, however, wired Johnson congratulations on his speech;[75] yet observers noted a marked difference of approach between the Secretary and the President. A friend wrote Seward that he had read his speech with gratitude; "but what shall I say of the speech of the President!"[76] Bryant's *Evening Post* remarked sadly that Johnson seemed to forget what Seward had emphasized, that the difference between the President and certain leading Republicans "is a question of methods and not one of different ends." The *Post* trusted that Johnson would apologize for the "shocking imputation that Stevens, Sumner and others were seeking to incite assassination."[77] Johnson himself never repudiated his statement; indeed, he subsequently insisted in connection with the Connecticut gubernatorial election that those who wished

[72] These generalizations are based primarily upon the letters-received file of the Johnson MSS, Feb. 23, 1866 to March 26, 1866.

[73] Andrew to Blair, March 18, 1866, Johnson MSS. For a perceptive account of Andrew's position, *see* McKitrick, *Andrew Johnson and Reconstruction*, pp. 217–38.

[74] Barlow to Blair, April 9, 1866, quoting a recent letter from McClellan. General McClellan's one condition was that Johnson turn out Stanton. *See also* Barlow to Blair, July 16, 1866, Barlow MSS.

[75] Seward to Johnson, Feb. 23, 1866; Weed to Johnson, Feb. 23, 1866, Johnson MSS.

[76] M. Perry to Seward, Feb. 23, 1866, Seward MSS.

[77] New York *Evening Post*, reprinted in Philadelphia *Evening Telegraph*, clippings on Freedmen's Bureau veto, Scrapbook, Johnson MSS.

his support must sustain the controversial speech as well as his various messages to Congress.[78]

Johnson's veto and speech aroused excitement, concern, and indignation among Republicans. John W. Forney of the Washington *Chronicle* and Philadelphia *Press* had been publishing strong statements of confidence and denouncing Democratic efforts to "fabricate opinion" for the President.[79] With the announcement of the veto, he turned upon Johnson with bitterness. He revealed that despite his earlier declarations of faith in the President, he had been apprehensive when Johnson had failed to declare for the Union party prior to the New York and Pennsylvania elections, had received Democratic leaders "almost in state," and had for a time made John Van Buren a "confidant daily." The veto would, according to Forney, postpone or defeat "every essential amendment of the National Constitution," remand the freedmen to new horrors, lead to the merciless proscription of "independent and earnest men," and to the "resuscitation by federal patronage of the entire Copperhead party." The nation's leading Radical paper, the Chicago *Tribune,* which had long since lost its early confidence in Johnson, now attacked relentlessly, not hesitating to accuse the President of "deep hypocrisy" in respect to Negro rights and of deliberate intent to cement the loyalty of Southern states whose votes he expected to make him President. The *Tribune's* attack was echoed by a number of papers of the Midwest, where there was an acute awareness that Vallandigham, the notorious Ohio Copperhead, was claiming the President as a convert to his platform. Greeley's *Tribune* was firm in opposition, but spoke more in stern sorrow than in anger.[80] These papers accepted the challenge of the veto.

More of the Republican press, however, refused to acknowledge the Presidential declaration of war. They did not damn the veto entirely but saw in it a balance of valid and invalid argument, some tipping the scale for Johnson, others against him. A number accepted the Seward position that the difference between Executive and Congress was a matter not of ends, but of means. There was a general expectation that a modified version of the Bureau bill would receive the President's assent. Many papers ignored the President's denial to Congress of any authority to set conditions before a restoration of the former rebel states to full participation in the nation's councils. With notable exceptions, the pervasive tone of the Republican press was one of respect, a refusal to follow Forney and the Chicago *Tribune* in impugning the motives of the President. The dominant sentiment among Republicans was still one of accepting Johnson as *their* president and scorning Democratic claims that he was theirs or that a chasm had been opened between the Chief Executive and the Union-Republican party.

Evidence of this moderation and openness to conciliation is certain beyond question. The *Herald's* Washington correspondent sent word that the Republican caucus held the evening after the President's speech was a "singular" affair, without the passion and "spicy time" anticipated. A majority had not been willing "to declare an open war against Andrew Johnson." He predicted that since the congressional

[78] *See* Chapter 7, footnote 77.

[79] Washington *Chronicle,* Feb. 17, 1866.

[80] The principal source for the conclusions and quotations in this and the following paragraph is the extensive collection of newspaper clippings on the Freedmen's Bureau veto in the presidential Scrapbook, Johnson MSS.

majority would not declare war then, when excitement was at its height, they would not be able to do so later, for with time the moderate men of the party would be increasingly "inclined to go with Johnson." [81] The *World* cynically remarked that "the Radicals rather than give up the offices, are preparing to surrender at discretion." [82]

The President still enjoyed the support of influential and articulate moderates, notably that of Senator John Sherman and Governor Jacob D. Cox of Ohio. Governor Cox had talked with the President and released a reassuring letter to the press. Samuel Bowles, editor of the highly respected Springfield *Republican,* was in Washington and sent home reports of "A Lull in the Conflict at the Capital." He saw in the conversation between Governor Cox and the President a basis for "cooperation and harmony"; meantime, "Congress is doing nothing and saying nothing to aggravate matters." [83] By March 8, Senator Morgan was reporting to Weed: "We are gaining here, but our friends in the Senate were very angry for some time." [84] A week later, Representative Dawes was writing his wife that there would probably be no open rupture during the current session of Congress.[85] Henry Ward Beecher's support of the President in the Freedmen's Bureau veto must have led many an old Abolitionist to suspend judgment.[86] Charles Sumner, the most uncompromising of the Radicals, was weakening in his opposition to anything short of equal suffrage. Indeed, Wendell Phillips, in apprehension, tried to persuade Sumner that "this is no time to consult *harmony*." Phillips disparaged not only Doolittle and Raymond, avowed Johnson supporters, but also Senators Trumbull and Fessenden, moderates, and Henry Wilson of Massachusetts, a Radical, as examples of "cowardly Republicanism." [87] A compromise program for restoration of the Southern states suggested by Senator William M. Stewart of Nevada was receiving wide support.[88] Senator Trumbull believed that his Civil Rights Bill, which would protect Negro rights through regular court procedures rather than the extralegal agency of the Bureau and the Army, had the approval of the President. In short, to quote an authority on the work of the Joint Committee on Reconstruction, there was "much peace talk in and out of Congress." [89]

The conciliatory reaction of Republicans generally, the flood of approving letters that reached his desk, the overwhelming support indicated by the numerous press clippings which his staff assembled—all these may have given Andrew Johnson an unwarranted confidence that he was "master of the situation." To be certain, letters and clippings were weighted heavily by Northern Democratic opinion and Southern jubilation. The President, however, was not unmindful of the Democracy and the

[81] New York *Herald,* Feb. 26, 1866.

[82] New York *World,* March 1, 1866.

[83] Springfield *Republican,* March 1, 1866; *see also* Feb. 28, 1866.

[84] Morgan to Weed, March 8, 1866, Morgan MSS.

[85] Dawes to wife, March 16, 1866, Dawes MSS.

[86] Howard K. Beale reached the conclusion that the veto lost Johnson few friends. *The Critical Year,* p. 84.

[87] Phillips to Sumner, March 24, 1866, Charles Sumner MSS, Houghton Library of the Harvard College Library.

[88] Kendrick, *Journal of the Joint Committee on Reconstruction,* pp. 252–55; McKitrick, *Andrew Johnson and Reconstruction,* pp. 339–43; James, *Framing of the Fourteenth Amendment,* pp. 94–97.

[89] James, *Framing of the Fourteenth Amendment,* p. 96. On the desire for conciliation following the veto, see McKitrick, *Andrew Johnson and Reconstruction,* pp. 298–306.

THE PRESIDENT DECLARES WAR 387

South; and neither the South nor the Democracy wished compromise and reconciliation between the President and the congressional majority. Andrew Johnson
chose war, not peace. On March 27, 1866, he returned Trumbull's Civil Rights Bill
to the Senate with a Presidential veto.

25 / "Radicals" and Economic Policies: The Senate, 1861–1873

Glenn M. Linden

Who were the "Radicals" who opposed Johnson and were they extremists? Did they share common beliefs on issues other than Reconstruction? Did their racial views differ markedly from those of Johnson and other conservatives in the North? Did they have goals beyond those they professed?

These questions are not easy to answer, and for several generations historians have puzzled over them. In the early part of the century when Reconstruction studies were dominated by the students of William A. Dunning at Columbia University, historians condemned the Radical governments of the South and blamed "the Tragic Era" on Northern Republican leaders. Some were pictured as being vindictive, self-serving, and corrupt; others, such as Stevens and Sumner, who could not easily be accused of insincerity or dishonesty, were pilloried for fanaticism. Employing labels such as "truculent," "vindictive," "cynical," "hard," "merciless," and "demagogic," Dunning and his disciples consigned the Radicals to the lowest level of the American political inferno.

With the advent of Charles A. Beard and his school, an important additional item was added to the indictment. Not only were the Radicals power-hungry and vengeful, they were also greedy and were seeking to create a plutocracy in America. As agents of Northeastern industrialism the Radicals feared a revived conservative South because a Democratic "solid South" would jeopardize the economic gains of the war years. Democratic majorities in Congress and a Democratic administration would attack the protective tariff, the national banking system, the federal subsidies to railroads, and might even repudiate the sacred wartime debt.

In recent years both the Dunningites and the Beardians have fallen out of favor. We are no longer impressed by the "vindictiveness" of the Radicals. Considering the passions and angers of civil war, the North was remarkably forbearing in its treatment of Confederate leaders. With the single exception of Jefferson Davis, no Confederate leader, either civil or military, was jailed or even seriously threatened with punishment, and even Davis, after a period,

Journal of Southern History, XXXII, No. 2 (May 1966), 189–199. Copyright 1966 by the Southern Historical Association. Reprinted by permission of the Managing Editor.

was freed without trial. Ex-Confederates were deprived of various civil rights by Congressional and Presidential directive, but they were relatively few in number and seldom did their proscription last for very long.

Nor is the Radicals' concern for the freedmen as suspect as it once was. Admittedly, few Radicals were free from race prejudice and many seriously doubted the Negro's capacity for self-government. Their reluctance to support Negro suffrage in their own states lends support to charges of hypocrisy in imposing black suffrage on the white South. Yet surely there were considerations at stake in this matter of Negro suffrage that were not self-serving. How were the freedmen to protect themselves against the powerful, educated, self-confident white community in the South without the elementary right to vote? Actually the freedmen probably could have protected themselves better against their enemies by having a "stake in society" than by the ballot. In these states where they were a minority and could never hope by themselves to overcome a hostile white majority, land was clearly more important than the franchise. Nevertheless, in the end, most of the Republican Congressional leaders accepted the nineteenth-century liberal idea that a man armed with the vote and equal before the law could take care of himself. It was an unimaginative, easy, and unfortunate conclusion, perhaps, but it was not necessarily cynical or insincere, and it certainly was not vindictive.

Finally, the Radicals have been accused of being servants of the predatory new business classes anxious to further Northern industrial capitalism. Recent studies of the views of both businessmen and Radical politicians indicate that businessmen generally opposed Radical insistence on a firm policy in the South and deplored the use of federal power to protect the freedmen. Moreover, the Northern business community scarcely had an identifiable program that any group of politicians could have championed. Deeply divided on almost all of the economic issues of the day, it did not present the united front that the Beardian thesis presupposes.

In the following article, Glenn Linden examines the proposition that there was a unified Radical position on the major economic issues of the Second American Revolution. In this article, and a companion piece dealing with the House of Representatives, Linden uses some of the newer, quantitative techniques of political history and demonstrates their usefulness.

For further reading: Glenn M. Linden, "Radicals and Economic Policies: The House of Representatives, 1861–1873," *Civil War History*, XIV (September 1968); Stanley Coben, "Northeastern Business and Radical Reconstruction: A Re-examination," *Mississippi Valley Historical Review*, XLVI (June 1959); Peter Kolchin, "The Business Press and Reconstruction, 1865–1868," *Journal of Southern History*, XXXIII (May 1967); * David Donald, *The Politics of Reconstruction, 1863–1867* (Baton Rouge, La.: Louisiana State University Press, 1965); * Robert Sharkey, *Money, Class and Party: An Economic Study of Civil War and Reconstruction* (Baltimore, Md.: The Johns Hopkins Press, 1959); * Irwin Unger, *The Greenback Era: A Social and Political History of American Finance, 1865–1879* (Princeton, N. J.: Princeton University Press, 1964).

In a volume published in 1963 with the title *Generalization in the Writing of History,* Professor David M. Potter quoted a generalization concerning the "Radical Republicans": " 'The Radical Republicans defeated Lincoln's mild program and inaugurated the era of drastic reconstruction.' " In analyzing that generalization, Professor Potter expressed the conclusion that

> This relatively simple sentence, though apparently devoid of theory, contains at least three very broad generalizations, each one treacherous in the extreme. First is a generalization which ascribes to an unstated number of individuals a common identity strong enough to justify classifying them as a group—namely, the Radical Republicans—and ascribes to this group a crucial role in defeating one policy and implementing another. Yet, in terms of analysis historians have had great difficulty either in defining what constituted a Radical or in proving that any given aggregate of individuals formed a truly cohesive Radical bloc.[1]

Historians have indeed had "great difficulty either in defining what constituted a Radical or in proving that any given aggregate of individuals formed a truly cohesive Radical bloc." One example of this difficulty may be seen in the continuing exchange of views on the subject between Professors T. Harry Williams and David Donald; and their dialogue may suggest one possibly fruitful way of approaching the complex problem posed by Professor Potter.[2] Professors Williams and Donald, in their most recently published essays on the subject, present contrasting descriptions and interpretations of Radical Republicans. In so doing, they point up the problems involved in classifying individuals as members of the group.[3] Moreover, Professor Donald suggests one way of identifying the political position of individuals in his statement that "Too many historians have failed to look at the voting patterns of the Civil War Congresses." [4] The identification of individual Radicals by name through analysis of votes and the identification of specific policies or actions as "Radical" seems to be one of the most fruitful avenues for future studies of Radicalism.

This article attempts to use quantitative methods to test certain historical generalizations—particularly that there was a group of "Radical Republicans" in the Civil War and Reconstruction period and that these Radicals tended to support economic measures favorable to big business. Although the word "Radical" has had many different meanings, it is safe to say that most historians have equated it with severity towards former Confederates and support for Negroes in the political area and with support of dominant Republican industrial and business interests in the economic area. The present author has collected records of the voting behavior of congressmen

---

[1] David M. Potter, "Explicit Data and Implicit Assumptions in Historical Study," in Louis Gottschalk (ed.), *Generalization in the Writing of History* (Chicago, 1963), 184.

[2] T. Harry Williams, *Lincoln and the Radicals* ([Madison], 1941) and "Lincoln and the Radicals: An Essay in Civil War History and Historiography," in Grady McWhiney (ed.), *Grant, Lee, Lincoln and the Radicals* (Evanston, 1964), 92–117; David Donald, "Devils Facing Zionward," *ibid.,* 72–91, and "The Radicals and Lincoln," in Donald, *Lincoln Reconsidered* (New York, 1956), 103–27.

[3] Although neither author was attempting to provide a complete listing of the Radicals and they did not restrict themselves to senators and congressmen, each mentioned Zachariah Chandler, James A. Garfield, George W. Julian, Wendell Phillips, Thaddeus Stevens, Charles Sumner, and Benjamin F. Wade as Radicals. Donald also named John A. Andrew, Benjamin F. Butler, Salmon P. Chase, Henry Winter Davis, James W. Grimes, and Horace Greeley; Williams referred to Lydia Maria Child, Joshua Giddings, Owen Lovejoy, and Henry Wilson.

[4] Donald, "Devils Facing Zionward," 79.

from July 1861 to March 1873 (the Thirty-seventh through the Forty-second Congress) and has sought to identify "Radicals" by name.[5] Evidence drawn from only one source, the votes in Congress, and reflecting the views of only the senators and congressmen, obviously cannot provide a picture of the entire society and of the entire range of behavior. Such evidence may, however, throw at least some light on the society and on the range of behavior by providing as precise an identification and description as possible of the particular group based on the one type of evidence.

In seeking to identify "Radicals" in Congress by name during the era of Civil War and Reconstruction, the writer analyzed eighty-two roll-call votes in the Senate from the Confiscation Act of 1862 through the resolutions on Arkansas and Louisiana in 1873.[6] These votes constituted the writer's test of "Radicalism" in Congress from 1861 to 1873. On this total of eighty-two votes (thirty-two final votes and fifty votes on amendments), the senators were classified as supporters or opponents of "Radical" measures. A list was compiled of thirty-two Republican senators and one Democratic senator who supported "Radical" measures (1) in at least 75 percent of the votes they cast on the eighty-two roll-call votes described above and (2) for all the terms they served in the Senate from 1861 to 1873. These thirty-three senators, who constitute the writer's list of "Radical" senators as determined by roll-call votes for the period from 1861 to 1873, are presented in Table I.

Senator John B. Henderson, Democrat from Missouri, voted in support of all "Radical" measures under consideration here during the period May 1865 to November 1866. During the period December 1866 to March 1873 Henderson voted in favor of "Radical" measures in 78 percent of the votes he cast, but he voted in only nine of the sixty-five roll calls under consideration during this period and for this reason he is not identified by the writer as a "Radical." [7]

A list of "Non-Radical" senators was also compiled—those who voted in favor of

---

[5] See Glenn M. Linden, "Congressmen, 'Radicalism,' and Economic Issues, 1861–1873" (unpublished Ph.D. dissertation, University of Washington, 1963). This study includes both senators and representatives, and it reaches essentially the same conclusions for both houses, suggesting that any differences in the rules and procedure of the Senate and the House of Representatives did not reflect themselves in the roll-call vote. The present article restricts itself to a consideration of senators because of the limitations of space.

[6] The writer compiled his list of test measures from those mentioned in fifteen standard histories of the period. A complete list of the eighty-two roll calls is given in Linden, "Congressmen, 'Radicalism,' and Economic Issues," 119–26. For charts showing the vote of each senator on each of the roll calls, see *ibid.*, 127–33. Among the key measures used were: Confiscation Act, *Congressional Globe*, 37 Cong., 2 Sess., 3276 (July 12, 1862); Thirteenth Amendment, *ibid.*, 1490 (April 8, 1864); Wade-Davis Bill, *ibid.*, 38 Cong., 1 Sess., 3461 (July 1, 1864); Freedmen's Bureau Bill, *ibid.*, 39 Cong., 1 Sess., 421 (January 25, 1866); Civil Rights Bill, *ibid.*, 606–607 (February 2, 1866); Fourteenth Amendment, *ibid.*, 3041 (June 8, 1866); Reconstruction Act over veto, *ibid.*, 2 Sess., 1976 (March 2, 1867); Omnibus Bill over veto, *ibid.*, 40 Cong., 2 Sess., 3466 (June 25, 1868); Fifteenth Amendment, *ibid.*, 3 Sess., 1641 (February 26, 1869); bill to admit Virginia, Mississippi, and Texas, *ibid.*, 41 Cong., 1 Sess., 656 (April 9, 1869); bill to admit Georgia, *ibid.*, 2 Sess., 2829 (April 19, 1870); Enforcement Act, *ibid.*, 3 Sess., 1655 (February 24, 1871); Ku Klux Klan Act., *ibid.*, 42 Cong., 1 Sess., 709 (April 14, 1871).

[7] Linden, "Congressmen, 'Radicalism,' and Economic Issues," 131. In addition many senators did not vote on enough measures to be classified in any one of the three categories during a given period. If they did not participate in one-third of the votes of a period, they were not included in that period. Several senators voted on enough economic measures to be included in Table 4 but not on enough political measures to be included in Tables 1, 2, or 3. They are S. G. Arnold, J. F. Simmons, P. King, A. Kennedy, and M. S. Latham.

TABLE I*

"RADICAL" SENATORS

	State	July 1861– April 1865	May 1865– Nov. 1866	Dec. 1866 March 1873
Republicans:				
Buckingham, W. A.	Conn.			X
Cameron, S.	Pa.			X
Carpenter, M. H.	Wis.			X
Cattell, A. G.	N. J.			X
Chandler, Z.	Mich.	X	X	X
Conness, J.	Calif.	X	X	X
Corbett, H. W.	Ore.			X
Cragin, A. H.	N. H.		X	X
Creswell, J. A. J.	Md.		X	X
Edmunds, G. F.	Vt.		X	X
Ferry, T. W.	Mich.			X
Fogg, G. G.	N. H.			X
Frelinghuysen, F. T.	N. J.			X
Hale, J. P.	N. H.	X		
Hamlin, H.	Me.			X
Harlan, J.	Iowa	X		X
Kirkwood, S. J.	Iowa		X	X
Lane, J. H.	Kan.	X	X	
Morrill, J. S.	Vt.			X
Morton, O. H. P. T.	Ind.			X
Patterson, J. W.	N. H.			X
Poland, L. P.	Vt.		X	X
Pomeroy, S. C.	Kan.	X	X	X
Pratt, D. D.	Ind.			X
Ramsey, A.	Minn.	X	X	X
Sherman, J.	Ohio	X	X	X
Sumner, C.	Mass.	X	X	X
Thayer, J. M.	Neb.			X
Wade, B. F.	Ohio	X	X	X
Wilkinson, M. S.	Minn.	X		
Wilson, H.	Mass.	X	X	X
Windom, W.	Minn.			X
Democrats:				
Brown, B. G.	Mo.	X	X	X

* X indicates the period in which the senator was in office and voted sufficiently to be classified

"Radical" measures on the eighty-two roll-call votes less than 50 percent of the time during their terms in the Senate from 1861 through 1873. This "Non-Radical" list included the names of twenty-eight senators shown in Table II.

Those senators whose voting records were neither "Radical" nor "Non-Radical" (as defined above) were classified as "Unaligned." These thirty-nine senators are shown in Table III.

Analysis of the voting records thus provides *one* basis for classifying senators. It is not maintained here that this is the only basis on which senators can or should be classified—instead, this classification is seen as a supplement to existing studies—a supplement, it is hoped, which supports efforts for a more specific and a more com-

TABLE II*

"NON-RADICAL" SENATORS

	State	July 1861–April 1865	May 1865–Nov. 1866	Dec. 1866–March 1873
Republicans:				
Cowan, E.	Pa.	X	X	X
Dixon, J.	Conn.		X	X
Doolittle, J. R.	Wis.		X	X
Hitchcock, P. W.	Neb.			X
Democrats:				
Bayard, J. A.	Del.			X
Blair, F. P.	Mo.			X
Buckalew, C. R.	Pa.	X	X	X
Casserly, E.	Calif.			X
Davis, G.	Ky.			X
Davis, H. G.	W. Va.			X
Guthrie, J.	Ky.		X	
Hamilton, W. T.	Md.			X
Hendricks, T. A.	Ind.	X	X	X
Johnson, R.	Md.		X	X
Johnston, J. W.	Va.			X
Kelly, J. K.	Ore.			X
Machen, W. B.	Ky.			X
McCreery, T. C.	Ky.			X
McDougall, J. A.	Calif.	X	X	
Nesmith, J. W.	Ore.		X	X
Powell, L. W.	Ky.	X		
Riddle, G. R.	Del.	X	X	
Saulsbury, W.	Del.	X	X	X
Stevenson, J. W.	Ky.			X
Stockton, J. P.	N. J.		X	X
Thurman, A. G.	Ohio			X
Vickers, G.	Md.			X
Whyte, W. P.	Md.			X

* X indicates the period in which the senator was in office and voted sufficiently to be classified

TABLE III

"UNALIGNED" SENATORS

Senator	State	Senator	State	Senator	State
Anthony, H. B.	R. I.	Foster, L. S.	Conn.	Schurz, C.	Mo.
Boreman, A. I.	W. Va.	Grimes, J. W.	Iowa	Scott, J.	Pa.
Browning, O. H.	Ill.	Harris, I.	N. Y.	Sprague, W.	R. I.
Caldwell, A.	Kan.	Howard, J. M.	Mich.	Stewart, W. M.	Nev.
Carlile, J. S.	Va.	Howe, T. O.	Wis.	Ten Eyck, J. C.	N. J.
Clark, D.	N. H.	Howell, J. B.	Iowa	Tipton, T. W.	Neb.
Cole, C.	Calif.	Lane, H. S.	Ind.	Trumbull, L.	Ill.
Conkling, R.	N. Y.	Logan, J. A.	Ill.	Van Winkle, P. G.	W. Va.
Drake, C. D.	Mo.	Morgan, E. D.	N. Y.	Willey, W. T.	W. Va.
Fenton, R. E.	N. Y.	Morrill, L. M.	Me.	Williams, G. H.	Ore.
Ferry, O. S.	Conn.	Norton, D. S.	Minn.	Wilson, R.	Mo.
Fessenden, W. P.	Me.	Nye, J. W.	Nev.	Wright, G. G.	Iowa
Foot, S.	Vt.	Ross, E. G.	Kan.	Yates, R.	Ill.

prehensive identification of individuals by name as "Radical," "Non-Radical," or "Unaligned." [8]

Once the senators have been identified in the manner described above, it is possible to use the identifications to examine one of the major disagreements in the descriptions and interpretations of "Radicals" by historians—the disagreement concerning the economic policies and programs advocated and supported by "Radicals."

Historians have presented varied descriptions and interpretations of the economic policies and programs of "Radicals" during the years of Civil War and Reconstruction. Some have pictured the "Radicals" as a group of individuals in general agreement on economic policies, policies which were designed to benefit industrial and business interests (with the implication that most industrial and business interests favored similar economic policies). Two historians who have made influential interpretations of this sort are Professor T. Harry Williams and the late Howard K. Beale. According to Professor Beale, in a volume published in 1930 and reprinted in 1958, ". . . in general, the Radical Party represented Big Business, railroads, manufacturers, and monopolists. . . ." [9] Professor David Donald, some of his former students, and Professor Robert P. Sharkey have expressed a different conclusion. "The charge," Professor Donald has written, "that they [the Radicals] were spokesmen for the business interests of the North presupposes a degree of unity among these antislavery leaders

---

[8] An article by Edward L. Gambill, "Who Were the Senate Radicals?" *Civil War History,* XI (September 1965), 237–44, seeks to identify Radicals in the Thirty-ninth Congress, March 4, 1865, to March 3, 1867. His findings are similar to those stated above, though the selection of a shorter period and the establishing of a minimum percentage of 83.3 for "Radicalism" results in some significant differences. He includes parts of moderate and Radical Reconstruction together —December 1865 to November 1866 and December 1866 to March 1867—while the present writer has divided them at the election of 1866. Also he has focused on political Radicalism, whereas the present article is concerned with both political and economic Radicalism. The differences are as follows: (1) Anthony of Rhode Island, Howard of Michigan, and Yates of Illinois appear as "Radical" in Gambill's findings, whereas this writer considers them "Unaligned," since their voting records in the July 1861 to April 1865 and December 1866 to March 1873 periods were less than 75 percent in support of "Radical" measures. (2) Brown of Missouri, Conness of California, Cragin of New Hampshire, and Poland of Vermont are classified as Moderate Republicans by Gambill; this writer classified them as "Radical," since each supported "Radical" measures in at least 75 percent of the votes they cast. (The dividing line between "Radicals" and Moderate Republicans is not easy to determine, but 75 percent seems more realistic than 83.3 percent.) (3) Creswell of Maryland, Kirkwood of Iowa, Lane of Kansas, and Sherman of Ohio are considered Moderate Republicans by Gambill in his findings; this writer considers them "Radicals" because of their 80 percent or higher support of "Radical" measures during all of their terms in the Senate from 1861 to 1873. (4) Norton of Minnesota and Van Winkle of West Virginia are classified as Conservative Republicans by Gambill, whereas this writer considers them "Unaligned." Cowan of Pennsylvania, Dixon of Connecticut, and Doolittle of Wisconsin are also classified as Conservative Republicans by Gambill and as "Non-Radical" by this writer. These differences may be largely semantic and of doubtful importance. It might be mentioned that it is difficult to determine which specific measures Gambill used in his scales and whether they do effectively measure Radicalism.

[9] Howard K. Beale, *The Critical Year: A Study of Andrew Johnson and Reconstruction* (New York, 1930), 263; see also Beale, "The Tariff and Reconstruction," *American Historical Review,* XXXV (January 1930), 276–94, and Williams, *Lincoln and the Radicals.* A possible modification of Williams' views is presented in his essay, "Lincoln and the Radicals: An Essay in Civil War History and Historiography," which discusses Radical economic views on pages 99–100 and in note 10, page 115.

which did not, in fact, exist." [10] Professor Sharkey, referring to his book, *Money, Class, and Party,* has stated, "Among the more important results of this study is the conclusion that among the so-called Radical Republicans there were serious cleavages on financial questions." [11]

In analyzing these two contrasting descriptions of the economic policies of "Radicals," the previous identification of senators as "Radical," "Non-Radical," or "Unaligned" can be used. Did, for example, the senators identified in Table I as "Radical" vote alike on economic issues in the Senate during the years from 1861 through March 1873? In order to determine which economic issues in the Senate should be considered in answering that question, the writer analyzed ninety-five roll-call votes (nineteen final votes and seventy-six votes on amendments) ranging from the Legal Tender Act of 1862 to the Supplementary National Currency Bill of 1873. [12]

To see if the "Radical" senators voted alike on these ninety-five roll calls on economic issues, the vote of the majority of "Radical" senators on each roll call was computed and designated "yea" or "nay" as the "majority Radical vote" for that particular roll call. Then the voting record of each senator in the ninety-five roll calls was compared with the "majority Radical vote." Earlier, thirty-three "Radical" senators were identified on the basis that on eighty-two roll-call votes they had voted the "Radical" position on at least 75 percent of the votes they cast and for all the terms they served in the Senate from 1861 through March 1873. Applying the same standard to the ninety-five roll calls on economic issues, only ten of the thirty-three "Radical" senators voted in accord with the "majority Radical vote" on at least 75 percent of the roll calls and for all the terms they served in the Senate from 1861 through March 1873. [13] Thus the evidence from the total of 177 roll-call votes seems to indicate that the "Radical" senators who voted together on noneconomic issues did not vote together to any marked extent on economic issues. [14]

[10] Donald, *Lincoln Reconsidered,* 110; Stanley Coben, "Northeastern Business and Radical Reconstruction: A Re-examination," *Mississippi Valley Historical Review,* XLVI (June 1959), 67–90; Irwin Unger, "Business and Currency in the Ohio Gubernatorial Campaign of 1875," *Mid-America,* XLI (January 1959), 27–39, and "Business Men and Specie Resumption," *Political Science Quarterly,* LXXIV (March 1959), 46–70.

[11] Robert P. Sharkey, *Money, Class, and Party: An Economic Study of Civil War and Reconstruction* (Baltimore, 1959), 279.

[12] A list of the measures considered and the issues involved in the ninety-five roll calls may be found in Linden, "Congressmen, 'Radicalism,' and Economic Issues," 142–44, 149, 152–56; charts showing the vote of each senator on each of the roll calls appear on pages 145–48, 150–51, 157–59. Among the measures considered were the following: Legal Tender Act, *Cong. Globe,* 37 Cong., 2 Sess., 804 (February 13, 1862); Homestead Bill, *ibid.,* 1951 (May 6, 1862); National Currency Bill, *ibid.,* 3 Sess., 897 (February 13 [12?], 1863); Internal Revenue Bill, *ibid.,* 38 Cong., 1 Sess., 2770 (June 6, 1864); Loan Bill, *ibid.,* 39 Cong., 1 Sess., 1854 (April 9, 1866); Contraction Bill, *ibid.,* 40 Cong., 2 Sess., 537 (January 15, 1868); Tax on Manufacturers, *ibid.,* 1992 (March 19, 1868); Supplementary Currency Bill, *ibid.,* 3223 (June 17, 1868); Bill to Strengthen Public Credit, *ibid.,* 41 Cong., 1 Sess., 70 (March 15, 1869); Funding Bill, *ibid.,* 2 Sess., 1884 (March 11, 1870); Coinage Bill, *ibid.,* 3 Sess., 399 (January 10, 1871); Tax and Tariff Bill, *ibid.,* 42 Cong., 2 Sess., 4088 (May 30, 1872); Supplementary National Currency Bill, *ibid.,* 3 Sess., 1107 (February 5, 1873).

[13] The ten senators were Conness of California, Cragin of New Hampshire, Ferry of Michigan, Hale of New Hampshire, Hamlin of Maine, Kirkwood of Iowa, Lane of Kansas, Thayer of Nebraska, Wade of Ohio, and Wilkinson of Minnesota.

[14] Charles Sumner voted in agreement with the "majority Radical vote" 60 percent of the time from December 1866 to March 1873.

In order to see if there were some more pronounced pattern in the voting on economic issues, the same ninety-five votes on economic issues were rearranged according to the geographic section represented by the senators. On this basis fifty-seven senators voted in agreement with the other senators from their geographic

TABLE IV*

SENATORS ALIGNED GEOGRAPHICALLY ON ECONOMIC ISSUES

	Classi-fication	State	July 1861–April 1865	May 1865–Nov. 1866	Dec. 1866–March 1873
NEW ENGLAND STATES					
Republicans:					
Anthony, H. B.	(U)	R. I.	X	X	X
Arnold, S. G.		R. I.	X		
Buckingham, W. A.	(R)	Conn.			X
Clark, D.	(U)	N. H.	X		
Dixon, J.	(NR)	Conn.	X		X
Edmunds, G. F.	(R)	Vt.		X	X
Ferry, O. S.	(U)	Conn.			X
Hale, J. P.	(R)	N. H.	X		
Hamlin, H.	(R)	Me.			X
Patterson, J. W.	(R)	N. H.			X
Poland, L. P.	(R)	Vt.		X	X
Simmons, J. F.		R. I.	X		
MID-ATLANTIC STATES					
Republicans:					
Cameron, S.	(R)	Pa.			X
Conkling, R.	(U)	N. Y.			X
Cowan, E.	(NR)	Pa.	X	X	
Fenton, R. E.	(U)	N. Y.			X
Frelinghuysen, F. T.	(R)	N. J.			X
King, P.		N. Y.	X		
Scott, J.	(U)	Pa.			X
Ten Eyck, J. C.	(U)	N. J.	X		
MIDDLE WESTERN STATES					
Democrats:					
Norton, D. S.	(U)	Minn.			X
Tipton, T. W.	(U)	Neb.			X
Wright, G. G.	(U)	Iowa			X
Republicans:					
Harlan, J.	(R)	Iowa	X		X
Hitchcock, P. W.	(NR)	Neb.			X
Howell, J. B.	(U)	Iowa			X
Lane, H. S.	(U)	Ind.	X	X	X
Lane, J. H.	(R)	Kan.	X		
Logan, J. A.	(U)	Ill.			X
Morton, O. H. P. T.	(R)	Ind.			X
Pratt, D. D.	(R)	Ind.			X
Ramsey, A.	(R)	Minn.	X	X	X
Sherman, J.	(R)	Ohio	X	X	X
Thayer, J. M.	(R)	Neb.			X
Wade, B. F.	(R)	Ohio	X	X	X
Windom, W.	(R)	Minn.			X
Yates, R.	(U)	Ill.		X	X

TABLE IV (Continued)

	Classi-fication	State	July 1861–April 1865	May 1865–Nov. 1866	Dec. 1866–March 1873
BORDER STATES					
Democrats:					
Bayard, J. A.	(NR)	Del.			X
Davis, H. G.	(NR)	W. Va.			X
Hamilton, W. T.	(NR)	Md.			X
Henderson, J. B.		Mo.	X		X
Johnson, R.	(NR)	Md.	X	X	X
McCreery, T. C.	(NR)	Ky.			X
Powell, L. W.	(NR)	Ky.	X		
Riddle, G. R.	(NR)	Del.	X		
Saulsbury, W.	(NR)	Del.	X	X	X
Stevenson, J. W.	(NR)	Ky.			X
Vickers, G.	(NR)	Md.			X
Republicans:					
Creswell, J. A. J.	(R)	Md.		X	
Schurz, C.	(U)	Mo.			X
Van Winkle, P. G.	(U)	W. Va.	X	X	
Unionists:					
Carlile, J. S.	(U)	Va.	X		
Kennedy, A.		Md.	X		
PACIFIC COAST STATES					
Democrats:					
Latham, M. S.		Calif.	X		
McDougall, J. A.	(NR)	Calif.	X		
Republicans:					
Cole, C.	(U)	Calif.			X
Williams, G. H.	(U)	Ore.		X	X

* X indicates the period in which the senator was in office and voted sufficiently to be classified. The letters in parentheses indicate the classification of the senator as "Radical," "Non-Radical," or "Unaligned" in terms of voting on political measures.

A few senators did not vote on sufficient political measures to be classified.

section on at least 75 percent of the votes they cast on the ninety-five roll-call votes described above and for all the terms they served in the Senate from 1861 to 1873. In the first period, from 1861 to 1865, thirty-five of fifty-seven senators had a voting position 75 percent or more in agreement with members of their own geographic section. In the second period, from May 1865 to November 1866, thirty-one out of forty senators, and in the third period, from December 1866 to March 1873, forty-eight out of eighty-two senators possessed this same degree of voting unity. These results are shown in Table IV.

Table IV thus indicates that on the ninety-five roll calls on economic issues, senators from the same geographic region voted together more frequently than did "Radical" senators. Many senators from the same geographic region tended to vote together on the economic issues in question, whether the senators were "Radical," "Non-Radical," or "Unaligned," and whether the senators were Republicans or Democrats. Republican and Democratic senators from the Middle Western and Pacific Coast regions, in particular, voted like their colleagues from their sections on the roll calls on economic measures.

The evidence described above from the 177 roll-call votes in the Senate and the analysis of that evidence provide the basis for the following conclusions:

1. Thirty-three senators have been identified as "Radicals," twenty-eight as "Non-Radical," and thirty-nine as "Unaligned" for the period from July 1861 through March 1873, in terms of their voting records in eighty-two roll-call votes on measures pertaining to the reconstruction of the Southern States and to Negroes.[15] Those eighty-two roll-call votes provide one definition of "Radicalism" in specific terms, with the generalized definition being that "Radicalism" consisted in support for Negroes and for restrictions on former Confederates.

2. "Radical" senators, as defined above, did not vote alike in ninety-five roll-call votes on such economic issues as the tariff, currency, and banking, nor did "Non-Radical" senators vote alike. Instead, when these economic issues came before the Congress for decision, senators ("Radical" or "Non-Radical," Democrat or Republican) tended to vote with other senators from the same geographic section. This suggests that the definition of "Radicalism" in the Civil War and Reconstruction years should not specify a particular stand on economic questions so far as the voting of "Radical" senators is concerned.

The identification of individual "Radicals" by name, and of specific measures as "Radical," may provide a fruitful method for tackling the difficult problem described by Professor Potter at the beginning of this article.

[15] This quantitative voting analysis sustains Professors Donald and Williams in classifying Senators Zachariah Chandler, Charles Sumner, and Benjamin F. Wade as "Radicals," but it does not sustain the classification by Donald of James W. Grimes as a "Radical," since his voting record in the period from December 1866 to March 1873 was only 58 percent "Radical." See note 3 above.

26 / The Revolution of 1875

Vernon L. Wharton

"Redemption" meant the restoration of the Southern states to conservative white control. It is a term that implies a return to virtue and better times, and of course it is consistent with the older views of Reconstruction. It is clearly a serious misnomer.

It ignores the solid accomplishments of the Radical governments of the South. It also misleadingly suggests a peaceful process. At times, in the older descriptions of Redemption, it seems as if the conservative forces won their victory by sheer moral superiority and some good natured manipulation of the blacks. Another version of the Redemption story concedes its violent character but justifies it as a spontaneous uprising of the outraged and indignant "people" against insupportable Radical barbarity.

Redemption took place in different ways in different places. Several states —Tennessee, Virginia, North Carolina, and Georgia—were controlled by Republicans for only a short period. Elsewhere Radical rule was relatively weak and the restoration of conservative governments was simple. In the states of the deep South—Florida, Louisiana, South Carolina, and Mississippi, in particular—where the proportion of Negroes was high and the Radicals well-entrenched, the process was often disorderly and brutally coercive.

One of the major instruments of this violent reaction was the Ku Klux Klan. Organized by Confederate veterans in 1865, the Klan quickly became a weapon of white supremacy. Between 1865 and 1871 it grew rapidly as a counterweight to the Radical Loyal Leagues, and employed its members, decked out in weird, ghostlike regalia, to attack Negro and Radical leaders, break up Radical political rallies, and whip Negro militiamen. In 1871 and 1872 the federal government, following an extensive investigation, initiated a series of legal prosecutions to end the Klan's reign of terror.

But violence as a conservative weapon did not cease with the decline of the Klan; it merely altered its form. One of the more effective schemes for restoring conservative control was the so-called Mississippi Plan of 1875. Mississippi had not fared badly under Radical rule. Unlike South Carolina and Louisiana where peculation and venality had been pervasive, the state had enjoyed relatively honest, efficient government. But this meant little to

The Negro in Mississippi, 1865–1890 (Chapel Hill, N. C.: University of North Carolina Press, 1947), Chap. XIII. Reprinted by permission.

the white conservatives who were clearly more deeply offended by the "up-pity" black man than by thievery—if it was carried out by their own kind. In the following piece written by a Southern liberal, Vernon Wharton of Millsaps College in Jackson, Mississippi, we find a vivid picture of the combined trickery, physical intimidation, and economic pressure that successfully returned the state to conserv ive rule.

For further reading: Stanley Horn, *Invisible Empire: The Story of the Ku Klux Klan, 1866–1871* (Boston, Mass.: Houghton Mifflin Company, 1939); Francis B. Simkins, "The Ku Klux Klan in South Carolina, 1868–1871," *Journal of Negro History,* XII (October 1927); Garnie W. McGinty, *Louisiana Redeemed: The Overthrow of Carpetbag Rule, 1876–1880* (New Orleans: Pelican Publishing Company, 1941); William J. Cooper, Jr., *The Conservative Regime: South Carolina, 1877–1890* (Baltimore, Md.: The Johns Hopkins Press, 1968).

From the beginning of Reconstruction, there were in Mississippi a large number of white men who insisted upon the necessity of accepting the results of the war and of complying with the requirements of the national government. This group, made up largely of old Whigs, and generally men of property, desired above all else order, prosperity, and harmonious relations within the Union. Guaranteeing to the Negro those minimum rights set up in the amendments to the Constitution, they would seek to gain his confidence and his vote by convincing him that their leadership was for the best interests of both races. Such distinguished citizens as A. G. Brown, C. C. Shackleford, H. F. Simrall, Amos R. Johnston, J. A. P. Campbell, Joshua Morris, and J. L. Alcorn were by temperament members of this group, although some worked with the Democratic party and some with the Republican. The essence of their failure lay in the fact that almost none of them could bring himself to deal with a Negro, however able or honest that Negro might be, as a political or social equal. In later years, J. L. Alcorn often declared that he had never been a "negro Republican." [1] Exactly the same was true of such Northern leaders as H. R. Pease, George C. McKee, and R. C. Powers. By 1874, men of this class had to recognize either their failure to make Democrats of the Negroes, or the repudiation of their leadership in the Republican party. Given the assurance that the national government would not intervene, most of these conservatives were then ready to join the mass of the white Democrats in any methods they might use to drive the Negroes from power.

The majority of the white citizens, brought up on the belief that the Negro was an inferior creature who must be kept in subjection, found themselves unable from the beginning to endorse the program of the Conservatives. In December, 1869, the editor of the Columbus *Index* made a bid for the leadership of this group with the declaration: "We have given the negro a fair trial. He has voted solidly against us, and we hoist, from this day, the white man's flag, and will never take it down so long as we have a voice in the government of the State." [2] The year 1870 saw

[1] Jackson *Clarion-Ledger,* November 27, 1890.
[2] Hinds County *Gazette,* December 15, 1869, quoting the Columbus *Index.*

the organization of a number of "White Men's Clubs" throughout the state. One at Bellefontaine, with 152 members, pledged its subscribers to a perpetual and un-compromising opposition to social and political equality of the white and black races, and to all measures tending thereto. Believing that Negro suffrage was "wrong in principle and disastrous in effect," they pledged themselves to labor unceasingly, from year to year, for the restoration of white supremacy in Mississippi and in the United States.[3] A similar club at West Point agreed to follow a policy that would ignore the Negro as a voter and as an element in politics.[4] The Columbus *Democrat*, advocating the union of these groups in a revitalized Democratic party, declared:

> . . . Its leading ideas are, that white men shall govern, that niggers are not rightly entitled to vote, and that when it gets into power, niggers will be placed upon the same footing with white minors who do not vote or hold office.
>
> There are professed Democrats who do not understand Democratic principles, that want the party mongrelized, thinking that the less difference between the two parties will give them a better chance for the spoils. They are willing for the niggers to vote, but not to hold office. . . .
>
> Nigger voting, holding office and sitting in the jury box, are all wrong, and against the sentiment of the country. There is nothing more certain to occur than that these outrages upon justice and good government will soon be re-moved, and the unprincipled men who are now their advocates will sink lower in the social scale than the niggers themselves.[5]

Here was sheer racial antagonism. There was no consideration of the undesirability of the participation of ignorant and poverty-stricken masses in the government of the state; the line was drawn on the basis of race.

In the face of the decrepitude of the Democratic party, and of the certainty of Federal intervention in case of a state-wide movement based on violence, the program was held in check during 1871, 1872, and 1873. But with the rejection of Alcorn in the election of 1873, and the great increase in office holding by Negroes after that election, the movement gained new strength. Native and Northern whites whose leadership had been rejected by the Negroes now joined in the demand for white supremacy. The great financial depression of 1873 was reflected in the state by increased unpleasantness in political and social relations, and in the nation by a decline of interest in affairs of the South. Furthermore this financial collapse, along with the discovery of scandals in the Federal government, served greatly to weaken the power of the Republican party in the nation. There were predictions of a Democratic president in 1876. When these predictions were strengthened by the great Democratic victories which gained control of the House of Representatives in 1874, conservative leaders in Mississippi at last agreed to abandon their caution. The word went out that the time for revolution was at hand, and the efforts of such men as A. G. Brown and L. Q. C. Lamar to halt the movement were of no avail.

Greater and greater numbers of white Republicans in Mississippi were now desert-ing the party and joining the opposing conventions. As Charles Nordhoff was told in the spring of 1875, the Democrats were making it "too damned hot for them to stay out." [6] Economic pressure and threats of physical violence were used, but the

[3] Mississippi *Weekly Pilot,* July 30, August 12, 1870.
[4] *Ibid.,* November 26, 1870.
[5] *Ibid.,* December 24, 1870, quoting the Columbus *Democrat.*
[6] Charles Nordhoff, *The Cotton States,* p. 77.

most powerful force was that of social ostracism. Colonel James A. Lusk, a prominent native Republican, said to a Negro leader: "No white man can live in the South in the future and act with any other than the Democratic party unless he is willing and prepared to live a life of social isolation and remain in political oblivion." In consideration of the future happiness of his sons and daughters, he felt it necessary to announce his renunciation of all Republican connections.[7] The Canton *Mail* published the names of those whites who must no longer be recognized on the streets, and whose attentions must be scorned by "every true woman." [8]

At the same time that white Republicans were abandoning their party, more and more of the conservative Democratic leaders and newspapers were accepting the "white-line" program. The transition could be seen clearly in most cases. Editors who for several years had written of the Negroes in terms of sympathy, impatience, or friendly ridicule, and who had even praised them at times in an effort to gain their votes, came to speak of them during the summer of 1874 with open dislike, and finally with hatred.[9] By May of 1875, such original color liners as the Vicksburg *Herald*, Columbus *Index*, Handsboro *Democrat*, Yazoo City *Banner*, Vicksburg *Monitor*, and Okolona *Southern States*, had been joined by the conservative Hinds County *Gazette*, Newton *Ledger*, Brandon *Republican*, Forest *Register*, and Jackson *Clarion*, and by the Republican Meridian *Gazette*.

The general charge made by papers and individuals in renouncing their former conservatism was that the color line had already been drawn by the Negro. As evidence, they offered the fact that almost none of the Negroes ever voted with the whites [Democrats],[10] that in some of the counties the Negroes had taken most of the offices,[11] that in the Republican convention of 1873 Negroes had absolutely demanded three of the seven state offices,[12] and that, on such questions as the reduction of the tax for schools, Negroes in the legislature had voted almost as a unit against the whites.[13] In making these charges, the Democrats ignored the fact that the Negroes had from the beginning welcomed the leadership of almost any white who would serve with them, that in so doing they had taken into their party from ten to twenty thousand white Mississippians and that they could not be expected to join in any numbers a party which had from the beginning opposed all of the rights upon which their hopes were built.

As time went on the attack became more and more bitter. The Forest *Register* carried at its masthead the slogan: "A white man in a white man's place. A black man in a black man's place. Each according to the 'eternal fitness of things.' " The Yazoo City *Banner* declared, *"Mississippi is a white man's country, and by the Eternal God we'll rule it."* [14] The Handsboro *Democrat* called for *"A white man's Government, by white men, for the benefit of white men."* [15] All of these papers justified

---

[7] John R. Lynch, *The Facts of Reconstruction*, p. 122.

[8] Mississippi *Weekly Pilot*, September 4, 1875 and September 11, 1875, quoting the Canton *Mail*.

[9] This transition is especially noticeable in the Hinds County *Gazette* and the Jackson *Clarion*.

[10] Vicksburg *Daily Herald*, November 29, 1874; Hinds County *Gazette*, September 23, 1874.

[11] Hinds County *Gazette*, August 26, 1874.

[12] Columbus *Press*, August 7, 1875.

[13] Hinds County *Gazette*, May 5, 1875.

[14] Mississippi *Weekly Pilot*, July 31, 1875, quoting Yazoo City *Banner*.

[15] *Ibid.*, April 10, 1875, quoting the Handsboro *Democrat*.

their stand in editorials describing the depravity and innate bestiality of the Negro. These reached a climax in one published by the Forest *Register*.

> A negro preacher is an *error loci*. God Almighty, in farming out his privileges to mankind, drew a line as to qualifications.
>
> He never exacted from a nation or tribe an impossibility. . . . Does any sane man believe the negro capable of comprehending the ten commandments? The miraculous conception and the birth of our Savior? The high moral precepts taught from the temple on the mount?
>
> Every effort to inculcate these great truths but tends to bestialize his nature, and by obfuscating his little brain unfits him for the duties assigned him as a hewer of wood and drawer of water. The effort makes him a demon of wild, fanatical destruction, and consigns him to the fatal shot of the white man.[16]

Declarations by the rapidly dwindling group of conservative Democrats that the votes of the Negroes could be secured by treating them fairly and reasoning with them met the scorn of the white liners. The editor of the Newton *Democrat* declared that he would just as soon try to reason with a shoal of crocodiles or a drove of Kentucky mules.[17] From Colonel McCardle of the Vicksburg *Herald* came the answer: "The way to treat Sambo is not to argue to him or to reason with him. If you do that, it puffs his vanity and it only makes him insolent. Say to him, 'Here, we are going to *carry* this election; you may vote as you like; but we *are* going to carry it. Then we are going to look after ourselves and our friends; you can look after yourself,' and he will vote with you." [18] Furthermore, when Lamar succeeded in inserting in the Democrat-Conservative platform a vague statement recognizing "the civil and political equality of all men," and inviting the Negroes to vote with the party for good government, the white liners were quick to deny any allegiance.[19] As a Democratic leader declared the following year, ". . . [The] only issue in the election was whether the whites or the blacks should predominate; there was no other politics that I could see in it. Men that had been republicans all their lives just laid aside republicanism and said that they had to go into the ranks then." [20] In the words of J. S. McNeily, "It was a part of the creed of a desperate condition, one easily understood, that any white man, however odious, was preferable . . . to any negro however unobjectionable individually." [21]

Once the general policy had been adopted that Negro and Republican control of the state government was to be broken at any cost, a number of methods were followed for its accomplishment. One of these involved the intimidation of those whites who still worked with the Republican party. There was a general understanding that in the case of the outbreak of a "race war," carpet-baggers would be the first to be killed.[22] As early as December, 1874, the Hinds County *Gazette* declared that death should be meted out to those who continued their opposition. "All other means having been exhausted to abate the horrible condition of things, the thieves

---

[16] Forest *Register,* September 15, 1875.

[17] James B. Ranck, *Albert Gallatin Brown,* p. 275.

[18] Mississippi *Weeky Pilot,* May 29, 1875, quoting the Vicksburg *Herald.*

[19] Columbus *Democrat,* August 21, 1875; Mississippi *Weekly Pilot,* September 4, 1875, quoting the Columbus *Democrat.*

[20] Testimony of W. A. Montgomery, *Senate Reports,* no. 527, 44th Congress, 1st session, p. 542.

[21] J. S. McNeily, "War and Reconstruction in Mississippi," *P.M.H.S.C.S.,* II, 417.

[22] J. S. McNeily, "Climax and Collapse of Reconstruction in Mississippi," *P.M.H.S.,* XII, 405.

and robbers, and scoundrels, white and black, deserve death and ought to be killed. . . . The thieves and robbers kept in office by Governor Ames and his robber associates . . . ought to be compelled to leave the State, or abide the consequences." [23] After the Clinton "riot," Colonel McCardle of the *Herald* urged that in future cases of violence white Republicans be killed and the deluded Negroes spared.[24] At the same time, the editor of the Columbus *Index* announced, "The White League is resolved to kill hereafter only those white wretches who incite negroes to riot and murder." [25] According to J. S. McNeily, "There is no doubt that this sentiment made for peace, in the campaign." [26] There is also no doubt that as time went by the Negroes found fewer and fewer white leaders at their meetings.

Against the Negroes themselves one of the most powerful forces used was economic pressure. All over the state, Democratic clubs announced that no Negro who voted Republican could hope for any form of employment the following year. It was also urged that the boycott be extended to the wives of Negro Republicans.[27] In some cases, doctors announced that they would no longer serve Negroes who did not vote the Democratic ticket.[28] Lists of Negroes who were pledged for or against the party were prepared, and arrangements were made for checkers to be present at the polls. After the election, the names of Negroes marked for discharge were printed in the various papers, along with the names of those who deserved special consideration for having refrained from voting or for having worked with the Democrats.[29]

At the same time, except in the counties where the Democrats had a safe majority, strenuous efforts were being made to get the Negroes into the various Democratic clubs. For those Negroes who would take this step, and participate in the processions and other functions of the clubs, there were pledges of protection and of continued employment. There were also abundant supplies of flags, transparencies, uniforms, and badges. The Democratic badge in Lafayette County not only protected the wearer from physical violence, but also allowed him to "boss" other Negroes. There were numerous barbecues and picnics at which Negro bands and glee clubs furnished entertainment, and at which Negroes either volunteered or were hired to speak.[30] In some of the counties, no expense was spared. In Monroe, the candidates for the legis-

---

[23] Hinds County *Gazette*, December 30, 1874.

[24] Mississippi *Weekly Pilot*, October 9, 1875, quoting the Vicksburg *Herald*.

[25] Columbus *Index*, October 8, 1875.

[26] J. S. McNeily, "Climax and Collapse of Reconstruction in Mississippi," *P.M.H.S.*, XII, 405.

[27] Mississippi *Weekly Pilot*, January 30, 1875, quoting the Newton *Ledger*; Aberdeen *Examiner*, September 4, November 4, 1875; Hinds County *Gazette*, November 18, 1874, August 25, September 15, October 27, December 1, 1875; Julia Kendel, "Reconstruction in Lafayette County," *P.M.H.S.*, XIII, 251; E. F. Puckett, "Reconstruction in Monroe County," *P.M.H.S.*, XI, 145, 146, 153; *Senate Reports*, no. 527, 44th Congress, 1st session, p. xiv; Mississippi *Weekly Pilot*, September 11, 1875, quoting the Canton *Mail*.

[28] E. F. Puckett, *op. cit.*, XI, 145.

[29] Hinds County *Gazette*, August 4, 11, November 10, 17, December 1, 1875; Aberdeen *Examiner*, November 11, 1875; Meridian *Mercury*, November 6, 1875; Mississippi *Weekly Pilot*, November 13, 1875.

[30] Hinds County *Gazette*, July 28, August 11, September 1, 15, 1875; R. Watkins, "Reconstruction in Marshall County," *P.M.H.S.*, XII, 177, 185, 189; J. Kendel, *op. cit.*, XIII, 250, 251; Fred Z. Browne, "Reconstruction in Yalobusha and Grenada Counties," *P.M.H.S.*, XII, 251, 252; Fred Witty, "Reconstruction in Carroll and Montgomery Counties," *P.M.H.S.*, X, 126; John W. Kyle, "Reconstruction in Panola County," *P.M.H.S.*, XIII, 73; E. F. Puckett, *op. cit.*, XI, 144.

lature gave $1,000.00 each, and subscriptions from private citizens ranged up to $500.00.[31] In Panola, the Democratic committee supplied $5,000.00 in addition to subscriptions from individuals. According to one of the leaders in that county, "Our purpose was to overawe the negroes and exhibit to them the ocular proof of our power . . . by magnificent torchlight processions at night and in the day by special trains of cars . . . loaded down with white people with flags flying, drums beating, and bands playing, the trains being chartered and free for everybody." [32]

However pleasing these affairs may have been to those who participated, they had little effect on the campaign. Negro attendance was usually disappointingly small. Most of the Negro speakers and entertainers either had to be hired, or were "Uncle Toms" who had no standing with their fellows. At many of the barbecues, the Negroes were placed at separate tables, and at others many of the whites felt that the whole affair was "ridiculous," and refused to enter into the spirit of the occasion.[33] Of the two methods that were used by the more conservative Democrats to persuade the Negroes to vote away their political power, then, only that involving economic pressure had any appreciable success.

Much more successful was the use of threats and actual violence. It is not to be imagined that this campaign of violence involved all who called themselves Democrats. Many members of the party undoubtedly opposed it, and many more probably considered it regrettable but necessary. It did involve directly thousands of young men and boys of all classes, a large part of the poor white element, and many local political leaders of some importance. Furthermore, it must be admitted that the Democratic leaders of the state, while they often denied the existence of violence, or tried to shift the blame for it to the Negroes, never actually repudiated its use, and in some cases encouraged it. In the meantime, the Democratic press adopted the slogan, "Carry the election peaceably if we can, forcibly if we must." [34] Urged on by newspapers and political leaders, young men all over the state formed militia companies, and Democratic clubs provided themselves with the latest style of repeating rifles.[35] By September, 1875, the Hinds County *Gazette* could announce, "The people of this State are now fully armed, equipped, and drilled. . . ." [36] As described later by the Aberdeen *Examiner,* the situation was well under control in Monroe County:

> . . . the firmest word was "victory"—to be achieved by arms if necessary. When the central power made treaties in Jackson involving the laying down or stacking of arms, the people in this part of the state burnished their arms and bought more cartridges, and each county conducted the campaign upon its own plan . . . each looking to winning its own home fight in its own home way, and each ready and willing to support its neighbors physically and morally whenever the emergency demanded aid, as was not unfrequently the case.

[31] E. F. Puckett, *op. cit.,* XI, 144.

[32] J. W. Kyle, *op. cit.,* XIII, 73.

[33] Hinds County *Gazette,* July 28, August 11, October 27, 1875; R. Watkins, *op. cit.,* XII, 177, 189; F. M. Witty, *op. cit.,* X, 126, 127; J. W. Kyle, *op. cit.,* XIII, 73; F. Z. Browne, *op. cit.,* XII, 251, 252.

[34] Yazoo City *Democrat,* September 14, 1875; Hinds County *Gazette,* August 4, 1875; Aberdeen *Examiner,* August 2, 1883.

[35] Vicksburg *Times and Republican,* May 28, 29, June 3, 21, 1873; Hinds County *Gazette,* December 16, 1874; Vicksburg *Herald,* February 26, 1875; Mississippi *Weekly Pilot,* December 26, 1874, quoting the Brandon *Republican;* J. W. Kyle, *op. cit.,* XIII, 75.

[36] Hinds County *Gazette,* September 29, 1875.

... here and elsewhere in the dark counties we guaranteed peace by thoroughly organising for war; and . . . at the call of the County Executive Committee it was easy—as demonstrated on several occasions—to put seventeen hundred well-mounted horsemen into line, that could be transposed into a brigade of cavalry at a moment's notice, to say nothing of a thoroughly organized artillery company and a company of Infantry armed with needle guns, purchased by our citizens, for home service. In addition to this, our eight hundred square miles of territory was so thoroughly connected by courier lines and posts, that we could communicate with every voter within its borders within a few hours.[37]

With this powerful military force at its command, the white Democracy was ready for its campaign against a mass of Negroes who were timorous, unarmed, and largely unorganized. The program involved extensive processions and drills, and much firing of cannon, at least one of which was owned by every club of any importance. As the campaign of intimidation went on, Negro Republicans were ostentatiously enrolled in "dead books."[38] Negro political leaders were warned that another speech would mean death.[39] Republican political meetings were broken up by violent attacks, or prevented by armed force.[40] Committees of "active young men" waited on Negroes who tried to prevent others of their race from deserting their party.[41] Negroes were prevented from registering by sham battles and the firing of pistols at registration points, or by armed pickets who met them on the roads.[42] Democrats adopted a policy of appearing in force at all Republican meetings, demanding the privilege of presenting Democratic speakers, and compelling Republican speakers to "tell the truth or quit the stand."[43]

In the political, economic, and social subjugation of the freedmen, the most effective weapon ever developed was the "riot." Because this fact was discovered in the Meridian riot of 1871, that incident deserves some attention. In the spring of 1871, Meridian, a rapidly growing railroad town in the eastern part of the state, was under the control of white Republicans appointed to office by Governor Alcorn, and of Negro leaders including J. Aaron Moore, William Clopton, and Warren Tyler. The population of this new town could best be described as "tough," and relations between the races were bad. For the purpose of discussing the situation, the Negroes were brought together in a mass meeting early in March, and were addressed by the three Negro leaders and William Sturgis, the white Republican mayor. While the meeting was going on, a fire alarm was heard, and it was discovered that a store owned by Sturgis was on fire. In the resultant excitement, there was further unpleasantness between the whites and the blacks. On the following morning, white citizens persuaded a lawyer who had not been present at the Republican meeting to prepare an affidavit to the effect that the speeches of Warren Tyler, Bill Dennis

---

[37] Aberdeen *Examiner*, August 2, 1883.

[38] W. Calvin Wells, "Reconstruction in Hinds County," *P.M.H.S.*, IX, 102.

[39] J. W. Kyle, *op. cit.*, XIII, 71.

[40] F. M. Witty, *op. cit.*, X, 123; Mississippi *Weekly Pilot*, October 2, 1875; *Senate Reports*, no. 527, 44th Congress, 1st session, pp. 196–197.

[41] Hinds County *Gazette*, July 28, August 18, September 23, 1875.

[42] Mississippi *Weekly Pilot*, October 9, 1875; *Senate Reports*, no. 527, 44th Congress, 1st session, p. 1718.

[43] J. W. Kyle, *op. cit.*, XIII, 72; J. Kendel, *op. cit.*, XIII, 244; Hinds County *Gazette*, August 4, 1875.

[Clopton], and Aaron Moore had been of an incendiary character.[44] The trial of these men was held the following Sunday afternoon before Judge Bramlette, a native white Republican, in a crowded court room. According to the prosecutor, one of the Negroes, Warren Tyler, interrupted James Brantley, a white witness, to say, "I want three colored men summoned to impeach your testimony." Brantley then seized the city marshal's stick and started toward the Negro. Tyler, moving toward a side door, reached back as though to draw a pistol, and general firing immediately began in the rear of the court room.[45] Although it seems that no one actually saw Tyler fire, and although Negroes stoutly denied that he did so, the available evidence indicates that he probably shot at the advancing Brantley and, missing him, killed Judge Bramlette.[46] W. H. Hardy, a local Democratic leader, later wrote a description of the affair in which he attributed the shot that killed Bramlette to the Negro Bill Dennis. In this he was probably incorrect, but to the rest of his story there is general agreement.

> As quick as a flash the white men sitting in the rear drew their pistols and fired upon Dennis. [Tyler had run through the side door and leaped to the ground from a second-floor veranda.] By the time the smoke cleared away the court room had but few people left in it. Judge Bramlette was found dead and Bill Dennis mortally wounded. The riot [sic] was on and white men and negroes were seen running in every direction; the white men to get their arms and the negroes in mortal terror to seek a place of hiding. Every man that could do so got a gun or a pistol and went on the hunt for negroes. The two men left to guard the wounded Bill Dennis in the sheriff's office grew tired of their job and threw him from the balcony into the middle of the street, saying that their services were needed elsewhere, and they could not waste time guarding a wounded negro murderer. Warren Tyler was found concealed in a shack and shot to death. Aaron Moore had escaped from the courthouse in the confusion and lay out in the woods that night, and the next day made his way to Jackson. . . . It was not known how many negroes were killed by the enraged whites, but the number has been estimated at from twenty-five to thirty. . . .
>
> The mayor, Bill Sturgis, was thoroughly overcome with terror at the vengeance of the people and concealed himself in the garret of his boarding house. Being a member of the Odd Fellows' order he opened communication with a member of the lodge, and it resulted in a cartel by which Sturgis was to resign the office of mayor and was to leave the State in twenty-four hours. . . .[47]

This affair marked the end of Republican control in the area surrounding Meridian. According to Dunbar Rowland, "The Meridian riot marks an epoch in the transition period of reconstruction, and was a forecast of the end of carpetbag rule in Mississippi." [48] His opinion endorses that of W. H. Hardy:

> It [the Meridian riot] demonstrated the cowardice of both the carpetbaggers and the negro, and that in danger, either real or imaginary, they took counsel

[44] J. S. McNeily, "The Enforcement Act of 1871 and the Ku-Klux Klan in Mississippi," *P.M.H.S.*, IX, 128–130; *House Reports*, no. 41, 42d Congress, 1st session, pt. i, pp. 479–480; *ibid.*, pt. ii, pp. 97–98.

[45] *Ibid.*, pt. i, pp. 480–481; pt. ii, pp. 97–99.

[46] *Ibid.*, pt. i, p. 127; pt. ii, pp. 10, 70, 99, 176, 182, 210, 221.

[47] W. H. Hardy, "Recollections of Reconstruction in East and Southeast Mississippi," *P.M.H.S.*, VII, 205–206.

[48] J. Dunbar Rowland, *History of Mississippi*, II, 172.

of their fear. When the white people failed, after every reasonable appeal to argument, to reason, to justice, to a sense of the public weal, they brought into full play the lessons learned in the Meridian riot, and it proved efficient in the campaign of 1875.[49]

The lesson learned was that the Negroes, largely unarmed, economically dependent, and timid and unresourceful after generations of servitude, would offer no effective resistance to violence. Throughout the period, any unpleasant incident was likely to produce such a "riot." During the bad feeling of 1874 and 1875 there were a great number of unpleasant incidents, and after each resulting riot Negro resistance to white domination in the surrounding area completely collapsed.

With the development of the white-line program in the summer of 1874, the newspapers began to carry a constantly increasing number of stories about clashes between the races. Some of these were reports of real incidents growing out of increasing bitterness; others seem to have been the product of exaggerated rumors, or of an effort to arouse feeling against the Negroes. Soon blood began to flow. In Austin, Negroes raised violent objections to the release of a white man who, in shooting at a Negro man, had killed a Negro girl. In the quarrel which followed, six Negroes were killed; no whites were wounded.[50] In Vicksburg, where the white militia had overthrown Republican control in the municipal election, a number of Negroes prepared to come into town in answer to a call from the Negro sheriff. After they had agreed to go back to their homes, firing started. About thirty-five Negroes were killed. Two whites met death, one possibly by accident.[51] This was in December, 1874. Three months later, the Vicksburg *Monitor* announced, *"The same tactics that saved Vicksburg will surely save the State, and no other will."* [52] In the same city, in the following July, the Republicans held a celebration of Independence Day. Trouble developed with white Democrats. Two Negroes were killed; no whites were wounded. Water Valley was disturbed by a rumor that Negroes were going to attack the town. An exploring party found a group of Negroes concealed under a cliff. An unknown number of Negroes were killed; no whites were wounded.[53] In August, Negroes at a Republican meeting in Louisville "succeeded in raising a disturbance." "Result, two negroes wounded, no white men hurt. Will the negro never learn that he is always sure to be the sufferer in these riots?" [54] Late in the same month, a group of whites near Macon, including more than a hundred horsemen from Alabama, were out looking for a Negro political meeting. After they had failed to find one, they were told by a runner that several hundred Negroes had gathered at a church, where they were preparing to carry aid to those of their race in Vicksburg, on the other side of the state. When the church was found, the Alabamians disobeyed the order of the deputy sheriff and fired into the crowd. Twelve or thirteen Negroes were killed; no white was hurt.[55]

A few nights later, the Republicans endeavored to hold a meeting in Yazoo City.

[49] W. H. Hardy, *op. cit.*, VII, 206.

[50] Hinds County *Gazette,* August 19, 1874.

[51] *Ibid.,* December 9, 1874; Vicksburg *Herald,* December, 1874; Mississippi *Weekly Pilot,* March 6, 1875.

[52] Mississippi *Weekly Pilot,* March 20, 1875, quoting the Vicksburg *Monitor.*

[53] J. C. Brown, *op. cit.,* XII, 257.

[54] Hinds County *Gazette,* August 25, 1875, quoting the Kosciusko *Star.*

[55] *Senate Reports,* no. 527, 44th Congress, 1st session, pp. 1176–1177; Hinds County *Gazette,* September 1, 1875.

Their hall was invaded by a number of Democrats, led by their "rope-bearer," H. M. Dixon. In the confusion which followed, a native white Republican was killed, and several Negroes were wounded. The white sheriff escaped with his life by fleeing to Jackson. White militia then took charge of the county, and systematically lynched the Negro leaders in each supervisor's district.[56] Three days later, Democrats obtained their customary division of time at a large Republican meeting and picnic at Clinton. Trouble developed between a Negro policeman and a young white who was drunk. In the shooting which followed, two young white Democrats and a white Republican were killed. The number of Negroes killed is unknown; estimates varied from ten to thirty. Two thousand Negroes in wild panic rushed to the woods or to Jackson. By nightfall, armed whites, including the Vicksburg "Modocs," had control of the entire area. During the next four days they scoured the surrounding country, killing Negro leaders. Estimates of the number killed varied between ten and fifty.[57] On the day of the Clinton affair, white Democrats captured a Republican meeting at Utica and compelled a thousand Negroes to listen to Democratic speakers for several hours. There seems to have been no bloodshed.[58] A few days later, there was a minor skirmish at Satartia in which one Negro was killed.[59] Early in the following month, the Negro sheriff was run out of Coahoma County after an encounter in which five Negroes were killed and five wounded. One white was killed from ambush; another shot himself by accident.[60] The final clash of the campaign came at Columbus, a large town with a heavy Negro majority, on the night before the election. A crowd of young whites rushed from a drug store to attack a Negro parade, cutting the heads out of the drums and scattering the marchers. About an hour later, two old sheds in the Negro section were found to be burning, and the rumor was spread that the blacks were trying to burn the town. The Columbus Riflemen and a large number of visiting Alabamians immediately took charge, and Negroes began to flee for safety. Those who refused to halt were fired upon; four men were killed, and several men and one woman were wounded. No whites were hurt.[61]

Long before the day of the election, a Democratic victory was assured. In many of the counties, all efforts to hold Republican meetings were abandoned. In several of the black counties, the sheriffs had fled or were powerless. White military units held the towns, and pickets patrolled the roads. The Negroes, with many of their leaders either dead or in hiding, faced the proposition of voting with the Democrats or staying away from the polls.

Letters to Governor Ames revealed the panic of the Negroes. From Yazoo City came the plea, "I beg you most fulley to send the United soldiers here; they have hung six more men since the killing of Mr. Fawn; they wont let the republican have

[56] A. T. Morgan, *Yazoo*, pp. 465–484; Mississippi *Weekly Pilot*, September 4, 25, October 2, 1875; Jackson *Weekly Clarion*, August 27, 1879; Yazoo City *Herald*, October 15, 1875; Elizabeth Caldwell, "Reconstruction in Yazoo County," unpublished master's thesis, University of North Carolina, 1931, pp. 55–56. Dixon's title of "rope-bearer" was gained through his leadership in lynching expeditions.

[57] *Senate Reports*, no. 527, 44th Congress, 1st session, pp. 321, 368, 501, 544; Mississippi *Weekly Pilot*, September 11, 25, 1875; Hinds County *Gazette*, September 15, 1875; C. H. Brough, "The Clinton Riot," *P.M.H.S.*, VI, 62.

[58] C. H. Brough, *op. cit.*, VI, 54.

[59] Hinds County *Gazette*, September 15, 1875.

[60] *Ibid.*, October 13, 1875; *Senate Reports*, no. 527, 44th Congress, 1st session, pp. 69–70.

[61] Mississippi *Weekly Pilot*, November 13, 1875; *Senate Reports*, no. 527, 44th Congress, 1st session, pp. 805–820.

no ticket . . . ; fighting comemense just I were closuing, 2 two killed . . . help; send troop and arms pleas. . . . Send help, help, troops. . . ." [62] From Noxubee County came the cry:

> Last Saturday, the 30th, the democrats was in Macon town in high rage, raring around and shooting of their cannons all up and down the street, and shooting all their pistols also, and which they have already sword to you for peace; and I don't think they act much in that way last Saturday, for there was Richard Gray shot down walking on the pavements, shot by the democrats, and he was shot five times, four times after he fell, and was said shot because he was nominated for treasurer, and forher more, because he made a speech and said he never did expect to vote a democrate ticket, and also advised the colored citizens to do the same.[63]

From Warren County came a letter from 108 Negroes who could not and would not register and vote, "for we cannot hold a meeting of no description without being molested and broken up; and further our lives are not safe at nor in our cabins, and therefore we deem it unwise to make a target of our body to be shot down like dogs and have no protection. . . ." [64] From Vicksburg came the plea, "The rebles turbulent; are aiming themselves here now to-day to go to Sartartia to murder more poor negroes. Gov., aint the no pertiction?" [65]

There was not any protection. In January, the administration had endeavored to secure the passage of a bill to allow the governor to set up special police bodies in towns where they were needed. Passed in the house by a vote of forty to thirty-eight, it was killed on a color-line vote in the senate.[66] In the desperate days of September, Governor Ames made the formal gesture of commanding the private military bands to disperse. From the *Clarion*, there came a scornful answer that was echoed all over the state: " 'Now, therefore, I, A.A., do hereby command all persons belonging to such organizations to disband.' Ha! ha!! ha!!! 'Command.' 'Disband.' That's good." [67]

The Governor then turned to the Federal government, although he knew his request would be unpopular, even in the North. To Attorney-General Edward Pierrepont, he wrote: "Let the odium, in all its magnitude descend on me. I cannot escape. I am conscious in the discharge of my duty toward a class of American citizens whose only offense consists in their color, and which I am powerless to protect." [68] The plea was hopeless. Negro suffrage, or even Negro freedom, had never been really popular with the masses in the North. Negro suffrage had appeared to be necessary, and had been accepted as such. It had been inaugurated to save a party that a majority of the voters in a number of the Northern states now considered hardly worth saving. Its maintenance had proved to be a troublesome problem. Why should the Negro majority in Mississippi be constantly crying for help? The sending of Federal troops into a state simply to prevent white men from ruling Negroes was distasteful to the average

[62] *Senate Reports*, no. 527, 44th Congress, 1st session, "Documentary Evidence," p. 99.

[63] *Ibid.*, p. 73.

[64] *Ibid.*, p. 88.

[65] *Ibid.*, p. 89.

[66] Mississippi *Senate Journal*, 1875, p. 302. See also Hinds County *Gazette*, March 3, 1875.

[67] Mississippi *Weekly Pilot*, September 11, 1875, quoting the Jackson *Clarion*.

[68] Mississippi *Weekly Pilot*, September 11, 18, 1875.

Northern voter.[69] In the final moment of his decision, Grant was visited by a delegation of politicians from Ohio, a pivotal state which was to have an election in October. Mississippi, these visitors declared, was already lost to the party; troops would arrive too late to save the state. Even worse, the order that sent troops to Mississippi would mean the loss of Ohio to the party. The Negroes must be sacrificed.[70] Grant's answer to Ames was a statement that aid could not be sent until all local resources had been exhausted. In the midst of the negotiations, Pierrepont declared, "The whole public are tired of these annual autumnal outbreaks in the South." "This flippant utterance of Attorney-General Edward Pierrepont," wrote Adelbert Ames twenty years later, "was the way the executive branch of the National government announced that it had decided that the reconstruction acts of congress were a failure." [71]

As a last hope, Ames turned to the organization of a state militia, placing at its head Brigadier General William F. Fitzgerald, an ex-Confederate who had become a Republican. It was the Governor's idea to organize equal companies of whites and blacks, and at first many of the Democrats, under the leadership of J. Z. George, proclaimed their willingness to join. It quickly became apparent, however, that the great mass of the party was absolutely opposed to such a move.[72] If the militia was to be formed, it must be made up almost entirely of Negroes. Difficulties rapidly increased. Democrats secured two blanket injunctions against any further use of the funds which the legislature had appropriated.[73] In several places, state arms were seized by the White Leagues.[74] The refugee sheriff of Yazoo County was convinced that an attempt to use the militia there would bring open war, and finally refused to recommend it.[75] A caucus of the Republican legislators found the Negro members almost as a unit opposed to the plan.[76] By October 15, only two companies, one of whites and the other of Negroes, had been organized. Both of these were at the state capital.

In the meantime, it had become apparent both to Governor Ames and to the Democratic leaders that any activity by a Negro militia would bring immediate conflict. Both parties were anxious to avoid this, Ames for the sake of the Negroes, and the Democratic committeemen because they feared it would bring Federal intervention.[77] The result was a conference between the governor on one side and J. Z. George and his colleagues on the other. Out of this conference came an agreement that Ames should immediately abandon all efforts to form a militia. On their side, the Democratic leaders guaranteed a fair and peaceful election.[78]

There are some aspects of this agreement that are difficult to understand. Ames'

[69] J. S. McNeily, "Climax and Collapse of Reconstruction in Mississippi," *P.M.H.S.*, XII, 402, quoting the New York *Herald*; *Senate Reports*, no. 527, 44th Congress, 1st session, p. 377, quoting the Chicago *Tribune*.

[70] John R. Lynch, *The Facts of Reconstruction*, pp. 150–151.

[71] Adelbert Ames to E. Benjamin Andrews, May 24, 1895, J. W. Garner Papers, Mississippi State Archives.

[72] J. S. McNeily, "Climax and Collapse of Reconstruction in Mississippi," *P.M.H.S.*, XII, 396–398; Mississippi *Weekly Pilot*, October 16, 1875; *ibid.*, quoting the Meridian *Mercury*.

[73] Mississippi *Weekly Pilot*, October 16, 1875.

[74] *Ibid.*, September 4, 1875, October 2, 1875.

[75] J. S. McNeily, "Climax and Collapse of Reconstruction in Mississippi," *P.M.H.S.*, XII, 407.

[76] A. T. Morgan, *Yazoo*, pp. 456–457.

[77] Frank Johnston, "The Conference of October 15, 1875," *P.M.H.S.*, VI, 69.

[78] Mississippi *Weekly Pilot*, October 16, 23, 1875.

report to Pierrepont included the lines: "I have full faith in their honor, and implicit confidence that they can accomplish all they undertake. Consequently, I believe that we shall have peace, order, and a fair election." [79] This does not ring entirely true. It seems more probable that the Governor had fought a hopeless fight as long as he dared, and was ready to seize an opportunity for an honorable surrender. More genuine was his remark to George K. Chase, as report after report of breaches of the peace agreement continued to come in: "I wish you would go to see them [J. Z. George and Ethelbert Barksdale], and get this thing fixed, and see what it means, and let us have quiet anyhow; no matter if they are going to carry the State, let them carry it, and let us be at peace and have no more killing." [80]

The Democratic guarantee of peace and a fair election is also hard to understand. There can be little doubt that such men as J. Z. George, Joshua Green, and Frank Johnston were anxious for peace. They were convinced that intimidation had already been carried far enough to guarantee Democratic control of the legislature. Any further violence might serve to reverse Grant's decision in regard to the sending of troops. From telegrams sent by George before and during the election, it appears that he made a real effort to preserve order; although in some cases, notably in that of Yazoo County, he seems to have sought, for political purposes, pledges which he knew would not be carried out.[81] The essential difficulty lay in the fact that leaders in some of the black counties were determined to gain redemption not only for the state but also for their local governments. They felt that the work must be carried on through the day of the election. As a result, a large section of the Democratic press immediately repudiated the peace agreement,[82] and local White Leagues "burnished up their arms and bought more cartridges." [83]

On the day of the election, a peculiar quiet prevailed in many of the counties. "It was a very quiet day in Jackson—fearfully quiet." [84] According to a witness at Yazoo City, "Hardly anybody spoke aloud." [85] In Columbus, where many of the Negroes were still in the swamps as a result of the riot on the preceding night, the Democratic mayor reported everything as "quiet as a funeral." [86] Similar reports came from Bolton, Lake, and Boswell. At Holly Springs, about 250 Negroes voted with the Democrats, offering their open ballots as proof.[87] At Meridian, the White League seized the polls, while the Negroes, "sullen and morose," gathered in a mass across the street. Any Negro who approached without a white Democrat at his side was immediately crowded away from the ballot box.[88]

In other sections, the day was not so peaceful. In Scott County, Negroes who were carrying the Republican tickets for distribution at the polls were fired on "by accident" by Democratic squirrel hunters. They fled, abandoning both the tickets and their mules. At Forest, the county seat, it was arranged for boys with whips to rush suddenly into the crowd of Negroes. The voters, already frightened and nervous, feared that

---

[79] J. W. Garner, op. cit., p. 389.

[80] Senate Reports, no. 527, 44th Congress, 1st session, p. 1807.

[81] Ibid., pp. 380–420.

[82] Mississippi Weekly Pilot, October 23, 1875.

[83] Aberdeen Examiner, August 2, 1883.

[84] Senate Reports, no. 527, 44th Congress, 1st session, p. 539.

[85] Ibid., p. 527.

[86] Ibid., pp. 800, 805.

[87] Vicksburg Herald, November 3, 1875.

[88] W. H. Hardy, op. cit., IV, 129.

this was the beginning of an outbreak, and left in a panic.[89] In Monroe County, on the day before the election, the Negro candidate for chancery clerk saved himself and several friends by a promise to leave the state and not to return.[90] At Okolona, the Negroes, with women and children, gathered at a church in the edge of town, intending to go from there to the polls in groups. The Democratic army marched up and formed near the church. When guns went off by accident, the Negroes stampeded, paying no attention to Democratic invitations for them to come back and vote. At Aberdeen, in spite of the fact that the heavy Negro population in the eastern part of the county was cut off by an open bridge and pickets along the Tombigbee, a large number gathered at the polls early in the morning. E. O. Sykes, in charge of the Democratic war department, posted the cavalry he had imported from Alabama, surrounded the Negroes with infantry, loaded a cannon with chains and slugs, and then sent a strong-arm squad into the crowd to beat the Negroes over the head. They broke and ran, many of them swimming the river in search of safety. The Republican sheriff, an ex-Confederate, locked himself in his own jail. The Democrats then carried the box "very quietly," turning a Republican majority of 648 in 1871 into a Democratic majority of 1,175.[91]

At Grenada, trouble developed between a white and a Negro at the polls. While the Democrat was beating the Negro over the head with an axe handle, the Democratic captain called for the cannon, and his men ran for their guns, which they had left at a neighboring store. General E. C. Walthall quieted the crowd, but the Negroes had stampeded, and would not return.[92] At Port Gibson, there was trouble between a young white man and a young Negro. General firing began, resulting in the death of "an old, inoffensive negro man," and the wounding of four or five others. The Negroes scattered, and few of them returned to vote.[93] In general, however, it can be said that the election was quiet, as elections went in Mississippi, and that the Republicans polled a heavy vote in many sections.

The Democrats came very close to sweeping the state. In some places they used fraud,[94] but this method was generally unnecessary. In Yazoo County, the center of an overwhelming Negro majority, Republican candidates received only seven votes. In Kemper they received four, and in Tishomingo twelve.[95] They received two votes at Utica, in the black county of Hinds, and none at Auburn.[96] Democrats carried the first, third, fourth, and fifth congressional districts. The second went to G. Wiley Wells, renegade Republican who was working with the Democrats. In the sixth, John R. Lynch, with much white support, held his majorities in the black counties of Adams, Jefferson, and Wilkinson to win by a slim margin over Roderick Seal.[97]

[89] Forrest Cooper, "Reconstruction in Scott County," *P.M.H.S.*, XIII, 175–176.

[90] Aberdeen *Examiner*, November 11, 1875.

[91] *Senate Reports*, no. 527, 44th Congress, 1st session, pp. 1029–1030, 1103–1105, 1107; Aberdeen *Examiner*, November 11, 1875; E. F. Puckett, "Reconstruction in Monroe County," *P.M.H.S.*, XI, 153–155.

[92] Julia C. Brown, "Reconstruction in Yalobusha and Grenada Counties," *P.M.H.S.*, XII, 255–256.

[93] *Senate Reports*, no. 527, 44th Congress, 1st session, pp. 201–202; Vicksburg *Herald*, November 3, 1875.

[94] Hinds County *Gazette*, November 10, 17, 1875; W. Calvin Wells, "Reconstruction in Hinds County," *P.M.H.S.*, IX, 104; E. F. Puckett, *op. cit.*, XI, 135.

[95] J. W. Garner, *op. cit.*, p. 395.

[96] Hinds County *Gazette*, November 10, 1875.

[97] *Ibid.*, November 24, December 1, 1875.

In the state senate, of which only half the members had been involved in the election, there were now twenty-six Democrats and ten Republicans. Only five, all of them hold-overs, were Negroes. In the new house of representatives, there were twenty Republicans and ninety-five Democrats. Sixteen of the representatives were Negroes; of these, fifteen were Republicans and one was a Democrat.[98] Sixty-two of the seventy-four counties elected Democrats as their local officials.[99] In the only race for a state office, that for state treasurer, the Democrat, W. L. Hemingway, polled 96,596 votes to 66,155 for George M. Buchanan, a popular and widely known ex-Confederate who was his Republican opponent.

When the Democratic legislature met in the following January, it quickly completed the work by impeaching and removing the Lieutenant-Governor, and by securing the resignations of the Governor and the Superintendent of Education. Thus ended the successful revolution of 1875. In its preparation and execution, economic and political motives played a large part. Essentially, however, it was a racial struggle. This was expressed most clearly, twenty years later, by Adelbert Ames:

> There was a time when policy made it advisable for the white men of Mississippi to advance "corruption," "negro mobs," anything and everything but the true reason for their conduct. That time has long since passed. There is no good reason why the truth should not be stated in plain terms.

> It is this—they are white men, Anglo-Saxons—a dominant race—educated to believe in negro slavery. To perpetuate the then existing order of things they ventured everything and lost. An unjust and tyrannical power (from their standpoint) had filled their state with mourning, beggared them, freed their slaves and as a last insult and injury made the ex-slave a political equal. They resisted by intimidation, violence and murder. Excuses by the way of justification were given while the powerful hand of the national government was to be feared. Soon the national government and public opinion ceased to be dreaded. They then announced boldly that this is a white man's government and that the negro and ex-slave should, forever, form no part of it.

> This determination has been proclaimed time and again and what is more to the purpose has been acted on. With an excess of 60,000 colored people Mississippi became the seat of a white man's government.[100]

Altogether, it is well that the Federal government did not intervene to protect the Negroes in 1875. The entire process would have been repeated a few years later, with increased animosity and violence. Social revolutions are not accomplished by force, unless that force is overwhelming, merciless, and continued over a long period. The Negro, returned to a status intermediate between that of slavery and that of full citizenship, now finds in education and hard work opportunities for slow but certain advancement. On the other hand, the dominant race, dominant through tradition, education, and superior economic and legal advantages, yields more and more to the promptings of humanitarianism and enlightened self-interest. With each generation there is less violence and injustice, and more recognition of interdependence and of common needs and interests. There are retrogressions, but it is easy to believe that a gradual, healthy progress will be maintained.

[98] *Senate Reports*, no. 527, 44th Congress, 1st session, part IV, pp. 147–148; Mississippi *Senate Journal*, 1876, pp. 690–691; Mississippi *House Journal*, 1876, pp. 678–682.

[99] J. W. Garner, *op. cit.*, p. 395.

[100] Adelbert Ames to E. Benjamin Andrews, May 24, 1895, J. W. Garner Papers.

27 / The Forked Road to Reunion

C. Vann Woodward

The closing act of Reconstruction took place in Washington rather than in the deep South. By the fall of 1876, only three states were as yet unredeemed —South Carolina, Louisiana, and Florida, where federal troops sustained the Radical regimes in the face of a united white opposition, willing, as in Mississippi, to resort to fraud and intimidation.

The stakes of power in the fall of 1876 were particularly high. Control of state administrations in the South was not merely a local concern—1876 was a Presidential election year and every electoral vote seemed likely to count. Nationally the Republicans were a minority. In 1868 and 1872, Grant had won by substantial popular majorities but it had been against notably weak opponents. In 1874 the Democrats had swept the Congressional elections and it seemed entirely possible that running against such a strong candidate as Samuel J. Tilden of New York, the Republican, Rutherford B. Hayes, would be badly beaten.

The contest produced one of the most acute constitutional crises in the country's history. On election night it seemed as if Tilden had edged out his opponent by a respectable popular majority and had for certain only one vote less than the majority needed in the electoral college. Unfortunately in the three unredeemed Southern states, both parties claimed popular majorities for their ticket and the right to cast the state's full electoral vote for its own candidate. On whichever set of returns was valid rode the choice of President, and, incidently, the fate of Reconstruction.

The following months were a time of extreme political uncertainty and disquiet. Public anxiety rose to an almost unbearable pitch as it became more and more uncertain whether the dispute would be settled by Inauguration Day. Both sides, of course, charged fraud, and a few hot-tempered Democrats, certain that their first chance to win the Presidency in more than a decade would be stolen from them, threatened to march on Washington and place Tilden in office by force. Meanwhile an Electoral Commission had been selected by Congress to investigate the disputed returns and had, by strict party vote, endorsed the Republican electors. But would Congress now accept the Commission's conclusions? The Democrats controlled the House of Representatives and could easily prevent a final decision by March 4.

Origins of the New South, 1877–1913; vol. IX of *A History of the South* (Baton Rouge, La.: Louisiana State University Press, 1951). Reprinted by permission.

At this point a bargain ended the dispute and cleared the way for a peaceful settlement and the inauguration of Hayes. As the story usually goes, Southern Democrats, reluctant to stir up further sectional acrimony and convinced that Hayes was not a Radical, agreed to accept his election in exchange for a withdrawal of the remaining troops from the South, thus allowing the conservative forces to triumph. Conservative restoration in the South was to be the price for electing Hayes President.

According to C. Vann Woodward, even more was at stake. If the removal of the federal troops was all that was at issue, Tilden and the Democrats would have served conservative purposes as well, if not better, than Hayes and the Republicans. But the Democrats would not grant the South certain economic favors closely connected with the ambitions of the South's business classes, often ex-Whigs, who wanted federal subsidies for internal improvements. Particularly enticing was a large federal land grant for the grandiose and overblown Texas-Pacific Railroad. Northern Democrats with their Jeffersonian scruples would not endorse such government largesse. The Republicans, on the other hand, with their Whiggish tradition, had already demonstrated their paternalistic bent and would prove far more friendly to the new Southern yen for federal subsidies. In the end, with certain added promises of patronage for Southerners, the bargain was struck, and Hayes was inaugurated President.

In the following chapter from his outstanding study, *Origins of the New South*, Woodward summarizes the "Compromise of 1877," which he developed more fully in his monograph *Reunion and Reaction*. The reader will note the strong Beardian coloration of Woodward's interpretation, and indeed, in many ways, his Compromise of 1877 complements and rounds off Beard's Second American Revolution thesis.

For further reading: C. Vann Woodward, *Reunion and Reaction: The Compromise of 1877 and the End of Reconstruction* (Boston, Mass.: Little, Brown and Company, 1951); Paul L. Haworth, *The Hayes-Tilden Disputed Presidential Election of 1876* (Cleveland, Ill.: The Burrows Brothers Company, 1906); Patrick W. Riddleberger, "The Radicals' Abandonment of the Negro during Reconstruction," *Journal of Negro History*, XLV (April 1960); Stanley P. Hirshson, *Farewell to the Bloody Shirt: Northern Republicans and the Southern Negro, 1877–1893* (Bloomington, Ind.: Indiana University Press, 1962); Vincent P. De Santis, *Republicans Face the Southern Question: The New Departure Years, 1877–1897* (Baltimore, Md.: The Johns Hopkins University Press, 1959).

Decisions of great moment confronted the South in the winter that brought the end of Reconstruction.[1] They were decisions that affected the welfare and future course not merely of the South alone but of the nation as a whole. The occasion for

[1] This chapter is based on the author's *Reunion and Reaction: The Compromise of 1877 and the End of Reconstruction* (Boston, 1951), in which the story is much more fully elaborated and documented. Permission was kindly granted by Little, Brown and Company.

these decisions, the thing that gave the South, for the first time in years, a measure of freedom to choose her course, was the disputed Presidential election of 1876.

A great deal more was at stake in the winter of 1876–1877 than the question of which of two citizens, Samuel J. Tilden or Rutherford B. Hayes, would occupy the White House. To many Northerners it seemed that all the hard-won fruits of the Civil War and Reconstruction were in jeopardy. On one plane there were the North's more idealistic war aims, those centered about the freeing and protecting of the Negro and reflected in the new amendments of the Constitution. On a different plane there were the less idealistic, less publicized war aims, those centered around the protection of the peculiar interests and privileges of a sectional economy. They were reflected in new statutes regarding money, banks, tariffs, land, railroads, subsidies—all placed on the lawbooks while the South was out of the Union. People who thought of themselves as realists were already talking of saving the fruits of Northern victory on one plane by sacrificing those on the other.

It was a depression year, the worst year of a bad depression. In the East radical labor elements and unemployed were working themselves into a violent temper that foreshadowed the insurrectionary riots of the summer. In the West a tide of agrarian radicalism was rising in the shape of Granger, Greenback, and silverite doctrines. From both East and West came threats against the elaborate structure of protective tariffs, railroad subsidies, banking privileges, and monetary arrangements upon which the new economic order was founded.

And now the South, kept at bay for sixteen years, presented a third threat to the New Order. Traditionally hostile to the new capitalistic legislation, believed to be nursing bitter grievances, and suspected of all manner of mischief, the South was at last returning in full force, united as never before, to upset the sectional balance of power. Which way would the South throw her weight in the impending struggle over national issues? Would she make common cause with other rebellious elements? Would she join hands with restless labor in the East as she once had? Or would she rush into the arms of her ante-bellum ally, the agrarian West, break up the East-West alliance that won the war, and leave the East once more an isolated minority section? Or could the South be induced to combine with Northern conservatives and become a bulwark instead of a danger to the new capitalistic order? If the South were given a share in some of the more tangible fruits of the New Order, might she not prove more friendly toward it? And if so, what inducements would be found necessary?

These questions loomed large in the deliberations of those who sought a practical solution to the Presidential election crisis and had an important influence upon the Compromise of 1877.

The circumstances of the national electoral crisis will be readily recalled. A closely contested election gave Tilden and the Democratic ticket more than a quarter of a million more popular votes than Hayes received and 184 uncontested electoral votes, or just one short of the number required to elect. Hayes trailed with only 166 undisputed electoral votes, but Republican managers immediately laid claim to the 19 doubtful votes of South Carolina, Florida, and Louisiana. Democratic managers laid a counterclaim to one Oregon vote on the ground that the elector was a Federal officeholder and therefore disqualified. There seems to be no positive way of determining what the results of a perfectly fair election in the three Southern states would have been. The consensus of recent historians is that Tilden deserved the 4 electoral votes of Florida and was therefore elected.[2] Republican returning boards in each of the three states "canvassed" the returns, however, and under pressure of visiting Republican delegations certified all electoral votes for Hayes. Rival Democratic state authorities at the same time certified another set of returns for Tilden. Congress was therefore presented with conflicting returns for 20 electoral votes, including the one from Oregon. Hayes would have to be awarded every one of these votes to win, while Tilden required only one to complete a majority.

The question was, who was to count the votes? Neither the Constitution, nor the law and rules, nor precedent and custom offered an acceptable solution. The strongly Democratic House of Representatives and a stanchly Republican Senate were completely at odds on methods proposed. A deadlock ensued, and as the weeks slipped by without prospect of agreement, tension mounted in Washington and gripped the nation. It had been only sixteen years since a Presidential election had precipitated a civil war, and each quadrennial election since then had turned, in the last analysis, on the employment of military force or the threat of it. It remained to be seen whether the country could regain the ability to choose a President without resort to force. To Abram S. Hewitt, national Democratic chairman, a peaceful solution seemed extremely doubtful in 1876. He knew of fifteen states in which Democratic war veterans were organizing for military resistance to the election "fraud," and to him "it seemed as if the terrors of civil war were again to be renewed."[3] One historian concluded that more people expected a bloody outbreak in the crisis of 1876–1877 than had anticipated such an outcome in the crisis of 1860–1861.[4]

In the meantime, as soon as Congress convened in December, friends of Governor Hayes discerned a difference between the attitudes of Northern and Southern Democrats on the subject of the electoral crisis. The Southerners, "especially those who were old Whigs," observed James A. Garfield, counseled peace and moderation, deplored the violent talk of Northern Tildenites, and seemed less zealous for Tilden's cause. Garfield urged that "in some discreet way" overtures be made to the Southerners immediately.[5] Murat Halstead had already attempted unsuccessfully to get L. Q. C. Lamar to visit Hayes, and in lieu of that he arranged a long interview between Hayes and Lamar's friend W. H. Roberts, editor of the New Orleans *Times*. The talk was gratifying but inconclusive.[6]

What was needed was negotiators who were on easier personal terms than were Northern Republican and Southern Democratic politicians at that particular time. Just such men were the officials of the Western Associated Press, a nonpartisan organization of which the leading newspapers of the Mississippi Valley, North and South, were members. Halstead of the Cincinnati *Commercial* was president, and William

[2] Among historians holding that Tilden carried Florida are Allan Nevins, *Abram S. Hewitt, With Some Account of Peter Cooper* (New York, 1935), 373; H. J. Eckenrode, *Rutherford B. Hayes, Statesman of Reunion* (New York, 1930), 227; Alexander C. Flick, *Samuel J. Tilden, A Study in Political Sagacity* (New York, 1939), 415–16; Leon B. Richardson, *William E. Chandler, Republican* (New York, 1940), 193. The older historians, James Schouler, William A. Dunning, and James Ford Rhodes, also put Louisiana in Tilden's column.

[3] Allan Nevins (ed.), *Selected Writings of Abram S. Hewitt* (New York, 1937), 177–78.

[4] Paul L. Haworth, *The Hayes-Tilden Disputed Presidential Election of 1876* (Cleveland, 1906), 168.

[5] James A. Garfield to Rutherford B. Hayes, December 12, 1876, in Rutherford B. Hayes Papers (Hayes Memorial Library, Fremont, Ohio).

[6] Murat Halstead to Hayes, November 30, 1876, *ibid.*; Cincinnati *Enquirer*, December 2, 1876; New York *Herald*, December 4, 1876.

Henry Smith of Chicago, Hayes's closest personal friend and political adviser, was general agent. On the board of directors sat Joseph Medill of the Chicago *Tribune,* Colonel Andrew J. Kellar of the Memphis *Avalanche,* Richard Smith of the Cincinnati *Gazette,* and W. N. Haldeman, publisher of Watterson's Louisville *Courier-Journal.* William Henry Smith and Colonel Kellar called a meeting of several of these men in Cincinnati on December 14. Smith reported to Hayes that they had "arranged a programme" for splitting the Southern Democrats from their party and that Kellar was leaving at once for Washington to "enter zealously on the great work." [7]

Smith believed that Kellar was "an admirable man" for the job, that he was "discreet and wise and fully sympathizes with us." [8] A Douglas Democrat and a Union man, Kellar nevertheless fought for the Confederacy. After the war he entered newspaper work in Memphis and identified himself with the Whig-industrialist wing of the Tennessee Democrats led by Colonel Colyar of Nashville. Kellar was to collaborate with General Henry Van Ness Boynton, Washington representative of the Cincinnati *Gazette* and one of the Capital's most distinguished newspapermen. Of New England abolitionist background, the General had won his rank on the opposite side of the firing line from Colonel Kellar. Union general and Confederate colonel admired each other enthusiastically from the start and worked in complete harmony. Boynton wrote Smith that the Colonel was "able to do that part of the work which was most difficult for us, namely sounding certain Southern men. He has their confidence & he easily got near them." [9]

Under the guidance of Kellar and Boynton the Republican strategists conducted the most searching analysis ever made of the mind of the Redeemers, and the correspondence and journals that record their findings constitute the richest available source of information on the nature of the New Order in the South. Garfield's diary records his first interview with Kellar, in which the Colonel demonstrated that the so-called "Solid South" was weakest along the seams where the old Whigs and Unionists had been forcibly joined with Democrats and Secessionists. If Hayes could break the South along those seams by detaching the old Whig element he could not only gain support in the current crisis from the South but "build up a sound Republican party there" in the future. [10]

The forgotten history of Southern Whiggery became a subject of absorbing interest to practical politicians. State by state they canvassed the South to tabulate the antebellum voting power of Whig and Unionist elements that now voted Democratic. [11] They derived great comfort from the fact that these elements had cast a majority of Southern votes in 1860. Hayes's friends were enormously gratified to note the remarkable proportion of old Whigs and Unionists among the new Southern Senators, Congressmen, governors, and Democratic leaders. Approaches were made to many

[7] William Henry Smith to Hayes, December 14, 1876, in Hayes Papers. On the origins of the plan, see Andrew J. Kellar to William Henry Smith, November 14, December 10, 1876, in William Henry Smith Papers (William Henry Smith Memorial Library, Indiana State Historical Society, Indianapolis; copies in Hayes Memorial Library).
[8] Smith to Hayes, December 14, 1876, in Hayes Papers.
[9] Henry V. Boynton to Smith, December 18, 1876, in Smith Papers.
[10] Garfield Diary, December 17, 18, 1876, in James A. Garfield Papers (Division of Manuscripts, Library of Congress).
[11] New York *Times,* January 11, 1877; Chicago *Tribune,* January 3, 1877; Cincinnati *Daily Gazette,* December 19, 1876.

Southern leaders—to Governor Augustus H. Garland of Arkansas, Senator David M. Key and two other Congressmen of Tennessee, Hampton of South Carolina, Benjamin H. Hill and Gordon of Georgia, Lamar of Mississippi, and several Congressmen from Louisiana and Texas. One of Hayes's advisers counted twenty-six Southern members of Congress "who before Secession were Whigs" and who were pledged "to resist all extreme measures, and who are at least desirous that you may be inaugurated." [12] One thing the Republicans learned about these Redeemers was that whether they were old Whigs or not, they were not the old ante-bellum planter type of conservative. They spoke for much the same type of railroad and industrial interests as did the Republicans and took a "practical" view of things. The various business alliances and lobbies with which Southern Congressmen were identified were carefully noted by Boynton and Kellar for future reference.

Republicans began to see the Southern problem and the Redeemers with new eyes, and the more they saw the more anachronistic seemed the Southern policy of the Republican party. It dated back to the revolutionary days of Thaddeus Stevens and Charles Sumner. The party of abolitionist radicalism had now became the party of vested interests and big business; the old Whig element was on top, its program had been enacted, and its leader was Rutherford B. Hayes, an ex-Whig and a stanch conservative. Yet in the South the party still appealed for the votes of a propertyless electorate of manumitted slaves with a platform of radical equalitarianism. The contradiction was obvious. And while the Northern Whigs were taking over leadership of the Republican party from Free-Soilers and Radicals, Southern Whigs and conservative Democrats had to a considerable extent replaced Jacksonians as leaders of the Democracy of their region. In the old days Federalists and Whigs had combined naturally, without regard to sectional barriers, but now that the Northern conservatives were sorely pressed by radical farmers and laborers in West and East, they found themselves estranged from their normal allies in the South. This was the more regrettable in view of the demonstrable futility of leaning on black labor votes. "We have tried for eight years to uphold Negro rule in the South officered by carpet baggers," lamented Medill, "but without exception it has resulted in failure." [13] Medill and large numbers of Hayes's advisers in North and South urged him to abandon the Carpetbaggers, place the Negro under political fealty to his former master, and appeal to the latter along the lines of the old Whig conservatism. The revolution in Republican policy was debated publicly and privately and was eventually adopted. "The whole subject is a constant theme of earnest talk in Washington," reported the New York Times.[14]

Hayes was advised by realists, however, who knew that practical politics is not based merely on appeals to tradition. "Just what sort of assurances the South wants is not quite so clear," Garfield wrote Hayes, "for they are a little vague in their expressions." [15] Kellar and Boynton set out to clear up that vagueness. It was obvious that the Southerners wanted to get rid of the last Carpetbaggers, but Tilden could do that. Hayes would have to go further. A little discreet inquiry indicated the lay of the land.

The South's extreme poverty and her hunger for capital were the basic considera-

[12] A. H. Markland to Hayes, January 5, 1877, in Hayes Papers.
[13] Joseph Medill to Richard Smith, February 17, 1877, ibid.
[14] New York Times, January 11, 1877.
[15] Garfield to Hayes, December 12, 1876, in Hayes Papers.

tions. They were no mere sociological abstractions but powerfully felt needs of a dominant class and of many of the plain people. No ruling class of our history ever found itself so completely stripped of its economic foundations as did that of the South in this period. Involved in the downfall of the old planter class were the leading financial, commercial, and industrial families of the region. The hard struggle of these people to get back on their feet and recoup their losses took on a measure of desperation. Early in 1877 the more desperate of them were said by one of their number to be "willing for almost anything to turn up which gives promise or possibility of change." [16] Numerous leaders of old families attached themselves to Yankee capitalists, economic Carpetbaggers who came South for profits. These adventurers often prospered with the aid of extravagant subsidies from Carpetbag state governments. But the Panic of 1873 forced the economic Carpetbaggers to retreat on their home bases, and the political Carpetbaggers left the states that they turned over to the Redeemers impoverished or bankrupt.

As a last resort the South turned to the Federal treasury, and as the depression deepened to its gloomiest year that seemed the only hope left. The Southerners could make a respectable case for government aid. They pointed to the flood of subsidies, grants, bonds, and appropriations bestowed upon Northern enterprise during the South's absence and asked why, since they were taxed to pay for them, they could not ask for a share of these blessings. Surely the clearing of the fine harbors of Savannah, Mobile, and New Orleans, still choked with wartime obstructions or mud, meant improvements of national interest. And there were millions of acres of the richest lands in four states annually subject to floods for lack of an adequate system of levees and flood control along the Mississippi. The South's uncompleted railway system, one of the victims of war and invasion, was surely as worthy of Federal subsidies as were the new railroads that wandered among the buffalo over the uninhabited plains of the West. Deteriorating public buildings, fallen bridges, choked canals, unbuilt waterways, and obstructed river channels all waited their turn for an appropriation. For the construction of such projects a corporation had usually been organized and stock floated, and usually operations had been suspended in the Panic of 1873 to await news of the earnestly petitioned bill for a Federal subsidy. Popular support for many of the bills was not wanting, for they often promised to fulfill real needs. Around each of these bills—and there were hundreds of them— gathered a group of capitalists, politicians, and civil leaders—a lobby. And on the progress of that lobby sometimes hung the hopes of rebuilding the fortunes of once-mighty families.

No sooner had the Southerners returned to Washington and presented their internal-improvement bills, however, than they were informed that the Great Barbecue was over and they were too late. It was now time for reform. Northern leaders of their own party adopted the slogan "Retrenchment and Reform" and greeted their returning friends from the South with lectures on economy. One Northern Democratic reformer introduced a resolution forbidding all future subsidies and grants to private enterprises. Introduced on the eve of an election, the bill passed by 223 to 33. All but seven of the opposition votes came from the South.[17] Colonel Kellar's Memphis paper called the bill "an insult to the South," and noted that "When a practical

[16] J. L. M. Curry, "The South, Her Condition and Needs," in *Galaxy* (New York), XXIII (1877), 544, 548.
[17] *Congressional Record*, 44 Cong., 1 Sess., 227.

question like paying a Southern claim, or assisting an internal improvement such as the Texas and Pacific Railroad or the Mississippi levees came up," Yankee Democrats "could be relied on to take the extreme Northern ground of opposition." [18] The New Orleans *Times* marveled that "an excessive fit of economy should have seized the country when the North was gorged and the hungry South was begging a modicum of the same fostering generosity." And the worst offenders were the perfidious Northern Democrats.[19] By comparison the Republicans showed a sympathetic understanding. Garfield wrote Hayes that numerous Southerners had told him that "in the matter of internal improvements they had been better treated by the Republicans than they were likely to be by Democrats." [20] He thought this point worth developing in the current crisis.

General Boynton and Colonel Kellar quickly fixed upon the South's hunger for Federal money as one of the means of solving the national political crisis. This hunger took as many forms as there were Southern bills for internal improvements in Congress. None of the lobbies behind these bills, however, was so well organized, shrewdly directed, liberally financed, and widely supported in the South as that demanding a Federal subsidy for the Texas and Pacific Railway Company. The president of the Texas and Pacific was Colonel Thomas A. Scott of Philadelphia, who was also president of the Pennsylvania Railroad, the biggest freight carrier in the world and probably the most powerful corporation in America at that time. Seeking to round out a nationwide system and to challenge the transcontinental monopoly of the Union Pacific and Central Pacific, Scott entered Texas in 1872 to build a southern route to the Pacific coast. His resources included claims to some 16,000,000 acres of public lands in New Mexico, Arizona, and California, the last great land grant made to a railroad by the Federal government. Scott also had a large grant of land in Texas made by that state to two companies acquired by the Texas and Pacific, plus a grant of $6,000,000 in bonds by the Reconstruction legislature of Texas, passed over the Republican governor's veto.[21]

Construction was placed in charge of General Grenville M. Dodge, already famous as chief engineer of the Union Pacific and known as one of the ablest railroad lobbyists in the country. The Panic of 1873 brought construction to a sudden halt, prevented Scott from floating bonds in Europe, and confronted both the Texas and Pacific and Scott with financial disaster. In this plight Scott turned to the Federal treasury as the means of repairing his fortunes and sought the advice of General Dodge with regard to securing a subsidy.[22] Dodge pointed out that the Crédit Mobilier scandal had discredited railroad subsidies, that both major parties had forsworn the policy, and that the West, where he had once mobilized great support, was under Granger influence. The South, he thought, was the only hope. "Every convention in the Northwest is putting resolutions in their platforms against that class of legislation," Dodge wrote Scott, "so that our fight has got to be made by the combined

[18] Memphis *Daily Avalanche*, January 11, 1877.
[19] New Orleans *Times*, February 25, 1877.
[20] Garfield to Hayes, December 12, 1876, in Hayes Papers.
[21] Charles S. Potts, *Railroad Transportation in Texas*, University of Texas *Bulletin*, No. 119 (Austin, 1909), 95; Charles W. Ramsdell, *Reconstruction in Texas* (New York, 1910), 307–308.
[22] Jacob R. Perkins, *Trails, Rails and Wars; The Life of General G. M. Dodge* (Indianapolis, 1929), 257.

South and what votes we can get from the middle and eastern states." [23] The General, with this program in mind, plunged into the task of mobilizing the South for the Texas and Pacific bill.

A formidable part of the army Dodge and Scott enlisted were the four projected eastern branches of the Texas and Pacific, all of which were incorporated in Scott's bill, and all likewise asking subsidies. One of the three southernmost branches was to connect the eastern termini of the Texas and Pacific in east Texas with New Orleans, one with Vicksburg, and one with Memphis. Each of the companies incorporated to build these branches claimed a land grant but boasted few other assets save large stock issues of dubious worth that would be greatly enhanced by the passage of the Scott bill. Two rival companies, one affiliated with the Carpetbaggers and one with the Redeemers, were ready to build the New Orleans branch. A fourth branch was projected to leave the Texas and Pacific in west Texas and wander for 436 miles through uninhabited plains, much of it in Indian Territory that was closed to settlement, to Vinita, where it was to connect with a line to St. Louis.[24] In all, the branch lines amounted to more mileage than the Texas and Pacific trunk line. Around each branch was grouped a collection of interests—holders of the relatively worthless paper of the corporations who hoped to build the line, landlocked towns awaiting the "great day," and numerous politicians, some of them personally interested. Eight states and three territories were directly touched, and eastward from the terminal cities of the branches stretched railroads through other states seeking outlet to the west. The Vinita branch alone, Dodge estimated, controlled twenty-five votes in Congress.[25] One Arkansas Senator was president of the Memphis branch and the other a director. "Each branch," observed the Nation, "represents so many Congressional Districts and so many votes, and it represents so many thousands of tons of iron which are to be manufactured in so many other districts which have so many more votes." [26] If the branches were incomprehensible from the viewpoint of railway economics, they were thoroughly understandable from the viewpoint of railway politics.

General Dodge did not rely upon the branches alone for Southern support. "There was no success here," he wrote in 1875, "until I changed my whole policy, by reaching men from their homes not in Washington." [27] To do this he used the press of the South. Early in his campaign he was able to list forty-two Southern newspapers from Virginia to Texas, among them the most influential journals of the region, that were lending him strong support.[28] "The people behind the press at home is what has done this work," declared Dodge, explaining his success.[29] But not altogether. For

[23] Grenville M. Dodge to Thomas A. Scott, June 16, 1874, letter-book in Box No. 346, in Grenville M. Dodge Papers (Iowa Historical and Memorial Building, Des Moines).

[24] Railroad Gazette (New York, Chicago), IX (January 19, 1877), 29–30; New York Times, January 22, 1877; House of Representatives, Reports of Committees, 44 Cong., 2 Sess., No. 139, Pt. II, 4.

[25] Dodge to Scott, January 12, 1875, letter-book in Box No. 346, in Dodge Papers.

[26] Nation (New York), XXIV (1877), 24.

[27] Dodge to Frank S. Bond, vice-president of the Texas and Pacific, March 1, 1875, letter-book in Box No. 346, in Dodge Papers.

[28] The Press and the People on the Importance of a Southern Line Railway to the Pacific and in Favor of Government Aid to the Texas and Pacific Railway Co. (Philadelphia, 1875), 25–47.

[29] Dodge to Bond, March 1, 1875, letter-book in Box No. 346, in Dodge Papers.

Dodge also undertook to secure formal endorsement of the Texas and Pacific bill by all of the state legislatures of the South, and was successful in all states save Virginia and Louisiana.[30] State action usually took the form of a resolution instructing Senators and requesting Representatives to vote for Scott's bill. Chambers of commerce in Atlanta, Augusta, Louisville, Macon, Memphis, Nashville, New Orleans, Richmond, Vicksburg, and other cities of the South petitioned Congress for passage of the Scott bill. Of all his achievements, Dodge was proudest of securing the endorsement of the National Grange itself, a stronghold of opposition, at its convention in Charleston.[31] The prestige of old Confederate chieftains was too strong in the era of Redemption to be neglected, and Dodge was able to secure the active support of Jefferson Davis, Stephens, General Beauregard, and R. M. T. Hunter. Two former governors, James W. Throckmorton of Texas and John C. Brown of Tennessee, both old Whigs turned Democrats, were elected officials of the Texas and Pacific.

In November, 1875, a national railroad convention met in St. Louis to organize pressure in support of the Texas and Pacific bill. It was attended by 869 delegates from thirty-one states and territories, the largest number from the South.[32] President of the convention was Stanley Matthews, kinsman of Governor Hayes, counsel to Tom Scott, and later Senator from Ohio. Older members recalled the St. Louis convention of 1849, also held to urge a Federal subsidy for a Pacific railroad. Jefferson Davis, chairman of the Mississippi delegation, was present in 1875 to defend his report of 1855 on the route that Scott later adopted. The road to the Pacific had been one of the favorite panaceas for the South's ills in the fifties. The movement stirred historical memories of earlier sectional disputes and compromises.[33] Scott's plan revived the Cotton Kingdom's ante-bellum impulse to expand the Southern system westward and make colonies of the territories between Texas and California. It promised realization of the old planter-statesmen's dreams of a Southern route to the Pacific. It offered "justice to the South" in the form of subsidies that other regions had enjoyed, and it accommodated itself perfectly to the ground swell of reviving Whiggery in the region.

Despairing of aid from Northern Democrats, the Southern Congressmen returned to Washington in December, 1876, determined "not to wait any longer for outside help, but help themselves in the matter of internal improvements." They were said to be "a unit upon two questions": Mississippi levees and the Texas and Pacific. On "the very best authority," a Washington correspondent reported, "They mean to have these things." [34] The New Orleans *Times* saw in the "presidential complication" the South's opportunity, because the crisis had "made a 'new departure' of some sort necessary to both parties of the North, in order to secure the favor of the South." [35]

[30] *Resolutions of the Legislatures, Boards of Trade, State Granges, Etc., Favoring Government Aid to the Texas & Pacific Railway* (Philadelphia, 1874), 35–38; *Press and People on the Importance of a Southern Line Railway*, 6–10.

[31] *House Miscellaneous Documents*, 43 Cong., 2 Sess., No. 89, *passim*.

[32] *Proceedings of the National Railroad Convention at St. Louis, Mo., November 23 and 24, 1875, in Regard to the Construction of the* TEXAS & PACIFIC RAILWAY *as a Southern Trans-Continental Railway Line from the Mississippi Valley to the Pacific Ocean on the Thirty-Second Parallel of Latitude* (St. Louis, 1875), vii–viii, 45–57.

[33] Robert R. Russel, *Improvement of Communication with the Pacific Coast as an Issue in American Politics, 1783–1864* (Cedar Rapids, 1948), 25–26, and *passim*.

[34] St. Louis *Post-Dispatch*, January 15, 1877.

[35] New Orleans *Times*, February 24, 1877.

"What we want for *practical* success," General Boynton wrote William Henry Smith on December 20, a week after Kellar had arrived in Washington, "is thirty or thirty-six votes. West Tennessee, Arkansas, a large Kentucky element, Louisiana, Texas, Mississippi *and Tom Scott* want help for the Texas & Pacific Road." He proceeded to outline "strong arguments" in favor of Scott's bill. "If such arguments & views commend themselves to Gov. Hayes," he continued, "& Tom Scott, & the prominent representatives of the States I have named could *know* this, Scott with his whole force would come here, & get those votes in spite of all human power, & all the howlings which blusterers North & South could put up. . . . If Gov. H. feels disposed toward this enterprise as many of the best & most honest men of the republican party do—there would certainly be no impropriety for some recognized friend of his giving *Scott* to understand it." [36]

Smith showed Boynton's proposal to Medill, who pronounced it "of grave importance" and asked Smith to tell Hayes that he did "not think the price too high for the end proposed to be accomplished." Smith thought the Boynton letter "of great interest" and forwarded it to Hayes with Medill's opinion.[37] Hayes's reaction was guarded but encouraging. "I do not wish to be committed to details," he wrote. "It is so desirable to restore peace and prosperity to the South that I have given a good deal of thought to it. The two things I would be exceptionally liberal about are education and internal improvements of a national character." He continued with the reflection that the South needed to put business above politics, and asked Smith to meet him in Xenia, Ohio.[38] A few days after the conference Hayes wrote Smith that he doubted "the trustworthyness [*sic*] of the forces you hope to rally." [39] Smith replied that he was puzzled by the statement, but would pursue the Southern policy on his "own responsibility." [40] Boynton was satisfied with Hayes's statement that he would be "exceptionally liberal" about internal improvements, and continued his work. Hayes was kept fully informed.

In the meantime, three simultaneous developments were increasing pressure for a drastic departure in the strategy of the Hayes men. The first was a serious threat of defection from Hayes's cause among Republican Congressmen that alarmed Hayes's most trusted advisers.[41] The second was an intensification of the threat of violent or revolutionary tactics on the part of Democrats. This came mainly from the North, but a few Southerners participated. Watterson called for 100,000 Democrats to march on Washington and ensure Tilden's inauguration.[42] The third development lay in railroad politics. For four years the most effective opposition to Scott's bill had come from the powerful lobby of Collis P. Huntington, who sought to block Scott's challenge of the transcontinental monopoly and get government consent to build the southern route himself. Using the same methods as Scott, Huntington complained

[36] Boynton to Smith, December 20, 1876, in Smith Papers.

[37] Smith to Hayes, December 22, 1876, in Hayes Papers.

[38] Hayes to Smith, December 24, 1876 (presumably a copy), *ibid.*

[39] Hayes to Smith, January 3, 1877 (presumably a copy), *ibid.*

[40] Smith to Hayes, January 5, 1877, *ibid.*

[41] John Sherman to Hayes, January 3, 1877, in Charles R. Williams, *The Life of Rutherford Birchard Hayes, Nineteenth President of the United States* (Boston, 1914), I, 521; Garfield Diary, January 5, 1877, in Garfield Papers; James M. Comly to Hayes, January 8, 1877 (copy), in Hayes Papers.

[42] Louisville *Courier-Journal*, January 8, 1877; New York *Times*, January 7, 8, 9, 1877; Washington *National Republican*, January 9, 1877.

that the Forty-fourth Congress was "composed of the hungriest set of men that ever got together," and that "It costs money to fix things so that I would know his [Scott's] bill would not pass." [43] The two men fought each other to a deadlock, but on December 24, 1876, they met in Philadelphia and agreed upon a compromise of mutual advantage.[44] Then during the first week in January the House Committee on Pacific Railroads, of which Lamar was chairman and Garfield a member, agreed to report a subsidy bill in which both Scott and Huntington would share benefits.[45] Thenceforth the two great antagonistic lobbies would join forces, and their combined power would be formidable indeed. General Dodge, director and lobbyist for the Union Pacific as well as for the Texas and Pacific, saw to it that the lobbies of Jay Gould and Sidney Dillon, which were seeking passage of Senator John B. Gordon's sinking-fund bill, were co-ordinated politically with the lobbies of Huntington and Scott.[46]

General Boynton had been seeking for some time "a perfectly *safe* way" to approach Scott. Finally, on January 14 Dodge brought Scott to Boynton's home and the three had a long talk. "Col Scott feels sure," Boynton reported to William Henry Smith, "that the attitude of Gov H towards the South, & his willingness to help them in their material interests can be so used here among prominent Southern democrats as to effectively kill all measures looking toward revolution. He will go to work in the matter *personally*, & with the skill & *directness* for which he is justly celebrated. The talk we had was a long one, covering all the ground, & I am sure you would have been much pleased & encouraged by it. From today there will be no lack of help, for Scott's whole powerful machinery will be set in motion at once, & I am sure you will be able to detect the influence of it in *votes* within ten days. . . . This is a short letter, but it weighs a *ton*." [47] According to Boynton, Scott had "the *very greatest confidence*" in his ability to bring the Southerners into line. A few days later, reporting on Scott's progress, Boynton wrote Smith: "You would not guess in some time who was the first man to surrender without hesitation to Scott after the talk I wrote you about. You will hardly believe it but it *was* Watterson." [48] Whether for this reason or not, Watterson's Louisville *Courier-Journal* suddenly changed from the most bellicose to one of the most moderate papers in the South. Medill's *Tribune* congratulated Watterson on the alteration.[49]

On January 24 Lamar arose in the House in the midst of debate on the Electoral Commission and reported, with cordial endorsement for passage, the Texas and Pacific bill. It was a remarkable proposal. The government was asked to guarantee for fifty years the annual payment of 5 percent interest on bonds of 1,187 miles of trunk line

[43] Collis P. Huntington to David D. Colton, November 20, 1874, and January 17, 1876, in Chicago *Tribune*, December 27, 1883.

[44] Huntington to Colton, December 25, 1876, *ibid*. On Scott's side the compromise was foreseen in Dodge to James A. Evans, November 6, 1876, letter-book in Box No. 384, in Dodge Papers.

[45] Garfield Diary, January 11, 1877, in Garfield Papers; New York *Times*, January 5, 13, 1877.

[46] Dodge to Bond, March 1, 1876, letter-book in Box No. 346; Dodge to Sidney Dillon, December 14, 1876, letter-book in Box No. 382; Dodge to Jay Gould, February 12, 1877, letter-book in Box No. 384, in Dodge Papers.

[47] Boynton to Smith, January 14, 1877, in Smith Papers. As usual, Boynton wrote two letters to Smith on the same date, covering the same ground. Why this was his practice the writer cannot imagine.

[48] Boynton to Smith, January 26, 1877, *ibid*.

[49] Chicago *Tribune*, February 13, 1877. Compare the tone of the Louisville *Courier-Journal*, January 24, 1877, with issues in the weeks following.

at $40,000 a mile and a possible 1,378 miles of branches at $30,000 to $35,000 a mile. The annual interest came to $4,473,500 and the aggregate for fifty years to $223,675,-000. The security offered left much to be desired, while the profits all went to the railroads.[50] Realizing that he was speaking in "the midst of serious political perplexity and threatened danger," Lamar offered the Texas and Pacific bill as "one of the simplest and yet surest means of reconciling the interests and harmonizing the sentiment of this whole country." It would promote not only "reconciliation" of the sections but "material reconstruction" of the South, and "mutual respect and affection" at a time they were desperately needed.[51]

William S. Holman of Indiana, Democratic chairman of the House Committee on Appropriations, was immediately on his feet with objections to Lamar's request for unanimous consent to give the bill priority. This was no surprise, for Holman had introduced the resolution against subsidies and a later one calling for an investigation of alleged shady practices used to put the original charter of the Texas and Pacific through Congress.[52] The latter resolution was a slap in the face of Southern Democrats and a notice that the Democracy was the party of reform and not of Whiggery and revived Grantism. Other Northern Democratic Congressmen joined Holman in denouncing subsidies, railroad jobbery, and the Texas and Pacific bill.[53] Scott's Southern friends got no comfort for their "reconciliation" scheme from Northern members of their own party.

The Northern Democratic press took up the outcry against the Texas and Pacific "job" and heaped merciless criticism upon its Southern Democratic supporters. The New York *Sun*, popularly believed to be the mouthpiece of Tilden, pronounced Lamar's bill "the most nefarious railroad jobbery yet attempted in this country," a revival of Crédit Mobilier tactics.[54] The *Nation*, voice of liberal Republicans and reformers, had hoped to find "in Southern politicians like Mr. Lamar himself and Senator Gordon of Georgia, powerful assistance in ridding the Government of the corrupt and jobbing practices," and declared it "almost incredible that they should be seen rising up in company with Mr. Tom Scott and his kind." The editor was particularly concerned about Lamar, "representative, *par excellence*, of the South in the new order of things," and warned him "that suspicion of bribery will just as naturally rest on the supporters of a Texas and Pacific as of a Union Pacific job." [55] More galling to Southern Congressmen than anything else were the bitter attacks of the Democratic Washington *Union* and its editor Montgomery Blair. As Tilden's counsel and editorial voice in the Capital, Blair was extremely well informed and merciless in his attacks on "*Southern* Democrats—Tom Scott's Democrats." To Blair it seemed that Scott's subsidy was playing the role that Biddle's bank had played in Jackson's time and was being used to revive Southern Whiggery in the guise of Democracy.[56] He wrote Tilden of connivance "between the Radicals & the men of the Lamar order," and warned, "you will be defeated by the lobbies." [57]

[50] House of Representatives, *Reports of Committees*, 44 Cong., 2 Sess., No. 139, Pt. II, 4.

[51] *Ibid.*, Pt. I, 8; *Congressional Record*, 44 Cong., 2 Sess., 924.

[52] *Congressional Record*, 44 Cong., 1 Sess., 598.

[53] *Ibid.*, 2 Sess., 922–24.

[54] New York *Sun*, January 9, February 6, 13, 16, 1877.

[55] *Nation*, XXIV (1877), 65–66, 82–83.

[56] Washington *Union*, February 19, 20, 1877.

[57] Montgomery Blair to Samuel J. Tilden, February 8, 1877, in Samuel J. Tilden Papers (New York Public Library).

The Texas and Pacific subsidy was only one of numerous issues that illustrate the cleavage between Northern and Southern Democrats. The Southerners got more aid from the Republicans than from Northerners of their own party in their drive for money to free the mouth of the Mississippi from mud bars.[58] And again, almost twice as many Republicans as Northern Democrats voted with the South in favor of an appropriation for repairing Mississippi levees and reclaiming flooded lands.[59] Time and again the South would gain Republican support in the Senate or on the floor of the House for an appropriation—for the Galveston harbor, for a Southern steamship line, or for some other local bill—only to have it killed by the Democratic Committee on Appropriations.[60] The Washington *National Republican* openly urged Republican Congressmen to vote with the South in order to compel a roll call on the Texas and Pacific bill and fix responsibility for its defeat on "the Tilden wing" of Democrats.[61] Friends of the bill, however, were unable to force a roll call. The lobbies of Scott, Gould, and Huntington brazenly invaded the House, creating such confusion at times as to stop proceedings on the electoral crisis.[62]

Meanwhile, it began to seem that a peaceful solution had been found for the dispute over the counting of the electoral votes in the Electoral Commission, which had been created with bipartisan support the last week in January. But as soon as the Commission cast its first vote on February 8 it became clear that the decision was going against the Democrats by a vote of eight to seven. Then the Democrats heard that Justice Joseph P. Bradley, who cast the deciding vote on the Commission, had suddenly changed his opinion the night before he cast his first vote. When it was charged that he had been influenced by Scott and other Pacific railroad lobbyists, they raised the cry of "conspiracy" and refused to abide by the Commission's decision.[63] Northern Democrats at once opened a filibuster in the House that was designed to prevent completion of the count of electoral votes. It could prevent Hayes's election, and it could lead to violence, even revolution. Its success would depend upon the support of the Southern Democrats.

Boynton, Kellar, and Dodge all expressed confidence that the Southerners could be dissuaded from joining the filibuster. "I shall expect to see hard & effective work there," wrote Boynton, referring to the "Scott help." For the Southerners the problem had been "much simplified" since "they have only to say that good faith, honor, & respect for law all bind them not to impede the execution of the new law for the counting." [64] As tension mounted in Washington over the threat of the filibuster, however, some of Hayes's advisers, including Boynton, urged him to give the South

[58] *Congressional Record,* 44 Cong., 2 Sess., 1066–73, 1086, 1347; *Letter from James B. Eads to Hon. W. S. Holman, January 29, 1877* (Washington, 1877), a pamphlet.

[59] *Congressional Record,* 44 Cong., 2 Sess., 2232.

[60] James M. Comly to Hayes, January 8, 1877 (copy), in Hayes Papers. Referring to the defeat of a ship subsidy, the New Orleans *Times* warned: "These repeated rejections of similar bills for Southern aid or relief on the part of a strongly Democratic House may prove at last to much for patient endurance." Quoted in Memphis *Avalanche,* March 1, 1877.

[61] Washington *National Republican,* January 29, 1877.

[62] Chicago *Tribune,* January 31, 1877.

[63] On Joseph P. Bradley's change of opinion, see Nevins (ed.), *Selected Writings of Abram S. Hewitt,* 173; Charles Bradley (ed.), *Miscellaneous Writings of the Late Hon. Joseph P. Bradley* (Newark, 1902), 220–22; on the influence of Scott and the railroads, see New York *Sun,* February 20, 1877.

[64] Boynton to Smith, February 11, 1877, in Smith Papers; Dodge to Gould, February 12, 1877, letter-book in Box No. 384, in Dodge Papers.

additional assurances. Hayes wrote John Sherman that the Senator could assure Southerners that he would live up to his promises and that Sherman could "not express that too strongly." [65] But by this time the South was asking for something more. Shortly after the filibuster opened, a group of Southern Congressmen met in Washington and dispatched a messenger to Chicago to present Medill and William Henry Smith with the request that Hayes appoint Kellar's friend Senator Key of Tennessee postmaster general. The portfolio of the traditional cabinet dispenser of patronage was a high price for Democrats to demand of Republicans—an unprecedented price. But the Southern bargainers had it in their power to deliver in exchange two prizes denied the Republicans by a majority of the electorate in 1876: the Presidency and control of the House. The election had narrowed the Democratic majority in the new House to about eight votes. The messenger of the Southern Democratic caucus told Smith that nine of their number were "pledged to aid in giving the Republicans the organization of the new House by electing Garfield, Speaker." These elaborations of the Compromise were enthusiastically endorsed by Medill, Halstead, Boynton, William Henry Smith, and Richard Smith, who urged them upon Hayes. Henceforth the additions were referred to as part of "the purely political plan," as distinguished from "the Scott plan." [66]

At a Democratic caucus on February 17 the Northern filibusters sought to get the official endorsement of the party for their movement to stop "the inauguration of the usurper." Their support in a stormy session came "almost entirely from the North and West," while "the South was almost a unit" against the filibuster. Southern leaders succeeded in passing a motion by a vote of sixty-eight to forty-nine in favor of completing the count.[67] At a second caucus two days later the filibuster met another defeat in spite of a fire-eating speech by Speaker Samuel J. Randall, in which he accused the Southerners of disloyalty and warned them that Hayes would revive bayonet rule in the South and "overwhelm any southern man in ruin who aided in carrying out their agreement in good faith." [68] Though visibly shaken, the Southern ranks held firm. The caucus did agree to put a clause in the army appropriation bill forbidding the President to intervene in the South with troops. When the Senate refused to agree, the House eventually adjourned without passing the bill, thus leaving Hayes without pay for the army. That action put "teeth" and "sanctions" in the Compromise.[69]

When Boynton learned that the Southerners had stood their ground in the caucus he was overjoyed. "It is difficult," he wrote William Henry Smith, "to distinguish between the comparative effect produced by the two elements—the purely political, & the Scott forces." He doubted that either could have held the South in line alone. "I am sure," he added, "the Scott force has performed enough of the work to entitle it to claims the execution of which appeared in the letters I received." [70] General

[65] Hayes to John Sherman, February 15, 1877, in Hayes Papers.

[66] William Henry Smith to Hayes, February 17, 1877; Joseph Medill to Richard Smith, February 17, 1877; Boynton to William Henry Smith, February 27, 1877, *ibid.*

[67] Cincinnati *Enquirer,* February 19, 1877. New York *Times,* February 19, 1877, reports fifty-six negative votes.

[68] Charles Foster to Hayes, February 21, 1877, in Hayes Papers; Albert V. House, Jr., "The Political Career of Samuel J. Randall" (Ph.D. dissertation, University of Wisconsin, 1934), 98–99.

[69] New York *Times,* February 20, 1877; *Congressional Record,* 44 Cong., 2 Sess., 2248–52.

[70] Boynton to William Henry Smith, February 18, 22, 1877, in Smith Papers.

Dodge, from a less disinterested point of view, wrote Tom Scott attributing the stand of the Southerners entirely to the fact that he had "come to a very clear understanding with those people." Dodge thought he and Scott should see Hayes, who had "a clear understanding" that he was to give them aid in his inaugural, as soon as the President-elect reached Washington. It was even more important for "our Southern friends" to see the President, since "Lamar and a few of that class of men would have great weight with him." [71]

As soon as the South's defection became known, all the leading Republican papers, including those that had for years, and as recently as the summer campaign, pictured the South as treasonous, brutal, and disloyal, broke into effusions of praise for the "decency," "statesmanship," "honor," and "immovable good faith and loyalty of the South." [72] The *National Republican* called the South's vote against the filibuster on February 20 "the bravest and wisest act that has been recorded in the annals of political history for half a century." To the editor it appeared but natural and proper that the "governing classes" in the South should combine with like elements in the North against the Northern Democratic "riff-raff" and assume leadership over "the native menial classes" of the South, especially since the latter had proved "incapable of the intelligent exercise of the privileges of citizenship." [73] To Northern Democrats the South's course seemed more like apostasy, if not something worse. "Thus jobbery can effect reconstruction and *'conciliation'* when the military failed," brooded Montgomery Blair, "and we are enabled to see that it was not Wells, Packard, Kellogg, Stearns & Co. [Carpetbaggers] who gave Southern votes to Hayes, but *Southern Democrats—Tom Scott's Democrats!*" [74]

Then on February 22, when all seemed to be settled, the Columbus *Ohio State Journal*, edited by a close friend of Hayes, came forth with a typical bloody-shirt editorial attacking Louisiana Democrats in contemptuous terms. The editorial was quickly disavowed, but the excitement over the incident created a temporary diversion. Seizing upon this opportunity, three Louisiana Congressmen with Major E. A. Burke, the personal representative of the Democratic claimant for the Louisiana governorship, succeeded in arranging what became famous as the "Wormley House Bargain." Using the threat of a renewed filibuster, Burke and his friends managed to frighten Sherman, Charles Foster, Matthews, and Garfield into repeating such pledges of Hayes's good intentions toward the South as had already been given, and in pinning down somewhat more definitely the understanding about withdrawing troops from Louisiana and South Carolina. John Young Brown of Kentucky and Senator Gordon independently wrung written and signed versions of these pledges from Matthews and Foster.[75] Since these pledges were well publicized they may have helped in weakening Republican resistance to Hayes's policy.

The importance of the Wormley Bargain, however, has been greatly exaggerated. Major Burke later admitted under oath that he was playing a "bluff game," that he could not have held his temporary recruits from the South in the filibuster, that his "bargain" had no appreciable effect on the outcome of the electoral crisis, that the

[71] Dodge to Scott, February 20, 1877, letter-book in Box No. 384, in Dodge Papers.

[72] New York *Times*, February 19, 1877; Chicago *Tribune*, February 19, 1877; New York *Herald*, February 19, 1877.

[73] Washington *National Republican*, February 19, 20, 21, 1877.

[74] Washington *Union*, February 20, 1877.

[75] "Presidential Election Investigation," in *House Miscellaneous Documents*, 45 Cong., 3 Sess., No. 31, I, 974–81; III, 619–29.

South would have helped complete the electoral count anyway, and that Hayes was already committed to the policy he pursued "before these negotiations were entered into." [76] But as an explanation to offer angry and puzzled constituents for the apostasy of Southern representatives the Bargain had its uses. Pictured as a knightly deed, the rescue of distressed sister states from the heel of the Carpetbagger, it was much easier to explain than complicated arrangements regarding patronage, postmasters general, speakerships, control of the House, railroad subsidies, branch roads, and internal improvements. The story also served to enhance the reputation of certain politicians as "Redeemers," though Lamar, Watterson, Hill, Brown, John Hancock, and other leaders who shared the enhanced reputation, never once broke rank and joined the filibuster with other Southerners to assist Major Burke's maneuver. [77] When that maneuver was completed the filibuster suddenly ceased, the count was completed, and Hayes was peacefully inaugurated. [78]

Then began a period of eight months during which "reconciliation" flourished, and Hayes, with the co-operation of Southern conservatives, launched his policy to win support in the South. The inaugural address contained a boost for Southern internal improvements. The President told Garfield and Matthews that he favored Scott's bill "if that will bring Southern support to the Administration to make it worth while." [79] To the press he "expressed himself in very decided terms in favor of a system of internal improvements calculated to benefit and develop the South, and especially of such Government aid as may be appropriate to secure the completion of the Texas and Pacific Railway." [80] Hayes promptly sent in the nomination of Senator Key for postmaster general, and when Republican Senators resisted this and other appointments, Hayes was glad to note that "the resolute support of the Southern Senators like Gordon, Lamar, and Hill" overcame the opposition. [81] After a brief delay and some awkwardness the President removed the troops from the statehouses of Louisiana and South Carolina, and the last Carpetbag regimes immediately collapsed.

In spite of the need for an army appropriation, Hayes postponed the calling of an extra session of Congress until fall in order to give the South time to respond to his new policy. Postmaster General Key, with Hayes's blessing, began rapidly filling post offices and higher posts with ex-Confederates, old-line Whigs, Douglas Democrats, and plain Democrats. According to a Southern paper friendly to Hayes, one third of his Southern appointments of the first five months were Democrats. [82] So encouraging were the letters Hayes received from Southern conservatives, businessmen, and politicians in praise of his policy that in May he wrote: "I am confident it will secure North Carolina, with a fair chance in Maryland, Virginia, Tennessee, and Arkansas, and am not without hopes of Louisiana, South Carolina, and Florida." [83] With mem-

[76] *Ibid.*, I, 990, 1015.

[77] *Congressional Record*, 44 Cong., 2 Sess., 2007–2009, 2025, 2030, 2048–49.

[78] Meantime, Samuel J. Randall turned against the filibuster. Hewitt and other New York Democrats also joined in opposing it.

[79] Garfield Diary, April 3, 1877, in Garfield Papers.

[80] Louisville *Courier-Journal*, April 26, 1877.

[81] Hayes Diary, March 14, 1877, in Charles R. Williams (ed.), *Diary and Letters of Rutherford Birchard Hayes* (Columbus, 1922–1926), III, 427. L. Q. C. Lamar and Benjamin H. Hill entered the Senate in March, 1877.

[82] Louisville *Commercial* (Republican paper), August 21, 1877.

[83] Hayes to W. D. Bickam, May 3, 1877, in Williams (ed.), *Diary and Letters of Rutherford Birchard Hayes*, III, 432.

bers of his family and cabinet, accompanied by Wade Hampton, the President made a triumphant speaking tour through the Southeast in September. In Atlanta he told Negroes that their "rights and interests would be safer" in the hands of the Southern white man than in the care of the Federal government. Southern exponents of the Compromise of 1877, Gordon, Lamar, Hill, Hampton, and Stephens, made speeches in the North that assisted in the rituals of reconciliation and gratified conservative opinion in the Northeast. "If this is Southern Democracy," exclaimed the ex-Radical *Harper's Weekly*, "it is wonderfully like the best Northern Republicanism." [84] So long as this mood prevailed the rejuvenation of Whiggery proceeded apace, and the South was drawn closer into alliance with the conservative Northeast.

The first serious breach in the Compromise of 1877 occurred on October 15, 1877, when the Southern Congressmen failed to deliver the votes necessary to elect Garfield speaker and organize the House for the Republicans.[85] Hayes's policy of conciliation began to deteriorate from that point, for a large wing of his own party came forth in open revolt against it. Opponents of the policy found one vulnerable point of attack in the enormous number of internal-improvement bills pressed by Southern Congressmen. "We must conciliate the Solid South, undoubtedly," remarked the New York *Tribune*. "But what will it cost?" [86] The cost added up to national bankruptcy, in the editor's opinion. The second breach of the Compromise came at the hands of the President himself in December when he publicly expressed "grave doubt" regarding the Texas and Pacific bill and declared against "any more Credit Mobilier operations." [87] Scott continued to pile up political victories with the aid of Southern Democrats, but in the meantime Huntington, once more at war with Scott, was laying rails eastward over the same route—without subsidy and with Hayes's blessing.[88] The South got her road to the Pacific, but not in the way she had planned.

The Whiggish alliance between Republicans and Southern conservatives might have survived these breaches of the Compromise had it not been for a sudden wave of agrarian radicalism in 1878 that swept the South out of control of conservative leaders and into temporary alliance with the West. Southern farmers of the Jacksonian tradition who had submitted to the leadership of the Whig-Democrats only in the emergency of Redemption now grew restive and unhappy. The millennium of subsidies promised by the Redeemers failed to materialize, and the depression deepened. Desperate for relief, the agrarian debtors embraced the Greenbacker, silverite, and antimonopoly doctrines of the West and called for the regulation instead of the subsidization of railroads. Yielding to this sentiment in spite of all that Lamar, Hill, Stephens, and other conservatives could do to prevent it, the Southern delegation in the House voted solidly with the West against Eastern opposition to pass Richard P. Bland's free coinage bill and the Bland-Allison silver purchase bill, to repass the

[84] *Harper's Weekly*, XXI (1877), 343. For a full discussion of the mood of reconciliation, see Paul H. Buck, *The Road to Reunion, 1865–1900* (Boston, 1937), 100–106.

[85] Garfield had been skeptical of the plan from the start. See Garfield Diary, April 6, 1877, in Garfield Papers.

[86] New York *Tribune*, December 19, 1877.

[87] General Boynton, who reported this story in the Cincinnati *Daily Gazette*, December 22, 1877, was "both surprised & disgusted" at Hayes's change of position. He thought of publishing his correspondence regarding the Texas and Pacific deal, but never did. Boynton to Benjamin H. Bristow, December 24, 1877, in Benjamin H. Bristow Papers (Division of Manuscripts, Library of Congress).

[88] Huntington to Colton, October 10, 1877, in Chicago *Tribune*, December 28, 1883.

latter over Hayes's indignant veto, and to repeal the law for the resumption of specie payments.[89] In the South powerful movements got underway in a majority of states to repudiate state bonds worth millions of dollars, held largely by Northeastern capitalists.

Agrarian leaders of the South revived the ante-bellum sectional diplomacy of a Western alliance. They dusted off the old arguments for unity between the agrarian sections—the geographic and ethnic ties, the "natural" system of river, versus the "artificial" system of railroad, transportation, the common cause of farming economies against an industrial economy. Senator John T. Morgan of Alabama declared that a community of interest would "draw the South and West together . . . beyond the power of resistance or of future disseverance."[90] "United politically, they are invincible," contended a Mississippian. "They can defy the world, the flesh, and the devil."[91] Toombs of Georgia swore that the West always had been the South's "most valuable ally."[92] Facing West, the Southern Democrats wrote state platforms for the campaign of 1878 that flamed forth defiance of Eastern capitalism, its banks, monetary system, railroads, and monopolies. The election resulted in the first "Solid South." Not one of the states that Hayes had courted did he win.

As soon as the West-South combination became apparent and the South began voting for agrarian money and antimonopoly bills and repudiating state bonds, the spirit of conciliation vanished among Republican circles. The *National Republican*, which had praised the South as the home of honor and loyalty in 1877, discovered in 1878 that "the spirit of rebellion still lives and is liable at any moment to be again entrenched in arms."[93] The Southern ideas regarding money, debts, banks, and state bonds proved to the New York *Tribune* that "the South is not yet ready for the new civilization," that it "still stands in need of reconstruction," and that between it and the North there was "a radical, irrepressible conflict."[94] Wendell Phillips thought that since "the South and West are naturally allies" on the "material question" and the East and West on "moral issues," the Republicans blundered in dropping issues of the latter type in 1877. "The Southern question . . . properly treated, ight have delayed this material question for some years," he believed.[95] William byd Garrison declared that the lesson of the 1878 campaign was plain: " 'The bdy shirt!' *In hoc signo vinces!*"[96] By that time the party had rejected Hayes's ty and returned to the bloody shirt.

general debate over sectional diplomacy took place in the South after the election 78. Because the West had proved more responsive to the bloody-shirt issue than eals for agrarian unity, the Southern advocates of a Western alliance were ited and on the defensive. Lamar and the conservatives, "who persistently

essional Record, 45 Cong., 1 Sess., 241; *ibid.*, 2 Sess., 1112, 1410–11, 1420; *ibid.*, 1 33.

. Morgan, "The Political Alliance of the South with the West," in *North American* w York), CXXVI (1878), 318.

Jackson *Weekly Clarion-Ledger*, February 6, 1878.

oombs to Alexander H. Stephens, March 25, 1880, in Ulrich B. Phillips (ed.), idence of Robert Toombs, Alexander H. Stephens, and Howell Cobb, in American :iation, *Annual Report*, 1911, II (Washington, 1913), 740.

 National Republican, June 13, 1878.

ribune, January 4, February 4, March 27, 1879.

llips, "The Outlook," in *North American Review*, CXXVII (1878), 102.

w York *Tribune*, January 4, 1879.

resisted this movement," maintained stoutly that they had been "justified by events" and that "a further Western alliance is now out of the question." It was plain that the road to reunion was a forked road, that the right fork led to the East and the left fork to the West. Between the right-forkers and the left-forkers the debate raged for months.[97] It was to break out intermittently again and again over the years, but in the immediate issue the counsel of the right-fork conservatives—the architects of the Compromise of 1877—was to prevail. There is no better statement of their position than one found in the Charleston *News and Courier*:

"We see no hope that a platform will be framed that is acceptable to both East and West. . . . With one section or the other the South must go, and our fixed opinion is that the *permanent interests of the South lie with the East rather than with the West*. The aim of the South being to . . . avoid whatever is revolutionary in politics, sociology or finance, the South must go with the East, despite its aggregating self-assertion, rather than join hands with the West, which is learning the A, B, C, of statesmanship." [98]

The partners of the South's Eastern alliance were Democrats instead of the Republicans Hayes had hoped they would be, but they were quite as conservative. Meekly the South lined up in 1880 behind a national Democratic platform reported by Henry Watterson that contained the phrase "strict maintenance of the public faith" twice in one sentence. And in the successive Cleveland campaigns the South submitted tamely to doctrine dictated by the sectional interests of the Northeastern economy. The reconstructed South came to be regarded in the eighties as a bulwark of, instead of a menace to, the new economic order. "For actual sectional issues," observed the New York *Journal of Commerce*, "we must look north of Mason and Dixon's line. Future storms will come not from the South, but from the West." [99] The Southern states, agreed the *Industrial South*, were the "breakwater for all fanaticism. They are the bulwark against all the storms of political passion. They send forth conservative influences." [100]

It took a lot of hallooing and heading off by the conservative leaders to keep the mass of Southerners herded up the right fork. Agrarian mavericks were eternally taking off up the left fork followed by great droves that they had stampeded. With the aid of the New-South propagandists, however, and by frequent resort to repressive or demagogic devices, the right-forkers contrived to keep the South fairly faithful to the Eastern alignment—until the advent of the Populists.

[97] For an illuminating discussion of the debate, see Charles Nordhoff in New York *Herald,* November 19, 1878.

[98] Charleston *News and Courier,* December 13, 1878. A similar treatment of the question i in the Richmond *Dispatch,* October 22, 1878.

[99] Quoted in Galveston *Daily News,* January 4, 1885.

[100] *Industrial South* (Richmond), VI (June 3, 1886), 247.